Federal Habeas Corpus

Federal Habeas Corpus

Cases and Materials

SECOND EDITION

Andrea D. Lyon
Clinical Professor of Law,
Associate Dean for Clinical Programs
Director, The Center for Justice in Capital Cases
DePaul University College of Law

Emily Hughes
Associate Professor of Law
Washington University in St. Louis School of Law

Mary Prosser
Clinical Assistant Professor of Law
Frank J. Remington Center
University of Wisconsin Law School

Justin Marceau
Assistant Professor of Law
University of Denver, Sturm College of Law

Carolina Academic Press
Durham, North Carolina

Paperback ISBN: 978-1-5310-1235-9
Hardback ISBN 978-1-59460-866-7
LCCN 2010938806

Carolina Academic Press
700 Kent Street
Durham, NC 27701
Telephone (919) 489-7486
Fax (919)493-5668
www.cap-press.com

Printed in the United States of America
2021 Printing

We dedicate this book to
Arnold, John, and Rebecca,
Samantha, Will, Molly, Hannah, Ella and Zach,
Harvey T. Lyon and in fond and grateful memory of Yolanda Lyon Miller 1930–2010,
and to the many colleagues and clients who have
generously shared their knowledge and their stories with us.

Contents

Foreword

Why Is Habeas Corpus Important?

By John C. Tucker

"Would you write a short introduction for our casebook about why habeas corpus is important?" Professor Lyon asked. "I'd be glad to," I said.

The problem, I soon realized, is how to write anything short about something as fundamental to our legal system as habeas corpus—the law which Blackstone described as "the stable bulwark of our liberties," and which American courts commonly refer to as simply "The Great Writ."

In talking about habeas corpus we can't avoid starting nearly 800 years ago at Runnymede, with the most famous provision of Magna Carta: "No freeman shall be taken or imprisoned except by the lawful judgement of his peers or by the law of the land." Magna Carta Art. 39 (1215). For the next 467 years, English kings periodically ignored that stricture and imprisoned their subjects without due process of law, while English parliaments passed laws designed to prevent it—laws referred to by the Latin phrase "habeas corpus"—loosely, "you have the person, now show a legal justification for keeping him or let him go." Finally, the Habeas Corpus Act of 1679 (the statute Blackstone was talking about) pretty much settled the matter. Unless parliament passed a law temporarily suspending habeas, no citizen of England could be imprisoned without a formal charge and an opportunity to contest it.

Given the importance of habeas corpus as a check on the power of the English monarch, it is not surprising that the American colonists also saw it as their most important guarantee of due process, and were enraged when royal authorities sometimes refused to afford its protections to colonists who challenged their arbitrary conduct. Thus, in Federalist 84, Alexander Hamilton declared that habeas corpus was "the bulwark of the British Constitution" and essential to the protection of liberty in the new nation. Habeas corpus became the only English common-law process explicitly written into our own Constitution, and jurisdiction to enforce the Great Writ was granted to American courts in the first Judiciary Act in 1789, even before the adoption of the Bill of Rights.

From that time forward, the Great Writ has been seen as a cornerstone of American justice. As the Supreme Court declared in *Fay v. Noia,* "there is no higher duty than to maintain it unimpaired."

It was *Gideon v. Wainwright,* another habeas case, which, with the book and movie *Gideon's Trumpet,* became the most famous of the decisions which marked the Warren Court's post World War II effort to extend the protections of the United States Constitution to criminal defendants whose due process rights had previously been left to the less-than-rigorous care of state courts. And while many important cases of that era were decided on direct appeal from state supreme courts, the protections established by cases like *Grif-*

fin v. Illinois (free transcript), *Mapp v. Ohio* (exclusionary rule), *Brady v. Maryland* (exculpatory evidence), *Miranda v. Arizona* (warning of rights) and *Malloy v. Hogan* (Fifth Amendment) were initially most often vindicated by a federal petition for writ of habeas corpus.

If you really want to understand why habeas corpus is so important, the people to talk to are the thousands of criminal defendants who have found themselves convicted and imprisoned in state penitentiaries—sometimes on death row—because of ineffective assistance of counsel, or the concealment of exculpatory evidence, or a confession obtained by artifice or coercion. In the roughly two decades following reinstatement of the death penalty in America, nearly 50% of the cases in which a verdict and sentence of death was imposed and approved by the state courts were set aside in federal court by petition for writ of habeas corpus. And while it is probably impossible to give definitive numbers, there is no question that a majority of the 114 men and women who have been released from death row as a result, in part, of the development of DNA testing which proved them innocent, would have died had their executions not been delayed by operation of the Great Writ. Sometimes a life was saved by a finding that the original verdict or sentence was constitutionally defective, sometimes it was delay alone that saved an innocent life until DNA testing was perfected. Such a result would only be decried by the posturing politicians who in recent years have sought to weaken the protections of habeas corpus as a way of demonstrating their supposed "toughness on crime." The founding fathers—whom such politicians shamelessly invoke at every opportunity—would weep.

As lawyers who will handle criminal cases, whether as a significant element of your practice or simply to fulfill your obligation to the profession by accepting appointed cases at the trial or post-trial levels, an understanding of the law of habeas corpus is as essential as anything the users of this book will learn in law school. Indeed, with the increasingly restrictive and complex procedural requirements which have been imposed on the exercise of the writ in recent years by legislators and the Rehnquist Court, an understanding of the intricacies of habeas corpus law is more important than ever, lest the protections of the Great Writ be lost to a client by ignorance or inadvertence.

Finally, we cannot ignore the frontal assault on the writ which our current royalty has mounted in the name of national security and the "war on terror." As I write, the detainee cases are awaiting decision in the Supreme Court. By the time you read this introduction they will have been decided. If the Court rules for the Government, non-citizens may no longer have access to the protections of the writ at all, even when held on American-controlled soil. Even citizens, if arbitrarily designated "enemy combatants," may see the protections of the Great Writ fade like the grin of the Cheshire Cat, until nothing of practical importance remains.

In these times, the ghosts of Runnymede are not grinning, and protection of the Great Writ has never been more important. Whatever is decided in the detainee cases, for ordinary citizens, the Great Writ must remain as a bulwark of our liberties, the ultimate vehicle for protecting our Constitutional rights against the power of government. A lawyer who does not know how to preserve the rights guaranteed by the Writ and to invoke them for her clients is not fully educated in the law.

John Tucker, a lawyer and the author of May God Have Mercy: A True Story of Crime and Punishment *and* Trial and Error: The Education of a Courtroom Lawyer, passed away on October 9, 2010.

Preface

We undertook this book in hopes of helping students understand and critically examine the political, legal, and pragmatic effects of the role of habeas corpus in our criminal justice system. At the same time, we hope this book may also be useful to attorneys who wish to familiarize themselves with habeas corpus jurisprudence. While we have tried to fairly present the competing concerns that inform this complex and evocative area of the law, because we are defense attorneys, our experiences representing individual—rather than governmental—interests have undoubtedly shaped our personal perspectives. As we finished reading each case, we would often wonder what happened to the person behind the case, the person whose life and liberty the Court's decision most immediately affected. Many of the cases are thus followed by a brief synopsis of what happened to the defendant after the case was over.

We want to acknowledge the support and assistance our schools provided us while writing this book: DePaul University College of Law and Interim Dean Warren Wolfson, University of Denver Sturm College of Law and Dean Marty Katz, University of Wisconsin Law School and Dean Ken Davis, and Washington University in St. Louis School of Law and Dean Kent Syverud, as well as the Israel Treiman Fellowship at Washington University School of Law. In addition, we would like to thank the University of Iowa College of Law and Dean Gail Agrawal for supporting final editing for this project during the fall of 2010. We also acknowledge the important work of Professors James Liebman, Randy Hertz, Eric Freedman, Larry Yackle, and many others whose treatises, articles, books, and research continue to be both groundbreaking and foundational. In addition, we sincerely thank Professors Susan Bandes, Keith Findley, Samuel R. Gross, James Liebman, Meredith Ross, and Marc Weber, as well as Grant Sovern, for their insightful comments and suggestions. A number of current and former law students also assisted us with various phases of the book, including Kelly Brunie, Delilah Catalan, Julie Darr, Erin Hairoupoulos, Glenn Hui, Elizabeth Klein, Bryon Lichstein, Sarah Mease, Matthew Mulder, Annie O'Reilly, Joshua Pierson, Daniel Rabinovitz, Maryam Toghraee, and Evan Weitz. And finally, we extend a special thanks to our assistants, Mary Bandstra, Lisa Lammey, and Pam Finnigan, and to our proofreader, Susan Burgess, for their patience and diligence.

Permissions

Thanks to the following authors and copyright holders for permission to use their materials:

Various case opinions, contained within the text, are reprinted and/or adapted with the permission of LexisNexis.

Bator, Paul M., *Finality in Criminal Law and Federal Habeas Corpus for State Prisoners*, 76 Harv. L. Rev. 441 (1963). Reprinted with permission.

The Conviction that Keeps on Hurting—Drug Offenders and Federal Benefits, Drug War Chronicle #471 (February 5th, 2007). Reprinted with permission.

Friendly, Henry J., *Is Innocence Irrelevant? Collateral Attack on Criminal Judgments*, 38 U. Chi. L. Rev. 142 (1970). Reprinted with permission.

Goodman, Leonard. *Reflections from a Guantanamo Detainee Lawyer.* Printed with permission of the author.

Hertz, Randy, and James S. Liebman, Appendix A, Reprinted with permission from Federal Habeas Corpus Practice and Procedure, 4th Ed. Copyright 2001, Matthew Bender & Company, Inc., a member of the LexisNexis Group. All rights reserved.

Liebman, James S., Jeffrey Fagan and Valerie West, A Broken System: Error Rates in Capital Cases, 1973–1995 (Executive Summary) (June 12, 2000). Reprinted with permission of the author.

Liebman, James S., Jeffrey Fagan, Andrew Gelman, Valerie West, Garth Davies, and Alexander Kiss, A Broken System, Part II: Why There Is So Much Error in Capital Cases, and What Can Be Done About It (Executive Summary) (February 11, 2002). Reprinted with permission of the author.

PART I
Introduction

Chapter 1

The Great Writ

A. What Is Habeas Corpus?

Habeas review, or the *Great Writ* as it is often called, is the legal process through which a convicted prisoner may challenge the legality of his or her conviction or sentence. When we talk about habeas review in America we generally are referring to *federal* habeas corpus review, and in this book the phrase habeas review will refer to federal habeas corpus, unless otherwise specified. Habeas is a vehicle for challenging *final* convictions; it is not a readjudication of guilt. This means that if the defendant prevails, he most likely will obtain a new trial rather than release from prison.

The terms habeas corpus review, collateral proceedings, and post-conviction litigation are closely related, and they overlap to a greater or lesser degree depending on how states choose to define the two latter terms (the definition of habeas corpus review is fixed by federal statute). Their practical application and import to our Constitution and our system of federalism are the topics discussed at length in the chapters that follow. A substantial portion of this text is devoted to the procedural complexities and hurdles that are designed to facilitate comity and finality in state criminal cases by preventing federal courts from routinely undermining state convictions. Chapter 1 begins by looking at a more fundamental and antecedent question: How is federal habeas corpus distinct from and different than any other form of litigation?

Even though habeas litigation ultimately may be resolved through an adversarial trial-type presentation of evidence, it is unlike the trial process of determining the guilt or sentence for a particular defendant. In fact, federal habeas proceedings might not commence until more than a decade has passed since the defendant was found guilty and sentenced. Likewise, habeas review must not be confused with a defendant's attempts to have his sentence or conviction overturned through direct appeals, because a prisoner may not even pursue habeas corpus relief until all of the direct appeals have been completed and the convictions have been affirmed and rendered final. In short, habeas review is a unique synthesis of trial and appellate practice; it is neither purely appellate nor purely trial work.

Even recognizing that habeas corpus practice is self-contained in the sense that it is composed of its own set of trials, procedures, and appeals, what the writ of habeas corpus actually covers is not easily answerable. Indeed, the law of habeas corpus is riddled with paradoxes. For example, habeas practice is simultaneously civil and criminal. At stake in habeas litigation is whether the prisoner is "in custody in violation of the Constitution or laws or treaties of the United States." 28 U.S.C. § 2254(a). This means that claims regarding the conditions of confinement or abuse suffered by the prisoner are not cognizable on habeas review; only claims regarding the validity of the criminal conviction or sentence may be litigated. Nonetheless, federal habeas proceedings are considered non-criminal and, therefore, are understood best as civil actions because they are not an adjudication of guilt or innocence. Additionally, while the prosecutor bears the burden of proof in a criminal trial, in a habeas corpus action "the petitioner generally bears the burden of proof."[1]

Indeed, the writ has a unique place in our system of adjudication. Habeas actions are nominally civil in the sense that the Rules of Criminal Procedure do not apply and the Rules of Civil Procedure *may* apply. However, quite often the Rules of Civil Procedure also do not apply. There are many situations in which the Rules of Civil Procedure are trumped by a distinct set of rules promulgated specifically for habeas litigation, The Rules Governing Section 2254 Cases.[2] Perhaps the Supreme Court put it best when it said that "habeas corpus proceedings are characterized as 'civil' [b]ut the label is gross and inexact. Essentially, the proceeding is unique."[3]

Even the type of lawyering necessary to prevail in habeas litigation is chameleon-like. On the one hand, federal habeas litigation is rightly regarded as the critical frontier of constitutional litigation for many of the protections enshrined in the Bill of Rights. This is because federal habeas review is likely the only opportunity a prisoner will have to present and litigate his federal constitutional claims. The underlying merits of a federal habeas case therefore turn on constitutional interpretation and analysis. At the same time, there are few areas of the law in which statutory interpretation is more determinative of the actual outcome of the litigation. As discussed throughout this book, following the enactment of the Anti-Terrorism and Effective Death Penalty Act (AEDPA) in 1996, statutory interpretation has dominated the Supreme Court's habeas docket and, in turn, habeas practice as well.

In short, federal habeas corpus law is *sui generis*. The practices, procedures, and applicable law have no necessary or automatic connection to either conventional criminal or civil litigation. The best we can say is that the *Great Writ* is a profoundly important legal process by which a convicted prisoner may challenge the legality of his or her detention.[4] Thus, understanding the substance of habeas corpus law involves an understanding of the circumstances in which a habeas challenge may be brought as well as the ability to trace the procedural life of a habeas corpus case.

B. *When* Is Habeas Corpus?

As one commentator aptly noted, "[habeas] has ... historically not been a substantive 'right' that someone possesses so much as it has been an evolving set of procedures through

1. *Garlotte v. Fordice*, 515 U.S. 39, 46 (1995). Actions under 42 U.S.C. § 1983 are the appropriate vehicle for a prisoner seeking monetary damages or injunctive relief for a constitutional violation; however, habeas corpus is the only process through which a prisoner may challenge the fact or duration of his imprisonment with the goal of securing his release.

2. The Federal Rules of Civil Procedure provide that "[t]hese rules apply to proceedings for habeas corpus ... to the extent that the practice in those proceedings is not specified in a federal statute, the Rules Governing Section 2254 Cases, or the Rules Governing Section 2255 Cases." FED. R. CIV. P. 81(a)(4)(A).

3. *Harris v. Nelson*, 394 U.S. 286, 293–94 (1969).

4. The writ of habeas corpus may provide a vehicle for challenging the legality of a variety of noncriminal government detentions. *See, e.g., Hopkins v. Lynn*, 888 F.2d 35 (5th Cir. 1989) (challenging a civil commitment order); *Ohio Adult Parole Authority v. Woodard*, 523 U.S. 272 (1998) (challenging the denial of parole); *INS. v. St. Cyr*, 533 U.S. 289 (2001) (confirming the writ's role in preventing unlawful deportation proceedings). *See also Murphy v. Garrett*, 729 F. Supp. 461 (W.D. Pa. 1990) (holding that a federal court had habeas jurisdiction over a conviction by a military court). *See also* Chapter 14, *infra*, discussing the role of habeas corpus in executive detentions such as Guantánamo Bay.

which the right to be free from illegal detention may be vindicated."[5] Consequently, to understand federal habeas review, it is essential to have a working knowledge of when and how a prisoner's petition for habeas corpus relief is reviewed by the federal courts.

(1) The Stages of a Criminal Case

In order to understand the holding of a habeas corpus case, it is necessary to have a firm grasp of the stages of a criminal trial. Each habeas case alleges some fundamental (typically constitutional) defect that occurred in one or more of the stages of the criminal case that are outlined in Chart 1.1 on the next page.

(2) The Three Phases of Review

After the defendant has been convicted, sentenced, and begun his term of incarceration, he can assert that he is being detained in violation of the Constitution based on a defect that occurred during any of the stages of a trial listed in Chart 1.1. He litigates this claim during three distinct phases of appeals, as explained first in words and then in a chart below.

Once a defendant is found guilty in state court, he may appeal to the state court of appeals and, if unsuccessful, to the state supreme court.[6] This level of appeal—referred to as "direct review" or "direct appeal"—is generally limited to claims of legal error that can be identified from the trial record alone.

If relief is denied on direct review, the prisoner may seek collateral review in the state courts.[7] Collateral attacks typically consist of claims that require factual development beyond the record. Collateral review (also called post-conviction review) begins in the state trial court (often with the same judge who presided over the original trial). Appeals following the litigation in the state trial court follow the same route as a state direct appeal. As discussed in Chapter 7 (Exhaustion), simply bypassing the state post-conviction procedures and pleading one's new facts or new claims in federal court is not an option.

If the highest court in the state denies relief, a petitioner is entitled to seek *discretionary* review by the United States Supreme Court both on direct review and on collateral review. If the state supreme court denies the collateral petition and the U.S. Supreme Court does not grant *certiorari*, then the defendant can file a federal habeas petition.[8] A federal habeas

5. Marc D. Falkoff, *Back to Basics: Habeas Corpus Procedures and Long-Term Executive Detention*, 86 Denv. U. L. Rev. 961, 966 (2009) (tracing the history of the habeas writ in order to articulate standards for habeas review of executive detentions). *See* Clarke D. Forsythe, *The Historical Origins of Broad Federal Habeas Review Reconsidered*, 70 Notre Dame L. Rev. 1079 (1995) (noting the debate over the origins of habeas corpus and its historical meaning).

6. If the defendant is sentenced to death, the appeal goes directly to the state supreme court.

7. Some states collapse the two layers of appeal into what is referred to as a unitary review system. In a unitary system direct review and collateral review take place concurrently such that all claims must be raised in a single appeal. *See, e.g., Slusher v. State*, 823 N.E.2d 1219, 1222 (Ind. Ct. App. 2005).

8. Under 28 U.S.C.A. § 2244(d)(2), the time limit on filing a federal habeas petition is tolled by a properly filed application for state post-conviction relief. The Supreme Court, however, has held that a petition for certiorari to the United States Supreme Court seeking review of denial of state post-conviction relief does not toll the time period for filing a federal habeas petition. *Lawrence v. Florida*, 549 U.S. 327, 334 (2007) (noting that it is possible for a state prisoner to be in the "awkward" situation of having to file a federal habeas petition in the district court while a certiorari petition from state post-conviction proceedings is pending before the U.S. Supreme Court).

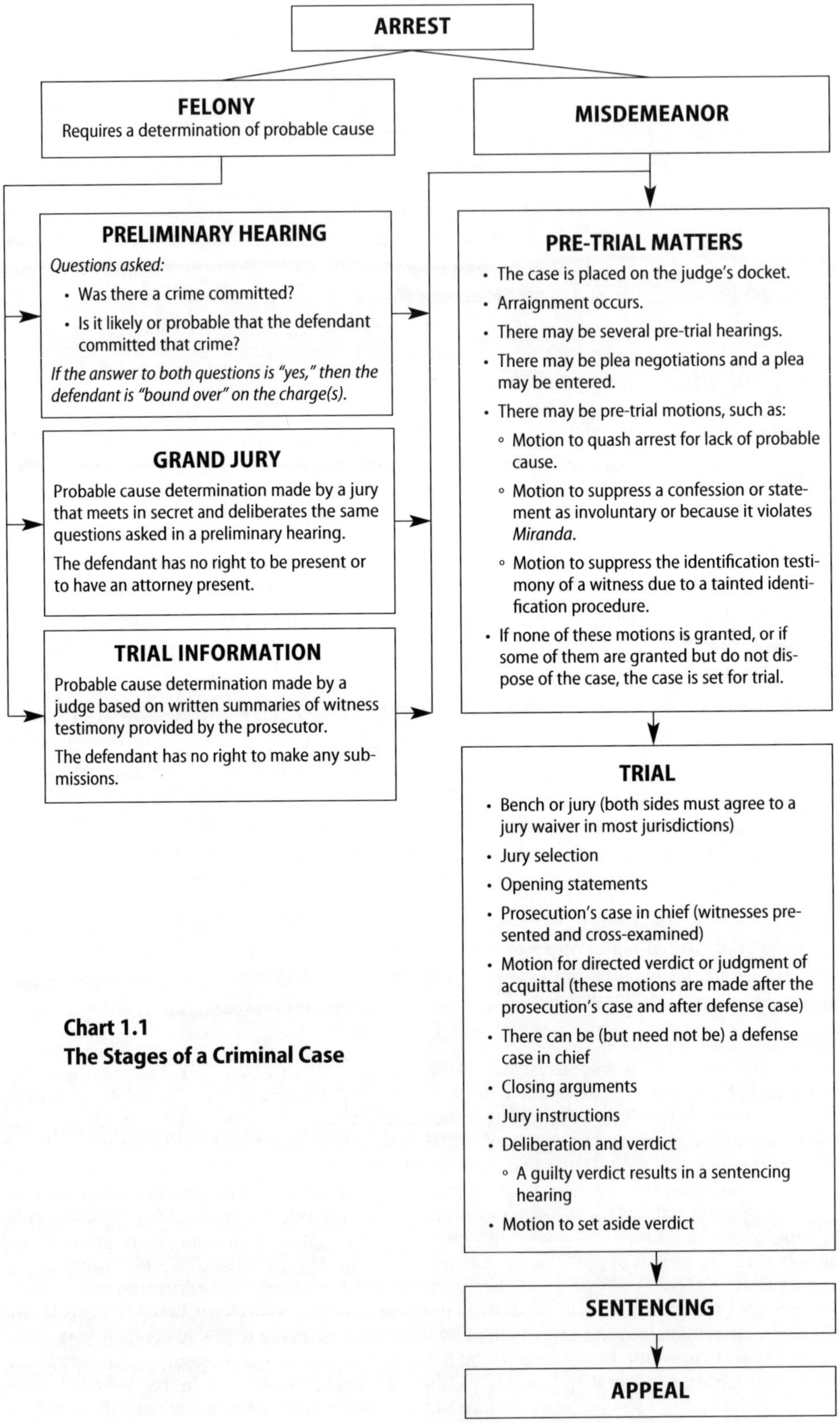

ARREST

FELONY
Requires a determination of probable cause

MISDEMEANOR

PRELIMINARY HEARING

Questions asked:

- Was there a crime committed?
- Is it likely or probable that the defendant committed that crime?

If the answer to both questions is "yes," then the defendant is "bound over" on the charge(s).

GRAND JURY

Probable cause determination made by a jury that meets in secret and deliberates the same questions asked in a preliminary hearing.

The defendant has no right to be present or to have an attorney present.

TRIAL INFORMATION

Probable cause determination made by a judge based on written summaries of witness testimony provided by the prosecutor.

The defendant has no right to make any submissions.

PRE-TRIAL MATTERS

- The case is placed on the judge's docket.
- Arraignment occurs.
- There may be several pre-trial hearings.
- There may be plea negotiations and a plea may be entered.
- There may be pre-trial motions, such as:
  - Motion to quash arrest for lack of probable cause.
  - Motion to suppress a confession or statement as involuntary or because it violates *Miranda*.
  - Motion to suppress the identification testimony of a witness due to a tainted identification procedure.
- If none of these motions is granted, or if some of them are granted but do not dispose of the case, the case is set for trial.

TRIAL

- Bench or jury (both sides must agree to a jury waiver in most jurisdictions)
- Jury selection
- Opening statements
- Prosecution's case in chief (witnesses presented and cross-examined)
- Motion for directed verdict or judgment of acquittal (these motions are made after the prosecution's case and after defense case)
- There can be (but need not be) a defense case in chief
- Closing arguments
- Jury instructions
- Deliberation and verdict
  - A guilty verdict results in a sentencing hearing
- Motion to set aside verdict

SENTENCING

APPEAL

Chart 1.1
The Stages of a Criminal Case

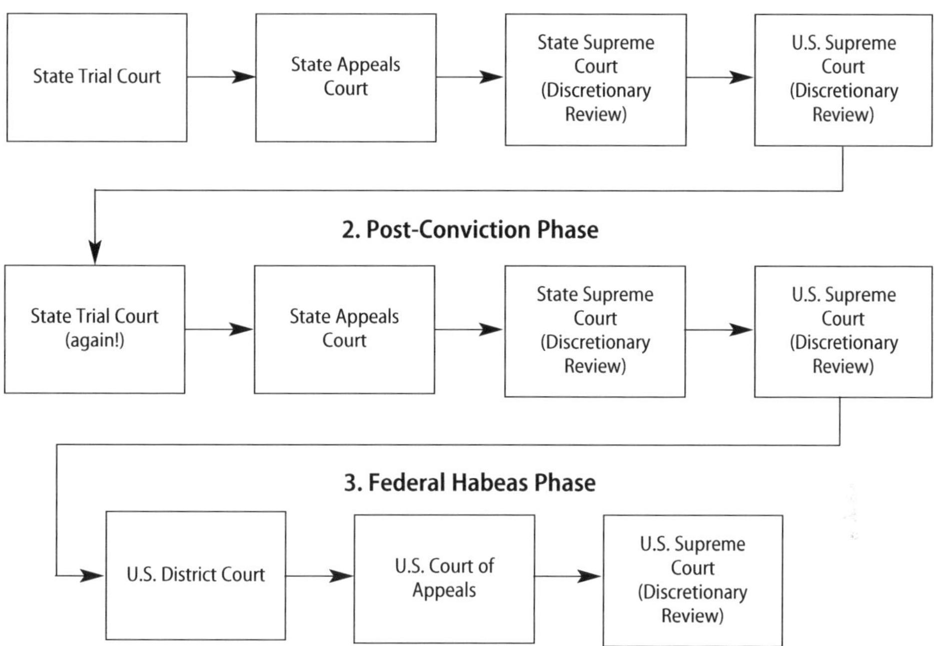

Chart 1.2 The Three Phases of Review

petition is filed in the U.S. District Court in the district where the petitioner is imprisoned. A denial of relief by the district court can be appealed to the federal circuit court with jurisdiction over that district. And if the federal circuit court denies relief, then once again discretionary review may be sought in the U.S. Supreme Court. Chart 1.2 illustrates the three phases of review.

C. Habeas in Context: The History and Evolution of the Writ

Modern habeas case law and scholarship are not developing in a vacuum; they are a direct product of (or in some instances a reaction to) a longstanding debate about the role that federal courts should play in reviewing state convictions. This section identifies and discusses four points in the historical development of habeas corpus doctrine that are relevant to the development of federal habeas corpus doctrine in the United States: (1) The Origins of Habeas Corpus; (2) Habeas Corpus Recognized in the United States; (3) The Warren Era and the Habeas Trinity; and (4) the Anti-Warren Federalist Revolution. While reading this chapter, it is important to bear in mind that the 1996 AEDPA significantly altered federal habeas law. Chapter Two introduces some of the relevant provisions of AEDPA, then discusses the seismic shift generated by the Act.

(1) The Origins of Habeas Corpus

Habeas corpus enjoys a substantial historical pedigree, but the nature of the procedures that comprise the habeas right have evolved considerably over the centuries. Scholars have traced the origins of the Great Writ to the Magna Carta, England's original charter of rights from 1215, and, indeed, there is substantial authority suggesting that the writ became a critical mechanism in safeguarding some of the rights promised by the Magna Carta.[9] As initially conceived and applied, however, the writ's protections were considerably more modest than the modern protections associated with habeas corpus.

Habeas corpus often is translated as "produce the body" or "you have the body."[10] At common law, the scope of the writ was quite literal and therefore narrow—it required that a prisoner be produced or brought before the court, and often nothing more.[11] The authority detaining the prisoner did not have to provide an explanation or justification for the detention. It was not until at least the Fourteenth Century that habeas corpus began to be understood as including both a right to be physically present as well as a right to have the imprisonment explained or defended. By the Eighteenth Century, habeas corpus had evolved in stature to such a degree that William Blackstone would remark in his Commentaries on the Laws of England that habeas corpus is "the great and efficacious writ" which was "directed to the person detaining another, and commanding him to produce the body of the prisoner with the day and cause of his caption and detention...."[12] Blackstone's pronouncement that habeas corpus is the Great Writ is oft repeated, and in many ways Blackstone is just as correct today as he was almost three hundred years ago. But Blackstone's summary is not the final word on habeas corpus; it simply is the most common springboard for analyzing modern federal habeas review.

(2) Habeas Corpus Recognized in the United States

The United States Constitution gives explicit recognition to the writ of habeas corpus. Article 1, the Suspension Clause, states, "The Privilege of the Writ of Habeas Corpus shall not be suspended, unless when in cases of Rebellion or Invasion public safety may require it."[13] In addition, habeas corpus law is codified at 28 U.S.C. §§ 2241, 2254–55, which set forth the general jurisdictional requirements for a successful petition and the specific conditions required for federal courts to entertain, alternatively, state and federal prisoners' petitions.[14]

In the most basic sense, a prisoner's entitlement to habeas corpus review is relatively uncontroversial. The controversial aspect of federal habeas review relates to the questions of whether and to what extent federal courts sitting in habeas are permitted (and required) to review state criminal convictions. The Suspension Clause does not specify whether federal courts are permitted, as a matter of constitutional right, to review the

---

9. John Meador, Habeas Corpus and Magna Carta: Dualism of Power and Liberty (1966).

10. In keeping with this translation, the named party against whom the defendant files his petition must be his actual custodian, i.e., the individual in charge of the prison or facility in which he is held, as opposed to a government entity or public officer. *See Rumsfeld v. Padilla*, 542 U.S. 426, 447 (2004).

11. W.S. Holdsworth, A History of English Law 97 (1903).

12. William Blackstone, 3 Commentaries 129–37.

13. U.S. Const. art. I, § 9, cl. 2.

14. 28 U.S.C. §§ 2241, 2254, 2255 (2006).

final judgments of lower state courts of competent jurisdiction. At the time when Blackstone composed his Commentaries celebrating the significance of the writ, habeas corpus was largely a remedy for extrajudicial imprisonment or detention without trial. That is to say, the "historical core" of the writ is tethered to the notion that non-judicial—i.e., executive or legislative—detentions warrant substantive review and oversight by a neutral judicial branch.[15] Given this history the most pressing question for the last century was whether federal review of state-authorized custody is a permissible application of the writ of habeas corpus.

If federal oversight is warranted, then to what extent and to what end? Are federal courts entitled to review the merits of state adjudications and order the release of state prisoners? *Frank v. Mangum* is an important starting point for understanding the current debate over the scope of federal habeas review. *Frank* is one of the earliest cases to expressly address the question of whether federal courts are permitted to exercise authority under the writ of habeas corpus to reverse a state conviction.

Frank v. Mangum

237 U.S. 309 (1915)

Statement by MR. JUSTICE PITNEY:

Leo M. Frank, the present appellant, being a prisoner in the custody of the sheriff in the jail of Fulton County, Georgia, presented to the district court of the United States for the northern district of Georgia his petition for a writ of habeas corpus under U. S. Rev. Stat. § 753, Comp. Stat. 1913, § 1281, upon the ground that he was in custody in violation of the Constitution of the United States, especially that clause of the 14th Amendment which declares that no state shall deprive any person of life, liberty, or property without due process of law. The district court, upon consideration of the petition and accompanying exhibits, deeming that, upon his own showing, petitioner was not entitled to the relief sought, refused to award the writ. Whether this refusal was erroneous is the matter to be determined upon the present appeal.

From the petition and exhibits it appears that in May, 1913, Frank was indicted by the grand jury of Fulton County for the murder of one Mary Phagan; he was arraigned before the superior court of that county, and, on August 25, 1913, after a trial lasting four weeks, in which he had the assistance of several attorneys, the jury returned a verdict of guilty. On the following day, the court rendered judgment, sentencing him to death, and remanding him, meanwhile, to the custody of the sheriff and jailer, the present appellee. * * *

* * *

Thereupon his application for a writ of habeas corpus was made to the district court, with the result already mentioned. The petition purports to set forth the criminal proceedings pursuant to which appellant is detained in custody, including the indictment, the trial and conviction, the motions, and the appeals above set forth. It contains a statement in narrative form of the alleged course of the trial, including allegations of disorder and manifestations of hostile sentiment in and about the court room, and states that Frank was absent at the time the verdict was rendered without his consent, pursuant to a suggestion from the trial judge to his counsel to the effect that there was probable danger of

15. *INS v. St. Cyr*, 533 U.S. 289, 301 (2001).

violence to Frank and to his counsel if he and they were present and there should be a verdict of acquittal or a disagreement of the jury; and that under these circumstances they consented (but without Frank's authority) that neither he nor they should be present at the rendition of the verdict. From the averments of the petition it appears that the same allegations were made the basis of the first motion for a new trial, and also for the motion of April 16, 1914, to set aside the verdict. * * *

MR. JUSTICE PITNEY, after making the foregoing statement, delivered the opinion of the court:

The points raised by the appellant may be reduced to the following:

(1) It is contended that the disorder in and about the court room during the trial and up to and at the reception of the verdict amounted to mob domination, that not only the jury, but the presiding judge, succumbed to it, and that this in effect wrought a dissolution of the court, so that the proceedings were *coram non judice.*

* * *

In dealing with these contentions, we should have in mind the nature and extent of the duty that is imposed upon a Federal court on application for the writ of habeas corpus under § 753, Rev. Stat. Comp. Stat. 1913, § 1281. Under the terms of that section, in order to entitle the present appellant to the relief sought, it must appear that he is held in custody in violation of the Constitution of the United States. Moreover, if he is held in custody by reason of his conviction upon a criminal charge before a court having plenary jurisdiction over the subject-matter or offense, the place where it was committed, and the person of the prisoner, it results from the nature of the writ itself that he cannot have relief on habeas corpus. Mere errors in point of law, however serious, committed by a criminal court in the exercise of its jurisdiction over a case properly subject to its cognizance, cannot be reviewed by habeas corpus. That writ cannot be employed as a substitute for the writ of error.

As to the 'due process of law' that is required by the 14th Amendment, it is perfectly well settled that a criminal prosecution in the courts of a state, based upon a law not in itself repugnant to the Federal Constitution, and conducted according to the settled course of judicial proceedings as established by the law of the state, so long as it includes notice and a hearing, or an opportunity to be heard, before a court of competent jurisdiction, according to established modes of procedure, is 'due process' in the constitutional sense.

It is therefore conceded by counsel for appellant that, in the present case, we may not review irregularities or erroneous rulings upon the trial, however serious, and that the writ of habeas corpus will lie only in case the judgment under which the prisoner is detained is shown to be absolutely void for want of jurisdiction in the court that pronounced it, either because such jurisdiction was absent at the beginning, or because it was lost in the course of the proceedings. And since no question is made respecting the original jurisdiction of the trial court, the contention is and must be that by the conditions that surrounded the trial, and the absence of defendant when the verdict was rendered, the court was deprived of jurisdiction to receive the verdict and pronounce the sentence.

But it would be clearly erroneous to confine the inquiry to the proceedings and judgment of the trial court. The laws of the state of Georgia (as will appear from decisions elsewhere cited) provide for an appeal in criminal cases to the supreme court of that state upon divers grounds, including such as those upon which it is here asserted that the trial court was lacking in jurisdiction. And while the 14th Amendment does not require that a state shall provide for an appellate review in criminal cases, it is perfectly obvious that where such an appeal is provided for, and the prisoner has had the benefit of it, the proceedings in the appellate tribunal are to be regarded as a part of the process of law under which he is held in custody by the state, and to be considered in determining any question of alleged deprivation of his life or liberty contrary to the 14th Amendment.

In fact, such questions as are here presented under the due process clause of the 14th Amendment, though sometimes discussed as if involving merely the jurisdiction of some court or other tribunal, in a larger and more accurate sense involve the power and authority of the state itself. The prohibition is addressed to the state; if it be violated, it makes no difference in a court of the United States by what agency of the state this is done; so, if a violation be threatened by one agency of the state, but prevented by another agency of higher authority, there is no violation by the state. It is for the state to determine what courts or other tribunals shall be established for the trial of offenses against its criminal laws, and to define their several jurisdictions and authority as between themselves. And the question whether a state is depriving a prisoner of his liberty without due process of law, where the offense for which he is prosecuted is based upon a law that does no violence to the Federal Constitution, cannot ordinarily be determined, with fairness to the state, until the conclusion of the course of justice in its courts.

It is indeed, settled by repeated decisions of this court that where it is made to appear to a court of the United States that an applicant for habeas corpus is in the custody of a state officer in the ordinary course of a criminal prosecution, under a law of the state not in itself repugnant to the Federal Constitution, the writ, in the absence of very special circumstances, ought not to be issued until the state prosecution has reached its conclusion, and not even then until the Federal questions arising upon the record have been brought before this court upon writ of error.

It follows as a logical consequence that where, as here, a criminal prosecution has proceeded through all the courts of the state, including the appellate as well as the trial court, the result of the appellate review cannot be ignored when afterwards the prisoner applies for his release on the ground of a deprivation of Federal rights sufficient to oust the state of its jurisdiction to proceed to judgment and execution against him. This is not a mere matter of comity, as seems to be supposed. The rule stands upon a much higher plane, for it arises out of the very nature and ground of the inquiry into the proceedings of the state tribunals, and touches closely upon the relations between the state and the Federal governments. * * * 'The forbearance which courts of co-ordinate jurisdiction, administered under a single system, exercise towards each other, whereby conflicts are avoided by avoiding interference with the process of each other, is a principle of comity, with perhaps no higher sanction than the utility which comes from concord; but between state courts and those of the United States, it is something more. It is a principle of right and of law, and therefore, of necessity.'

* * *

* * * [A] prisoner in custody pursuant to the final judgment of a state court of criminal jurisdiction may have a judicial inquiry in a court of the United States into the very truth and substance of the causes of his detention, although it may become necessary to look behind and beyond the record of his conviction to a sufficient extent to test the jurisdiction of the state court to proceed to judgment against him.

In the light, then, of these established rules and principles: that the due process of law guaranteed by the 14th Amendment has regard to substance of right, and not to matters of form or procedure; that it is open to the courts of the United States, upon an application for a writ of habeas corpus, to look beyond forms and inquire into the very substance of the matter, to the extent of deciding whether the prisoner has been deprived of his liberty without due process of law, and for this purpose to inquire into jurisdictional facts, whether they appear upon the record or not; that an investigation into the case of a prisoner held in custody by a state on conviction of a criminal offense must take into consideration the entire course of proceedings in the courts of the state, and not merely a single step in those proceedings; and that it is incumbent upon the prisoner to set forth in his application a sworn statement of the facts concerning his detention and by virtue of what claim or authority he is detained, we proceed to consider the questions presented.

1. And first, the question of the disorder and hostile sentiment that are said to have influenced the trial court and jury to an extent amounting to mob domination.

The district court having considered the case upon the face of the petition, we must do the same, treating it as if demurred to by the sheriff. There is no doubt of the jurisdiction to issue the writ of habeas corpus. The question is as to the propriety of issuing it in the present case. Under § 755, Rev. Stat. Comp. Stat. 1913, § 1283, it was the duty of the court to refuse the writ if it appeared from the petition itself that appellant was not entitled to it.

* * *

It is a fundamental principle of jurisprudence, arising from the very nature of courts of justice and the objects for which they are established, that a question of fact or of law distinctly put in issue and directly determined by a court of competent jurisdiction cannot afterwards be disputed between the same parties. * * *

* * * To do this, as we have already pointed out, would be not merely to disregard comity, but to ignore the essential question before us, which is not the guilt or innocence of the prisoner, or the truth of any particular fact asserted by him, but whether the state, taking into view the entire course of its procedure, has deprived him of due process of law. This familiar phrase does not mean that the operations of the state government shall be conducted without error or fault in any particular case, nor that the Federal courts may substitute their judgment for that of the state courts, or exercise any general review over their proceedings, but only that the fundamental rights of the prisoner shall not be taken from him arbitrarily or without the right to be heard according to the usual course of law in such cases.

We, of course, agree that if a trial is in fact dominated by a mob, so that the jury is intimidated and the trial judge yields, and so that there is an actual interference with the course of justice, there is, in that court, a departure from due process of law in the proper sense of that term. And if the state, supplying no corrective process, carries into execution a judgment of death or imprisonment based upon a verdict thus produced by mob domination, the state deprives the accused of his life or liberty without due process of law.

But the state may supply such corrective process as to it seems proper. Georgia has adopted the familiar procedure of a motion for a new trial, followed by an appeal to its supreme court, not confined to the mere record of conviction, but going at large, and upon evidence adduced outside of that record, into the question whether the processes of justice have been interfered with in the trial court. Repeated instances are reported of verdicts and judgments set aside and new trials granted for disorder or mob violence interfering with the prisoner's right to a fair trial.

Such an appeal was accorded to the prisoner in the present case, in a manner and under circumstances already stated, and the Supreme Court, upon a full review, decided appellant's allegations of fact, so far as matters now material are concerned, to be unfounded.

Owing to considerations already adverted to (arising not out of comity merely, but out of the very right of the matter to be decided, in view of the relations existing between the states and the Federal government), we hold that such a determination of the facts as was thus made by the court of last resort of Georgia respecting the alleged interference with the trial through disorder and manifestations of hostile sentiment cannot, in this collateral inquiry, be treated as a nullity, but must be taken as setting forth the truth of the matter; certainly until some reasonable ground is shown for an inference that the court which rendered it either was wanting in jurisdiction, or at least erred in the exercise of its jurisdiction; and that the mere assertion by the prisoner that the facts of the matter are other than the state court, upon full investigation, determined them to be, will not be deemed sufficient to raise an issue respecting the correctness of that determination; especially not, where the very evidence upon which the determination was rested is withheld by him who attacks the finding.

It is argued that if in fact there was disorder such as to cause a loss of jurisdiction in the trial court, jurisdiction could not be restored by any decision of the Supreme Court. This, we think, embodies more than one error of reasoning. It regards a part only of the judicial proceedings, instead of considering the entire process of law. It also begs the question of the existence of such disorder as to cause a loss of jurisdiction in the trial court, which should not be assumed, in the face of the decision of the reviewing court, without showing some adequate ground for disregarding that decision. And these errors grow out of the initial error of treating appellant's narrative of disorder as the whole matter, instead of reading it in connection with the context. The rule of law that in ordinary cases requires a prisoner to exhaust his remedies within the state before coming to the courts of the United States for redress would lose the greater part of its salutary force if the prisoner's mere allegations were to stand the same in law after as before the state courts had passed judgment upon them.

We are very far from intimating that manifestations of public sentiment, or any other form of disorder, calculated to influence court or jury, are matters to be lightly treated. The decisions of the Georgia courts in this and other cases show that such disorder is repressed, where practicable, by the direct intervention of the trial court and the officers under its command; and that other means familiar to the common-law practice, such as postponing the trial, changing the venue, and granting a new trial, are liberally resorted to in order to protect persons accused of crime in the right to a fair trial by an impartial jury. The argument for appellant amounts to saying that this is not enough; that by force of the 'due process of law' provision of the 14th Amendment, when the first attempt at a fair trial is rendered abortive through outside interference, the state, instead of allowing a new trial under better auspices, must abandon jurisdiction over the accused, and refrain from further inquiry into the question of his guilt.

To establish this doctrine would, in a very practical sense, impair the power of the states to repress and punish crime; for it would render their courts powerless to act in opposition to lawless public sentiment. The argument is not only unsound in principle, but is in conflict with the practice that prevails in all of the states, so far as we are aware. The cases cited do not sustain the contention that disorder or other lawless conduct calculated to overawe the jury or the trial judge can be treated as a dissolution of the court, or as rendering the proceedings *coram non judice*, in any such sense as to bar further proceedings. * * *

The Georgia courts, in the present case, proceeded upon the theory that Frank would have been entitled to this relief had his charges been true, and they refused a new trial only because they found his charges untrue save in a few minor particulars not amounting to more than irregularities, and not prejudicial to the accused. There was here no denial of due process of law.

* * *

4. To conclude: Taking appellant's petition as a whole, and not regarding any particular portion of it to the exclusion of the rest, dealing with its true and substantial meaning, and not merely with its superficial import, it shows that Frank, having been formally accused of a grave crime, was placed on trial before a court of competent jurisdiction, with a jury lawfully constituted; he had a public trial, deliberately conducted, with the benefit of counsel for his defense; he was found guilty and sentenced pursuant to the laws of the state; twice he has moved the trial court to grant a new trial, and once to set aside the verdict as a nullity; three times he has been heard upon appeal before the court of last resort of that state, and in every instance the adverse action of the trial court has been affirmed; his allegations of hostile public sentiment and disorder in and about the court room, improperly influencing the trial court and the jury against him, have been rejected because found untrue in point of fact upon evidence presumably justifying that finding, and which he has not produced in the present proceeding; his contention that his lawful rights were infringed because he was not permitted to be present when the jury rendered its verdict has been set aside because it was waived by his failure to raise the objection in due season when fully cognizant of the facts. In all of these proceedings the state, through its courts, has retained jurisdiction over him, has accorded to him the fullest right and opportunity to be heard according to the established modes of procedure, and now holds him in custody to pay the penalty of the crime of which he has been adjudged guilty. In our opinion, he is not shown to have been deprived of any right guaranteed to him by the 14th Amendment or any other provision of the Constitution or laws of the United States; on the contrary, he has been convicted, and is now held in custody, under 'due process of law' within the meaning of the Constitution.

The final order of the District Court, refusing the application for a writ of habeas corpus, is affirmed.

MR. JUSTICE HOLMES, dissenting:

Mr. JUSTICE HUGHES and I are of opinion that the judgment should be reversed. The only question before us is whether the petition shows on its face that the writ of habeas corpus should be denied, or whether the district court should have proceeded to try the facts. The allegations that appear to us material are these: The trial began on July 28, 1913, at Atlanta, and was carried on in a court packed with spectators and surrounded by a crowd outside, all strongly hostile to the petitioner. On Saturday, August 23, this hostility was sufficient to lead the judge to confer in the presence of the jury with the chief of police of Atlanta and the colonel of the Fifth Georgia Regiment, stationed in that city, both of whom were known to the jury. On the same day, the evidence seemingly having been closed, the public press, apprehending danger, united in a request to the court that the proceedings should not continue on that evening. Thereupon the court adjourned until Monday morning. On that morning, when the solicitor general entered the court, he was greeted with applause, stamping of feet and clapping of hands, and the judge, before beginning his charge, had a private conversation with the petitioner's counsel in which he expressed the opinion that there would be 'probable danger of violence' if there should be an acquittal or a disagreement, and that it would be safer for not only the petitioner but his counsel to be absent from court when the verdict was brought in. At the judge's request they agreed that the petitioner and they should be absent, and they kept their word. When the verdict was rendered, and before more than one of the jurymen had been polled, there was such a roar of applause that the polling could not go on until order was restored. The noise outside was such that it was difficult for the judge to hear the answers of the jurors, although he was only 10 feet from them. With these specifications of fact, the petitioner alleges that the trial was dominated by a hostile mob and was nothing but an empty form.

* * *

The argument for the appellee in substance is that the trial was in a court of competent jurisdiction, that it retains jurisdiction although, in fact, it may be dominated by a mob, and that the rulings of the state court as to the fact of such domination cannot be reviewed. But the argument seems to us inconclusive. Whatever disagreement there may be as to the scope of the phrase 'due process of law,' there can be no doubt that it embraces the fundamental conception of a fair trial, with opportunity to be heard. Mob law does not become due process of law by securing the assent of a terrorized jury. We are not speaking of mere disorder, or mere irregularities in procedure, but of a case where the processes of justice are actually subverted. In such a case, the Federal court has jurisdiction to issue the writ. The fact that the state court still has its general jurisdiction and is otherwise a competent court does not make it impossible to find that a jury has been subjected to intimidation in a particular case. The loss of jurisdiction is not general, but particular, and proceeds from the control of a hostile influence.

* * *

Notes

1. *Subsequent case history*

Frank was convicted of the murder of one of his factory workers, 13-year-old Mary Phagan. The case is widely regarded—now—as having been a miscarriage of justice. Frank, who was Jewish, became the focus of many conflicting cultural pressures, and the jury's conclusion represented, in part, class and regional resentment of educated Northern industrialists who were perceived to be wielding too much power in the South. The media sensationalized the trial. Shortly after Frank's conviction, new evidence emerged that cast doubt on his guilt, so the governor commuted his death sentence to life. But Frank was kidnapped from prison and lynched by a group of citizens who called themselves the Knights of Mary Phagan. The ringleaders included a former governor, a senator's son, a Methodist minister, a state legislator, and a former state Superior Court judge. In 1913, in response to Frank's conviction, the B'nai B'rith founded the Anti-Defamation League. Ultimately, in 1986, "[w]ithout attempting to address the question of guilt or innocence," Georgia granted Frank a pardon. *See* The New Georgia Encyclopedia, available at http://www.georgiaencyclopedia.org/nge/Article.jsp?id=h-906.

2. *Defense perspective*

From the prisoner's perspective, which would the prisoner rather have the court do, and why: Review the merits of the state court decision? Assess only whether the state court had jurisdiction? Something else altogether? Which is the *Frank* court doing?

(3) The Warren Era and the Habeas Trinity

In the wake of *Frank v. Mangum*, the dispositive inquiry regarding whether the prisoner was entitled to federal habeas relief was essentially procedural: Did the state court provide a process that, consistent with due process, was full and fair? As in *Frank*, federal review of the constitutional question was foreclosed when the state review was deemed sufficiently procedurally robust. For almost fifty years following *Frank*, the Court did not engage in any comprehensive reassessment of the scope of the writ. During Earl Warren's tenure as the Chief Justice of the Supreme Court, however, the procedural limitations on federal habeas review became significantly less important. The Warren Court, guided by visionaries like William Brennan, reframed the debate over the appropriate scope of federal habeas review.[1] Under Warren's leadership, the Court simultaneously expanded the scope of protections derived from the Bill of Rights and the availability of federal habeas review as a forum for vindicating the newly minted rights.

In what has been called the Habeas Trinity, the Warren Court handed down three landmark decisions that clarified the role of federal habeas corpus as an enforcement mechanism for the Bill of Rights: *Fay v. Noia*, 372 U.S. 391 (1963) (*see infra*, Chapter 8); *Townsend v. Sain*, 372 U.S. 293 (1963) (*see infra*, Chapter 11); and *Brown v. Allen* (below). To this day, litigation ensues as to the continued vitality of various aspects of these decisions. These cases often are regarded as the beginning of modern habeas corpus jurisprudence. They established a mechanism for vindicating federal rights that state courts previously had been unwilling or unable to enforce.[2]

Brown v. Allen

344 U.S. 443 (1953)

JUSTICE REED delivered the opinion of the Court

Certiorari was granted to review judgments of the United States Court of Appeals for the Fourth Circuit. These cases were argued last year. As the records raised serious federal constitutional questions upon which the carrying out of death sentences depended and procedural issues of importance in the relations between states and the federal government upon which there was disagreement in this Court, we decided to set the cases for reargument. 343 U.S. 973, 72 S.Ct. 1072, 96 L.Ed. 1366. We have now heard the cases again. [The case involved the consolidated appeals of several prisoners.]

* * *

II. Effect of Former Proceedings.

The effect to be given this Court's former refusal of certiorari in these cases was presented to the District Court which heard the applications for federal habeas corpus upon full records of the state proceedings in the trial and appellate courts. * * *

* * *

A. *Effect of Denial of Certiorari.* [Writing for a minority of the Court, Justice Reed expressed his view that lower federal courts should give consideration or deference to prior denials of *certiorari* for the same case.]

---

1. The authors of this book do not purport to resolve the longstanding conflict as to whether the Warren Court dramatically expanded or merely transformatively reinvigorated the Great Writ. Current litigation regarding the scope of federal habeas review continues the debate of whether Warren's vision of habeas corpus was coterminous with the constitutional grant of the privilege or whether the constitutional protections are actually much narrower than those recognized in the landmark habeas corpus cases from the 1960s.

2. *See, e.g., Gideon v. Wainright*, 372 U.S. 335 (1963) (applying for the first time the Sixth Amendment right to counsel to the states through federal habeas review of a state conviction).

* * *

B. *Effect of State Court Adjudications.* With the above statement of the position of the minority on the weight to be given our denial of certiorari, we turn to another question. The fact that no weight is to be given by the Federal District Court to our denial of certiorari should not be taken as an indication that similar treatment is to be accorded to the orders of the state courts. So far as weight to be given the proceedings in the courts of the state is concerned, a United States district court, with its familiarity with state practice is in a favorable position to recognize adequate state grounds in denials of relief by state courts without opinion. *A fortiori*, where the state action was based on an adequate state ground, no further examination is required, unless no state remedy for the deprivation of federal constitutional rights ever existed. Furthermore, where there is material conflict of fact in the transcripts of evidence as to deprivation of constitutional rights, the District Court may properly depend upon the state's resolution of the issue. In other circumstances the state adjudication carries the weight that federal practice gives to the conclusion of a court of last resort of another jurisdiction on federal constitutional issues. It is not *res judicata*.

Furthermore, in view of the consideration that was given by the District Court to our denial of certiorari in these cases, should we return them to that court for reexamination in the light of this Court's ruling upon the effect to be given to the denial? We think not. From the findings of fact and the judgments of the District Court we cannot see that such consideration as was given by that court to our denials of certiorari could have had any effect on its conclusions as to whether the respective defendants had been denied federal constitutional protection. It is true, under the Court's ruling today, that the District Court in each of the three cases erroneously gave consideration to our denial of certiorari. It is also true that its rulings, set out above, show that without that consideration, it found from its examination of the state records and new evidence presented that the conduct of the respective state proceedings was in full accord with due process. Such conclusions make immaterial the fact that the trial court gave consideration to our denial of certiorari.

The District Court and the Court of Appeals recognized the power of the District Court to reexamine federal constitutional issues even after trial and review by a state and refusal of certiorari in this Court. The intimation to the contrary in *Speller v. Allen* must be read as the Court's opinion after the hearing. "In the review of judicial proceedings the rule is settled that, if the decision below is correct, it must be affirmed, although the lower court relied upon a wrong ground or gave a wrong reason." Certainly the consideration given by the District Court to our former refusals of certiorari on the issues presented cannot affect its determinations that there was no merit in any of the applications for habeas corpus. Where it is made to appear affirmatively, as here, that the alleged error could not affect the result, such errors may be disregarded even in the review of criminal trials. Whether we affirm or reverse in these cases, therefore, does not depend upon the trial court‘s consideration of our denial of certiorari but upon the soundness of its decisions upon the issues of alleged violation of federal procedural requirements or of petitioner's constitutional rights by the North Carolina proceedings. We now take up those problems.

* * *

IV. Disposition of Constitutional Issues.

Next we direct our attention to the records which were before the District Court in order to review that court's conclusions that North Carolina accorded petitioners a fair adjudication of their federal questions. Questions of discrimination and admission of coerced confessions lie in the compass of the Due Process and Equal Protection Clauses of the Fourteenth Amendment. Have petitioners received hearings consonant with standards accepted by this Nation as adequate to justify their convictions?

[The Court proceeds to discuss and ultimately agree with the district court's denial of the writ based on unconstitutional exclusions of black jurors from juries in *Brown v. Allen*. The Court then examines and agrees with the district court's rejection of Brown's claim of unconstitutional use of a coerced confession. Next, the Court turns to *Speller v. Allen* and affirms the district court's rejection of Speller's claim of unconstitutional exclusion of black jurors.]

* * *

This situation confronts us. North Carolina furnished a criminal court for the trial of those charged with crime. Petitioners at all times had counsel, chosen by themselves and recognized by North Carolina as competent to conduct the defense. In that court all petitioners' objections and proposals, whether of jury discrimination, admission of confessions, instructions or otherwise, were heard and decided against petitioners. The state furnished an adequate and easily-complied-with method of appeal. This included a means to serve the statement of the case on appeal in the absence of the prosecutor from his office. Yet petitioners' appeal was not taken and the State of North Carolina, although the full trial record and statement on appeal were before it, refused to consider the appeal on its merits.

The writ of habeas corpus in federal courts is not authorized for state prisoners at the discretion of the federal court. It is only authorized when a state prisoner is in custody in violation of the Constitution of the United States. That fact is not to be tested by the use of habeas corpus in lieu of an appeal. To allow habeas corpus in such circumstances would subvert the entire system of state criminal justice and destroy state energy in the detection and punishment of crime.

Of course, federal habeas corpus is allowed where time has expired without appeal when the prisoner is detained without opportunity to appeal because of lack of counsel, incapacity, or some interference by officials. Also, this Court will review state habeas corpus proceedings even though no appeal was taken, if the state treated habeas corpus as permissible. Federal habeas corpus is available following our refusal to review such state habeas corpus proceedings. Failure to appeal is much like a failure to raise a known and existing question of unconstitutional proceeding or action prior to conviction or commitment. Such failure, of course, bars subsequent objection to conviction on those grounds.

North Carolina has applied its law in refusing this out-of-time review. This Court applies its jurisdictional statute in the same manner. We cannot say that North Carolina's action in refusing review after failure to perfect the case on appeal violates the Federal Constitution. A period of limitation accords with our conception of proper procedure.

Finally, federal courts may not grant habeas corpus for those convicted by the state except pursuant to § 2254. We have interpreted § 2254 as not requiring repetitious applications to state courts for collateral relief, but clearly the state's procedure for relief must be employed in order to avoid the use of federal habeas corpus as a matter of procedural routine to review state criminal rulings. A failure to use a state's available remedy, in the absence of some interference or incapacity, bars federal habeas corpus. The statute requires that the applicant exhaust available state remedies. To show that the time has passed for appeal is not enough to empower the Federal District Court to issue the writ. The judgments must be affirmed.

* * *

JUSTICE BLACK, with whom JUSTICE DOUGLAS concurs, dissenting.

The four petitioners in these cases are under sentences of death imposed by North Carolina state courts. All are Negroes. Brown and Speller were convicted of raping white women; the two Daniels, aged 17 when arrested, were convicted of murdering a white man. The State Supreme Court affirmed and we denied certiorari in all the cases. These are habeas corpus proceedings which challenge the validity of the convictions.

I agree with the Court that the District Court had habeas corpus jurisdiction in all the cases including power to release either or all of the prisoners if held as a result of violation of constitutional rights. This I understand to be a reaffirmance of the principle embodied in *Moore v. Dempsey*. I also agree that in the exercise of this jurisdiction the District Court had power to hear and consider all relevant facts bearing on the constitutional contentions asserted in these cases. I disagree with the Court's conclusion that petitioners failed to establish those contentions. * * *

* * *

I read *Moore v. Dempsey, supra*, as standing for the principle that it is never too late for courts in habeas corpus proceedings to look straight through procedural screens in order to prevent forfeiture of life or liberty in flagrant defiance of the Constitution. Perhaps there is no more exalted judicial function. I am willing to agree that it should not be exercised in cases like these except under special circumstances or in extraordinary situations. But I cannot join in any opinion that attempts to confine the Great Writ within rigid formalistic boundaries.

Notes

1. *Subsequent case history*

Clyde Brown and Raleigh Speller were both executed in North Carolina on May 29, 1953. Bennie Daniels and Lloyd Ray Daniels were both executed in North Carolina on November 6, 1953.

2. *The standard of review*

Brown v. Allen is considered a seminal case in announcing the standard of review that federal courts apply when reviewing state convictions. Does Justice Reed's majority opinion dictate a standard of review? Is the standard of review the same for questions of law as for questions of fact? What is the practical effect of the standard of review in federal habeas cases?

3. *Supremacy of the Constitution*

Under *Brown v. Allen*, what role do federal courts play in ensuring that the Bill of Rights is uniformly applied? Is this exercise of judicial authority consistent with federalism and separation of powers concerns?

4. *Dissent*

What does the dissent mean when it writes that it is "never too late for courts in habeas corpus proceedings to look straight through procedural screens..."?

(4) The Anti-Warren Counter-Revolution

The *Brown v. Allen* decision and its progeny are among the cases credited with spurring the anti-Warren, or Federalist, counter-revolution. The first indications of change came from scholarly articles and academic debates. Political outcry, calls for reform, appointments to the federal judiciary and decisions of the judiciary followed suit.[1] As one commentator has summarized the post-Warren context:

> Richard M. Nixon relentlessly attacked the Court's criminal procedure decisions during his 1968 campaign for president and pledged to appoint Justices who would not "handcuff" the police. Nixon was swept into the White House, and he and his Republican successors named the next eleven Justices to the Supreme Court, including Warren E. Burger (to replace Warren) and William H. Rehnquist (to replace Burger) as Chief Justices in 1969 and 1986 respectively. Over the next three decades, the Burger and Rehnquist Courts fundamentally reworked constitutional criminal procedure.[2]

As expected, the Burger and Rehnquist Courts imposed significant hurdles to the efforts by state prisoners to secure federal habeas corpus review. Some of these cases are discussed elsewhere in the book. However, in assessing the forces that motivated fundamental change in the modern habeas landscape, the work of Professor Paul Bator should be carefully considered. Professor Bator's influential article, *Finality in Criminal Law and Federal Habeas Corpus for State Prisoners*, has shaped the Court's debate over habeas rights and has framed the legislative debate over the scope and importance of federal habeas review. Bator challenged the analytic underpinnings of cases like *Brown v. Allen* and called for their reversals. Since its publication in 1963, the Article has assumed a foundational role in the habeas debate. Scholars, judges, and members of Congress often refer to the article, either attacking or defending the paper's central propositions depending on their own views of the proper scope of federal habeas review. Although published almost a half-century ago, the article continues to play an important role in the development of and debate over modern habeas law.

Finality in Criminal Law and Federal Habeas Corpus for State Prisoners

Paul M. Bator

76 Harvard Law Review 441 (1963)

* * *

The problem of finality in criminal law raises acute tensions in our society. This should not, of course, occasion surprise. For the processes of the criminal law are, after all, purposefully and designedly awful. Through them society purports to bring citizens to the bar of judgment for condemnation, and those condemned become for that reason subject to governmental power exercised in its acutest forms: loss of property, of liberty, even life. No wonder that our instinct is that we must be sure before we proceed to the end, that we will not write an irrevocable finis on the page until we are somehow truly satisfied that justice has been done.

* * *

1. *See generally* William J. Stuntz, *The Uneasy Relationship Between Criminal Procedure and Criminal Justice*, 107 YALE L.J. 1, 3–4, n.1 (1997); Carol Steiker, *Counter-Revolution in Constitutional Criminal Procedure? Two Audiences, Two Answers*, 94 MICH. L. REV. 2466, 2466–67 n.5 (1996).

2. Stephen F. Smith, *Activism as Restraint: Lessons from Criminal Procedure*, 80 TEX. L. REV. 1057, 1060 (2002).

It is thus not surprising to find that turbulence surrounds the doctrines of the criminal law which determine when, if ever, a judgment of conviction assumes finality. One of the areas of acutest controversy, namely, the proper reach of the federal habeas corpus jurisdiction for state prisoners, is the subject of this essay. The problems created by this jurisdiction are peculiarly difficult because underlying dilemmas with respect to finality in criminal cases are here compounded by the complex demands of a federal system with its two sets of courts applying law derived from two sovereignties. Imbedded in this often murky and technical field of law are fundamental problems about justice: what processes and institutions in a federal system can best assure that the exercise of the powers invoked by a judgment of conviction will be based on premises acceptable politically and morally? When has justice been done?

The ultimate issue I propose to treat is this: under what circumstances should a federal district court on habeas corpus have the power to redetermine the merits of federal questions decided by the state courts in the course of state criminal cases?

Let us briefly review the structure within which this problem arises. A defendant is tried in a state court for an offense against state law. A variety of federal questions may arise in the course of the litigation; thus the accused may claim that the federal constitution precludes the state from introducing a confession which, he alleges, was forcibly extracted from him. It is, of course, the duty of the state court conscientiously to decide this federal question in accordance with the governing federal law, which the command of the supremacy clause makes applicable to the case. Let us assume that the state court does so: its decision will turn on findings of fact as to what phenomena existed or occurred bearing on the making of the confession, and on the application of federal legal standards to these facts. Alleged error in the disposition of the federal question may be and is, I further assume, properly raised for appellate review in the state system. On affirmance, the federal issue is subject to direct review by the United States Supreme Court, usually on certiorari, sometimes on appeal. In case of affirmance by that Court or a denial of the writ, the judgment, in the normal operations of the legal system, becomes final and binding. Should then a federal district court, in the face of such a judgment, have jurisdiction in a collateral habeas corpus proceeding to redetermine the federal question which the state court has already decided and which the Supreme Court has had an opportunity to review? The law today seems squarely to answer "yes"; the reigning principle is the striking one that a state prisoner may seek and automatically obtain federal district court collateral review of the merits of all federal (at least constitutional) questions, no matter how fully and fairly these have been litigated in the state-court system.

One word of reservation: I assume, in this article, that the defendant in the state case has not forfeited his right to litigate his federal claim by procedural default; in other words, I do not propose to deal with the vexing question whether a state prisoner who fails to raise his federal contentions in accordance with state procedural law loses his right to raise them on federal habeas corpus.

I. SOME GENERAL CONSIDERATIONS

A. Finality in Criminal Litigation

The federal writ of habeas corpus has its roots in the common law. * * * Its function, in the great phrase, is to test "the legality of the detention of one in the custody of another." * * * In our constitutional context this refers, of course, to detentions made illegal by federal law. Power to issue the writ is conferred, and this limitation made explicit, in section 2241 of the Judicial Code.

* * *

When is a state prisoner held in "violation" of federal law? I suppose that the answer that may first suggest itself is that one is held in violation of federal law whenever the state courts have erroneously decided a federal question bearing dispositively on the judgment authorizing the detention. And if this is the case, the proper reach of the jurisdiction can be tersely summarized: the writ should test the merits of every dispositive federal question in the case.

I do not claim that such a *result* is necessarily unsound. The conclusion that a federal court should, at some point, have the power to decide the merits of all federal constitutional questions arising in state criminal proceedings (with a habeas court doing so if the Supreme Court has failed to review the issue) may be a sound one, resting on the specific institutional and political premises of our constitutional federalism. The fourteenth amendment does, after all, direct supervening commands to the states in the management of their criminal law; the Constitution does not accept the state process as "complete." The creation of a remedial framework to ensure effective implementation of these commands is, therefore, one of the important tasks of our system. It is the purpose of the main body of this essay to analyze habeas corpus in terms of this task, to weigh the strength of the claim that federal rights should be tested by federal courts.

In these introductory pages, however, I want to ignore the special demands for a specifically federal forum to which habeas corpus may be responsive, and direct my attention more generally to the problem of finality as it bears on the great task of creating rational institutional schemes for the administration of the criminal law. More particularly, consider some of the general premises which may underlie the demand for relitigation of constitutional questions on habeas corpus. The fundamental assumption often seems to be a generalized version of the notion adverted to above: a prisoner is obviously held in violation of law if the decision to detain was "wrong." It would follow that a detention may not be considered lawful unless the proceedings leading to it were, in some ultimate sense, free of error, unless the facts as found were "really" true and the law "really" correctly applied. If a tribunal finds that the prisoner was not whipped in order to procure a confession, but, in fact, he actually was whipped, he is detained illegally. If the court determines that on the facts as found the confession was admissible, but the "correct" view of the law is that such a confession is not admissible, he is detained illegally. Underlying all the processes is the ultimate reality that he was wrongly condemned. And thus to determine the legality of the detention one must, evidently, determine whether the committing tribunal fell into error.

What must be noted, however, is that on this underlying premise the conclusion is inescapable that no detention can ever be finally determined to be lawful; for if legality turns on "actual" freedom from errors of either fact or law, whenever error is alleged the court passing on legality will necessarily have to satisfy itself by determining the merits whether in fact error occurred. After all, there is no ultimate guarantee that *any* tribunal arrived at the correct result; the conclusions of a habeas corpus court, or of any number of habeas corpus courts, that the facts were X and that on X facts Y law applies are not infallible; if the existence *vel non* of mistake determines the lawfulness of the judgment, there can be no escape from a literally endless relitigation of the merits because the possibility of mistake always exists.

In fact, doesn't the dilemma go deeper? As Professor Jaffe has taught us, if the lawfulness of the exercise of the power to detain turns on whether the facts which validate its exercise "actually" happened in some ultimate sense, power can never be exercised lawfully at all, because we can never absolutely recreate past phenomena and thus can never have final certainty as to their existence:

A court cannot any more than any other human agency break down the barrier between appearance and reality. In short, the court can be wrong.

* * *

* * * [I]f a criminal judgment is ever to be final, the notion of legality must at some point include the assignment of final competences to determine legality. But, it may be asked, why should we seek a point at which such a judgment becomes final? Conceding that no process can assure ultimate truth, will not repetition of inquiry stand a better chance of approximating it? In view of the awesomeness of the consequences of conviction, shouldn't we allow redetermination of the merits in an attempt to make sure that no error has occurred?

Surely the answer runs, in the first place, in terms of conservation of resources—and I mean not only simple economic resources, but all of the intellectual, moral, and political resources involved in the legal system. The presumption must be, it seems to me, that if a job can be well done once, it should not be done twice. * * *

Mere iteration of process can do other kinds of damage. I could imagine nothing more subversive of a judge's sense of responsibility, of the inner subjective conscientiousness which is so essential a part of the difficult and subtle art of judging well, than an indiscriminate acceptance of the notion that all the shots will always be called by someone else. Of course this does not mean that we should not have appeals. As we shall see, important functional and ethical purposes are served by allowing recourse to an appellate court in a unitary system, and to a federal supreme court in a federal system. The acute question is the effect it will have on a trial judge if we then allow still further recourse where these purposes may no longer be relevant. What seems so objectionable is second-guessing merely for the sake of second-guessing, in the service of the illusory notion that if we only try hard enough we will find the "truth."

Another point, too, should be remembered. The procedural arrangements we create for the adjudication of criminal guilt have an important bearing on the effectiveness of the substantive commands of the criminal law. I suggest that finality may be a crucial element of this effectiveness. Surely it is essential to the educational and deterrent functions of the criminal law that we be able to say that one violating that law will swiftly and certainly become subject to punishment, just punishment. Yet this threat may be undermined if at the same time we so define the processes leading to just punishment that it can really never be finally imposed at all. A procedural system which permits an endless repetition of inquiry into facts and law in a vain search for ultimate certitude implies a lack of confidence about the possibilities of justice that cannot but war with the effectiveness of the underlying substantive commands. Furthermore, we should at least tentatively inquire whether an endless reopening of convictions, with its continuing underlying implication that perhaps the defendant can escape from corrective sanctions after all, can be consistent with the aim of rehabilitating offenders. The first step in achieving that aim may be a realization by the convict that he is justly subject to sanction, that he stands in need of rehabilitation; and a process of reeducation cannot, perhaps, even begin if we make sure that the cardinal moral predicate is missing, if society itself continuously tells the convict that he may not be justly subject to reeducation and treatment in the first place. The idea of just condemnation lies at the heart of the criminal law, and we should not lightly create processes which implicitly belie its possibility.

One further point should be made in this canvass of the general policies which support doctrines of finality in the criminal law. It is a point difficult to formulate because so easily twisted into an expression of mere complacency. Repose is a psychological necessity in a secure and active society, and it should be one of the aims—though, let me make explicit, not the sole aim—of a procedural system to devise doctrines which, in the end, do give us repose, do embody the judgment that we have tried hard enough and thus may take it that justice has been done. There comes a point where a procedural system which leaves matters perpetually open no longer reflects humane concern but merely anxiety and a desire for immobility. Somehow, somewhere, we must accept the fact that human institutions are short of infallible; there is reason for a policy which leaves well enough alone and which channels our limited resources of concern toward more productive ends. I want to be careful to stress that I do not counsel a smug acceptance of injustice merely because it is disturbing to worry whether injustice has been done. What I do seek is a general procedural system which does not cater to a perpetual and unreasoned anxiety that there is a possibility that error has been made in every criminal case in the legal system.

B. Limitations on the Policies of Finality

I am aware that my argument may seem to go too far. Nobody contends, and I would not do so either, that the legal system would be better served if all courts of original jurisdiction had final competence to decide all cases. The possibilities of error, oversight, arbitrariness and even venality in any human institution are such that subjecting decisions to review of some kind answers a felt need: it would simply go against the grain, today, to make a matter as sensitive as a criminal conviction subject to unchecked determination by a single institution.

* * *

Let me repeat, then, that the point is not that no court should review any other court. Nor do I suggest at this stage that a federal habeas corpus court should not review the merits of all federal questions litigated in the state court, that valid justifications, rooted in our federalism, of such a jurisdiction may not be forthcoming. All I say is that it is not enough to validate the jurisdiction to assert that some error of fact or law as to the federal question may in fact occur in a state litigation. The point can be put in terms of a limiting (rather than defining) principle: if one set of institutions has been granted the task of finding the facts and applying the law and does so in a manner rationally adapted to the task, in the absence of institutional or functional reasons to the contrary we should accept a presumption against mere repetition of the process on the alleged ground that, after all, error could have occurred.

I should like now to set forth certain limiting principles at the other extreme: general categories where it seems to me plain that the first go-around, whether in a unitary or a federal system, should not count, and where relitigation serves obvious and appropriate ends.

1. *Failure of Process.*—The first category has been implicit throughout the discussion. I have said that, presumptively, a process fairly and rationally adapted to the task of finding the facts and applying the law should not be repeated. This suggests that it is always an appropriate inquiry whether previous process was meaningful process, that is, whether the conditions and tools of inquiry were such as to assure a reasoned probability that the facts were correctly found and the law correctly applied. At the very least if no opportunity at all was provided to litigate a question which the applicable law makes relevant to the disposition of the case, it is just and useful to have a subsequent "supervisory" jurisdiction, as it were, to furnish such an opportunity. Similarly, if the conditions under which

a question was litigated were not fairly and rationally adapted for the reaching of a correct solution of any issue of fact or law, there would seem to be no reason of principle to immunize the solution reached; that issue should be redetermined. Suppose that well-supported allegations are made on collateral attack that the trial judge in a criminal trial was bribed to convict (and that the prisoner did not discover this until the time for appeal had expired). The appropriateness of exercising a collateral jurisdiction would seem beyond question: a "trial" under such circumstances is not a rational method of inquiry into questions of fact or law, and no reason exists to respect its conclusions. The same would be true of a case where a mob is alleged to have dominated the trial court and jury, and no remedy was provided on appeal to test this allegation itself. Again, suppose a prisoner alleges that he was, through torture, forced to plead guilty. Such a finding of "guilt" manifestly should not "count" as a full and fair litigation which forecloses further inquiry; and, if no remedy exists by appeal (as it would not if the coercion was "successful" enough), it is plainly appropriate to test it on collateral attack.

What binds these cases together is that in all of them the inquiry is, initially directed, not at the question whether substantive error of fact or law occurred, but at whether the processes previously employed for determination of questions of fact and law were fairly and rationally adapted to that task. * * *

* * *

We must therefore be wary before assuming too easily that the absence of state process should be cured by using the federal habeas jurisdiction as a backstop, as it were, rather than exercising a more direct control by an affirmative command that the state may not imprison the defendant without itself providing such process. What we have is a question, to be answered in light of the political, institutional and functional considerations, as to which route we should take.

One more caution should be added. Even if we conclude that we should have a federal collateral jurisdiction to test the integrity of previous state proceedings, this does not mean that such a jurisdiction should assume the precise form which has been associated traditionally with the writ of habeas corpus. Most significantly, we should be aware that the policies we have been discussing do not support the notion that federal collateral attack should be available without limit of time. The fact that a forum is called for to test an allegation of coercion of a guilty plea or prosecution perjury does not tell us that a prisoner should be free to wait to raise these at his pleasure. The policies of finality and repose must surely play a role even when there has been failure of process, though the role may be the more limited one of placing on the prisoner the obligation to make his allegations within a reasonable time after they have become available to him.

2. *Failure of Jurisdiction.*—The second category which furnishes appropriate limitation on notions of finality in the criminal law is the most traditional one of all, involving the concept, so vexing and difficult on its edges, yet so useful at the core, of "jurisdiction." It is black-letter in civil as well as criminal law that the judgment of a court without at least colorable jurisdiction or competence to deal with the issue it is purporting to decide enjoys no immunity from collateral attack. The reason must be plain: it is not that the decision may be erroneous, but that allowing it to "count" would violate the political rules allocating institutional competences to deal with various matters. * * *

* * *

Let me now summarize my conclusions. It has not been my purpose to set up hard and fast touchstones for the habeas corpus jurisdiction. More particularly let me again warn the reader explicitly that what has gone before does not purport to be an analysis of the possible roles which such a jurisdiction can play in a constitutional federalism. It may be entirely justified and appropriate that the question whether a defendant has been deprived of federal constitutional rights should always be decided by a federal constitutional court. That is the question which I will treat in detail in the latter parts of this essay. What I have tried to do so far is simply to canvass some of the underlying general problems of finality, without reference to the special institutional and functional claims of federalism, and to establish a set of limiting notions. In these terms, then, I see the need for a tentative presumption that questions fairly and fully canvassed by institutions with general competence to deal with such questions and making use of processes fairly and rationally adapted to the function of deciding them should not be relitigated *unless* felt functional or institutional requirements call for the repetition. On the other hand, as the proposition implies, subsequent jurisdictions should be free to ignore decisions previously made by institutions without colorable competence in the premises; and should in any event be free to direct inquiry into the question whether the totality of previous proceedings furnished the defendant with a full and fair opportunity to litigate his case.

With this general introduction I turn now to a study of the law of federal habeas corpus itself. The next section of this article describes and analyzes the development of the jurisdiction up to the decision in *Brown v. Allen*, which explicitly enthroned the principle that all federal constitutional questions decided in state criminal cases may be redetermined on the merits on federal habeas corpus. The remainder of the article is then devoted to an analysis of the doctrine of that case.

[Section II, wherein Professor Bator discusses the history and body of law pertaining to habeas, is omitted.]

III. *BROWN V. ALLEN* AND ITS JUSTIFICATIONS

A. The Decision and Its Problems

Brown v. Allen reached the Supreme Court in the 1951 Term and was decided in 1953. It involved three proceedings: Brown's, Speller's, and Daniels'; only the first two need concern us here. Brown was convicted of rape by a North Carolina court and sentenced to death. In his appeal to the state supreme court he claimed his conviction violated the federal constitution because of the admission of a coerced confession and racial discrimination in the selection of grand and petit juries. These issues had been fully litigated, with the aid of counsel, in the trial court through procedures not themselves alleged to have been in any way unfair. The state supreme court affirmed the conviction, rejecting the defendant's federal contentions on the merits in a reasoned opinion. Certiorari was denied. The prisoner then sought federal habeas corpus. The district court denied the writ without holding a hearing, and the court of appeals affirmed.

Speller, also a capital case, likewise involved a claim of racial discrimination in jury selections which had been fully litigated in the state system. (Indeed, the state courts had twice previously reversed Speller's convictions, first on the ground that such discrimination was shown, and then after retrial because his counsel had not been furnished adequate opportunity to test the question; this was, therefore, Speller's third trial.) The state supreme court rejected the allegation on the merits, and certiorari was denied. Now Speller, too, sought habeas. The district court took testimony on the discrimination issue in addition to considering the state record, and denied the writ. Again, the court of appeals affirmed.

The Supreme Court granted certiorari in both cases and affirmed the convictions. It did so, however, not on the basis of *Frank v. Mangum*, that the state had provided adequate corrective process, but by reaching and rejecting on the merits the federal claims presented which had been previously adjudicated by the state courts. The Court did so without any explicit discussion of the question of jurisdiction or any apparent understanding of how radical this step was: with only Mr. Justice Jackson disagreeing, eight of nine Justices assumed that on habeas corpus federal district courts must provide review of the merits of constitutional claims fully litigated in the state-court system. As Professor Hart says, the decision thus "manifestly broke new ground." It seems to say,

> that due process of law in the case of state prisoners is not primarily concerned with the adequacy of the state's corrective process or of the prisoner's personal opportunity to avail himself of this process ... but relates essentially to the avoidance in the end of any underlying constitutional error....

And ever since *Brown v. Allen* the Supreme Court has continued to assume, without discussion, that it is the purpose of the federal habeas corpus jurisdiction to redetermine the merits of federal constitutional questions decided in state criminal proceedings.

What is the basis of *Brown v. Allen*? The opinions do not cast much light on that question. Mr. Justice Frankfurter, in one of the two opinions of the Court in the case, repeatedly asserts, without discussion, that the act of 1867 compels the conclusion that state consideration "cannot foreclose" federal determination of the merits of constitutional claims; he says that as to all legal issues (such as the admissibility of a confession) the district judge "must" exercise his own judgment, that Congress has "seen fit" to "give to the lower federal courts power to inquire into federal claims, by way of habeas corpus," and that it would be "inadmissible to deny the use of the writ merely because a State court has passed on a federal constitutional issue." But these are mere statements of conclusion; they ignore completely that such a purpose cannot be derived automatically from either the language or history of the 1867 act, and that the act was not so understood in the first eighty years of its history; they ignore, too, the explicit ruling in *In re Wood* that at least the question of jury discrimination in violation of the Constitution is not a question open on collateral attack if opportunity to litigate it was afforded in the state system and on direct review.

Oddly enough, much of the discussion in the two majority opinions in *Brown* deals not with the question why a state's adjudication of the law should be disregarded, but why the state's adjudication of the facts should not necessarily be disregarded. Mr. Justice Reed states that no new hearing as to the facts is necessary if the district court is satisfied that the state process has given them "fair consideration" and resulted in a "satisfactory conclusion," if no "unusual circumstances" are present and the record "affords an adequate opportunity" to test the merits of the claim. The taking of new evidence by the district court is "in its discretion." Mr. Justice Frankfurter says that as to the facts, the state's conclusions "may" be accepted by the district judge "unless a vital flaw be found in the process of ascertaining such facts." These ambiguous formulations have created vexing problems as to the scope of review on habeas corpus which I need not canvass here. I do suggest, however, that the basic reason why the courts have had such difficulties in defining the scope of review on habeas is that the Court in *Brown* did not provide a principled rationalization of the purpose being served by affording the federal court the right to review the determination of the state court in the first instance. If it is the purpose of the habeas jurisdiction to assure that no error has been made, then there is no reason why the state courts' determinations of fact should be any more sacred than their conclusions of law. In view of the function of appellate courts to make pronouncements of law, it is manifestly sensible to restrict their review to issues of law. But district court jurisdiction on habeas certainly does not serve that purpose; and if the purpose is to assure "correct" determinations, that purpose should not be disregarded when the allegation is that the state court has erred in finding the facts bearing on a constitutional claim. On the other hand, if meaningful process serves as an adequate guarantee of the probability of the correctness of factfindings, we are entitled to some explanation why it does not satisfy us with respect to legal conclusions.

There is another aspect of this question which should be noticed. The Court in *Brown* made much of the notion that the integrity of a state's process with respect to factfinding should be respected. But it made clear that this is solely a matter of discretion, that the district judge may redetermine the facts even where there is no "unusual circumstance" or "vital flaw" which casts doubt on the adequacy of those findings; and the Court went out of its way to reaffirm this grant of discretion a few years later. But if the federal judge has an impeccable record before him, that is, he has no reason to believe that the factfinding processes of the state courts were in any way inadequate to the task at hand, on what principle should he decide whether to exercise such a discretion? Note that if he does exercise it, he would seem to be completely free to disregard the state-court findings even though the issue may turn on an assessment of the veracity of witnesses; in such a case we have the startling result that a state prisoner is deemed to be held in violation of the Constitution of the United States because a state judge believed the prosecution's witnesses and the federal judge believes those of the defendant.

Nor do the opinions in *Brown v. Allen* deal adequately with the grave problems of federalism created by the doctrine of that case. It is fashionable today to dismiss the resentments created in the states by the existence of an indiscriminate federal habeas jurisdiction; we are told that complaints about intrusion by federal habeas courts into state criminal processes are disingenuous, directed not at the remedy but at the substantive due process doctrines enforced thereby; we are further assured that such complaints are in any event beside the mark since very few prisoners are actually released by the federal courts. But the very unanimity of the resentment among state law-enforcement officials and judges, many of them, surely, as conscientious in their adherence to the Constitution and as intellectually honest as their critics, counsels, not against the jurisdiction, but against its indiscriminate expansion without principled justification. Note further that it was not state officials but the Judicial Conference of the United States, headed by Chief Justice Warren, which in 1955 adopted a report of a committee consisting of Circuit Judges Parker, Phillips and Stephens and District Judges Hooper, Vaught and Wyzanski, which stated that the expansion of the habeas jurisdiction has:

> greatly interfered with the procedure of the State courts, delaying in many cases the proper enforcement of their judgments. Where adequate procedure is provided by State law for the handling of such matters, it is clear that the remedy should be sought in the State courts with any review ... only by the Supreme Court....

and recommended, *inter alia*, statutory preclusion of the writ where a federal question was "raised and determined" in the state-court system.

The point is not that it is unseemly for a federal district judge to reverse the action of the highest court of the state, but that it is unseemly for him to do so without principled institutional justification for his power. This justification was simply not provided by the opinions in *Brown v. Allen*. * * *

* * *

B. The Right to a Federal Forum

* * *

In fact the result of the rather wooden differentiation we now make between constitutional and nonconstitutional questions is not without its ironies. Why is it, for instance, that we go so far to allow relitigation of constitutional questions (even where the particular issue is closely balanced and technical) and yet do not allow any relitigation of the fundamental question of the factual guilt or innocence of the accused? If a state prisoner claims that he confessed after he was interrogated for six hours, not (as the state court found) for four, the law says he may relitigate the issue and, perhaps, gain release as a consequence, even though the evidence of guilt may be overwhelming. But if a defendant is convicted of murder and ten years later another person confesses to the crime, so that we can be absolutely certain that the defendant was innocent all the time, the law says that he must rely on executive clemency. Why? Why should we pay so little attention to finality with respect to constitutional questions when, in general, the law is so unbending with respect to other questions which, nevertheless, may bear as crucially on justice as any constitutional issue in the case?

In any event, even if we assume that issues bearing on constitutional rights are necessarily "important," this does not automatically validate the claim to a federal forum. Why should a federal court hear cases even if they do involve these important rights? The answer is, of course, clear where state courts will not—and are not compelled to—hear them at all or under fair circumstances. But what if a state court has done so? Is there any sense in which the federal courts will, in the abstract, be more "correct" with respect to issues of federal law than state courts? Surely not. There is no intrinsic reason why the fact that a man is a federal judge should make him more competent, or conscientious, or learned with respect to the applicable federal law than his neighbor in the state courthouse. The federal judge is more "correct" under the present system only because our institutional arrangements make him authoritative. As Justice Jackson pointed out about the Supreme Court itself:

> [R]eversal by a higher court is not proof that justice is thereby better done. There is no doubt that if there were a super-Supreme Court, a substantial proportion of our reversals of state courts would also be reversed. We are not final because we are infallible, but we are infallible only because we are final.

* * *

I do not wish to overstate the argument. Important values may be served by having federal judges pass on federal issues. Even in a very general sense a federal judge, operating within a different system and with a differently defined set of institutional responsibilities, may bring to bear on such issues an objectivity, a freshness and insight which may have been denied to the state judge, no matter how conscientious, whose perspective will be subtly shaped by implicit presumptions derived from his responsibilities within the state institutional framework, who stands within *that* system. More particular considerations may be mentioned too. The federal judge is independent by constitutional guarantee; the state judge may not be. The difference surely does bear on conditions necessary for principled judging; it is, at least, a common assumption—perhaps implicit in the Constitution itself—that state courts may be more responsive to local pressures, local prejudices, local politics, than federal judges. And there is, too, the fear that state officials, including judges, will somehow be less sympathetic or generous with respect to federal claims raised by state prisoners than federal judges.

* * *

* * * If the purpose of the certiorari jurisdiction is to settle conflicts and decide important cases, the mere fact that in the process the Supreme Court (infallible only because it is

final) has authority to make decisions which will be deemed right does not prove that its jurisdiction is also necessary for the doing of justice, and therefore does not tell us that without federal review the probabilities that the states will do justice are unacceptably low.

What it comes down to, really, is that the state prisoner in an important case does have one more chance to persuade a set of judges—and judges, perhaps, of superior objectivity and fresher perspective with respect to matters of federal law—to see the case his way than the prisoner in an unimportant case. And this is a real difference. The sense of inequality created by the discretionary certiorari jurisdiction does seem to me a weighty and important consideration. Whether it serves in itself to justify *Brown v. Allen*, in view of all the problems created, I am not at all sure. But at least it helps rationalize and explain it.

B.The Problem of Inadequate Supreme Court Supervision

Another line of argument to support the present structure of the habeas corpus jurisdiction rests on the proposition that direct review by the Supreme Court provides inadequate supervision of the state courts' adjudications with respect to state defendants' federal constitutional rights. Of course, whether supervision is "adequate" turns on how one defines the purposes being served by such supervision. Insofar as we are told that habeas corpus is necessary because the overcrowding of the Supreme Court's docket makes it impossible for the Court to consider the merits of every case where a prisoner alleges that he has been deprived of a constitutional right, this is but another version of the assertion that a federal court should decide the merits of every such case. But there does exist another, rather different, problem. It stems from the well-known fact that the typical certiorari petition from a state prisoner, and the record, if any, that accompanies it, are often wholly inadequate to inform the Supreme Court whether the case should be reviewed. The petitions, we are told, drafted usually without a lawyer, are frequently unintelligible and rarely clear; certified records are "almost unknown" and,

> the number of cases in which most of the papers necessary to prove what happened in the State proceedings are not filed is striking. Whether there has been an adjudication or simply a perfunctory denial of a claim below is rarely ascertainable. Seldom do we have enough on which to base a solid conclusion as to the adequacy of the State adjudication. Even if we are told something about a trial of the claims the applicant asserts, we almost never have a transcript of these proceedings to assist us in determining whether the trial was adequate.

And these messy and often inscrutable petitions come before the Court in very large numbers indeed.

* * *

D. Some Cautions: The Inadequate State Process

The existence, notorious and oft-exhibited, of grave inadequacies in the states' criminal procedures, both original and post-conviction, makes the federal habeas corpus jurisdiction a present necessity. On this bedrock proposition I agree with the writ's defenders. These inadequacies have been explicitly acknowledged by distinguished state judges, including a committee of the Conferences of Chief Justices, whose report, recommending many improvements in state procedures, states that:

> responsibility for the unfortunate conditions prevailing in habeas corpus litigation rests upon the State as well as upon the Federal judicial systems, and ... the

evils presently prevailing can be reduced substantially by action taken at the State level.

If any doubt remains as to this point, it should be allayed by Professor Curtis Reitz's admirable article in the University of Pennsylvania Law Review, [*Federal Habeas Corpus*, 108 U. Pa. L. Rev. 461 (1960)], in which he reports on a painstaking canvass of some thirty-five cases from a ten-year period involving state prisoners in which habeas corpus was ultimately granted by a federal court. These cases show beyond a doubt that the states frequently fail to provide a fair and rational setting for the litigation of claims of federal constitutional right, so that habeas turns out to be the only available remedy for the vindication of such claims.

What is, however, so hard for me to grasp is why the existence of habeas to cure failures of state process justifies its present reach to cases where there has not been such a failure of process. Inadequacies of state procedure do not validate the status quo. The issue is not whether the jurisdiction should be abolished but whether its expansion to cases where there is no reasoned basis to suspect failure to provide a rational trial of the federal question, before an unbiased tribunal and through fair procedures, is justified.* * *

* * *

IV. CONCLUSION: THE ROLE OF DISCRETION

What should we conclude about *Brown v. Allen*? I do not pretend to find the answer easy, nor the claims for federal supervision unweighty. Their strength derives from our own historical experience. The last twenty-five years have seen rapid and tremendous expansion and movement in the substantive doctrines derived from the due process clause which limit the power of the states in their administration of criminal justice. It is natural that, in an era of such rapid growth in the substantive federal law, there should be a demand that the remedial system keep pace, that federal supervision be expanded to make sure that the states receive the new doctrines hospitably. And there is, of course, the underlying suspicion that in fact the states have not done so, that if we do not keep a sharp eye out, federal rights will be subtly eroded, verbal respect paid to the principles but the substance robbed of meaning through astringent and unsympathetic application. (The suspicion is surely fed by the knowledge that a substantial proportion of those accused of crime, particularly in the Southern States, will be Negroes.)

Yet we must remember that the remedial system we construct must be tailored for tomorrow as well as today. It is not fanciful to suppose that the law of due process for criminal defendants will, in the foreseeable future, reach a resting point, will become stabilized. * * *

Similarly, I resist the notion that sound remedial institutions can be built on the premise that state judges are not in sympathy with federal law. Again we must think in terms of tomorrow as well as today. Hopefully we will reach the day when the suspicion will no longer be justified that state judges—especially Southern state judges—evade their responsibilities by giving only the appearance of fairness in their rulings as to state defendants' federal rights. The unification of the country is, after all, in progress; the day when Southern justice is like Northern justice, justice for the Negro like justice for the white, is no longer out of sight. And our remedial system ought to take account of this motion.

The crucial point, it is worth reiterating, is that the question before us is *not* whether federal supervision of the states' administration of criminal justice is necessary. The question is whether such supervision is inadequate if limited to the very sweeping powers of the Supreme Court on direct review, and of the district courts on habeas to inquire into the fairness of the state's process. Is more than this needed? Must there be further supervision if the Supreme Court has had a chance to review the case and has chosen not to, and if the federal district court finds that the state has afforded fair process for the litigation of federal rights?

True, it will be argued that such supervision cannot ensure that in each case the federal right has in fact been conscientiously protected; it does not guard against cases where there has been the appearance of fairness but not its inner essence. But is it so clear that it is the function of judicial review to give us this ultimate guarantee? *Can* the legal system assure us in any event of this ultimate inner conscientiousness? And may one not speculate that perhaps conscientiousness is a by-product not only of supervision from above but also of responsibility, that it is not the best way to assure honest respect for federal law to relieve the state judge of responsibility?

In sum, it seems to me that the proper verdict on the case made for *Brown v. Allen* is "not proven"—and I do think the burden of proof is on the proponents. I rest partly on the federalist premise, that the abrasions and conflicts created by federal interference with the states' administration of criminal justice should be avoided in the absence of felt need, where the institutional necessities are as dubious as they seem to me to be in this case. I also reason from the very real claims which the need for finality and repose seem to me to make on the criminal process, claims particularly strong in view of what I consider to be philosophically faulty premises about justice which are often at the heart of the demand that we repeat inquiry endlessly to make sure that no mistake has been made. And, finally, *Brown v. Allen* seems to me to be unresponsive to (and even subversive of) what should be our central aim: encouraging reform and improvement in state criminal procedures.

Nevertheless, I cannot pretend that the case the other way is weightless. Our traditional doctrines of judicial review do rest on the premise of good-faith judging. Whenever good faith is questioned, strain is put on the ordinary rules of review; and maybe untraditional and extraordinary accommodations should therefore be made. There is surely appeal in the notion, and perhaps it makes sense at a time when there still is a justified suspicion and distrust of state-court rulings as to federal constitutional rights, to have a jurisdiction with a large and roving commission "to prevent a complete miscarriage of justice"; maybe,

> it is well that a writ the historic purpose of which is to furnish "a swift and imperative remedy in all cases of illegal restraint" ... should be left fluid and free from the definiteness appropriate to ordinary jurisdictional doctrines.

Of course we should not forget that there is already in existence an instrument in the administration of criminal justice whose very purpose is to assure relief where there has been a miscarriage of justice: the power of executive clemency supposedly already gives us a roving commission, usually free of technicalities and jurisdictional limitations, to seek out and right injustice. In fact it is striking how often we lose sight of the pardon as an integral part of the administration of criminal justice; in many cases where judicial relief is sought by way of collateral attack, the question that leaps to mind is: why is not pardon the obvious and sound solution here? Why wasn't executive clemency exercised? Surely it is a sorry thing that in so many states the pardoning power has been allowed to atrophy, and is reserved for highly extraordinary (usually death) cases. And again we have the striking phenomenon that the states' own failure to provide, through the pardon, an effective instrument of justice has prompted a search for a federal substitute, in this case in the form of habeas corpus.

In any event, *Brown v. Allen* may be justified in terms of a need for an extraordinary roving jurisdiction to make sure once more that there has not been, with respect to constitutional rights, a miscarriage of justice; perhaps we do need to grant federal courts the power to redetermine the merits to assure that covert unfairness does not lurk behind the appearance of fairness. But if this is the theory of the jurisdiction, then what is called for, I submit, is a decision, based on all the facts, whether justice really does call for release in the particular case. Suppose, for instance, that a federal district judge finds (1) that the admissibility of a confession has been fully and fairly litigated in the state courts, on an impeccable record giving the Supreme Court a full opportunity to review if it so chooses; (2) that on the merits he disagrees with the state judges as to admissibility; and (3) that the evidence in the record apart from the confession, or, indeed, the trustworthiness of the confession itself, makes it absolutely clear that the defendant was guilty as charged. It is (today's) hornbook law that on direct review there would be automatic reversal, that neither the trustworthiness of the confession nor the other evidence of guilt can cure the error; let us, further, assume the soundness of this doctrine. But is it absolutely clear that the reasons which have moved us to so astringent a rule of law on the merits, as it were, should necessarily apply in a jurisdiction which is concededly extraordinary, the existence of which is justified by the need to make sure once more that justice in the particular case has indeed been done? Remember that I assume that full corrective process has been afforded in the original litigation: the defendant has had a fair opportunity to establish his federal claim. We now give him one more chance, in the fear that justice has miscarried. But has it miscarried if he has had one meaningful go-around and the district judge can be morally assured that he was guilty? I acknowledge that the purpose of the rule of automatic reversal is to deter uncivilized police behavior and to keep the courts' own processes unsullied; but the claims for deterrence do not strike me as so inexorable that we must honor them in cases where our fundamental purpose, in fact our justification for inquiry, is, after all, to do our best by the defendant; nor can I take too seriously the idea that the integrity of the legal process will be sullied if a court in effect finds that for purposes of the extraordinary habeas jurisdiction the admission of the confession—previously tested by fair process—was harmless error.

I continue to resist, in sum, the notion that the inquiry on habeas should be mere repetition, an exact replica, of what has gone before. I do not see that as institutionally justified. If we wish to have an ultimate recourse, if we want to grant the federal courts a roving extraordinary commission to undo injustice, then, it seems to me, all the factors which bear on justice should be put on the scales. If *Brown v. Allen* is to remain the law, it should be modified to make clear that where a federal constitutional question has been fully canvassed by fair state process, and meaningfully submitted for possible Supreme Court review, then the federal district judge on habeas, though entitled to redetermine the merits, has a large discretion to decide whether the federal error, if any, was prejudicial, whether justice will be served by releasing the prisoner, taking into account in the largest sense all the relevant factors, including his conscientious appraisal of the guilt or innocence of the accused on the basis of the full record before him.

Notes

1. *Critiquing* Brown v. Allen

What is Professor Bator's basic objection to *Brown v. Allen*?

2. *"Extraordinary roving jurisdiction"*

Toward the end of the article, Professor Bator states, "In any event, *Brown v. Allen* may be justified in terms of a need for an extraordinary roving jurisdiction to make sure once more that there has not been, with respect to constitutional rights, a miscarriage of justice." What is the proper role of federal habeas review? Is federal habeas review necessary in the 21st century?

3. *Conscientiousness and habeas corpus*

Discussing the relationship between state and federal authority over federal questions, Bator asks, "[M]ay one not speculate that perhaps the conscientiousness is a by-product not only of supervision from above but also of responsibility?" Is Bator suggesting that unfair state processes are a natural product of our federal system? How does this relate to Bator's thesis that "truth" cannot be found through the justice system but, rather, the best we can strive for are unbiased and procedurally fair processes?

4. *The role of an elected judiciary*

To what degree do you think that the judiciary standing for election affects their decision-making? Might this be one of Professor Bator's concerns? Since standing down from the Supreme Court in 2006, Justice O'Connor has become more vocal about expressing her opposition to judicial elections, advocating for a system of appointment, coupled with subsequent performance evaluation.[1] Would O'Connor's approach be sufficient to allay concerns about the effect of public opinion on the judicial decision-making process?

1. Sandra Day O'Connor, *Taking Justice Off the Ballot*, N.Y. Times, May 21, 2010.

Chapter 2

Introduction to AEDPA

Unhappy with decisions like *Brown v. Allen* and motivated by the work of scholars like Professor Bator, Congress sought to legislatively curtail the reach of federal habeas corpus review. After decades of legislative failure, during which attempts to redu ce the scope of federal habeas review were rejected, in 1996 Congress passed, and President Bill Clinton signed into law, the Anti-Terrorism and Effective Death Penalty Act (AEDPA).

As two commentators summarized the events:

> Criminals are not popular. No politician in recent memory has lost an election for being too tough on crime. In 1996, the Republican Congress and the Democratic President collaborated on two major statutes affecting the legal protections available to criminals. The Antiterrorism and Effective Death Penalty Act of 1996 (AEDPA) modifies the habeas corpus statute in a number of ways, affecting the disposition of federal post-conviction challenges to all criminal convictions, not just those resulting in death sentences.[1]

The remainder of this chapter is devoted to highlighting some of the major changes introduced by AEDPA.

A. When Do the Restrictions Announced in AEDPA Apply?

The focus of this book is the procedures and rights associated with federal habeas corpus review of a state conviction. The limitations contained in AEDPA discussed in this chapter apply to every federal habeas petition filed by a state prisoner.[2] Accordingly, the question of whether AEDPA's limitations can be applied retroactively was one of the first major issues litigated under the new act. This question was resolved in *Lindh v. Murphy*, 521 U.S. 320 (1997). In *Lindh*, the Court held that AEDPA applies only to cases that were not pending when the legislation was enacted on April 24, 1996.

If AEDPA applies to all federal habeas actions that were not pending on April 24, 1996, then a critical question is what constitutes a pending petition. The Ninth Circuit addressed this question in *Calderon v. U.S. Dist. Court for the Cent. Dist. of Cal.*, 128 F.3d 1283 (9th Cir. 1997). When AEDPA was enacted on April 24, 1996, Rodney Gene Beeler had filed

1. Mark Tushnet & Larry Yackle, *Symbolic Statutes and Real Laws: The Pathologies of the Antiterrorism and Effective Death Penalty Act and the Prison Litigation Reform Act*, 47 Duke L.J. 1, 1 (1997).

2. Later in the book certain procedural and fact-finding aspects of federal habeas litigation are discussed. Aspects of the procedural analysis seem to dictate that certain of the limitations on constitutional relief contained in AEDPA will not always apply.

his request for appointment of counsel and stay of execution but not his application for a writ of habeas corpus. Judge Kozinski addressed Beeler's argument that "filing the request for appointment of counsel commenced his case" for purposes of AEDPA applicability. Judge Kozinski noted that "Rule 11 of the Rules Governing § 2254 Cases says '[t]he Federal Rules of Civil Procedure, to the extent that they are not inconsistent with these rules, may be applied, when appropriate, to petitions filed under these rules.'" He reasoned that "[f]iling an application for a writ is analogous to filing a complaint, which commences a civil case under Fed. R. Civ. P. 3." Requesting counsel, even if it is a required preliminary step, is not functionally analogous to "filing a complaint." Instead, the court concluded that "for purposes of determining cases to which the AEDPA applies, a case is pending when the application for a writ of habeas corpus is filed." *See Calderon*, 128 F.3d at 1287 and n.3.

The Ninth Circuit subsequently took up this issue sitting *en banc* and held, "[A] petition for the appointment of counsel to prepare and file a petition for a writ of habeas corpus, accompanied by a motion for a stay of execution * * * is a threshold action that presents a 'case' to the district court." *Calderon*, 163 F.3d 530, 540 (9th Cir. 1998) (en banc). In so doing, they overruled the previous circuit court decision.

The Ninth Circuit's internal disagreement was, however, made moot by the Supreme Court's ruling in *Woodford v. Garceau*, 538 U.S. 20 (2003). In *Woodford* the Court settled the question and held that "an application filed after AEDPA's effective date should be reviewed under AEDPA, even if other filings by that same applicant—such as, for example, a request for the appointment of counsel or a motion for a stay of execution—were presented to a federal court prior to AEDPA's effective date."

The question of when a case is "pending" also is significant for determining whether the statute of limitations on filing a habeas action has run. This is because the time limit for filing a federal habeas petition is tolled while a properly filed state petition is pending in the state court, as the next section explains.

B. Statute of Limitations

There has long been debate about the equity and proper application of a statute of limitations imposed on prisoners that forever forecloses the vindication of constitutional violations. Recall that Professor Bator noted, "Even if we conclude that we should have a federal collateral jurisdiction to test the integrity of previous state proceedings ... we should be aware that the policies we have been discussing do not support the notion that federal collateral attack should be available without limit of time."[3] For decades Congressional efforts to impose a statute of limitations proved fruitless. In *Vasquez v. Hillery*, 474 U.S. 254, 265 (1986), for example, the Court commented that "despite many attempts in recent years, Congress has yet to create a statute of limitations for federal habeas corpus actions." And in an appendix to its opinion in *Lonchar v. Thomas*, 517 U.S. 314 (1996),

3. *See also*, U.S. Judicial Conference Ad Hoc Committee on Federal Habeas Corpus in Capital Cases, Committee Report and Proposal 6, 18–21 (1989) (Powell Committee Report) (recommending a statute of limitations); Ira P. Robbins, Toward a More Just and Effective System of Review in State Death Penalty Cases: Recommendations and Report to the American Bar Association Task Force on Death Penalty Habeas Corpus 29–30 (1990) (also recommending a statute of limitations).

the Court listed more than 80 bills proposing statutes of limitations for federal habeas cases that Congress had introduced but had not adopted over the previous ten years.

Proponents of more limited access to federal habeas review were successful in large part due to the statute of limitations in AEDPA. Section 2244(d) provides:

> (1) A 1-year period of limitation shall apply to an application for a writ of habeas corpus by a person in custody pursuant to the judgment of a State court. The limitation period shall run from the latest of—
>
> (A) the date on which the judgment became final by the conclusion of direct review or the expiration of the time for seeking such review;
>
> (B) the date on which the impediment to filing an application created by State action in violation of the Constitution or laws of the United States is removed, if the applicant was prevented from filing by such State action;
>
> (C) the date on which the constitutional right asserted was initially recognized by the Supreme Court, if the right has been newly recognized by the Supreme Court and made retroactively applicable to cases on collateral review; or
>
> (D) the date on which the factual predicate of the claim or claims presented could have been discovered through the exercise of due diligence.
>
> (2) The time during which a properly filed application for State post-conviction or other collateral review with respect to the pertinent judgment or claim is pending shall not be counted toward any period of limitation under this subsection.

Notes

1. What is the purpose of imposing a statute of limitations on the ability of a prisoner to challenge the constitutionality of his or her detention? The Conference Committee Report provides an insight into the thinking of the members of Congress who supported the Act:

> This title incorporates reforms to curb the abuse of the statutory writ of habeas corpus, and to address the acute problems of unnecessary delay and abuse in capital cases. It sets a one year limitation on an application for a habeas writ and revises the procedures for consideration of a writ in federal court.

H.R. Rep. No. 104-518, at 111 (1996) (Conf. Rep.).

2. Under § 2244 a prisoner has one year in which to file a federal habeas corpus petition. At what point in the case does the one-year time limit begin to run? What happens if the state post-conviction court fails to complete its review of the state petition within a year? What happens if the state post-conviction lawyer takes a full year to prepare and file the state post-conviction petition?

3. A conviction becomes final at the conclusion of direct review. This means that the time permitted for seeking direct review in the U.S. Supreme Court does not count against the one-year time limit.

4. What if a federal habeas petition is filed within the one-year time limit but the prisoner attempts to add additional claims after the one-year limit? Should it matter whether the new claims are "tied to a common core of operative facts" in the original pleading

and thus relate back under Fed. R. Civ. P. 15(c)? *See Mayle v. Felix*, 545 U.S. 644, 664 (2005) (applying the civil procedure doctrine of relation back to federal habeas proceedings).

C. 28 U.S.C. § 2254

The revisions to § 2254, in particular § 2254(d), have rightly been called the centerpiece of AEDPA. Many habeas lawyers make the mistake of turning only to the current version of § 2254, but understanding the current version requires a familiarity with how the statute read before AEDPA was enacted. Both versions of the statute are provided below. Take several minutes to review and compare the pre-AEDPA and AEDPA versions.

28 U.S.C. § 2254 (1948–1996)

(a) The Supreme Court, a Justice thereof, a circuit judge, or a district court shall entertain an application for a writ of habeas corpus in behalf of a person in custody pursuant to the judgment of a State court only on the ground that he is in custody in violation of the Constitution or laws or treaties of the United States.

(b) An application for a writ of habeas corpus in behalf of a person in custody pursuant to the judgment of a State court shall not be granted unless it appears that the applicant has exhausted the remedies available in the courts of the State, or that there is either an absence of available State corrective process or the existence of circumstances rendering such process ineffective to protect the rights of the prisoner.

28 U.S.C. § 2254 (as amended in 1996)

(a) The Supreme Court, a Justice thereof, a circuit judge, or a district court shall entertain an application for a writ of habeas corpus in behalf of a person in custody pursuant to the judgment of a State court only on the ground that he is in custody in violation of the Constitution or laws or treaties of the United States.

(b) (1) An application for a writ of habeas corpus on behalf of a person in custody pursuant to the judgment of a State court shall not be granted unless it appears that—

(A) the applicant has exhausted the remedies available in the courts of the State; or

(B) (i) there is an absence of available State corrective process; or

(ii) circumstances exist that render such process ineffective to protect the rights of the applicant.

(2) An application for a writ of habeas corpus may be denied on the merits, notwithstanding the failure of the applicant to exhaust the remedies available in the courts of the State.

(3) A State shall not be deemed to have waived the exhaustion requirement or be estopped from reliance upon the requirement unless the State,

(c) An applicant shall not be deemed to have exhausted the remedies available in the courts of the State, within the meaning of this section, if he has the right under the law of the State to raise, by any available procedure, the questions presented.

(d) In any proceeding instituted in a Federal court by an application for a writ of habeas corpus by a person in custody pursuant to the judgment of a State court, a determination after a hearing on the merits of a factual issue, made by a State court of competent jurisdiction in a proceeding to which the applicant for the writ and the State or an officer or agent thereof were parties, evidenced by a written finding, written opinion, or other reliable and adequate written indicia, shall be presumed to be correct, unless the applicant shall establish or it shall otherwise appear, or the respondent shall admit

(1) that the merits of the factual dispute were not resolved in the State court hearing;

(2) that the factfinding procedure employed by the State court was not adequate to afford a full and fair hearing;

(3) that the material facts were not adequately developed at the State court hearing;

(4) that the State court lacked jurisdiction of the subject matter or over the person of the applicant in the State court proceeding;

(5) that the applicant was an indigent and the State court, in deprivation of his constitutional right, failed to appoint counsel to represent him in the State court proceeding

(6) that the applicant did not receive a full, fair, and adequate hearing in the state court proceeding[;] or

through counsel, expressly waives the requirement.

(c) An applicant shall not be deemed to have exhausted the remedies available in the courts of the State, within the meaning of this section, if he has the right under the law of the State to raise, by any available procedure, the question presented.

(d) An application for a writ of habeas corpus on behalf of a person in custody pursuant to the judgment of a State court shall not be granted with respect to any claim that was adjudicated on the merits in State court proceedings unless the adjudication of the claim—

(1) resulted in a decision that was contrary to, or involved an unreasonable application of, clearly established Federal law, as determined by the Supreme Court of the United States; or

(2) resulted in a decision that was based on an unreasonable determination of the facts in light of the evidence presented in the State court proceeding.

(7) that the applicant was otherwise denied due process of law in the State court proceeding;

(8) or unless that part of the record of the State court proceeding in which the determination of such factual issue

(e) If the applicant challenges the sufficiency of the evidence adduced in such State court proceeding to support the State court's determination of a factual issue made therein, the applicant, if able, shall produce that part of the record pertinent to a determination of the sufficiency of the evidence to support such determination. If the applicant, because of indigency or other reason is unable to produce such part of the record, then the State shall produce such part of the record and the Federal court shall direct the State to do so by order directed to an appropriate State official. If the State cannot provide such pertinent part of the record, then the court shall determine under the existing facts and circumstances what weight shall be given to the State court's factual determination.

(e) (1) In a proceeding instituted by an application for a writ of habeas corpus by a person in custody pursuant to the judgment of a State court, a determination of a factual issue made by a State court shall be presumed to be correct. The applicant shall have the burden of rebutting the presumption of correctness by clear and convincing evidence.

(2) If the applicant has failed to develop the factual basis of a claim in State court proceedings, the court shall not hold an evidentiary hearing on the claim unless the applicant shows that—

(A) the claim relies on—

(i) a new rule of constitutional law, made retroactive to cases on collateral review by the Supreme Court, that was previously unavailable; or

(ii) a factual predicate that could not have been previously discovered through the exercise of due diligence; and

(B) the facts underlying the claim would be sufficient to establish by clear and convincing evidence that but for constitutional error, no reasonable factfinder would have found the applicant guilty of the underlying offense.

(f) A copy of the official records of the State court, duly certified by the clerk of such court to be a true and correct copy of a finding, judicial opinion, or other reliable written indicia showing such a factual determination by the State court

(f) If the applicant challenges the sufficiency of the evidence adduced in such State court proceeding to support the State court's determination of a factual issue made therein, the applicant, if able, shall produce that part of the record

shall be admissible in the Federal court proceeding.

pertinent to a determination of the sufficiency of the evidence to support such determination. If the applicant, because of indigency or other reason is unable to produce such part of the record, then the State shall produce such part of the record and the Federal court shall direct the State to do so by order directed to an appropriate State official. If the State cannot provide such pertinent part of the record, then the court shall determine under the existing facts and circumstances what weight shall be given to the State court's factual determination.

(g) A copy of the official records of the State court, duly certified by the clerk of such court to be a true and correct copy of a finding, judicial opinion, or other reliable written indicia showing such a factual determination by the State court shall be admissible in the Federal court proceeding.

(h) Except as provided in section 408 of the Controlled Substances Act, in all proceedings brought under this section, and any subsequent proceedings on review, the court may appoint counsel for an applicant who is or becomes financially unable to afford counsel, except as provided by a rule promulgated by the Supreme Court pursuant to statutory authority. Appointment of counsel under this section shall be governed by section 3006A of title 18.

(i) The ineffectiveness or incompetence of counsel during Federal or State collateral post-conviction proceedings shall not be a ground for relief in a proceeding arising under section 2254.

Notes

1. *Comparing pre- and post-AEDPA*

What are some of the key differences between the two statutes? Why do you think Congress made these changes?

2. *Bator's influence*

Do you think Professor Bator would be pleased with the 1996 Amendments? Does the new statute address his concerns regarding federal review of state convictions?

3. *Section 2254(i)*

What is the significance of this provision? Does this section preclude a prisoner from asserting a constitutional right to effective post-conviction representation?

(1) Making Sense of § 2254(d)

A considerable amount of current, and likely future, federal habeas litigation centers around the question of whether the limitations on relief contained in the 1996 version of § 2254(d)(1) apply to a particular case. The state has an interest in construing this provision as broadly as possible in order to shield the state conviction from federal review. By contrast, counsel for the prisoner typically argues that § 2254(d)(1) is facially unconstitutional, that § 2254(d)(1) is unconstitutional as applied to the current case, or (perhaps more pragmatically) that as a matter of statutory interpretation and/or constitutional avoidance, the limitations on relief announced through AEDPA do not apply to the case at hand.

Why is litigation over the applicability of (d)(1) so ubiquitous? *Williams v. Taylor* is the Court's first extended explanation on the proper application of (d)(1). The Court's interpretations of the provision make it clear why applicability is a critical threshold question in modern habeas litigation.

Williams v. Taylor

529 U.S. 362 (2000)

JUSTICE STEVENS announced the judgment of the Court and delivered the opinion of the Court with respect to Parts I, III, and IV, and an opinion with respect to Parts II and V. JUSTICE SOUTER, JUSTICE GINSBURG, and JUSTICE BREYER join this opinion in its entirety. JUSTICE O'CONNOR and JUSTICE KENNEDY join Parts I, III, and IV of this opinion.

The questions presented are whether Terry Williams' constitutional right to the effective assistance of counsel as defined in *Strickland v. Washington* was violated, and whether the judgment of the Virginia Supreme Court refusing to set aside his death sentence "was contrary to, or involved an unreasonable application of, clearly established Federal law, as determined by the Supreme Court of the United States," within the meaning of 28 U.S.C. § 2254(d)(1) (1994 ed., Supp. III). We answer both questions affirmatively.

I

On November 3, 1985, Harris Stone was found dead in his residence on Henry Street in Danville, Virginia. Finding no indication of a struggle, local officials determined that the cause of death was blood alcohol poisoning, and the case was considered closed. Six months after Stone's death, Terry Williams, who was then incarcerated in the "I" unit of the city jail for an unrelated offense, wrote a letter to the police stating that he had killed "'that man down on Henry Street'" and also stating that he "'did it'" to that "'lady down on West Green Street'" and was "'very sorry.'" The letter was unsigned, but it closed with a reference to "I cell." The police readily identified Williams as its author, and, on April 25, 1986, they obtained several statements from him. In one Williams admitted that, after Stone refused to lend him "'a couple of dollars,'" he had killed Stone with a mattock and taken the money from his wallet. In September 1986, Williams was convicted of robbery and capital murder.

At Williams' sentencing hearing, the prosecution proved that Williams had been convicted of armed robbery in 1976 and burglary and grand larceny in 1982. The prosecution also introduced the written confessions that Williams had made in April. The prosecution described two auto thefts and two separate violent assaults on elderly victims perpetrated after the Stone murder. On December 4, 1985, Williams had started a fire outside one victim's residence before attacking and robbing him. On March 5, 1986, Williams had brutally assaulted an elderly woman on West Green Street—an incident he had mentioned in his letter to the police. That confession was particularly damaging because other evidence established that the woman was in a "vegetative state" and not expected to recover. Williams had also been convicted of arson for setting a fire in the jail while awaiting trial in this case. Two expert witnesses employed by the State testified that there was a "high probability" that Williams would pose a serious continuing threat to society.

The evidence offered by Williams' trial counsel at the sentencing hearing consisted of the testimony of Williams' mother, two neighbors, and a taped excerpt from a statement by a psychiatrist. One of the neighbors had not been previously interviewed by defense counsel, but was noticed by counsel in the audience during the proceedings and asked to testify on the spot. The three witnesses briefly described Williams as a "nice boy" and not a violent person. The recorded psychiatrist's testimony did little more than relate Williams' statement during an examination that in the course of one of his earlier robberies, he had removed the bullets from a gun so as not to injure anyone.

In his cross-examination of the prosecution witnesses, Williams' counsel repeatedly emphasized the fact that Williams had initiated the contact with the police that enabled them to solve the murder and to identify him as the perpetrator of the recent assaults, as well as the car thefts. In closing argument, Williams' counsel characterized Williams' confessional statements as "dumb," but asked the jury to give weight to the fact that he had "turned himself in, not on one crime but on four ... that the [police otherwise] would not have solved." The weight of defense counsel's closing, however, was devoted to explaining that it was difficult to find a reason why the jury should spare Williams' life.

The jury found a probability of future dangerousness and unanimously fixed Williams' punishment at death. The trial judge concluded that such punishment was "proper" and "just" and imposed the death sentence. The Virginia Supreme Court affirmed the conviction and sentence. It rejected Williams' argument that when the trial judge imposed sentence, he failed to give mitigating weight to the fact that Williams had turned himself in.

State Habeas Corpus Proceedings

In 1988 Williams filed for state collateral relief in the Danville Circuit Court. The petition was subsequently amended, and the Circuit Court (the same judge who had presided over Williams' trial and sentencing) held an evidentiary hearing on Williams' claim that trial counsel had been ineffective. Based on the evidence adduced after two days of hearings, Judge Ingram found that Williams' conviction was valid, but that his trial attorneys had been ineffective during sentencing. Among the evidence reviewed that had not been presented at trial were documents prepared in connection with Williams' commitment when he was 11 years old that dramatically described mistreatment, abuse, and neglect during his early childhood, as well as testimony that he was "borderline mentally retarded," had suffered repeated head injuries, and might have mental impairments organic in origin. The habeas hearing also revealed that the same experts who had testified on the State's behalf at trial believed that Williams, if kept in a "structured environment," would not pose a future danger to society.

Counsel's failure to discover and present this and other significant mitigating evidence was "below the range expected of reasonable, professional competent assistance of counsel." Counsel's performance thus "did not measure up to the standard required under the holding of *Strickland v. Washington*, and [if it had,] there is a reasonable probability that the result of the sentencing phase would have been different." Judge Ingram therefore recommended that Williams be granted a rehearing on the sentencing phase of his trial.

The Virginia Supreme Court did not accept that recommendation. * * *

* * *

Federal Habeas Corpus Proceedings

Having exhausted his state remedies, Williams sought a federal writ of habeas corpus pursuant to 28 U.S.C. § 2254 (1994 ed. and Supp. III). After reviewing the state habeas hearing transcript and the state courts' findings of fact and conclusions of law, the federal trial judge agreed with the Virginia trial judge: The death sentence was constitutionally infirm.

After noting that the Virginia Supreme Court had not addressed the question whether trial counsel's performance at the sentencing hearing fell below the range of competence demanded of lawyers in criminal cases, the judge began by addressing that issue in detail. He identified five categories of mitigating evidence that counsel had failed to introduce, and he rejected the argument that counsel's failure to conduct an adequate investigation had been a strategic decision to rely almost entirely on the fact that Williams had voluntarily confessed.

* * *

The Federal Court of Appeals reversed. It construed § 2254(d)(1) as prohibiting the grant of habeas corpus relief unless the state court "'decided the question by interpreting or applying the relevant precedent in a manner that reasonable jurists would all agree is unreasonable.'" Applying that standard, it could not say that the Virginia Supreme Court's decision on the prejudice issue was an unreasonable application of the tests developed in either *Strickland* or *Lockhart*. It explained that the evidence that Williams presented a future danger to society was "simply overwhelming," it endorsed the Virginia Supreme Court's interpretation of *Lockhart*, and it characterized the state court's understanding of the facts in this case as "reasonable."

We granted certiorari and now reverse.

II

In 1867, Congress enacted a statute providing that federal courts "shall have power to grant writs of habeas corpus in all cases where any person may be restrained of his or her liberty in violation of the constitution, or of any treaty or law of the United States...." Act of Feb. 5, 1867, ch. 28, § 1, 14 Stat. 385. Over the years, the federal habeas corpus statute has been repeatedly amended, but the scope of that jurisdictional grant remains the same. It is, of course, well settled that the fact that constitutional error occurred in the proceedings that led to a state-court conviction may not alone be sufficient reason for concluding that a prisoner is entitled to the remedy of habeas. On the other hand, errors that undermine confidence in the fundamental fairness of the state adjudication certainly justify the issuance of the federal writ. *See, e.g., Teague v. Lane*. The deprivation of the right to the effective assistance of counsel recognized in *Strickland* is such an error.

The warden here contends that federal habeas corpus relief is prohibited by the amendment to 28 U.S.C. § 2254 (1994 ed., Supp. III), enacted as a part of the Antiterrorism and Effective Death Penalty Act of 1996 (AEDPA). The relevant portion of that amendment provides:

> (d) An application for a writ of habeas corpus on behalf of a person in custody pursuant to the judgment of a State court shall not be granted with respect to any claim that was adjudicated on the merits in State court proceedings unless the adjudication of the claim—
>
> > (1) resulted in a decision that was contrary to, or involved an unreasonable application of, clearly established Federal law, as determined by the Supreme Court of the United States;....

In this case, the Court of Appeals applied the construction of the amendment [incorrectly]. [The Court then sets forth the lower court's application, and explained why it was incorrect].

* * *

As the Fourth Circuit would have it, a state-court judgment is "unreasonable" in the face of federal law only if all reasonable jurists would agree that the state court was unreasonable. Thus, in this case, for example, even if the Virginia Supreme Court misread our opinion in *Lockhart*, we could not grant relief unless we believed that none of the judges who agreed with the state court's interpretation of that case was a "reasonable jurist." But the statute says nothing about "reasonable judges," presumably because all, or virtually all, such judges occasionally commit error; they make decisions that in retrospect may be characterized as "unreasonable." Indeed, it is most unlikely that Congress would deliberately impose such a requirement of unanimity on federal judges. As Congress is acutely aware, reasonable lawyers and lawgivers regularly disagree with one another. Congress surely did not intend that the views of one such judge who might think that relief is not warranted in a particular case should always have greater weight than the contrary, considered judgment of several other reasonable judges.

The inquiry mandated by the amendment relates to the way in which a federal habeas court exercises its duty to decide constitutional questions; the amendment does not alter the underlying grant of jurisdiction in § 2254(a). When federal judges exercise their federal-question jurisdiction under the "judicial Power" of Article III of the Constitution, it is "emphatically the province and duty" of those judges to "say what the law is." *Marbury v. Madison*, 5 U.S. 137 (1803). At the core of this power is the federal courts' independent responsibility—independent from its coequal branches in the Federal Government, and independent from the separate authority of the several States—to interpret federal law. A construction of AEDPA that would require the federal courts to cede this authority to the courts of the States would be inconsistent with the practice that federal judges have traditionally followed in discharging their duties under Article III of the Constitution. If Congress had intended to require such an important change in the exercise of our jurisdiction, we believe it would have spoken with much greater clarity than is found in the text of AEDPA.

This basic premise informs our interpretation of both parts of § 2254(d)(1): first, the requirement that the determinations of state courts be tested only against "clearly established Federal law, as determined by the Supreme Court of the United States," and second, the prohibition on the issuance of the writ unless the state court's decision is "contrary to, or involved an unreasonable application of," that clearly established law. We address each part in turn.

The "clearly established law" requirement

In *Teague v. Lane*, we held that the petitioner was not entitled to federal habeas relief because he was relying on a rule of federal law that had not been announced until after his state conviction became final. The antiretroactivity rule recognized in *Teague*, which prohibits reliance on "new rules," is the functional equivalent of a statutory provision commanding exclusive reliance on "clearly established law." Because there is no reason to believe that Congress intended to require federal courts to ask both whether a rule sought on habeas is "new" under *Teague*—which remains the law—and also whether it is "clearly established" under AEDPA, it seems safe to assume that Congress had congruent concepts in mind. It is perfectly clear that AEDPA codifies *Teague* to the extent that *Teague* requires federal habeas courts to deny relief that is contingent upon a rule of law not clearly established at the time the state conviction became final.

* * *

To this, AEDPA has added, immediately following the "clearly established law" requirement, a clause limiting the area of relevant law to that "determined by the Supreme Court of the United States." If this Court has not broken sufficient legal ground to establish an asked-for constitutional principle, the lower federal courts cannot themselves establish such a principle with clarity sufficient to satisfy the AEDPA bar. * * *

* * *

In the context of this case, we also note that, as our precedent interpreting *Teague* has demonstrated, rules of law may be sufficiently clear for habeas purposes even when they are expressed in terms of a generalized standard rather than as a bright-line rule. As JUSTICE KENNEDY has explained:

> If the rule in question is one which of necessity requires a case-by-case examination of the evidence, then we can tolerate a number of specific applications without saying that those applications themselves create a new rule.... Where the beginning point is a rule of this general application, a rule designed for the specific purpose of evaluating a myriad of factual contexts, it will be the infrequent case that yields a result so novel that it forges a new rule, one not dictated by precedent. *Wright v. West*, 505 U.S. 277, 308–309 (1992) (opinion concurring in judgment).

Moreover, the determination whether or not a rule is clearly established at the time a state court renders its final judgment of conviction is a question as to which the "federal courts must make an independent evaluation." *Id.* at 305 (O'CONNOR, J., concurring in judgment).

It has been urged, in contrast, that we should read *Teague* and its progeny to encompass a broader principle of deference requiring federal courts to "validate 'reasonable, good-faith interpretations' of the law" by state courts. * * *

Teague, however, does not extend this far. The often repeated language that *Teague* endorses "reasonable, good-faith interpretations" by state courts is an explanation of policy, not a statement of law. The *Teague* cases reflect this Court's view that habeas corpus is not to be used as a second criminal trial, and federal courts are not to run roughshod over the considered findings and judgments of the state courts that conducted the original trial and heard the initial appeals. On the contrary, we have long insisted that federal habeas courts attend closely to those considered decisions, and give them full effect when their findings and judgments are consistent with federal law. But as JUSTICE O'CONNOR explained [in her concurring judgment] in *Wright*:

> [T]he duty of the federal court in evaluating whether a rule is "new" is not the same as deference; ... *Teague* does not direct federal courts to spend less time or effort scrutinizing the existing federal law, on the ground that they can assume the state courts interpreted it properly.
>
> [T]he maxim that federal courts should "give great weight to the considered conclusions of a coequal state judiciary" ... does not mean that we have held in the past that federal courts must presume the correctness of a state court's legal conclusions on habeas, or that a state court's incorrect legal determination has ever been allowed to stand because it was reasonable. We have always held that federal courts, even on habeas, have an independent obligation to say what the law is.

We are convinced that in the phrase, "clearly established law," Congress did not intend to modify that independent obligation.

The "contrary to, or an unreasonable application of," requirement

The message that Congress intended to convey by using the phrases, "contrary to" and "unreasonable application of" is not entirely clear. The prevailing view in the Circuits is that the former phrase requires de novo review of "pure" questions of law and the latter requires some sort of "reasonability" review of so-called mixed questions of law and fact.

We are not persuaded that the phrases define two mutually exclusive categories of questions. Most constitutional questions that arise in habeas corpus proceedings—and therefore most "decisions" to be made—require the federal judge to apply a rule of law to a set of facts, some of which may be disputed and some undisputed. For example, an erroneous conclusion that particular circumstances established the voluntariness of a confession, or that there exists a conflict of interest when one attorney represents multiple defendants, may well be described either as "contrary to" or as an "unreasonable application of" the governing rule of law. In constitutional adjudication, as in the common law, rules of law often develop incrementally as earlier decisions are applied to new factual situations. But rules that depend upon such elaboration are hardly less lawlike than those that establish a bright-line test.

Indeed, our pre-AEDPA efforts to distinguish questions of fact, questions of law, and "mixed questions," and to create an appropriate standard of habeas review for each, generated some not insubstantial differences of opinion as to which issues of law fell into which category of question, and as to which standard of review applied to each. * * *

The statutory text likewise does not obviously prescribe a specific, recognizable standard of review for dealing with either phrase. Significantly, it does not use any term, such as "de novo" or "plain error," that would easily identify a familiar standard of review. Rather, the text is fairly read simply as a command that a federal court not issue the habeas writ unless the state court was wrong as a matter of law or unreasonable in its application of law in a given case. The suggestion that a wrong state-court "decision"—a legal judgment rendered "after consideration of facts, and ... law," Black's Law Dictionary 407 (6th ed.1990)—may no longer be redressed through habeas (because it is unreachable under the "unreasonable application" phrase) is based on a mistaken insistence that the § 2254(d)(1) phrases have not only independent, but mutually exclusive, meanings. Whether or not a federal court can issue the writ "under [the] 'unreasonable application' clause," the statute is clear that habeas may issue under § 2254(d)(1) if a state court "decision" is "contrary to ... clearly established Federal law." We thus anticipate that there will be a variety of cases, like this one, in which both phrases may be implicated.

Even though we cannot conclude that the phrases establish "a body of rigid rules," they do express a "mood" that the federal judiciary must respect. In this respect, it seems clear that Congress intended federal judges to attend with the utmost care to state-court decisions, including all of the reasons supporting their decisions, before concluding that those proceedings were infected by constitutional error sufficiently serious to warrant the issuance of the writ. Likewise, the statute in a separate provision provides for the habeas remedy when a state-court decision "was based on an unreasonable determination of the facts *in light of the evidence presented in the State court proceeding*." While this provision is not before us in this case, it provides relevant context for our interpretation of § 2254(d)(1); in this respect, it bolsters our conviction that federal habeas courts must make as the starting point of their analysis the state courts' determinations of fact, including that aspect of a "mixed question" that rests on a finding of fact. AEDPA plainly sought to ensure a level of "deference to the determinations of state courts," provided those determinations did not conflict with federal law or apply federal law in an unreasonable way. Congress wished to curb delays, to prevent "retrials" on federal habeas, and to give effect to state convictions to the extent possible under law. When federal courts are able to fulfill these goals within the bounds of the law, AEDPA instructs them to do so.

On the other hand, it is significant that the word "deference" does not appear in the text of the statute itself. Neither the legislative history, nor the statutory text suggests any difference in the so-called "deference" depending on which of the two phrases is implicated. Whatever "deference" Congress had in mind with respect to both phrases, it surely is not a requirement that federal courts actually defer to a state-court application of the federal law that is, in the independent judgment of the federal court, in error. As Judge Easterbrook noted with respect to the phrase "contrary to":

> Section 2254(d) requires us to give state courts' opinions a respectful reading, and to listen carefully to their conclusions, but when the state court addresses a legal question, it is the law "as determined by the Supreme Court of the United States" that prevails.

* * *

In sum, the statute directs federal courts to attend to every state-court judgment with utmost care, but it does not require them to defer to the opinion of every reasonable state-court judge on the content of federal law. If, after carefully weighing all the reasons for accepting a state court's judgment, a federal court is convinced that a prisoner's custody—or, as in this case, his sentence of death—violates the Constitution, that independent judgment should prevail. Otherwise the federal "law as determined by the Supreme Court of the United States" might be applied by the federal courts one way in Virginia and another way in California. In light of the well-recognized interest in ensuring that federal courts interpret federal law in a uniform way, we are convinced that Congress did not intend the statute to produce such a result.

III

In this case, Williams contends that he was denied his constitutionally guaranteed right to the effective assistance of counsel when his trial lawyers failed to investigate and to present substantial mitigating evidence to the sentencing jury. The threshold question under AEDPA is whether Williams seeks to apply a rule of law that was clearly established at the time his state-court conviction became final. That question is easily answered because the merits of his claim are squarely governed by our holding in *Strickland v. Washington.*

* * *

It is past question that the rule set forth in *Strickland* qualifies as "clearly established Federal law, as determined by the Supreme Court of the United States." That the *Strickland* test "of necessity requires a case-by-case examination of the evidence," *Wright*, 505 U.S. at 308 (KENNEDY, J., concurring), obviates neither the clarity of the rule nor the extent to which the rule must be seen as "established" by this Court. This Court's precedent "dictated" that the Virginia Supreme Court apply the *Strickland* test at the time that court entertained Williams' ineffective-assistance claim. And it can hardly be said that recognizing the right to effective counsel "breaks new ground or imposes a new obligation on the States." Williams is therefore entitled to relief if the Virginia Supreme Court's decision rejecting his ineffective-assistance claim was either "contrary to, or involved an unreasonable application of," that established law. It was both.

* * *

[T]he judgment of the Court of Appeals is reversed, and the case is remanded for further proceedings consistent with this opinion.

It is so ordered.

JUSTICE O'CONNOR delivered the opinion of the Court with respect to Part II (except as to the footnote), concurred in part, and concurred in the judgment.

In 1996, Congress enacted the Antiterrorism and Effective Death Penalty Act (AEDPA). In that Act, Congress placed a new restriction on the power of federal courts to grant writs of habeas corpus to state prisoners. The relevant provision, 28 U.S.C. § 2254(d)(1) (1994 ed., Supp. III), prohibits a federal court from granting an application for a writ of habeas corpus with respect to a claim adjudicated on the merits in state court unless that adjudication "resulted in a decision that was contrary to, or involved an unreasonable application of, clearly established Federal law, as determined by the Supreme Court of the United States." The Court holds today that the Virginia Supreme Court's adjudication of Terry Williams' application for state habeas corpus relief resulted in just such a decision. I agree with that determination.... Because I disagree, however, with the interpretation of § 2254(d)(1) set forth in Part II of JUSTICE STEVENS' opinion, I write separately to explain my views.

I

Before 1996, this Court held that a federal court entertaining a state prisoner's application for habeas relief must exercise its independent judgment when deciding both questions of constitutional law and mixed constitutional questions (i.e., application of constitutional law to fact). In other words, a federal habeas court owed no deference to a state court's resolution of such questions of law or mixed questions. In 1991, in the case of *Wright v. West*, we revisited our prior holdings by asking the parties to address the following question in their briefs:

> In determining whether to grant a petition for writ of habeas corpus by a person in custody pursuant to the judgment of a state court, should a federal court give deference to the state court's application of law to the specific facts of the petitioner's case or should it review the state court's determination de novo?

* * *

I wrote separately in *Wright* because I believed JUSTICE THOMAS had "understate[d] the certainty with which *Brown v. Allen* rejected a deferential standard of review of issues of law." I also explained that we had considered the standard of review applicable to mixed constitutional questions on numerous occasions and each time we concluded that federal habeas courts had a duty to evaluate such questions independently. With respect to JUSTICE THOMAS' suggestion that *Teague* and its progeny called into question the vitality of the independent-review rule, I noted that "*Teague* did not establish a 'deferential' standard of review" because "[i]t did not establish a standard of review at all." While *Teague* did hold that state prisoners could not receive "the retroactive benefit of new rules of law," it "did *not* create any deferential standard of review with regard to old rules." [*Wright*] 505 U.S. at 304 (emphasis in original).

Finally, and perhaps most importantly for purposes of today's case, I stated my disagreement with JUSTICE THOMAS' suggestion that de novo review is incompatible with the maxim that federal habeas courts should "give great weight to the considered conclusions of a coequal state judiciary," *Miller* [474 U.S. 104, 112 (1985)]. Our statement in *Miller* signified only that a state-court decision is due the same respect as any other "persuasive, well-reasoned authority." *Wright*, 505 U.S. at 305. "But this does not mean that we have held in the past that federal courts must presume the correctness of a state court's legal conclusions on habeas, or that a state court's incorrect legal determination has ever been allowed to stand because it was reasonable. We have always held that federal courts, even on habeas, have an independent obligation to say what the law is." Under the federal habeas statute as it stood in 1992, then, our precedents dictated that a federal court should grant a state prisoner's petition for habeas relief if that court were to conclude in its independent judgment that the relevant state court had erred on a question of constitutional law or on a mixed constitutional question.

If today's case were governed by the federal habeas statute prior to Congress' enactment of AEDPA in 1996, I would agree with JUSTICE STEVENS that Williams' petition for habeas relief must be granted if we, in our independent judgment, were to conclude that his Sixth Amendment right to effective assistance of counsel was violated.

II

A

Williams' case is *not* governed by the pre-1996 version of the habeas statute. Because he filed his petition in December 1997, Williams' case is governed by the statute as amended by AEDPA. * * *

* * *

Accordingly, for Williams to obtain federal habeas relief, he must first demonstrate that his case satisfies the condition set by § 2254(d)(1). That provision modifies the role of federal habeas courts in reviewing petitions filed by state prisoners.

JUSTICE STEVENS' opinion in Part II essentially contends that § 2254(d)(1) does not alter the previously settled rule of independent review. Indeed, the opinion concludes its statutory inquiry with the somewhat empty finding that § 2254(d)(1) does no more than express a "'mood' that the Federal Judiciary must respect." For JUSTICE STEVENS, the congressionally enacted "mood" has two important qualities. First, "federal courts [must] attend to every state-court judgment with utmost care" by "carefully weighing all the reasons for accepting a state court's judgment." Second, if a federal court undertakes that careful review and yet remains convinced that a prisoner's custody violates the Constitution, "that independent judgment should prevail."

One need look no further than our decision in *Miller* to see that JUSTICE STEVENS' interpretation of § 2254(d)(1) gives the 1996 amendment no effect whatsoever. The command that federal courts should now use the "utmost care" by "carefully weighing" the reasons supporting a state court's judgment echoes our pre-AEDPA statement in *Miller* that federal habeas courts "should, of course, give great weight to the considered conclusions of a coequal state judiciary." Similarly, the requirement that the independent judgment of a federal court must in the end prevail essentially repeats the conclusion we reached in the very next sentence in *Miller* with respect to the specific issue presented there: "But, as we now reaffirm, the ultimate question whether, under the totality of the circumstances, the challenged confession was obtained in a manner compatible with the requirements of the Constitution is a matter for independent federal determination."

That JUSTICE STEVENS would find the new § 2254(d)(1) to have no effect on the prior law of habeas corpus is remarkable given his apparent acknowledgment that Congress wished to bring change to the field. ("Congress wished to curb delays, to prevent 'retrials' on federal habeas, and to give effect to state convictions to the extent possible under law"). That acknowledgment is correct and significant to this case. It cannot be disputed that Congress viewed § 2254(d)(1) as an important means by which its goals for habeas reform would be achieved.

JUSTICE STEVENS arrives at his erroneous interpretation by means of one critical misstep. He fails to give independent meaning to both the "contrary to" and "unreasonable application" clauses of the statute. By reading § 2254(d)(1) as one general restriction on the power of the federal habeas court, JUSTICE STEVENS manages to avoid confronting the specific meaning of the statute's "unreasonable application" clause and its ramifications for the independent-review rule. It is, however, a cardinal principle of statutory construction that we must "'give effect, if possible, to every clause and word of a statute.'" Section 2254(d)(1) defines two categories of cases in which a state prisoner may obtain federal habeas relief with respect to a claim adjudicated on the merits in state court. Under the statute, a federal court may grant a writ of habeas corpus if the relevant state-court decision was either (1) "*contrary to* ... clearly established Federal law, as determined by the Supreme Court of the United States," or (2) "*involved an unreasonable application of* ... clearly established Federal law, as determined by the Supreme Court of the United States."

* * *

The word "contrary" is commonly understood to mean "diametrically different," "opposite in character or nature," or "mutually opposed." Webster's Third New International Dictionary 495 (1976). The text of § 2254(d)(1) therefore suggests that the state court's decision must be substantially different from the relevant precedent of this Court. The Fourth Circuit's interpretation of the "contrary to" clause accurately reflects this textual meaning. A state-court decision will certainly be contrary to our clearly established precedent if the state court applies a rule that contradicts the governing law set forth in our cases. Take, for example, our decision in *Strickland v. Washington*. If a state court were to reject a prisoner's claim of ineffective assistance of counsel on the grounds that the prisoner had not established by a preponderance of the evidence that the result of his criminal proceeding would have been different, that decision would be "diametrically different," "opposite in character or nature," and "mutually opposed" to our clearly established precedent because we held in *Strickland* that the prisoner need only demonstrate a "reasonable probability that ... the result of the proceeding would have been different." A state-court decision will also be contrary to this Court's clearly established precedent if the state court confronts a set of facts that are materially indistinguishable from a decision of this Court and nevertheless arrives at a result different from our precedent. Accordingly, in either of these two scenarios, a federal court will be unconstrained by § 2254(d)(1) because the state-court decision falls within that provision's "contrary to" clause.

On the other hand, a run-of-the-mill state-court decision applying the correct legal rule from our cases to the facts of a prisoner's case would not fit comfortably within § 2254(d)(1)'s "contrary to" clause. Assume, for example, that a state-court decision on a prisoner's ineffective-assistance claim correctly identifies *Strickland* as the controlling legal authority and, applying that framework, rejects the prisoner's claim. Quite clearly, the state-court decision would be in accord with our decision in *Strickland* as to the legal prerequisites for establishing an ineffective-assistance claim, even assuming the federal court considering the prisoner's habeas application might reach a different result applying the *Strickland* framework itself. It is difficult, however, to describe such a run-of-the-mill state-court decision as "diametrically different" from, "opposite in character or nature" from, or "mutually opposed" to *Strickland*, our clearly established precedent. Although the state-court decision may be contrary to the federal court's conception of how *Strickland* ought to be applied in that particular case, the decision is not "mutually opposed" to *Strickland* itself.

JUSTICE STEVENS would instead construe § 2254(d)(1)'s "contrary to" clause to encompass such a routine state-court decision. That construction, however, saps the "unreasonable application" clause of any meaning. If a federal habeas court can, under the "contrary to" clause, issue the writ whenever it concludes that the state court's application of clearly established federal law was incorrect, the "unreasonable application" clause becomes a nullity. We must, however, if possible, give meaning to every clause of the statute. JUSTICE STEVENS not only makes no attempt to do so, but also construes the "contrary to" clause in a manner that ensures that the "unreasonable application" clause will have no independent meaning. We reject that expansive interpretation of the statute. Reading § 2254(d)(1)'s "contrary to" clause to permit a federal court to grant relief in cases where a state court's error is limited to the manner in which it applies Supreme Court precedent is suspect given the logical and natural fit of the neighboring "unreasonable application" clause to such cases.

The Fourth Circuit's interpretation of the "unreasonable application" clause of § 2254(d)(1) is generally correct. That court held in *Green* [*v. French*, 148 F.3d 865 (1998)] that a state-court decision can involve an "unreasonable application" of this Court's clearly established precedent in two ways. First, a state-court decision involves an unreasonable application of this Court's precedent if the state court identifies the correct governing legal rule from this Court's cases but unreasonably applies it to the facts of the particular state prisoner's case. Second, a state-court decision also involves an unreasonable application of this Court's precedent if the state court either unreasonably extends a legal principle from our precedent to a new context where it should not apply or unreasonably refuses to extend that principle to a new context where it should apply.

A state-court decision that correctly identifies the governing legal rule but applies it unreasonably to the facts of a particular prisoner's case certainly would qualify as a decision "involv[ing] an unreasonable application of ... clearly established Federal law." Indeed, we used the almost identical phrase "application of law" to describe a state court's application of law to fact in the certiorari question we posed to the parties in *Wright*.[a]

a. The legislative history of § 2254(d)(1) also supports this interpretation. *See, e.g.*, 142 Cong. Rec. 7799 (1996) (remarks of Sen. Specter) ("[U]nder the bill deference will be owed to State courts' decisions on the application of Federal law to the facts. Unless it is unreasonable, a State court's decision

The Fourth Circuit also held in *Green* that state-court decisions that unreasonably extend a legal principle from our precedent to a new context where it should not apply (or unreasonably refuse to extend a legal principle to a new context where it should apply) should be analyzed under § 2254(d)(1)'s "unreasonable application" clause. Although that holding may perhaps be correct, the classification does have some problems of precision. Just as it is sometimes difficult to distinguish a mixed question of law and fact from a question of fact, it will often be difficult to identify separately those state-court decisions that involve an unreasonable application of a legal principle (or an unreasonable failure to apply a legal principle) to a new context. Indeed, on the one hand, in some cases it will be hard to distinguish a decision involving an unreasonable extension of a legal principle from a decision involving an unreasonable application of law to facts. On the other hand, in many of the same cases it will also be difficult to distinguish a decision involving an unreasonable extension of a legal principle from a decision that "arrives at a conclusion opposite to that reached by this Court on a question of law." Today's case does not require us to decide how such "extension of legal principle" cases should be treated under § 2254(d)(1). For now it is sufficient to hold that when a state-court decision unreasonably applies the law of this Court to the facts of a prisoner's case, a federal court applying § 2254(d)(1) may conclude that the state-court decision falls within that provision's "unreasonable application" clause.

B

There remains the task of defining what exactly qualifies as an "unreasonable application" of law under § 2254(d)(1). The Fourth Circuit held in *Green* that a state-court decision involves an "unreasonable application of ... clearly established Federal law" only if the state court has applied federal law "in a manner that reasonable jurists would all agree is unreasonable." * * *

Defining an "unreasonable application" by reference to a "reasonable jurist," however, is of little assistance to the courts that must apply § 2254(d)(1) and, in fact, may be misleading. Stated simply, a federal habeas court making the "unreasonable application" inquiry should ask whether the state court's application of clearly established federal law was objectively unreasonable. The federal habeas court should not transform the inquiry into a subjective one by resting its determination instead on the simple fact that at least one of the Nation's jurists has applied the relevant federal law in the same manner the state court did in the habeas petitioner's case. The "all reasonable jurists" standard would tend to mislead federal habeas courts by focusing their attention on a subjective inquiry rather than on an objective one. For example, the Fifth Circuit appears to have applied its "reasonable jurist" standard in just such a subjective manner. * * *

The term "unreasonable" is no doubt difficult to define. That said, it is a common term in the legal world and, accordingly, federal judges are familiar with its meaning. For purposes of today's opinion, the most important point is that an unreasonable application of federal law is different from an incorrect application of federal law. Our opinions in *Wright*, for example, make that difference clear. JUSTICE THOMAS' criticism of this Court's subsequent reliance on *Brown* turned on that distinction. The Court in *Brown*, JUSTICE THOMAS contended, held only that a federal habeas court must determine whether the

applying the law to the facts will be upheld"); 141 Cong. Rec. 14666 (1995) (remarks of Sen. Hatch) ("[W]e allow a Federal court to overturn a State court decision only if it is contrary to clearly established Federal law or if it involves an 'unreasonable application' of clearly established Federal law to the facts").

relevant state-court adjudication resulted in a "'satisfactory conclusion.'" In JUSTICE THOMAS' view, *Brown* did not answer "the question whether a 'satisfactory' conclusion was one that the habeas court considered correct, as opposed to merely reasonable." In my separate opinion in *Wright*, I made the same distinction, maintaining that "a state court's incorrect legal determination has [never] been allowed to stand because it was reasonable. We have always held that federal courts, even on habeas, have an independent obligation to say what the law is." In § 2254(d)(1), Congress specifically used the word "unreasonable," and not a term like "erroneous" or "incorrect." Under § 2254(d)(1)'s "unreasonable application" clause, then, a federal habeas court may not issue the writ simply because that court concludes in its independent judgment that the relevant state-court decision applied clearly established federal law erroneously or incorrectly. Rather, that application must also be unreasonable.

* * *

Throughout this discussion the meaning of the phrase "clearly established Federal law, as determined by the Supreme Court of the United States" has been put to the side. That statutory phrase refers to the holdings, as opposed to the dicta, of this Court's decisions as of the time of the relevant state-court decision. In this respect, the "clearly established Federal law" phrase bears only a slight connection to our *Teague* jurisprudence. With one caveat, whatever would qualify as an old rule under our *Teague* jurisprudence will constitute "clearly established Federal law, as determined by the Supreme Court of the United States" under § 2254(d)(1). The one caveat, as the statutory language makes clear, is that § 2254(d)(1) restricts the source of clearly established law to this Court's jurisprudence.

In sum, § 2254(d)(1) places a new constraint on the power of a federal habeas court to grant a state prisoner's application for a writ of habeas corpus with respect to claims adjudicated on the merits in state court. Under § 2254(d)(1), the writ may issue only if one of the following two conditions is satisfied—the state-court adjudication resulted in a decision that (1) "was contrary to ... clearly established Federal law, as determined by the Supreme Court of the United States," or (2) "involved an unreasonable application of ... clearly established Federal law, as determined by the Supreme Court of the United States." Under the "contrary to" clause, a federal habeas court may grant the writ if the state court arrives at a conclusion opposite to that reached by this Court on a question of law or if the state court decides a case differently than this Court has on a set of materially indistinguishable facts. Under the "unreasonable application" clause, a federal habeas court may grant the writ if the state court identifies the correct governing legal principle from this Court's decisions but unreasonably applies that principle to the facts of the prisoner's case.

III

Although I disagree with JUSTICE STEVENS concerning the standard we must apply under § 2254(d)(1) in evaluating Terry Williams' claims on habeas, I agree with the Court that the Virginia Supreme Court's adjudication of Williams' claim of ineffective assistance of counsel resulted in a decision that was both contrary to and involved an unreasonable application of this Court's clearly established precedent. * * *

* * *

Accordingly, although I disagree with the interpretation of § 2254(d)(1) set forth in Part II of JUSTICE STEVENS' opinion, I join Parts I, III, and IV of the Court's opinion and concur in the judgment of reversal.

[Omitted: CHIEF JUSTICE REHNQUIST, joined by SCALIA and THOMAS, JJ., concurring in part, dissenting in part.]

Notes

1. *Subsequent case history*

While Terry Williams' case was pending retrial, on November 14, 2000, Williams accepted a life sentence without the possibility of parole. In exchange, the prosecution agreed not to pursue the death penalty. Brooke A. Master, *Deal Gets Inmate Off Death Row*, The Washington Post, Nov. 15, 2000, at B1.

2. *Justice O'Connor's footnote*

Section II of Justice O'Connor's opinion garnered a bare majority (Justices O'Connor, Scalia, Thomas, Kennedy, and Rehnquist). As the caption notes, however, the footnote in her opinion was rejected by Justice Scalia and thus was not endorsed by a majority of the Court. Why do you suppose Justice Scalia would join the entire section, including the sentence attached to the footnote, but oppose the footnote?

3. *"No reasonable jurist"*

What does "no reasonable jurist" mean? Why does the majority reject the Fourth Circuit's "no reasonable jurist" interpretation of (d)(1)'s unreasonable application clause?

4. *Justice O'Connor versus Justice Stevens—determining AEDPA's destiny by a single vote*

Although Justice Stevens announced the judgment of the Court and wrote for the majority as to several sections of his opinion, he was unable to garner five votes for the key interpretive analysis under AEDPA (Section II). Instead, Justice O'Connor wrote for a five Justice majority regarding the meaning and scope of some of AEDPA's key provisions. What are the principle differences between Justice Stevens' reading of (d)(1) and that offered by Justice O'Connor?

In a footnote to Section II of his opinion, Justice Stevens, quoting an influential lower court judge, wrote:

> It does not tell us to "defer" to state decisions, as if the Constitution means one thing in Wisconsin and another in Indiana. Nor does it tell us to treat state courts the way we treat federal administrative agencies. Deference after the fashion of *Chevron U.S.A. Inc. v. Natural Resources Defense Council, Inc.*, 467 U.S. 837 (1984), depends on delegation. Congress did not delegate either interpretive or executive power to the state courts. They exercise powers under their domestic law, constrained by the Constitution of the United States. "Deference" to the jurisdictions bound by those constraints is not sensible.

Is it Justice Stevens' view that states cannot be the final arbiter of the Constitution dictated by the Constitution itself? Does Justice O'Connor reject this view? *See* Justin F. Marceau, *Un-Incorporating the Bill of Rights: The Tension between the Fourteenth Amendment and the Federalism Concerns that Underlie Modern Criminal Procedure Reforms*, 98 J. Crim. L. & Criminology 1231 (2008) (arguing that the purpose of selective incorporation under the Fourteenth Amendment and the Supremacy Clause—achieving a uniformity of constitutional rights so as to prevent a patchwork of rights among the several states—is undermined by the currently accepted interpretation of § 2254(d)).

Is Justice Stevens' reading of § 2254(d)(1) plausible? Is his reading faithful to the text of the statute? What is the net effect of Justice O'Connor's interpretation of § 2254(d)(1)? What is the standard for reviewing an alleged error of law? What is the standard for reviewing mixed questions of law and fact?

(2) "Clearly Established Federal Law"

Justice O'Connor's majority opinion regarding the proper application of § 2254(d)(1) remains controversial as a matter of textual and historical interpretation. In subsequent decisions, however, the Court has reaffirmed and elaborated on Justice O'Connor's view of (d)(1). In *Carey v. Musladin*, the Court elaborated on the threshold inquiry under (d)(1), the "clearly established law" analysis. *Musladin*'s definition of "clearly established law" has substantially limited the lower court's ability to interpret the federal constitution, and it has the potential to substantially limit the number of state prisoners who will be entitled to federal habeas relief.

Carey v. Musladin

549 U.S. 70 (2006)

JUSTICE THOMAS delivered the opinion of the Court, joined by *ROBERTS, C. J.*, AND *SCALIA, GINSBURG, BREYER,* AND *ALITO, JJ.*

This Court has recognized that certain courtroom practices are so inherently prejudicial that they deprive the defendant of a fair trial. In this case, a state court held that buttons displaying the victim's image worn by the victim's family during respondent's trial did not deny respondent his right to a fair trial. We must decide whether that holding was contrary to or an unreasonable application of clearly established federal law, as determined by this Court. We hold that it was not.

I

On May 13, 1994, respondent Mathew Musladin shot and killed Tom Studer outside the home of Musladin's estranged wife, Pamela. At trial, Musladin admitted that he killed Studer but argued that he did so in self-defense. A California jury rejected Musladin's self-defense argument and convicted him of first-degree murder and three related offenses.

During Musladin's trial, several members of Studer's family sat in the front row of the spectators' gallery. On at least some of the trial's 14 days, some members of Studer's family wore buttons with a photo of Studer on them. Prior to opening statements, Musladin's counsel moved the court to order the Studer family not to wear the buttons during the trial. The court denied the motion, stating that it saw "no possible prejudice to the defendant."

Musladin appealed his conviction to the California Court of Appeal in 1997. He argued that the buttons deprived him of his Fourteenth Amendment and Sixth Amendment rights. At the outset of its analysis, the Court of Appeal stated that Musladin had to show actual or inherent prejudice to succeed on his claim.... The Court of Appeal ... made clear that it "consider[ed] the wearing of photographs of victims in a courtroom to be an 'impermissible factor coming into play,' the practice of which should be discouraged." Nevertheless, the court concluded that the buttons had not "branded defendant 'with an unmistakable mark of guilt' in the eyes of the jurors" because "[t]he simple photograph of Tom Studer was unlikely to have been taken as a sign of anything other than the normal grief occasioned by the loss of [a] family member."

At the conclusion of the state appellate process, Musladin filed an application for writ of habeas corpus in Federal District Court pursuant to § 2254. In his application, Musladin argued that the buttons were inherently prejudicial and that the California Court of Appeal erred by holding that the Studers' wearing of the buttons did not deprive him of a fair trial. The District Court denied habeas relief but granted a certificate of appealability on the buttons issue.

The Court of Appeals for the Ninth Circuit reversed and remanded for issuance of the writ, finding that under § 2254 the state court's decision "was contrary to, or involved an unreasonable application of, clearly established Federal law, as determined by the Supreme Court of the United States." According to the Court of Appeals, this Court's decisions in *Williams* and *Flynn* clearly established a rule of federal law applicable to Musladin's case. Specifically, the Court of Appeals cited its own precedent in support of its conclusion that *Williams* and *Flynn* clearly established the test for inherent prejudice applicable to spectators' courtroom conduct. The Court of Appeals held that the state court's application of a test for inherent prejudice that differed from the one stated in *Williams* and *Flynn* "was contrary to clearly established federal law and constituted an unreasonable application of that law." We granted certiorari and now vacate.

II

* * *

In *Williams v. Taylor*, we explained that "clearly established Federal law" in § 2254(d)(1) "refers to the holdings, as opposed to the dicta, of this Court's decisions as of the time of the relevant state-court decision." Therefore, federal habeas relief may be granted here if the California Court of Appeal's decision was contrary to or involved an unreasonable application of this Court's applicable holdings.

A

In *Estelle v. Williams* ["*Williams*"] and *Flynn*, this Court addressed the effect of courtroom practices on defendants' fair-trial rights. In *Williams*, the Court considered "whether an accused who is compelled to wear identifiable prison clothing at his trial by a jury is denied due process or equal protection of the laws." The Court stated that "the State cannot, consistently with the Fourteenth Amendment, compel an accused to stand trial before a jury while dressed in identifiable prison clothes," but held that the defendant in that case had waived any objection to being tried in prison clothes by failing to object at trial.

In *Flynn*, the Court addressed whether seating "four uniformed state troopers" in the row of spectators' seats immediately behind the defendant at trial denied the defendant his right to a fair trial. The Court held that the presence of the troopers was not so inherently prejudicial that it denied the defendant a fair trial. In reaching that holding, the Court stated that "the question must be ... whether 'an unacceptable risk is presented of impermissible factors coming into play.'"

Both *Williams* and *Flynn* dealt with government-sponsored practices: In *Williams*, the State compelled the defendant to stand trial in prison clothes, and in *Flynn*, the State seated the troopers immediately behind the defendant. Moreover, in both cases, this Court noted that some practices are so inherently prejudicial that they must be justified by an "essential state" policy or interest.

B

In contrast to state-sponsored courtroom practices, the effect on a defendant's fair-trial rights of the spectator conduct to which Musladin objects is an open question in our jurisprudence. This Court has never addressed a claim that such private-actor courtroom conduct was so inherently prejudicial that it deprived a defendant of a fair trial. And although the Court articulated the test for inherent prejudice that applies to state conduct in *Williams* and *Flynn*, we have never applied that test to spectators' conduct. Indeed, part of the legal test of *Williams* and *Flynn*—asking whether the practices furthered an essential state interest—suggests that those cases apply only to state-sponsored practices.

Reflecting the lack of guidance from this Court, lower courts have diverged widely in their treatment of defendants' spectator-conduct claims. Some courts have applied *Williams* and *Flynn* to spectators' conduct. Other courts have declined to extend *Williams* and *Flynn* to spectators' conduct. Other courts have distinguished *Flynn* on the facts. And still other courts have ruled on spectator-conduct claims without relying on, discussing, or distinguishing *Williams* or *Flynn*.

Given the lack of holdings from this Court regarding the potentially prejudicial effect of spectators' courtroom conduct of the kind involved here, it cannot be said that the state court "unreasonabl[y] appli[ed] clearly established Federal law." § 2254(d)(1). No holding of this Court required the California Court of Appeal to apply the test of *Williams* and *Flynn* to the spectators' conduct here. Therefore, the state court's decision was not contrary to or an unreasonable application of clearly established federal law.

III

The Court of Appeals improperly concluded that the California Court of Appeal's decision was contrary to or an unreasonable application of clearly established federal law as determined by this Court. For these reasons, the judgment of the Court of Appeals is vacated, and the case is remanded for further proceedings consistent with this opinion.

It is so ordered.

JUSTICE STEVENS, concurring in the judgment.

In *Williams v. Taylor*, this Court issued two opinions announcing two separate holdings. In Part II-B of Justice O'Connor's opinion, the Court held that an incorrect application of federal law was not necessarily an "'unreasonable application of ... clearly established Federal law'" within the meaning of 28 U.S.C. § 2254(d)(1). In Parts III and IV of my opinion, in which Justice O'Connor joined, the Court held that the Virginia Supreme Court's rejection of the petitioner's claim that he had received ineffective assistance of counsel was both contrary to and an unreasonable application of law as determined by our earlier opinion in *Strickland v. Washington*.

In *Strickland*, we held that the petitioner had not been denied the effective assistance of counsel and upheld his sentence of death. While our ultimate *holding* rejected the petitioner's ineffective assistance claim, the reasoning in our opinion (including carefully considered dicta) set forth the standards for evaluating such claims that have been accepted as "clearly established law" for over 20 years. Nevertheless, in a somewhat ironic dictum in her *Williams* [*v. Taylor*] opinion, JUSTICE O'CONNOR stated that the statutory phrase "clearly established Federal law, as determined by the Supreme Court of the United States," refers to "the holdings, as opposed to the dicta, of this Court's decisions as of the time of the relevant state-court decision." That dictum has been repeated in three subsequent opinions in which a bare majority of the Court rejected constitutional claims that four of us would have upheld. Because I am persuaded that JUSTICE O'CONNOR's dictum about dicta represents an incorrect interpretation of the statute's text, and because its repetition today is wholly unnecessary, I do not join the Court's opinion.

* * *

Ultimately, [i]n my opinion, there is no merit whatsoever to the suggestion that the First Amendment may provide some measure of protection to spectators in a courtroom who engage in actual or symbolic speech to express any point of view about an ongoing proceeding.

JUSTICE KENNEDY, concurring in the judgment.

Trials must be free from a coercive or intimidating atmosphere. T his fundamental principle of due process is well established. It was recognized in *Frank v. Mangum*, 237 U.S. 309 (1915), though the Court credited the determination of the state court and granted no relief; and it was the square holding in *Moore v. Dempsey*, 261 U.S. 86 (1923), though the Court remanded for factfinding rather than for a new trial. The disruptive presence of the press required reversal in *Sheppard v. Maxwell*, 384 U.S. 333, 600 (1966), where "newsmen took over practically the entire courtroom, hounding most of the participants in the trial," and *Estes v. Texas*, 381 U.S. 532, 550 (1965), where the presence of cameras distracted jurors throughout the proceedings.

The rule against a coercive or intimidating atmosphere at trial exists because "we are committed to a government of laws and not of men," under which it is "of the utmost importance that the administration of justice be absolutely fair and orderly," and "[t]he constitutional safeguards relating to the integrity of the criminal process attend every stage of a criminal proceeding ... culminating with a trial 'in a courtroom presided over by a judge.'"

The rule settled by these cases requires a court, on either direct or collateral review, to order a new trial when a defendant shows his conviction has been obtained in a trial tainted by an atmosphere of coercion or intimidation similar to that documented in the foregoing cases. This would seem to be true whether the pressures were from partisans, or, as seems to have been the case in *Sheppard*, from persons reacting to the drama of the moment who created an environment so raucous that calm deliberation by the judge or jury was likely compromised in a serious way. If, in a given case, intimidation of this nature was brought about by the wearing of buttons, relief under the Antiterrorism and Effective Death Penalty Act of 1996 (AEDPA) would likely be available even in the absence of a Supreme Court case addressing the wearing of buttons. While general rules tend to accord courts "more leeway ... in reaching outcomes in case-by-case determinations," AEDPA does not require state and federal courts to wait for some nearly identical factual pattern before a legal rule must be applied.

In the case before us there is no indication the atmosphere at respondent's trial was one of coercion or intimidation to the severe extent demonstrated in the cases just discussed. The instant case does present the issue whether as a preventative measure, or as a general rule to preserve the calm and dignity of a court, buttons proclaiming a message relevant to the case ought to be prohibited as a matter of course. That rule has not been clearly established by our cases to date. It may be that trial judges as a general practice already take careful measures to preserve the decorum of courtrooms, thereby accounting for the lack of guiding precedents on this subject.

In all events, it seems to me the case as presented to us here does call for a new rule, perhaps justified as much as a preventative measure as by the urgent needs of the situation. That rule should be explored in the court system, and then established in this Court before it can be grounds for relief in the procedural posture of this case.

For these reasons, I concur in the judgment of the Court.

[Concurrence of SOUTER, J., omitted.]

Notes

1. *Subsequent case history*

In 2009, the Ninth Circuit denied relief on Musladin's remaining issues and affirmed the District Court's denial of habeas relief. *Musladin v. Lamarque*, 555 F.3d 830 (9th Cir. 2009). Mathew Musladin is serving a life sentence in a minimum security medical facility in Vacaville, California.

2. *Ironic dictum?*

What portion of Justice O'Connor's controlling opinion in *Williams* does Justice Stevens consider ironic? Why? And why does Justice Kennedy concur in the judgment when he seems to believe that events such as these "call for a new rule"?

3. *New rule's effect*

Assume that all nine Justices joined a separate opinion in *Musladin* that concluded that wearing buttons did violate due process. In other words, assume they concluded that relief is not available to Musladin because the meaning of due process was not "clearly established" at the time of his case, but the Court is nonetheless able to agree on the proper scope of due process moving forward. In a future case (say, for example, by a prisoner challenging his conviction this year), would habeas relief be available on the exact same facts as Musladin's case?

4. *Controlling precedent*

What about lower court precedent? Does circuit court law constitute clearly established law, or is it irrelevant to the determination of whether a prisoner is entitled to habeas relief? Does it matter if the proposition a lower court adopts is entirely uncontroversial and accepted by every federal circuit? For example, assume that every federal circuit court has held that the use of preemptory challenges to exclude members of a certain religion violates equal protection. Does this mean that the law is clearly established as to this point even though the Supreme Court has never directly addressed the issue?

5. *Shadow law*

Is there any danger of confusion when the nation's high court denies relief in a case like *Musladin* without *actually* addressing the underlying propriety of the constitutional claim?

Professor Alan Chen predicts that:

> Some state courts may reasonably misread these decisions as affecting not only federal habeas review, but also the course of constitutional development. Accordingly, a state court might read a federal court's decision concluding that another state court had not erred unreasonably as an endorsement of that state court's actual doctrinal conclusion.

Alan K. Chen, *Shadow Law: Reasonable Unreasonableness, Habeas Theory, and the Nature of Legal Rules*, 2 Buff. Crim. L. Rev. 535, 628 (1999). What is the import of Chen's concern?

6. *What if the prisoner is subject to an entirely new form of abuse?*

Due process prohibits the use of involuntary confessions. In addressing the issue of voluntariness, the Court has on a few occasions stated that certain forms of abuse or deception are sufficient to render a confession involuntary. Assume, however, that the local police engage in a newly invented method of interrogation that, though heinous and cruel, has never been addressed directly by the Supreme Court. Is the prisoner entitled to relief under *Musladin*?

In his concurrence, Kennedy explained, "While general rules tend to accord courts 'more leeway ... in reaching outcomes in case-by-case determinations,' the AEDPA does not require state and federal courts to wait for some nearly identical factual pattern before a legal rule must be applied." Justice Kennedy's concern foreshadows analysis subsequently provided by a majority of the Court in *Panetti v. Quarterman*, 551 U.S. 930, 953 (2007), where the Supreme Court explained the meaning of "clearly established" in the following passage:

> That the standard is stated in general terms does not mean the application was reasonable. AEDPA does not "require state and federal courts to wait for some nearly identical factual pattern before a legal rule must be applied." Nor does AEDPA prohibit a federal court from finding an application of a principle unreasonable when it involves a set of facts "different from those of the case in which the principle was announced." The statute recognizes, to the contrary, that even a general standard may be applied in an unreasonable manner. These principles guide a reviewing court that is faced, as we are here, with a record that cannot, under any reasonable interpretation of the controlling legal standard, support a certain legal ruling.

(3) "Contrary to" and "Unreasonable Application of"

In addition to imposing a new requirement that state prisoners demonstrate clearly established law, recall that § 2254(d)(1) simultaneously limits relief unless the prisoner can establish that the state court's analysis was "contrary to, or involved an unreasonable application of," the clearly established law, as defined in *Musladin*. In *Williams v. Taylor*, Justice O'Connor's majority opinion concluded that "Justice Stevens arrives at his erroneous interpretation [of (d)(1)] by means of one critical misstep. He fails to give independent meaning to both the 'contrary to' and 'unreasonable application' clauses of the statute."

Although the two standards have remained somewhat opaque in the years since Justice O'Connor's observation, subsequent case law has provided some content to these two "independent" concepts. In *Woodford v. Visciotti*, the Court delivered a unanimous opinion regarding the meaning of the "unreasonable application" clause of § 2254(d)(1).

Woodford v. Visciotti

537 U.S. 19 (2002)

PER CURIAM.

The United States Court of Appeals for the Ninth Circuit affirmed the grant of habeas relief to respondent John Visciotti after concluding that he had been prejudiced by ineffective assistance of counsel at trial. Because this decision exceeds the limits imposed on federal habeas review by 28 U.S.C. § 2254(d), we reverse.

I

Respondent and a co-worker, Brian Hefner, devised a plan to rob two fellow employees, Timothy Dykstra and Michael Wolbert, on November 8, 1982, their payday. They invited the pair to join them at a party. As the four were driving to that supposed destination in Wolbert's car, respondent asked Wolbert to stop in a remote area so that he could relieve himself. When all four men had left the car, respondent pulled a gun, demanded the victims' wallets (which turned out to be almost empty), and got Wolbert to tell him where in the car the cash was hidden. After Hefner had retrieved the cash, respondent walked over to the seated Dykstra and killed him with a shot in the chest from a distance of three or four feet. Respondent then raised the gun in both hands and shot Wolbert three times, in the torso and left shoulder, and finally, from a distance of about two feet, in the left eye. Respondent and Hefner fled the scene in Wolbert's car. Wolbert miraculously survived to testify against them.

Respondent was convicted by a California jury of first-degree murder, attempted murder, and armed robbery, with a special-circumstance finding that the murder was committed during the commission of a robbery. The same jury determined that respondent should suffer death. The California Supreme Court affirmed the conviction and sentence.

Respondent filed a petition for a writ of habeas corpus in the California Supreme Court, alleging ineffective assistance of counsel. That court appointed a referee to hold an evidentiary hearing and make findings of fact—after which, and after briefing on the merits, it denied the petition in a lengthy opinion. The California Supreme Court assumed that respondent's trial counsel provided constitutionally inadequate representation during the penalty phase, but concluded that this did not prejudice the jury's sentencing decision.

Respondent filed a federal habeas petition in the United States District Court for the Central District of California. That court determined that respondent had been denied effective assistance of counsel during the penalty phase of his trial, and granted the habeas petition as to his sentence. The State appealed to the Court of Appeals for the Ninth Circuit.

The Court of Appeals correctly observed that a federal habeas application can only be granted if it meets the requirements of 28 U.S.C. § 2254(d) ... * * *

* * *

The Court of Appeals found that the California Supreme Court decision ran afoul of both the "contrary to" and the "unreasonable application" conditions of § 2254(d)(1), and affirmed the District Court's grant of relief. The State of California petitioned for a writ of certiorari, which we now grant along with respondent's motion for leave to proceed *in forma pauperis.*

II

* * *

B.

The Court of Appeals ... held that, regardless of whether the California Supreme Court applied the proper standard for determining prejudice under *Strickland*, its decision involved an unreasonable application of our clearly established precedents. Specifically, the Ninth Circuit concluded that the determination that Visciotti suffered no prejudice as a result of his trial counsel's deficiencies was "objectively unreasonable." Under § 2254(d)'s "unreasonable application" clause, a federal habeas court may not issue the writ simply because that court concludes in its independent judgment that the state-court decision applied *Strickland* incorrectly. Rather, it is the habeas applicant's burden to show that the state court applied *Strickland* to the facts of his case in an objectively unreasonable manner. An "unreasonable application of federal law is different from an incorrect application of federal law." The Ninth Circuit did not observe this distinction, but ultimately substituted its own judgment for that of the state court, in contravention of 28 U.S.C. § 2254(d).

The Ninth Circuit based its conclusion of "objective unreasonableness" upon its perception (1) that the California Supreme Court failed to "take into account" the totality of the available mitigating evidence, and "to consider" the prejudicial impact of certain of counsel's actions, and (2) that the "aggravating factors were not overwhelming." * * *

* * *

The Court of Appeals disagreed with this [the state court's] assessment, suggesting that the fact that the jury deliberated for a full day and requested additional guidance on the meaning of "moral justification" and "extreme duress" meant that the "aggravating factors were not overwhelming." Perhaps so. However, "under § 2254(d)(1), it is not enough to convince a federal habeas court that, in its independent judgment, the state-court decision applied Strickland incorrectly." The federal habeas scheme leaves primary responsibility with the state courts for these judgments, and authorizes federal-court intervention only when a state-court decision is objectively unreasonable. It is not that here. Whether or not we would reach the same conclusion as the California Supreme Court, "we think at the very least that the state court's contrary assessment was not 'unreasonable.'" Habeas relief is therefore not permissible under § 2254(d).

The judgment of the Court of Appeals for the Ninth Circuit is reversed.

Notes

1. *Subsequent case history*

The Ninth Circuit denied petitioner's motion for oral argument on post-remand briefing and remanded the case to the district court for further proceedings, consistent with the above opinion. *Visciotti v. Brown*, 406 F.3d 1131 (9th Cir. 2005).

2. *Stare decisis*

Is *Visciotti* consistent with Justice O'Connor's opinion in *Williams*? Is it consistent with Justice Stevens' opinion in *Williams*?

3. *Does the Supreme Court disagree with the Ninth Circuit's legal analysis?*

More recently, in *Schriro v. Landrigan*, 550 U.S. 465, 473 (2007), the Court reiterated the fact that the applicability of § 2254(d)(1) will, in many cases, be dispositive as to the question of whether a state prisoner is entitled to relief for an otherwise meritorious constitutional claim:

> AEDPA, however, changed the standards for granting federal habeas relief. Under AEDPA, Congress prohibited federal courts from granting habeas relief unless a state court's adjudication of a claim "resulted in a decision that was contrary to, or involved an unreasonable application of, clearly established Federal law, as determined by the Supreme Court of the United States," § 2254(d)(1).... The ques-

> tion under AEDPA is not whether a federal court believes the state court's determination was incorrect but whether that determination was unreasonable—a substantially higher threshold.

During an oral argument for another case, Chief Justice Roberts explained his understanding of the unreasonable application clause in mathematical terms: "[A]ll you have to do is say: 2 plus 2 is somewhere between 3 and 5." (Oral Argument Transcript, *Berghuis v. Smith*, 08-1402, Jan. 20, 2010).

4. *Contrary to clearly established federal law*

Unlike the definition of "unreasonable application of" as used in (d)(1), Justice O'Connor's understanding of the "contrary to" clause of § 2254(d)(1) has remained largely unchallenged. It is well established that "a decision by a state court is 'contrary to' [the] clearly established law [of the Supreme Court] if it 'applies a rule that contradicts the governing law set forth in [Supreme Court] cases.'" *Price v. Vincent*, 538 U.S. 634, 640 (2003) (quoting *Williams v. Taylor*, 529 U.S. 362 (2000)). *See also Frantz v. Hazey*, 533 F.3d 724, 734 (9th Cir. 2008) (en banc) ("[e]xcept in the extremely rare circumstance in which a state case presents facts that are materially identical to those in a Supreme Court case, it is difficult to imagine many situations in which the result of a state court adjudication could be contrary to clearly established Supreme Court precedent.").

5. *Questions regarding the proper application of § 2254(d)(1)*

A. How should a federal court decide a habeas petition when the state court's adjudication constituted an unreasonable application of clearly established federal law, but not an application of the law that is clearly contrary to binding Supreme Court precedent?

B. If a prisoner establishes that the state court adjudicated his claim in a manner that is contrary to clearly established federal law, is he automatically entitled to habeas relief?

In *Frantz*, the en banc Court of the Ninth Circuit reviewed the decisions of other circuits and addressed this question:

> Section 2254 presumes that federal courts already have the authority to issue the writ of habeas corpus to a state prisoner.... [I]t is not itself a grant of habeas authority, let alone a discrete and independent source of post-conviction relief." ... In turn, § 2254(d), like other subsections of § 2254, implements and limits the authority granted in § 2241 for "a person in custody pursuant to the judgment of a State court." [In other words,] Section 2254 is properly seen as a limitation on the general grant of habeas authority in § 2241. Just as, for example, § 2254(b) restricts our underlying § 2241 and constitutional authority by creating an exhaustion requirement, § 2254(d) establishes certain kinds of state court error as a predicate to habeas relief "with respect to any claim that was adjudicated on the merits in State court.
>
> Where, as here, the limitations established by other subsections of § 2254 are satisfied, § 2254(a) sets out the general standard that must be satisfied by a petition "for a writ of habeas corpus in behalf of a person in custody pursuant to the judgment of a State court": The petition must rely "on the ground that he is in custody in violation of the Constitution or laws or treaties of the United States." * * *
>
> * * *
>
> Moreover, "AEDPA does not require a federal habeas court to adopt any one methodology in deciding the only question that matters under § 2254(d)(1)."

> Nor does it require any particular methodology for ordering the § 2254(d) and § 2254(a) determination. Sometimes, we may be able to decide the § 2254(d)(1) issue better by deciding the constitutional issue de novo first, when doing so would illuminate the § 2254(d)(1) analysis. In other cases, it may make sense to address § 2254(d)(1) first.
>
> In sum, where the analysis on federal habeas, in whatever order conducted, results in the conclusion that § 2254(d)(1) is satisfied, then federal habeas courts must review the substantive constitutionality of the state custody de novo.

Frantz, 533 F.3d at 735–37.

C. Should a federal habeas court defer to a state court judgment as required by (d)(1) when the state court judgment fails to provide any explanation or reasoning in support of the judgment? For example, should a federal court defer to a state court judgment when the state court merely provides a two-word "postcard" denial, "RELIEF DENIED"? Is this an adjudication on the merits as required by (d)(1)?

See generally Early v. Packer, 537 U.S. 3, 8 (2002) (per curiam) ("Avoiding these pitfalls [a 'contrary to' error] does not require citation ... [or] awareness of [Supreme Court] cases, so long as neither the reasoning nor the result of the state-court decision contradicts them."). Several circuits have adopted the position that a summary denial of relief is sufficient for purposes of triggering the limitations contained in § 2254(d)(1). *See* Evan Tsen Lee, *Section 2254(d) of the Federal Habeas Statute: Is It Beyond Reason?*, 56 Hastings L.J. 283, 285–86 (2004)(cataloguing the various approaches among circuits to summary or "silent" state court judgments).

But see Knowles v. Mirzayance, 129 S.Ct. 1411 (2009), *rehearing denied*, 129 S.Ct. 2426 (2009) (suggesting that summary judgments by a state court may not warrant deference). The Court noted that one might "question whether the California Court of Appeal's denial of [a] claim should receive as much deference as the 'prototypical' state-court adjudication 'involv[ing] both a reasoned, written opinion and an adequate development of the factual record in support of the claims.'" *Mirzayance*, 129 S.Ct. at 1418 n.2.

D. Might the limitations on relief contained in § 2254(d) be challenged on constitutional grounds? The Supreme Court has not directly addressed the question. Many commentators have argued that the provision is unconstitutional on a variety of grounds. One of the more common arguments is presented in a concurring opinion by Judge Noonan:

> AEDPA does operate over the whole class of cases of habeas corpus. It does not require a result in any particular case. What it does do is to strike at the center of the judge's process of reasoning. It shuts the judge off from the judge's normal sources of law and curbs that use of analogy which is the way the mind of a judge works. In our system of law where precedent prevails and is developed, AEDPA denies the judge the use of circuit precedent, denies development of Supreme Court and circuit precedent, denies the deference due the penumbra and emanations of precedent, and even denies the courts the power to follow the law as now determined by the Supreme Court—the precedent to be applied must have been in existence at the earlier moment when a state decision occurred. A more blinkered concept of law cannot be imagined—law, particularly constitutional law—is treated as what once was the law. The development of doctrine is despised. That despisal is a direct legislative interference in the independence of the judiciary....

* * *

Federal judges have taken an oath to uphold the Constitution of the United States. That oath has always been understood to mean the Constitution as it is interpreted by the courts. It is, of course, a grade school fiction that the Constitution does not change. It changes constantly: by constitutional amendment, by decisions of the Supreme Court, and by the invention of such things as the airplane, automobile, and internet. For a judge to be frustrated in following the most recent decision of the Supreme Court is perilously close to forcing the judge to violate his oath to uphold the Constitution as it presently is understood.

* * *

Can the constitutionality of AEDPA be sustained? Our circuit [the Ninth Circuit] has so ruled. I am bound by this decision. Moreover, the Supreme Court has upheld the application of AEDPA in a multitude of cases, tacitly assuming its constitutionality. Yet if I cannot depart from the law of the circuit, I may still ask the question as to constitutionality in the light of governing decisions by the Supreme Court.

As every law school student knows, *Marbury v. Madison* held unconstitutional an Act of Congress that attempted to confer jurisdiction on the Supreme Court. Writing for the unanimous court, Chief Justice Marshall declared:

> The judicial power of the United States is extended to all cases arising under the constitution. Could it be the intention of those who gave this power, to say that, in using it, the constitution should not be looked into? That a case arising under the constitution should be decided without examining the instrument under which it arises? This is too extravagant to be maintained.... *Marbury*, 5 U.S. at 178–80.

* * *

As recently as 1995, the Supreme Court held ... :

> Congress has exceeded its authority by requiring the federal courts to exercise "the judicial power of the United States," U.S. Const., Art. III, § 1, in a manner repugnant to the text, structure, and traditions of Article III.
>
> ...
>
> ... Article III establishes a "judicial department" with the "province and duty ... to say what the law is" in particular cases and controversies. The record of history shows that the Framers crafted this charter of the judicial department with an expressed understanding that it gives the Federal Judiciary the power, not merely to rule on cases, but to decide them, subject to review only by superior courts in the Article III hierarchy—with an understanding, in short, that "a judgment conclusively resolves the case" because "a 'judicial Power' is one to render dispositive judgments."...
>
> Almost two centuries after Marbury, Chief Justice Marshall's reasoning was once more applied ... :
>
> * * *
>
> Our national experience teaches that the Constitution is preserved best when each part of the government respects both the Constitution and the proper ac-

> tions and determinations of the other branches. When the Court has interpreted the Constitution, it has acted within the province of the Judicial Branch, which embraces the duty to say what the law is.

Irons v. Carey, 479 F.3d 658, 667–670 (9th Cir. 2007) (Noonan, J. concurring).

Chapter 3

The Statute of Limitations

The filing of a habeas petition that might ultimately secure one's release from prison presents a bit of a Goldilocks problem for a state prisoner—the petition can't be too early and it can't be too late; it must be *just right*. The doctrine of exhaustion (discussed in Chapter 8) dictates that a federal habeas petition will be deemed premature, or the claims therein unexhausted, if it is filed in federal court before the state court system has had a full opportunity to adjudicate the claims. A statute of limitations, by contrast, dictates that a prisoner who delays too long in filing his federal habeas petition also will be ineligible for federal relief. This chapter discusses the issues raised by the federal statute of limitations and the exceptions to the statute of limitations.

Many scholars and judges have questioned the equity of a habeas corpus statute of limitations insofar as such a limitation could serve as a permanent barrier to prisoners whose convictions in fact rest on unconstitutional practices. For most of the Writ's history, there was no formal time limitation for the filing of a habeas corpus petition. So long as the State could not prove undue prejudice from the delay, a prisoner was permitted to seek habeas corpus review. But the longstanding practice of refusing to allow claims challenging the constitutionality of a conviction or sentence to expire became increasingly unpopular in the latter half of the twentieth century.[1] For decades there were concerted legislative efforts to impose a statute of limitations. In *Vasquez v. Hillery*, 474 U.S. 254, 265 (1986), for example, the Court commented that "despite many attempts in recent years, Congress has yet to create a statute of limitations for federal habeas corpus actions." And in an appendix to its opinion in *Lonchar v. Thomas*, 517 U.S. 314 (1996), the Court listed more than 80 bills proposing statutes of limitations for federal habeas cases that Congress had introduced but had not adopted over the previous ten years.

Proponents of a statute of limitations finally succeeded when in 1996, as part of the Anti-Terrorism and Effective Death Penalty Act (AEDPA), a one-year statute of limitations was imposed on the filing of a federal habeas petition.

1. *See also*, U.S. Judicial Conference Ad Hoc Committee on Federal Habeas Corpus in Capital Cases, Committee Report and Proposal 6, 18–21 (1989) (Powell Committee Report) (recommending a statute of limitations); Ira P. Robbins, Toward a More Just and Effective System of Review in State Death Penalty Cases: Recommendations and Report to the American Bar Association Task Force on Death Penalty Habeas Corpus 29–30 (1990) (also recommending a statute of limitations).

A. The One-Year Statute of Limitations

Section 2244(d)(1) provides for a "1-year period of limitation" within which a state prisoner must seek federal habeas corpus review.[2] The one-year statute of limitations begins to run from the "latest of" four circumstances enumerated in the statute:

> A. [T]he date on which the judgment became final by the conclusion of direct review or the expiration of the time for seeking such review.
>
> B. [T]he date on which the impediment to filing an application created by State action in violation of the Constitution or laws of the United States is removed, if the applicant was prevented from filing by such State action.
>
> C. [T]he date on which the constitutional right asserted was initially recognized by the Supreme Court, if the right has been newly recognized by the Supreme Court and made retroactively applicable to cases on collateral review.
>
> D. [T]he date on which the factual predicate of the claim or claims presented could have been discovered through the exercise of due diligence.

Notes

1. *Rationale*

The Conference Committee Report provides the following explanation for the Act's statute of limitations:

> This title incorporates reforms to curb the abuse of the statutory writ of habeas corpus, and to address the acute problems of unnecessary delay and abuse in capital cases. It sets a one year limitation on an application for a habeas writ and revises the procedures for consideration of a writ in federal court.

H.R. Rep. No. 104-518, at 111 (1996) (Conf. Rep.). Who among their constituents would most likely be concerned about "unnecessary delay and abuse in capital cases"? Is it a reasonable concern?

2. *Finality of conviction*

The first trigger for the statute of limitations listed above (§ 2244(d)(1)(A)) applies in the vast majority of federal habeas cases. Under this provision, the one-year statute of limitations is understood to commence from the date when the conviction becomes final. Generally, this dictates two conclusions: (i) the time for seeking direct review does not count against the one-year limit; and (ii) a conviction becomes final when the United States Supreme Court denies certiorari on direct review. If, however, the defendant does not seek certiorari, then the judgment is said to be "final" and the statute of limitations runs from the deadline for seeking certiorari in the Supreme Court. Stated another way, "the running of the statute of limitations imposed by § 2244(d)(1)(A) is triggered by either (i) the conclusion of all direct criminal appeals in the state system, followed by either the completion or denial of certiorari proceedings before the United States Supreme Court; or (ii) if certiorari was not sought, then by the conclusion of all direct criminal appeals in the state system followed by the expiration of the time allotted for filing a petition for the writ." *Smith v. Bowersox*, 159 F.3d 345, 348 (8th Cir. 1998).

---

2. Federal prisoners seeking relief under 28 U.S.C. § 2255 must comply with an analogous one-year statute of limitations. 28 U.S.C. § 2255(f).

3. *Brady violations*

In Chapter 5, the cognizability of prosecutorial misconduct on habeas review—including the failure to disclose exculpatory evidence—is discussed. Assuming that a petitioner has a colorable *Brady* claim but the prosecutor's failure to disclose does not become apparent until after the conviction has become final, has the statute of limitations expired? How should a court calculate the statute of limitations in these circumstances? Is it also plausible to argue that a *Brady* violation is a state-created "impediment" to filing a state post-conviction petition?

4. *State-created impediments to filing for relief*

What sort of state action is required in order to delay the running of the statute of limitations under this statutorily enumerated exception to the normal operation of the one-year limit? Section 2244(d)(1)(B) has been limited primarily to instances of "direct interference" such as when a state denies the prisoner access to legal materials. *See Shannon v. Newland*, 410 F.3d 1083, 1087 (9th Cir. 2005) (observing that most of the §2244(d)(1)(B) cases are of this genre). On the other hand, courts have recognized the possibility of broader application of this provision by noting that "the word 'impediment' is not defined in the statute itself, nor is it self-elucidating." *Wood v. Spencer*, 487 F.3d 1, 6 (1st Cir. 2007).

5. *Retroactively applicable*

Section 2244(d)(1)(C) provides that the one-year limitation period begins to run "on the date on which the constitutional right asserted was initially recognized by the Supreme Court, if the right has been newly recognized by the Supreme Court and made retroactively applicable to cases on collateral review." What if a new right is recognized but the right is not expressly made retroactive for another year? In such a case, when does the statute of limitations begin to run for a prisoner? Applying similar statutory language from §2255, the Supreme Court has held:

> We believe that the text ... settles this dispute. It unequivocally identifies one, and only one, date from which the 1-year limitation period is measured: "the date on which the right asserted was initially recognized by the Supreme Court." We "must presume that [the] legislature says in a statute what it means and means in a statute what it says there." ... An applicant has one year from the date on which the right he asserts was initially recognized by this Court.

Dodd v. United States, 545 U.S. 353, 357 (2005).

6. *Opt-in provisions—a shorter statute of limitations*

In addition to the new one-year limitation, AEDPA provides for "Special Habeas Procedures in Capital Cases," which, among other things, impose an even shorter statute of limitations (180 days) if the state satisfies certain conditions. 28 U.S.C. §§2261–2266. These provisions often are referred to as the opt-in provisions because they establish a sort of quid pro quo for the states: a state can "opt-in" and benefit from the truncated federal statute of limitations (and other benefits) if the state provides competent counsel and related resources during state collateral proceedings. *See* 28 U.S.C. §2261(b) and (c) (setting forth the requirements that states must meet in order to opt-in).

Although several states have attempted to qualify for opt-in status, federal courts have read the opt-in requirements strictly and to date only Arizona's system has been deemed adequate. *See Spears v. Stewart*, 267 F.3d 1026, 1041–42 (9th Cir. 2001) (recognizing that

Arizona's system facially qualified for opt-in status but that it was inadequate as applied). Presently, even Arizona's system has not qualified for the special benefits of opt-in status.

B. Statutory Tolling of the Statute of Limitations

Even after the one-year limitation is triggered by one of the four circumstances set forth in 28 U.S.C. § 2244(d)(1), that provision is softened considerably by the statutory tolling language of 28 U.S.C. § 2244(d)(2). The relevant language provides that "[t]he time during which a properly filed application for State post-conviction or other collateral review with respect to the pertinent judgment or claim is pending shall not be counted toward any period of limitation under this subsection." The critical issue, of course, is what is a "properly filed" state post-conviction petition.

There is substantial agreement among lower courts that ministerial events distinct from the merits of the case do not constitute a "properly filed" petition. For example, a prisoner's request for appointment of post-conviction counsel in state court has been roundly regarded as insufficient to toll the federal statute of limitations. *See Doyle v. Archuleta*, No. 10-1013, 2010 U.S. App. LEXIS 6744 (10th Cir. Mar. 31, 2010) ("[n]either a request for counsel, nor actual appointment of counsel, qualifies as a 'properly filed application for State post-conviction relief.'"). Lower court judges disagree, however, regarding the degree to which a prisoner must detail the merits of his claims in order to constitute a properly filed petition. *Compare Woodford v. Garceau*, 538 U.S. 202, 210 (2003) (suggesting that a degree of detail analogous to a civil complaint is needed to commence post-conviction proceedings), *with Isley v. Arizona Dep't of Corr.*, 383 F.3d 1054, 1056 (9th Cir. 2004) (holding that the filing of a pro-forma state "Notice of Post-Conviction Relief" is sufficient for statutory tolling under § 2244(d)(2)).

In *Pace v. DiGuglielmo*, the Court considered the applicability of § 2244's tolling provision when a prisoner filed a complete post-conviction petition that failed to comply with a particular condition of filing, the state statute of limitations. Later, in *Lawrence v. Florida*, the Supreme Court rejected a reading of § 2244(d) that would treat appeals to the United States Supreme Court following state post-conviction as proceedings that constitute a "properly filed" petition for purposes of statutory tolling.

Pace v. DiGuglielmo

544 U.S. 408 (2005)

CHIEF JUSTICE REHNQUIST delivered the opinion of the Court.

The federal Antiterrorism and Effective Death Penalty Act of 1996 (AEDPA) establishes a 1-year statute of limitations for filing a federal habeas corpus petition. 28 U.S.C. § 2244(d)(1). That limitations period is tolled, however, while "a properly filed application for State post-conviction or other collateral review with respect to the pertinent judgment or claim is pending." § 2244(d)(2). This case requires us to decide whether a state postconviction petition rejected by the state court as untimely nonetheless is "properly filed" within the meaning of § 2244(d)(2). We conclude that it is not, and hold that petitioner John Pace's federal petition is time barred.

In February 1986, petitioner pleaded guilty to second-degree murder and possession of an instrument of crime in a Pennsylvania state court. He was sentenced to life in prison without the possibility of parole. Petitioner did not file a motion to withdraw his guilty plea, and he did not file a direct appeal. In August 1986, he filed a petition under the Pennsylvania Post Conviction Hearing Act (PCHA), 42 Pa. Cons. Stat. § 9541 et seq. (1988) (amended and renamed by Act No. 1988-47, §§ 3, 6, 1988 Pa. Laws pp. 337–342). These proceedings concluded in September 1992, when the Pennsylvania Supreme Court denied petitioner's untimely request for discretionary review.

Over four years later, on November 27, 1996, petitioner filed another state postconviction petition, this time under the Pennsylvania Post Conviction Relief Act (PCRA), 42 Pa. Cons. Stat. § 9541 et seq. (1998). The PCRA had replaced the PCHA in 1988 and was amended in 1995 to include, for the first time, a statute of limitations for state postconviction petitions, with three exceptions. Although petitioner's PCRA petition was filed after the date upon which the new time limits became effective, the petition said nothing about timeliness.

After reviewing petitioner's PCRA petition, appointed counsel submitted a "no-merit" letter. On July 23, 1997, the Court of Common Pleas dismissed the petition, without calling for a response from the Commonwealth. The court noted that petitioner's claims previously had been litigated and were meritless. Petitioner appealed. On May 6, 1998, the Commonwealth filed a brief in response, asserting that petitioner's PCRA petition was untimely under the PCRA's time bar, § 9545(b) * * * On May 28, 1998, petitioner responded by arguing that the time limit was inapplicable to him. The Superior Court dismissed his petition as untimely on December 3, 1998. The Superior Court reasoned that petitioner's PCRA petition did not come within the statutory note following § 9545(b), and that petitioner had "neither alleged nor proven" that he fell within any statutory exception, see §§ 9545(b)(1)(i)–(iii). The Pennsylvania Supreme Court denied review on July 29, 1999.

On December 24, 1999, petitioner filed a federal habeas petition under 28 U.S.C. § 2254 in the District Court for the Eastern District of Pennsylvania. The Magistrate Judge recommended dismissal of the petition under AEDPA's statute of limitations, § 2244(d)(1), but the District Court rejected that recommendation. The District Court recognized that, without tolling, petitioner's petition was time barred. But it held that petitioner was entitled to both statutory and equitable tolling for the time during which his PCRA petition was pending—November 27, 1996 to July 29, 1999. Beginning with statutory tolling, the District Court held that, even though the state court rejected his PCRA petition as untimely, that did not prevent the petition from being "properly filed" within the meaning of § 2244(d)(2). It reasoned that because the PCRA set up judicially reviewable exceptions to the time limit, the PCRA time limit was not a "condition to filing" but a "condition to obtaining relief" as we described those distinct concepts in *Artuz v. Bennett*, 531 U.S. 4, 11 (2000). The District Court alternatively found extraordinary circumstances justifying equitable tolling.

The Court of Appeals for the Third Circuit reversed. With regard to statutory tolling, it relied on a line of Third Circuit cases to conclude that the PCRA time limit constitutes a "condition to filing" and that, when a state court deems a petition untimely, it is not "properly filed." With regard to equitable tolling, it held that there were not extraordinary circumstances justifying that remedy. Because Circuits have divided over whether a state postconviction petition that the state court has rejected as untimely nonetheless may be "properly filed," we granted certiorari. We now affirm.

In *Artuz v. Bennett*, *supra*, we held that time limits on postconviction petitions are "condition[s] to filing," such that an untimely petition would not be deemed "properly filed."

("[A]n application is 'properly filed' when its delivery and acceptance are in compliance with the applicable laws and rules governing filings" including "time limits upon its delivery"). However, we reserved the question we face here: "whether the existence of certain exceptions to a timely filing requirement can prevent a late application from being considered improperly filed." Having now considered the question, we see no grounds for treating the two differently.

As in *Artuz*, we are guided by the "common usage" and "commo[n] underst[anding]" of the phrase "properly filed." In common understanding, a petition filed after a time limit, and which does not fit within any exceptions to that limit, is no more "properly filed" than a petition filed after a time limit that permits no exception. The purpose of AEDPA's statute of limitations confirms this commonsense reading. On petitioner's theory, a state prisoner could toll the statute of limitations at will simply by filing untimely state postconviction petitions. This would turn § 2244(d)(2) into a de facto extension mechanism, quite contrary to the purpose of AEDPA, and open the door to abusive delay.

Carey v. Saffold, 536 U.S. 214 (2002), points to the same conclusion. In *Saffold*, we considered whether § 2244(d)(2) required tolling during the 4½ months between the California appellate court's denial of Saffold's postconviction petition and his further petition in the California Supreme Court. The California Supreme Court denied the petition "on the merits and for lack of diligence," which raised the question whether that court had dismissed for lack of merit, for untimeliness, or for both. Although we ultimately remanded, we explained that, "[i]f the California Supreme Court had clearly ruled that Saffold's 4½-month delay was 'unreasonable,'" i.e., untimely, "*that would be the end of the matter*, regardless of whether it also addressed the merits of the claim, or whether its timeliness ruling was 'entangled' with the merits." *[S]ee also id.* (KENNEDY, J., dissenting) ("If the California court held that all of [Saffold's] state habeas petitions were years overdue, then they were not 'properly filed' at all, and there would be no tolling of the federal limitations period"). What we intimated in *Saffold* we now hold: When a postconviction petition is untimely under state law, "that [is] the end of the matter" for purposes of § 2244(d)(2).

Petitioner makes three principal arguments against this reading. First, he asserts that "condition[s] to filing" are merely those conditions necessary to get a clerk to accept the petition, as opposed to conditions that require some judicial consideration. Respondent David DiGuglielmo (hereinafter respondent) characterizes petitioner's position, which the dissent also appears to embrace, as a juridical game of "hot potato," in which a petition will be "properly filed" so long as a petitioner is able to hand it to the clerk without the clerk tossing it back. Be that as it may, petitioner's theory is inconsistent with *Artuz*, where we explained that jurisdictional matters and fee payments, both of which often necessitate judicial scrutiny, are "condition[s] to filing." We fail to see how timeliness is any less a "filing" requirement than the mechanical rules that are enforceable by clerks, if such rules exist. For example, Pennsylvania Rule of Criminal Procedure 901 (2005), which is entitled "Initiation of Post-Conviction Collateral Proceedings," lists two mandatory conditions: (A) the petition "shall" be filed within the time limit, and (B) the proceedings "shall be initiated by filing" a verified petition and "3 copies with the clerk of the court in which the defendant was convicted and sentenced." The natural reading is that (A) is every bit as much of a "condition to filing" as (B).

* * *

Finally, petitioner challenges the fairness of our interpretation. He claims that a "petitioner trying in good faith to exhaust state remedies may litigate in state court for years only to find out at the end that he was never 'properly filed,'" and thus that his federal habeas petition is time barred. A prisoner seeking state postconviction relief might avoid this predicament, however, by filing a "protective" petition in federal court and asking the federal court to stay and abey the federal habeas proceedings until state remedies are exhausted. *See Rhines v. Weber*, 544 U.S. [269], 278 (2005). A petitioner's reasonable confusion about whether a state filing would be timely will ordinarily constitute "good cause" for him to file in federal court. ("[I]f the petitioner had good cause for his failure to exhaust, his unexhausted claims are potentially meritorious, and there is no indication that the petitioner engaged in intentionally dilatory tactics," then the district court likely "should stay, rather than dismiss, the mixed petition").

The dissent suggests that our conclusion in *Artuz*, that state procedural bars "prescrib[ing] a rule of decision for a court" confronted with certain claims previously adjudicated or not properly presented are not "filing" conditions, requires the conclusion that the time limit at issue here also is not a "filing" condition. The dissent ignores the fact that *Artuz* itself distinguished between time limits and procedural bars. For purposes of determining what are "filing" conditions, there is an obvious distinction between time limits, which go to the very initiation of a petition and a court's ability to consider that petition, and the type of "rule of decision" procedural bars at issue in *Artuz*, which go to the ability to obtain relief. Far from requiring "verbal gymnastics," it must be the case that a petition that cannot even be initiated or considered due to the failure to include a timely claim is not "properly filed."

For these reasons, we hold that time limits, no matter their form, are "filing" conditions. Because the state court rejected petitioner's PCRA petition as untimely, it was not "properly filed," and he is not entitled to statutory tolling under § 2244(d)(2).

[The Court then discussed equitable tolling, assuming without deciding that equitable tolling was available but holding that the requirements for such tolling were not satisfied on these facts].

* * *

It is so ordered.

[The dissenting opinion of JUSTICE STEVENS, joined by SOUTER, GINSBERG, & BREYER, JJ., is omitted].

Lawrence v. Florida

549 U.S. 327 (2007)

JUSTICE THOMAS delivered the opinion of the Court.

Congress established a 1-year statute of limitations for seeking federal habeas corpus relief from a state-court judgment, 28 U.S.C. § 2244(d), and further provided that the limitations period is tolled while an "application for State post-conviction or other collateral review" "is pending," § 2244(d)(2). We must decide whether a state application is still "pending" when the state courts have entered a final judgment on the matter but a petition for certiorari has been filed in this Court. We hold that it is not.

I

Petitioner Gary Lawrence and his wife used a pipe and baseball bat to kill Michael Finken. A Florida jury convicted Lawrence of first-degree murder, conspiracy to commit murder, auto theft, and petty theft. The trial court sentenced Lawrence to death. The Florida Supreme Court affirmed Lawrence's conviction and sentence on appeal, and this Court denied certiorari on January 20, 1998.

On January 19, 1999, 364 days later, Lawrence filed an application for state postconviction relief in a Florida trial court. The court denied relief, and the Florida Supreme Court affirmed, issuing its mandate on November 18, 2002. Lawrence sought review of the denial of state postconviction relief in this Court. We denied certiorari on March 24, 2003.

While Lawrence's petition for certiorari was pending, he filed the present federal habeas application. The Federal District Court dismissed it as untimely under § 2244(d)'s 1-year limitations period. All but one day of the limitations period had lapsed during the 364 days between the time Lawrence's conviction became final and when he filed for state postconviction relief. The limitations period was then tolled while the Florida courts entertained his state application. After the Florida Supreme Court issued its mandate, Lawrence waited another 113 days—well beyond the one day that remained in the limitations period—to file his federal habeas application. As a consequence, his federal application could be considered timely only if the limitations period continued to be tolled during this Court's consideration of his petition for certiorari. Then-applicable Eleventh Circuit precedent foreclosed any argument that § 2244's statute of limitations was tolled by the pendency of a petition for certiorari seeking review of a state postconviction proceeding. Accordingly, the District Court concluded that Lawrence had only one day to file a federal habeas application after the Florida Supreme Court issued its mandate. The Eleventh Circuit affirmed. We granted certiorari, and now affirm.

II

The Antiterrorism and Effective Death Penalty Act of 1996 (AEDPA) sets a 1-year statute of limitations for seeking federal habeas corpus relief from a state-court judgment. 28 U.S.C. § 2244(d)(1). This limitations period is tolled while a state prisoner seeks postconviction relief in state court:

> The time during which a properly filed application for State post-conviction or other collateral review with respect to the pertinent judgment or claim is pending shall not be counted toward any period of limitation under this subsection. § 2244(d)(2).

Based on this provision, the parties agree that AEDPA's limitations period was tolled from the filing of Lawrence's petition for state postconviction relief until the Florida Supreme Court issued its mandate affirming the denial of that petition. At issue here is whether the limitations period was also tolled during the pendency of Lawrence's petition for certiorari to this Court seeking review of the denial of state postconviction relief. If it was tolled, Lawrence's federal habeas application was timely. So we must decide whether, according to § 2244(d)(2), an "application for State post-conviction or other collateral review" "is pending" while this Court considers a certiorari petition.

Read naturally, the text of the statute must mean that the statute of limitations is tolled only while state courts review the application. * * * After the State's highest court has issued its mandate or denied review, no other state avenues for relief remain open. And an application for state postconviction review no longer exists. All that remains is a separate certiorari petition pending before a *federal* court. The application for state postconviction review is therefore not "pending" after the state court's postconviction review is complete, and § 2244(d)(2) does not toll the 1-year limitations period during the pendency of a petition for certiorari.

* * *

Contrary to Lawrence's suggestion, our interpretation of § 2244(d)(2) results in few practical problems. As JUSTICE STEVENS has noted, "this Court rarely grants review at this stage of the litigation even when the application for state collateral relief is supported by arguably meritorious federal constitutional claims," choosing instead to wait for "federal habeas proceedings." *Kyles v. Whitley*, 498 U.S. 931, 932 (1990) (opinion concurring in denial of stay of execution). Thus, the likelihood that the District Court will duplicate work or analysis that might be done by this Court if we granted certiorari to review the state postconviction proceeding is quite small. And in any event, a district court concerned about duplicative work can stay the habeas application until this Court resolves the case or, more likely, denies the petition for certiorari.

Lawrence argues that even greater anomalies result from our interpretation when the state court grants relief to a prisoner and the state petitions for certiorari. In that hypothetical, Lawrence maintains that the prisoner would arguably lack standing to file a federal habeas application immediately after the state court's judgment (because the state court granted him relief) but would later be time barred from filing a federal habeas application if we granted certiorari and the State prevailed. Again, this particular procedural posture is extremely rare. Even so, equitable tolling may be available, in light of the arguably extraordinary circumstances and the prisoner's diligence. See *Pace v. DiGuglielmo*, 544 U.S. 408, 418 and n. 8 (2005). We cannot base our interpretation of the statute on an exceedingly rare inequity that Congress almost certainly was not contemplating and that may well be cured by equitable tolling.

* * *

III

Lawrence also argues that equitable tolling applies to his otherwise untimely claims. We have not decided whether § 2244(d) allows for equitable tolling. Because the parties agree that equitable tolling is available, we assume without deciding that it is. To be entitled to equitable tolling, Lawrence must show "(1) that he has been pursuing his rights diligently, and (2) that some extraordinary circumstance stood in his way" and prevented timely filing.

Lawrence makes several arguments in support of his contention that equitable tolling applies to his case. First, he argues that legal confusion about whether AEDPA's limitations period is tolled by certiorari petitions justifies equitable tolling. But at the time the limitations period expired in Lawrence's case, the Eleventh Circuit and every other Circuit to address the issue agreed that the limitations period was not tolled by certiorari petitions. The settled state of the law at the relevant time belies any claim to legal confusion.

Second, Lawrence argues that his counsel's mistake in miscalculating the limitations period entitles him to equitable tolling. If credited, this argument would essentially equitably toll limitations periods for every person whose attorney missed a deadline. Attorney miscalculation is simply not sufficient to warrant equitable tolling. * * *

Third, Lawrence argues that his case presents special circumstances because the state courts appointed and supervised his counsel. But a State's effort to assist prisoners in postconviction proceedings does not make the State accountable for a prisoner's delay. Lawrence has not alleged that the State prevented him from hiring his own attorney or from representing himself. * * *

Fourth, Lawrence argues that his mental incapacity justifies his reliance upon counsel and entitles him to equitable tolling. Even assuming this argument could be legally credited, Lawrence has made no factual showing of mental incapacity. In sum, Lawrence has fallen far short of showing "extraordinary circumstances" necessary to support equitable tolling.

IV

The Court of Appeals correctly determined that the filing of a petition for certiorari before this Court does not toll the statute of limitations under § 2244(d)(2). It also correctly declined to equitably toll the limitations period in the factual circumstances of Lawrence's case. For these reasons, the judgment of the Court of Appeals is affirmed.

It is so ordered.

JUSTICE GINSBURG with whom JUSTICE STEVENS, JUSTICE SOUTER, and JUSTICE BREYER join, dissenting.

The Court today concludes that an application for state postconviction review "no longer exists"—and therefore is not "pending"—once it has been decided by a State's highest court. What remains, the majority reasons, is a "separate" certiorari proceeding pending before this Court. But petitions for certiorari do not exist in a vacuum; they arise from actions instituted in lower courts. When we are asked to review a state court's denial of habeas relief, we consider an application for that relief—not an application for federal habeas relief. Until we have disposed of the petition for certiorari, the application remains live as one for state postconviction relief; it is not transformed into a federal application simply because the state-court applicant petitions for this Court's review.

I would therefore hold that 28 U.S.C. § 2244(d)'s statute of limitations is tolled during the pendency of a petition for certiorari. Congress instructed that the one-year limitation period for filing a habeas petition in the appropriate federal district court does not include "[t]he time during which a properly filed application for State post-conviction or other collateral review ... is pending." § 2244(d)(2). That provision can and should be read to continue statutory tolling until this Court has either decided or denied a petition for certiorari addressed to the state court's disposition of an application for postconviction relief. * * * Lawrence timely sought this Court's review of the denial of state postconviction relief.

I

Two other provisions in AEDPA ... bear on the proper interpretation of § 2244(d)(2). The first of these, § 2244(d)(1)(A), tells us when AEDPA's statute of limitations begins to run; it states that the trigger is the "the date on which the judgment [of conviction] became final by the conclusion of direct review or the expiration of the time for seeking such review." Congress thus explicitly ordered that the clock starts, following a state conviction, when the time to file a petition for certiorari expires or, if a petition is filed, when it is decided or denied.

* * *

The majority maintains that if an application for state postconviction review were considered to be "pending" while a certiorari petition remained before this Court, then a state prisoner could not exhaust state postconviction remedies without filing a petition for certiorari. But exhaustion and tolling serve discrete functions and need not be synchronized. The former is a prerequisite to filing for habeas relief in federal court. Exhaustion promotes principles of comity and federalism by giving state courts the first opportunity to adjudicate claims of state prisoners; that doctrine, however, does not necessitate this Court's review of the state court's determination. *See O'Sullivan v. Boerckel*, 526 U.S. 838, 844

(1999). Tolling, in contrast, concerns the time within which a procedural move must be made, not the issues that must be raised before a particular tribunal. And while one purpose of tolling is to allow adequate time for exhaustion, that is not the sole objective. Tolling in the context here involved also protects a litigant's ability to pursue his or her federal claims in a federal forum and avoids simultaneous litigation in more than one court—objectives undercut by today's decision.

* * *

II

Not only is the majority's reading of § 2244(d)(2) unwarranted, it will also spark the simultaneous filing of two pleadings seeking essentially the same relief. A petitioner denied relief by a State's highest court will now have to file, contemporaneously, a petition for certiorari in this Court and a habeas petition in federal district court. Only by expeditiously filing for federal habeas relief will a prisoner ensure that the limitation period does not run before we have disposed of his or her petition for certiorari. Protective petitions will be essential, too, when we grant review of a state court's ruling on a state habeas petition, for many months can elapse between the date we agree to hear a case and the date we issue an opinion. Consequently, the same claims will be pending in two courts at once, and the duplication will occasion administrative problems; for example, no decision, law, or rule tells us in which court the record in the case should be lodged. There is no indication that Congress intended to burden the court system or litigants with such premature filings.

The anticipatory filing in a federal district court will be all the more anomalous when a habeas petitioner prevails in state court and the State petitions for certiorari. * * *

Though recognizing this problem, the majority suggests that equitable tolling may provide a solution. But in the next breath, the majority hastens to clarify that the Court does not hold that equitable tolling is available under AEDPA.

By contrast, no similar problems, practical or jurisdictional, would result from a determination that an application for state postconviction review remains "pending" while a petition for certiorari from the state court's decision is before this Court. Nor would such a determination create an untoward opportunity for abuse of the writ. The majority's suggestion that prisoners would have an incentive to petition for certiorari as a delay tactic has no basis in reality in the mine run of cases. Most prisoners want to be released from custody as soon as possible, not to prolong their incarceration. They are therefore interested in the expeditious resolution of their claims.

* * *

In sum, the majority's reading is neither compelled by the text of § 2244(d)(2) nor practically sound. By cutting off tolling before this Court has had an opportunity to consider a pending petition for certiorari, the Court's holding will unnecessarily encumber the federal courts with anticipatory filings and deprive unwitting litigants of the opportunity to pursue their constitutional claims—all without furthering the purposes of AEDPA.

For the reasons stated, I would hold that petitioner Lawrence qualifies for statutory tolling under § 2244(d)(2), and would therefore reverse the Eleventh Circuit's judgment.

Notes

1. *Subsequent histories*

John Pace's request for a rehearing was denied, 545 U.S. 1135 (2005), and he currently is serving his life sentence in the Pennsylvania State Correctional Institution at Graterford. *See* http://inmatelocator.cor.state.pa.us. Gary Lawrence is incarcerated at the Union Correctional Institution in Raiford, Florida, awaiting the imposition of his death sentence. *See* www.dc.state.fl.us/ActiveInmates.

2. *Litigation costs*

What are the costs associated with having to litigate if one can litigate? What are the costs of having to litigate whether one even has the right to litigate?

3. *Good faith*

Under the old standard in *Fay v. Noia*, 372 U.S. 391 (1963), the courts had discretion to decline to entertain a petition when it was found that the defendant deliberately bypassed remedies in state court. Provided the petition was filed in good faith, the petitioner was entitled to consideration of his claims. Should good faith matter?

In an often cited case, the Ninth Circuit held in *Roy v. Lampert*, 465 F.3d 964 (9th Cir. 2006), that two petitioners whose habeas petitions were filed late were entitled to the benefits of equitable tolling because they had been housed in prisons out of state and had been unable to gain access to records or libraries needed to file on time. In both cases, the Court found that once both were returned to their home state they acted promptly and that the delay was basically outside their control. What other kinds of factors should a court take into account in deciding if there is equitable tolling?

4. *Amending a habeas petition and the statute of limitations*

Under 28 U.S.C. § 2242, a petitioner is permitted to amend or supplement his federal habeas petition. In *Mayle v. Felix*, 545 U.S. 644 (2005), the Court held that a prisoner may amend his petition after the expiration of the statute of limitations but only to the extent permitted under the civil rules governing when a claim "relates back."

Under the relation back doctrine, an amendment is said to relate back to the date of the original pleading when the amendment arises "out of the conduct, transaction, or occurrence" at issue in the original pleading. In *Mayle*, the Court specifically rejected the view that because a federal habeas petition challenges the constitutionality of a conviction or sentence, *any* new claim relating to the constitutionality of the trial—the "conduct" or "transaction"—necessarily relates back. Instead, relying on AEDPA's focus on finality, the Court explained, "Felix's approach, the approach that prevailed in the Ninth Circuit, is boundless.... A miscellany of claims for relief could be raised later rather than sooner and relate back, for 'conduct, transaction, or occurrence' would be defined to encompass any pretrial, trial, or post-trial error that could provide a basis for challenging the conviction. An approach of that breadth ... 'views "occurrence" at too high a level of generality.'... If claims asserted after the one-year period could be revived simply because they relate to the same trial, conviction, or sentence as a timely filed claim, AEDPA's limitation period would have slim significance." *Id.* at 661–662.

C. Equitable Tolling of the Statute of Limitations

In both *Pace v. DiGuglielmo* and *Lawrence v. Florida* the Court assumed without deciding that equitable tolling of AEDPA's statute limits was permitted. Finally, in 2010, the Court directly addressed the issue of equitable tolling in *Holland v. Florida*.

Holland v. Florida

130 S.Ct. 2549 (2010)

JUSTICE BREYER delivered the opinion of the Court.

We here decide that the timeliness provision in the federal habeas corpus statute is subject to equitable tolling. *See* 28 U.S.C. § 2244(d). We also consider its application in this case. In the Court of Appeals' view, when a petitioner seeks to excuse a late filing on the basis of his attorney's unprofessional conduct, that conduct, even if it is "negligent" or "grossly negligent," cannot "rise to the level of egregious attorney misconduct" that would warrant equitable tolling unless the petitioner offers "proof of bad faith, dishonesty, divided loyalty, mental impairment or so forth." 539 F.3d 1334, 1339 (C.A.11 2008) (per curiam). In our view, this standard is too rigid. See *Irwin v. Department of Veterans Affairs*, 498 U.S. 89, 96 (1990); see also *Lawrence v. Florida*, 549 U.S. 327, 336 (2007). We therefore reverse the judgment of the Court of Appeals and remand for further proceedings.

I

AEDPA states that "[a] 1-year period of limitation shall apply to an application for a writ of habeas corpus by a person in custody pursuant to the judgment of a State court." § 2244(d)(1). It also says that "[t]he time during which a properly filed application for State post-conviction ... review" is "pending shall not be counted" against the 1-year period. § 2244(d)(2).

On January 19, 2006, Albert Holland filed a *pro se* habeas corpus petition in the Federal District Court for the Southern District of Florida. Both Holland (the petitioner) and the State of Florida (the respondent) agree that, unless equitably tolled, the statutory limitations period applicable to Holland's petition expired approximately five weeks before the petition was filed. Holland asked the District Court to toll the limitations period for equitable reasons. We shall set forth in some detail the record facts that underlie Holland's claim.

A

In 1997, Holland was convicted of first-degree murder and sentenced to death. The Florida Supreme Court affirmed that judgment. On October 1, 2001, this Court denied Holland's petition for certiorari. And on that date—the date that our denial of the petition ended further direct review of Holland's conviction—the 1-year AEDPA limitations clock began to run. See 28 U.S.C. § 2244(d)(1)(A); *Jimenez v. Quarterman*, 129 S.Ct. 681 (2009).

Thirty-seven days later, on November 7, 2001, Florida appointed attorney Bradley Collins to represent Holland in all state and federal postconviction proceedings. By September 19, 2002—316 days after his appointment and 12 days before the 1-year AEDPA limitations period expired—Collins, acting on Holland's behalf, filed a motion for postconviction relief in the state trial court. That filing automatically stopped the running of the AEDPA limitations period, § 2244(d)(2), with, as we have said, 12 days left on the clock.

For the next three years, Holland's petition remained pending in the state courts. During that time, Holland wrote Collins letters asking him to make certain that all of his claims would be preserved for any subsequent federal habeas corpus review. Collins wrote back, stating, "I would like to reassure you that we are aware of state-time limitations and federal exhaustion requirements." He also said that he would "presen[t] ... to the ... federal courts" any of Holland's claims that the state courts denied. In a second letter Collins added, "should your Motion for Post-Conviction Relief be denied" by the state courts, "your state habeas corpus claims will then be ripe for presentation in a petition for writ of habeas corpus in federal court."

In mid-May 2003 the state trial court denied Holland relief, and Collins appealed that denial to the Florida Supreme Court. Almost two years later, in February 2005, the Florida Supreme Court heard oral argument in the case. But during that 2-year period, relations between Collins and Holland began to break down. Indeed, between April 2003 and January 2006, Collins communicated with Holland only three times—each time by letter.

Holland, unhappy with this lack of communication, twice wrote to the Florida Supreme Court, asking it to remove Collins from his case. In the second letter, filed on June 17, 2004, he said that he and Collins had experienced "a complete breakdown in communication." Holland informed the court that Collins had "not kept [him] updated on the status of [his] capital case" and that Holland had "not seen or spoken to" Collins "since April 2003." He wrote, "Mr. Collins has abandoned [me]" and said, "[I have] no idea what is going on with [my] capital case on appeal." He added that "Collins has never made any reasonable effort to establish any relationship of trust or confidence with [me]," and stated that he "does not trust" or have "any confidence in Mr. Collin's ability to represent [him]," Holland concluded by asking that Collins be "dismissed (removed) off his capital case" or that he be given a hearing in order to demonstrate Collins' deficiencies. The State responded that Holland could not file any *pro se* papers with the court while he was represented by counsel, including papers seeking new counsel. The Florida Supreme Court agreed and denied Holland's requests.

During this same period Holland wrote various letters to the Clerk of the Florida Supreme Court. In the last of these he wrote, "[I]f I had a competent, conflict-free, post-conviction, appellate attorney representing me, I would not have to write you this letter. I'm not trying to get on your nerves. I just would like to know exactly what is happening with my case on appeal to the Supreme Court of Florida." During that same time period, Holland also filed a complaint against Collins with the Florida Bar Association, but the complaint was denied.

Collins argued Holland's appeal before the Florida Supreme Court on February 10, 2005. Shortly thereafter, Holland wrote to Collins emphasizing the importance of filing a timely petition for habeas corpus in federal court once the Florida Supreme Court issued its ruling. Specifically, on March 3, 2005, Holland wrote:

> "Dear Mr. Collins, P. A.:
>
> "How are you? Fine I hope.
>
> "I write this letter to ask that you please write me back, as soon as possible to let me know what the status of my case is on appeal to the Supreme Court of Florida.

> "If the Florida Supreme Court denies my [postconviction] and State Habeas Corpus appeals, please file my 28 U.S.C. 2254 writ of Habeas Corpus petition, before my deadline to file it runs out (expires).
>
> "Thank you very much.
>
> "Please have a nice day."

Collins did not answer this letter.

On June 15, 2005, Holland wrote again:

> "Dear Mr. Collins:
>
> "How are you? Fine I hope.
>
> "On March 3, 2005 I wrote you a letter, asking that you let me know the status of my case on appeal to the Supreme Court of Florida.
>
> "Also, have you begun preparing my 28 U.S.C. § 2254 writ of Habeas Corpus petition? Please let me know, as soon as possible.
>
> "Thank you."

But again, Collins did not reply.

Five months later, in November 2005, the Florida Supreme Court affirmed the lower court decision denying Holland relief. Three weeks after that, on December 1, 2005, the court issued its mandate, making its decision final. At that point, the AEDPA federal habeas clock again began to tick—with 12 days left on the 1-year meter. *See Coates v. Byrd*, 211 F.3d 1225 (11th Cir. 2000) (per curiam) (AEDPA clock restarts when state court completes postconviction review). Twelve days later, on December 13, 2005, Holland's AEDPA time limit expired.

B

Four weeks after the AEDPA time limit expired, on January 9, 2006, Holland, still unaware of the Florida Supreme Court ruling issued in his case two months earlier, wrote Collins a third letter:

> "Dear Mr. Bradley M. Collins:
>
> "How are you? Fine I hope.
>
> "I write this letter to ask that you please let me know the status of my appeals before the Supreme Court of Florida. Have my appeals been decided yet?
>
> "Please send me the [necessary information] ... so that I can determine when the deadline will be to file my 28 U.S.C. Rule 2254 Federal Habeas Corpus Petition, in accordance with all United States Supreme Court and Eleventh Circuit case law and applicable 'Antiterrorism and Effective Death Penalty Act,' if my appeals before the Supreme Court of Florida are denied.
>
> "Please be advised that I want to preserve my privilege to federal review of all of my state convictions and sentences.
>
> "Mr. Collins, would you please also inform me as to which United States District Court my 28 U.S.C. Rule 2254 Federal Habeas Corpus Petition will have to be timely filed in and that court's address?
>
> "Thank you very much."

Collins did not answer.

Nine days later, on January 18, 2006, Holland, working in the prison library, learned for the first time that the Florida Supreme Court had issued a final determination in his case and that its mandate had issued—five weeks prior. He immediately wrote out his own *pro se* federal habeas petition and mailed it to the Federal District Court for the Southern District of Florida the next day. The petition begins by stating,

> "Comes now Albert R. Holland, Jr., a Florida death row inmate and states that court appointed counsel has failed to undertake timely action to seek Federal Review in my case by filing a 28 U.S.C. Rule 2254 Petition for Writ of Habeas Corpus on my behalf."

It then describes the various constitutional claims that Holland hoped to assert in federal court.

The same day that he mailed that petition, Holland received a letter from Collins telling him that Collins intended to file a petition for certiorari in this Court from the State Supreme Court's most recent ruling. Holland answered immediately:

> "Dear Mr. Bradley M. Collins:
>
> .....
>
> "Since recently, the Supreme Court of Florida has denied my [postconviction] and state writ of Habeas Corpus Petition. I am left to understand that you are planning to seek certiorari on these matters.
>
> "It's my understanding that the AEDPA time limitations is not tolled during discretionary appellate reviews, such as certiorari applications resulting from denial of state post conviction proceedings.
>
> "Therefore, I advise you not to file certiorari if doing so affects or jeopardizes my one year grace period as prescribed by the AEDPA.
>
> "Thank you very much."

Holland was right about the law. *See Coates*, *supra*, at 1226–1227 (AEDPA not tolled during pendency of petition for certiorari from judgment denying state postconviction review).

On January 26, 2006, Holland tried to call Collins from prison. But he called collect and Collins' office would not accept the call. Five days later, Collins wrote to Holland and told him for the very first time that, as Collins understood AEDPA law, the limitations period applicable to Holland's federal habeas application had in fact expired in 2000—before Collins had begun to represent Holland. Specifically, Collins wrote:

> "Dear Mr. Holland:
>
> "I am in receipt of your letter dated January 20, 2006 concerning operation of AEDPA time limitations. One hurdle in our upcoming efforts at obtaining federal habeas corpus relief will be that the one-year statutory time frame for filing such a petition began to run after the case was affirmed on October 5, 2000 [when your] Judgment and Sentence ... were affirmed by the Florida Supreme Court. However, it was not until November 7, 2001, that I received the Order appointing me to the case. As you can see, I was appointed about a year after your case became final....
>
> "[T]he AEDPA time period [thus] had run before my appointment and therefore before your [postconviction] motion was filed."

Collins was wrong about the law. As we have said, Holland's 1-year limitations period did not begin to run until *this* Court denied Holland's petition for certiorari from the state courts' denial of relief on direct review, which occurred on October 1, 2001. *See* 28 U.S.C. § 2244(d)(1)(A). And when Collins was appointed (on November 7, 2001) the AEDPA clock therefore had 328 days left to go.

Holland immediately wrote back to Collins, pointing this out.

> "Dear Mr. Collins:
>
> "I received your letter dated January 31, 2006. You are incorrect in stating that 'the one-year statutory time frame for filing my 2254 petition began to run after my case was affirmed on October 5, 2000, by the Florida Supreme Court.' As stated on page three of [the recently filed] Petition for a writ of certiorari, October 1, 2001 is when the United States Supreme Court denied my initial petition for writ of certiorari and that is when my case became final. That meant that the time would be tolled once I filed my [postconviction] motion in the trial court.
>
> "Also, Mr. Collins you never told me that my time ran out (expired). I told you to timely file my 28 U.S.C. 2254 Habeas Corpus Petition before the deadline, so that I would not be time-barred.
>
> "You never informed me of oral arguments or of the Supreme Court of Florida's November 10, 2005 decision denying my postconviction appeals. You never kept me informed about the status of my case, although you told me that you would immediately inform me of the court's decision as soon as you heard anything.
>
> "Mr. Collins, I filed a motion on January 19, 2006 [in federal court] to preserve my rights, because I did not want to be time-barred. Have you heard anything about the aforesaid motion? Do you know what the status of aforesaid motion is?
>
> "Mr. Collins, please file my 2254 Habeas Petition immediately. Please do not wait any longer, even though it will be untimely filed at least it will be filed without wasting anymore time. (valuable time).
>
> "Again, please file my 2254 Petition at once.
>
> "Your letter is the first time that you have ever mentioned anything to me about my time had run out, before you were appointed to represent me, and that my one-year started to run on October 5, 2000.
>
> "Please find out the status of my motion that I filed on January 19, 2006 and let me know.
>
> "Thank you very much."

Collins did not answer this letter. Nor did he file a federal habeas petition as Holland requested.

On March 1, 2006, Holland filed another complaint against Collins with the Florida Bar Association. This time the bar asked Collins to respond, which he did, through his own attorney, on March 21. And the very next day, over three months after Holland's AEDPA statute of limitations had expired, Collins mailed a proposed federal habeas petition to Holland, asking him to review it.

But by that point Holland had already filed a *pro se* motion in the District Court asking that Collins be dismissed as his attorney. The State responded to that request by arguing once again that Holland could not file a *pro se* motion seeking to have Collins removed while he was represented by counsel, *i.e.*, represented by Collins. But this time the court considered Holland's motion, permitted Collins to withdraw from the case, and appointed a new lawyer for Holland. And it also received briefing on whether the circumstances of the case justified the equitable tolling of the AEDPA limitations period for a sufficient period of time (approximately five weeks) to make Holland's petition timely.

C

After considering the briefs, the Federal District Court held that the facts did not warrant equitable tolling and that consequently Holland's petition was untimely. * * *

On appeal, the Eleventh Circuit agreed with the District Court that Holland's habeas petition was untimely. The Court of Appeals first agreed with Holland that "'[e]quitable tolling can be applied to ... AEDPA's statutory deadline.'" But it also held that equitable tolling could not be applied in a case, like Holland's, that involves no more than "[p]ure professional negligence" on the part of a petitioner's attorney because such behavior can never constitute an "extraordinary circumstance." * * *

* * *

Holland petitioned for certiorari. Because the Court of Appeals' application of the equitable tolling doctrine to instances of professional misconduct conflicts with the approach taken by other Circuits, we granted the petition.

II

We have not decided whether AEDPA's statutory limitations period may be tolled for equitable reasons. *See Lawrence*, 549 U.S., at 336. Now, like all 11 Courts of Appeals that have considered the question, we hold that § 2244(d) is subject to equitable tolling in appropriate cases.

We base our conclusion on the following considerations. First, the AEDPA "statute of limitations defense ... is not 'jurisdictional.'" *Day v. McDonough*, 547 U.S. 198, 205 (2006). It does not set forth "an inflexible rule requiring dismissal whenever" its "clock has run."

We have previously made clear that a nonjurisdictional federal statute of limitations is normally subject to a "rebuttable presumption" in *favor* "of equitable tolling."

In the case of AEDPA, the presumption's strength is reinforced by the fact that "'equitable principles'" have traditionally "'governed'" the substantive law of habeas corpus, *Munaf v. Geren*, 553 U.S. 674, 693 (2008), for we will "not construe a statute to displace courts' traditional equitable authority absent the 'clearest command,'" *Miller v. French*, 530 U.S. 327, 340 (2000). The presumption's strength is yet further reinforced by the fact that Congress enacted AEDPA after this Court decided *Irwin* and therefore was likely aware that courts, when interpreting AEDPA's timing provisions, would apply the presumption. *See, e.g., Merck & Co. v. Reynolds*, 130 S.Ct. 1784 (2010).

Second, the statute here differs significantly from the statutes at issue in *United States v. Brockamp*, 519 U.S. 347 (1997), and *United States v. Beggerly*, 524 U.S. 38 (1998), two cases in which we held that *Irwin*'s presumption had been overcome. In *Brockamp*, we interpreted a statute of limitations that was silent on the question of equitable tolling as foreclosing application of that doctrine. But in doing so we emphasized that the statute at issue (1) "se[t] forth its time limitations in unusually emphatic form"; (2) used "highly detailed" and "technical" language "that, linguistically speaking, cannot easily be read as containing implicit exceptions"; (3) "reiterate[d] its limitations several times in several different ways"; (4) related to an "underlying subject matter," nationwide tax collection, with respect to which the practical consequences of permitting tolling would have been substantial; and (5) would, if tolled, "require tolling, not only procedural limitations, but also substantive limitations on the amount of recovery—a kind of tolling for which we ...

found no direct precedent." And in *Beggerly* we held that *Irwin*'s presumption was overcome where (1) the 12-year statute of limitations at issue was "unusually generous" and (2) the underlying claim "deal[t] with ownership of land" and thereby implicated landowners' need to "know with certainty what their rights are, and the period during which those rights may be subject to challenge."

By way of contrast, AEDPA's statute of limitations, unlike the statute at issue in *Brockamp*, does not contain language that is "unusually emphatic," nor does it "re-iterat[e]" it's time limitation. Neither would application of equitable tolling here affect the "substance" of a petitioner's claim. Moreover, in contrast to the 12-year limitations period at issue in *Beggerly*, AEDPA's limitations period is not particularly long. And unlike the subject matters at issue in both *Brockamp* and *Beggerly*—tax collection and land claims—AEDPA's subject matter, habeas corpus, pertains to an area of the law where equity finds a comfortable home. In short, AEDPA's 1-year limit reads like an ordinary, run-of-the-mill statute of limitations.

Respondent, citing *Brockamp*, argues that AEDPA should be interpreted to foreclose equitable tolling because the statute sets forth "explicit exceptions to its basic time limits" that do "not include 'equitable tolling.'" The statute does contain multiple provisions relating to the events that trigger its running. *See* § 2244(d)(1); *Clay v. United States*, 537 U.S. 522, 529 (2003). And we concede that it is silent as to equitable tolling while containing one provision that expressly refers to a different kind of tolling. *See* § 2244(d)(2) (stating that "[t]he time during which" a petitioner has a pending request for state post-conviction relief "shall not be counted toward" his "period of limitation" under AEDPA). But the fact that Congress expressly referred to tolling during state collateral review proceedings is easily explained without rebutting the presumption in favor of equitable tolling. A petitioner cannot bring a federal habeas claim without first exhausting state remedies—a process that frequently takes longer than one year. *See Rose v. Lundy*, 455 U.S. 509 (1982); § 2254(b)(1)(A). Hence, Congress had to explain how the limitations statute accounts for the time during which such state proceedings are pending. This special need for an express provision undermines any temptation to invoke the interpretive maxim *inclusio unius est exclusio alterius* (to include one item (*i.e.*, suspension during state-court collateral review) is to exclude other similar items (*i.e.*, equitable tolling)).

Third, and finally, we disagree with respondent that equitable tolling undermines AEDPA's basic purposes. We recognize that AEDPA seeks to eliminate delays in the federal habeas review process. *See Day*, 547 U.S. [198], 205–206. But AEDPA seeks to do so without undermining basic habeas corpus principles and while seeking to harmonize the new statute with prior law, under which a petition's timeliness was always determined under equitable principles. See *Slack v. McDaniel*, 529 U.S. 473, 483 (2000) ("AEDPA's present provisions ... incorporate earlier habeas corpus principles"). When Congress codified new rules governing this previously judicially managed area of law, it did so without losing sight of the fact that the "writ of habeas corpus plays a vital role in protecting constitutional rights." *Slack*, 529 U.S. at 483. It did not seek to end every possible delay at all costs. The importance of the Great Writ, the only writ explicitly protected by the Constitution, Art. I, § 9, cl. 2, along with congressional efforts to harmonize the new statute with prior law, counsels hesitancy before interpreting AEDPA's statutory silence as indicating a congressional intent to close courthouse doors that a strong equitable claim would ordinarily keep open.

For these reasons we conclude that neither AEDPA's textual characteristics nor the statute's basic purposes "rebut" the basic presumption set forth in *Irwin*. And we therefore join the Courts of Appeals in holding that § 2244(d) is subject to equitable tolling.

III

We have previously made clear that a "petitioner" is "entitled to equitable tolling" only if he shows "(1) that he has been pursuing his rights diligently, and (2) that some extraordinary circumstance stood in his way" and prevented timely filing. *Pace*, 544 U.S. at 418 (emphasis deleted). In this case, the "extraordinary circumstances" at issue involve an attorney's failure to satisfy professional standards of care. The Court of Appeals held that, where that is so, even attorney conduct that is "grossly negligent" can never warrant tolling absent "bad faith, dishonesty, divided loyalty, mental impairment or so forth on the lawyer's part." But in our view, the Court of Appeals' standard is too rigid.

* * *

We recognize that, in the context of procedural default, we have previously stated, without qualification, that a petitioner "must 'bear the risk of attorney error.'" *Coleman v. Thompson*, 501 U.S. 722, 752–753 (1991). But *Coleman* was "a case about federalism," in that it asked whether federal courts may excuse a petitioner's failure to comply with a state court's procedural rules, notwithstanding the state court's determination that its own rules had been violated. Equitable tolling, by contrast, asks whether federal courts may excuse a petitioner's failure to comply with federal timing rules, an inquiry that does not implicate a state court's interpretation of state law. Cf. *Lawrence*, 549 U.S., at 341 (Ginsburg, J., dissenting). Holland does not argue that his attorney's misconduct provides a substantive ground for relief, nor is this a case that asks whether AEDPA's statute of limitations should be recognized at all. *Day, supra.* Rather, this case asks how equity should be applied once the statute is recognized. And given equity's resistance to rigid rules, we cannot read *Coleman* as requiring a *per se* approach in this context.

In short, no pre-existing rule of law or precedent demands a rule like the one set forth by the Eleventh Circuit in this case. That rule is difficult to reconcile with more general equitable principles in that it fails to recognize that, at least sometimes, professional misconduct that fails to meet the Eleventh Circuit's standard could nonetheless amount to egregious behavior and create an extraordinary circumstance that warrants equitable tolling. And, given the long history of judicial application of equitable tolling, courts can easily find precedents that can guide their judgments. Several lower courts have specifically held that unprofessional attorney conduct may, in certain circumstances, prove "egregious" and can be "extraordinary" even though the conduct in question may not satisfy the Eleventh Circuit's rule.

We have previously held that "a garden variety claim of excusable neglect," *Irwin*, 498 U.S., at 96, such as a simple "miscalculation" that leads a lawyer to miss a filing deadline, *Lawrence, supra*, at 336, does not warrant equitable tolling. But the case before us does not involve, and we are not considering, a "garden variety claim" of attorney negligence. Rather, the facts of this case present far more serious instances of attorney misconduct. And, as we have said, although the circumstances of a case must be "extraordinary" before equitable tolling can be applied, we hold that such circumstances are not limited to those that satisfy the test that the Court of Appeals used in this case.

IV

The record facts that we have set forth in Part I of this opinion suggest that this case may well be an "extraordinary" instance in which petitioner's attorney's conduct constituted far more than "garden variety" or "excusable neglect." To be sure, Collins failed to file Holland's petition on time and appears to have been unaware of the date on which the limitations period expired—two facts that, alone, might suggest simple negligence. But, in these circumstances, the record facts we have elucidated suggest that the failure amounted to more: Here, Collins failed to file Holland's federal petition on time despite Holland's many letters that repeatedly emphasized the importance of his doing so. Collins apparently did not do the research necessary to find out the proper filing date, despite Holland's letters that went so far as to identify the applicable legal rules. Collins failed to inform Holland in a timely manner about the crucial fact that the Florida Supreme Court had decided his case, again despite Holland's many pleas for that information. And Collins failed to communicate with his client over a period of years, despite various pleas from Holland that Collins respond to his letters.

A group of teachers of legal ethics tells us that these various failures violated fundamental canons of professional responsibility, which require attorneys to perform reasonably competent legal work, to communicate with their clients, to implement clients' reasonable requests, to keep their clients informed of key developments in their cases, and never to abandon a client. See Brief for Legal Ethics Professors *et al.* as *Amici Curiae* (describing ethical rules set forth in case law, the Restatements of Agency, the Restatement (Third) of the Law Governing Lawyers (1998), and in the ABA Model Rules of Professional Conduct (2009)). And in this case, the failures seriously prejudiced a client who thereby lost what was likely his single opportunity for federal habeas review of the lawfulness of his imprisonment and of his death sentence.

We do not state our conclusion in absolute form, however, because more proceedings may be necessary. The District Court rested its ruling not on a lack of extraordinary circumstances, but rather on a lack of diligence—a ruling that respondent does not defend. We think that the District Court's conclusion was incorrect. The diligence required for equitable tolling purposes is "'reasonable diligence,'" see, *e.g.*, *Lonchar*, 517 U.S., at 326, not "'maximum feasible diligence,'" *Starns v. Andrews*, 524 F.3d 612, 618 (5th Cir. 2008). Here, Holland not only wrote his attorney numerous letters seeking crucial information and providing direction; he also repeatedly contacted the state courts, their clerks, and the Florida State Bar Association in an effort to have Collins—the central impediment to the pursuit of his legal remedy—removed from his case. And, the very day that Holland discovered that his AEDPA clock had expired due to Collins' failings, Holland prepared his own habeas petition *pro se* and promptly filed it with the District Court.

Because the District Court erroneously relied on a lack of diligence, and because the Court of Appeals erroneously relied on an overly rigid *per se* approach, no lower court has yet considered in detail the facts of this case to determine whether they indeed constitute extraordinary circumstances sufficient to warrant equitable relief.... Thus, because we conclude that the District Court's determination must be set aside, we leave it to the Court of Appeals to determine whether the facts in this record entitle Holland to equitable tolling, or whether further proceedings, including an evidentiary hearing, might indicate that respondent should prevail.

The judgment below is reversed, and the case is remanded for further proceedings consistent with this opinion.

It is so ordered.

[Concurring opinion by JUSTICE ALITO is omitted].

[Dissent by JUSTICE SCALIA is omitted.]

Notes

1. *Subsequent case history*

Albert Holland's case was remanded for further proceedings, and at the time this book was published, he was still incarcerated at Union Correctional Facility in Raiford, Florida. www.dc.state.fl.us/ActiveInmates.

2. "*Some extraordinary circumstance stood in his way*"

Short of facts as extreme as those in *Holland*, what other circumstances might justify the equitable tolling of AEDPA's statute of limitations? Should *Lawrence v. Florida* have come out differently after *Holland*, since it was simply counsel's mistake as to the relevant tolling of the statute of limitations that adversely affected both clients?

Would the result in *Holland* have been different if counsel had miscalculated the state post-conviction statute of limitations and filed an untimely state petition? Would the result have been different if counsel had otherwise procedurally defaulted one of Holland's claims?

PART II
Cognizable Claims

Chapter 4

When Is a Claim Cognizable?

The very essence of the words *habeas corpus*—"that you have the body"—signifies that when filing a petition for writ of habeas corpus, a person asserts he is in custody. Given the essence of the Great Writ, it comes as no surprise that one of the jurisdictional requirements for habeas review is that the petitioner be "in custody."

Section 2254(a) specifically states:

> The Supreme Court, a Justice thereof, a circuit judge, or a district court shall entertain an application for a writ of habeas corpus in behalf of a person in custody pursuant to the judgment of a State court only on the ground that he is in custody in violation of the Constitution or laws or treaties of the United States.

Although the issue of "custody" may seem simple to resolve, it is more complex than it first appears.

In *Carafas v. LaVallee*, the Court examined whether federal jurisdiction exists when a person who is in custody when he applies for a writ of habeas corpus is discharged before the Court issues its writ of certiorari. In deciding that such a person can pursue his claim, the Court pointed to amendments to the habeas corpus statute that specifically contemplate the possibility of relief other than immediate release from physical custody. A few days after *Carafas*, the Court stated in *Sibron v. New York* that a person who has completed his six-month sentence can continue to pursue a habeas petition he filed before completing his sentence. In so deciding, the Court relied on its holding in *Carafas*. The Court also explained that important constitutional problems sometimes occur in the context of minor offenses that carry short sentences and collateral consequences, and that people should be able to avail themselves of constitutional protections and remedies, even if they have completed their sentences before their petitions wind their way through the court process. The final case in this chapter, *Lane v. Williams*, also discusses collateral consequences of a conviction, but it does so in the context of a petitioner challenging his sentence, rather than the conviction itself. The Court found that when a person only challenges his sentence, expiration of that sentence renders the habeas petition moot.

Carafas v. LaVallee

391 U.S. 234 (1968)

JUSTICE FORTAS delivered the opinion of the Court.

This case has a lengthy procedural history. In 1960, petitioner was convicted of burglary and grand larceny in New York state court proceedings and was sentenced to concurrent terms of three to five years. On direct appeal (following *Mapp v. Ohio*, 367 U.S. 643 (1961)), petitioner claimed that illegally obtained evidence had been introduced against him at trial. The Appellate Division affirmed the conviction without opinion, as did the New York Court of Appeals. This Court denied a petition for a writ of certiorari.

Thereafter, complex proceedings took place in which petitioner sought in both federal and state courts to obtain relief by writ of habeas corpus, based on his claim that illegally seized evidence was used against him. On November 5, 1965, the United States District Court, as directed by the United States Court of Appeals for the Second Circuit, heard petitioner's claim on the merits. It dismissed his petition on the ground that he had failed to show a violation of his Fourth Amendment rights. Petitioner appealed in circumstances hereinafter related. The Court of Appeals for the Second Circuit dismissed the appeal. * * * We granted the petition [for a writ of certiorari.] * * * [F]irst we must consider the State's contention that this case is now moot because petitioner has been unconditionally released from custody.

Petitioner applied to the United States District Court for a writ of habeas corpus in June 1963. He was in custody at that time. On March 6, 1967, petitioner's sentence expired, and he was discharged from the parole status in which he had been since October 4, 1964. We issued our writ of certiorari on October 16, 1967.

The issue presented, then, is whether the expiration of petitioner's sentence, before his application was finally adjudicated and while it was awaiting appellate review, terminates federal jurisdiction with respect to the application. Respondent relies upon *Parker v. Ellis*, 362 U.S. 574 (1960), and unless this case is overruled, it stands as an insuperable barrier to our further consideration of petitioner's cause or to the grant of relief upon his petition for a writ of habeas corpus.

Parker v. Ellis held that when a prisoner was released from state prison after having served his full sentence, this Court could not proceed to adjudicate the merits of the claim for relief on his petition for habeas corpus which he had filed with the Federal District Court. This Court held that upon petitioner's unconditional release the case became "moot." Parker was announced in a *per curiam* decision.

It is clear that petitioner's cause is not moot. In consequence of his conviction, he cannot engage in certain businesses; he cannot serve as an official of a labor union for a specified period of time; he cannot vote in any election held in New York State; he cannot serve as a juror. Because of these "disabilities or burdens (which) may flow from" petitioner's conviction, he has "a substantial stake in the judgment of conviction which survives the satisfaction of the sentence imposed on him." *Fiswick v. United States*, 329 U.S. 211, 222 (1946). On account of these "collateral consequences," the case is not moot. *Ginsberg v. New York*, 390 U.S. 629, 633–634 n.2 (1968); *Fiswick v. United States, supra*, 329 U.S. at 222, n. 10; *United States v. Morgan*, 346 U.S. 502, 512–513 (1954).

The substantial issue, however, which is posed by *Parker v. Ellis*, is not mootness in the technical or constitutional sense, but whether the statute defining the habeas corpus jurisdiction of the federal judiciary in respect of persons in state custody is available here. In *Parker v. Ellis*, as in the present case, petitioner's application was filed in the Federal District Court when he was in state custody, and in both the petitioner was unconditionally released from state custody before his case could be heard in this Court. For the reasons which we here summarize and which are stated at length in the dissenting opinions in *Parker v. Ellis*, we conclude that under the statutory scheme, once the federal jurisdiction has attached in the District Court, it is not defeated by the release of the petitioner prior to completion of proceedings on such application.

The federal habeas corpus statute requires that the applicant must be "in custody" when the application for habeas corpus is filed. This is required not only by the repeated references in the statute, but also by the history of the great writ. Its province, shaped to guarantee the most fundamental of all rights, is to provide an effective and speedy instrument by which judicial inquiry may be had into the legality of the detention of a person. *See Peyton v. Rowe*, [391 U.S. 54 (1968)].

But the statute does not limit the relief that may be granted to discharge of the applicant from physical custody. Its mandate is broad with respect to the relief that may be granted. It provides that "[t]he court shall ... dispose of the matter as law and justice require." 28 U.S.C. § 2243. The 1966 amendments to the habeas corpus statute seem specifically to contemplate the possibility of relief other than immediate release from physical custody. At one point, the new § 2244(b) (1964 ed., Supp. II), speaks in terms of "release from custody or other remedy." *See Peyton v. Rowe, supra*; *Walker v. Wainwright*, 390 U.S. 335 (1968). *Cf. Ex Parte Hull*, 312 U.S. 546 (1941).

In the present case, petitioner filed his application shortly after June 20, 1963, while he was in custody. He was not released from custody until March 6, 1967, two weeks before he filed his petition for certiorari here. During the intervening period his application was under consideration in various courts. Petitioner is entitled to consideration of his application for relief on its merits. He is suffering, and will continue to suffer, serious disabilities because of the law's complexities and not because of his fault, if his claim that he has been illegally convicted is meritorious. There is no need in the statute, the Constitution, or sound jurisprudence for denying to petitioner his ultimate day in court. [The Court goes on to hold that because the district court had issued a certificate of probable cause to appeal and waived the filing fee, it was error for the appeals court to deny him the right to appeal in forma pauperis. In so doing, the Court also overrules *Parker v. Ellis*.]

* * *

Accordingly, the judgment below is vacated and the case is remanded to the United States Court of Appeals for the Second Circuit for further proceedings consistent with this opinion.

It is so ordered.

Judgment vacated and case remanded.

[JUSTICE MARSHALL took no part in the consideration or decision of this case. JUSTICE HARLAN and JUSTICE STEWART concurred.]

Notes

1. *Adverse effects of convictions*

In order for a habeas petitioner to be successful if he is no longer in custody he must have filed the petition prior to being released and be able to show that he has an actual, legal interest in the result of the habeas proceeding. *Broughton v. North Carolina*, 717 F.2d 147 (4th Cir. 1983), is an example of the necessity of this second requirement. Because of an outburst during a civil trial, the petitioner in *Broughton* was sentenced to thirty days of jail for criminal contempt of court. She ultimately sought a writ of habeas corpus from federal district court. The court dismissed her claim, however, because she had procedurally defaulted at the state level. She was released five days after the dismissal but nonetheless sought an appeal. The Fourth Circuit did not reach the procedural default issue and instead called her claim moot and remanded with instructions to the district court to dismiss.

> It is true that unconditional release from state custody will not always moot a claim for habeas relief, for the collateral consequences of a criminal conviction

> may create "a substantial stake in the ... conviction which survives the satisfaction of the sentence." *Carafas v. LaVallee*, 391 U.S. 234, 237 [(citation omitted)].
>
> * * *
>
> Broughton [will not suffer] collateral consequences as a result of her misdemeanor contempt conviction. The contempt conviction, for example, will not prevent her from voting, serving on a jury, obtaining a license to practice law, becoming an official of a labor union, or qualifying for state elective offices. Nor will the criminal conviction expose her to the possibility of an enhanced sentence if she commits a later criminal act. In sum, Broughton will suffer no collateral legal consequences as a result of her challenged conviction; hence, her unconditional release from state custody has ended the controversy.

Broughton, 717 F.2d at 149–150.

Sibron v. New York
Peters v. New York

Nos. 63 & 74
392 U.S. 40 (1968)

CHIEF JUSTICE WARREN delivered the opinion of the Court.

These are companion cases to No. 67, *Terry v. Ohio*, 392 U.S. 1 (1968), decided today. They present related questions under the Fourth and Fourteenth Amendments, but the cases arise in the context of New York's "stop-and-frisk" law, N.Y. Code Crim. Proc. § 180-a. This statute provides:

> 1. A police officer may stop any person abroad in a public place whom he reasonably suspects is committing, has committed or is about to commit a felony or any of the offenses specified in section five hundred fifty-two of this chapter, and may demand of him his name, address and an explanation of his actions.
>
> 2. When a police officer has stopped a person for questioning pursuant to this section and reasonably suspects that he is in danger of life or limb, he may search such person for a dangerous weapon. If the police officer finds such a weapon or any other thing the possession of which may constitute a crime, he may take and keep it until the completion of the questioning, at which time he shall either return it, if lawfully possessed, or arrest such person.

The appellants, Sibron and Peters, were both convicted of crimes in New York state courts on the basis of evidence seized from their persons by police officers. The Court of Appeals of New York held that the evidence was properly admitted, on the ground that the searches which uncovered it were authorized by the statute. * * *

* * * Sibron, the appellant in No. 63, was convicted of the unlawful possession of heroin. He moved before trial to suppress the heroin seized from his person by the arresting officer, Brooklyn Patrolman Anthony Martin. After the trial court denied his motion, Sibron pleaded guilty to the charge, preserving his right to appeal the evidentiary ruling. At the hearing on the motion to suppress, Officer Martin testified that while he was patrolling his beat in uniform on March 9, 1965, he observed Sibron "continually from the hours of 4:00 P.M. to 12:00, midnight ... in the vicinity of 742 Broadway." He stated that during this period of time he saw Sibron in conversation with six or eight persons whom he (Patrolman Martin) knew from past experience to be narcotics addicts. The officer testified

that he did not overhear any of these conversations, and that he did not see anything pass between Sibron and any of the others. Late in the evening Sibron entered a restaurant. Patrolman Martin saw Sibron speak with three more known addicts inside the restaurant. Once again, nothing was overheard and nothing was seen to pass between Sibron and the addicts. Sibron sat down and ordered pie and coffee, and, as he was eating, Patrolman Martin approached him and told him to come outside. Once outside, the officer said to Sibron, "You know what I am after." According to the officer, Sibron "mumbled something and reached into his pocket." Simultaneously, Patrolman Martin thrust his hand into the same pocket, discovering several glassine envelopes, which, it turned out, contained heroin.

The State has had some difficulty in settling upon a theory for the admissibility of these envelopes of heroin. In his sworn complaint Patrolman Martin stated:

> As the officer approached the defendant, the latter being in the direction of the officer and seeing him, he did put his hand in his left jacket pocket and pulled out a tinfoil envelope and did attempt to throw same to the ground. The officer never losing sight of the said envelope seized it from the defendant's left hand, examined it and found it to contain ten glascine [sic] envelopes with a white substance alleged to be Heroin.

This version of the encounter, however, bears very little resemblance to Patrolman Martin's testimony at the hearing on the motion to suppress. In fact, he discarded the abandonment theory at the hearing. Nor did the officer ever seriously suggest that he was in fear of bodily harm and that he searched Sibron in self-protection to find weapons.

The prosecutor's theory at the hearing was that Patrolman Martin had probable cause to believe that Sibron was in possession of narcotics because he had seen him conversing with a number of known addicts over an eight-hour period. In the absence of any knowledge on Patrolman Martin's part concerning the nature of the intercourse between Sibron and the addicts, however, the trial court was inclined to grant the motion to suppress. * * *

* * *

I

At the outset we must deal with the question whether we have jurisdiction in No. 63. It is asserted that because Sibron has completed service of the six-month sentence imposed upon him as a result of his conviction, the case has become moot under *St. Pierre v. United States*, 319 U.S. 41 (1943). We have concluded that the case is not moot.

In the first place, it is clear that the broad dictum with which the Court commenced its discussion in *St. Pierre*—that "the case is moot because, after petitioner's service of his sentence and its expiration, there was no longer a subject matter on which the judgment of this Court could operate" (319 U.S. at 42)—fails to take account of significant qualifications recognized in *St. Pierre* and developed in later cases. Only a few days ago we held unanimously that the writ of habeas corpus was available to test the constitutionality of a state conviction where the petitioner had been in custody when he applied for the writ, but had been released before this Court could adjudicate his claims. *Carafas v. LaVallee*, 391 U.S. 234 (1968). On numerous occasions in the past this Court has proceeded to adjudicate the merits of criminal cases in which the sentence had been fully served or the probationary period during which a suspended sentence could be reimposed had terminated. Thus mere release of the prisoner does not mechanically foreclose consideration of the merits by this Court.

St. Pierre itself recognized two possible exceptions to its "doctrine" of mootness, and both of them appear to us to be applicable here. The Court stated that "[I]t does not appear that petitioner could not have brought his case to this Court for review before the expiration of his sentence," noting also that because the petitioner's conviction was for contempt and because his controversy with the Government was a continuing one, there was a good chance that there would be "ample opportunity to review" the important question presented on the merits in a future proceeding. 319 U.S. at 43. This was a plain recognition of the vital importance of keeping open avenues of judicial review of deprivations of constitutional right. There was no way for Sibron to bring his case here before his six-month sentence expired. By statute he was precluded from obtaining bail pending appeal, and by virtue of the inevitable delays of the New York court system, he was released less than a month after his newly appointed appellate counsel had been supplied with a copy of the transcript and roughly two months before it was physically possible to present his case to the first tier in the state appellate court system. This was true despite the fact that he took all steps to perfect his appeal in a prompt, diligent, and timely manner.

Many deep and abiding constitutional problems are encountered primarily at a level of "low visibility" in the criminal process—in the context of prosecutions for "minor" offenses which carry only short sentences. We do not believe that the Constitution contemplates that people deprived of constitutional rights at this level should be left utterly remediless and defenseless against repetitions of unconstitutional conduct. A State may not cut off federal review of whole classes of such cases by the simple expedient of a blanket denial of bail pending appeal. As *St. Pierre* clearly recognized, a State may not effectively deny a convict access to its appellate courts until he has been released and then argue that his case has been mooted by his failure to do what it alone prevented him from doing.

The second exception recognized in *St. Pierre* permits adjudication of the merits of a criminal case where "under either state or federal law further penalties or disabilities can be imposed ... as a result of the judgment which has ... been satisfied." 319 U.S. at 43. Subsequent cases have expanded this exception to the point where it may realistically be said that inroads have been made upon the principle itself. *St. Pierre* implied that the burden was upon the convict to show the existence of collateral legal consequences. Three years later in *Fiswick v. United States*, 329 U.S. 211 (1946), however, the Court held that a criminal case had not become moot upon release of the prisoner, noting that the convict, an alien, might be subject to deportation for having committed a crime of "moral turpitude"—even though it had never been held (and the Court refused to hold) that the crime of which he was convicted fell into this category. The Court also pointed to the fact that if the petitioner should in the future decide he wanted to become an American citizen, he might have difficulty proving that he was of "good moral character."

* * *

[I]n *Pollard v. United States*, 352 U.S. 354 (1957), the Court abandoned all inquiry into the actual existence of specific collateral consequences and in effect presumed that they existed. * * *

This case certainly meets that test for survival. Without pausing to canvass the possibilities in detail, we note that New York expressly provides by statute that Sibron's conviction may be used to impeach his character should he choose to put it in issue at any future criminal trial, N.Y. Code Crim. Proc. § 393-c, and that it must be submitted to a trial judge for his consideration in sentencing should Sibron again be convicted of a crime, N.Y. Code Crim. Proc.§ 482. There are doubtless other collateral consequences. Moreover, we see no relevance in the fact that Sibron is a multiple offender. * * * A judge or jury faced with a question of character, like a sentencing judge, may be inclined to forgive or at least discount a limited number of minor transgressions, particularly if they occurred at some time in the relatively distant past. It is impossible for this Court to say at what point the number of convictions on a man's record renders his reputation irredeemable. And even if we believed that an individual had reached that point, it would be impossible for us to say that he had no interest in beginning the process of redemption with the particular case sought to be adjudicated. We cannot foretell what opportunities might present themselves in the future for the removal of other convictions from an individual's record. The question of the validity of a criminal conviction can arise in many contexts, compare *Burgett v. Texas*, 389 U.S. 109 (1967), and the sooner the issue is fully litigated the better for all concerned. It is always preferable to litigate a matter when it is directly and principally in dispute, rather than in a proceeding where it is collateral to the central controversy. Moreover, litigation is better conducted when the dispute is fresh and additional facts may, if necessary, be taken without a substantial risk that witnesses will die or memories fade. And it is far better to eliminate the source of a potential legal disability than to require the citizen to suffer the possibly unjustified consequences of the disability itself for an indefinite period of time before he can secure adjudication of the State's right to impose it on the basis of some past action.

None of the concededly imperative policies behind the constitutional rule against entertaining moot controversies would be served by a dismissal in this case. There is nothing abstract, feigned, or hypothetical about Sibron's appeal. Nor is there any suggestion that either Sibron or the State has been wanting in diligence or fervor in the litigation. We have before us a fully developed record of testimony about contested historical facts, which reflects the "impact of actuality" to a far greater degree than many controversies accepted for adjudication as a matter of course under the Federal Declaratory Judgment Act, 28 U.S.C. § 2201.

* * * Sibron "has a substantial stake in the judgment of conviction which survives the satisfaction of the sentence imposed on him." *Fiswick v. United States*, *supra*, [329 U.S.] at 222. The case is not moot.

* * *

[The Court upheld Peters' conviction but reversed Sibron's conviction on the ground that the heroin was unconstitutionally admitted as evidence against him.]

[JUSTICE DOUGLAS concurred in both Peters' and Sibron's cases; JUSTICES FORTAS and WHITE concurred; JUSTICE HARLAN concurred in the result; and JUSTICE BLACK concurred in Peters' case but dissented in Sibron's case.]

Notes

1. *Burden of proof*

The Court in *Sibron* stated, "[A] criminal case is moot only if it is shown that there is no possibility that any collateral legal consequences will be imposed on the basis of the challenged conviction." *Sibron*, 392 U.S. at 57. This subsequently has been interpreted to mean that if a petitioner files for habeas relief and then is released before the end of the proceedings, it is assumed that she will continue to suffer sufficiently adverse consequences to justify federal habeas jurisdiction and, therefore, it is the State's burden to show otherwise. *D.S.A. v. Circuit Court Branch 1*, 942 F.2d 1143, 1146 n.3 (7th Cir. 1991).

What should be done in a situation where the petitioner was convicted of multiple offenses, has been subsequently released from incarceration, and is seeking a writ of habeas corpus for only one of the convictions? Does it matter for which offense he is continuing to suffer the adverse effects of his conviction? *See Malloy v. Purvis*, 681 F.2d 736 (11th Cir. 1982).

Lane v. Williams

455 U.S. 624 (1982)

JUSTICE STEVENS delivered the opinion of the Court.

In 1975, respondents pleaded guilty in Illinois state court to a charge of burglary, an offense punishable at that time by imprisonment for an indeterminate term of years and a mandatory 3-year parole term. We granted certiorari to consider whether the failure of the trial court to advise respondents of that mandatory parole requirement before accepting their guilty pleas deprived them of due process of law. We are unable to reach that question, however, because we find that respondents' claims for relief are moot.

I

On March 11, 1975, respondent Lawrence Williams appeared in Illinois state court and pleaded guilty to a single count of burglary. Before accepting the guilty plea, the trial judge elicited Williams' understanding of the terms of a plea agreement, in which his attorney and the prosecutor had agreed that Williams would receive an indeterminate sentence of from one to two years in prison in exchange for pleading guilty. The judge informed Williams that he would impose the bargained sentence, and advised him of both the nature of the charge against him and the constitutional rights that he would waive by pleading guilty. After the prosecutor established a factual basis for the plea, Williams indicated that he understood his rights and wished to plead guilty.

At the time that Williams pleaded guilty, Illinois law required every indeterminate sentence for certain felonies, including burglary, to include a special parole term in addition to the term of imprisonment. During the plea acceptance hearing, neither the trial judge, the prosecutor, nor defense counsel informed Williams that his negotiated sentence included a mandatory parole term of three years.

Williams was discharged from prison on May 20, 1976, and released on parole. On March 3, 1977, he was arrested for reasons that do not appear in the record and, on March 16, 1977, he was returned to prison as a parole violator. While in custody, Williams filed a petition for a writ of habeas corpus in the United States District Court for the Northern District of Illinois. He alleged that he "was not informed" that a mandatory parole term had attached to his sentence until two months before his discharge from prison and that "his present incarceration is therefore in violation of the Due Process Clause of the 14th Amendment to the U. S. Constitution." Williams' petition did not ask the federal court to set aside his conviction and allow him to plead anew. It requested an order "freeing him from the present control" of the Warden and from "all future liability" under his original sentence.

On January 4, 1978, the District Court found that Williams' guilty plea had been induced unfairly in violation of the Due Process Clause of the Fourteenth Amendment and ordered Williams released from custody. *United States ex rel. Williams v. Morris*, 447 F. Supp. 95 ([N.D. Ill.] 1978). The court expressly "opted for specific performance" of the plea bargain "rather than nullification of the guilty plea." *Id.* at 101. The relief granted was precisely what Williams had requested.

Williams was not, however, immediately released from custody. The District Court entered a stay to give the State an opportunity to file a motion for reconsideration. Before that stay was lifted, Williams was released from prison on a special 6-month "supervisory release term." The District Court subsequently denied the State's motion to reconsider and the State appealed. While that appeal was pending, Williams' 6-month release term expired and he was released from the custody of the Illinois Department of Corrections.

[The Court then explained the facts concerning the other respondent, Southall, which were similar to Williams's case.]

* * *

II

Respondents claim that their constitutional rights were violated when the trial court accepted their guilty pleas without informing them of the mandatory parole requirement. Assuming, for the sake of argument, that the court's failure to advise respondents of this consequence rendered their guilty pleas void, respondents could seek to remedy this error in two quite different ways. They might ask the District Court to set aside their convictions and give them an opportunity to plead anew; in that event, they might either plead not guilty and stand trial or they might try to negotiate a different plea bargain properly armed with the information that any sentence they received would include a special parole term. Alternatively, they could seek relief in the nature of "special enforcement" of the plea agreement as they understood it; in that event, the elimination of the mandatory parole term from their sentences would remove any possible harmful consequence from the trial court's incomplete advice.

If respondents had sought the opportunity to plead anew, this case would not be moot. Such relief would free respondents from all consequences flowing from their convictions, as well as subject them to reconviction with a possibly greater sentence. *Cf. North Carolina v. Pearce*, 395 U.S. 711 [(1969)]. Thus, a live controversy would remain to determine whether a constitutional violation in fact had occurred and whether respondents were entitled to the relief that they sought.

Since respondents had completed their previously imposed sentences, however, they did not seek the opportunity to plead anew. Rather, they sought to remedy the alleged constitutional violation by removing the consequence that gave rise to the constitutional harm. In the course of their attack, that consequence expired of its own accord. Respondents are no longer subject to any direct restraint as a result of the parole term. They may not be imprisoned on the lesser showing needed to establish a parole violation than to prove a criminal offense. Their liberty or freedom of movement is not in any way curtailed by a parole term that has expired.

Since respondents elected only to attack their sentences, and since those sentences expired during the course of these proceedings, this case is moot. "Nullification of a conviction may have important benefits for a defendant ... but urging in a habeas corpus proceeding the correction of a sentence already served is another matter." *North Carolina v. Rice*, 404 U.S. 244, 248 [(1971)].

* * *

Respondents have never attacked, on either substantive or procedural grounds, the finding that they violated the terms of their parole. Respondent Williams simply sought an order "freeing him from the present control" of the Warden and from "all future liability" under his original sentence; Southall sought his "immediate release" from custody.

Through the mere passage of time, respondents have obtained all the relief that they sought. In these circumstances, no live controversy remains.

The Court of Appeals also held that this case was not moot because it was "capable of repetition, yet evading review." *Southern Pacific Terminal Co. v. ICC*, 219 U.S. 498, 515 [(1911)]. That doctrine, however, is applicable only when there is "a reasonable expectation that the same complaining party would be subjected to the same action again." *Weinstein v. Bradford*, 423 U.S. 147, 149 [(1975)]; *Murphy v. Hunt*, [455 U.S. 478,] 482 [(1982)]. Respondents are now acutely aware of the fact that a criminal sentence in Illinois will include a special parole term; any future guilty plea will not be open to the same constitutional attack. The possibility that other persons may litigate a similar claim does not save this case from mootness.

The judgment of the Court of Appeals is vacated. The case should be dismissed as moot.

It is so ordered.

[JUSTICE MARSHALL, with whom JUSTICES BRENNAN AND BLACKMUN joined, dissented.]

Notes

1. *Dissenting opinion by Justice Marshall (joined by Justice Brennan and Justice Blackmun)*

The dissenting opinion by Justice Marshall includes the following observation:

> The majority announces today that this case is moot because, in its view, no collateral consequences flow from respondents' parole revocations, which were based on findings that respondents had violated the conditions of parole terms declared void by the courts below. I dissent from this holding because I believe it is contrary to this Court's precedents and because it ignores the fact that the State of Illinois does attach collateral consequences to parole revocations, a fact recognized both in the State's brief to the Court of Appeals on the issue of mootness and in state-court decisions in analogous cases.

In light of the Court's discussion of collateral consequences in *Sibron*, do you agree with Justice Marshall that the holding in *Lane v. Williams* is contrary to the Court's precedent? Why or why not?

2. *Collateral consequences under the Federal Sentencing Guidelines*

Lane v. Williams predates the enactment of the Federal Sentencing Guidelines, wherein an individual sentenced to even a short period of time (*i.e.*, more than 60 days) is subject to a two point increase of his criminal history score instead of the one point increase to which he would be subject if he had he been sentenced to a term of probation. *See United States v. Chavez-Palacios*, 30 F.3d 1290, 1293 (10th Cir. 1994) (discussing sections 4A1.1(b) and (c) of the Federal Sentencing Guidelines). Should such collateral consequences of a sentence already served still render the appeal moot? *See Chavez-Palacios*, 30 F.3d at 1293 (finding the appeal not moot); *United States v. Dickey*, 924 F.2d 836 (9th Cir.), *cert. denied*, 502 U.S. 943 (1991) (same).

3. *Immigration consequences of a conviction*

In *Padilla v. Kentucky*, 130 S.Ct. 1473 (2009), the Supreme Court addressed the obligation of defense counsel to inform her client of the immigration consequences of a criminal conviction, in the context of a Sixth Amendment claim of ineffective assistance of counsel. Padilla, a permanent resident for 40 years, pleaded guilty to transporting drugs, an offense that automatically made him subject to deportation. Padilla alleged that his lawyer had erroneously advised him that he did not have to worry about deportation because of his long residence in the U.S. and that he had relied on his lawyer's advice in pleading guilty. In seeking to withdraw his guilty plea, Padilla claimed that he would have gone to trial if he had known the true immigration consequences of his plea. According to the Kentucky Supreme Court, neither a failure to advise Padilla of the deportation consequences nor misadvice about the deportation consequences was a basis for relief. The Supreme Court of Kentucky denied post-conviction relief, without an evidentiary hearing, on the ground that the guarantee of effective assistance of counsel "does not protect a criminal defendant from erroneous advice about deportation because it is merely a 'collateral' consequence of his conviction." *Id.* at 1478.

Without deciding whether Padilla had been prejudiced, and thus able to withdraw his plea, the Supreme Court held that constitutionally competent counsel must inform a defendant of whether his plea carries a risk of deportation. The Court specifically included in this mandate a duty not to misinform the client as to the immigration consequences, as well as the duty to affirmatively inform the client when there are possible deportation consequences. The Court reversed the Supreme Court of Kentucky and remands for further proceedings.

Emphasizing that "[t]he landscape of federal immigration law has changed dramatically over the past 90 years," the Court described in some detail how the U.S. moved from "a period of unimpeded immigration," to legislation in 1917 authorizing deportation on the basis of conduct in the U.S. while still allowing a sentencing judge to make a binding judicial recommendation against deportation (JRAD), to restrictions on and then elimination of JRAD (1990), to elimination of most of the Attorney General's authority to grant discretionary relief (1996). Thus, with removal of a non-citizen "practically inevitable" after the 1996 amendments, "accurate legal advice for noncitizens accused of crimes has never been more important." *Id.* at 1478–1480.

The Court declined to define deportation as either a direct or a collateral consequence of a conviction, while noting the disagreement among courts as to how to distinguish between collateral and direct consequences, and the agreement of many federal courts with the view taken by the Supreme Court of Kentucky. Instead, the Court found that "advice regarding deportation is not categorically removed from the ambit of the Sixth Amendment right to counsel," and thus Padilla's claim would be evaluated under *Strickland* v. *Washington*, 466 U.S. 68, the seminal case setting out the standard for evaluating Sixth Amendment claims of ineffective assistance of counsel. [1] *Id.* at 1482.

The Court concluded that it was easy to find deficiency of counsel's performance in Padilla's case because the deportation consequences could easily have been determined by reading the relevant immigration statutes. When the deportation consequence is "truly clear," counsel has a duty to give correct advice. *Id.* at 1483. In contrast, counsel's duty is more limited when the law is less "succinct and straightforward." In the latter situation, a lawyer "need do no more than advise a noncitizen that pending criminal charges may carry a risk of adverse immigration consequences." *Id.*

A. Justice Alito, in a concurrence, took issue with the majority's holding that counsel must not only avoid misadvising a client as to immigration consequences but also must

1. *Strickland v. Washington* is discussed in Chapter 5.

affirmatively inform his client as to the immigration consequences of a plea. Although he concurred in the judgment and appears to acknowledge that immigration consequences are "exceptionally important collateral matters," he would limit the holding to a rule governing affirmative misadvice. *Id.* at 1493. He emphasized the complexity of immigration law and the difficulty of determining, for example, if a particular offense is a "crime of moral turpitude" or an "aggravated felony," either of which could constitute grounds for removal. In his view, it is "unrealistic" to expect criminal defense lawyers to "provide expert advice on matters that lie outside their area of training and experience," including deportation and a wide range of other collateral consequences. *Id.* at 1487–88.

B. Which view of defense counsel's legal obligation is most persuasive? What might be the ramifications of these different views of the role of defense counsel?

4. *Consequences of convictions for sex offenses*

In recent years Congress and state legislatures have passed legislation that impacts persons convicted of sexual offenses even after completion of their sentences and periods of supervision. One example is a sex offender registry statute, often referred to as Megan's Law, which requires persons convicted of certain sex offenses to register with a specified public or law enforcement agency over a certain number of years or for life.[2] These registry laws have a corresponding community notification component, which provides for access by the public to information about the offender and his or her crimes. In addition, failure to comply with the law subjects the offender to criminal prosecution. Many of these laws expressly apply to persons convicted prior to the registration legislation. In *Smith v. John Doe*, 538 U.S. 84 (2003), the Supreme Court considered a challenge to the Alaska Sex Offender Registration Act, which requires certain convicted sex offenders to register with local law enforcement and to provide verification of personal information on an ongoing basis. Local law enforcement forwards offender information to the Department of Public Safety, which maintains a central data base of sex offenders. Some of the information the registry keeps, such as driver's license numbers, information about medical treatment, and fingerprints, is kept confidential. Other personal information, such as the offender's name, address, photograph, place of employment, date of birth, crime, and details of the convictions and sentences, are published on the Internet. The Act's notification and registration requirements are retroactive. *Id.* at 90–91.

The respondents brought a 42 U.S.C. § 1983 action to declare the Act void as to them on the ground that the registration requirement is a retroactive punishment that violates the *Ex Post Facto* Clause. The district court granted summary judgment for the petitioners, but the Ninth Circuit concluded that the Act violated the *Ex Post Facto* Clause because its effects were punitive, even though the legislature intended the Act to be nonpunitive. *Id.* at 91–92. The Supreme Court concluded that the legislature intended to create a "civil, nonpunitive regime" and that the respondents failed to override legislative intent by the

2. In 1994, Congress passed the Jacob Wetterling Crimes Against Children and Sexually Violent Offender Registration Act, codified as amended in 42 U.S.C. § 14071 (2000), which made federal crime prevention funds available to the states on the condition they pass sex offender registration and community notification legislation. Congress amended the Wetterling Act in 1996 by passing Megan's Law (codified as amended at 42 U.S.C. § 14071(e)), which removed a requirement of the Wetterling Act that registry information be kept confidential and added a mandatory community notification provision. Every state now has a version of Megan's Law. In 2006, Congress passed the Adam Walsh Child Protection and Safety Act of 2006, P.L. 109-248, one provision of which establishes a national sex offender registry, which will include state court convictions. SORNA, the Sex Offender Registration and Notification Act, is Title I of the Adam Walsh Act.

"clearest proof" that the Act is punitive. "[D]issemination of truthful information in furtherance of a legitimate governmental objective" is not punishment. *Id.* at 96, 98. Although publicity may cause adverse consequences for the offender, stigma is not an integral part of the regulatory scheme. *Id.* at 98. The Court viewed the respondents' arguments that the Act makes the covered offender "completely unemployable" as speculative. While access of the public to this information may have a "lasting and painful impact" on the offender, the Court stated this impact flows from the conviction, not from operation of the Act. *Id.* at 100–101. Key to the majority's conclusion that the registration requirements do not impose punitive restraints in violation of the *Ex Post Facto* Clause, was the "Act's rational connection to a nonpunitive purpose—public safety and concern about recidivism. *Id.* at 102–103.

In dissent, Justice Stevens (joined by Justice Ginsberg) applied a Due Process analysis and concluded that the Act "unquestionably" affects a constitutionally protected interest in liberty. The statutes "impose significant affirmative obligations and a severe stigma on every person to whom they apply." In addition to providing the information described above, registrants "may not shave their beards, color their hair, change their employer, or borrow a car without reporting those events to the authorities." *Id.* at 111. Justice Stevens also found these consequences to be punitive because they are imposed on everyone who commits a certain offense, are not imposed on anyone else, and severely impair a person's liberty. Thus, retroactive application of these statutes "constitutes a flagrant violation of the protections afforded by the Double Jeopardy and *Ex Post Facto* Clauses of the Constitution." *Id.* at 114. Stevens agreed with the majority that such statutes are constitutional if applied to post-enactment offenses. *Id.*

Justice Ginsberg, in a separate dissent joined by Justice Breyer, found the Act punitive in effect. In her view, the scope of the legislation exceeds its purpose because its application and duration do not depend upon future dangerousness or individualized risk assessments, and no amount of proof of rehabilitation or incapacitation can shorten the registration or notification periods. *Id.* at 116–117. Ginsberg noted that one of the petitioners had completed treatment and been released early based on his conduct and on psychiatric assessments that he posed low risk of reoffending. That petitioner had married and been granted custody of a child following a court determination that he had been rehabilitated. Nonetheless, under the Act he has to register as a sex offender for life. *Id.* at 117–118.

A. Justice Souter, concurring in the judgment, describes the consequences of the sex offender registration laws:

> [T]here is significant evidence of onerous practical effects of being listed on a sex offender registry. *See, e.g., Doe v. Pataki*, 120 F.3d 1263, 1279 (2d Cir. 1997) (noting "numerous instances in which sex offenders have suffered harm in the aftermath of notification—ranging from public shunning, picketing, press vigils, ostracism, loss of employment, and eviction, to threats of violence, physical attacks, and arson"); *E.B. v. Verniero*, 119 F.3d 1077, 1102 (3d Cir. 1997) ("The record documents that registrants and their families have experienced profound humiliation and isolation as a result of the reaction of those notified. Employment and employment opportunities have been jeopardized or lost. Housing and housing opportunities have suffered a similar fate. Family and other personal relationships have been destroyed or severely strained. Retribution has been visited by private, unlawful violence and threats and, while such incidents of 'vigilante justice' are not common, they happen with sufficient frequency and publicity that registrants justifiably live in fear of them"); Brief for the Office of the

Public Defender for the State of New Jersey et al. as Amici Curiae 7-21 (describing specific incidents).

Smith, 538 U.S. at 109, n.* (Souter, J., concurring).

Given his description of the consequences of registration, why does Justice Souter concur in the result?

B. *Must defense counsel notify his client of the sex offender registration and notification laws before a guilty plea?*

The Supreme Court has not decided whether the requirements of sex offender registration and notification laws are of such consequence that the Sixth Amendment requires counsel to advise a defendant if they apply to him prior to a guilty plea. Lower courts taking the view that these laws are collateral consequences have denied relief to defendants claiming ineffective assistance of counsel because of counsel's failure to advise them of the registry and notification laws prior to a guilty plea. For example, in *Virsnieks v. Smith*, 521 F.3d 707 (7th Cir. 2008), the Seventh Circuit Court of Appeals rejected a claim that Virsnieks' plea had not been knowing or voluntary because he did not know he could be ordered to register as a sex offender. Explaining that while the Supreme Court has not comprehensively delineated what constitutes direct consequences of a plea, of which the defendant must be notified,[3] and what are collateral consequences for purposes of evaluating the voluntariness of a plea, the court concluded that "no clearly established federal law requires that defendants be informed of the possibility that they could be ordered to register as sexual offenders." *Id.* at 716. Thus, the issue of whether the requirement to register as a sex offender is a direct or collateral consequence of a plea was not "sufficiently clear" to allow the federal court to conclude that the state court's decision that his plea was knowing and voluntary was contrary to or an unreasonable application of the Supreme Court's decision in *Brady v. United States.*

C. *Is a challenge to the application of the sex offender registration and notification laws cognizable in habeas?*

Lower courts frequently have concluded that a challenge to the constitutionality or application of a sexual offender registration statute is not cognizable in habeas because the habeas petitioner cannot satisfy the "in-custody" requirement of the habeas statute. *Williamson v. Gregoire*, 151 F.3d 1180 (9th Cir. 1998). In *Leslie v. Randle*, 296 F.3d 518 (6th Cir. 2002), the United States Court of Appeals for the Sixth Circuit concluded that the registration requirements are not the kind of severe restraint on liberty that constitute "custody," even if the petitioner is still serving a sentence for the offense requiring registration. Rather, they are more akin to collateral consequences, such as the loss of the right to vote, and thus insufficient to amount to "custody." *Id.* at 522. Similarly, the possibility of incarceration for failure to comply with the registration requirements at some time in the future has been held to be insufficient to satisfy the in-custody requirement because it is too remote and speculative. *Virsnieks, supra*, at 720. The *Virsnieks* court concluded: "Given the habeas statute's 'in-custody' requirement, courts have rejected uniformly the argument that a challenge to a sentence of registration under a sexual offender statute is cognizable in habeas." *Id.* at 718.

3. For a plea to be voluntary and intelligent, and thus meet constitutional requirements, the defendant must have full knowledge of the direct consequences of his plea. *Brady v. United States*, 397 U.S. 742, 755 (1970).

The Supreme Court has not decided whether the consequences of sex offender registration and notification laws can meet the "in-custody" standard of *Spencer v. Kemna*, 523 U.S. 1 (1998), a case in which the Supreme Court applied *Lane v. Williams, supra*, in holding that a revoked parolee could not use habeas to attack the validity of the revocation of his parole after his sentence had expired because he could not establish the kind of collateral consequences sufficient to state an Article III case or controversy. In a per curiam decision in *United States v. Juvenile Male*, No. 09-940, 2010 U.S. LEXIS 4565 (June 7, 2010), the Court postponed answering this question.

In 2006, Congress passed The Sexual Offender Registration and Notification Act (SORNA), which requires persons convicted of certain sex offenses, including qualifying offenses under state law, to register and continue to register in every jurisdiction where they live, work, or attend school. SORNA applies to juvenile adjudications as well as to adult convictions. In 2007 the Attorney General issued an interim rule applying SORNA to sex offenders convicted of qualifying offenses prior to passage of SORNA. In *United States v. Juvenile Male*, a juvenile adjudicated delinquent in a federal prosecution of a qualifying sexual offense challenged the application of SORNA to preenactment offenses. The Ninth Circuit found that retroactive application of SORNA in the context of a juvenile adjudication violates the *Ex Post Facto* Clause and vacated the sex offender registration requirements that the district court had imposed as a condition of respondent's supervision. Before the case reached the Supreme Court, respondent completed his supervision.

On the application of the United States to grant certiorari, the Supreme Court stated that, because the respondent's sex offender registration duty expired with his supervision, the case was moot unless the respondent could show that a decision to invalidate the registration conditions of his supervision would be likely to redress collateral consequences adequate to meet Article III's injury-in-fact requirement." *Id.* at *3–*4. The Court noted that the most likely collateral consequence that a decision favorable to the respondent could address is "the requirement that respondent remain registered as a sex offender" under state law. The Court certified to the Montana Supreme Court the question of whether the respondent's current and continuing duty to register as a sex offender in that state depends upon the validity of the prior federal juvenile supervision order or is based on an independent duty imposed by state law. *Id.* at *5–*6.

5. *Further reading*

There is reason to debate the wisdom of federal courts staying out of cases when the petitioner no longer is in the custody or control of the State. For a thorough examination of the subject, see Marc Mauer, *The Intended and Unintended Consequences of Incarceration-based Sentencing Policies*, 16 T.M. Cooley L. Rev. 47 (1999).

6. *Other collateral consequences*

Consider the following article from the *Drug War Chronicle* and consider whether the concept of "custody" should be expanded. Do collateral consequences of criminal convictions, such as effectively barring a person from holding certain jobs, voting in certain states, or obtaining student loans, warrant expansion of the concept of custody? What would be the cost to such an expansion?

* * *

The Conviction That Keeps on Hurting—Drug Offenders and Federal Benefits

Drug War Chronicle (The world's leading drug policy newsletter)
February 5th, 2007, Issue #471

Some 15 to 20 million people have been arrested on drug charges and subjected to the tender mercies of the criminal justice system in the past two decades. But, thanks to congressional drug warriors, the punishments drug offenders face often extend far beyond the prison walls or the parole officer's office. A number of federal laws ostensibly aimed at reducing drug use block people with drug convictions from gaining access to federal benefits and services. These laws have a disproportionate impact on society's most vulnerable or marginalized members—the poor, people of color, and women with children—and in some cases, do not even require that a person actually be convicted of a drug offense to be punished. No conviction is needed to be evicted from public housing for drugs—even someone else's.

A growing number of groups and individuals ranging from the American Bar Association to welfare rights organizations, public health and addiction groups, drug reform organizations, and elected officials have called for changes in these laws or their outright repeal, saying they are cruel, inhumane, counterproductive, and amount to "double jeopardy" for drug offenders trying to become productive members of society.

"We feel that these laws are discriminatory and tend to focus on an illness as opposed to a crime," said Alexa Eggleston of the Legal Action Center, one of the key groups in the movement to adjust those laws. "We also think that if you have a conviction, you should be able to serve your time and come out and resume your life. We say we want people to get sober, get treatment, get a job, get housing, but then we set up all these barriers and roadblocks that seem designed to stop them from moving forward. These lifetime bans are very destructive of people's ability to reintegrate into society and move forward with their lives as productive citizens."

"These discriminatory laws represent incredible barriers in terms of people getting on with their lives, which is why they are part of our platform for change," said Pat Taylor, director of Faces and Voices of Recovery, a national alliance of individuals and organizations committed to securing the rights of people with addictions. "If you can't get housing, can't get a job, it's really hard to get your life back on track." (The article then goes on to list laws that restrict benefits even to people whose arrests or convictions are decades old.)

* * *

While GAO notes that "thousands of persons were denied postsecondary education benefits, federally assisted housing, or selected licenses and contracts as a result of federal laws that provide for denying benefits to drug offenders," it is low-balling the real figure, which, according to its own numbers, is in the hundreds of thousands. Additionally, the GAO report does not factor in the number of people who simply did not apply for housing, welfare benefits, or student loans because they knew or believed they were ineligible.

* * *

Chapter 5

Types of Cognizable Claims

The following sections outline two common claims litigants raise in habeas corpus petitions: ineffective assistance of counsel and withholding exculpatory evidence. In addition to discussing the seminal cases in these two areas, this section introduces issues of race and politics in the criminal justice system through an examination of challenges to peremptory strikes in jury selection and imposition of the death penalty.

A. Ineffective Assistance of Counsel

The cases in this section outline the Supreme Court's standards for deciding when the Constitution requires a conviction or death sentence to be set aside because counsel's assistance at either the trial or the sentencing was ineffective. In *Strickland v. Washington*, 466 U.S. 668 (1984), the Court set forth the seminal standard for deciding what constitutes ineffective assistance of counsel and found that trial counsel was not ineffective.

> First, the defendant must show that counsel's performance was deficient. This requires showing that counsel made errors so serious that counsel was not functioning as the "counsel" guaranteed the defendant by the Sixth Amendment. Second, the defendant must show that the deficient performance prejudiced the defense. This requires showing that counsel's errors were so serious as to deprive the defendant of a fair trial, a trial whose result is reliable. Unless a defendant makes both showings, it cannot be said that the conviction or death sentence resulted from a breakdown in the adversary process that renders the result unreliable.

Id. at 687.

In *Williams v. Taylor*, the Court applied the *Strickland* standard and determined that trial counsel were ineffective because they failed both to investigate and to present substantial mitigating evidence during the sentencing portion of the defendant's capital murder trial. In *Wiggins v. Smith*, the court defined what is meant by an adequate investigation, and it found ineffective assistance of counsel.

Williams v. Taylor

529 U.S. 362 (2000)

* * *

The questions presented are whether Terry Williams' constitutional right to the effective assistance of counsel as defined in *Strickland v. Washington* was violated, and whether the judgment of the Virginia Supreme Court refusing to set aside his death sentence "was contrary to, or involved an unreasonable application of, clearly established Federal law, as determined by the Supreme Court of the United States," within the meaning of 28 U.S.C. § 2254(d)(1) (1994 ed., Supp. III). We answer both questions affirmatively.

[The portion of the case containing the factual basis for Williams' conviction and addressing the applicability of § 2254(d)(1) may be found in Chapter 2.]

I

* * *

The evidence offered by Williams' trial counsel at the sentencing hearing consisted of the testimony of Williams' mother, two neighbors, and a taped excerpt from a statement by a psychiatrist. One of the neighbors had not been previously interviewed by defense counsel, but was noticed by counsel in the audience during the proceedings and asked to testify on the spot. The three witnesses briefly described Williams as a "nice boy" and not a violent person. The recorded psychiatrist's testimony did little more than relate Williams' statement during an examination that in the course of one of his earlier robberies, he had removed the bullets from a gun so as not to injure anyone.

In his cross-examination of the prosecution witnesses, Williams' counsel repeatedly emphasized the fact that Williams had initiated the contact with the police that enabled them to solve the murder and to identify him as the perpetrator of the recent assaults, as well as the car thefts. In closing argument, Williams' counsel characterized Williams' confessional statements as "dumb," but asked the jury to give weight to the fact that he had "turned himself in, not on one crime but on four ... that the [police otherwise] would not have solved." The weight of defense counsel's closing, however, was devoted to explaining that it was difficult to find a reason why the jury should spare Williams' life.

The jury found a probability of future dangerousness and unanimously fixed Williams' punishment at death. The trial judge concluded that such punishment was "proper" and "just" and imposed the death sentence. The Virginia Supreme Court affirmed the conviction and sentence. It rejected Williams' argument that when the trial judge imposed sentence, he failed to give mitigating weight to the fact that Williams had turned himself in.

State Habeas Corpus Proceedings

In 1988 Williams filed for state collateral relief in the Danville Circuit Court. The petition was subsequently amended, and the Circuit Court (the same judge who had presided over Williams' trial and sentencing) held an evidentiary hearing on Williams' claim that trial counsel had been ineffective. Based on the evidence adduced after two days of hearings, Judge Ingram found that Williams' conviction was valid, but that his trial attorneys had been ineffective during sentencing. Among the evidence reviewed that had not been presented at trial were documents prepared in connection with Williams' commitment when he was 11 years old that dramatically described mistreatment, abuse, and neglect during his early childhood, as well as testimony that he was "borderline mentally retarded," had suffered repeated head injuries, and might have mental impairments organic in origin. The habeas hearing also revealed that the same experts who had testified on the State's behalf at trial believed that Williams, if kept in a "structured environment," would not pose a future danger to society.

Counsel's failure to discover and present this and other significant mitigating evidence was "below the range expected of reasonable, professional competent assistance of counsel." Counsel's performance thus "did not measure up to the standard required under the holding of *Strickland v. Washington*, and [if it had,] there is a reasonable probability that the result of the sentencing phase would have been different." Judge Ingram therefore recommended that Williams be granted a rehearing on the sentencing phase of his trial.

The Virginia Supreme Court did not accept that recommendation. * * *

* * *

Federal Habeas Corpus Proceedings

Having exhausted his state remedies, Williams sought a federal writ of habeas corpus pursuant to 28 U.S.C. § 2254 (1994 ed. and Supp. III). After reviewing the state habeas hearing transcript and the state courts' findings of fact and conclusions of law, the federal trial judge agreed with the Virginia trial judge: The death sentence was constitutionally infirm.

After noting that the Virginia Supreme Court had not addressed the question whether trial counsel's performance at the sentencing hearing fell below the range of competence demanded of lawyers in criminal cases, the judge began by addressing that issue in detail. He identified five categories of mitigating evidence that counsel had failed to introduce, and he rejected the argument that counsel's failure to conduct an adequate investigation had been a strategic decision to rely almost entirely on the fact that Williams had voluntarily confessed.

* * *

The Federal Court of Appeals reversed. It construed § 2254(d)(1) as prohibiting the grant of habeas corpus relief unless the state court "'decided the question by interpreting or applying the relevant precedent in a manner that reasonable jurists would all agree is unreasonable.'" Applying that standard, it could not say that the Virginia Supreme Court's decision on the prejudice issue was an unreasonable application of the tests developed in either *Strickland* or *Lockhart*[*v. Fretwell*, 506 U.S. 364 (1993)]. It explained that the evidence that Williams presented a future danger to society was "simply overwhelming," it endorsed the Virginia Supreme Court's interpretation of *Lockhart*, and it characterized the state court's understanding of the facts in this case as "reasonable."

We granted certiorari and now reverse.

II

In 1867, Congress enacted a statute providing that federal courts "shall have power to grant writs of habeas corpus in all cases where any person may be restrained of his or her liberty in violation of the constitution, or of any treaty or law of the United States...." Act of Feb. 5, 1867, ch. 28, § 1, 14 Stat. 385. * * * [E]rrors that undermine confidence in the fundamental fairness of the state adjudication certainly justify the issuance of the federal writ. *See, e.g.*, *Teague v. Lane*, 489 U.S. 288 (1989). The deprivation of the right to the effective assistance of counsel recognized in *Strickland* is such an error. *Strickland*, 466 U.S. at 686, 697–698.

* * *

III

In this case, Williams contends that he was denied his constitutionally guaranteed right to the effective assistance of counsel when his trial lawyers failed to investigate and to present substantial mitigating evidence to the sentencing jury. The threshold question under AEDPA is whether Williams seeks to apply a rule of law that was clearly established at the time his state-court conviction became final. That question is easily answered because the merits of his claim are squarely governed by our holding in *Strickland v. Washington*.

* * *

To establish ineffectiveness, a "defendant must show that counsel's representation fell below an objective standard of reasonableness." To establish prejudice he "must show that there is a reasonable probability that, but for counsel's unprofessional errors, the result of the proceeding would have been different. A reasonable probability is a probability sufficient to undermine confidence in the outcome."

It is past question that the rule set forth in *Strickland* qualifies as "clearly established Federal law, as determined by the Supreme Court of the United States." That the *Strickland* test "of necessity requires a case-by-case examination of the evidence," *Wright* (KENNEDY, J., concurring), obviates neither the clarity of the rule nor the extent to which the rule must be seen as "established" by this Court. This Court's precedent "dictated" that the Virginia Supreme Court apply the *Strickland* test at the time that court entertained Williams' ineffective-assistance claim. *Teague*. And it can hardly be said that recognizing the right to effective counsel "breaks new ground or imposes a new obligation on the States." Williams is therefore entitled to relief if the Virginia Supreme Court's decision rejecting his ineffective-assistance claim was either "contrary to, or involved an unreasonable application of," that established law. It was both.

IV

The Virginia Supreme Court erred in holding that our decision in *Lockhart v. Fretwell* modified or in some way supplanted the rule set down in *Strickland*. It is true that while the *Strickland* test provides sufficient guidance for resolving virtually all ineffective-assistance-of-counsel claims, there are situations in which the overriding focus on fundamental fairness may affect the analysis. * * *

* * *

* * * In the instant case, it is undisputed that Williams had a right—indeed, a constitutionally protected right—to provide the jury with the mitigating evidence that his trial counsel either failed to discover or failed to offer.

* * *

Unlike the Virginia Supreme Court, the state trial judge omitted any reference to *Lockhart* and simply relied on our opinion in *Strickland* as stating the correct standard for judging ineffective-assistance claims. * * * The trial judge analyzed the ineffective-assistance claim under the correct standard; the Virginia Supreme Court did not.

We are likewise persuaded that the Virginia trial judge correctly applied both components of that standard to Williams' ineffectiveness claim. Although he concluded that counsel competently handled the guilt phase of the trial, he found that their representation during the sentencing phase fell short of professional standards—a judgment barely disputed by the State in its brief to this Court. The record establishes that counsel did not begin to prepare for that phase of the proceeding until a week before the trial. They failed to conduct an investigation that would have uncovered extensive records graphically describing Williams' nightmarish childhood, not because of any strategic calculation but because they incorrectly thought that state law barred access to such records. Had they done so, the jury would have learned that Williams' parents had been imprisoned for the criminal neglect of Williams and his siblings, that Williams had been severely and repeatedly beaten by his father, that he had been committed to the custody of the social services bureau for two years during his parents' incarceration (including one stint in an abusive foster home), and then, after his parents were released from prison, had been returned to his parents' custody.

Counsel failed to introduce available evidence that Williams was "borderline mentally retarded" and did not advance beyond sixth grade in school. They failed to seek prison records recording Williams' commendations for helping to crack a prison drug ring and for returning a guard's missing wallet, or the testimony of prison officials who described Williams as among the inmates "least likely to act in a violent, dangerous or provocative way." Counsel failed even to return the phone call of a certified public accountant who had offered to testify that he had visited Williams frequently when Williams was incarcerated as part of a prison ministry program, that Williams "seemed to thrive in a more regimented and structured environment," and that Williams was proud of the carpentry degree he earned while in prison.

Of course, not all of the additional evidence was favorable to Williams. The juvenile records revealed that he had been thrice committed to the juvenile system—for aiding and abetting larceny when he was 11 years old, for pulling a false fire alarm when he was 12, and for breaking and entering when he was 15. But as the Federal District Court correctly observed, the failure to introduce the comparatively voluminous amount of evidence that did speak in Williams' favor was not justified by a tactical decision to focus on Williams' voluntary confession. Whether or not those omissions were sufficiently prejudicial to have affected the outcome of sentencing, they clearly demonstrate that trial counsel did not fulfill their obligation to conduct a thorough investigation of the defendant's background.

We are also persuaded, unlike the Virginia Supreme Court, that counsel's unprofessional service prejudiced Williams within the meaning of *Strickland.* After hearing the additional evidence developed in the postconviction proceedings, the very judge who presided at Williams' trial and who once determined that the death penalty was "just" and "appropriate," concluded that there existed "a reasonable probability that the result of the sentencing phase would have been different" if the jury had heard that evidence. We do not agree with the Virginia Supreme Court that Judge Ingram's conclusion should be discounted because he apparently adopted "a *per se* approach to the prejudice element" that placed undue "emphasis on mere outcome determination." Judge Ingram did stress the importance of mitigation evidence in making his "outcome determination," but it is clear that his predictive judgment rested on his assessment of the totality of the omitted evidence rather than on the notion that a single item of omitted evidence, no matter how trivial, would require a new hearing.

The Virginia Supreme Court's own analysis of prejudice reaching the contrary conclusion was thus unreasonable in at least two respects. First, as we have already explained, the State Supreme Court mischaracterized at best the appropriate rule, made clear by this Court in *Strickland*, for determining whether counsel's assistance was effective within the meaning of the Constitution. While it may also have conducted an "outcome determinative" analysis of its own, it is evident to us that the court's decision turned on its erroneous view that a "mere" difference in outcome is not sufficient to establish constitutionally ineffective assistance of counsel. Its analysis in this respect was thus not only "contrary to," but also, inasmuch as the Virginia Supreme Court relied on the inapplicable exception recognized in *Lockhart*, an "unreasonable application of" the clear law as established by this Court.

Second, the State Supreme Court's prejudice determination was unreasonable insofar as it failed to evaluate the totality of the available mitigation evidence—both that adduced at trial, and the evidence adduced in the habeas proceeding—in reweighing it against the evidence in aggravation. See *Clemons v. Mississippi*, 494 U.S. 738, 751–752 (1990). This error is apparent in its consideration of the additional mitigation evidence developed in the postconviction proceedings. The court correctly found that as to "the factual part of the mixed question," there was "really ... no ... dispute" that available mitigation evidence was not presented at trial. As to the prejudice determination comprising the "legal part" of its analysis, it correctly emphasized the strength of the prosecution evidence supporting the future dangerousness aggravating circumstance.

But the state court failed even to mention the sole argument in mitigation that trial counsel did advance—Williams turned himself in, alerting police to a crime they otherwise would never have discovered, expressing remorse for his actions, and cooperating with the police after that. While this, coupled with the prison records and guard testimony, may not have overcome a finding of future dangerousness, the graphic description of Williams' childhood, filled with abuse and privation, or the reality that he was "borderline mentally retarded," might well have influenced the jury's appraisal of his moral culpability. See *Boyde v. California*, 494 U.S. 370, 387 (1990). The circumstances recited in his several confessions are consistent with the view that in each case his violent behavior was a compulsive reaction rather than the product of cold-blooded premeditation. Mitigating evidence unrelated to dangerousness may alter the jury's selection of penalty, even if it does not undermine or rebut the prosecution's death-eligibility case. The Virginia Supreme Court did not entertain that possibility. It thus failed to accord appropriate weight to the body of mitigation evidence available to trial counsel.

V

In our judgment, the state trial judge was correct both in his recognition of the established legal standard for determining counsel's effectiveness, and in his conclusion that the entire postconviction record, viewed as a whole and cumulative of mitigation evidence presented originally, raised "a reasonable probability that the result of the sentencing proceeding would have been different" if competent counsel had presented and explained the significance of all the available evidence. It follows that the Virginia Supreme Court rendered a "decision that was contrary to, or involved an unreasonable application of, clearly established Federal law." Williams' constitutional right to the effective assistance of counsel as defined in *Strickland v. Washington* was violated.

Accordingly, the judgment of the Court of Appeals is reversed, and the case is remanded for further proceedings consistent with this opinion.

It is so ordered.

Notes

1. *Subsequent case history*

On November 14, 2000, Terry Williams accepted a life sentence without the possibility of parole. In exchange, the prosecution agreed not to pursue the death penalty. Brooke A. Master, *Deal Gets Inmate Off Death Row*, The Washington Post, Nov. 15, 2000, at B1.

2. *The first reversal*

Although the Court decided *Strickland* in 1984, *Williams* was the first case in which the Court found ineffective assistance of counsel under the two-prong *Strickland* standard. Jenny Roberts, *Too Little, Too Late: Ineffective Assistance of Counsel, the Duty to Investigate, and Pretrial Discovery in Criminal Cases*, 331 Fordham Urb. L. J. 1097 (2004). Why do you think it took the Court sixteen years to find ineffective assistance of counsel under *Strickland*?

3. *A note about deference*

Justice Stevens observes in Section II:

> We all agree that state-court judgments must be upheld unless, after the closest examination of the state-court judgment, a federal court is firmly convinced that a federal constitutional right has been violated. Our difference is as to the cases in which, at first-blush, a state-court judgment seems entirely reasonable, but thorough analysis by a federal court produces a firm conviction that that judgment is infected by constitutional error. In our view, such an erroneous judgment is "unreasonable" within the meaning of the act even though that conclusion was not immediately apparent.

If you were a state court judge reading this excerpt, how would you understand its application to you?

Wiggins v. Smith

539 U.S. 510 (2003)

JUSTICE O'CONNOR delivered the opinion of the Court.

Petitioner, Kevin Wiggins, argues that his attorneys' failure to investigate his background and present mitigating evidence of his unfortunate life history at his capital sentencing proceedings violated his Sixth Amendment right to counsel. In this case, we consider whether the United States Court of Appeals for the Fourth Circuit erred in upholding the Maryland Court of Appeals' rejection of this claim.

I.

A

On September 17, 1988, police discovered 77-year-old Florence Lacs drowned in the bathtub of her ransacked apartment in Woodlawn, Maryland. The State indicted petitioner for the crime on October 20, 1988, and later filed a notice of intention to seek the death penalty. Two Baltimore County public defenders, Carl Schlaich and Michelle Nethercott, assumed responsibility for Wiggins' case. In July 1989, petitioner elected to be tried before a judge in Baltimore County Circuit Court. On August 4, after a 4-day trial, the court found petitioner guilty of first-degree murder, robbery, and two counts of theft.

After his conviction, Wiggins elected to be sentenced by a jury, and the trial court scheduled the proceedings to begin on October 11, 1989. On September 11, counsel filed a motion for bifurcation of sentencing in hopes of presenting Wiggins' case in two phases. Counsel intended first to prove that Wiggins did not act as a "principal in the first degree,"—*i.e.*, that he did not kill the victim by his own hand. Counsel then intended, if necessary, to present a mitigation case. In the memorandum in support of their motion, counsel argued that bifurcation would enable them to present each case in its best light; separating the two cases would prevent the introduction of mitigating evidence from diluting their claim that Wiggins was not directly responsible for the murder.

On October 12, the court denied the bifurcation motion, and sentencing proceedings commenced immediately thereafter. In her opening statement, Nethercott told the jurors they would hear evidence suggesting that someone other than Wiggins actually killed Lacs. Counsel then explained that the judge would instruct them to weigh Wiggins' clean record as a factor against a death sentence. She concluded: "You're going to hear that Kevin Wiggins has had a difficult life. It has not been easy for him. But he's worked. He's tried to be a productive citizen, and he's reached the age of 27 with no convictions for prior crimes of violence and no convictions, period.... I think that's an important thing for you to consider." During the proceedings themselves, however, counsel introduced no evidence of Wiggins' life history.

Before closing arguments, Schlaich made a proffer to the court, outside the presence of the jury, to preserve bifurcation as an issue for appeal. He detailed the mitigation case counsel would have presented had the court granted their bifurcation motion. He explained that they would have introduced psychological reports and expert testimony demonstrating Wiggins' limited intellectual capacities and childlike emotional state on the one hand, and the absence of aggressive patterns in his behavior, his capacity for empathy, and his desire to function in the world on the other. At no point did Schlaich proffer any evidence of petitioner's life history or family background. On October 18, the court instructed the jury on the sentencing task before it, and later that afternoon, the jury returned with a sentence of death. A divided Maryland Court of Appeals affirmed.

B

In 1993, Wiggins sought postconviction relief in Baltimore County Circuit Court. With new counsel, he challenged the adequacy of his representation at sentencing, arguing that his attorneys had rendered constitutionally defective assistance by failing to investigate and present mitigating evidence of his dysfunctional background. To support his claim, petitioner presented testimony by Hans Selvog, a licensed social worker certified as an expert by the court. Selvog testified concerning an elaborate social history report he had prepared containing evidence of the severe physical and sexual abuse petitioner suffered at the hands of his mother and while in the care of a series of foster parents. Relying on state social services, medical, and school records, as well as interviews with petitioner and numerous family members, Selvog chronicled petitioner's bleak life history.

According to Selvog's report, petitioner's mother, a chronic alcoholic, frequently left Wiggins and his siblings home alone for days, forcing them to beg for food and to eat paint chips and garbage. Mrs. Wiggins' abusive behavior included beating the children for breaking into the kitchen, which she often kept locked. She had sex with men while her children slept in the same bed and, on one occasion, forced petitioner's hand against a hot stove burner—an incident that led to petitioner's hospitalization. At the age of six, the State placed Wiggins in foster care. Petitioner's first and second foster mothers abused him physically, and, as petitioner explained to Selvog, the father in his second foster home repeatedly molested and raped him.

During the postconviction proceedings, Schlaich testified that he did not remember retaining a forensic social worker to prepare a social history, even though the State made funds available for that purpose. He explained that he and Nethercott, well in advance of trial, decided to focus their efforts on "retrying the factual case" and disputing Wiggins' direct responsibility for the murder. In April 1994, at the close of the proceedings, the judge observed from the bench that he could not remember a capital case in which counsel had not compiled a social history of the defendant, explaining, "not to do a social history, at least to see what you have got, to me is absolute error. I just—I would be flabbergasted if the Court of Appeals said anything else." In October 1997, however, the trial court denied Wiggins' petition for postconviction relief. The court concluded that "when the decision not to investigate ... is a matter of trial tactics, there is no ineffective assistance of counsel."

The Maryland Court of Appeals affirmed the denial of relief, concluding that trial counsel had made "a deliberate, tactical decision to concentrate their effort at convincing the jury" that appellant was not directly responsible for the murder. The court observed that counsel knew of Wiggins' unfortunate childhood. They had available to them both the presentence investigation (PSI) report prepared by the Division of Parole and Probation, as required by Maryland law, as well as "more detailed social service records that recorded incidences of physical and sexual abuse, an alcoholic mother, placements in foster care, and borderline retardation." The court acknowledged that this evidence was neither as detailed nor as graphic as the history elaborated in the Selvog report but emphasized that "counsel *did* investigate and *were* aware of appellant's background." Counsel knew that at least one uncontested mitigating factor—Wiggins' lack of prior convictions—would be before the jury should their attempt to disprove Wiggins' direct responsibility for the murder fail. As a result, the court concluded, Schlaich and Nethercott "made a reasoned choice to proceed with what they thought was their best defense."

C

In September 2001, Wiggins filed a petition for writ of habeas corpus in Federal District Court. The trial court granted him relief, holding that the Maryland courts' rejection of his ineffective assistance claim "involved an unreasonable application of clearly established federal law." *Wiggins v. Corcoran*, 164 F.Supp.2d 538, 557 (2001) (citing *Williams v. Taylor*, 529 U.S. 362 (2000)). The court rejected the State's defense of counsel's "tactical" decision to "'retry guilt,'" concluding that for a strategic decision to be reasonable, it must be "based upon information the attorney has made after conducting a reasonable investigation." The court found that though counsel were aware of some aspects of Wiggins' background, that knowledge did not excuse them from their duty to make a "fully informed and deliberate decision" about whether to present a mitigation case. In fact, the court concluded, their knowledge triggered an obligation to look further.

Reviewing the District Court's decision *de novo*, the Fourth Circuit reversed, holding that counsel had made a reasonable strategic decision to focus on petitioner's direct responsibility. The court contrasted counsel's complete failure to investigate potential mitigating evidence in *Williams* with the fact that Schlaich and Nethercott knew at least some details of Wiggins' childhood from the PSI and social services records. The court acknowledged that counsel likely knew further investigation "would have resulted in more sordid details surfacing," but agreed with the Maryland Court of Appeals that counsel's knowledge of the avenues of mitigation available to them "was sufficient to make an informed strategic choice" to challenge petitioner's direct responsibility for the murder. The court emphasized that conflicting medical testimony with respect to the time of death, the absence of direct evidence against Wiggins, and unexplained forensic evidence at the crime scene supported counsel's strategy.

We granted certiorari and now reverse.

II

A

Petitioner renews his contention that his attorneys' performance at sentencing violated his Sixth Amendment right to effective assistance of counsel. The amendments to 28 U.S.C. § 2254, enacted as part of the Antiterrorism and Effective Death Penalty Act of 1996 (AEDPA), circumscribe our consideration of Wiggins' claim and require us to limit our analysis to the law as it was "clearly established" by our precedents at the time of the state court's decision. * * * We have made clear that the "unreasonable application" prong of § 2254(d)(1) permits a federal habeas court to "grant the writ if the state court identifies the correct governing legal principle from this Court's decisions but unreasonably applies that principle to the facts" of petitioner's case. *Williams*, 529 U.S. at 413. * * *

We established the legal principles that govern claims of ineffective assistance of counsel in *Strickland v. Washington*. An ineffective assistance claim has two components: A petitioner must show that counsel's performance was deficient, and that the deficiency prejudiced the defense. To establish deficient performance, a petitioner must demonstrate that counsel's representation "fell below an objective standard of reasonableness." We have declined to articulate specific guidelines for appropriate attorney conduct and instead have emphasized that "the proper measure of attorney performance remains simply reasonableness under prevailing professional norms."

In this case, as in *Strickland*, petitioner's claim stems from counsel's decision to limit the scope of their investigation into potential mitigating evidence. Here, as in *Strickland*, counsel attempt to justify their limited investigation as reflecting a tactical judgment not to present mitigating evidence at sentencing and to pursue an alternate strategy instead. In rejecting Strickland's claim, we defined the deference owed such strategic judgments in terms of the adequacy of the investigations supporting those judgments:

> Strategic choices made after thorough investigation of law and facts relevant to plausible options are virtually unchallengeable; and strategic choices made after less than complete investigation are reasonable precisely to the extent that reasonable professional judgments support the limitations on investigation. In other words, counsel has a duty to make reasonable investigations or to make a reasonable decision that makes particular investigations unnecessary. In any ineffectiveness case, a particular decision not to investigate must be directly assessed for reasonableness in all the circumstances, applying a heavy measure of deference to counsel's judgments.

* * *

In light of these standards, our principal concern in deciding whether Schlaich and Nethercott exercised "reasonable professional judgment" is not whether counsel should have presented a mitigation case. Rather, we focus on whether the investigation supporting counsel's decision not to introduce mitigating evidence of Wiggins' background *was itself reasonable*. * * *

B

1

The record demonstrates that counsel's investigation drew from three sources. Counsel arranged for William Stejskal, a psychologist, to conduct a number of tests on petitioner. Stejskal concluded that petitioner had an IQ of 79, had difficulty coping with demanding situations, and exhibited features of a personality disorder. These reports revealed nothing, however, of petitioner's life history.

With respect to that history, counsel had available to them the written PSI, which included a one-page account of Wiggins' "personal history" noting his "misery as a youth," quoting his description of his own background as "'disgusting,'" and observing that he spent most of his life in foster care. Counsel also "tracked down" records kept by the Baltimore City Department of Social Services (DSS) documenting petitioner's various placements in the State's foster care system. In describing the scope of counsel's investigation into petitioner's life history, both the Fourth Circuit and the Maryland Court of Appeals referred only to these two sources of information.

Counsel's decision not to expand their investigation beyond the PSI and the DSS records fell short of the professional standards that prevailed in Maryland in 1989. As Schlaich acknowledged, standard practice in Maryland in capital cases at the time of Wiggins' trial included the preparation of a social history report. Despite the fact that the Public Defender's office made funds available for the retention of a forensic social worker, counsel chose not to commission such a report. Counsel's conduct similarly fell short of the standards for capital defense work articulated by the American Bar Association (ABA)—standards to which we long have referred as "guides to determining what is reasonable." The ABA Guidelines provide that investigations into mitigating evidence "should comprise efforts to discover *all reasonably available* mitigating evidence and evidence to rebut any aggravating evidence that may be introduced by the prosecutor." Despite these well-defined norms, however, counsel abandoned their investigation of petitioner's background after having acquired only rudimentary knowledge of his history from a narrow set of sources.

The scope of their investigation was also unreasonable in light of what counsel actually discovered in the DSS records. The records revealed several facts: Petitioner's mother was a chronic alcoholic; Wiggins was shuttled from foster home to foster home and displayed some emotional difficulties while there; he had frequent, lengthy absences from school; and, on at least one occasion, his mother left him and his siblings alone for days without food. As the Federal District Court emphasized, any reasonably competent attorney would have realized that pursuing these leads was necessary to making an informed choice among possible defenses, particularly given the apparent absence of any aggravating factors in petitioner's background. Indeed, counsel uncovered no evidence in their investigation to suggest that a mitigation case, in its own right, would have been counterproductive, or that further investigation would have been fruitless; this case is therefore distinguishable from our precedents in which we have found limited investigations into mitigating evidence to be reasonable.* * *

The record of the actual sentencing proceedings underscores the unreasonableness of counsel's conduct by suggesting that their failure to investigate thoroughly resulted from inattention, not reasoned strategic judgment. Counsel sought, until the day before sentencing, to have the proceedings bifurcated into a retrial of guilt and a mitigation stage. On the eve of sentencing, counsel represented to the court that they were prepared to come forward with mitigating evidence and that they intended to present such evidence in the event the court granted their motion to bifurcate. In other words, prior to sentencing, counsel never actually abandoned the possibility that they would present a mitigation defense. Until the court denied their motion, then, they had every reason to develop the most powerful mitigation case possible.

What is more, during the sentencing proceeding itself, counsel did not focus exclusively on Wiggins' direct responsibility for the murder. After introducing that issue in her opening statement, Nethercott entreated the jury to consider not just what Wiggins "is found to have done," but also "who [he] is." Though she told the jury it would "hear that Kevin Wiggins has had a difficult life," counsel never followed up on that suggestion with details of Wiggins' history. At the same time, counsel called a criminologist to testify that inmates serving life sentences tend to adjust well and refrain from further violence in prison—testimony with no bearing on whether petitioner committed the murder by his own hand. Far from focusing exclusively on petitioner's direct responsibility, then, counsel put on a halfhearted mitigation case, taking precisely the type of "shotgun" approach the Maryland Court of Appeals concluded counsel sought to avoid. When viewed in this light, the "strategic decision" the state courts and respondents all invoke to justify counsel's limited pursuit of mitigating evidence resembles more a *post-hoc* rationalization of counsel's conduct than an accurate description of their deliberations prior to sentencing.

In rejecting petitioner's ineffective assistance claim, the Maryland Court of Appeals appears to have assumed that because counsel had *some* information with respect to petitioner's background—the information in the PSI and the DSS records—they were in a position to make a tactical choice not to present a mitigation defense. In assessing the reasonableness of an attorney's investigation, however, a court must consider not only the quantum of evidence already known to counsel, but also whether the known evidence would lead a reasonable attorney to investigate further. Even assuming Schlaich and Nethercott limited the scope of their investigation for strategic reasons, *Strickland* does not establish that a cursory investigation automatically justifies a tactical decision with respect to sentencing strategy. Rather, a reviewing court must consider the reasonableness of the investigation said to support that strategy.

The Maryland Court of Appeals' application of *Strickland*'s governing legal principles was objectively unreasonable. Though the state court acknowledged petitioner's claim that counsel's failure to prepare a social history "did not meet the minimum standards of the profession," the court did not conduct an assessment of whether the decision to cease all investigation upon obtaining the PSI and the DSS records actually demonstrated reasonable professional judgment. * * *

Additionally, the court based its conclusion, in part, on a clear factual error—that the "social service records ... recorded incidences of ... sexual abuse." As the State and the United States now concede, the records contain no mention of sexual abuse, much less of the repeated molestations and rapes of petitioner detailed in the Selvog report. The state court's assumption that the records documented instances of this abuse has been shown to be incorrect by "clear and convincing evidence," 28 U.S.C. § 2254(e)(1), and reflects "an unreasonable determination of the facts in light of the evidence presented in the State court proceeding," § 2254(d)(2). This partial reliance on an erroneous factual finding further highlights the unreasonableness of the state court's decision.

The dissent insists that this Court's hands are tied, under § 2254(d), "by the state court's factual determinations that Wiggins' trial counsel '*did* investigate and *were* aware of [Wiggins'] background.'" But as we have made clear, the Maryland Court of Appeals' conclusion that the *scope* of counsel's investigation into petitioner's background met the legal standards set in *Strickland* represented an objectively unreasonable application of our precedent. § 2254(d)(1). Moreover, the court's assumption that counsel learned of a major aspect of Wiggins' background, *i.e.*, the sexual abuse, from the DSS records was clearly erroneous. The requirements of § 2254(d) thus pose no bar to granting petitioner habeas relief.

2

* * *

We therefore must determine, *de novo*, whether counsel reached beyond the PSI and the DSS records in their investigation of petitioner's background. The record as a whole does not support the conclusion that counsel conducted a more thorough investigation than the one we have described. * * *

The State maintained at oral argument that Schlaich's reference to "other people's reports" indicated that counsel learned of the sexual abuse from sources other than the PSI and the DSS records. But when pressed repeatedly to identify the sources counsel might have consulted, the State acknowledged that no written reports documented the sexual abuse and speculated that counsel must have learned of it through "oral reports" from Wiggins himself. Not only would the phrase "other people's reports" have been an unusual way for counsel to refer to conversations with his client, but the record contains no evidence that counsel ever pursued this line of questioning with Wiggins. For its part, the United States emphasized counsel's retention of the psychologist. But again, counsel's decision to hire a psychologist sheds no light on the extent of their investigation into petitioner's social background. Though Stejskal based his conclusions on clinical interviews with Wiggins, as well as meetings with Wiggins' family members, his final report discussed only petitioner's mental capacities and attributed nothing of what he learned to Wiggins' social history.

To further underscore that counsel did not know, prior to sentencing, of the sexual abuse, as well as of the other incidents not recorded in the DSS records, petitioner directs us to the content of counsel's October 17, 1989, proffer. Before closing statements and outside the presence of the jury, Schlaich proffered to the court the mitigation case counsel would have introduced had the court granted their motion to bifurcate. In his statement, Schlaich referred only to the results of the psychologist's test and mentioned nothing of Wiggins' troubled background. Given that the purpose of the proffer was to preserve their pursuit of bifurcation as an issue for appeal, they had every incentive to make their mitigation case seem as strong as possible. Counsel's failure to include in the proffer the powerful evidence of repeated sexual abuse is therefore explicable only if we assume that counsel had no knowledge of the abuse.

Contrary to the dissent's claim, we are not accusing Schlaich of lying. His statements at the postconviction proceedings that he knew of this abuse, as well as of the hand-burning incident, may simply reflect a mistaken memory shaped by the passage of time. After all, the state postconviction proceedings took place over four years after Wiggins' sentencing. Ultimately, given counsel's likely ignorance of the history of sexual abuse at the time of sentencing, we cannot infer from Schlaich's postconviction testimony that counsel looked further than the PSI and the DSS records in investigating petitioner's background. Indeed, the record contains no mention of sources other than those it is undisputed counsel possessed. We therefore conclude that counsel's investigation of petitioner's background was limited to the PSI and the DSS records.

3

In finding that Schlaich and Nethercott's investigation did not meet *Strickland*'s performance standards, we emphasize that *Strickland* does not require counsel to investigate every conceivable line of mitigating evidence no matter how unlikely the effort would be to assist the defendant at sentencing. Nor does *Strickland* require defense counsel to present mitigating evidence at sentencing in every case. Both conclusions would interfere with the "constitutionally protected independence of counsel" at the heart of *Strickland*. We base our conclusion on the much more limited principle that "strategic choices made after less than complete investigation are reasonable" only to the extent that "reasonable professional judgments support the limitations on investigation." A decision not to investigate thus "must be directly assessed for reasonableness in all the circumstances."

* * *

III

In order for counsel's inadequate performance to constitute a Sixth Amendment violation, petitioner must show that counsel's failures prejudiced his defense. In *Strickland*, we made clear that, to establish prejudice, a "defendant must show that there is a reasonable probability that, but for counsel's unprofessional errors, the result of the proceeding would have been different. A reasonable probability is a probability sufficient to undermine confidence in the outcome." In assessing prejudice, we reweigh the evidence in aggravation against the totality of available mitigating evidence. In this case, our review is not circumscribed by a state court conclusion with respect to prejudice, as neither of the state courts below reached this prong of the *Strickland* analysis.

The mitigating evidence counsel failed to discover and present in this case is powerful. As Selvog reported based on his conversations with Wiggins and members of his family, Wiggins experienced severe privation and abuse in the first six years of his life while in the custody of his alcoholic, absentee mother. He suffered physical torment, sexual molestation, and repeated rape during his subsequent years in foster care. The time Wiggins spent homeless, along with his diminished mental capacities, further augment his mitigation case. Petitioner thus has the kind of troubled history we have declared relevant to assessing a defendant's moral culpability. *Penry v. Lynaugh*, 492 U.S. 302, 319 (1989) ("'[E]vidence about the defendant's background and character is relevant because of the belief, long held by this society, that defendants who commit criminal acts that are attributable to a disadvantaged background ... may be less culpable than defendants who have no such excuse'"); see also *Eddings v. Oklahoma*, 455 U.S. 104, 112 (1982) (noting that consideration of the offender's life history is a "'part of the process of inflicting the penalty of death'"); *Lockett v. Ohio*, 438 U.S. 586, 604 (1978) (invalidating Ohio law that did not permit consideration of aspects of a defendant's background).

Given both the nature and the extent of the abuse petitioner suffered, we find there to be a reasonable probability that a competent attorney, aware of this history, would have introduced it at sentencing in an admissible form. While it may well have been strategically defensible upon a reasonably thorough investigation to focus on Wiggins' direct responsibility for the murder, the two sentencing strategies are not necessarily mutually exclusive. Moreover, given the strength of the available evidence, a reasonable attorney may well have chosen to prioritize the mitigation case over the direct responsibility challenge, particularly given that Wiggins' history contained little of the double edge we have found to justify limited investigations in other cases.

* * *

We further find that had the jury been confronted with this considerable mitigating evidence, there is a reasonable probability that it would have returned with a different sentence. In reaching this conclusion, we need not, as the dissent suggests, make the state-law evidentiary findings that would have been at issue at sentencing. Rather, we evaluate the totality of the evidence—"both that adduced at trial, *and the evidence adduced in the habeas proceeding[s]*."

* * *

* * * Accordingly, the judgment of the United States Court of Appeals for the Fourth Circuit is reversed, and the case is remanded for further proceedings consistent with this opinion.

It is so ordered.

JUSTICE SCALIA, with whom JUSTICE THOMAS joins, dissenting:

The Court today vacates Kevin Wiggins' death sentence on the ground that his trial counsel's investigation of potential mitigating evidence was "incomplete." Wiggins' trial counsel testified under oath, however, that he was aware of the basic features of Wiggins' troubled childhood that the Court claims he overlooked. The Court chooses to disbelieve this testimony for reasons that do not withstand analysis. Moreover, even if this disbelief could plausibly be entertained, that would certainly not establish (as 28 U.S.C. § 2254(d) requires) that the Maryland Court of Appeals was *unreasonable* in believing it, and in therefore concluding that counsel adequately investigated Wiggins' background. The Court also fails to observe § 2254(e)(1)'s requirement that federal habeas courts respect state-court factual determinations not rebutted by "clear and convincing evidence." The decision sets at naught the statutory scheme we once described as a "highly deferential standard for evaluating state-court rulings." *Lindh v. Murphy*, 521 U.S. 320, 333, n.7 (1997). I respectfully dissent.

* * *

II

* * *

There is no "reasonable probability" that a social-history investigation would have altered the chosen strategy of Wiggins' trial counsel. As noted earlier, Schlaich was well aware—without the benefit of a "social history" report—that Wiggins had a troubled childhood and background. And the Court remains bound, *even after* concluding that Wiggins has satisfied the standards of §§ 2254(d)(1) and (d)(2), by the state court's factual determination that Wiggins' trial attorneys "*were* aware of [Wiggins'] background" and "were aware that Wiggins had a most unfortunate childhood." See 28 U.S.C. § 2254(e)(1). Wiggins' trial attorneys chose, however, not to present evidence of Wiggins' background to the jury because of their "deliberate, tactical decision to concentrate their effort at convincing the jury that appellant was not a principal in the killing of Ms. Lacs."

Wiggins has not shown that the incremental information in Hans Selvog's social-history report would have induced counsel to change this course. * * *

* * *

Today's decision is extraordinary—even for our "death is different" jurisprudence. It fails to give effect to § 2254(e)(1)'s requirement that state court factual determinations be presumed correct, and disbelieves the sworn testimony of a member of the bar while treating hearsay accounts of statements of a convicted murderer as established fact. I dissent.

Notes

1. *Subsequent case history*

In 2004, Kevin Wiggins' attorneys negotiated a plea deal with the state of Maryland. Wiggins accepted an offer of life in prison. Although he was eligible for parole within four months of his sentencing, Maryland inmates sentenced to life in prison are rarely paroled. *See* Jennifer McMenamin, *Wiggins accepts offer of life term; Death sentence was overturned by Supreme Court last year; Eligible for parole hearing soon*, The Baltimore Sun, Oct. 8, 2004, at B1.

2. *Considering the term "unreasonableness"*

What is your response to Justice Scalia's remark that the Maryland Court of Appeals was not unreasonable in believing the testimony of Wiggins' attorney? Would you agree with Justice Scalia that the Court's decision in *Wiggins* was "extraordinary"?

3. *How far is the Court willing to take the analysis in* Wiggins?

In October 2003, the Supreme Court issued a *per curiam* opinion in *Yarborough v. Gentry*, 540 U.S. 1 (2003), a case in which the Ninth Circuit granted habeas corpus relief on the basis of ineffective assistance of counsel during the closing argument at trial. Lionel

Gentry was convicted in a California state court of assault with a deadly weapon for stabbing his girlfriend, who testified against him at trial. The Ninth Circuit reviewed Gentry's attorney's closing argument and criticized him for such errors as not highlighting certain potentially exculpatory pieces of evidence, criticizing his own client, failing to demand that the jury acquit Gentry, and confessing that he could not tell who was telling the truth, either. In reversing the Ninth Circuit's decision, the Supreme Court stated that the "Ninth Circuit's conclusion—not only that [counsel's] performance was deficient, but that any disagreement with that conclusion would be objectively unreasonable—gives too little deference to the state courts that have primary responsibility for supervising defense counsel in state criminal trials."

Based on the bare facts outlined in this note about Gentry's closing argument, what are the main differences between Gentry's case and Wiggins' case that enabled the Court to reach such different results?

4. *What constitutes a strategic decision and how reasonable must it be?*

In *Wood v. Allen*, 130 S.Ct. 841 (2010), the Court affirmed the denial of habeas relief to a petitioner sentenced to death for the murder of his ex-girlfriend in Alabama. After losing his direct appeal, Holly Wood sought state post-conviction relief, alleging in one of his claims that trial counsel were ineffective for not investigating and presenting evidence of his mental deficiencies. At the state post-conviction evidentiary hearing, Wood's counsel presented evidence that he had an IQ in the borderline range of functioning and could read only at a third grade level. The jury had never heard evidence of these facts at either the guilt or penalty phase. The state trial court found that counsel had made a strategic decision not to pursue evidence of Wood's retardation, and therefore counsels' performance was not deficient and had not prejudiced Wood's defense. The trial court also found if the evidence developed at the evidentiary hearing had been presented to the jury, there was no reasonable probability of a different outcome. Wood then sought habeas relief. The federal district court granted the habeas petition on the ground that the state court's determination that counsel had made a strategic decision was an unreasonable determination of the facts. Two more experienced defense counsel had assigned the penalty phase to a third attorney with little experience. That attorney testified he had seen references to mental deficiency in an expert's report but could not remember if he had considered pursuing the issue of retardation as mitigation evidence. In addition, this attorney had not succeeded in getting Wood's school records and had not talked to Wood's teachers. Finding both deficient performance and prejudice, the federal district court concluded that the state court holding was an unreasonable application of federal law. The Eleventh Circuit reversed, concluding that the state trial court's findings were neither an unreasonable application of federal law nor grounded on an unreasonable determination of the facts.

The Supreme Court found that counsel could have made "a deliberate decision to focus on other defenses" rather than pursuing and presenting evidence of mental deficiencies. The Court cited testimony that the more experienced attorneys had read the expert's report and that one of them had told the trial judge that they would not introduce the report to the jury. It thus held that "even under petitioner's reading of § 2254(d)(2), the state court's conclusion that Wood's counsel made a strategic decision not to pursue or present evidence of his mental deficiencies was not an unreasonable determination of the facts."

Why did the Court find counsels' strategic choice unreasonable in *Wiggins* but not in *Wood*?

5. *Prevailing professional norms*

In *Rompilla v. Beard*, 545 U.S. 374 (2005), the Supreme Court again assessed the effectiveness of defense counsel's investigation of evidence for the sentencing phase of a capital case. While defense counsel had sought mitigating evidence from the defendant, family members, and mental health professionals, they had not examined the public records relating to their client's prior convictions even though they knew the prosecutor would try to show violent character through the defendant's prior felony convictions. The Court found that even where the defendant and family members had suggested that no mitigating evidence was available, counsel was nonetheless "bound to make reasonable efforts to obtain and review materials that counsel knows the prosecution will probably rely on as evidence of aggravation." In finding counsel to have been ineffective in this case, the Court held that counsel's performance should be judged by prevailing professional norms, specifically referring to the ABA Guidelines for the Appointment and Performance of Counsel in Death Penalty Cases and to the following provision of the American Bar Association's Standards for Criminal Justice:

> It is the duty of the lawyer to conduct a prompt investigation of the circumstances of the case and to explore all avenues leading to facts relevant to the merits of the case and the penalty in the event of conviction. The investigation should always include efforts to secure information in the possession of the prosecution and law enforcement authorizes. The duty to investigate exists regardless of the accused's admissions or statements to the lawyer of facts constituting guilt or the accused's stated desire to plead guilty.

Contrast the Court's reliance on professional organization rules in *Wiggins* and *Rompilla* with its statement in *Strickland* that "[p]revailing norms of practice as reflected in American Bar Association standards ... are guides to determining what is reasonable, but they are only guides." *Strickland*, *supra*, at 688.

Five years after *Rompilla*, the Court referred to prevailing professional norms in finding defense counsel deficient for providing erroneous advice about the deportation consequences of a plea of guilty. In *Padilla v. Kentucky*, discussed in Chapter 4, the Court again emphasized the link between "constitutional deficiency" in representation and "prevailing professional norms" and found that "[t]he weight of prevailing professional norms supports the view that counsel must advise her client regarding the risk of deportation." 130 S.Ct. 1473, 1482 (2010).

Justice Alito, concurring in the judgment because of the affirmative misadvice given to Padilla, noted that *Strickland* held that prevailing norms are only guidelines. He asserted that the Court's decision to impose an affirmative duty on defense counsel to advise clients if there might be immigration consequences of a plea "marks a major upheaval in Sixth Amendment law." *Id.* at 1491.

What is your assessment of Justice Alito's points of disagreement?

B. Withholding Exculpatory Evidence

In the landmark case *Brady v. Maryland*, 373 U.S. 83 (1963), the United States Supreme Court ruled that a prosecutor has a duty to turn over to the defendant material exculpatory evidence. After separate trials, petitioner Brady and a co-defendant, Boblit, were found guilty of murder in the first degree and sentenced to death. At Brady's trial, which took place first, Brady took the stand and admitted his participation in the crime but claimed that Boblit did the actual killing. Defense counsel even conceded in closing argument that Brady was guilty of first-degree murder, asking only that the jury return the verdict "without capital punishment." Prior to trial, defense counsel had asked the prosecution to allow him to examine Boblit's extra-judicial statements, and several of those statements were shown to him. Although defense counsel had read several of Boblit's statements, the prosecution withheld a key statement in which Boblit admitted the actual homicide. Brady was not aware of Boblit's admission until after his conviction had been affirmed. When he later appealed to the United States Supreme Court, the Court held that prosecutorial suppression of evidence favorable to an accused—when the accused had requested such discovery—violates due process if the evidence is material either to guilt or punishment, irrespective of the good faith or bad faith of the prosecution.[1]

In *Strickler v. Greene*, the Court applied a more modern analysis of a *Brady* violation in another capital case.

Strickler v. Greene

527 U.S. 263 (1999)

JUSTICE STEVENS delivered the opinion of the Court.

The District Court for the Eastern District of Virginia granted petitioner's application for a writ of habeas corpus and vacated his capital murder conviction and death sentence on the grounds that the Commonwealth had failed to disclose important exculpatory evidence and that petitioner had not, in consequence, received a fair trial. The Court of Appeals for the Fourth Circuit reversed because petitioner had not raised his constitutional claim at his trial or in state collateral proceedings. In addition, the Fourth Circuit concluded that petitioner's claim was, "in any event, without merit." Finding the legal question presented by this case considerably more difficult than the Fourth Circuit, we granted certiorari to consider (1) whether the State violated *Brady v. Maryland* and its progeny; (2) whether there was an acceptable "cause" for petitioner's failure to raise this claim in state court; and (3), if so, whether he suffered prejudice sufficient to excuse his procedural default.

I

In the early evening of January 5, 1990, Leanne Whitlock, an African-American sophomore at James Madison University, was abducted from a local shopping center and robbed and murdered. In separate trials, both petitioner and Ronald Henderson were

1. *Brady* and its progeny represent an exception to the rule that there is no general constitutional right to discovery in criminal cases. *Wardius v. Orgeon*, 412 U.S. 470 (1973); *United States v. Ruiz*, 536 U.S. 622 (2002); *Weatherford v. Bursey*, 429 U.S. 545 (1977). Most states have discovery rules or statutes setting out what information the prosecution must disclose to the defendant, at what point in the proceedings, and under what circumstances. Increasingly, states have adopted "reciprocal discovery" rules that require the defense to provide discovery to the prosecution. A defendant's entitlement to discovery under these formal rules varies greatly across jurisdictions, from very restrictive to broad. Even in those jurisdictions with liberal discovery rules, a criminal defendant's access to information known to the prosecution is far more limited than is a litigant's access in civil cases. Many commentators have called for reforms to the discovery process in criminal cases. *See e.g.*, Mary Prosser, *Reforming Criminal Discovery: Why Old Objections Must Yield to New Realities*, 2006 Wis. L. Rev. 541 (2006).

convicted of all three offenses. Henderson was convicted of first-degree murder, a non-capital offense, whereas petitioner was convicted of capital murder and sentenced to death.

At both trials, a woman named Anne Stoltzfus testified in vivid detail about Whitlock's abduction. The exculpatory material that petitioner claims should have been disclosed before trial includes documents prepared by Stoltzfus, and notes of interviews with her, that impeach significant portions of her testimony. We begin, however, by noting that, even without the Stoltzfus testimony, the evidence in the record was sufficient to establish petitioner's guilt on the murder charge. Whether petitioner would have been convicted of capital murder and received the death sentence if she had not testified, or if she had been sufficiently impeached, is less clear. To put the question in context, we review the trial testimony at some length.

The Testimony at Trial

At about 4:30 p.m. on January 5, 1990, Whitlock borrowed a 1986 blue Mercury Lynx from her boyfriend, John Dean, who worked in the Valley Shopping Mall in Harrisonburg, Virginia. At about 6:30 or 6:45 p.m., she left her apartment, intending to return the car to Dean at the mall. She did not return the car and was not again seen alive by any of her friends or family.

Petitioner's mother testified that she had driven petitioner and Henderson to Harrisonburg on January 5. She also testified that petitioner always carried a hunting knife that had belonged to his father. Two witnesses, a friend of Henderson's and a security guard, saw petitioner and Henderson at the mall that afternoon. The security guard was informed around 3:30 p.m. that two men, one of whom she identified at trial as petitioner, were attempting to steal a car in the parking lot. She had them under observation during the remainder of the afternoon but lost sight of them at about 6:45.

At approximately 7:30 p.m., a witness named Kurt Massie saw the blue Lynx at a location in Augusta County about 25 miles from Harrisonburg and a short distance from the cornfield where Whitlock's body was later found. Massie identified petitioner as the driver of the vehicle; he also saw a white woman in the front seat and another man in the back. Massie noticed that the car was muddy, and that it turned off Route 340 onto a dirt road.

At about 8 p.m., another witness saw the Lynx at Buddy's Market, with two men sitting in the front seat. The witness did not see anyone else in the car. At approximately 9 p.m., petitioner and Henderson arrived at Dice's Inn, a bar in Staunton, Virginia, where they stayed for about four or five hours. They danced with several women, including four prosecution witnesses: Donna Kay Tudor, Nancy Simmons, Debra Sievers, and Carolyn Brown. While there, Henderson gave Nancy Simmons a watch that had belonged to Whitlock. Petitioner spent most of his time with Tudor, who was later arrested for grand larceny based on her possession of the blue Lynx.

These four women all testified that Tudor had arrived at Dice's at about 8 p.m. Three of them noticed nothing unusual about petitioner's appearance, but Tudor saw some blood on his jeans and a cut on his knuckle. Tudor also testified that she, Henderson, and petitioner left Dice's together after it closed to search for marijuana. Henderson was driving the blue Lynx, and petitioner and Tudor rode in back. Tudor related that petitioner was leaning toward Henderson and talking with him; she overheard a crude conversation that could reasonably be interpreted as describing the assault and murder of a black person with a "rock crusher." Tudor stated that petitioner made a statement that implied that he had killed someone, so they "wouldn't give him no more trouble." Tudor testified that while she, petitioner, and Henderson were driving around, petitioner took out his knife and threatened to stab Henderson because he was driving recklessly. Petitioner then began driving.

At about 4:30 or 5 a.m. on January 6, petitioner drove Henderson to Kenneth Workman's apartment in Timberville. Henderson went inside to get something, and petitioner and Tudor drove off without waiting for him. Workman testified that Henderson had blood on his pants and stated he had killed a black person.

Petitioner and Tudor then drove to a motel in Blue Ridge. A day or two later they went to Virginia Beach, where they spent the rest of the week. Petitioner gave Tudor pearl earrings that Whitlock had been wearing when she was last seen. Tudor saw Whitlock's driver's license and bank card in the glove compartment of the car. Tudor testified that petitioner unsuccessfully attempted to use Whitlock's bank card when they were in Virginia Beach.

When petitioner and Tudor returned to Augusta County, they abandoned the blue Lynx. On January 11, the police identified the car as Dean's, and found petitioner's and Tudor's fingerprints on both the inside and the outside of the car. They also found shoe impressions that matched the soles of shoes belonging to petitioner. Inside the car, they retrieved a jacket that contained identification papers belonging to Henderson.

The police also recovered a bag at petitioner's mother's house that Tudor testified she and petitioner had left when they returned from Virginia Beach. The bag contained, among other items, three identification cards belonging to Whitlock and a black "tank top" shirt that was later found to have human blood and semen stains on it.

On January 13, a farmer called the police to advise them that he had found Henderson's wallet; a search of the area led to the discovery of Whitlock's frozen, nude, and battered body. A 69-pound rock, spotted with blood, lay nearby. Forensic evidence indicated that Whitlock's death was caused by "multiple blunt force injuries to the head." The location of the rock and the human blood on the rock suggested that it had been used to inflict these injuries. Based on the contents of Whitlock's stomach, the medical examiner determined that she died fewer than six hours after she had last eaten.

A number of Caucasian hair samples were found at the scene, three of which were probably petitioner's. Given the weight of the rock, the prosecution argued that one of the killers must have held the victim down while the other struck her with the murder weapon.

Donna Tudor's estranged husband, Jay Tudor, was called by the defense and testified that in March she had told him that she was present at the murder scene and that petitioner did not participate in the murder. Jay Tudor's testimony was inconsistent in several respects with that of other witnesses. For example, he testified that several days elapsed between the time that petitioner, Henderson, and Donna Tudor picked up Whitlock and the time of Whitlock's murder.

Anne Stoltzfus' Testimony

Anne Stoltzfus testified that on two occasions on January 5 she saw petitioner, Henderson, and a blonde girl inside the Harrisonburg mall, and that she later witnessed their abduction of Whitlock in the parking lot. She did not call the police, but a week and a half after the incident she discussed it with classmates at James Madison University, where both she and Whitlock were students. One of them called the police. The next night a detective visited her, and the following morning she went to the police station and told her story to Detective Claytor, a member of the Harrisonburg City Police Department. Detective Claytor showed her photographs of possible suspects, and she identified petitioner and Henderson "with absolute certainty" but stated that she had a slight reservation about her identification of the blonde woman.

At trial, Stoltzfus testified that, at about 6 p.m. on January 5, she and her 14-year-old daughter were in the Music Land store in the mall looking for a compact disc. While she was waiting for assistance from a clerk, petitioner, whom she described as "Mountain Man," and the blonde girl entered. Because petitioner was "revved up" and "very impatient," she was frightened and backed up, bumping into Henderson (whom she called "Shy Guy"), and thought she felt something hard in the pocket of his coat.

Stoltzfus left the store, intending to return later. At about 6:45, while heading back toward Music Land, she again encountered the threesome: "Shy Guy" walking by himself, followed by the girl, and then "Mountain Man" yelling "Donna, Donna, Donna." The girl bumped into Stoltzfus and then asked for directions to the bus stop. The three then left.

At first Stoltzfus tried to follow them because of her concern about petitioner's behavior, but she "lost him" and then headed back to Music Land. The clerk had not returned, so she and her daughter went to their car. While driving to another store, they saw a shiny dark blue car. The driver was "beautiful," "well dressed and she was happy, she was singing...." When the blue car was stopped behind a minivan at a stop sign, Stoltzfus saw petitioner for the third time. She testified:

> "'Mountain Man' came tearing out of the Mall entrance door and went up to the driver of the van and ... was just really mad and ran back and banged on back of the backside of the van and then went back to the Mall entrance wall where 'Shy Guy' and 'Blonde Girl' was standing ... then we left [and before the van and a white-pickup truck could turn] 'Mountain Man' came out again...."

After first going to the passenger side of the pickup truck, petitioner came back to the black girl's car, "pounded on" the passenger window, shook the car, yanked the door open and jumped in. When he motioned for "Blonde Girl" and "Shy Guy" to get in, the driver stepped on the gas and "just laid on the horn" but she could not go because there were people walking in front of the car. The horn "blew a long time" and petitioner "started hitting her ... on the left shoulder, her right shoulder and then it looked like to me that he started hitting her on the head and I was, I just became concerned and upset. So I beeped, honked my horn and then she stopped honking the horn and he stopped hitting her and opened the door again and the 'Blonde Girl' got in the back and 'Shy Guy' followed and got behind him."

Stoltzfus pulled her car up parallel to the blue car, got out for a moment, got back in, and leaned over to ask repeatedly if the other driver was "O.K." The driver looked "frozen" and mouthed an inaudible response. Stoltzfus started to drive away and then realized "the only word that it could possibly be, was help." The blue car then drove slowly around her, went over the curb with its horn honking, and headed out of the mall. Stoltzfus briefly followed, told her daughter to write the license number on a "3x4 [inch] index card," and then left for home because she had an empty gas tank and "three kids at home waiting for supper."

At trial Stoltzfus identified Whitlock from a picture as the driver of the car and pointed to petitioner as "Mountain Man." When asked if pretrial publicity about the murder had influenced her identification, Stoltzfus replied "absolutely not." She explained: "First of all, I have an exceptionally good memory. I had very close contact with [petitioner] and he made an emotional impression with me because of his behavior and I, he caught my attention and I paid attention. So I have absolutely no doubt of my identification."

The Commonwealth did not produce any other witnesses to the abduction. Stoltzfus' daughter did not testify.

The Stoltzfus Documents

The materials that provide the basis of petitioner's *Brady* claim consist of notes taken by Detective Claytor during his interviews with Stoltzfus, and letters written by Stoltzfus to Claytor. They cast serious doubt on Stoltzfus' confident assertion of her "exceptionally good memory." Because the content of the documents is critical to petitioner's procedural and substantive claims, we summarize their content.

Exhibit 1 is a handwritten note prepared by Detective Claytor after his first interview with Stoltzfus on January 19, 1990, just two weeks after the crime. The note indicates that she could not identify the black female victim. The only person Stoltzfus apparently could identify at this time was the white female.

Exhibit 2 is a document prepared by Detective Claytor some time after February 1. It contains a summary of his interviews with Stoltzfus conducted on January 19 and January 20, 1990. At that time "she was not sure whether she could identify the white males but felt sure she could identify the white female."

Exhibit 3 is entitled "Observations" and includes a summary of the abduction.

Exhibit 4 is a letter written by Stoltzfus to Claytor three days after their first interview "to clarify some of my confusion for you." The letter states that she had not remembered being at the mall, but that her daughter had helped jog her memory. Her description of the abduction includes the comment: "I have a very vague memory that I'm not sure of. It seems as if the wild guy that I saw had come running through the door and up to a bus as the bus was pulling off.... Then the guy I saw came running up to the black girl's window? Were those 2 memories the same person?" In a postscript she noted that her daughter "doesn't remember seeing the 3 people get into the black girl's car...."

Exhibit 5 is a note to Claytor captioned "My Impressions of 'The Car,'" which contains three paragraphs describing the size of the car and comparing it with Stoltzfus' Volkswagen Rabbit, but not mentioning the license plate number that she vividly recalled at the trial.

Exhibit 6 is a brief note from Stoltzfus to Claytor dated January 25, 1990, stating that after spending several hours with John Dean, Whitlock's boyfriend, "looking at current photos," she had identified Whitlock "beyond a shadow of a doubt." The district court noted that by the time of trial her identification had been expanded to include a description of her clothing and her appearance as a college kid who was "singing" and "happy."

Exhibit 7 is a letter from Stoltzfus to Detective Claytor, dated January 16, 1990, in which she thanks him for his "patience with my sometimes muddled memories." She states that if the student at school had not called the police, "I never would have made any of the associations that you helped me make."

In Exhibit 8, which is undated and summarizes the events described in her trial testimony, Stoltzfus commented: "So where is the 3x4 card? ... It would have been very nice if I could have remembered all this at the time and had simply gone to the police with the information. But I totally wrote this off as a trivial episode of college kids carrying on and proceeded with my own full-time college load at JMU.... Monday, January 15th. I was cleaning out my car and found the 3x4 card. I tore it into little pieces and put it in the bottom of a trash bag."

There is a dispute between the parties over whether petitioner's counsel saw Exhibits 2, 7, and 8 before trial. The prosecuting attorney conceded that he himself never saw Exhibits 1, 3, 4, 5, and 6 until long after petitioner's trial, and they were not in the file he made available to petitioner. For purposes of this case, therefore, we assume that petitioner proceeded to trial without having seen Exhibits 1, 3, 4, 5, and 6.

State Proceedings

Petitioner was tried in Augusta County, where Whitlock's body was found, on charges of capital murder, robbery, and abduction. Because the prosecutor maintained an open file policy, which gave petitioner's counsel access to all of the evidence in the Augusta County prosecutor's files, petitioner's counsel did not file a pretrial motion for discovery of possible exculpatory evidence. In closing argument, petitioner's lawyer effectively conceded that the evidence was sufficient to support the robbery and abduction charges, as well as the lesser offense of first-degree murder, but argued that the evidence was insufficient to prove that petitioner was guilty of capital murder.

The judge instructed the jury that petitioner could be found guilty of the capital charge if the evidence established beyond a reasonable doubt that he "jointly participated in the fatal beating" and "was an active and immediate participant in the act or acts that caused the victim's death." The jury found petitioner guilty of abduction, robbery, and capital murder. After listening to testimony and arguments presented during the sentencing phase, the jury made findings of "vileness" and "future dangerousness," and unanimously recommended the death sentence that the judge later imposed.

The Virginia Supreme Court affirmed the conviction and sentence. It held that the trial court had properly instructed the jury on the "joint perpetrator" theory of capital murder and that the evidence, viewed most favorably in support of the verdict, amply supported the prosecution's theory that both petitioner and Henderson were active participants in the actual killing.

In December 1991, the Augusta County Circuit Court appointed new counsel to represent petitioner in state habeas corpus proceedings. State habeas counsel advanced an ineffective-assistance-of-counsel claim based, in part, on trial counsel's failure to file a motion under *Brady v. Maryland* "to have the Commonwealth disclose to the defense all exculpatory evidence known to it—or in its possession." In answer to that claim, the Commonwealth asserted that such a motion was unnecessary because the prosecutor had maintained an open file policy. The Circuit Court dismissed the petition, and the State Supreme Court affirmed.

Federal Habeas Corpus Proceedings

In March 1996, petitioner filed a federal habeas corpus petition in the Eastern District of Virginia. The district court entered a sealed, *ex parte* order granting petitioner's counsel the right to examine and to copy all of the police and prosecution files in the case. That order led to petitioner's counsel's first examination of the Stoltzfus materials, described above.

* * *

After reviewing the Stoltzfus materials, and making the assumption that the three disputed exhibits had been available to the defense, the district court concluded that the failure to disclose the other five was sufficiently prejudicial to undermine confidence in the jury's verdict. It granted summary judgment to petitioner and granted the writ.

The Court of Appeals vacated in part and remanded. It held that petitioner's *Brady* claim was procedurally defaulted because the factual basis for the claim was available to him at the time he filed his state habeas petition. * * *

* * *

As an alternative basis for decision, the Court of Appeals also held that petitioner could not establish prejudice because "the Stoltzfus materials would have provided little or no help ... in either the guilt or sentencing phases of the trial." With respect to guilt, the court noted that Stoltzfus' testimony was not relevant to petitioner's argument that he was only guilty of first-degree murder rather than capital murder because Henderson, rather than he, actually killed Whitlock. With respect to sentencing, the court concluded that her testimony "was of no import" because the findings of future dangerousness and vileness rested on other evidence. Finally, the court noted that even if it could get beyond the procedural default, the *Brady* claim would fail on the merits because of the absence of prejudice. The Court of Appeals, therefore, reversed the district court's judgment and remanded the case with instructions to dismiss the petition.

II

The first question that our order granting certiorari directed the parties to address is whether the State violated the *Brady* rule. We begin our analysis by identifying the essential components of a *Brady* violation.

In *Brady* this Court held "that the suppression by the prosecution of evidence favorable to an accused upon request violates due process where the evidence is material either to guilt or to punishment, irrespective of the good faith or bad faith of the prosecution." *Brady v. Maryland.* We have since held that the duty to disclose such evidence is applicable even though there has been no request by the accused, *United States v. Agurs*, 427 U.S. 97 (1976), and that the duty encompasses impeachment evidence as well as exculpatory evidence, *United States v. Bagley*, 473 U.S. 667 (1985). Such evidence is material "if there is a reasonable probability that, had the evidence been disclosed to the defense, the result of the proceeding would have been different." Moreover, the rule encompasses evidence "known only to police investigators and not to the prosecutor." In order to comply with *Brady*, therefore, "the individual prosecutor has a duty to learn of any favorable evidence known to the others acting on the government's behalf in this case, including the police."

* * *

* * * Thus the term "*Brady* violation" is sometimes used to refer to any breach of the broad obligation to disclose exculpatory evidence—that is, to any suppression of so-called "*Brady* material"—although, strictly speaking, there is never a real "*Brady* violation" unless the nondisclosure was so serious that there is a reasonable probability that the suppressed evidence would have produced a different verdict. There are three components of a true *Brady* violation: The evidence at issue must be favorable to the accused, either because it is exculpatory, or because it is impeaching; that evidence must have been suppressed by the State, either willfully or inadvertently; and prejudice must have ensued.

Two of those components are unquestionably established by the record in this case. The contrast between (a) the terrifying incident that Stoltzfus confidently described in her testimony and (b) her initial perception of that event "as a trivial episode of college kids carrying on" that her daughter did not even notice, suffices to establish the impeaching character of the undisclosed documents. Moreover, with respect to at least five of those documents, there is no dispute about the fact that they were known to the State but not disclosed to trial counsel. It is the third component—whether petitioner has established the prejudice necessary to satisfy the "materiality" inquiry—that is the most difficult element of the claimed *Brady* violation in this case.

* * *

III

* * *

[The Court begins its analyses of whether the petitioner has shown cause to excuse his failure to raise a *Brady* claim at trial and concludes that he has established sufficient reasons for this failure. The concept of procedural default, including cause and prejudice, are discussed, *infra*, in Chapter 9.]

IV

The differing judgments of the district court and the Court of Appeals attest to the difficulty of resolving the issue of prejudice. Unlike the Fourth Circuit, we do not believe that "the Stolzfus*[sic]* materials would have provided little or no help to Strickler in either the guilt or sentencing phases of the trial." Without a doubt, Stoltzfus' testimony was prejudicial in the sense that it made petitioner's conviction more likely than if she had not testified, and discrediting her testimony might have changed the outcome of the trial.

That, however, is not the standard that petitioner must satisfy in order to obtain relief. He must convince us that "there is a reasonable probability" that the result of the trial would have been different if the suppressed documents had been disclosed to the defense. * * *

The Court of Appeals' negative answer to that question rested on its conclusion that, without considering Stoltzfus' testimony, the record contained ample, independent evidence of guilt, as well as evidence sufficient to support the findings of vileness and future dangerousness that warranted the imposition of the death penalty. The standard used by that court was incorrect. As we made clear in *Kyles* [*v. Whitley*, 514 U.S. 419 (1995)], the materiality inquiry is not just a matter of determining whether, after discounting the inculpatory evidence in light of the undisclosed evidence, the remaining evidence is sufficient to support the jury's conclusions. Rather, the question is whether "the favorable evidence could reasonably be taken to put the whole case in such a different light as to undermine confidence in the verdict."

* * *

Given the record evidence involving Henderson, the district court concluded that, without Stoltzfus' testimony, the jury might have been persuaded that Henderson, rather than petitioner, was the ringleader. He reasoned that a "reasonable probability of conviction" of first-degree, rather than capital, murder sufficed to establish the materiality of the undisclosed Stoltzfus materials and, thus, a *Brady* violation.

* * *

Even if Stoltzfus and her testimony had been entirely discredited, the jury might still have concluded that petitioner was the leader of the criminal enterprise because he was the one seen driving the car by Kurt Massie near the location of the murder and the one who kept the car for the following week. In addition, Tudor testified that petitioner threatened Henderson with a knife later in the evening.

More importantly, however, petitioner's guilt of capital murder did not depend on proof that he was the dominant partner: Proof that he was an equal participant with Henderson was sufficient under the judge's instructions. Accordingly, the strong evidence that Henderson was a killer is entirely consistent with the conclusion that petitioner was also an actual participant in the killing.

Furthermore, there was considerable forensic and other physical evidence linking petitioner to the crime. The weight and size of the rock, and the character of the fatal injuries to the victim, are powerful evidence supporting the conclusion that two people acted jointly to commit a brutal murder.

We recognize the importance of eyewitness testimony; Stoltzfus provided the only disinterested, narrative account of what transpired on January 5, 1990. However, Stoltzfus' vivid description of the events at the mall was not the only evidence that the jury had before it. Two other eyewitnesses, the security guard and Henderson's friend, placed petitioner and Henderson at the Harrisonburg Valley Shopping Mall on the afternoon of Whitlock's murder. One eyewitness later saw petitioner driving Dean's car near the scene of the murder.

The record provides strong support for the conclusion that petitioner would have been convicted of capital murder and sentenced to death, even if Stoltzfus had been severely impeached. The jury was instructed on two predicates for capital murder: robbery with a deadly weapon and abduction with intent to defile. * * *

* * *

Petitioner also maintains that he suffered prejudice from the failure to disclose the Stoltzfus documents because her testimony impacted on the jury's decision to impose the death penalty. Her testimony, however, did not relate to his eligibility for the death sentence and was not relied upon by the prosecution at all during its closing argument at the penalty phase. With respect to the jury's discretionary decision to impose the death penalty, it is true that Stoltzfus described petitioner as a violent, aggressive person, but that portrayal surely was not as damaging as either the evidence that he spent the evening of the murder dancing and drinking at Dice's or the powerful message conveyed by the 69-pound rock that was part of the record before the jury. Notwithstanding the obvious significance of Stoltzfus' testimony, petitioner has not convinced us that there is a reasonable probability that the jury would have returned a different verdict if her testimony had been either severely impeached or excluded entirely.

Petitioner has satisfied two of the three components of a constitutional violation under *Brady*: exculpatory evidence and nondisclosure of this evidence by the prosecution. Petitioner has also demonstrated cause for failing to raise this claim during trial or on state postconviction review. However, petitioner has not shown that there is a reasonable probability that his conviction or sentence would have been different had these materials been disclosed. He therefore cannot show materiality under *Brady* or prejudice from his failure to raise the claim earlier. Accordingly, the judgment of the Court of Appeals is

Affirmed.

[A concurrence, in part, by JUSTICE SOUTER is omitted, as is a dissent, in part, by JUSTICE SOUTER, joined in part by JUSTICE KENNEDY.]

Notes

1. *Subsequent case history*

Tony Strickler was executed by lethal injection on July 21, 1999.

2. *Other opinions*

Justice Souter, with whom Justice Kennedy joined in part, concurred with the Court's opinion in Part III and otherwise dissented. He agreed with the Court that Strickler failed to establish a reasonable probability that, had the materials withheld been disclosed, he would not have been found guilty of capital murder. Justice Souter then emphasized that the prejudice inquiry does not stop at the conviction but also goes to each step of the sentencing process—and there, Justice Souter believed that Strickler had carried his burden. Specifically, Justice Souter believed there was a reasonable probability (which he took to mean a "significant possibility") that disclosure of the Stoltzfus materials would have led the jury to recommend life, not death.

In explaining his position, Justice Souter stated:

> Ultimately, I cannot accept the Court's discount of Stoltzfus in the *Brady* sentencing calculus for the reason I have repeatedly emphasized, the undeniable narrative force of what she said. Against this, it does not matter so much that other witnesses could have placed Strickler at the shopping mall on the afternoon of the murder, or that the Stoltzfus testimony did not directly address the aggravating factors found. What is important is that her evidence presented a gripping story. Its message was that Strickler was the madly energetic leader of two morally apathetic accomplices, who were passive but for his direction. One cannot be reasonably confident that not a single juror would have had a different perspective after an impeachment that would have destroyed the credibility of that story. I would accordingly vacate the sentence and remand for reconsideration, and to that extent I respectfully dissent.

3. *The influence of* Giglio, Agurs, and Bagley

In addition to *Brady v. Maryland*, another seminal case that informed the Court's opinion in *Strickler* is *Giglio v. United States*, 405 U.S. 150 (1972). In *Giglio*, petitioner was convicted of passing forged money orders and sentenced to five years in prison, based largely on the testimony of a co-conspirator, Taliento. On cross-examination, defense counsel had sought to discredit Taliento by eliciting testimony about promises made by the government to secure his testimony, but Taliento denied that he had made a deal with the government. While an appeal was pending, defense counsel discovered new evidence indicating that the government had failed to disclose an alleged promise made to Taliento—a promise that Taliento would not be prosecuted if he testified for the government. The government conceded that the promise had been made, although there was dispute among various prosecutors as to the extent of the leniency offered to Taliento. The Court found credible the claim that the initial prosecution had in fact offered some level of leniency to Taliento. The issue before the Court was whether the undisclosed evidence relating to the credibility of the witness was such as to require a new trial under the due process criteria of precedent such as *Brady v. Maryland*, 373 U.S. 83 (1963).

The Court held that a new trial is not automatically required when evidence useful to the defense is discovered after trial if it would not likely have changed the verdict. The Court further stated that whether the nondisclosure of the evidence was purposeful or not does not matter—the prosecutor ultimately is held responsible. Because the government's case against Giglio depended almost entirely on the witness's testimony, without which there would have been insufficient evidence for an indictment or a jury determination, the witness' credibility was an important issue. In ordering a new trial, the Court found that the government's promises regarding future prosecution of the witness were relevant to his credibility and the jury should have known about them. Thus, the Court made clear that impeachment evidence is covered by the *Brady* rule.

The decisions in *United States v. Agurs*, 427 U.S. 97 (1976), and *United States v. Bagley*, 473 U.S. 667 (1985), also informed the Court's discussion of whether the undisclosed evidence in *Strickler* was "material." Agurs was convicted of second degree murder for killing Sewell by stabbing him with a knife during a fight at a motel. Witnesses found Sewell on top of Agurs struggling for possession of a bowie knife, which Sewall had carried on his person along with another knife. Agurs had possession of the knife; one witness testified Sewell was trying to jam the knife into Agurs' chest. Agurs alleged she acted in self-defense. Sewell died of multiple stab wounds to his chest and abdomen, and he had several slash wounds on his arms characterized by a pathologist as defensive wounds. Prior to trial, defense counsel did not make a specific request for Sewell's prior criminal record. After trial, defense counsel discovered that Sewall had a prior record of assault and carrying a dangerous weapon (knives). The government opposed Agurs' postconviction motion for a new trial on the grounds that there was no duty to disclose without a specific request, that the evidence could have been discovered before trial, and that the evidence was not material. The district court denied Agurs' motion on the grounds it was not material. The Court of Appeals reversed, finding no misconduct by the prosecutor nor lack of diligence by the defense, but concluding that the undisclosed evidence was material because it might have affected the jury's verdict.

The Court described three situations in which the principles of *Brady* might apply and defined the standard of materiality for two of these categories. First, where the undisclosed evidence reveals the government used perjured testimony that it knew, or should have known, was false, a conviction must be set aside if there is any reasonable likelihood that the untruthful testimony could have had an impact on the jury's decision. The second situation is where counsel has made a specific pretrial request for the undisclosed evidence, as in *Brady*, thereby putting the prosecutor on notice of what the defense is seeking. The third category is where counsel either makes no request for the evidence or only a general request for exculpatory material. The Court found no significant difference between the "no request" and general request categories because it found that any duty to disclose arises from the character of the evidence, not from the conduct of counsel.

The Court decided for the first time whether a prosecutor has the duty to disclose exculpatory evidence in the absence of a request by the defense and defined the standard of materiality that creates such a duty. The Court rejected the view of the Court of Appeals that the duty to disclose arises when a prosecutor has information that might affect the jury's verdict—in essence, a harmless-error standard. The Court attempted to differentiate the standard for a new trial based on newly discovered evidence from a neutral source—where the defendant must satisfy "the severe burden of demonstrating that the newly discovered evidence probably would have resulted in an acquittal"—from the situation where the evidence has been in the government's possession. *Id.* at 111. The Court held that if the withheld evidence, evaluated in the context of the whole record, creates a reasonable doubt that did not otherwise exist, the evidence is material and reversal is required. Applying this standard of materiality to *Agurs*, and reversing the Court of Appeals, the Court found the trial court's assessment of the evidence to have been thorough and "entirely reasonable." It reached this decision by noting the view of the trial court that Agurs' theory of self-defense was inconsistent with Sewell's wounds, that Sewell's prior record did not contradict any prosecutorial evidence, that the withheld evidence was cumulative of other evidence presented regarding Sewell's possession of weapons, and that the trial judge unqualifiedly believed that Agurs was guilty. While the Court did not define the standard of materiality for the situation in which a specific request has been made, the Court suggested that there might be a more lenient standard when no request or only a general request for exculpatory evidence is made.

Almost a decade later, the Court in *Bagley* readdressed the materiality standard of *Agurs*. Bagley was charged with numerous drug and firearms offenses. Prior to trial, his lawyers asked for evidence of promises made to witnesses in exchange for their testimony for the government. The prosecutor provided counsel with affidavits of government witnesses asserting that no promises had been made to them. These same witnesses testified at Bagley's bench trial, where he was found guilty of the narcotics offenses. Bagley's post-trial FOIA requests revealed contracts between a law enforcement agency (ATF) and the witnesses, by which the witnesses were to be paid for their services. Bagley moved to vacate his sentence under 28 U.S.C. § 2255, alleging a *Brady* violation. The district court denied the motion, finding that the witnesses had expected to be paid, but that even if the evidence had been disclosed at trial, the impeachment evidence would not have affected the outcome of the trial. The Court of Appeals reversed on the grounds that the government's failure to provide requested *Brady* information required automatic reversal.

The Supreme Court cited *Agurs* as standing for the proposition that constitutional error occurs "only if the evidence is material in the sense that its suppression undermines confidence in the outcome of a trial." *Id.* at 678. The Court then turned to the definition of materiality when a specific request for the undisclosed evidence has been made. Rejecting the government's suggestion that a more lenient standard might be appropriate in specific request cases, the Court instead found the *Strickland* formulation of the *Agurs* materiality test to be "sufficiently flexible" to cover all of the *Agurs* categories: "no request," general request, and specific request. Thus, "evidence is material only if there is a reasonable probability that, had the evidence been disclosed to the defense, the result of the proceeding would have been different. A 'reasonable probability' is a probability sufficient to undermine confidence in the outcome." *Id.* at 682. While the court recognized that the government's failure to respond to a specific request may be interpreted as a representation that the evidence does not exist, and thus might change defense counsel's plans for investigation or trial, the Court asserted that the materiality test it adopts allows a reviewing court to consider such adverse consequences to the preparation and presentation of the defense.

4. *Practical and political implications*

What practical limitations might come into play in identifying any exculpatory evidence that might exist in a case? What political considerations might affect a prosecutor's determination of what evidence should be turned over to the defense? What are the political and practical considerations of *Strickler* on habeas practice for the prosecution? For the defense?

5. *"Others acting on the government's behalf"*

In *Kyles v. Whitley*, 514 U.S. 419 (1995), the Court discussed the circumstances under which exculpatory evidence that may or may not have been known to the prosecution becomes the prosecution's responsibility. After two trials, Curtis Lee Kyles was convicted and sentenced to death for the murder of 60-year-old Dolores Dye during a carjacking outside of a grocery store. Throughout their investigation, the police relied heavily on an informant named "Beanie" who implicated Kyles in the murder. The state informed the defense that there was no exculpatory evidence, despite knowledge of several evidentiary items that undermined both the eyewitness' and Beanie's credibility.

The State argued that "it should not be held accountable ... for evidence known only to police investigators and not to the prosecutor." *Id.* at 438. The Court responded:

> [T]he individual prosecutor has a duty to learn of any favorable evidence known to the others acting on the government's behalf ... including the police. But whether the prosecutor succeeds or fails in meeting this obligation (whether, that is, a failure to disclose is in good faith or bad faith) the prosecution's responsi-

> bility for failing to disclose known, favorable evidence rising to a material level of importance is inescapable.

Id. at 437–38.

The Court noted several possible findings the jury could have made after considering the exculpatory evidence and ordered a new trial. Kyles was tried three more times. Each time the jury hung and the court declared a mistrial. In 1998, the prosecution decided not to try Kyles a sixth time. Nina Rivkind and Steven F. Shatz, Cases and Materials on the Death Penalty 396 (2001), *citing* J. Gill, *Murder Trial's Inglorious End*, The New Orleans Times-Picayune, Feb. 20, 1998, at B7.

C. Politics and Race

Discussions of comity and finality in case law often are present in response not only to legal doctrine but also to perceived political consequences. This section provides a brief introduction that explores how politics and race interweave with habeas corpus jurisprudence. Because appealing capital sentences is an important function of habeas corpus litigation, the seminal study by James Liebman et al., *A Broken System: Part I and Part II*, included below in subsection 1, highlights some of the political dimensions in both capital cases and habeas corpus jurisprudence. The first statistical study ever undertaken of modern American capital appeals, Liebman's report goes beyond simply documenting that capital appeals take a long time to wind through the system because American capital sentences are replete with error. He observes that "capital trials produce so many mistakes that it takes three judicial inspections to catch them—leaving grave doubt whether we *do* catch them all." Liebman also notes that some of the "disturbing sources of pressure to overuse the death penalty are political pressures on elected judges, well-founded doubts about the state's ability to convict serious criminals, and the race of the state's residents and homicide victims."

Subsection 2 explores the issue of race through both *McCleskey v. Kemp* and *Miller-El v. Cockrell.* While acknowledging that a study conducted by Professor David Baldus et al., widely referred to as the "Baldus Study," indicates a disparity in the imposition of the death sentence in Georgia based on the race of the victim, *McCleskey* finds that "apparent disparities in sentencing are an inevitable part of our criminal justice system" and that constitutional guarantees were met in McCleskey's case because the state attempted to make his sentencing "as fair as possible." In *Miller-El*, the Court examines when a state prisoner can appeal the denial or dismissal of his petition for writ of habeas corpus within the context of a claim that includes district attorneys using peremptory strikes to exclude 10 of the 11 African-Americans eligible to serve on Miller-El's jury.

(1) Politics

A Broken System: Error Rates in Capital Cases, 1973–1995

James S. Liebman, Jeffrey Fagan, and Valerie West
June 12, 2000 Executive Summary

There is a growing bipartisan consensus that flaws in America's death-penalty system have reached crisis proportions. Many fear that capital trials put people on death row who don't belong there. Others say capital appeals take too long. This report—the first statistical study ever undertaken of modern American capital appeals (4,578 of them in state capital cases between 1973 and 1995)—suggests that *both* claims are correct.

Capital sentences do spend a long time under judicial review. As this study documents, however, **judicial review takes so long precisely *because* American capital sentences are so persistently and systematically fraught with error that seriously undermines their reliability.**

Our 23 years worth of results reveal a death penalty system collapsing under the weight of its own mistakes. They reveal a system in which lives and public order are at stake, yet for decades has made more mistakes than we would tolerate in far less important activities. They reveal a system that is wasteful and broken and needs to be addressed.

Our central findings are as follows:

- Nationally, during the 23-year study period, **the overall rate of prejudicial error in the American capital punishment system was 68%.** In other words, courts found **serious, reversible error in nearly 7 of every 10 of the thousands of capital sentences that were fully reviewed during the period.**
- Capital trials produce **so many mistakes** that it takes three judicial inspections to catch them—leaving **grave doubt whether we *do* catch them all.** After state courts threw out **47%** of death sentences due to serious flaws, a later federal review found "serious error"—error undermining the reliability of the outcome—in **40%** of the *remaining* sentences.
- Because state courts come first and see *all* the cases, they do most of the work of correcting erroneous death sentences. Of the **2,370 death sentences** thrown out due to serious error, **90%** were overturned by **state judges**—many of whom were the very judges who imposed the death sentence in the first place; nearly all of whom were directly beholden to the electorate; and none of whom, consequently, were disposed to overturn death sentences except for very good reason. This does not mean that federal review is unnecessary. Precisely *because* of the huge amounts of serious capital error that state appellate judges are called upon to catch, it is not surprising that **a substantial number of the capital judgments they let through to the federal stage are still seriously flawed.**
- To lead to reversal, error must be serious, indeed. The most common errors—prompting a **majority of reversals** at the state post-conviction stage—are (1) **egregiously incompetent defense lawyers who didn't even look for—*and demonstrably missed*—important evidence that the defendant was innocent or did not deserve to die; and (2) police or prosecutors who *did* discover that kind of evidence but *suppressed* it, again keeping it from the jury.** [Hundreds of examples of these and other serious errors are collected in Appendix C and D to this Report.]

- High error rates put many individuals at risk of wrongful execution: **82%** of the people whose capital judgments were overturned by state post-conviction courts due to serious error were found to deserve a sentence **less than death** when the errors were cured on retrial; ***7% were found to be innocent of the capital crime.***
- High error rates persist over time. More than **50%** of all cases reviewed were found seriously flawed in **20 of the 23 study years**, including 17 of the last 19. In **half** the years, including the **most recent one**, the error rate was **over 60%.**
- High error rates exist across the country. **Over 90%** of American death-sentencing states have overall error rates of **52% or higher.** 85% have error rates of **60% or higher. Three-fifths** have error rates of **70% or higher.**
- Illinois (whose governor recently declared a moratorium on executions after a spate of death-row exonerations) does not produce atypically faulty death sentences. **The overall rate of serious error found in Illinois capital sentences (66%) is very close to—and slightly *lower* than—the national average (68%).**
- Catching so much error takes time—a national average of **9 years** from death sentence to the last inspection and execution. By the end of the study period, that average had risen to **10.6 years. In *most* cases, death row inmates wait for years for the lengthy review procedures needed to uncover all this error. Then, their death sentences are *reversed.***
- This much error, and the time needed to cure it, impose **terrible costs on taxpayers, victims' families, the judicial system, and the wrongly condemned. And it renders unattainable the finality, retribution and deterrence that are the reasons usually given for having a death penalty.**

Erroneously trying capital defendants the first time around, operating the multi-tiered inspection process needed to catch the mistakes, warehousing thousands under costly death row conditions in the meantime, and having to try **two out of three cases *again*** is irrational.

This report describes the extent of the problem. A subsequent report will examine its causes and their implications for resolving the death penalty crisis.

A Broken System, Part II: Why There Is So Much Error in Capital Cases, and What Can Be Done About It

James S. Liebman, Jeffrey Fagan, Andrew Gelman, Valerie West, Garth Davies, and Alexander Kiss

February 11, 2002 Executive Summary

Copyright ©2002 by James S. Liebman, et al.

There is growing awareness that serious, reversible error permeates America's death penalty system, putting innocent lives at risk, heightening the suffering of victims, leaving killers at large, wasting tax dollars, and failing citizens, the courts and the justice system.

Our June 2000 Report shows how often mistakes occur and how serious it is: 68% of all death verdicts imposed and fully reviewed during the 1973–1995 study period were reversed by courts due to serious errors.

Analyses presented for the first time here reveal that 76% of the reversals at the two appeal stages where data are available for study were because defense lawyers had been egregiously incompetent, police and prosecutors had suppressed exculpatory evidence or committed other professional misconduct, jurors had been misinformed about the law, or judges and jurors had been biased. Half of those reversals tainted the verdict finding the defendant guilty of a capital crime as well as the verdict imposing the death penalty. *82%* of the cases sent back for retrial at the second appeal phase ended in sentences less than death, including 9% that ended in *not guilty verdicts.*

Part II of our study addresses two critical questions: Why does our death penalty system make so many mistakes? How can these mistakes be prevented, if at all? Our findings are based on the most comprehensive set of data ever assembled on factors related to capital error—or other trial error.

Our main finding indicates that if we are going to have the death penalty, it should be reserved for the worst of the worst: **Heavy and indiscriminate use of the death penalty creates a high risk that mistakes will occur**. The more often officials use the death penalty, the wider the range of crimes to which it is applied, and the more it is imposed for offenses that are not highly aggravated, the greater the risk that capital convictions and sentences will be seriously flawed.

Most disturbing of all, we find that **the conditions evidently pressuring counties and states to overuse the death penalty and thus increase the risk of unreliability and error include *race*, *politics* and *poorly performing law enforcement systems*.** Error also is linked to overburdened and underfunded state courts.

MAIN FINDING

The higher the rate at which a state imposes death verdicts, the greater the probability that *each* death verdict will have to be reversed because of serious error.

- The overproduction of death penalty verdicts has a powerful effect in increasing the risk of error. Our best analysis predicts that:
- Capital error rates more than *triple* when the death-sentencing rate increases from a quarter of the national average to the national average, holding other factors constant.
- When death sentencing increases from a quarter of the national average to the highest rate for a state in our study, the predicted increase in reversal rates is *six-fold*—to *about 80%*.

In particular, the more often states impose death sentences in cases that are not highly aggravated, the higher the risk of serious error.

- At the federal habeas stage, the probability of reversal grows substantially as the crimes resulting in capital verdicts are less aggravated. For each additional aggravating factor, the probability of reversal drops by about 15%, when other conditions are held constant at their averages. Imposing the death penalty in cases that are not the worst of the worst is a recipe for unreliability and error.

Comparisons of particular states' capital-sentencing and capital-error rates illustrate the strong relationship between frequent death sentencing and error. * * *

- All but one of the 10 states with the highest death-sentencing rates during the 23-year study period had overall capital reversal rates at or above the average rate of 68%.

PRESSURES ASSOCIATED WITH OVERUSE OF THE DEATH PENALTY

Four disturbing conditions are strongly associated with high rates of serious capital error. Their common capacity to pressure officials to use the death penalty aggressively in response to fears about crime and regardless of how weak any particular case for a death verdict is, may explain their relationship to high capital error rates.

- **The closer the homicide risk to whites in a state comes to equaling or surpassing the risk to blacks, the higher the error rate.** Other things equal, reversal rates are *twice as high* where homicides are most heavily concentrated on whites compared to blacks, than where they are the most heavily concentrated on blacks.
- **The higher the proportion of African-Americans in a state—and in one analysis, the more welfare recipients in a state—the higher the rate of serious capital error.** Because this effect has to do with traits of the population at large, not those of particular trial participants, it appears to be an indicator of crime fears driven by racial and economic conditions.
- **The lower the rate at which states apprehend, convict and imprison serious criminals, the higher their capital error rates.** Predicted capital error rates for states with only 1 prisoner per 100 FBI Index Crimes are about 75%, holding other factors constant. Error rates drop to 36% for states with 4 prisoners per 100 crimes, and to 13% for those with the highest rate of prisoners to crimes. Evidently, officials who do a poor job fighting crime also conduct poor capital investigations and trials. Well-founded doubts about a state's ability to catch criminals may lead officials to extend the death penalty to a wider array of weaker cases—at huge cost in error and delay.
- **The more often and directly state trial judges are subject to popular election, and the more partisan those elections are, the higher the state's rate of serious capital error.**

ADDITIONAL FINDINGS

Heavy use of the death penalty causes delay, increases cost, and keeps the system from doing its job. High numbers of death verdicts waiting to be reviewed paralyze appeals. Holding other factors constant, the process of moving capital verdicts from trial to a final result seems to come to a halt in states with more than 20 verdicts under review at one time.

Poor quality trial proceedings increase the risk of serious, reversible error. Poorly funded courts, high capital and non-capital caseloads, and unreliable procedures for finding the facts all increase the chance that serious error will be found. In contrast, high quality, well-funded private lawyers from out of state significantly increase a defendant's chance of showing a federal court that his death verdict is seriously flawed and has to be retried.

Chronic capital error rates have persisted over time. Overall reversal rates were high and fairly steady throughout the second half of the 23-year study period, averaging 60%. When all significant factors are considered, state high courts on direct appeal—where 79% of the 2349 reversals occurred—found significantly more reversible error in *recent* death verdicts than in verdicts imposed earlier in the study period. Other things equal, direct appeal reversal rates were increasing 9% a year during the study period.

State and federal appeals judges cannot be relied upon to catch all serious trial errors in capital cases. Like trial judges, appeals judges are susceptible to political pressure and make mistakes. And the rules appeals judges use to decide whether errors are serious enough to require death verdicts to be reversed are so strict that egregious errors slip through. We study four illustrative cases in which *the courts approved the convictions and death sentences of innocent men* despite a full set of appeals. These case studies show that judges repeatedly recognized that the proceedings were marred by error but affirmed anyway because of stringent rules limiting reversals.

SUMMARY EXPLANATION

The lower the rate at which a state imposes death sentences—and the more it confines those verdicts to the worst of the worst—the less likely it is that serious error will be found. The fewer death verdicts a state imposes, the less overburdened its capital appeal system is, and the more likely it is to carry out the verdicts it imposes. The more often states succumb to pressures to inflict capital sentences in marginal cases, the higher is the risk of error and delay, the lower is the chance verdicts will be carried out, and the greater is the temptation to approve flawed verdicts on appeal. Among the disturbing sources of pressure to overuse the death penalty are political pressures on elected judges, well-founded doubts about the state's ability to convict serious criminals, and the race of the state's residents and homicide victims.

METHODS

We employ an array of statistical methods to identify factors that predict where and when death verdicts are more likely to be found to be seriously flawed, and to assure that the analyses are comprehensive, conservative and reliable: We use several statistical methods with different assumptions about the arrangement of capital reversals and reversal rates to ensure that results are driven by relationships in the data, not statistical methods. We analyze reversals at each separate review stage and at all three stages combined. We use multiple regression to analyze the simultaneous effect on reversal rates of important general factors (state, county, year and time trend) and specific conditions that may explain error rates. We examine factors operating at the state, county and case level. And we check for consistency of results across analyses to determine which factors and sets of significant factors are the most robust and warrant the most confidence.

POLICY OPTIONS

The harms resulting from chronic capital error are costly. Many of its evident causes are not easily addressed head-on (*e.g.*, the complex interaction of a state's racial make-up, its welfare burden and the efficacy of its law enforcement policies). And indirect remedies are unreliable because they demand self-restraint by officials who in the past have succumbed to pressures to extend the death penalty to cases that are not highly aggravated. As a result, some states and counties may conclude that the only answer to chronic capital error is to stop using the death penalty, or to limit it to the very small number of prospective offenses where there is something approaching a social consensus that only the death penalty will do.

In other states and counties, a set of carefully targeted reforms based upon careful study of local conditions might seek to achieve the central goal of limiting the death penalty to "the worst of the worst"—to defendants who can be shown without doubt to have committed an egregiously aggravated murder without extenuating factors. Ten reforms that might help accomplish this goal are:

- Requiring proof beyond *any* doubt that the defendant committed the capital crime.
- Requiring that aggravating factors substantially outweigh mitigating ones before a death sentence may be imposed.
- Barring the death penalty for defendants with inherently extenuating conditions—mentally retarded persons, juveniles, severely mentally ill defendants.

- Making life imprisonment without parole an alternative to the death penalty and clearly informing juries of the option.
- Abolishing judge overrides of jury verdicts imposing life sentences.
- Using comparative review of murder sentences to identify what counts as "the worst of the worst" in the state, and overturning outlying death verdicts.
- Basing charging decisions in potentially capital cases on full and informed deliberations.
- Making all police and prosecution evidence bearing on guilt vs. innocence, and on aggravation vs. mitigation available to the jury at trial.
- Insulating capital-sentencing and appellate judges from political pressure.
- Identifying, appointing and compensating capital defense counsel in ways that attract an adequate number of well-qualified lawyers to do the work.

CONCLUSION

Over decades and across dozens of states, large numbers and proportions of capital verdicts have been reversed because of serious error. The capital system is collapsing under the weight of that error, and the risk of executing the innocent is high. Now that explanations for the problem have been identified and a range of options for responding to it are available, the time is ripe to fix the death penalty, or if it can't be fixed, to end it.

Notes

1. *The long road to justice*

Liebman's report documents not only the startlingly high error rate in capital convictions but the fact that "[c]atching so much error takes time.... In *most* cases, death row inmates wait for years for the lengthy review procedures needed to uncover all this error. Then, their death sentences are *reversed.*" What is your assessment of Liebman's observation that "[t]his much error, and the time needed to cure it, impose terrible costs on taxpayers, victims' families, the judicial system, and the wrongly condemned. And it renders unattainable the finality, retribution and deterrence that are the reasons usually given for having a death penalty"?

Can you envision any way that habeas corpus jurisprudence could be changed in order to address these issues?

2. *Judges and the politics of death*

In their article *Judges and the Politics of Death: Deciding Between the Bill of Rights and the Next Election in Death Penalty Cases*, 75 B.U. L. Rev. 759 (1995), Stephen B. Bright and Patrick J. Keenan examine the influence of the politics of crime on judicial behavior in capital cases. They observe that in jurisdictions where judges stand for election, judges face the same "hydraulic pressure" of public opinion to which publicly elected prosecutors are subjected. "As a result of the increasing prominence of the death penalty in judicial elections as well as other campaigns for public office," Bright and Keenan maintain, "judges are well aware of the consequences to their careers of unpopular decisions in capital cases."

Assuming that Bright and Keenan are correct, in what ways could the "hydraulic pressure" of public opinion influence the outcome of habeas petitions in capital cases?

(2) Race

McCleskey v. Kemp

481 U.S. 279 (1987)

JUSTICE POWELL delivered the opinion of the Court.

This case presents the question whether a complex statistical study that indicates a risk that racial considerations enter into capital sentencing determinations proves that petitioner McCleskey's capital sentence is unconstitutional under the Eighth or Fourteenth Amendment.

I

McCleskey, a black man, was convicted of two counts of armed robbery and one count of murder in the Superior Court of Fulton County, Georgia, on October 12, 1978. McCleskey's convictions arose out of the robbery of a furniture store and the killing of a white police officer during the course of the robbery. The evidence at trial indicated that McCleskey and three accomplices planned and carried out the robbery. All four were armed. McCleskey entered the front of the store while the other three entered the rear. McCleskey secured the front of the store by rounding up the customers and forcing them to lie face down on the floor. The other three rounded up the employees in the rear and tied them up with tape. The manager was forced at gunpoint to turn over the store receipts, his watch, and $6. During the course of the robbery, a police officer, answering a silent alarm, entered the store through the front door. As he was walking down the center aisle of the store, two shots were fired. Both struck the officer. One hit him in the face and killed him.

Several weeks later, McCleskey was arrested in connection with an unrelated offense. He confessed that he had participated in the furniture store robbery, but denied that he had shot the police officer. At trial, the State introduced evidence that at least one of the bullets that struck the officer was fired from a .38 caliber Rossi revolver. This description matched the description of the gun that McCleskey had carried during the robbery. The State also introduced the testimony of two witnesses who had heard McCleskey admit to the shooting.

The jury convicted McCleskey of murder. At the penalty hearing, the jury heard arguments as to the appropriate sentence. Under Georgia law, the jury could not consider imposing the death penalty unless it found beyond a reasonable doubt that the murder was accompanied by one of the statutory aggravating circumstances. The jury in this case found two aggravating circumstances to exist beyond a reasonable doubt: the murder was committed during the course of an armed robbery, and the murder was committed upon a peace officer engaged in the performance of his duties. In making its decision whether to impose the death sentence, the jury considered the mitigating and aggravating circumstances of McCleskey's conduct. McCleskey offered no mitigating evidence. The jury recommended that he be sentenced to death on the murder charge and to consecutive life sentences on the armed robbery charges. The court followed the jury's recommendation and sentenced McCleskey to death.

On appeal, the Supreme Court of Georgia affirmed the convictions and the sentences. This Court denied a petition for a writ of certiorari. The Superior Court of Fulton County denied McCleskey's extraordinary motion for a new trial. McCleskey then filed a petition for a writ of habeas corpus in the Superior Court of Butts County. After holding an evidentiary hearing, the Superior Court denied relief. The Supreme Court of Georgia denied McCleskey's application for a certificate of probable cause to appeal the Superior Court's denial of his petition, and this Court again denied certiorari.

McCleskey next filed a petition for a writ of habeas corpus in the Federal District Court for the Northern District of Georgia. His petition raised 18 claims, one of which was that the Georgia capital sentencing process is administered in a racially discriminatory manner in violation of the Eighth and Fourteenth Amendments to the United States Constitution. In support of his claim, McCleskey proffered a statistical study performed by Professors David C. Baldus, Charles Pulaski, and George Woodworth, (the Baldus study) that purports to show a disparity in the imposition of the death sentence in Georgia based on the race of the murder victim and, to a lesser extent, the race of the defendant. The Baldus study is actually two sophisticated statistical studies that examine over 2,000 murder cases that occurred in Georgia during the 1970's. The raw numbers collected by Professor Baldus indicate that defendants charged with killing white persons received the death penalty in 11% of the cases, but defendants charged with killing blacks received the death penalty in only 1% of the cases. The raw numbers also indicate a reverse racial disparity according to the race of the defendant: 4% of the black defendants received the death penalty, as opposed to 7% of the white defendants.

Baldus also divided the cases according to the combination of the race of the defendant and the race of the victim. He found that the death penalty was assessed in 22% of the cases involving black defendants and white victims; 8% of the cases involving white defendants and white victims; 1% of the cases involving black defendants and black victims; and 3% of the cases involving white defendants and black victims. Similarly, Baldus found that prosecutors sought the death penalty in 70% of the cases involving black defendants and white victims; 32% of the cases involving white defendants and white victims; 15% of the cases involving black defendants and black victims; and 19% of the cases involving white defendants and black victims.

Baldus subjected his data to an extensive analysis, taking account of 230 variables that could have explained the disparities on nonracial grounds. One of his models concludes that, even after taking account of 39 nonracial variables, defendants charged with killing white victims were 4.3 times as likely to receive a death sentence as defendants charged with killing blacks. According to this model, black defendants were 1.1 times as likely to receive a death sentence as other defendants. Thus, the Baldus study indicates that black defendants, such as McCleskey, who kill white victims have the greatest likelihood of receiving the death penalty.

* * *

The district court held an extensive evidentiary hearing on McCleskey's petition. Although it believed that McCleskey's Eighth Amendment claim was foreclosed by the Fifth Circuit's decision in *Spinkellink v. Wainwright*, it nevertheless considered the Baldus study with care. It concluded that McCleskey's "statistics do not demonstrate a prima facie case in support of the contention that the death penalty was imposed upon him because of his race, because of the race of the victim, or because of any Eighth Amendment concern." As to McCleskey's Fourteenth Amendment claim, the court found that the methodology of the Baldus study was flawed in several respects. Because of these defects, the court held that the Baldus study "fail[ed] to contribute anything of value" to McCleskey's claim. Accordingly, the court denied the petition insofar as it was based upon the Baldus study.

The Court of Appeals for the Eleventh Circuit, sitting en banc, carefully reviewed the district court's decision on McCleskey's claim. It assumed the validity of the study itself and addressed the merits of McCleskey's Eighth and Fourteenth Amendment claims. That is, the court assumed that the study "showed that systematic and substantial disparities existed in the penalties imposed upon homicide defendants in Georgia based on race of the homicide victim, that the disparities existed at a less substantial rate in death sentencing based on race of defendants, and that the factors of race of the victim and defendant were at work in Fulton County." Even assuming the study's validity, the Court of Appeals found the statistics "insufficient to demonstrate discriminatory intent or unconstitutional discrimination in the Fourteenth Amendment context, [and] insufficient to show irrationality, arbitrariness and capriciousness under any kind of Eighth Amendment analysis." The court noted:

> The very exercise of discretion means that persons exercising discretion may reach different results from exact duplicates. Assuming each result is within the range of discretion, all are correct in the eyes of the law. It would not make sense for the system to require the exercise of discretion in order to be facially constitutional, and at the same time hold a system unconstitutional in application where that discretion achieved different results for what appear to be exact duplicates, absent the state showing the reasons for the difference....
>
> The Baldus approach ... would take the cases with different results on what are contended to be duplicate facts, where the differences could not be otherwise explained, and conclude that the different result was based on race alone.... This approach ignores the realities.... There are, in fact, no exact duplicates in capital crimes and capital defendants. The type of research submitted here tends to show which of the directed factors were effective, but is of restricted use in showing what undirected factors control the exercise of constitutionally required discretion.

* * *

The Court of Appeals affirmed the denial by the district court of McCleskey's petition for a writ of habeas corpus insofar as the petition was based upon the Baldus study, with three judges dissenting as to McCleskey's claims based on the Baldus study. We granted certiorari and now affirm.

II

McCleskey's first claim is that the Georgia capital punishment statute violates the Equal Protection Clause of the Fourteenth Amendment. He argues that race has infected the administration of Georgia's statute in two ways: persons who murder whites are more likely to be sentenced to death than persons who murder blacks, and black murderers are more likely to be sentenced to death than white murderers. As a black defendant who killed a white victim, McCleskey claims that the Baldus study demonstrates that he was discriminated against because of his race and because of the race of his victim. In its broadest form, McCleskey's claim of discrimination extends to every actor in the Georgia capital sentencing process, from the prosecutor who sought the death penalty and the jury that imposed the sentence, to the State itself that enacted the capital punishment statute and allows it to remain in effect despite its allegedly discriminatory application. We agree with the Court of Appeals, and every other court that has considered such a challenge, that this claim must fail.

A

Our analysis begins with the basic principle that a defendant who alleges an equal protection violation has the burden of proving "the existence of purposeful discrimination." *Whitus v. Georgia*, 385 U.S. 545, 550 (1967). A corollary to this principle is that a criminal defendant must prove that the purposeful discrimination "had a discriminatory effect" on him. *Wayte v. United States*, 470 U.S. 598, 608 (1985). Thus, to prevail under the Equal Protection Clause, McCleskey must prove that the decisionmakers in *his* case acted with discriminatory purpose. He offers no evidence specific to his own case that would support an inference that racial considerations played a part in his sentence. Instead, he relies solely on the Baldus study. McCleskey argues that the Baldus study compels an inference that his sentence rests on purposeful discrimination. McCleskey's claim that these statistics are sufficient proof of discrimination, without regard to the facts of a particular case, would extend to all capital cases in Georgia, at least where the victim was white and the defendant is black.

The Court has accepted statistics as proof of intent to discriminate in certain limited contexts. First, this Court has accepted statistical disparities as proof of an equal protection violation in the selection of the jury venire in a particular district. Although statistical proof normally must present a "stark" pattern to be accepted as the sole proof of discriminatory intent under the Constitution, *Arlington Heights v. Metropolitan Housing Dev. Corp.*, 429 U.S. 252, 266 "[b]ecause of the nature of the jury-selection task, ... we have permitted a finding of constitutional violation even when the statistical pattern does not approach [such] extremes." *Id.* at 266, n.13. Second, this Court has accepted statistics in the form of multiple-regression analysis to prove statutory violations under Title VII of the Civil Rights Act of 1964. *Bazemore v. Friday*, 478 U.S. 385, 400–01 (1986) (opinion of BRENNAN, J., concurring in part).

But the nature of the capital sentencing decision, and the relationship of the statistics to that decision, are fundamentally different from the corresponding elements in the venire-selection or Title VII cases. Most importantly, each particular decision to impose the death penalty is made by a petit jury selected from a properly constituted venire. Each jury is unique in its composition, and the Constitution requires that its decision rest on consideration of innumerable factors that vary according to the characteristics of the individual defendant and the facts of the particular capital offense. *See Hitchcock v. Dugger*; *Lockett v. Ohio*. Thus, the application of an inference drawn from the general statistics to a specific decision in a trial and sentencing simply is not comparable to the application of an inference drawn from general statistics to a specific venire-selection or Title VII case. In those cases, the statistics relate to fewer entities, and fewer variables are relevant to the challenged decisions.

Another important difference between the cases in which we have accepted statistics as proof of discriminatory intent and this case is that, in the venire-selection and Title VII contexts, the decisionmaker has an opportunity to explain the statistical disparity. Here, the State has no practical opportunity to rebut the Baldus study. "[C]ontrolling considerations of ... public policy," *McDonald v. Pless*, 238 U.S. 264, 267 (1915), dictate that jurors "cannot be called ... to testify to the motives and influences that led to their verdict." *Chicago, B. & Q. R. Co. v. Babcock*, 204 U.S. 585, 593 (1907). Similarly, the policy considerations behind a prosecutor's traditionally "wide discretion" suggest the impropriety of our requiring prosecutors to defend their decisions to seek death penalties, "often years after they were made." *See Imbler v. Pachtman*, 424 U.S. 409, 425–26 (1976). Moreover, absent far stronger proof, it is unnecessary to seek such a rebuttal, because a legitimate and unchallenged explanation for the decision is apparent from the record: McCleskey committed an act for which the United States Constitution and Georgia laws permit imposition of the death penalty.

Finally, McCleskey's statistical proffer must be viewed in the context of his challenge. McCleskey challenges decisions at the heart of the State's criminal justice system. "[O]ne of society's most basic tasks is that of protecting the lives of its citizens and one of the most basic ways in which it achieves the task is through criminal laws against murder." *Gregg v. Georgia*, 428 U.S. 153, 226 (1976) (WHITE, J., concurring). Implementation of these laws necessarily requires discretionary judgments. Because discretion is essential to the criminal justice process, we would demand exceptionally clear proof before we would infer that the discretion has been abused. The unique nature of the decisions at issue in this case also counsels against adopting such an inference from the disparities indicated by the Baldus study. Accordingly, we hold that the Baldus study is clearly insufficient to support an inference that any of the decisionmakers in McCleskey's case acted with discriminatory purpose.

B

McCleskey also suggests that the Baldus study proves that the State as a whole has acted with a discriminatory purpose. He appears to argue that the State has violated the Equal Protection Clause by adopting the capital punishment statute and allowing it to remain in force despite its allegedly discriminatory application. But "'[d]iscriminatory purpose'... implies more than intent as volition or intent as awareness of consequences. It implies that the decisionmaker, in this case a state legislature, selected or reaffirmed a particular course of action at least in part 'because of,' not merely 'in spite of,' its adverse effects upon an identifiable group." *Personnel Administrator of Massachusetts v. Feeney*, 442 U.S. 256, 279 (1979). For this claim to prevail, McCleskey would have to prove that the Georgia Legislature enacted or maintained the death penalty statute *because of* an anticipated racially discriminatory effect. In *Gregg v. Georgia*, this Court found that the Georgia capital sentencing system could operate in a fair and neutral manner. There was no evidence then, and there is none now, that the Georgia Legislature enacted the capital punishment statute to further a racially discriminatory purpose.

Nor has McCleskey demonstrated that the legislature maintains the capital punishment statute because of the racially disproportionate impact suggested by the Baldus study. As legislatures necessarily have wide discretion in the choice of criminal laws and penalties, and as there were legitimate reasons for the Georgia Legislature to adopt and maintain capital punishment, *see Gregg v. Georgia*, we will not infer a discriminatory purpose on the part of the State of Georgia. Accordingly, we reject McCleskey's equal protection claims.

III

McCleskey also argues that the Baldus study demonstrates that the Georgia capital sentencing system violates the Eighth Amendment. We begin our analysis of this claim by reviewing the restrictions on death sentences established by our prior decisions under that Amendment.

A

The Eighth Amendment prohibits infliction of "cruel and unusual punishments." This Court's early Eighth Amendment cases examined only the "particular methods of execution to determine whether they were too cruel to pass constitutional muster." *Gregg v. Georgia*, 428 U.S. at 170. Subsequently, the Court recognized that the constitutional prohibition against cruel and unusual punishments "is not fastened to the obsolete but may acquire meaning as public opinion becomes enlightened by a humane justice." *Weems v. United States*, 217 U.S. 349, 378 (1910). In *Weems*, the Court identified a second principle inherent in the Eighth Amendment, "that punishment for crime should be graduated and proportioned to offense."

Chief Justice Warren, writing for the plurality in *Trop v. Dulles*, 356 U.S. 86, 99 (1958), acknowledged the constitutionality of capital punishment. In his view, the "basic concept underlying the Eighth Amendment" in this area is that the penalty must accord with "the dignity of man." In applying this mandate, we have been guided by his statement that "[t]he Amendment must draw its meaning from the evolving standards of decency that mark the progress of a maturing society." Thus, our constitutional decisions have been informed by "contemporary values concerning the infliction of a challenged sanction." *Gregg v. Georgia*, 428 U.S. at 173. In assessing contemporary values, we have eschewed subjective judgment, and instead have sought to ascertain "objective indicia that reflect the public attitude toward a given sanction." First among these indicia are the decisions of state legislatures, "because the ... legislative judgment weighs heavily in ascertaining" contemporary standards. We also have been guided by the sentencing decisions of juries, because they are "a significant and reliable objective index of contemporary values." Most of our recent decisions as to the constitutionality of the death penalty for a particular crime have rested on such an examination of contemporary values. *E.g.*, *Enmund v. Florida*, 458 U.S. 782, 782–96 (1982) (felony murder); *Coker v. Georgia*, 433 U.S. 584, 592–97 (1977) (rape); *Gregg v. Georgia* (murder).

B

Two principal decisions guide our resolution of McCleskey's Eighth Amendment claim. In *Furman v. Georgia*, 408 U.S. 238 (1972), the Court concluded that the death penalty was so irrationally imposed that any particular death sentence could be presumed excessive. Under the statutes at issue in *Furman*, there was no basis for determining in any particular case whether the penalty was proportionate to the crime: "[T]he death penalty [was] exacted with great infrequency even for the most atrocious crimes and ... there [was] no meaningful basis for distinguishing the few cases in which it [was] imposed from the many cases in which it [was] not." *Id.* at 313 (WHITE, J., concurring).

In *Gregg*, the Court specifically addressed the question left open in *Furman*—whether the punishment of death for murder is "under all circumstances, 'cruel and unusual' in violation of the Eighth and Fourteenth Amendments of the Constitution." We noted that the imposition of the death penalty for the crime of murder "has a long history of acceptance both in the United States and in England." "The most marked indication of society's endorsement of the death penalty for murder [was] the legislative response to *Furman*." During the 4-year period between *Furman* and *Gregg*, at least 35 States had reenacted the death penalty, and Congress had authorized the penalty for aircraft piracy. The "actions of juries" were "fully compatible with the legislative judgments."

We noted that any punishment might be unconstitutionally severe if inflicted without penological justification, but concluded:

> Considerations of federalism, as well as respect for the ability of a legislature to evaluate, in terms of its particular State, the moral consensus concerning the death penalty and its social utility as a sanction, require us to conclude, in the absence of more convincing evidence, that the infliction of death as a punishment for murder is not without justification and thus is not unconstitutionally severe.

The second question before the Court in *Gregg* was the constitutionality of the particular procedures embodied in the Georgia capital punishment statute. We explained the fundamental principle of *Furman*, that "where discretion is afforded a sentencing body on a matter so grave as the determination of whether a human life should be taken or spared, that discretion must be suitably directed and limited so as to minimize the risk of wholly arbitrary and capricious action." Numerous features of the then new Georgia statute met the concerns articulated in *Furman*. The Georgia system bifurcates guilt and sentencing proceedings so that the jury can receive all relevant information for sentencing without the risk that evidence irrelevant to the defendant's guilt will influence the jury's consideration of that issue. The statute narrows the class of murders subject to the death penalty to cases in which the jury finds at least one statutory aggravating circumstance beyond a reasonable doubt. Conversely, it allows the defendant to introduce any relevant mitigating evidence that might influence the jury not to impose a death sentence. The procedures also require a particularized inquiry into "'the circumstances of the offense together with the character and propensities of the offender.'" Thus, "while some jury discretion still exists, 'the discretion to be exercised is controlled by clear and objective standards so as to produce non-discriminatory application.'" Moreover, the Georgia system adds "an important additional safeguard against arbitrariness and caprice" in a provision for automatic appeal of a death sentence to the State Supreme Court. The statute requires that court to review each sentence to determine whether it was imposed under the influence of passion or prejudice, whether the evidence supports the jury's finding of a statutory aggravating circumstance, and whether the sentence is disproportionate to sentences imposed in generally similar murder cases. To aid the court's review, the trial judge answers a questionnaire about the trial, including detailed questions as to "the quality of the defendant's representation [and] whether race played a role in the trial."

C

In the cases decided after *Gregg*, the Court has imposed a number of requirements on the capital sentencing process to ensure that capital sentencing decisions rest on the individualized inquiry contemplated in *Gregg*. In *Woodson v. North Carolina*, we invalidated a mandatory capital sentencing system, finding that the "respect for humanity underlying the Eighth Amendment requires consideration of the character and record of the individual offender and the circumstances of the particular offense as a constitutionally indispensable part of the process of inflicting the penalty of death." Similarly, a State must "narrow the class of murderers subject to capital punishment," *Gregg v. Georgia*, by providing "specific and detailed guidance" to the sentencer. *Proffitt v. Florida*, 428 U.S. 242, 253 (1976) (joint opinion of Stewart, POWELL, and STEVENS, JJ.).

In contrast to the carefully defined standards that must narrow a sentencer's discretion to *impose* the death sentence, the Constitution limits a State's ability to narrow a sentencer's discretion to consider relevant evidence that might cause it to *decline to impose* the death sentence. "[T]he sentencer ... [cannot] be precluded from considering, *as a mitigating factor*, any aspect of a defendant's character or record and any of the circumstances of the offense that the defendant proffers as a basis for a sentence less than death." *Lockett v. Ohio, Lockett v. Ohio,* 438 U.S., at 604; *See Skipper v. South Carolina*, 476 U.S. 1 (1986). Any exclusion of the "compassionate or mitigating factors stemming from the diverse frailties of humankind" that are relevant to the sentencer's decision would fail to treat all persons as "uniquely individual human beings." *Woodson v. North Carolina*, 428 U.S. at 304.

Although our constitutional inquiry has centered on the procedures by which a death sentence is imposed, we have not stopped at the face of a statute, but have probed the application of statutes to particular cases. For example, in *Godfrey v. Georgia*, 446 U.S. 420 (1980), the Court invalidated a Georgia Supreme Court interpretation of the statutory aggravating circumstance that the murder be "outrageously or wantonly vile, horrible or inhuman in that it involved torture, depravity of mind, or an aggravated battery to the victim." Although that court had articulated an adequate limiting definition of this phrase, we concluded that its interpretation in *Godfrey* was so broad that it may have vitiated the role of the aggravating circumstance in guiding the sentencing jury's discretion.

Finally, where the objective indicia of community values have demonstrated a consensus that the death penalty is disproportionate as applied to a certain class of cases, we have established substantive limitations on its application. In *Coker v. Georgia,* 433 U.S. 584 (1977), the Court held that a State may not constitutionally sentence an individual to death for the rape of an adult woman. In *Enmund v. Florida,* 458 U.S. 782 (1982), the Court prohibited imposition of the death penalty on a defendant convicted of felony murder absent a showing that the defendant possessed a sufficiently culpable mental state. Most recently, in *Ford v. Wainwright,* 477 U.S. 399 (1986), we prohibited execution of prisoners who are insane.

D

In sum, our decisions since *Furman* have identified a constitutionally permissible range of discretion in imposing the death penalty. First, there is a required threshold below which the death penalty cannot be imposed. In this context, the State must establish rational criteria that narrow the decisionmaker's judgment as to whether the circumstances of a particular defendant's case meet the threshold. Moreover, a societal consensus that the death penalty is disproportionate to a particular offense prevents a State from imposing the death penalty for that offense. Second, States cannot limit the sentencer's consideration of any relevant circumstance that could cause it to decline to impose the penalty. In this respect, the State cannot channel the sentencer's discretion, but must allow it to consider any relevant information offered by the defendant.

IV

A

In light of our precedents under the Eighth Amendment, McCleskey cannot argue successfully that his sentence is "disproportionate to the crime in the traditional sense." *See Pulley v. Harris,* 465 U.S. 37, 43 (1984). He does not deny that he committed a murder in the course of a planned robbery, a crime for which this Court has determined that the death penalty constitutionally may be imposed. *Gregg v. Georgia*, 428 at 187. His disproportionality claim "is of a different sort." *Pulley v. Harris,* 465 U.S. at 50–51. McCleskey argues that the sentence in his case is disproportionate to the sentences in other murder cases.

On the one hand, he cannot base a constitutional claim on an argument that his case differs from other cases in which defendants *did* receive the death penalty. On automatic appeal, the Georgia Supreme Court found that McCleskey's death sentence was not disproportionate to other death sentences imposed in the State. The court supported this conclusion with an appendix containing citations to 13 cases involving generally similar murders. Moreover, where the statutory procedures adequately channel the sentencer's discretion, such proportionality review is not constitutionally required. *Pulley v. Harris,* 465 U.S. at 50–51.

On the other hand, absent a showing that the Georgia capital punishment system operates in an arbitrary and capricious manner, McCleskey cannot prove a constitutional violation by demonstrating that other defendants who may be similarly situated did *not* receive the death penalty. In *Gregg,* the Court confronted the argument that "the opportunities for discretionary action that are inherent in the processing of any murder case under Georgia law," specifically the opportunities for discretionary leniency, rendered the capital sentences imposed arbitrary and capricious. We rejected this contention[.] * * *

Because McCleskey's sentence was imposed under Georgia sentencing procedures that focus discretion "on the particularized nature of the crime and the particularized characteristics of the individual defendant," we lawfully may presume that McCleskey's death sentence was not "wantonly and freakishly" imposed, and thus that the sentence is not disproportionate within any recognized meaning under the Eighth Amendment.

B

Although our decision in *Gregg* as to the facial validity of the Georgia capital punishment statute appears to foreclose McCleskey's disproportionality argument, he further contends that the Georgia capital punishment system is arbitrary and capricious in *application*, and therefore his sentence is excessive, because racial considerations may influence capital sentencing decisions in Georgia. We now address this claim.

To evaluate McCleskey's challenge, we must examine exactly what the Baldus study may show. Even Professor Baldus does not contend that his statistics prove that race enters into any capital sentencing decisions or that race was a factor in McCleskey's particular case. Statistics at most may show only a likelihood that a particular factor entered into some decisions. There is, of course, some risk of racial prejudice influencing a jury's decision in a criminal case. There are similar risks that other kinds of prejudice will influence other criminal trials. The question "is at what point that risk becomes constitutionally unacceptable." *Turner v. Murray,* 476 U.S. 28, 36, n.8 (1986). McCleskey asks us to accept the likelihood allegedly shown by the Baldus study as the constitutional measure of an unacceptable risk of racial prejudice influencing capital sentencing decisions. This we decline to do.

Because of the risk that the factor of race may enter the criminal justice process, we have engaged in "unceasing efforts" to eradicate racial prejudice from our criminal justice system. *Batson v. Kentucky,* 476 U.S. 79, 85 (1986). Our efforts have been guided by our recognition that "the inestimable privilege of trial by jury ... is a vital principle, underlying the whole administration of criminal justice," *Ex parte Milligan,* 4 Wall. 2, 123 (1866). *See Duncan v. Louisiana,* 391 U.S. 145, 155 (1968). Thus, it is the jury that is a criminal defendant's fundamental "protection of life and liberty against race or color prejudice." *Strauder v. West Virginia,* 100 U.S.303, 309 (1880). Specifically, a capital sentencing jury representative of a criminal defendant's community assures a "'diffused impartiality,'" *Taylor v. Louisiana,* 419 U.S. 522 (1975), in the jury's task of "express[ing] the conscience of the community on the ultimate question of life or death." *Witherspoon v. Illinois,* 391 U.S. 510, 519(1968).

Individual jurors bring to their deliberations "qualities of human nature and varieties of human experience, the range of which is unknown and perhaps unknowable." *Peters v. Kiff,* 407 U.S. 493, 503 (1972). The capital sentencing decision requires the individual jurors to focus their collective judgment on the unique characteristics of a particular criminal defendant. It is not surprising that such collective judgments often are difficult to explain. But the inherent lack of predictability of jury decisions does not justify their condemnation. On the contrary, it is the jury's function to make the difficult and uniquely human judgments that defy codification and that "buil[d] discretion, equity, and flexibility into a legal system."

McCleskey's argument that the Constitution condemns the discretion allowed decisionmakers in the Georgia capital sentencing system is antithetical to the fundamental role of discretion in our criminal justice system. Discretion in the criminal justice system offers substantial benefits to the criminal defendant. Not only can a jury decline to impose the death sentence, it can decline to convict or choose to convict of a lesser offense.

Whereas decisions against a defendant's interest may be reversed by the trial judge or on appeal, these discretionary exercises of leniency are final and unreviewable. Similarly, the capacity of prosecutorial discretion to provide individualized justice is "firmly entrenched in American law." As we have noted, a prosecutor can decline to charge, offer a plea bargain, * * * or decline to seek a death sentence in any particular case. Of course, "the power to be lenient [also] is the power to discriminate," but a capital punishment system that did not allow for discretionary acts of leniency "would be totally alien to our notions of criminal justice." *Gregg v. Georgia,* 428 U.S., at 200, n.50.

C

At most, the Baldus study indicates a discrepancy that appears to correlate with race. Apparent disparities in sentencing are an inevitable part of our criminal justice system. The discrepancy indicated by the Baldus study is "a far cry from the major systemic defects identified in *Furman,*" *Pulley v. Harris,* 465 U.S., at 54. As this Court has recognized, any mode for determining guilt or punishment "has its weaknesses and the potential for misuse." *Singer v. United States,* 380 U.S. 24, 35 (1965). Specifically, "there can be 'no perfect procedure for deciding in which cases governmental authority should be used to impose death.'" *Zant v. Stephens,* 462 U.S. 862, 884 (1983). Despite these imperfections, our consistent rule has been that constitutional guarantees are met when "the mode [for determining guilt or punishment] itself has been surrounded with safeguards to make it as fair as possible." *Singer v. United States,* 380 U.S. at 35. Where the discretion that is fundamental to our criminal process is involved, we decline to assume that what is unexplained is invidious. In light of the safeguards designed to minimize racial bias in the process, the fundamental value of jury trial in our criminal justice system, and the benefits that discretion provides to criminal defendants, we hold that the Baldus study does not demonstrate a constitutionally significant risk of racial bias affecting the Georgia capital sentencing process.

V

Two additional concerns inform our decision in this case. First, McCleskey's claim, taken to its logical conclusion, throws into serious question the principles that underlie our entire criminal justice system. The Eighth Amendment is not limited in application to capital punishment, but applies to all penalties. *Solem v. Helm,* 463 U.S. 277, 289–290 (1983); *see Rummel v. Estelle,* 445 U.S. 263, 293 (1980) (POWELL, J., dissenting). Thus, if we accepted McCleskey's claim that racial bias has impermissibly tainted the capital sentencing decision, we could soon be faced with similar claims as to other types of penalty. Moreover, the claim that his sentence rests on the irrelevant factor of race easily could be extended to apply to claims based on unexplained discrepancies that correlate to membership in other minority groups, and even to gender. Similarly, since McCleskey's claim relates to the race of his victim, other claims could apply with equally logical force to statistical disparities that correlate with the race or sex of other actors in the criminal justice system, such as defense attorneys or judges. Also, there is no logical reason that such a claim need be limited to racial or sexual bias. If arbitrary and capricious punishment is the touchstone under the Eighth Amendment, such a claim could—at least in theory—be based upon any arbitrary variable, such as the defendant's facial characteristics, or the physical attractiveness of the defendant or the victim, that some statistical study indicates may be influential in jury decisionmaking. As these examples illustrate, there is no limiting principle to the type of challenge brought by McCleskey. The Constitution does not require that a State eliminate any demonstrable disparity that correlates with a potentially irrelevant factor in order to operate a criminal justice system that includes capital punishment. As we have stated specifically in the context of capital punishment, the Constitution does not "plac[e] totally unrealistic conditions on its use." *Gregg v. Georgia*, 428 U.S at 199, n.50.

Second, McCleskey's arguments are best presented to the legislative bodies. It is not the responsibility—or indeed even the right—of this Court to determine the appropriate punishment for particular crimes. It is the legislatures, the elected representatives of the people, that are "constituted to respond to the will and consequently the moral values of the people." *Furman v. Georgia*, 408 U.S. at 383 (Burger, C.J., dissenting). Legislatures also are better qualified to weigh and "evaluate the results of statistical studies in terms of their own local conditions and with a flexibility of approach that is not available to the courts." *Gregg v. Georgia*, 428 U.S. at 186. Capital punishment is now the law in more than two-thirds of our States. It is the ultimate duty of courts to determine on a case-by-case basis whether these laws are applied consistently with the Constitution. Despite McCleskey's wide-ranging arguments that basically challenge the validity of capital punishment in our multiracial society, the only question before us is whether in his case the law of Georgia was properly applied. We agree with the district court and the Court of Appeals for the Eleventh Circuit that this was carefully and correctly done in this case.

VI

Accordingly, we affirm the judgment of the Court of Appeals for the Eleventh Circuit.

It is so ordered.

JUSTICE BRENNAN, with whom JUSTICE MARSHALL joins, and with whom JUSTICE BLACKMUN and JUSTICE STEVENS join in all but Part I, dissenting.

I

Adhering to my view that the death penalty is in all circumstances cruel and unusual punishment forbidden by the Eighth and Fourteenth Amendments, I would vacate the decision below insofar as it left undisturbed the death sentence imposed in this case. *Gregg v. Georgia*, 428 U.S. 153, 227 (1976) (BRENNAN, J., dissenting). The Court observes that "[t]he *Gregg*-type statute imposes unprecedented safeguards in the special context of capital punishment," which "ensure a degree of care in the imposition of the death penalty that can be described only as unique." Notwithstanding these efforts, murder defendants in Georgia with white victims are more than four times as likely to receive the death sentence as are defendants with black victims. Nothing could convey more powerfully the intractable reality of the death penalty: "that the effort to eliminate arbitrariness in the infliction of that ultimate sanction is so plainly doomed to failure that it—and the death penalty—must be abandoned altogether." *Godfrey v. Georgia*, 446 U.S. 420, 442 (1980) (MARSHALL, J., concurring in judgment).

Even if I did not hold this position, however, I would reverse the Court of Appeals, for petitioner McCleskey has clearly demonstrated that his death sentence was imposed in violation of the Eighth and Fourteenth Amendments. While I join Parts I through IV-A of JUSTICE BLACKMUN's dissenting opinion discussing petitioner's Fourteenth Amendment claim, I write separately to emphasize how conclusively McCleskey has also demonstrated precisely the type of risk of irrationality in sentencing that we have consistently condemned in our Eighth Amendment jurisprudence.

II

At some point in this case, Warren McCleskey doubtless asked his lawyer whether a jury was likely to sentence him to die. A candid reply to this question would have been disturbing. First, counsel would have to tell McCleskey that few of the details of the crime or of McCleskey's past criminal conduct were more important than the fact that his victim was white. Furthermore, counsel would feel bound to tell McCleskey that defendants charged with killing white victims in Georgia are 4.3 times as likely to be sentenced to death as defendants charged with killing blacks. In addition, frankness would compel the disclosure that it was more likely than not that the race of McCleskey's victim would determine whether he received a death sentence: 6 of every 11 defendants convicted of killing a white person would not have received the death penalty if their victims had been black, while, among defendants with aggravating and mitigating factors comparable to McCleskey's, 20 of every 34 would not have been sentenced to die if their victims had been black. Finally, the assessment would not be complete without the information that cases involving black defendants and white victims are more likely to result in a death sentence than cases featuring any other racial combination of defendant and victim. The story could be told in a variety of ways, but McCleskey could not fail to grasp its essential narrative line: there was a significant chance that race would play a prominent role in determining if he lived or died.

The Court today holds that Warren McCleskey's sentence was constitutionally imposed. It finds no fault in a system in which lawyers must tell their clients that race casts a large shadow on the capital sentencing process. The Court arrives at this conclusion by stating that the Baldus study cannot "*prove* that race enters into any capital sentencing decisions or that race was a factor in McCleskey's particular case." Since, according to Professor Baldus, we cannot say "to a moral certainty" that race influenced a decision, we can identify only "a likelihood that a particular factor entered into some decisions," and "a discrepancy that appears to correlate with race." This "likelihood" and "discrepancy," holds the Court, is insufficient to establish a constitutional violation. The Court reaches this conclusion by placing four factors on the scales opposite McCleskey's evidence: the desire to encourage sentencing discretion, the existence of "statutory safeguards" in the Georgia scheme, the fear of encouraging widespread challenges to other sentencing decisions, and the limits of the judicial role. The Court's evaluation of the significance of petitioner's evidence is fundamentally at odds with our consistent concern for rationality in capital sentencing, and the considerations that the majority invokes to discount that evidence cannot justify ignoring its force.

* * *

JUSTICE BLACKMUN, with whom JUSTICE MARSHALL and JUSTICE STEVENS join, and with whom JUSTICE BRENNAN joins in all but Part IV-B, dissenting.

The Court today sanctions the execution of a man despite his presentation of evidence that establishes a constitutionally intolerable level of racially based discrimination leading to the imposition of his death sentence. I am disappointed with the Court's action not only because of its denial of constitutional guarantees to petitioner McCleskey individually, but also because of its departure from what seems to me to be well-developed constitutional jurisprudence.

* * *

Yet McCleskey's case raises concerns that are central not only to the principles underlying the Eighth Amendment, but also to the principles underlying the Fourteenth Amendment. Analysis of his case in terms of the Fourteenth Amendment is consistent with this Court's recognition that racial discrimination is fundamentally at odds with our constitutional guarantee of equal protection. The protections afforded by the Fourteenth Amendment are not left at the courtroom door. *Hill v. Texas*, 316 U.S. 400, 406 (1942). Nor is equal protection denied to persons convicted of crimes. *Lee v. Washington*, 390 U.S. 333 (1968). The Court in the past has found that racial discrimination within the criminal justice system is particularly abhorrent: "Discrimination on the basis of race, odious in all aspects, is especially pernicious in the administration of justice." *Rose v. Mitchell*, 443 U.S. 545, 555 (1979). * * *

* * *

I

A

The Court today seems to give a new meaning to our recognition that death is different. Rather than requiring "a correspondingly greater degree of scrutiny of the capital sentencing determination," *California v. Ramos*, 463 U.S. 992, 998–99 (1983), the Court relies on the very fact that this is a case involving capital punishment to apply a *lesser* standard of scrutiny under the Equal Protection Clause. The Court concludes that "legitimate" explanations outweigh McCleskey's claim that his death sentence reflected a constitutionally impermissible risk of racial discrimination. The Court explains that McCleskey's evidence is too weak to require rebuttal "because a legitimate and unchallenged explanation for the decision is apparent from the record: McCleskey committed an act for which the United States Constitution and Georgia laws permit imposition of the death penalty." The Court states that it will not infer a discriminatory purpose on the part of the state legislature because "there were legitimate reasons for the Georgia Legislature to adopt and maintain capital punishment."

The Court's assertion that the fact of McCleskey's conviction undermines his constitutional claim is inconsistent with a long and unbroken line of this Court's case law. * * *

* * *

II

* * *

B

There can be no dispute that McCleskey has made the requisite showing under the first prong of the standard. The Baldus study demonstrates that black persons are a distinct group that are singled out for different treatment in the Georgia capital sentencing system. The Court acknowledges, as it must, that the raw statistics included in the Baldus study and presented by petitioner indicate that it is much less likely that a death sentence will result from a murder of a black person than from a murder of a white person. White-victim cases are nearly 11 times more likely to yield a death sentence than are black-victim cases. The raw figures also indicate that even within the group of defendants who are convicted of killing white persons and are thereby more likely to receive a death sentence, black defendants are more likely than white defendants to be sentenced to death.

With respect to the second prong, McCleskey must prove that there is a substantial likelihood that his death sentence is due to racial factors. *See Hunter v. Underwood*, 471 U.S. 222, 228 (1985). The Court of Appeals assumed the validity of the Baldus study and found that it "showed that systemic and substantial disparities existed in the penalties imposed upon homicide defendants in Georgia based on race of the homicide victim, that the disparities existed at a less substantial rate in death sentencing based on race of defendants, and that the factors of race of the victim and defendant were at work in Fulton County." The question remaining therefore is at what point does that disparity become constitutionally unacceptable. *See Turner v. Murray*, 476 U.S. 28, 36, n.8 (1986). * * *

* * *

IV

A

One of the final concerns discussed by the Court may be the most disturbing aspect of its opinion. Granting relief to McCleskey in this case, it is said, could lead to further constitutional challenges. That, of course, is no reason to deny McCleskey his rights under the Equal Protection Clause. If a grant of relief to him were to lead to a closer examination of the effects of racial considerations throughout the criminal justice system, the system, and hence society, might benefit. Where no such factors come into play, the integrity of the system is enhanced. Where such considerations are shown to be significant, efforts can be made to eradicate their impermissible influence and to ensure an evenhanded application of criminal sanctions.

B

Like JUSTICE STEVENS, I do not believe acceptance of McCleskey's claim would eliminate capital punishment in Georgia. JUSTICE STEVENS points out that the evidence presented in this case indicates that in extremely aggravated murders the risk of discriminatory enforcement of the death penalty is minimized. I agree that narrowing the class of death-eligible defendants is not too high a price to pay for a death penalty system that does not discriminate on the basis of race. Moreover, the establishment of guidelines for Assistant District Attorneys as to the appropriate basis for exercising their discretion at the various steps in the prosecution of a case would provide at least a measure of consistency. The Court's emphasis on the procedural safeguards in the system ignores the fact that there are none whatsoever during the crucial process leading up to trial. As JUSTICE WHITE stated for the plurality in *Turner v. Murray*, I find "the risk that racial prejudice may have infected petitioner's capital sentencing unacceptable in light of the ease with which that risk could have been minimized." I dissent.

JUSTICE STEVENS, with whom JUSTICE BLACKMUN joins, dissenting.

There "is a qualitative difference between death and any other permissible form of punishment," and hence, "'a corresponding difference in the need for reliability in the determination that death is the appropriate punishment in a specific case.'" *Zant v. Stephens*, 462 U.S. 862, 884–85 (1983) (quoting *Woodson v. North Carolina*, 428 U.S. 280, 305 (1976) (plurality opinion of Stewart, POWELL, and STEVENS, JJ.)). Even when considerations far less repugnant than racial discrimination are involved, we have recognized the "vital importance to the defendant and to the community that any decision to impose the death sentence be, and appear to be, based on reason rather than caprice or emotion." *Gardner v. Florida*, 430 U.S. 349, 358 (1977). "[A]lthough not every imperfection in the deliberative process is sufficient, even in a capital case, to set aside a state-court judgment, the severity of the sentence mandates careful scrutiny in the review of any colorable claim of error." *Zant*, 462 U.S. at 885.

In this case it is claimed—and the claim is supported by elaborate studies which the Court properly assumes to be valid—that the jury's sentencing process was likely distorted by racial prejudice. The studies demonstrate a strong probability that McCleskey's sentencing jury, which expressed "the community's outrage—its sense that an individual has lost his moral entitlement to live," *Spaziano v. Florida*, 468 U.S. 447, 469(1984) (STEVENS, J., dissenting)—was influenced by the fact that McCleskey is black and his victim was white, and that this same outrage would not have been generated if he had killed a member of his own race. This sort of disparity is constitutionally intolerable. It flagrantly violates the Court's prior "insistence that capital punishment be imposed fairly, and with reasonable consistency, or not at all." *Eddings v. Oklahoma,* 455 U.S. 104, 112 (1982).

The Court's decision appears to be based on a fear that the acceptance of McCleskey's claim would sound the death knell for capital punishment in Georgia. If society were indeed forced to choose between a racially discriminatory death penalty (one that provides heightened protection against murder "for whites only") and no death penalty at all, the choice mandated by the Constitution would be plain. *Eddings v. Oklahoma, supra.* But the Court's fear is unfounded. One of the lessons of the Baldus study is that there exist certain categories of extremely serious crimes for which prosecutors consistently seek, and juries consistently impose, the death penalty without regard to the race of the victim or the race of the offender. If Georgia were to narrow the class of death-eligible defendants to those categories, the danger of arbitrary and discriminatory imposition of the death penalty would be significantly decreased, if not eradicated. As JUSTICE BRENNAN has demonstrated in his dissenting opinion, such a restructuring of the sentencing scheme is surely not too high a price to pay.

Like JUSTICE BRENNAN, I would therefore reverse the judgment of the Court of Appeals. I believe, however, that further proceedings are necessary in order to determine whether McCleskey's death sentence should be set aside. First, the Court of Appeals must decide whether the Baldus study is valid. I am persuaded that it is, but orderly procedure requires that the Court of Appeals address this issue before we actually decide the question. Second, it is necessary for the district court to determine whether the particular facts of McCleskey's crime and his background place this case within the range of cases that present an unacceptable risk that race played a decisive role in McCleskey's sentencing.

Accordingly, I respectfully dissent.

Notes

1. *Subsequent case history*

Warren McCleskey was executed by electrocution on September 25, 1991.

2. *A fear of "too much justice"?*

In her introduction to the *Race to Execution Symposium Issue* published by the DePaul Law Review, Professor Susan Bandes wrote that "Bryan Stevenson spoke for many of us who work for reform in the death penalty context when he said: 'I have not yet recovered from reading the *McCleskey* decision.' He was deeply troubled by the Court's 'fear of too much justice,' its claim that it could not acknowledge racial bias in the capital context because it would then have to deal with racial bias in other criminal contexts as well. But, he went on:

> It was the second thing the Court said that broke my heart, that did something to me that I'm still trying to recover from. The second thing the Court said was a certain amount of bias, a certain quantum of discrimination ... is in the Court's opinion inevitable.... And so we are gathered in this room talking about race and the death penalty while the United States Supreme Court has already said it's pointless for you to be here."

Susan Bandes, *Introduction: Race to Execution Symposium*, 53 DePaul L. Rev. 4, 1403 (2004), *citing* Bryan Stevenson, *Keynote Address: Race to Execution Symposium*, 53 DePaul L. Rev. 4, 1699 (2004).[2]

Do you agree with the Court that a certain quantum of discrimination is "inevitable"? In what way does habeas corpus jurisprudence reinforce—or refute—the Court's assertion?

Can you think of other approaches to address racial discrimination in the criminal justice system?[3]

Miller-El v. Cockrell

537 U.S. 322 (2003)

JUSTICE KENNEDY delivered the opinion of the Court.

In this case we once again examine when a state prisoner can appeal the denial or dismissal of his petition for writ of habeas corpus. In 1986 two Dallas County assistant district attorneys used peremptory strikes to exclude 10 of the 11 African-Americans eligible to serve on the jury which tried petitioner Thomas Joe Miller-El. During the ensuing 17 years, petitioner has been unsuccessful in establishing, in either state or federal court, that his conviction and death sentence must be vacated because the jury selection procedures violated the Equal Protection Clause and our holding in *Batson v. Kentucky,* 476 U.S. 79 (1986). The claim now arises in a federal petition for writ of habeas corpus. The procedures and standards applicable in the case are controlled by the habeas corpus statute codified at Title 28, chapter 153 of the United States Code, most recently amended in a substantial manner by the Antiterrorism and Effective Death Penalty Act of 1996 (AEDPA). In the interest of finality AEDPA constrains a federal court's power to disturb state-court convictions.

The United States District Court for the Northern District of Texas, after reviewing the evidence before the state trial court, determined that petitioner failed to establish a constitutional violation warranting habeas relief. The Court of Appeals for the Fifth Circuit, concluding there was insufficient merit to the case, denied a certificate of appealability (COA) from the district court's determination. The COA denial is the subject of our decision.

At issue here are the standards AEDPA imposes before a court of appeals may issue a COA to review a denial of habeas relief in the district court. Congress mandates that a prisoner seeking postconviction relief under 28 U.S.C. § 2254 has no automatic right to appeal a district court's denial or dismissal of the petition. Instead, petitioner must first seek and obtain a COA. In resolving this case we decide again that when a habeas applicant seeks permission to initiate appellate review of the dismissal of his petition, the court of appeals should limit its examination to a threshold inquiry into the underlying merit of his claims. *Slack v. McDaniel,* 529 U.S. 473, 481 (2000). Consistent with our prior precedent and the text of the habeas corpus statute, we reiterate that a prisoner seeking a COA need

2. There have been many studies of racial discrimination in the criminal justice system, from arrest through sentencing. *See, e.g.*, www.sentencingproject.org and raceandjustice@sentencingproject.org for archived and ongoing accounts of such studies.

3. In 2009, North Carolina enacted the "Racial Justice Act," which provides murder suspects and death row inmates the right to try to prove that racial bias influenced the prosecutor's decision to seek the death penalty. Amanda Hendler-Voss, *NC Takes Moral Path On Racial Bias On Death Row*, Asheville Citizen-Times, Aug. 23, 2009, at 11.

only demonstrate "a substantial showing of the denial of a constitutional right." 28 U.S.C. § 2253(c)(2). A petitioner satisfies this standard by demonstrating that jurists of reason could disagree with the district court's resolution of his constitutional claims or that jurists could conclude the issues presented are adequate to deserve encouragement to proceed further. *Slack, supra* at 484. Applying these principles to petitioner's application, we conclude a COA should have issued.

I

A

Petitioner, his wife Dorothy Miller-El, and one Kenneth Flowers robbed a Holiday Inn in Dallas, Texas. They emptied the cash drawers and ordered two employees, Doug Walker and Donald Hall, to lie on the floor. Walker and Hall were gagged with strips of fabric, and their hands and feet were bound. Petitioner asked Flowers if he was going to kill Walker and Hall. When Flowers hesitated or refused, petitioner shot Walker twice in the back and shot Hall in the side. Walker died from his wounds.

The State indicted petitioner for capital murder. He pleaded not guilty, and jury selection took place during five weeks in February and March 1986. When *voir dire* had been concluded, petitioner moved to strike the jury on the grounds that the prosecution had violated the Equal Protection Clause of the Fourteenth Amendment by excluding African-Americans through the use of peremptory challenges. Petitioner's trial occurred before our decision in *Batson, supra*, and *Swain v. Alabama*, 380 U.S. 202 (1965), was then the controlling precedent. As *Swain* required, petitioner sought to show that the prosecution's conduct was part of a larger pattern of discrimination aimed at excluding African-Americans from jury service. In a pretrial hearing held on March 12, 1986, petitioner presented extensive evidence in support of his motion. The trial judge, however, found "no evidence ... that indicated any systematic exclusion of blacks as a matter of policy by the District Attorney's office; while it may have been done by individual prosecutors in individual cases." The state court then denied petitioner's motion to strike the jury. Twelve days later, the jury found petitioner guilty; and the trial court sentenced him to death.

Petitioner appealed to the Texas Court of Criminal Appeals. While the appeal was pending, on April 30, 1986, the Court decided *Batson v. Kentucky* and established its three-part process for evaluating claims that a prosecutor used peremptory challenges in violation of the Equal Protection Clause. First, a defendant must make a prima facie showing that a peremptory challenge has been exercised on the basis of race. Second, if that showing has been made, the prosecution must offer a race-neutral basis for striking the juror in question. Third, in light of the parties' submissions, the trial court must determine whether the defendant has shown purposeful discrimination.

After acknowledging petitioner had established an inference of purposeful discrimination, the Texas Court of Criminal Appeals remanded the case for new findings in light of *Batson*. A post-trial hearing was held on May 10, 1988 (a little over two years after petitioner's jury had been empaneled). There, the original trial court admitted all the evidence presented at the *Swain* hearing and further evidence and testimony from the attorneys in the original trial.

On January 13, 1989, the trial court concluded that petitioner's evidence failed to satisfy step one of *Batson* because it "did not even raise an inference of racial motivation in the use of the state's peremptory challenges" to support a prima facie case. Notwithstanding this conclusion, the state court determined that the State would have prevailed on steps two and three because the prosecutors had offered credible, race-neutral explanations for each African-American excluded. The court further found "no disparate prosecutorial examination of any of the venireman in question" and "that the primary reasons for the exercise of the challenges against each of the veniremen in question [was] their reluctance to assess or reservations concerning the imposition of the death penalty." There was no discussion of petitioner's other evidence.

The Texas Court of Criminal Appeals denied petitioner's appeal, and we denied certiorari. Petitioner's state habeas proceedings fared no better, and he was denied relief by the Texas Court of Criminal Appeals.

Petitioner filed a petition for writ of habeas corpus in federal district court pursuant to 28 U.S.C. § 2254. Although petitioner raised four issues, we concern ourselves here with only petitioner's jury selection claim premised on *Batson*. The Federal Magistrate Judge who considered the merits was troubled by some of the evidence adduced in the state-court proceedings. He, nevertheless, recommended, in deference to the state courts' acceptance of the prosecutors' race-neutral justifications for striking the potential jurors, that petitioner be denied relief. The United States District Court adopted the recommendation. Pursuant to § 2253, petitioner sought a COA from the district court, and the application was denied. Petitioner renewed his request to the Court of Appeals for the Fifth Circuit, and it also denied the COA.

The Court of Appeals noted that, under controlling habeas principles, a COA will issue "'only if the applicant has made a substantial showing of the denial of a constitutional right.'" *Miller-El v. Johnson*. Citing our decision in *Slack v. McDaniel*, the court reasoned that "[a] petitioner makes a 'substantial showing' when he demonstrates that his petition involves issues which are debatable among jurists of reason, that another court could resolve the issues differently, or that the issues are adequate to deserve encouragement to proceed further." The Court of Appeals also interjected the requirements of 28 U.S.C. § 2254 into the COA determination: "As an appellate court reviewing a federal habeas petition, we are required by § 2254(d)(2) to presume the state court findings correct unless we determine that the findings result in a decision which is unreasonable in light of the evidence presented. And the unreasonableness, if any, must be established by clear and convincing evidence. *See* 28 U.S.C. § 2254(e)(1)."

Applying this framework to petitioner's COA application, the Court of Appeals concluded "that the state court's findings are not unreasonable and that Miller-El has failed to present clear and convincing evidence to the contrary." As a consequence, the court "determined that the state court's adjudication neither resulted in a decision that was unreasonable in light of the evidence presented nor resulted in a decision contrary to clearly established federal law as determined by the Supreme Court," and it denied petitioner's request for a COA. We granted certiorari.

B

While a COA ruling is not the occasion for a ruling on the merit of petitioner's claim, our determination to reverse the Court of Appeals counsels us to explain in some detail the extensive evidence concerning the jury selection procedures. Petitioner's evidence falls into two broad categories. First, he presented to the state trial court, at a pretrial *Swain* hearing, evidence relating to a pattern and practice of race discrimination in the *voir dire*. Second, two years later, he presented, to the same state court, evidence that directly related to the conduct of the prosecutors in his case. We discuss the latter first.

A comparative analysis of the venire members demonstrates that African-Americans were excluded from petitioner's jury in a ratio significantly higher than Caucasians were. Of the 108 possible jurors reviewed by the prosecution and defense, 20 were African-American. Nine of them were excused for cause or by agreement of the parties. Of the 11

African-American jurors remaining, however, all but 1 were excluded by peremptory strikes exercised by the prosecutors. On this basis 91% of the eligible black jurors were removed by peremptory strikes. In contrast the prosecutors used their peremptory strikes against just 13% (4 out of 31) of the eligible nonblack prospective jurors qualified to serve on petitioner's jury.

These numbers, while relevant, are not petitioner's whole case. During *voir dire*, the prosecution questioned venire members as to their views concerning the death penalty and their willingness to serve on a capital case. Responses that disclosed reluctance or hesitation to impose capital punishment were cited as a justification for striking a potential juror for cause or by peremptory challenge. *Wainwright v. Witt*, 469 U.S. 412 (1985). The evidence suggests, however, that the manner in which members of the venire were questioned varied by race. To the extent a divergence in responses can be attributed to the racially disparate mode of examination, it is relevant to our inquiry.

Most African-Americans (53%, or 8 out of 15) were first given a detailed description of the mechanics of an execution in Texas:

> If those three [sentencing] questions are answered yes, at some point[,] Thomas Joe Miller-El will be taken to Huntsville, Texas. He will be placed on death row and at some time will be taken to the death house where he will be strapped on a gurney, an IV put into his arm and he will be injected with a substance that will cause his death ... as the result of the verdict in this case if those three questions are answered yes.

Only then were these African-American venire members asked whether they could render a decision leading to a sentence of death. Very few prospective white jurors (6%, or 3 out of 49) were given this preface prior to being asked for their views on capital punishment. Rather, all but three were questioned in vague terms: "Would you share with us ... your personal feelings, if you could, in your own words how you do feel about the death penalty and capital punishment and secondly, do you feel you could serve on this type of a jury and actually render a decision that would result in the death of the Defendant in this case based on the evidence?"

There was an even more pronounced difference, on the apparent basis of race, in the manner the prosecutors questioned members of the venire about their willingness to impose the minimum sentence for murder. Under Texas law at the time of petitioner's trial, an unwillingness to do so warranted removal for cause. *Huffman v. State*, 450 S.W.2d 858, 861 (Tex.Crim.App.1970)(vacated in part, 408 U.S. 936). This strategy normally is used by the defense to weed out pro-state members of the venire, but, ironically, the prosecution employed it here. The prosecutors first identified the statutory minimum sentence of five years' imprisonment to 34 out of 36 (94%) white venire members, and only then asked: "If you hear a case, to your way of thinking [that] calls for and warrants and justifies five years, you'll give it?" In contrast, only 1 out of 8 (12.5%) African-American prospective jurors were informed of the statutory minimum before being asked what minimum sentence they would impose. The typical questioning of the other seven black jurors was as follows:

> [Prosecutor]: Now, the maximum sentence for [murder] ... is life under the law. Can you give me an idea of just your personal feelings what you feel a minimum sentence should be for the offense of murder the way I've set it out for you?
>
> [Juror]: Well, to me that's almost like it's premeditated. But you said they don't have a premeditated statute here in Texas.

* * *

> [Prosecutor]: Again, we're not talking about self-defense or accident or insanity or killing in the heat of passion or anything like that. We're talking about the knowing—
>
> [Juror]: I know you said the minimum. The minimum amount that I would say would be at least twenty years.

Furthermore, petitioner points to the prosecution's use of a Texas criminal procedure practice known as jury shuffling. This practice permits parties to rearrange the order in which members of the venire are examined so as to increase the likelihood that visually preferable venire members will be moved forward and empaneled. With no information about the prospective jurors other than their appearance, the party requesting the procedure literally shuffles the juror cards, and the venire members are then reseated in the new order. Shuffling affects jury composition because any prospective jurors not questioned during *voir dire* are dismissed at the end of the week, and a new panel of jurors appears the following week. So jurors who are shuffled to the back of the panel are less likely to be questioned or to serve.

On at least two occasions the prosecution requested shuffles when there were a predominate number of African-Americans in the front of the panel. On yet another occasion the prosecutors complained about the purported inadequacy of the card shuffle by a defense lawyer but lodged a formal objection only after the postshuffle panel composition revealed that African-American prospective jurors had been moved forward.

Next, we turn to the pattern and practice evidence adduced at petitioner's pretrial *Swain* hearing. Petitioner subpoenaed a number of current and former Dallas County assistant district attorneys, judges, and others who had observed firsthand the prosecution's conduct during jury selection over a number of years. Although most of the witnesses denied the existence of a systematic policy to exclude African-Americans, others disagreed. A Dallas County district judge testified that, when he had served in the District Attorney's Office from the late-1950's to early-1960's, his superior warned him that he would be fired if he permitted any African-Americans to serve on a jury. Similarly, another Dallas County district judge and former assistant district attorney from 1976 to 1978 testified that he believed the office had a systematic policy of excluding African-Americans from juries.

Of more importance, the defense presented evidence that the District Attorney's Office had adopted a formal policy to exclude minorities from jury service. A 1963 circular by the District Attorney's Office instructed its prosecutors to exercise peremptory strikes against minorities: "'Do not take Jews, Negroes, Dagos, Mexicans or a member of any minority race on a jury, no matter how rich or how well educated.'" A manual entitled "Jury Selection in a Criminal Case" was distributed to prosecutors. It contained an article authored by a former prosecutor (and later a judge) under the direction of his superiors in the District Attorney's Office, outlining the reasoning for excluding minorities from jury service. Although the manual was written in 1968, it remained in circulation until 1976, if not later, and was available at least to one of the prosecutors in Miller-El's trial.

Some testimony casts doubt on the State's claim that these practices had been discontinued before petitioner's trial. For example, a judge testified that, in 1985, he had to exclude a prosecutor from trying cases in his courtroom for race-based discrimination in jury selection. Other testimony indicated that the State, by its own admission, once requested a jury shuffle in order to reduce the number of African-Americans in the venire. Concerns over the exclusion of African-Americans by the District Attorney's Office were echoed by Dallas County's Chief Public Defender.

This evidence had been presented by petitioner, in support of his *Batson* claim, to the state and federal courts that denied him relief. It is against this background that we examine whether petitioner's case should be heard by the Court of Appeals.

II

A

As mandated by federal statute, a state prisoner seeking a writ of habeas corpus has no absolute entitlement to appeal a district court's denial of his petition. 28 U.S.C. § 2253. Before an appeal may be entertained, a prisoner who was denied habeas relief in the district court must first seek and obtain a COA from a circuit justice or judge. This is a jurisdictional prerequisite because the COA statute mandates that "unless a circuit justice or judge issues a certificate of appealability, an appeal may not be taken to the court of appeals...." § 2253(c)(1). As a result, until a COA has been issued federal courts of appeals lack jurisdiction to rule on the merits of appeals from habeas petitioners.

A COA will issue only if the requirements of § 2253 have been satisfied. "The COA statute establishes procedural rules and requires a threshold inquiry into whether the circuit court may entertain an appeal." *Slack,* 529 U.S. at 482; *Hohn v. United States,* 524 U.S. 236, 248 (1998). As the Court of Appeals observed in this case, § 2253(c) permits the issuance of a COA only where a petitioner has made a "substantial showing of the denial of a constitutional right." In *Slack, supra,* at 483, we recognized that Congress codified our standard, announced in *Barefoot v. Estelle,* 463 U.S. 880 (1983), for determining what constitutes the requisite showing. Under the controlling standard, a petitioner must "show that reasonable jurists could debate whether (or, for that matter, agree that) the petition should have been resolved in a different manner or that the issues presented were 'adequate to deserve encouragement to proceed further.'" [*Slack*]

The COA determination under § 2253(c) requires an overview of the claims in the habeas petition and a general assessment of their merits. We look to the district court's application of AEDPA to petitioner's constitutional claims and ask whether that resolution was debatable amongst jurists of reason. This threshold inquiry does not require full consideration of the factual or legal bases adduced in support of the claims. In fact, the statute forbids it. When a court of appeals side steps this process by first deciding the merits of an appeal, and then justifying its denial of a COA based on its adjudication of the actual merits, it is in essence deciding an appeal without jurisdiction.

To that end, our opinion in *Slack* held that a COA does not require a showing that the appeal will succeed. Accordingly, a court of appeals should not decline the application for a COA merely because it believes the applicant will not demonstrate an entitlement to relief. The holding in *Slack* would mean very little if appellate review were denied because the prisoner did not convince a judge, or, for that matter, three judges, that he or she would prevail. It is consistent with § 2253 that a COA will issue in some instances where there is no certainty of ultimate relief. After all, when a COA is sought, the whole premise is that the prisoner "'has already failed in that endeavor.'" *Barefoot, supra,* at 893, n.4.

Our holding should not be misconstrued as directing that a COA always must issue. Statutes such as AEDPA have placed more, rather than fewer, restrictions on the power of federal courts to grant writs of habeas corpus to state prisoners. *Duncan v. Walker,* 533 U.S. 167, 178 (2001)("'AEDPA's purpose [is] to further the principles of comity, finality, and federalism'" (quoting *Williams v. Taylor,* 529 U.S. 420, 436(2000) (opinion of O'CONNOR, J.))). The concept of a threshold, or gateway, test was not the innovation of AEDPA. Congress established a threshold prerequisite to appealability in 1908, in large part because it was "concerned with the increasing number of frivolous habeas corpus petitions challenging capital sentences which delayed execution pending completion of the appellate process...." *Barefoot*. By enacting AEDPA, using the specific standards the Court had elaborated earlier for the threshold test, Congress confirmed the necessity and the requirement of differential treatment for those appeals deserving of attention from those that plainly do not. It follows that issuance of a COA must not be *pro forma* or a matter of course.

A prisoner seeking a COA must prove "'something more than the absence of frivolity'" or the existence of mere "good faith" on his or her part. *Barefoot*. We do not require petitioner to prove, before the issuance of a COA, that some jurists would grant the petition for habeas corpus. Indeed, a claim can be debatable even though every jurist of reason might agree, after the COA has been granted and the case has received full consideration, that petitioner will not prevail. As we stated in *Slack*, "where a district court has rejected the constitutional claims on the merits, the showing required to satisfy § 2253(c) is straightforward: The petitioner must demonstrate that reasonable jurists would find the district court's assessment of the constitutional claims debatable or wrong." [*Slack*]

B

Since Miller-El's claim rests on a *Batson* violation, resolution of his COA application requires a preliminary, though not definitive, consideration of the three-step framework mandated by *Batson* and reaffirmed in our later precedents. *E.g., Purkett v. Elem*, 514 U.S. 765 (1995); *Hernandez v. New York*, 500 U.S. 352 (1991). Contrary to the state trial court's ruling on remand, the State now concedes that petitioner, Miller-El, satisfied step one: "There is no dispute that Miller-El presented a prima facie claim" that prosecutors used their peremptory challenges to exclude venire members on the basis of race. Petitioner, for his part, acknowledges that the State proceeded through step two by proffering facially race-neutral explanations for these strikes. Under *Batson*, then, the question remaining is step three: whether Miller-El "has carried his burden of proving purposeful discrimination." *Hernandez, supra*, at 359.

As we confirmed in *Purkett v. Elem*, the critical question in determining whether a prisoner has proved purposeful discrimination at step three is the persuasiveness of the prosecutor's justification for his peremptory strike. At this stage, "implausible or fantastic justifications may (and probably will) be found to be pretexts for purposeful discrimination." *Ibid.* In that instance the issue comes down to whether the trial court finds the prosecutor's race-neutral explanations to be credible. Credibility can be measured by, among other factors, the prosecutor's demeanor; by how reasonable, or how improbable, the explanations are; and by whether the proffered rationale has some basis in accepted trial strategy.

In *Hernandez v. New York*, a plurality of the Court concluded that a state court's finding of the absence of discriminatory intent is "a pure issue of fact" accorded significant deference:

> Deference to trial court findings on the issue of discriminatory intent makes particular sense in this context because, as we noted in *Batson*, the finding "largely will turn on evaluation of credibility." In the typical peremptory challenge inquiry, the decisive question will be whether counsel's race-neutral explanation for a peremptory challenge should be believed. There will seldom be much evidence bearing on that issue, and the best evidence often will be the demeanor of the attorney who exercises the challenge. As with the state of mind of a juror, evaluation of the prosecutor's state of mind based on demeanor and credibility lies "peculiarly within a trial judge's province." *Wainwright v. Witt.*

Deference is necessary because a reviewing court, which analyzes only the transcripts from *voir dire*, is not as well positioned as the trial court is to make credibility determinations. "If an appellate court accepts a trial court's finding that a prosecutor's race-neutral explanation for his peremptory challenges should be believed, we fail to see how the appellate court nevertheless could find discrimination. The credibility of the prosecutor's explanation goes to the heart of the equal protection analysis, and once that has been settled, there seems nothing left to review."

In the context of direct review, therefore, we have noted that "the trial court's decision on the ultimate question of discriminatory intent represents a finding of fact of the sort accorded great deference on appeal" and will not be overturned unless clearly erroneous. A federal court's collateral review of a state-court decision must be consistent with the respect due state courts in our federal system. Where 28 U.S.C. § 2254 applies, our habeas jurisprudence embodies this deference. Factual determinations by state courts are presumed correct absent clear and convincing evidence to the contrary, § 2254(e)(1), and a decision adjudicated on the merits in a state court and based on a factual determination will not be overturned on factual grounds unless objectively unreasonable in light of the evidence presented in the state-court proceeding, § 2254(d)(2).

Even in the context of federal habeas, deference does not imply abandonment or abdication of judicial review. Deference does not by definition preclude relief. A federal court can disagree with a state court's credibility determination and, when guided by AEDPA, conclude the decision was unreasonable or that the factual premise was incorrect by clear and convincing evidence. In the context of the threshold examination in this *Batson* claim the issuance of a COA can be supported by any evidence demonstrating that, despite the neutral explanation of the prosecution, the peremptory strikes in the final analysis were race based. It goes without saying that this includes the facts and circumstances that were adduced in support of the prima facie case. Only after a COA is granted will a reviewing court determine whether the trial court's determination of the prosecutor's neutrality with respect to race was objectively unreasonable and has been rebutted by clear and convincing evidence to the contrary. At this stage, however, we only ask whether the district court's application of AEDPA deference, as stated in §§ 2254(d)(2) and (e)(1), to petitioner's *Batson* claim was debatable amongst jurists of reason.

C

Applying these rules to Miller-El's application, we have no difficulty concluding that a COA should have issued. We conclude, on our review of the record at this stage, that the district court did not give full consideration to the substantial evidence petitioner put forth in support of the prima facie case. Instead, it accepted without question the state court's evaluation of the demeanor of the prosecutors and jurors in petitioner's trial. The Court of Appeals evaluated Miller-El's application for a COA in the same way. In ruling that petitioner's claim lacked sufficient merit to justify appellate proceedings, the Court of Appeals recited the requirements for granting a writ under § 2254, which it interpreted as requiring petitioner to prove that the state court decision was objectively unreasonable by clear and convincing evidence.

This was too demanding a standard on more than one level. It was incorrect for the Court of Appeals, when looking at the merits, to merge the independent requirements of §§ 2254(d)(2) and (e)(1). AEDPA does not require petitioner to prove that a decision is objectively unreasonable by clear and convincing evidence. The clear and convincing evidence standard is found in § 2254(e)(1), but that subsection pertains only to state-court determinations of factual issues, rather than decisions. Subsection (d)(2) contains the unreasonable requirement and applies to the granting of habeas relief rather than to the granting of a COA.

The Court of Appeals, moreover, was incorrect for an even more fundamental reason. Before the issuance of a COA, the Court of Appeals had no jurisdiction to resolve the merits of petitioner's constitutional claims. True, to the extent that the merits of this case will turn on the agreement or disagreement with a state-court factual finding, the clear and convincing evidence and objective unreasonableness standards will apply. At the COA stage, however, a court need not make a definitive inquiry into this matter. As we have said, a COA determination is a separate proceeding, one distinct from the underlying merits. The Court of Appeals should have inquired whether a "substantial showing of the denial of a constitutional right" had been proved. Deciding the substance of an appeal in what should only be a threshold inquiry undermines the concept of a COA. The question is the debatability of the underlying constitutional claim, not the resolution of that debate.

In this case, the statistical evidence alone raises some debate as to whether the prosecution acted with a race-based reason when striking prospective jurors. The prosecutors used their peremptory strikes to exclude 91% of the eligible African-American venire members, and only one served on petitioner's jury. In total, 10 of the prosecutors' 14 peremptory strikes were used against African-Americans. Happenstance is unlikely to produce this disparity.

The case for debatability is not weakened when we examine the State's defense of the disparate treatment. The Court of Appeals held that "the presumption of correctness is especially strong, where, as here, the trial court and state habeas court are one and the same." As we have noted, the trial court held its *Batson* hearing two years after the *voir dire*. While the prosecutors had proffered contemporaneous race-neutral justifications for many of their peremptory strikes, the state trial court had no occasion to judge the credibility of these explanations at that time because our equal protection jurisprudence then, dictated by *Swain*, did not require it. As a result, the evidence presented to the trial court at the *Batson* hearing was subject to the usual risks of imprecision and distortion from the passage of time.

In this case, three of the State's proffered race-neutral rationales for striking African-American jurors pertained just as well to some white jurors who were not challenged and who did serve on the jury. The prosecutors explained that their peremptory challenges against six African-American potential jurors were based on ambivalence about the death penalty; hesitancy to vote to execute defendants capable of being rehabilitated; and the jurors' own family history of criminality. In rebuttal of the prosecution's explanation, petitioner identified two empaneled white jurors who expressed ambivalence about the death penalty in a manner similar to their African-American counterparts who were the subject of prosecutorial peremptory challenges. One indicated that capital punishment was not appropriate for a first offense, and another stated that it would be "difficult" to impose a death sentence. Similarly, two white jurors expressed hesitation in sentencing to death a defendant who might be rehabilitated; and four white jurors had family members with criminal histories. As a consequence, even though the prosecution's reasons for striking African-American members of the venire appear race neutral, the application of these rationales to the venire might have been selective and based on racial considerations. Whether a comparative juror analysis would demonstrate the prosecutors' rationales to have been pretexts for discrimination is an unnecessary determination at this stage, but the evidence does make debatable the district court's conclusion that no purposeful discrimination occurred.

We question the Court of Appeals' and state trial court's dismissive and strained interpretation of petitioner's evidence of disparate questioning. Petitioner argues that the prosecutors' sole purpose in using disparate questioning was to elicit responses from the African-American venire members that reflected an opposition to the death penalty or an unwillingness to impose a minimum sentence, either of which justified for-cause challenges by the prosecution under the then applicable state law. This is more than a remote possibility. Disparate questioning did occur. Petitioner submits that disparate questioning created the appearance of divergent opinions even though the venire members' views on the relevant subject might have been the same. It follows that, if the use of disparate questioning is determined by race at the outset, it is likely a justification for a strike based on the resulting divergent views would be pretextual. In this context the differences in the questions posed by the prosecutors are some evidence of purposeful discrimination.

As a preface to questions about views the prospective jurors held on the death penalty, the prosecution in some instances gave an explicit account of the execution process. Of those prospective jurors who were asked their views on capital punishment, the preface was used for 53% of the African-Americans questioned on the issue but for just 6% of white persons. The State explains the disparity by asserting that a disproportionate number of African-American venire members expressed doubts as to the death penalty on their juror questionnaires. This cannot be accepted without further inquiry, however, for the State's own evidence is inconsistent with that explanation. By the State's calculations, 10 African-American and 10 white prospective jurors expressed some hesitation about the death penalty on their questionnaires; however, of that group, 7 out of 10 African-Americans and only 2 out of 10 whites were given the explicit description.

There is an even greater disparity along racial lines when we consider disparate questioning concerning minimum punishments. Ninety-four percent of whites were informed of the statutory minimum sentence, compared to only twelve and a half percent of African-Americans. No explanation is proffered for the statistical disparity. Indeed, while petitioner's appeal was pending before the Texas Court of Criminal Appeals, that court found a *Batson* violation where this precise line of disparate questioning on mandatory minimums was employed by one of the same prosecutors who tried the instant case. It follows, in our view, that a fair interpretation of the record on this threshold examination in the COA analysis is that the prosecutors designed their questions to elicit responses that would justify the removal of African-Americans from the venire. *Batson* ("Circumstantial evidence of invidious intent may include proof of disproportionate impact.... We have observed that under some circumstances proof of discriminatory impact 'may for all practical purposes demonstrate unconstitutionality because in various circumstances the discrimination is very difficult to explain on nonracial grounds'").

We agree with petitioner that the prosecution's decision to seek a jury shuffle when a predominate number of African-Americans were seated in the front of the panel, along with its decision to delay a formal objection to the defense's shuffle until after the new racial composition was revealed, raise a suspicion that the State sought to exclude African-Americans from the jury. Our concerns are amplified by the fact that the state court also had before it, and apparently ignored, testimony demonstrating that the Dallas County District Attorney's Office had, by its own admission, used this process to manipulate the racial composition of the jury in the past. Even though the practice of jury shuffling might not be denominated as a *Batson* claim because it does not involve a peremptory challenge, the use of the practice here tends to erode the credibility of the prosecution's assertion that race was not a motivating factor in the jury selection.

Finally, in our threshold examination, we accord some weight to petitioner's historical evidence of racial discrimination by the District Attorney's Office. Evidence presented at the *Swain* hearing indicates that African-Americans almost categorically were excluded from jury service. *Batson* ("Proof of systematic exclusion from the venire raises an inference of purposeful discrimination because the 'result bespeaks discrimination.'"). Only the Federal Magistrate Judge addressed the import of this evidence in the context of a *Batson* claim; and he found it both unexplained and disturbing. Irrespective of whether the evidence could prove sufficient to support a charge of systematic exclusion of African-Americans, it reveals that the culture of the District Attorney's Office in the past was suffused with bias against African-Americans in jury selection. This evidence, of course, is relevant to the extent it casts doubt on the legitimacy of the motives underlying the State's actions in petitioner's case. Even if we presume at this stage that the prosecutors in Miller-El's case were not part of this culture of discrimination, the evidence suggests they were likely not ignorant of it. Both prosecutors joined the District Attorney's Office when assistant district attorneys received formal training in excluding minorities from juries. The supposition that race was a factor could be reinforced by the fact that the prosecutors marked the race of each prospective juror on their juror cards.

In resolving the equal protection claim against petitioner, the state courts made no mention of either the jury shuffle or the historical record of purposeful discrimination. We adhere to the proposition that a state court need not make detailed findings addressing all the evidence before it. This failure, however, does not diminish its significance. Our concerns here are heightened by the fact that, when presented with this evidence, the state trial court somehow reasoned that there was not even the inference of discrimination to support a prima facie case. This was clear error, and the State declines to defend this particular ruling. "If these general assertions were accepted as rebutting a defendant's prima facie case, the Equal Protection Clause 'would be but a vain and illusory requirement.'" *Batson,* 476 U.S. at 98 (quoting *Norris,* 294 U.S. at 598).

To secure habeas relief, petitioner must demonstrate that a state court's finding of the absence of purposeful discrimination was incorrect by clear and convincing evidence, 28 U.S.C. § 2254(e)(1), and that the corresponding factual determination was "objectively unreasonable" in light of the record before the court. The State represents to us that petitioner will not be able to satisfy his burden. That may or may not be the case. It is not, however, the question before us. The COA inquiry asks only if the district court's decision was debatable. Our threshold examination convinces us that it was.

The judgment of the Fifth Circuit is reversed, and the case is remanded for further proceedings consistent with this opinion.

It is so ordered.

JUSTICE SCALIA, concurring.

I join the Court's opinion, but write separately for two reasons: First, to explain why I believe the Court's willingness to consider the Antiterrorism and Effective Death Penalty Act of 1996's (AEDPA) limits on habeas relief in deciding whether to issue a certificate of appealability (COA) is in accord with the text of 28 U.S.C. § 2253(c). Second, to discuss some of the evidence on the State's side of the case—which, though inadequate (as the Court holds) to make the absence of a claimed violation of *Batson v. Kentucky*, undebatable, still makes this, in my view, a very close case.

I

* * *

Section 2253(c)(2) * * * provides that "[a] certificate of appealability *may issue ... only if* the applicant has made a substantial showing of the denial of a constitutional right." (Emphasis added). A "substantial showing" *does not entitle* an applicant to a COA; it is a necessary and not a sufficient condition. Nothing in the text of § 2253(c)(2) prohibits a circuit justice or judge from imposing additional requirements, and one such additional requirement has been approved by this Court. *See Slack v. McDaniel,* 529 U.S. 473, 484 (2000) (holding that a habeas petitioner seeking to appeal a district court's denial of habeas relief on procedural grounds must not only make a substantial showing of the denial of a constitutional right but *also* must demonstrate that jurists of reason would find it debatable whether the district court was correct in its procedural ruling).

The Court today imposes another additional requirement: a circuit justice or judge must deny a COA, even when the habeas petitioner has made a substantial showing that his constitutional rights were violated, if all reasonable jurists would conclude that a substantive provision of the federal habeas statute bars relief. To give an example, suppose a state prisoner presents a constitutional claim that reasonable jurists might find debatable, but is unable to find any "clearly established" Supreme Court precedent in support of that claim (which was previously rejected on the merits in state-court proceedings). Under the Court's view, a COA must be denied, *even if* the habeas petitioner satisfies the "substantial showing of the denial of a constitutional right" requirement of § 2253(c)(2), because all reasonable jurists would agree that habeas relief is impossible to obtain under § 2254(d). This approach is consonant with *Slack*, in accord with the COA's purpose of preventing meritless habeas appeals, and compatible with the text of § 2253(c), which does not make the "substantial showing of the denial of a constitutional right" a sufficient condition for a COA.

II

In applying the Court's COA standard to petitioner's case, we must ask whether petitioner has made a substantial showing of a *Batson* violation and also whether reasonable jurists could debate petitioner's ability to obtain habeas relief in light of AEDPA. The facts surrounding petitioner's *Batson* claims, when viewed in light of § 2254(e)(1)'s requirement that state-court factual determinations can be overcome only by clear and convincing evidence to the contrary, reveal this to be a close, rather than a clear, case for the granting of a COA.

Petitioner maintains that the following six African-American jurors were victims of racially motivated peremptory strikes: Edwin Rand, Wayman Kennedy, Roderick Bozeman, Billy Jean Fields, Joe Warren, and Carrol Boggess. As to each of them, the State proffered race-neutral explanations for its peremptory challenge. Five were challenged primarily because of their views on imposing the death penalty (Rand, Kennedy, Bozeman, Warren, and Boggess), and one (Fields) was challenged because (among other reasons) his brother had been convicted of drug offenses and served time in prison. By asserting race-neutral reasons for the challenges, the State satisfied step two of *Batson*. *See Purkett v. Elem*, 514 U.S. 765, 767–68 (1995). Unless petitioner can make a substantial showing that (*i.e.*, a showing that reasonable jurists could debate whether) the State fraudulently recited these explanations as pretext for race discrimination, he has not satisfied the requirement of § 2253(c)(2). Moreover, because the state court entered a finding of fact that the prosecution's purported reasons for exercising its peremptory challenges were not pretextual, a COA should not issue unless that finding can reasonably be thought to be contradicted by clear and convincing evidence. *See* § 2254(e)(1) ("[A] determination of a factual issue made by a State court shall be presumed to be correct. The applicant shall have the burden of rebutting the presumption of correctness by clear and convincing evidence").

The weakness in petitioner's *Batson* claims stems from his difficulty in identifying any unchallenged white venireman similarly situated to the six aforementioned African-American veniremen. Although petitioner claims that two white veniremen, Sandra Hearn and Marie Mazza, expressed views about the death penalty as ambivalent as those expressed by Rand, Kennedy, Bozeman, Warren, and Boggess, the *voir dire* transcripts do not clearly bear that out. Although Hearn initially stated that she thought the death penalty was inappropriate for first-time offenders, she also said, "I do not see any reason why I couldn't sit on a jury when you're imposing a death penalty." She further stated that someone who was an extreme child abuser deserved the death penalty, whether or not it was a first-time offense. Hearn also made pro-prosecution statements about her distaste for criminal defendants' use of psychiatric testimony to establish incompetency. As for Mazza, her stated views on the death penalty were as follows: "It's kind of hard determining somebody's life, whether they live or die, but I feel that is something that is accepted in our courts now and it is something that—a decision that I think I could make one way or the other."

Compare those statements with the sentiments expressed by the challenged African-American veniremen. Kennedy supported the death penalty only in cases of mass murder. "Normally I wouldn't say on just the average murder case—I would say no, not the death sentence." Bozeman supported the death penalty only "if there's no possible way to rehabilitate a person ... I would say somebody mentally disturbed or something like that or say a Manson type or something like that." When asked by the prosecutors whether repeated criminal violent conduct would indicate that a person was beyond rehabilitation, Bozeman replied, "No, not really." Warren refused to give any clear answer regarding his views on the death penalty despite numerous questions from the prosecutors. ("Well, there again, it goes back to the situation, you know, sometimes"). When asked whether the death penalty accomplishes anything, Warren answered, "Yes and no. Sometimes I think it does and sometimes I think it don't [*sic*]. Sometimes you have mixed feelings about things like that." When asked, "What do you think it accomplishes when you feel it does?," Warren replied, "I don't know." Boggess referred to the death penalty as "murder" and said, "whether or not I could actually go through with murder—with killing another person or taking another person's life, I just don't know. I'd have trouble with that." Rand is a closer case. His most ambivalent statement was "Can I do this? You know, right now I say I can, but tomorrow I might not." Later on Rand did say that he could impose the death penalty as a juror. But Hearn and Mazza (the white jurors who were seated) also said that they could sit on a jury that imposed the death penalty. At most, petitioner has shown that one of these African-American veniremen (Rand) may have been no more ambivalent about the death penalty than white jurors Hearn and Mazza. That perhaps would have been enough to permit the state trial court, deciding the issue *de novo* after observing the demeanor of the prosecutors and the disputed jurors, to find a *Batson* violation. But in a federal habeas case, where a state court has previously entered factfindings that the six African-American jurors were not challenged because of their race, petitioner must provide "clear and convincing evidence" that the state court erred, and, when requesting a COA, must demonstrate that jurists of reason could debate whether this standard was satisfied.

Fields, the sixth African-American venireman who petitioner claims was challenged because of his race, supported capital punishment. However, his brother had several drug convictions and had served time in prison. Warren and Boggess, two of the African-American veniremen previously discussed, also had relatives with criminal convictions—Warren's brother had been convicted of fraud in relation to food stamps, and Boggess had testified as a defense witness at her nephew's trial for theft and reported in her questionnaire that some of her cousins had problems with the law. Of the four white veniremen who petitioner claims also had relatives with criminal histories and therefore "should have been struck" by the prosecution—three (Noad Vickery, Cheryl Davis, and Chatta Nix) were actually so pro-prosecution that *they were struck by the petitioner*. The fourth, Joan Weiner, had a son who had shoplifted at the age of 10. That is hardly comparable to Fields's situation, and Weiner was a strong state's juror for other reasons: She had relatives who worked in law enforcement, and her support for the death penalty was clear and unequivocal.

For the above reasons, my conclusion that there is room for debate as to the merits of petitioner's *Batson* claim is far removed from a judgment that the State's explanations for its peremptory strikes were implausible.

With these observations, I join the Court's opinion.

JUSTICE THOMAS, dissenting.

Unpersuaded by petitioner's claims, the state trial court found that "there was no purposeful discrimination by the prosecution in the use of ... peremptory strikes." This finding established that petitioner had failed to carry his burden at step three of the inquiry set out in *Batson v. Kentucky*. Title 28 U.S.C. § 2254(e)(1) requires that a federal habeas court "presume" the state court's findings of fact "to be correct" unless petitioner can rebut the presumption "by clear and convincing evidence." The majority decides, without explanation, to ignore § 2254(e)(1)'s explicit command. I cannot. Because petitioner has not shown, by clear and convincing evidence, that any peremptory strikes of black veniremen were exercised because of race, he does not merit a certificate of appealability (COA). I respectfully dissent.

* * *

II

B

As noted, petitioner argues the prosecution struck six blacks—Rand, Kennedy, Bozeman, Fields, Warren, and Boggess—who were similarly situated to unstruck whites. I see no need to repeat JUSTICE SCALIA's dissection of petitioner's tales of white veniremen as ambivalent about the death penalty as Kennedy, Bozeman, Warren, and Boggess. However, the majority's cursory remark that "three of the State's proffered race-neutral rationales for striking [black] jurors pertained *just as well to some white jurors who were not challenged and who did serve on the jury*," (emphasis added), is flatly incorrect and deserves some discussion.

* * *

C

* * *

2

* * *

Quite simply, petitioner's arguments rest on circumstantial evidence and speculation that does not hold up to a thorough review of the record. Far from rebutting § 2254(e)(1)'s presumption, petitioner has perhaps not even demonstrated that reasonable jurists could debate whether he has provided the requisite evidence of purposeful discrimination—but that is the majority's inquiry, not mine. Because petitioner has not demonstrated by clear and convincing evidence that even one of the peremptory strikes at issue was the result of racial discrimination, I would affirm the denial of a COA.

Notes

1. *Subsequent case history*

On remand, the Fifth Circuit again found that prosecutors had not intentionally excluded African-Americans from Miller-El's capital jury. *Miller-El v. Cockrell*, 537 U.S. 322 (2003). The Supreme Court granted certiorari a second time and held that the state court wrongly concluded that the prosecution's strike of two of the black jurors was not racially motivated. *See Miller-El v. Dretke*, 545 U.S. 231 (2005).

After spending more than twenty years on death row, Thomas Miller-El pleaded guilty to capital murder and aggravated robbery on March 19, 2008, and received a life sentence for the murder and twenty years for the robbery. *See* Jennifer Emily, *Now off Texas Death Row, Inmate Talks of Jail, Not Crime*, The Dallas Morning News, Mar. 21, 2008.

2. *Statistics and race*

In *Miller-El*, the Court found that "the statistical evidence alone raises some debate as to whether the prosecution acted with a race-based reason when striking prospective jurors" and that "[h]appenstance is unlikely to produce this disparity." Why did the statistics in *Miller-El* affect the Court's ultimate decision, whereas the statistics in *McCleskey* did not?

3. Hernandez *and* Purkett

In reaching its decision in *Miller-El*, the Court referenced its prior decisions in *Hernandez v. New York*, 500 U.S. 352 (1991), and *Purkett v. Elem*, 514 U.S. 765 (1995) (*per curiam*).

Hernandez involved a state trial in New York where the prosecutor used four peremptory challenges to exclude Latino jurors. Although Hernandez eventually dropped his *Batson* claim for two of the four Latino jurors (because they had been convicted of crimes), he maintained his claim for the other two jurors. The prosecutor explained that he struck the jurors because they looked away from him and hesitated when he asked them whether they would be willing to accept the translator's rendition of witness testimony. The trial court and the state courts reviewing his direct appeal found that the prosecutor had offered a race-neutral basis for his peremptory challenges. The Court affirmed, noting the importance of deference to the trial judge's evaluation of the prosecutor's state of mind based on demeanor and credibility where the inferences drawn by the trial court find some support in the record. At the same time, however, the Court emphasized that "a policy of striking all who speak a given language, without regard to the particular circumstances of the trial or the individual responses of the jurors, may be found by the trial judge to be a pretext for racial discrimination." 500 U.S. at 371–72.

In *Purkett v. Elem*, Jimmy Elem filed a habeas petition in which he asserted that the prosecutor in his state trial in Missouri had improperly used a peremptory challenge to strike a potential black male juror. The race-neutral reason the prosecutor gave for excusing that juror was his "shoulder-length, curly, unkempt hair ... mustache and goatee type beard." 514 U.S. at 766. Although the trial judge, the state appellate courts, and the federal district court in which Elem filed his federal habeas petition all found that the proffered race-neutral reason was constitutionally acceptable, the Eighth Circuit Court of Appeals found that the prosecutor's reason for striking the juror was pretextual and that the state trial court had "'clearly erred' in finding that striking [the juror] had not been intentional discrimination." 514 U.S. at 767. The Court reversed, stating that a "legitimate reason" is "not a reason that makes sense, but a reason that does not deny equal protection." 514 U.S. at 769. The Court went on to note the following:

> In habeas proceedings in federal courts, the factual findings of state courts are presumed to be correct, and may be set aside, absent procedural error, only if they are "not fairly supported by the record." 28 U.S.C. § 2254(d)(8). Here the Court of Appeals did not conclude or even attempt to conclude that the state court's finding of no racial motive was not fairly supported by the record. For its whole focus was upon the *reasonableness* of the asserted nonracial motive (which it thought required by step two [of Batson]) rather than the *genuineness* of the motive. It gave no proper basis for overturning the state court's finding of no racial motive, a finding which turned primarily on an assessment of credibility.

514 U.S. at 769.

Given the backgrounds of both *Hernandez* and *Elem*, in which the Court deferred to the trial courts' factual findings regarding prosecutor credibility, what was it about Miller-El's case that enabled the Court to "have no difficulty concluding that a COA should have issued"? Similarly, what led the *Miller-El* Court to criticize the federal district court for "not giv[ing] full consideration to the substantial evidence petitioner put forth in support of the prima facie case" and "[i]nstead, ... [accepting] without question the state court's evaluation of the demeanor of the prosecutors and jurors in petitioner's trial"?

4. *A close case?*

Although concurring in the judgment, Justice Scalia stated that "some of the evidence on the State's side of the case—which, though inadequate (as the Court holds) to make the absence of a claimed violation of *Batson v. Kentucky*, 476 U.S. 79 (1986), undebatable, still makes this, in my view, a very close case." Based on the additional facts provided by Justice Scalia, what is your assessment of whether *Miller-El* was a "close case"?

5. *Was* Miller-El *a rare exception to* Hernandez's *highly deferential standard?*

In *Snyder v. Louisana*, 552 U.S. 472 (2008), a capital murder case, the Court relied significantly on *Miller-El* in holding that the trial court had committed clear error in making a factual determination that the prosecutor did not have discriminatory intent in striking a black juror. At Snyder's trial, the prosecutor used peremptory challenges on all of the black jurors remaining after for cause challenges—five of a pool of thirty-six prospective jurors. The prosecutor offered two race-neutral reasons in response to defense counsel's *Batson* objection to the challenge to one of the jurors: first, the juror looked very nervous; and second, the juror was going to miss student-teaching obligations. After the judge's law clerk called the dean of the juror's school and informed the court and the jurors what the dean had said—that his jury service would not be a problem—the juror did not express any further concern about serving on the jury and the prosecutor did not question him further about the matter. The trial judge gave no explanation for overruling the *Batson* objection as to this juror.

In reaching its decision, the Court analyzed the competing inferences and the evidentiary support for each reason the prosecutor had given. The Court agreed with the Louisiana Supreme Court that "deference is particularly appropriate where a trial judge has made a finding that an attorney credibly relied on demeanor in exercising a strike." *Id.* at 1209. At the same time, the Court noted that the trial judge had made no specific finding on the record about the juror's demeanor, so the Court could not conclude that the judge had considered the demeanor-based explanation in overruling the *Batson* challenge based on the juror's nervousness. As for the non-demeanor based reason (that the juror could not miss student teaching), the Court found that the record did not support this explanation even under a highly deferential standard of review.[4] The decision in *Snyder* was the first reversal by the Supreme Court of a state court factual finding due to the implausibility of the prosecutor's explanation for the strikes, where there was no prior history or pattern of discriminatory practices in the prosecutor's office (as there had been in *Miller-El*).[5] *Snyder*, however, was a direct appeal, without the statutory presumption of correctness of state court factual determinations that applies in habeas proceedings.[6]

In *Thaler v. Haynes*, 130 S.Ct. 1171 (2010), a *per curiam* decision, the Court addressed a demeanor-based *Batson* challenge in a habeas context. Defense counsel argued that a trial judge who had not personally observed a juror's demeanor could not, as a matter of law, fairly rule on a *Batson* challenge. The Court of Appeals overruled the district court's denial of Haynes' petition for habeas relief, under the view that *Batson*'s and *Snyder*'s "factual inquiry" requirement meant that a court (trial or appellate) could not rely on a paper record to adjudicate a demeanor-based *Batson* objection. Concluding that the strike violated *Batson* and that Haynes was entitled to a new trial, the Court of Appeals held that state courts are not entitled to "AEDPA deference" where the trial court is not able to verify the demeanor for which the jury was challenged. *Id.* at 1173.

The Supreme Court found that the Court of Appeals' reading of *Batson* and *Snyder* went too far: neither case held that a demeanor-based explanation for a peremptory challenge must be rejected unless the judge personally observed or recalled the relevant aspect of the prospective juror's demeanor. The Court noted, as it also did in *Snyder*, that even though the personal observations of the trial judge are of great importance, a trial judge may accept a prosecutor's demeanor-based explanation even if the judge cannot personally recall the prospective juror's demeanor. The Court also pointed out the unusual circumstances in *Haynes*: one judge had presided over the juror questioning and a different judge had presided over the exercise of peremptory challenges, so the judge who had ruled on the *Batson* objections had not seen the jurors' demeanor. Specifically not reaching a decision on the merits of the *Batson* challenge, the Court remanded to the Court of Appeals to apply the habeas statute's standard of review of a state court's determination of facts.

---

4. The Court found it unnecessary to decide whether once discriminatory intent is shown, the burden then shifts to the defending party to show that this was not determinative, a standard used in non-*Batson* contexts. The Court made clear that such a standard would be a minimum requirement.

5. John M. Castellano, *John M. Castellano on* Snyder v. Louisiana, 2008 Emerging Issues 2614 (2008).

6. Castellano, *supra* note 5.

Chapter 6

Limiting Access to Federal Review

In Chapter 12 ("Litigating Questions of Deference"), we will examine the relationship between one's opportunity for "full and fair" review of a claim in state court and the application of the deference prescribed by § 2254(d). This chapter, by contrast, considers whether there are situations in which it is permissible to deny federal habeas review altogether when the state process was "full and fair." In other words, the fundamental issue in this chapter is whether federal habeas review can be completely denied for a particular class of constitutional claims so long as the state review was full and fair.

Stone v. Powell presented the Court with a state prisoner's Fourth Amendment claim. After finding that the state court had provided a full and fair opportunity to litigate the Fourth Amendment claim, the Court held that the state prisoner may not be granted federal habeas corpus relief on the ground that evidence obtained in an unconstitutional search or seizure was introduced at his trial. *Kimmelman v. Morrison* shifts focus from a straight Fourth Amendment claim to a Sixth Amendment claim arising out of a Fourth Amendment claim. The Court decided whether a Sixth Amendment denial of effective representation claim, based on counsel's failure to file a timely motion to suppress evidence allegedly obtained in violation of the Fourth Amendment, may form the basis of a federal habeas claim. In the final case, *Withrow v. Williams*, the Court examined when federal courts can entertain a habeas petition based on a Fifth Amendment claim that a statement was obtained in violation of *Miranda*.

Stone v. Powell

428 U.S. 465 (1976)

JUSTICE POWELL delivered the opinion of the Court.

Respondents in these cases were convicted of criminal offenses in state courts, and their convictions were affirmed on appeal. The prosecution in each case relied upon evidence obtained by searches and seizures alleged by respondents to have been unlawful. Each respondent subsequently sought relief in a Federal District Court by filing a petition for a writ of federal habeas corpus under 28 U.S.C. § 2254. The question presented is whether a federal court should consider, in ruling on a petition for habeas corpus relief filed by a state prisoner, a claim that evidence obtained by an unconstitutional search or seizure was introduced at his trial, when he has previously been afforded an opportunity for full and fair litigation of his claim in the state courts. The issue is of considerable importance to the administration of criminal justice.

I

We summarize first the relevant facts and procedural history of these cases.

A

Respondent Lloyd Powell was convicted of murder in June 1968 after trial in a California state court. At about midnight on February 17, 1968, he and three companions entered the Bonanza Liquor Store in San Bernardino, Cal., where Powell became involved in an altercation with Gerald Parsons, the store manager, over the theft of a bottle of wine. In the scuffling that followed Powell shot and killed Parsons' wife. Ten hours later an officer of the Henderson, Nev., Police Department arrested Powell for violation of the Henderson vagrancy ordinance, and in the search incident to the arrest discovered a .38-caliber revolver with six expended cartridges in the cylinder.

Powell was extradited to California and convicted of second-degree murder in the Superior Court of San Bernardino County. Parsons and Powell's accomplices at the liquor store testified against him. A criminologist testified that the revolver found on Powell was the gun that killed Parsons' wife. The trial court rejected Powell's contention that testimony by the Henderson police officer as to the search and the discovery of the revolver should have been excluded because the vagrancy ordinance was unconstitutional. In October 1969, the conviction was affirmed by a California District Court of Appeal. Although the issue was duly presented, that court found it unnecessary to pass upon the legality of the arrest and search because it concluded that the error, if any, in admitting the testimony of the Henderson officer was harmless beyond a reasonable doubt under *Chapman v. California*, 386 U.S. 18 (1967). The Supreme Court of California denied Powell's petition for habeas corpus relief.

In August, 1971 Powell filed an amended petition for a writ of federal habeas corpus under 28 U.S.C. § 2254 in the United States District Court for the Northern District of California, contending that the testimony concerning the .38-caliber revolver should have been excluded as the fruit of an illegal search. He argued that his arrest had been unlawful because the Henderson vagrancy ordinance was unconstitutionally vague, and that the arresting officer lacked probable cause to believe that he was violating it. The District Court concluded that the arresting officer had probable cause and held that even if the vagrancy ordinance was unconstitutional, the deterrent purpose of the exclusionary rule does not require that it be applied to bar admission of the fruits of a search incident to an otherwise valid arrest. In the alternative, that court agreed with the California District Court of Appeal that the admission of the evidence concerning Powell's arrest, if error, was harmless beyond a reasonable doubt.

In December 1974, the Court of Appeals for the Ninth Circuit reversed. The court concluded that the vagrancy ordinance was unconstitutionally vague, that Powell's arrest was therefore illegal, and that although exclusion of the evidence would serve no deterrent purpose with regard to police officers who were enforcing statutes in good faith, exclusion would serve the public interest by deterring legislators from enacting unconstitutional statutes. After an independent review of the evidence the court concluded that the admission of the evidence was not harmless error since it supported the testimony of Parsons and Powell's accomplices.

B

Respondent David Rice was convicted of murder in April 1971 after trial in a Nebraska state court. At 2:05 a.m. on August 17, 1970, Omaha police received a telephone call that a woman had been heard screaming at 2867 Ohio Street. As one of the officers sent to that address examined a suitcase lying in the doorway, it exploded, killing him instantly. By August 22 the investigation of the murder centered on Duane Peak, a 15-year-old member of the National Committee to Combat Fascism (NCCF), and that afternoon a warrant was issued for Peak's arrest. The investigation also focused on other known members of the NCCF, including Rice, some of whom were believed to be planning to kill Peak before he could incriminate them. In their search for Peak, the police went to Rice's home at 10:30 that night and found lights and a television on, but there was no response to their repeated knocking. While some officers remained to watch the premises, a warrant was obtained to search for explosives and illegal weapons believed to be in Rice's possession. Peak was not in the house, but upon entering the police discovered, in plain view, dynamite, blasting caps, and other materials useful in the construction of explosive devices. Peak subsequently was arrested, and on August 27, Rice voluntarily surrendered. The clothes Rice was wearing at that time were subjected to chemical analysis, disclosing dynamite particles.

Rice was tried for first-degree murder in the District Court of Douglas County. At trial Peak admitted planting the suitcase and making the telephone call, and implicated Rice in the bombing plot. As corroborative evidence the State introduced items seized during the search, as well as the results of the chemical analysis of Rice's clothing. The court denied Rice's motion to suppress this evidence. On appeal the Supreme Court of Nebraska affirmed the conviction, holding that the search of Rice's home had been pursuant to a valid search warrant.

In September 1972 Rice filed a petition for a writ of habeas corpus in the United States District Court for Nebraska. Rice's sole contention was that his incarceration was unlawful because the evidence underlying his conviction had been discovered as the result of an illegal search of his home. The District Court concluded that the search warrant was invalid, as the supporting affidavit was defective under *Spinelli v. United States*, 393 U.S. 410 (1969), and *Aguilar v. Texas*, 378 U.S. 108 (1964). The court also rejected the State's contention that even if the warrant was invalid the search was justified because of the valid arrest warrant for Peak and because of the exigent circumstances.... The court reasoned that the arrest warrant did not justify the entry as the police lacked probable cause to believe Peak was in the house, and further concluded that the circumstances were not sufficiently exigent to justify an immediate warrantless search. The Court of Appeals for the Eighth Circuit affirmed, substantially for the reasons stated by the District Court.

Petitioners Stone and Wolff, the wardens of the respective state prisons where Powell and Rice are incarcerated, petitioned for review of these decisions, raising questions concerning the scope of federal habeas corpus and the role of the exclusionary rule upon collateral review of cases involving Fourth Amendment claims. We granted their petitions for certiorari. We now reverse.

II

The authority of federal courts to issue the writ of habeas corpus *ad subjiciendum* was included in the first grant of federal-court jurisdiction, made by the Judiciary Act of 1789, with the limitation that the writ extend only to prisoners held in custody by the United States. The original statutory authorization did not define the substantive reach of the writ. It merely stated that the courts of the United States "shall have power to issue writs of ... Habeas corpus...." The courts defined the scope of the writ in accordance with the common law and limited it to an inquiry as to the jurisdiction of the sentencing tribunal. *See, e.g., Ex parte Watkins*, 3 Pet. 193, 7 L. Ed. 650 (1830).

In 1867 the writ was extended to state prisoners. Under the 1867 Act federal courts were authorized to give relief in "all cases where any person may be restrained of his or her liberty in violation of the constitution, or of any treaty or law of the United States...." But the limitation of federal habeas corpus jurisdiction to consideration of the jurisdiction of the sentencing court persisted. And, although the concept of "jurisdiction" was subjected to considerable strain as the substantive scope of the writ was expanded, this expansion was limited to only a few classes of cases until *Frank v. Mangum*, 237 U.S. 309, in 1915. * * *

In the landmark decision in *Brown v. Allen*, the scope of the writ was expanded still further. In that case and its companion case, *Daniels v. Allen*, prisoners applied for federal habeas corpus relief claiming that the trial courts had erred in failing to quash their indictments due to alleged discrimination in the selection of grand jurors and in ruling certain confessions admissible. In *Brown*, the highest court of the State had rejected these claims on direct appeal, and this Court had denied certiorari. Despite the apparent adequacy of the state corrective process, the Court reviewed the denial of the writ of habeas corpus and held that Brown was entitled to a full reconsideration of these constitutional claims, including, if appropriate, a hearing in the Federal District Court. In *Daniels*, however, the State Supreme Court on direct review had refused to consider the appeal because the papers were filed out of time. This Court held that since the state-court judgment rested on a reasonable application of the State's legitimate procedural rules, a ground that would have barred direct review of his federal claims by this Court, the District Court lacked authority to grant habeas corpus relief. 344 U.S. 443, 458, 486.

This final barrier to broad collateral re-examination of state criminal convictions in federal habeas corpus proceedings was removed in *Fay v. Noia*. * * * This Court affirmed the grant of the writ, narrowly restricting the circumstances in which a federal court may refuse to consider the merits of federal constitutional claims.

During the period in which the substantive scope of the writ was expanded, the Court did not consider whether exceptions to full review might exist with respect to particular categories of constitutional claims. Prior to the Court's decision in *Kaufman v. United States*, 394 U.S. 217 (1969), however, a substantial majority of the Federal Courts of Appeals had concluded that collateral review of search-and-seizure claims was inappropriate on motions filed by federal prisoners under 28 U.S.C. § 2255, the modern postconviction procedure available to federal prisoners in lieu of habeas corpus. The primary rationale advanced in support of those decisions was that Fourth Amendment violations are different in kind from denials of Fifth or Sixth Amendment rights in that claims of illegal search and seizure do not "impugn the integrity of the fact-finding process or challenge evidence as inherently unreliable; rather, the exclusion of illegally seized evidence is simply a prophylactic device intended generally to deter Fourth Amendment violations by law enforcement officers." 394 U.S., at 224.

Kaufman rejected this rationale and held that search-and-seizure claims are cognizable in § 2255 proceedings. The Court noted that "the federal habeas remedy extends to state prisoners alleging that unconstitutionally obtained evidence was admitted against them at trial," and concluded, as a matter of statutory construction, that there was no basis for restricting "access by federal prisoners with illegal search-and-seizure claims to federal collateral remedies, while placing no similar restriction on access by state prisoners." Although in recent years the view has been expressed that the Court should re-examine the substantive scope of federal habeas jurisdiction and limit collateral review of search-and-seizure claims "solely to the question of whether the petitioner was provided a fair opportunity to raise and have adjudicated the question in state courts," *Schneckloth v. Bustamonte*, 412 U.S. 218, 250 (1973) (POWELL, J., concurring), the Court, without discussion or consideration of the issue, has continued to accept jurisdiction in cases raising such claims.

The discussion in *Kaufman* of the scope of federal habeas corpus rests on the view that the effectuation of the Fourth Amendment, as applied to the States through the Fourteenth Amendment, requires the granting of habeas corpus relief when a prisoner has been convicted in state court on the basis of evidence obtained in an illegal search or seizure since those Amendments were held in *Mapp v. Ohio*, 367 U.S. 643 (1961), to require exclusion of such evidence at trial and reversal of conviction upon direct review.

Until these cases we have not had occasion fully to consider the validity of this view. Upon examination, we conclude, in light of the nature and purpose of the Fourth Amendment exclusionary rule, that this view is unjustified. We hold, therefore, that where the State has provided an opportunity for full and fair litigation of a Fourth Amendment claim, the Constitution does not require that a state prisoner be granted federal habeas corpus relief on the ground that evidence obtained in an unconstitutional search or seizure was introduced at his trial.

III

The Fourth Amendment assures the "right of the people to be secure in their persons, houses, papers, and effects, against unreasonable searches and seizures." The Amendment was primarily a reaction to the evils associated with the use of the general warrant in England and the writs of assistance in the Colonies and was intended to protect the "sanctity of a man's home and the privacies of life," *Boyd v. United States*, 116 U.S. 616, 630 (1886), from searches under unchecked general authority.

The exclusionary rule was a judicially created means of effectuating the rights secured by the Fourth Amendment. Prior to the Court's decisions in *Weeks v. United States*, 232 U.S. 383 (1914), and *Gouled v. United States*, 255 U.S. 298 (1921), there existed no barrier to the introduction in criminal trials of evidence obtained in violation of the Amendment. *See Adams v. New York*, 192 U.S. 585 (1904). In *Weeks* the Court held that the defendant could petition before trial for the return of property secured through an illegal search or seizure conducted by federal authorities. In *Gouled* the Court held broadly that such evidence could not be introduced in a federal prosecution. *See Warden v. Hayden*, 387 U.S. 294 (1967). Thirty-five years after *Weeks* the Court held in *Wolf v. Colorado*, 338 U.S. 25 (1949), that the right to be free from arbitrary intrusion by the police that is protected by the Fourth Amendment is "implicit in 'the concept of ordered liberty' and as such enforceable against the States through the [Fourteenth Amendment] Due Process Clause." The Court concluded, however, that the *Weeks* exclusionary rule would not be imposed upon the States as "an essential ingredient of [that] right." The full force of *Wolf* was eroded in subsequent decisions, and a little more than a decade later the exclusionary rule was held applicable to the States in *Mapp v. Ohio*, 367 U.S. 643 (1961).

Decisions prior to *Mapp* advanced two principal reasons for application of the rule in federal trials. The Court in *Elkins*, for example, in the context of its special supervisory role over the lower federal courts, referred to the "imperative of judicial integrity," suggesting that exclusion of illegally seized evidence prevents contamination of the judicial process. 364 U.S. [206,] 222 (1960). But even in that context a more pragmatic ground was emphasized:

> The rule is calculated to prevent, not to repair. Its purpose is to deter—to compel respect for the constitutional guaranty in the only effectively available way—by removing the incentive to disregard it.

The *Mapp* majority justified the application of the rule to the States on several grounds, but relied principally upon the belief that exclusion would deter future unlawful police conduct.

Although our decisions often have alluded to the "imperative of judicial integrity," *e.g.*, *United States v. Peltier*, 422 U.S. 531, 536–39 (1975), they demonstrate the limited role of this justification in the determination whether to apply the rule in a particular context. Logically extended this justification would require that courts exclude unconstitutionally seized evidence despite lack of objection by the defendant, or even over his assent. *Cf. Henry v. Mississippi*, 379 U.S. 443 (1965). It also would require abandonment of the standing limitations on who may object to the introduction of unconstitutionally seized evidence, *Alderman v. United States*, 394 U.S. 165 (1969), and retreat from the proposition that judicial proceedings need not abate when the defendant's person is unconstitutionally seized, *Gerstein v. Pugh*, 420 U.S. 103, 119 (1975). Similarly, the interest in promoting judicial integrity does not prevent the use of illegally seized evidence in grand jury proceedings. *United States v. Calandra*, 414 U.S. 338 (1974). Nor does it require that the trial court exclude such evidence from use for impeachment of a defendant, even though its introduction is certain to result in conviction in some cases. *Walder v. United States*, 347 U.S. 62 (1954). The teaching of these cases is clear. While courts, of course, must ever be concerned with preserving the integrity of the judicial process, this concern has limited force as a justification for the exclusion of highly probative evidence. The force of this justification becomes minimal where federal habeas corpus relief is sought by a prisoner who previously has been afforded the opportunity for full and fair consideration of his search-and-seizure claim at trial and on direct review.

The primary justification for the exclusionary rule then is the deterrence of police conduct that violates Fourth Amendment rights. Post-*Mapp* decisions have established that the rule is not a personal constitutional right. It is not calculated to redress the injury to the privacy of the victim of the search or seizure, for any "[r]eparation comes too late." *Linkletter v. Walker*, 381 U.S. 618, 637 (1965). Instead, "the rule is a judicially created remedy designed to safeguard Fourth Amendment rights generally through its deterrent effect...." *United States v. Calandra, supra*, 414 U.S. at 348.

* * *

IV

We turn now to the specific question presented by these cases. Respondents allege violations of Fourth Amendment rights guaranteed them through the Fourteenth Amendment. The question is whether state prisoners—who have been afforded the opportunity for full and fair consideration of their reliance upon the exclusionary rule with respect to seized evidence by the state courts at trial and on direct review—may invoke their claim again on federal habeas corpus review. The answer is to be found by weighing the utility of the exclusionary rule against the costs of extending it to collateral review of Fourth Amendment claims.

The costs of applying the exclusionary rule even at trial and on direct review are well known: the focus of the trial, and the attention of the participants therein, are diverted from the ultimate question of guilt or innocence that should be the central concern in a criminal proceeding. Moreover, the physical evidence sought to be excluded is typically reliable and often the most probative information bearing on the guilt or innocence of the defendant. As Mr. JUSTICE BLACK emphasized in his dissent in *Kaufman*:

> A claim of illegal search and seizure under the Fourth Amendment is crucially different from many other constitutional rights; ordinarily the evidence seized can in no way have been rendered untrustworthy by the means of its seizure and indeed often this evidence alone establishes beyond virtually any shadow of a doubt that the defendant is guilty.

Application of the rule thus deflects the truth-finding process and often frees the guilty. The disparity in particular cases between the error committed by the police officer and the windfall afforded a guilty defendant by application of the rule is contrary to the idea of proportionality that is essential to the concept of justice. Thus, although the rule is thought to deter unlawful police activity in part through the nurturing of respect for Fourth Amendment values, if applied indiscriminately it may well have the opposite effect of generating disrespect for the law and administration of justice. These long-recognized costs of the rule persist when a criminal conviction is sought to be overturned on collateral review on the ground that a search-and-seizure claim was erroneously rejected by two or more tiers of state courts.

Evidence obtained by police officers in violation of the Fourth Amendment is excluded at trial in the hope that the frequency of future violations will decrease. Despite the absence of supportive empirical evidence, we have assumed that the immediate effect of exclusion will be to discourage law enforcement officials from violating the Fourth Amendment by removing the incentive to disregard it. More importantly, over the long term, this demonstration that our society attaches serious consequences to violation of constitutional rights is thought to encourage those who formulate law enforcement policies, and the officers who implement them, to incorporate Fourth Amendment ideals into their value system.

We adhere to the view that these considerations support the implementation of the exclusionary rule at trial and its enforcement on direct appeal of state-court convictions. But the additional contribution, if any, of the consideration of search-and-seizure claims of state prisoners on collateral review is small in relation to the costs. * * *

In sum, we conclude that where the State has provided an opportunity for full and fair litigation of a Fourth Amendment claim, a state prisoner may not be granted federal habeas corpus relief on the ground that evidence obtained in an unconstitutional search or seizure was introduced at his trial. In this context the contribution of the exclusionary rule, if any, to the effectuation of the Fourth Amendment is minimal and the substantial societal costs of application of the rule persist with special force.

Accordingly, the judgments of the Courts of Appeals are

Reversed.

[A concurring opinion by Chief JUSTICE BURGER, a dissenting opinion by JUSTICE BRENNAN, in which JUSTICE MARSHALL joined, and a dissenting opinion by JUSTICE WHITE are omitted.]

Notes

1. *Subsequent case history*

David Rice began serving a life sentence in Nebraska on April 17, 1971, and is still incarcerated. Nebraska Department of Correctional Services, http://www.corrections.state.ne.us (search David Rice on "Inmate Locator"). No information is available about Lloyd Powell.

2. *The rationale behind the exclusionary rule*

After stating that "despite the broad deterrent purpose of the exclusionary rule, it has never been interpreted to proscribe the introduction of illegally seized evidence in all proceedings or against all persons," Justice Powell cited the following observation by Professor Tony Amsterdam:

> The rule is unsupportable as reparation or compensatory dispensation to the injured criminal; its sole rational justification is the experience of its indispensability in "exert[ing] general legal pressures to secure obedience to the Fourth Amendment on the part of ... law-enforcing officers." As it serves this function,

> the rule is a needed, but grud[g]ingly taken, medicament; no more should be swallowed than is needed to combat the disease. Granted that so many criminals must go free as will deter the constables from blundering, pursuance of this policy of liberation beyond the confines of necessity inflicts gratuitous harm on the public interest....

428 U.S. at 487 n.24, quoting *Search, Seizure, and Section 2255: A Comment*, 112 U. Pa. L. Rev. 378, 388–389 (1964) (footnotes omitted).

Do you agree with Professor Amsterdam that the exclusionary rule is "unsupportable as reparation or compensatory dispensation to the injured criminal"? If one is to assume that the exclusionary rule should be applied only to the extent necessary to exert legal pressure on law enforcement to obey the Fourth Amendment, where should that line be drawn?

3. *Dissenting opinion by Justice Brennan*

In his dissenting opinion, with whom Justice Marshall concurred, Justice Brennan made the following observation:

> The Court's opinion does not specify the particular basis on which it denies federal habeas jurisdiction over claims of Fourth Amendment violations brought by state prisoners. The Court insists that its holding is based on the Constitution, but in light of the explicit language of 28 U.S.C. § 2254 (significantly not even mentioned by the Court), I can only presume that the Court intends to be understood to hold either that respondents are not, as a matter of statutory construction, "in custody in violation of the Constitution or laws ... of the United States," or that "'considerations of comity and concern for the orderly administration of criminal justice'" are sufficient to allow this Court to rewrite jurisdictional statutes enacted by Congress. Neither ground of decision is tenable; the former is simply illogical, and the latter is an arrogation of power committed solely to the Congress.

On what basis does the Court ground its decision? If you agree with Justice Brennan that one of the only rationales for the Court's holding is "considerations of comity and concern for the orderly administration of criminal justice," do you believe such concerns justify the result the Court reached? Why or why not?

4. *Dissenting opinion by Justice White*

Justice White's dissent begins with the following paragraph:

> For many of the reasons stated by MR. JUSTICE BRENNAN, I cannot agree that the writ of habeas corpus should be any less available to those convicted of state crimes where they allege Fourth Amendment violations than where other constitutional issues are presented to the federal court. Under the amendments to the habeas corpus statute, which were adopted after *Fay v. Noia*, and represented an effort by Congress to lend a modicum of finality to state criminal judgments, I cannot distinguish between Fourth Amendment and other constitutional issues.

What distinction does the Court draw between Fourth Amendment violations and other constitutional issues? What is your assessment of that distinction?

5. *What is "full and fair"?*

If a state court applies the wrong legal standard in adjudicating a constitutional claim, can the adjudication be considered an "opportunity for full and fair litigation" such that no federal review is required? What if the state court's adjudication of the claim is procedurally fair but utterly and incomprehensibly *incorrect* as a matter of law, *i.e.*, what if the adjudication is substantially flawed as a substantive matter?

Kimmelman v. Morrison

477 U.S. 365 (1986)

JUSTICE BRENNAN delivered the opinion of the Court.

The question we address in this case is whether the restrictions on federal habeas review of Fourth Amendment claims announced in *Stone v. Powell* should be extended to Sixth Amendment claims of ineffective assistance of counsel where the principal allegation and manifestation of inadequate representation is counsel's failure to file a timely motion to suppress evidence allegedly obtained in violation of the Fourth Amendment.

I

Respondent, Neil Morrison, was convicted by the State of New Jersey of raping a 15-year-old girl. The case presented by the State at respondent's bench trial consisted of scientific evidence and of the testimony of the victim, her mother, and the police officers who handled the victim's complaint.

The victim testified that Morrison, who was her employer, had taken her to his apartment, where he forced her onto his bed and raped her. Upon returning home, the girl related the incident to her mother, who, after first summoning Morrison and asking for his account of events, phoned the police. The police came to the victim's home and transported her to the hospital, where she was examined and tested for indicia of a sexual assault.

The State also called as a witness Detective Dolores Most, one of the officers who investigated the rape complaint. Most testified that she accompanied the victim to Morrison's apartment building a few hours after the rape. Morrison was not at home, but another tenant in the building let them into respondent's one-room apartment. While there, Most stated, she seized a sheet from respondent's bed.

At this point in the testimony respondent's counsel objected to the introduction of the sheet and to any testimony concerning it on the ground that Most had seized it without a search warrant. New Jersey Court Rules, however, require that suppression motions be made within 30 days of indictment unless the time is enlarged by the trial court for good cause. Because the 30-day deadline had long since expired, the trial judge ruled that counsel's motion was late. Defense counsel explained to the court that he had not heard of the seizure until the day before, when trial began, and that his client could not have known of it because the police had not left a receipt for the sheet. The prosecutor responded that defense counsel, who had been on the case from the beginning, had never asked for *any* discovery. Had trial counsel done so, the prosecutor observed, police reports would have revealed the search and seizure. The prosecutor stated further that one month before trial he had sent defense counsel a copy of the laboratory report concerning the tests conducted on stains and hairs found on the sheets.

Asked repeatedly by the trial court why he had not conducted any discovery, respondent's attorney asserted that it was the State's obligation to inform him of its case against his client, even though he made no request for discovery. The judge rejected this assertion and stated: "I hate to say it, but I have to say it, that you were remiss. I think this evidence was there and available to you for examination and inquiry." Defense counsel then attempted to justify his omission on the ground that he had not expected to go to trial because he had been told that the victim did not wish to proceed. The judge rejected this justification also, reminding counsel that once an indictment is handed down, the decision to go through with the complaint no longer belongs to the victim, and that it requires a court order to dismiss an indictment. While the judge agreed that defense counsel had "[brought] about a very valid basis ... for suppression ... if the motion had been brought and timely made," he refused "to entertain a motion to suppress in the middle of the trial."

The State then called a number of expert witnesses who had conducted laboratory tests on the stains and hairs found on the sheet, on a stain found on the victim's underpants, and on blood and hair samples provided by the victim and respondent. This testimony established that the bedsheet had been stained with semen from a man with type O blood, that the stains on the victim's underwear similarly exhibited semen from a man with type O blood, that the defendant had type O blood, that vaginal tests performed on the girl at the hospital demonstrated the presence of sperm, and that hairs recovered from the sheet were morphologically similar to head hair of both Morrison and the victim. Defense counsel aggressively cross-examined all of the expert witnesses.

The defense called four friends and acquaintances of the defendant and the defendant himself in an attempt to establish a different version of the facts. The defense theory was that the girl and her mother fabricated the rape in order to punish respondent for being delinquent with the girl's wages. According to Morrison, the girl and her mother had not intended to go through with the prosecution, but ultimately they found it impossible to extricate themselves from their lies. Morrison admitted that he had taken the girl to his apartment, but denied having had intercourse with her. He claimed that his sexual activity with other women accounted for the stains on his sheet, and that a hair from the girl's head was on his sheet because she had seated herself on his bed. Defense counsel also implied that the girl's underwear and vaginal secretions tested positive for semen and sperm because she probably had recently engaged in relations with the father of her baby. Counsel did not, however, call the girl's boyfriend to testify or have him tested for blood type, an omission upon which the prosecution commented in closing argument.

The trial judge, in rendering his verdict, noted: "As in most cases nothing is cut and dry. There are discrepancies in the State's case, there are discrepancies in the defense as it's presented." After pointing out some of the more troublesome inconsistencies in the testimony of several of the witnesses, the judge declared his conclusion that the State had proved its case beyond a reasonable doubt.

After trial, respondent dismissed his attorney and retained new counsel for his appeal. On appeal, respondent alleged ineffective assistance of counsel and error in the trial court's refusal to entertain the suppression motion during trial. The appeals court announced summarily that it found no merit in either claim and affirmed respondent's conviction. The Supreme Court of New Jersey subsequently denied respondent's petition for discretionary review. Respondent then sought postconviction relief in the New Jersey Superior Court, from the same judge who had tried his case. There Morrison presented the identical issues he had raised on direct appeal. The court denied relief on the ground that it was bound by the appellate court's resolution of those issues against respondent.

Respondent then sought a writ of habeas corpus in Federal District Court, again raising claims of ineffective assistance of counsel and erroneous admission of illegally seized evidence. The District Court ruled that because respondent did not allege that the State had denied him an opportunity to litigate his Fourth Amendment claim fully and fairly, direct consideration of this claim on federal habeas review was barred by *Stone v. Powell*. The District Court did find respondent's ineffective-assistance claim meritorious.

[The Court then discusses the fact that although this case was decided before *Strickland v. Washington*, 466 U.S. 668 (1984), the precedent relied on matched the reasoning in *Strickland.*]

* * *

The District Court then determined that, measured by the harmless-beyond-a-reasonable-doubt standard prescribed by [*United States v.*] *Baynes*, respondent had been prejudiced by counsel's ineffectiveness and issued a conditional writ of habeas corpus ordering Morrison's release unless New Jersey should retry him.

Although the District Court did not address the relevance of *Stone*, *supra*, to respondent's Sixth Amendment ineffective-assistance-of-counsel claim, the Court of Appeals did. Relying on both the language of *Stone* and the different natures of Fourth and Sixth Amendment claims, the Court of Appeals concluded that *Stone* should not be extended to bar federal habeas consideration of Sixth Amendment claims based on counsel's alleged failure competently to litigate Fourth Amendment claims. Because *Strickland* had recently been decided by this Court, the Court of Appeals reviewed the District Court's determination of ineffective assistance under *Strickland*'s test. The Court of Appeals determined that respondent's trial counsel had been "grossly ineffective" but vacated and remanded for the District Court to consider whether, under the standards set forth in *Strickland*, *supra*, respondent had been prejudiced by his attorney's incompetence.

Petitioners, the Attorney General of New Jersey and the Superintendent of Rahway State Prison, petitioned for certiorari. We granted their petition and now affirm.

II

Petitioners urge that the Sixth Amendment veil be lifted from respondent's habeas petition to reveal what petitioners argue it really is—an attempt to litigate his defaulted Fourth Amendment claim. They argue that because respondent's claim is in fact, if not in form, a Fourth Amendment one, *Stone* directly controls here. Alternatively, petitioners maintain that even if Morrison's Sixth Amendment claim may legitimately be considered distinct from his defaulted Fourth Amendment claim, the rationale and purposes of *Stone* are fully applicable to ineffective-assistance claims where the principal allegation of inadequate representation is counsel's failure to file a timely motion to suppress evidence allegedly obtained in violation of the Fourth Amendment. *Stone*, they argue, will be emasculated unless we extend its bar against federal habeas review to this sort of Sixth Amendment claim. Finally, petitioners maintain that consideration of defaulted Fourth Amendment claims in Sixth Amendment federal collateral proceedings would violate principles of comity and federalism and would seriously interfere with the State's interest in the finality of its criminal convictions.

A

We do not share petitioners' perception of the identity between respondent's Fourth and Sixth Amendment claims. While defense counsel's failure to make a timely suppression motion is the primary manifestation of incompetence and source of prejudice advanced by respondent, the two claims are nonetheless distinct, both in nature and in the requisite elements of proof.

Although it is frequently invoked in criminal trials, the Fourth Amendment is not a trial right; the protection it affords against governmental intrusion into one's home and affairs pertains to all citizens. The gravamen of a Fourth Amendment claim is that the complainant's legitimate expectation of privacy has been violated by an illegal search or seizure. *See, e.g., Katz v. United States*, 389 U.S. 347 (1967). In order to prevail, the complainant need prove only that the search or seizure was illegal and that it violated his reasonable expectation of privacy in the item or place at issue. *See, e.g., Rawlings v. Kentucky*, 448 U.S. 98, 104 (1980).

The right to counsel is a fundamental right of criminal defendants; it assures the fairness, and thus the legitimacy, of our adversary process. *E.g., Gideon v. Wainwright*, 372 U.S. 335 (1963). The essence of an ineffective-assistance claim is that counsel's unprofessional errors so upset the adversarial balance between defense and prosecution that the trial was rendered unfair and the verdict rendered suspect. *See, e.g., Strickland v. Washington*, 466 U.S., at 686; *United States v. Cronic*, 466 U.S. 648 (1984). In order to prevail, the defendant must show both that counsel's representation fell below an objective standard of reasonableness, *Strickland*, and that there exists a reasonable probability that, but for counsel's unprofessional errors, the result of the proceeding would have been different. Where defense counsel's failure to litigate a Fourth Amendment claim competently is the principal allegation of ineffectiveness, the defendant must also prove that his Fourth Amendment claim is meritorious and that there is a reasonable probability that the verdict would have been different absent the excludable evidence in order to demonstrate actual prejudice. Thus, while respondent's defaulted Fourth Amendment claim is one element of proof of his Sixth Amendment claim, the two claims have separate identities and reflect different constitutional values.

B

We also disagree with petitioners' contention that the reasoning and purposes of *Stone* are fully applicable to a Sixth Amendment claim which is based principally on defense counsel's failure to litigate a Fourth Amendment claim competently.

At issue in *Stone* was the proper scope of federal collateral protection of criminal defendants' right to have evidence, seized in violation of the Fourth Amendment, excluded at trial in state court. In determining that federal courts should withhold habeas review where the State has provided an opportunity for full and fair litigation of a Fourth Amendment claim, the Court found it crucial that the remedy for Fourth Amendment violations provided by the exclusionary rule "is not a personal constitutional right." The Court expressed the understanding that the rule "is not calculated to redress the injury to the privacy of the victim of the search or seizure;" instead, the Court explained, the exclusionary rule is predominately a "'judicially created'" structural remedy "'designed to safeguard Fourth Amendment rights generally through its deterrent effect.'" (quoting *United States v. Calandra*, 414 U.S. 338, 348 (1974)).

The Court further noted that "[as] in the case of any remedial device, 'the application of the rule has been restricted to those areas where its remedial objectives are thought most efficaciously served'" and that the rule has not been extended to situations such as grand jury proceedings, and impeachment of a defendant who testifies broadly in his own behalf, where the rule's costs would outweigh its utility as a deterrent to police misconduct. Applying this "pragmatic analysis" to the question whether prisoners who have been afforded a full and fair opportunity in state court to invoke the exclusionary rule may raise their Fourth Amendment claims on federal habeas review, the Court determined that they may not. While accepting that the exclusionary rule's deterrent effect outweighs its costs when enforced at trial and on direct appeal, the Court found any "additional contribution ... of the consideration of search-and-seizure claims ... on collateral review" to be too small in relation to the costs to justify federal habeas review.

In *Stone* the Court also made clear that its "decision ... [was] *not* concerned with the scope of the habeas corpus statute as authority for litigating constitutional claims generally." Rather, the Court simply "reaffirm[ed] that the exclusionary rule is a judicially created remedy rather than a personal constitutional right ... and ... emphasiz[ed] the minimal utility of the rule" in the context of federal collateral proceedings.

In contrast to the habeas petitioner in *Stone*, who sought merely to avail himself of the exclusionary rule, Morrison seeks direct federal habeas protection of his personal right to effective assistance of counsel.

The right of an accused to counsel is beyond question a fundamental right. *See, e.g.*, *Gideon* ("The right of one charged with crime to counsel may not be deemed fundamental and essential to fair trials in some countries, but it is in ours"). Without counsel the right to a fair trial itself would be of little consequence, for it is through counsel that the accused secures his other rights. The constitutional guarantee of counsel, however, "cannot be satisfied by mere formal appointment." *Avery v. Alabama*, 308 U.S. 444 (1940). "An accused is entitled to be assisted by an attorney, whether retained or appointed, who plays the role necessary to ensure that the trial is fair." *Strickland*. In other words, the right to counsel is the right to effective assistance of counsel.

[The Court then includes the following footnote: As we held only last Term, the right to effective assistance of counsel is not confined to trial, but extends also to the first appeal as of right. *Evitts v. Lucey*, 469 U.S. 387 (1985)]

Because collateral review will frequently be the only means through which an accused can effectuate the right to counsel, restricting the litigation of some Sixth Amendment claims to trial and direct review would seriously interfere with an accused's right to effective representation. A layman will ordinarily be unable to recognize counsel's errors and to evaluate counsel's professional performance; consequently a criminal defendant will rarely know that he has not been represented competently until after trial or appeal, usually when he consults another lawyer about his case. Indeed, an accused will often not realize that he has a meritorious ineffectiveness claim until he begins collateral review proceedings, particularly if he retained trial counsel on direct appeal. Were we to extend *Stone* and hold that criminal defendants may not raise ineffective-assistance claims that are based primarily on incompetent handling of Fourth Amendment issues on federal habeas, we would deny most defendants whose trial attorneys performed incompetently in this regard the opportunity to vindicate their right to effective trial counsel. We would deny all defendants whose appellate counsel performed inadequately with respect to Fourth Amendment issues the opportunity to protect their right to effective appellate counsel. Thus, we cannot say, as the Court was able to say in *Stone*, that restriction of federal habeas review would not severely interfere with the protection of the constitutional right asserted by the habeas petitioner.

Furthermore, while the Court may be free, under its analysis in *Stone*, to refuse for reasons of prudence and comity to burden the State with the costs of the exclusionary rule in contexts where the Court believes the price of the rule to exceed its utility, the Constitution constrains our ability to allocate as we see fit the costs of ineffective assistance. The Sixth Amendment mandates that the State bear the risk of constitutionally deficient assistance of counsel.

We also reject the suggestion that criminal defendants should not be allowed to vindicate through federal habeas review their right to effective assistance of counsel where counsel's primary error is failure to make a timely request for the exclusion of illegally seized evidence—evidence which is "typically reliable and often the most probative information bearing on the guilt or innocence of the defendant." *Stone*. While we have recognized that the "'premise of our adversary system of criminal justice ... that partisan advocacy ... will best promote the ultimate objective that the guilty be convicted and the innocent go free,'" *Evitts*, underlies and gives meaning to the right to effective assistance, we have never intimated that the right to counsel is conditioned upon actual innocence. The constitutional rights of criminal defendants are granted to the innocent and the guilty alike. Consequently, we decline to hold either that the guarantee of effective assistance of counsel belongs solely to the innocent or that it attaches only to matters affecting the determination of actual guilt. Furthermore, petitioners do not suggest that an ineffective-assistance claim asserted on direct review would fail for want of actual prejudice whenever counsel's primary error is failure to make a meritorious objection to the admission of reliable evidence the exclusion of which might have affected the outcome of the proceeding. We decline to hold that the scope of the right to effective assistance of counsel is altered in this manner simply because the right is asserted on federal habeas review rather than on direct review.

C

Stone's restriction on federal habeas review, petitioners warn, will be stripped of all practical effect unless we extend it to Sixth Amendment claims based principally on defense counsel's incompetent handling of Fourth Amendment issues. Petitioners predict that every Fourth Amendment claim that fails or is defaulted in state court will be fully litigated in federal habeas proceedings in Sixth Amendment guise and that, as a result, many state-court judgments will be disturbed. They seem to believe that a prisoner need only allege ineffective assistance, and if he has an underlying, meritorious Fourth Amendment claim, the writ will issue and the State will be obligated to retry him without the challenged evidence. Because it ignores the rigorous standard which *Strickland* erected for ineffective-assistance claims, petitioners' forecast is simply incorrect.

In order to establish ineffective representation, the defendant must prove both incompetence and prejudice. There is a strong presumption that counsel's performance falls within the "wide range of professional assistance;" the defendant bears the burden of proving that counsel's representation was unreasonable under prevailing professional norms and that the challenged action was not sound strategy. The reasonableness of counsel's performance is to be evaluated from counsel's perspective at the time of the alleged error and in light of all the circumstances, and the standard of review is highly deferential. The defendant shows that he was prejudiced by his attorney's ineffectiveness by demonstrating that "there is a reasonable probability that, but for counsel's unprofessional errors, the result of the proceeding would have been different." *See Strickland* (Where a defendant challenges his conviction, he must show that there exists "a reasonable probability that, absent the errors, the factfinder would have had a reasonable doubt respecting guilt"). And, in determining the existence *vel non* of prejudice, the court "must consider the totality of the evidence before the judge or jury." *Id.*

As is obvious, *Strickland*'s standard, although by no means insurmountable, is highly demanding. More importantly, it differs significantly from the elements of proof applicable to a straightforward Fourth Amendment claim. Although a meritorious Fourth Amendment issue is necessary to the success of a Sixth Amendment claim like respondent's, a good Fourth Amendment claim alone will not earn a prisoner federal habeas relief. Only those habeas petitioners who can prove under *Strickland* that they have been denied a fair trial by the gross incompetence of their attorneys will be granted the writ and will be entitled to retrial without the challenged evidence.

D

In summary, we reject petitioners' argument that *Stone*'s restriction on federal habeas review of Fourth Amendment claims should be extended to Sixth Amendment ineffective-assistance-of-counsel claims which are founded primarily on incompetent representation with respect to a Fourth Amendment issue. Where a State obtains a criminal conviction in a trial in which the accused is deprived of the effective assistance of counsel, the "State ... unconstitutionally deprives the defendant of his liberty." *Cuyler v. Sullivan*, 446 U.S. 335, 343 (1980). The defendant is thus "in custody in violation of the Constitution," 28 U.S.C. § 2254(a), and federal courts have habeas jurisdiction over his claim. We hold that federal courts may grant habeas relief in appropriate cases, regardless of the nature of the underlying attorney error.

III

Petitioners also argue that respondent has not satisfied either the performance or the prejudice prong of the test for ineffective assistance of counsel set forth in *Strickland*. We address each component of that test in turn.

A

With respect to the performance component of the *Strickland* test, petitioners contend that Morrison has not overcome the strong presumption of attorney competence established by *Strickland*. While acknowledging that this Court has said that a single, serious error may support a claim of ineffective assistance of counsel, petitioners argue that the mere failure to file a timely suppression motion alone does not constitute a *per se* Sixth Amendment violation. They maintain that the record "amply reflects that trial counsel crafted a sound trial strategy" and that, "[v]iewed in its entirety, counsel's pretrial investigation, preparation and trial performance were professionally reasonable." While we agree with petitioners' view that the failure to file a suppression motion does not constitute *per se* ineffective assistance of counsel, we disagree with petitioners' assessment of counsel's performance.

* * *

The trial record in this case clearly reveals that Morrison's attorney failed to file a timely suppression motion, not due to strategic considerations, but because, until the first day of trial, he was unaware of the search and of the State's intention to introduce the bedsheet into evidence. Counsel was unapprised of the search and seizure because he had conducted no pretrial discovery. Counsel's failure to request discovery, again, was not based on "strategy," but on counsel's mistaken beliefs that the State was obliged to take the initiative and turn over all of its inculpatory evidence to the defense and that the victim's preferences would determine whether the State proceeded to trial after an indictment had been returned.

Viewing counsel's failure to conduct any discovery from his perspective at the time he decided to forgo that stage of pretrial preparation and applying a "heavy measure of deference" to his judgment, we find counsel's decision unreasonable, that is, contrary to prevailing professional norms. The justifications Morrison's attorney offered for his omission betray a startling ignorance of the law—or a weak attempt to shift blame for inadequate preparation. "[C]ounsel has a duty to make reasonable investigations or to make a reasonable decision that makes particular investigations unnecessary." *Strickland*. Respondent's lawyer neither investigated, nor made a reasonable decision not to investigate, the State's case through discovery. Such a complete lack of pretrial preparation puts at risk both the defendant's right to an "'ample opportunity to meet the case of the prosecution,'" (quoting *Adams*), and the reliability of the adversarial testing process.

* * *

* * * We therefore agree with the District Court and the Court of Appeals that the assistance rendered respondent by his trial counsel was constitutionally deficient.

B

1

Petitioners also argue that respondent suffered no prejudice from his attorney's failure to make a timely suppression motion and that the Third Circuit erred in remanding the case to the District Court for a determination of prejudice under *Strickland*'s standard. * * *

* * *

Because it cannot fairly be said that the "merits of the factual dispute," § 2254(d)(1), regarding the existence of prejudice were resolved in the bail hearing, we conclude that the statements of the judge regarding the relative importance of the sheet are not findings of fact subject to § 2254(d) deference.

2

Respondent also criticizes the Court of Appeals' decision to remand for redetermination of prejudice. He argues that the record is sufficiently complete to enable this Court to apply *Strickland*'s prejudice prong directly to the facts of his case and urges that we do so.

We decline respondent's invitation. While the existing record proved adequate for our application of *Strickland*'s competency standard, it is incomplete with respect to prejudice. No evidentiary hearing has ever been held on the merits of respondent's Fourth Amendment claim. Because the State has not conceded the illegality of the search and seizure, it is entitled to an opportunity to establish that Officer Most's search came within one of the exceptions we have recognized to the Fourth Amendment's prohibition against warrantless searches. Even if not, respondent may be unable to show that absent the evidence concerning the bedsheet there is a reasonable probability that the trial judge would have had a reasonable doubt as to his guilt. If respondent could not make this showing, a matter on which we express no view, there would of course be no need to hold an evidentiary hearing on his Fourth Amendment claim.

The judgment of the Court of Appeals is

Affirmed.

[A concurring opinion by JUSTICE POWELL, in which CHIEF JUSTICE BURGER and JUSTICE REHNQUIST joined, is omitted.]

Notes

1. *Subsequent case history*

On remand, the district court granted Neil Morrison a new trial. *Morrison v. Kimmelman*, 650 F. Supp. 801 (D. N.J. 1986).

2. *Allocating costs of Fourth Amendment and Sixth Amendment violations*

In reaching its decision, the Court states that while it "may be free, under its analysis in *Stone*, to refuse for reasons of prudence and comity to burden the State with the costs of the exclusionary rule" in certain contexts, "[t]he Sixth Amendment mandates that the State bear the risk of constitutionally deficient assistance of counsel." What is your opinion of this distinction?

3. *Personal right versus fundamental rights*

Underlying the Court's rationale is the assessment that the exclusionary rule in *Stone* is a structural remedy created to protect Fourth Amendment rights, while the right to effective assistance of counsel in *Kimmelman* is a fundamental personal right. Do you agree with this assessment?

4. *"Sandbagging" critical claims*

Anticipating possible concerns that an attorney might "sandbag" an issue in hopes of gaining more favorable review of the claim in federal habeas corpus proceedings, Justice Brennan makes the following observation:

> We have no reason to believe that defense attorneys will "sandbag"—that is, consciously default or poorly litigate their clients' Fourth Amendment claims in state court in the hope of gaining more favorable review of these claims in Sixth Amendment federal habeas proceedings. First, it is virtually inconceivable that an attorney would deliberately invite the judgment that his performance was constitutionally deficient in order to win federal collateral review for his client. Second, counsel's client has little, if anything, to gain and everything to lose through such a strategy. It should be remembered that only incompetently litigated and defaulted Fourth Amendment claims that could lead to a reversal of the defendant's conviction on Sixth Amendment grounds are potentially outcome-determinative claims. No reasonable lawyer would forgo competent litigation of meritorious, possibly decisive claims on the remote chance that his deliberate dereliction might ultimately result in federal habeas review.

477 U.S. at 382 n.7. Is Justice Brennan's rationale describing why attorneys would not "sandbag" a Fourth Amendment issue reasonable?

Withrow v. Williams

507 U.S. 680 (1993)

JUSTICE SOUTER delivered the opinion of the Court.

In *Stone v. Powell*, we held that when a State has given a full and fair chance to litigate a Fourth Amendment claim, federal habeas review is not available to a state prisoner alleging that his conviction rests on evidence obtained through an unconstitutional search or seizure. Today we hold that *Stone*'s restriction on the exercise of federal habeas jurisdiction does not extend to a state prisoner's claim that his conviction rests on statements obtained in violation of the safeguards mandated by *Miranda v. Arizona*, 384 U.S. 436 (1966).

I

Police officers in Romulus, Michigan, learned that respondent, Robert Allen Williams, Jr., might have information about a double murder committed on April 6, 1985. On April 10, two officers called at Williams's house and asked him to the police station for questioning. Williams agreed to go. The officers searched Williams, but did not handcuff him, and they all drove to the station in an unmarked car. One officer, Sergeant David Early, later testified that Williams was not under arrest at this time, although a contemporaneous police report indicates that the officers arrested Williams at his residence.

At the station, the officers questioned Williams about his knowledge of the crime. Although he first denied any involvement, he soon began to implicate himself, and the officers continued their questioning, assuring Williams that their only concern was the identity of the "shooter." After consulting each other, the officers decided not to advise

Williams of his rights under *Miranda v. Arizona, supra*. When Williams persisted in denying involvement, Sergeant Early reproved him:

> You know everything that went down. You just don't want to talk about it. What it's gonna amount to is you can talk about it now and give us the truth and we're gonna check it out and see if it fits or else we're simply gonna charge you and lock you up and you can just tell it to a defense attorney and let him try and prove differently.

The reproof apparently worked, for Williams then admitted he had furnished the murder weapon to the killer, who had called Williams after the crime and told him where he had discarded the weapon and other incriminating items. Williams maintained that he had not been present at the crime scene.

Only at this point, some 40 minutes after they began questioning him, did the officers advise Williams of his *Miranda* rights. Williams waived those rights and during subsequent questioning made several more inculpatory statements. Despite his prior denial, Williams admitted that he had driven the murderer to and from the scene of the crime, had witnessed the murders, and had helped the murderer dispose of incriminating evidence. The officers interrogated Williams again on April 11 and April 12, and, on April 12, the State formally charged him with murder.

Before trial, Williams moved to suppress his responses to the interrogations, and the trial court suppressed the statements of April 11 and April 12 as the products of improper delay in arraignment under Michigan law. The court declined to suppress the statements of April 10, however, ruling that the police had given Williams a timely warning of his *Miranda* rights. A bench trial led to Williams's conviction on two counts each of first-degree murder and possession of a fire-arm during the commission of a felony and resulted in two concurrent life sentences. The Court of Appeals of Michigan affirmed the trial court's ruling on the April 10 statements, and the Supreme Court of Michigan denied leave to appeal. We denied the ensuing petition for writ of certiorari.

Williams then began this action *pro se* by petitioning for a writ of habeas corpus in the District Court, alleging a violation of his *Miranda* rights as the principal ground for relief. The District Court granted relief, finding that the police had placed Williams in custody for *Miranda* purposes when Sergeant Early had threatened to "lock [him] up," and that the trial court should accordingly have excluded all statements Williams had made between that point and his receipt of the *Miranda* warnings. The court also concluded, though neither Williams nor petitioner had addressed the issue, that Williams's statements after receiving the *Miranda* warnings were involuntary under the Due Process Clause of the Fourteenth Amendment and thus likewise subject to suppression. The court found that the totality of circumstances, including repeated promises of lenient treatment if he told the truth, had overborne Williams's will.

The Court of Appeals affirmed, holding the District Court correct in determining the police had subjected Williams to custodial interrogation before giving him the requisite *Miranda* advice, and in finding the statements made after receiving the *Miranda* warnings involuntary. The Court of Appeals summarily rejected the argument that the rule in *Stone v. Powell* should apply to bar habeas review of Williams's *Miranda* claim. We granted certiorari to resolve the significant issue thus presented.

II

We have made it clear that *Stone*'s limitation on federal habeas relief was not jurisdictional in nature, but rested on prudential concerns counseling against the application of the Fourth Amendment exclusionary rule on collateral review. We simply concluded in *Stone* that the costs of applying the exclusionary rule on collateral review outweighed any potential advantage to be gained by applying it there.

We recognized that the exclusionary rule, held applicable to the States in *Mapp v. Ohio*, 367 U.S. 643 (1961), "is not a personal constitutional right"; it fails to redress "the injury to the privacy of the victim of the search or seizure" at issue, "for any 'reparation comes too late.'" *Stone.* The rule serves instead to deter future Fourth Amendment violations, and we reasoned that its application on collateral review would only marginally advance this interest in deterrence. On the other side of the ledger, the costs of applying the exclusionary rule on habeas were comparatively great. We reasoned that doing so would not only exclude reliable evidence and divert attention from the central question of guilt, but would also intrude upon the public interest in "'(i) the most effective utilization of limited judicial resources, (ii) the necessity of finality in criminal trials, (iii) the minimization of friction between our federal and state systems of justice, and (iv) the maintenance of the constitutional balance upon which the doctrine of federalism is founded.'" *Stone*, quoting *Schneckloth v. Bustamonte*, 412 U.S. 218, 259 (1973) (Powell, J., concurring).

Over the years, we have repeatedly declined to extend the rule in *Stone* beyond its original bounds. In *Jackson v. Virginia*, 443 U.S. 307 (1979), for example, we denied a request to apply *Stone* to bar habeas consideration of a Fourteenth Amendment due process claim of insufficient evidence to support a state conviction. We stressed that the issue was "central to the basic question of guilt or innocence," unlike a claim that a state court had received evidence in violation of the Fourth Amendment exclusionary rule, and we found that to review such a claim on habeas imposed no great burdens on the federal courts.

After a like analysis, in *Rose v. Mitchell*, 443 U.S. 545 (1979), we decided against extending *Stone* to foreclose habeas review of an equal protection claim of racial discrimination in selecting a state grand-jury foreman. A charge that state adjudication had violated the direct command of the Fourteenth Amendment implicated the integrity of the judicial process, we reasoned, and failed to raise the "federalism concerns" that had driven the Court in *Stone.* Since federal courts had granted relief to state prisoners upon proof of forbidden discrimination for nearly a century, we concluded, "confirmation that habeas corpus remains an appropriate vehicle by which federal courts are to exercise their Fourteenth Amendment responsibilities" would not likely raise tensions between the state and federal judicial systems.

In a third instance, in *Kimmelman v. Morrison*, we again declined to extend *Stone*, in that case to bar habeas review of certain claims of ineffective assistance of counsel under the Sixth Amendment. We explained that unlike the Fourth Amendment, which confers no "trial right," the Sixth confers a "fundamental right" on criminal defendants, one that "assures the fairness, and thus the legitimacy, of our adversary process." We observed that because a violation of the right would often go unremedied except on collateral review, "restricting the litigation of some Sixth Amendment claims to trial and direct review would seriously interfere with an accused's right to effective representation."

In this case, the argument for extending *Stone* again falls short. To understand why, a brief review of the derivation of the *Miranda* safeguards, and the purposes they were designed to serve, is in order.

The Self-Incrimination Clause of the Fifth Amendment guarantees that no person "shall be compelled in any criminal case to be a witness against himself." U.S. Const., Amdt. 5. In *Bram v. United States*, 168 U.S. 532 (1897), the Court held that the Clause barred the introduction in federal cases of involuntary confessions made in response to custodial interrogation. We did not recognize the Clause's applicability to state cases until 1964, however, *see Malloy v. Hogan*, 378 U.S. 1 (1964); and, over the course of 30 years, beginning with the decision in *Brown v. Mississippi*, 297 U.S. 278 (1936), we analyzed the admissibility of confessions in such cases as a question of due process under the Fourteenth Amendment. Under this approach, we examined the totality of circumstances to determine whether a confession had been "'made freely, voluntarily and without compulsion or inducement of any sort.'" *Haynes v. Washington*, 373 U.S. 503, 513 (1963). Indeed, we continue to employ the totality-of-circumstances approach when addressing a claim that the introduction of an involuntary confession has violated due process. *E.g.*, *Arizona v. Fulminante*, 499 U.S. 279 (1991); *Miller v. Fenton*, 474 U.S. 194, 109–10 (1985). In *Malloy*, we recognized that the Fourteenth Amendment incorporates the Fifth Amendment privilege against self-incrimination, and thereby opened *Bram*'s doctrinal avenue for the analysis of state cases. So it was that two years later we held in *Miranda* that the privilege extended to state custodial interrogations. In *Miranda*, we spoke of the privilege as guaranteeing a person under interrogation "the right 'to remain silent unless he chooses to speak in the unfettered exercise of his own will,'" (quoting *Malloy*, *supra*) and held that "without proper safeguards the process of in-custody interrogation ... contains inherently compelling pressures which work to undermine the individual's will to resist and to compel him to speak where he would not otherwise do so freely." To counter these pressures we prescribed, absent "other fully effective means," the now-familiar measures in aid of a defendant's Fifth Amendment privilege. * * * Unless the prosecution can demonstrate the warnings and waiver as threshold matters, we held, it may not overcome an objection to the use at trial of statements obtained from the person in any ensuing custodial interrogation.

Petitioner, supported by the United States as *amicus curiae*, argues that *Miranda*'s safeguards are not constitutional in character, but merely "prophylactic," and that in consequence habeas review should not extend to a claim that a state conviction rests on statements obtained in the absence of those safeguards. We accept petitioner's premise for purposes of this case, but not her conclusion.

The *Miranda* Court did of course caution that the Constitution requires no "particular solution for the inherent compulsions of the interrogation process," and left it open to a State to meet its burden by adopting "other procedures ... at least as effective in apprising accused persons" of their rights. The Court indeed acknowledged that, in barring introduction of a statement obtained without the required warnings, *Miranda* might exclude a confession that we would not condemn as "involuntary in traditional terms," and for this reason we have sometimes called the *Miranda* safeguards "prophylactic" in nature. Calling the *Miranda* safeguards "prophylactic," however, is a far cry from putting *Miranda* on all fours with *Mapp*, or from rendering *Miranda* subject to *Stone*.

As we explained in *Stone*, the *Mapp* rule "is not a personal constitutional right," but serves to deter future constitutional violations; although it mitigates the juridical consequences of invading the defendant's privacy, the exclusion of evidence at trial can do nothing to remedy the completed and wholly extrajudicial Fourth Amendment violation. Nor can the *Mapp* rule be thought to enhance the soundness of the criminal process by improving the reliability of evidence introduced at trial. Quite the contrary, as we explained in *Stone*, the evidence excluded under *Mapp* "is typically reliable and often the most probative information bearing on the guilt or innocence of the defendant."

Miranda differs from *Mapp* in both respects. "Prophylactic" though it may be, in protecting a defendant's Fifth Amendment privilege against self-incrimination, *Miranda* safeguards "a fundamental *trial* right." *United States v. Verdugo-Urquidez*, 494 U.S. 259 (1990).

The privilege embodies "principles of humanity and civil liberty, which had been secured in the mother country only after years of struggle," *Bram,* and reflects

> many of our fundamental values and most noble aspirations: ... our preference for an accusatorial rather than an inquisitorial system of criminal justice; our fear that self-incriminating statements will be elicited by inhumane treatment and abuses; our sense of fair play which dictates "a fair state-individual balance by requiring the government to leave the individual alone until good cause is shown for disturbing him and by requiring the government in its contest with the individual to shoulder the entire load;" our respect for the inviolability of the human personality and of the right of each individual "to a private enclave where he may lead a private life;" our distrust of self-deprecatory statements; and our realization that the privilege, while sometimes "a shelter to the guilty," is often "a protection to the innocent." *Murphy v. Waterfront Comm'n of New York Harbor*, 378 U.S. 52, 55 (1964).

Nor does the Fifth Amendment "trial right" protected by *Miranda* serve some value necessarily divorced from the correct ascertainment of guilt. "'[A] system of criminal law enforcement which comes to depend on the "confession" will, in the long run, be less reliable and more subject to abuses' than a system relying on independent investigation." *Michigan v. Tucker*, 417 U.S. 433, 448 n.23 (1974). By bracing against "the possibility of unreliable statements in every instance of in-custody interrogation," *Miranda* serves to guard against "the use of unreliable statements at trial." *Johnson v. New Jersey*, 384 U.S. 719 (1966).

Finally, and most importantly, eliminating review of *Miranda* claims would not significantly benefit the federal courts in their exercise of habeas jurisdiction, or advance the cause of federalism in any substantial way. As one *amicus* concedes, eliminating habeas review of *Miranda* issues would not prevent a state prisoner from simply converting his barred *Miranda* claim into a due process claim that his conviction rested on an involuntary confession. Indeed, although counsel could provide us with no empirical basis for projecting the consequence of adopting petitioner's position, it seems reasonable to suppose that virtually all *Miranda* claims would simply be recast in this way.

If that is so, the federal courts would certainly not have heard the last of *Miranda* on collateral review. Under the due process approach, as we have already seen, courts look to the totality of circumstances to determine whether a confession was voluntary. Those potential circumstances include not only the crucial element of police coercion, *Colorado v. Connelly*, 479 U.S. 157 (1986); the length of the interrogation, *Ashcraft v. Tennessee*, 322 U.S. 143 (1944); its location, *see Reck v. Pate*, 367 U.S. 433 (1961); its continuity, *Leyra v. Denno*, 347 U.S. 556 (1954); the defendant's maturity, *Haley v. Ohio*, 332 U.S. 596 (1948) (opinion of Douglas, J.); education, *Clewis v. Texas*, 386 U.S. 707 (1967); physical condition, *Greenwald v. Wisconsin*, 390 U.S. 519 (1968) (*per curiam*); and mental health, *Fikes v. Alabama*, 352 U.S. 191 (1957). They also include the failure of police to advise the defendant of his rights to remain silent and to have counsel present during custodial interrogation. *Haynes v. Washington*, 373 U.S. 503 (1963). We could lock the front door against *Miranda*, but not the back.

We thus fail to see how abdicating *Miranda*'s bright-line (or, at least, brighter-line) rules in favor of an exhaustive totality-of-circumstances approach on habeas would do much of anything to lighten the burdens placed on busy federal courts. We likewise fail to see how purporting to eliminate *Miranda* issues from federal habeas would go very far to relieve such tensions as *Miranda* may now raise between the two judicial systems. Relegation of habeas petitioners to straight involuntariness claims would not likely reduce the amount of litigation, and each such claim would in any event present a legal question requiring an "independent federal determination" on habeas. *Miller v. Fenton*, 474 U.S., at 112.

One might argue that tension results between the two judicial systems whenever a federal habeas court overturns a state conviction on finding that the state court let in a voluntary confession obtained by the police without the *Miranda* safeguards. And one would have to concede that this has occurred in the past, and doubtless will occur again. It is not reasonable, however, to expect such occurrences to be frequent enough to amount to a substantial cost of reviewing *Miranda* claims on habeas or to raise federal-state tensions to an appreciable degree. We must remember in this regard that *Miranda* came down some 27 years ago. In that time, law enforcement has grown in constitutional as well as technological sophistication, and there is little reason to believe that the police today are unable, or even generally unwilling, to satisfy *Miranda*'s requirements. And if, finally, one should question the need for federal collateral review of requirements that merit such respect, the answer simply is that the respect is sustained in no small part by the existence of such review. "It is the occasional abuse that the federal writ of habeas corpus stands ready to correct." *Jackson*, 443 U.S., at 322.

III

One final point should keep us only briefly. As he had done in his state appellate briefs, on habeas Williams raised only one claim going to the admissibility of his statements to the police: that the police had elicited those statements without satisfying the *Miranda* requirements. In her answer, the petitioner addressed only that claim. The District Court, nonetheless, without an evidentiary hearing or even argument, went beyond the habeas petition and found the statements Williams made after receiving the *Miranda* warnings to be involuntary under due process criteria. Before the Court of Appeals, petitioner objected to the District Court's due process enquiry on the ground that the habeas petition's reference to *Miranda* rights had given her insufficient notice to address a due process claim.

Williams effectively concedes that his habeas petition raised no involuntariness claim, but he argues that the matter was tried by the implied consent of the parties under Federal Rule of Civil Procedure 15(b), and that petitioner can demonstrate no prejudice from the District Court's action. The record, however, reveals neither thought, word, nor deed of petitioner that could be taken as any sort of consent to the determination of an independent due process claim, and petitioner was manifestly prejudiced by the District Court's failure to afford her an opportunity to present evidence bearing on that claim's resolution. The District Court should not have addressed the involuntariness question in these circumstances.

IV

The judgment of the Court of Appeals is affirmed in part and reversed in part, and the case is remanded for further proceedings consistent with this opinion.

It is so ordered.

[An opinion by JUSTICE O'CONNOR, concurring in part and dissenting in part, in which CHIEF JUSTICE REHNQUIST joined, is omitted. An opinion by JUSTICE SCALIA, concurring in part and dissenting in part, in which JUSTICE THOMAS joined, also is omitted.]

Notes

1. *Subsequent case history*

No information is available about the status of Robert Allen Williams after remand and retrial.

2. *Justice O'Connor's observations*

Justice O'Connor, concurring in part and dissenting in part, joined by Chief Justice Rehnquist, makes the following observation:

> Today the Court permits the federal courts to overturn on habeas the conviction of a double murderer, not on the basis of an inexorable constitutional or statutory command, but because it believes the result desirable from the standpoint of equity and judicial administration. Because the principles that inform our habeas jurisprudence—finality, federalism, and fairness—counsel decisively against the result the Court reaches, I respectfully dissent from this holding.
>
> * * *
>
> In our federal system, state courts have primary responsibility for enforcing constitutional rules in their own criminal trials. When a case comes before the federal courts on habeas rather than on direct review, the judicial role is "significantly different." Most important here, federal courts on direct review adjudicate every issue of federal law properly presented; in contrast, "federal courts have never had a similar obligation on habeas corpus." As the Court explains today, federal courts exercising their habeas powers may refuse to grant relief on certain claims because of "prudential concerns" such as equity and federalism. This follows not only from the express language of the habeas statute, which directs the federal courts to "dispose of [habeas petitions] as law and justice require," 28 U.S.C. § 2243, but from our precedents as well. In *Francis v. Henderson*, 425 U.S. 536 (1976), we stated that "[t]his Court has long recognized that in some circumstances considerations of comity and concerns for the orderly administration of criminal justice require a federal court to forgo the exercise of its habeas corpus power." *Id.*; *Fay v. Noia*, *supra*, at 438 ("[H]abeas corpus has traditionally been regarded as governed by equitable principles").

507 U.S. at 697, 698–99.

Do you agree that habeas review should be more limited than other review? In your opinion, does the gravity of the offense inform the judicial reaction to issues presented in the case? Should it have any affect?

3. *The dependability of state courts*

Justice O'Connor also states:

> As the Court emphasizes today, *Miranda*'s prophylactic rule is now 27 years old; the police and the state courts have indeed grown accustomed to it. But it is precisely because the rule is well accepted that there is little further benefit to enforcing it on habeas. We can depend on law enforcement officials to administer warnings in the first instance and the state courts to provide a remedy when law enforcement officers err. None of the Court's asserted justifications for enforcing *Miranda*'s prophylactic rule through habeas—neither reverence for the Fifth Amendment nor the concerns of reliability, efficiency, and federalism—counsel in favor of the Court's chosen course. Indeed, in my view they cut in precisely the opposite direction. The Court may reconsider its decision when presented with empirical data. But I see little reason for such a costly delay. Logic and experience are at our disposal now. And they amply demonstrate that applying *Miranda*'s prophylactic rule on habeas does not increase the amount of justice dispensed; it only increases the frequency with which the admittedly guilty go free. * * *

507 U.S. at 714.

Do you agree with Justice O'Connor that "[w]e can depend on ... the state courts to provide a remedy when law enforcement officers err"? Why or why not? What do you think of Justice O'Connor's position that logic and experience "demonstrate that applying *Miranda*'s prophylactic rule on habeas does not increase the amount of justice dispensed"?

4. *Extending Stone v. Powell*

Justice Scalia argues in his dissent that the rule in *Stone v. Powell* should extend to all claims on federal habeas review, that is, that a fully litigated constitutional motion in state court should not be cognizable on habeas. What are the justifications for such a rule? The dangers?

Chapter 7

Innocence

This chapter explores the degree to which a habeas petitioner's claim of innocence factors into the petitioner's ability to receive relief through a federal habeas petition. The materials also reflect the advent of DNA testing, which has led to the exoneration of more than 250 persons since 1989,[1] and the impact that this developing forensic evidence has on post-conviction litigation.

Herrera v. Collins involved a petitioner who based his federal habeas petition on newly discovered evidence of actual innocence. The Court held that claims of actual innocence based on newly discovered evidence are not in and of themselves grounds for federal habeas relief: in addition to an innocence claim (whether based on newly discovered evidence or not), a successful petition must also include an independent constitutional violation from the underlying criminal proceeding. In *Schlup v. Delo*, the petitioner joined his innocence claim with a constitutional claim, alleging that his counsel was ineffective and that the prosecution withheld exculpatory evidence. Although Schlup could not meet the "cause and prejudice" standard for his successive habeas petition, because Schlup used his innocence claim as a gateway to litigate his constitutional claim, the Court distinguished *Schlup* from *Herrera* and said a habeas court can consider procedurally defaulted constitutional claims if the petitioner shows that it is more likely than not that no reasonable juror would have found him guilty beyond a reasonable doubt. In *House v. Bell*, the petitioner asserted his innocence as a freestanding claim and as a gateway through which to raise procedurally barred constitutional claims. The new evidence he offered to prove actual innocence included exculpatory DNA evidence. The Court found his case is the "extraordinary case" permitting habeas review under *Schlup*, but declined to decide if there is a freestanding innocence claim because House did not meet the threshold implied in *Herrera*. In *District Attorney's Office for the Third District v. Osborne*, the Court considered the claims of a prisoner who brought a federal civil rights action to gain access to evidence to conduct post-conviction DNA testing. Osborne made a due process claim as well as asserting his actual innocence. The Court did not answer the question of whether a defendant can gain access to evidence through a civil rights action or whether his claims are cognizable only in habeas. Rejecting the lower court's application of a *Brady v. Maryland* due process framework for granting Osborne's claim, the Court instead found that Alaska's post-conviction statutes are adequate on their face for those who seek access to DNA evidence. The Court refused to "constitutionalize" the issue by recognizing a freestanding right to access DNA evidence and again left open the question of whether there is a constitutional right to be released upon proof of "actual innocence." At the same time, the Court recognized, for the first time, that a convicted defendant can have a state-created, constitutionally protected liberty interest in proving his actual innocence that survives his conviction. In *In re: Troy Anthony Davis*, the Court took the unusual step of

1. The stories of these exonerations and analyses of the factors leading to wrongful convictions can be found at www.innocenceproject.org.

exercising original habeas jurisdiction to remand Davis's case to the federal district court for an evidentiary hearing to allow Davis to produce new evidence of actual innocence.

Herrera v. Collins

506 U.S. 390 (1993)

CHIEF JUSTICE REHNQUIST delivered the opinion of the Court.

Petitioner Leonel Torres Herrera was convicted of capital murder and sentenced to death in January 1982. He unsuccessfully challenged the conviction on direct appeal and state collateral proceedings in the Texas state courts, and in a federal habeas petition. In February 1992—10 years after his conviction—he urged in a second federal habeas petition that he was "actually innocent" of the murder for which he was sentenced to death, and that the Eighth Amendment's prohibition against cruel and unusual punishment and the Fourteenth Amendment's guarantee of due process of law therefore forbid his execution. He supported this claim with affidavits tending to show that his now-dead brother, rather than he, had been the perpetrator of the crime. Petitioner urges us to hold that this showing of innocence entitles him to relief in this federal habeas proceeding. We hold that it does not.

Shortly before 11 p.m. on an evening in late September 1981, the body of Texas Department of Public Safety Officer David Rucker was found by a passer-by on a stretch of highway about six miles east of Los Fresnos, Texas, a few miles north of Brownsville in the Rio Grande Valley. Rucker's body was lying beside his patrol car. He had been shot in the head.

At about the same time, Los Fresnos Police Officer Enrique Carrisalez observed a speeding vehicle traveling west towards Los Fresnos, away from the place where Rucker's body had been found, along the same road. Carrisalez, who was accompanied in his patrol car by Enrique Hernandez, turned on his flashing red lights and pursued the speeding vehicle. After the car had stopped briefly at a red light, it signaled that it would pull over and did so. The patrol car pulled up behind it. Carrisalez took a flashlight and walked toward the car of the speeder. The driver opened his door and exchanged a few words with Carrisalez before firing at least one shot at Carrisalez' chest. The officer died nine days later.

Petitioner Herrera was arrested a few days after the shootings and charged with the capital murder of both Carrisalez and Rucker. He was tried and found guilty of the capital murder of Carrisalez in January 1982, and sentenced to death. In July 1982, petitioner pleaded guilty to the murder of Rucker.

At petitioner's trial for the murder of Carrisalez, Hernandez, who had witnessed Carrisalez' slaying from the officer's patrol car, identified petitioner as the person who had wielded the gun. A declaration by Officer Carrisalez to the same effect, made while he was in the hospital, was also admitted. Through a license plate check, it was shown that the speeding car involved in Carrisalez' murder was registered to petitioner's "live-in" girlfriend. Petitioner was known to drive this car, and he had a set of keys to the car in his pants pocket when he was arrested. Hernandez identified the car as the vehicle from which the murderer had emerged to fire the fatal shot. He also testified that there had been only one person in the car that night.

The evidence showed that Herrera's Social Security card had been found alongside Rucker's patrol car on the night he was killed. Splatters of blood on the car identified as the vehicle involved in the shootings, and on petitioner's blue jeans and wallet were identified as type A blood—the same type which Rucker had. (Herrera has type O blood.) Similar evidence with respect to strands of hair found in the car indicated that the hair was

Rucker's and not Herrera's. A handwritten letter was also found on the person of petitioner when he was arrested, which strongly implied that he had killed Rucker. * * *

* * *

Petitioner * * * returned to state court and filed a second habeas petition, raising, among other things, a claim of "actual innocence" based on newly discovered evidence. In support of this claim petitioner presented the affidavits of Hector Villarreal, an attorney who had represented petitioner's brother, Raul Herrera, Sr., and of Juan Franco Palacious, one of Raul, Senior's former cellmates. Both individuals claimed that Raul, Senior, who died in 1984, had told them that he—and not petitioner—had killed Officers Rucker and Carrisalez. * * * The State District Court denied this application, finding that "no evidence at trial remotely suggest[ed] that anyone other than [petitioner] committed the offense." * * * The Texas Court of Criminal Appeals affirmed, * * * and we denied certiorari. * * *

In February 1992, petitioner lodged the instant habeas petition—his second—in federal court, alleging, among other things, that he is innocent of the murders of Rucker and Carrisalez, and that his execution would thus violate the Eighth and Fourteenth Amendments. In addition to proffering the above affidavits, petitioner presented the affidavits of Raul Herrera, Jr., Raul Senior's son, and Jose Ybarra, Jr., a schoolmate of the Herrera brothers. Raul, Junior, averred that he had witnessed his father shoot Officers Rucker and Carrisalez and petitioner was not present. Raul, Junior, was nine years old at the time of the killings. Ybarra alleged that Raul, Senior, told him one summer night in 1983 that he had shot the two police officers. * * * Petitioner alleged that law enforcement officials were aware of this evidence, and had withheld it in violation of *Brady v. Maryland*, 373 U.S. 83 (1963).

The District Court dismissed most of petitioner's claims as an abuse of the writ. * * * However, "in order to ensure that Petitioner can assert his constitutional claims and out of a sense of fairness and due process," the District Court granted petitioner's request for a stay of execution so that he could present his claim of actual innocence, along with the Raul, Junior, and Ybarra affidavits, in state court. * * * Although it initially dismissed petitioner's *Brady* claim on the ground that petitioner had failed to present "any evidence of withholding exculpatory material by the prosecution," * * * the District Court also granted an evidentiary hearing on this claim after reconsideration. * * *

The Court of Appeals vacated the stay of execution. * * * It agreed with the District Court's initial conclusion that there was no evidentiary basis for petitioner's *Brady* claim, and found disingenuous petitioner's attempt to couch his claim of actual innocence in *Brady* terms. * * * Absent an accompanying constitutional violation, the Court of Appeals held that petitioner's claim of actual innocence was not cognizable because, under *Townsend v. Sain*, 372 U.S. 293 (1963), "the existence merely of newly discovered evidence relevant to the guilt of a state prisoner is not a ground for relief on federal habeas corpus." * * * We granted certiorari, * * * and the Texas Court of Criminal Appeals stayed petitioner's execution. We now affirm.

Petitioner asserts that the Eighth and Fourteenth Amendments to the United States Constitution prohibit the execution of a person who is innocent of the crime for which he was convicted. This proposition has an elemental appeal, as would the similar proposition that the Constitution prohibits the imprisonment of one who is innocent of the crime for which he was convicted. After all, the central purpose of any system of criminal justice is to convict the guilty and free the innocent. * * * But the evidence upon which petitioner's claim of innocence rests was not produced at his trial, but rather eight years later. In any system of criminal justice, "innocence" or "guilt" must be determined in some sort of a judicial proceeding. Petitioner's showing of innocence, and indeed his constitutional claim for relief based upon that showing, must be evaluated in the light of the previous proceedings in this case, which have stretched over a span of 10 years.

A person when first charged with a crime is entitled to a presumption of innocence, and may insist that his guilt be established beyond a reasonable doubt. * * * Other constitutional provisions also have the effect of ensuring against the risk of convicting an innocent person. * * * In capital cases, we have required additional protections because of the nature of the penalty at stake. * * * All of these constitutional safeguards, of course, make it more difficult for the State to rebut and finally overturn the presumption of innocence which attaches to every criminal defendant. But we have also observed that "[d]ue process does not require that every conceivable step be taken, at whatever cost, to eliminate the possibility of convicting an innocent person." * * * To conclude otherwise would all but paralyze our system for enforcement of the criminal law.

Once a defendant has been afforded a fair trial and convicted of the offense for which he was charged, the presumption of innocence disappears. * * * Here, it is not disputed that the State met its burden of proving at trial that petitioner was guilty of the capital murder of Officer Carrisalez beyond a reasonable doubt. Thus, in the eyes of the law, petitioner does not come before the Court as one who is "innocent," but, on the contrary, as one who has been convicted by due process of law of two brutal murders.

Based on affidavits here filed, petitioner claims that evidence never presented to the trial court proves him innocent notwithstanding the verdict reached at his trial. Such a claim is not cognizable in the state courts of Texas. For to obtain a new trial based on newly discovered evidence, a defendant must file a motion within 30 days after imposition or suspension of sentence. * * * The Texas courts have construed this 30-day time limit as jurisdictional. * * *

Claims of actual innocence based on newly discovered evidence have never been held to state a ground for federal habeas relief absent an independent constitutional violation occurring in the underlying state criminal proceeding. * * * This rule is grounded in the principle that federal habeas courts sit to ensure that individuals are not imprisoned in violation of the Constitution—not to correct errors of fact. * * *

* * *

Our decision in *Jackson v. Virginia*, 443 U.S. 307 (1979), comes as close to authorizing evidentiary review of a state-court conviction on federal habeas as any of our cases. There, we held that a federal habeas court may review a claim that the evidence adduced at a state trial was not sufficient to convict a criminal defendant beyond a reasonable doubt. But in so holding, we emphasized:

> [T]his inquiry does not require a court to "ask itself whether *it* believes that the evidence at the trial established guilt beyond a reasonable doubt." Instead, the relevant question is whether, after viewing the evidence in the light most favorable to the prosecution, *any* rational trier of fact could have found the essential elements of the crime beyond a reasonable doubt. This familiar standard gives full play to the responsibility of the trier of fact fairly to resolve conflicts in the testimony, to weigh the evidence, and to draw reasonable inferences from basic facts to ultimate facts. * * *

We specifically noted that "the standard announced ... does not permit a court to make its own subjective determination of guilt or innocence." * * *

The type of federal habeas review sought by petitioner here is different in critical respects than that authorized by *Jackson*. First, the *Jackson* inquiry is aimed at determining whether there has been an independent constitutional violation—*i.e.*, a conviction based on evidence that fails to meet the *Winship* standard. Thus, federal habeas courts act in their historic capacity—to assure that the habeas petitioner is not being held in violation of his or her federal constitutional rights. Second, the sufficiency of the evidence review authorized by *Jackson* is limited to "record evidence." * * * *Jackson* does not extend to nonrecord evidence, including newly discovered evidence. Finally, the *Jackson* inquiry does not focus on whether the trier of fact made the *correct* guilt or innocence determination, but rather whether it made a *rational* decision to convict or acquit.

Petitioner is understandably imprecise in describing the sort of federal relief to which a suitable showing of actual innocence would entitle him. In his brief he states that the federal habeas court should have "an important initial opportunity to hear the evidence and resolve the merits of Petitioner's claim." * * * Acceptance of this view would presumably require the habeas court to hear testimony from the witnesses who testified at trial as well as those who made the statements in the affidavits which petitioner has presented, and to determine anew whether or not petitioner is guilty of the murder of Officer Carrisalez.

* * *

This is not to say that our habeas jurisprudence casts a blind eye toward innocence. In a series of cases culminating with *Sawyer v. Whitley*, 505 U.S. 333 (1992), decided last Term, we have held that a petitioner otherwise subject to defenses of abusive or successive use of the writ may have his federal constitutional claim considered on the merits if he makes a proper showing of actual innocence. This rule, or fundamental miscarriage of justice exception, is grounded in the "equitable discretion" of habeas courts to see that federal constitutional errors do not result in the incarceration of innocent persons. * * * But this body of our habeas jurisprudence makes clear that a claim of "actual innocence" is not itself a constitutional claim, but instead a gateway through which a habeas petitioner must pass to have his otherwise barred constitutional claim considered on the merits.

Petitioner in this case is simply not entitled to habeas relief based on the reasoning of this line of cases. For he does not seek excusal of a procedural error so that he may bring an independent constitutional claim challenging his conviction or sentence, but rather argues that he is entitled to habeas relief because newly discovered evidence shows that his conviction is factually incorrect. The fundamental miscarriage of justice exception is available "only where the prisoner *supplements* his constitutional claim with a colorable showing of factual innocence." * * * We have never held that it extends to freestanding claims of actual innocence. Therefore, the exception is inapplicable here.

Petitioner asserts that this case is different because he has been sentenced to death. But we have "refused to hold that the fact that a death sentence has been imposed requires a different standard of review on federal habeas corpus." * * *

* * *

In light of the historical availability of new trials, our own amendments to Rule 33, and the contemporary practice in the States, we cannot say that Texas' refusal to entertain petitioner's newly discovered evidence eight years after his conviction transgresses a principle of fundamental fairness "rooted in the traditions and conscience of our people." * * * This is not to say, however, that petitioner is left without a forum to raise his actual innocence claim. For under Texas law, petitioner may file a request for executive clemency. * * * Clemency * * * is deeply rooted in our Anglo-American tradition of law, and is the historic remedy for preventing miscarriages of justice where judicial process has been exhausted. * * *

* * *

Executive clemency has provided the "fail safe" in our criminal justice system. * * * It is an unalterable fact that our judicial system, like the human beings who administer it, is fallible. But history is replete with examples of wrongfully convicted persons who have been pardoned in the wake of after-discovered evidence establishing their innocence. In his classic work, Professor Edwin Borchard compiled 65 cases in which it was later determined that individuals had been wrongfully convicted of crimes. Clemency provided the relief mechanism in 47 of these cases; the remaining cases ended in judgments of acquittals after new trials. * * *Recent authority confirms that over the past century clemency has been exercised frequently in capital cases in which demonstrations of "actual innocence" have been made. * * *

In Texas, the Governor has the power, upon the recommendation of a majority of the Board of Pardons and Paroles, to grant clemency. * * * The board's consideration is triggered upon request of the individual sentenced to death, his or her representative, or the Governor herself. In capital cases, a request may be made for a full pardon, * * * a commutation of death sentence to life imprisonment or appropriate maximum penalty, * * * or a reprieve of execution. * * * The Governor has the sole authority to grant one reprieve in any capital case not exceeding 30 days. * * *

The Texas clemency procedures contain specific guidelines for pardons on the ground of innocence. The board will entertain applications for a recommendation of full pardon because of innocence upon receipt of the following: "(1) a written unanimous recommendation of the current trial officials of the court of conviction; and/or (2) a certified order or judgment of a court having jurisdiction accompanied by certified copy of the findings of fact (if any); and (3) affidavits of witnesses upon which the finding of innocence is based." * * * In this case, petitioner has apparently sought a 30-day reprieve from the Governor, but has yet to apply for a pardon, or even a commutation, on the ground of innocence or otherwise. * * *

As the foregoing discussion illustrates, in state criminal proceedings the trial is the paramount event for determining the guilt or innocence of the defendant. Federal habeas review of state convictions has traditionally been limited to claims of constitutional violations occurring in the course of the underlying state criminal proceedings. Our federal habeas cases have treated claims of "actual innocence," not as an independent constitutional claim, but as a basis upon which a habeas petitioner may have an independent constitutional claim considered on the merits, even though his habeas petition would otherwise be regarded as successive or abusive. History shows that the traditional remedy for claims of innocence based on new evidence, discovered too late in the day to file a new trial motion, has been executive clemency.

We may assume, for the sake of argument in deciding this case, that in a capital case a truly persuasive demonstration of "actual innocence" made after trial would render the execution of a defendant unconstitutional, and warrant federal habeas relief if there were no state avenue open to process such a claim. But because of the very disruptive effect that entertaining claims of actual innocence would have on the need for finality in capital cases, and the enormous burden that having to retry cases based on often stale evidence would place on the States, the threshold showing for such an assumed right would necessarily be extraordinarily high. The showing made by petitioner in this case falls far short of any such threshold.

Petitioner's newly discovered evidence consists of affidavits. In the new trial context, motions based solely upon affidavits are disfavored because the affiants' statements are obtained without the benefit of cross-examination and an opportunity to make credibility determinations. ** Petitioner's affidavits are particularly suspect in this regard because, with the exception of Raul Herrera, Jr.'s affidavit, they consist of hearsay. Likewise, in reviewing petitioner's new evidence, we are mindful that defendants often abuse new trial motions "as a method of delaying enforcement of just sentences." * * * Although we are not presented with a new trial motion *per se*, we believe the likelihood of abuse is as great—or greater—here.

* * *

This is not to say that petitioner's affidavits are without probative value. Had this sort of testimony been offered at trial, it could have been weighed by the jury, along with the evidence offered by the State and petitioner, in deliberating upon its verdict. Since the statements in the affidavits contradict the evidence received at trial, the jury would have had to decide important issues of credibility. But coming 10 years after petitioner's trial, this showing of innocence falls far short of that which would have to be made in order to trigger the sort of constitutional claim which we have assumed, *arguendo*, to exist.

The judgment of the Court of Appeals is

Affirmed.

JUSTICE O'CONNOR, with whom JUSTICE KENNEDY joins, concurring.

I cannot disagree with the fundamental legal principle that executing the innocent is inconsistent with the Constitution. Regardless of the verbal formula employed—"contrary to contemporary standards of decency," * * *—the execution of a legally and factually innocent person would be a constitutionally intolerable event. Dispositive to this case, however, is an equally fundamental fact: Petitioner is not innocent, in any sense of the word.

As the Court explains, * * *petitioner is not innocent in the eyes of the law because, in our system of justice, "the trial is the paramount event for determining the guilt or innocence of the defendant." * * * In petitioner's case, that paramount event occurred 10 years ago. He was tried before a jury of his peers, with the full panoply of protections that our Constitution affords criminal defendants. At the conclusion of that trial, the jury found petitioner guilty beyond a reasonable doubt. Petitioner therefore does not appear before us as an innocent man on the verge of execution. He is instead a legally guilty one who, refusing to accept the jury's verdict, demands a hearing in which to have his culpability determined once again. * * *

Consequently, the issue before us is not whether a State can execute the innocent. It is, as the Court notes, whether a fairly convicted and therefore legally guilty person is constitutionally entitled to yet another judicial proceeding in which to adjudicate his guilt anew, 10 years after conviction, notwithstanding his failure to demonstrate that constitutional error infected his trial. * * * In most circumstances, that question would answer itself in the negative. Our society has a high degree of confidence in its criminal trials, in no small part because the Constitution offers unparalleled protections against convicting the innocent. * * * The question similarly would be answered in the negative today, except for the disturbing nature of the claim before us. Petitioner contends not only that the Constitution's protections "sometimes fail" * * * but that their failure in his case will result in his execution—even though he is factually innocent and has evidence to prove it.

* * *

Nonetheless, the proper disposition of this case is neither difficult nor troubling. No matter what the Court might say about claims of actual innocence today, petitioner could not obtain relief. The record overwhelmingly demonstrates that petitioner deliberately shot and killed Officers Rucker and Carrisalez the night of September 29, 1981; petitioner's new evidence is bereft of credibility. Indeed, despite its stinging criticism of the Court's decision, not even the dissent expresses a belief that petitioner might possibly be actually innocent. Nor could it: The record makes it abundantly clear that petitioner is not somehow the future victim of "simple murder" * * * but instead himself the established perpetrator of two brutal and tragic ones.

* * *

Ultimately, two things about this case are clear. First is what the Court does *not* hold. Nowhere does the Court state that the Constitution permits the execution of an actually innocent person. Instead, the Court assumes for the sake of argument that a truly persuasive demonstration of actual innocence would render any such execution unconstitutional and that federal habeas relief would be warranted if no state avenue were open to process the claim. Second is what petitioner has not demonstrated. Petitioner has failed to make a persuasive showing of actual innocence. Not one judge—no state court judge, not the District Court Judge, none of the three judges of the Court of Appeals, and none of the Justices of this Court—has expressed doubt about petitioner's guilt. Accordingly, the Court has no reason to pass on, and appropriately reserves, the question whether federal courts may entertain convincing claims of actual innocence. That difficult question remains open. If the Constitution's guarantees of fair procedure and the safeguards of clemency and pardon fulfill their historical mission, it may never require resolution at all.

JUSTICE SCALIA, with whom JUSTICE THOMAS joins, concurring.

We granted certiorari on the question whether it violates due process or constitutes cruel and unusual punishment for a State to execute a person who, having been convicted of murder after a full and fair trial, later alleges that newly discovered evidence shows him to be "actually innocent." I would have preferred to decide that question, particularly since, as the Court's discussion shows, it is perfectly clear what the answer is: There is no basis in text, tradition, or even in contemporary practice (if that were enough) for finding in the Constitution a right to demand judicial consideration of newly discovered evidence of innocence brought forward after conviction. In saying that such a right exists, the dissenters apply nothing but their personal opinions to invalidate the rules of more than two-thirds of the States, and a Federal Rule of Criminal Procedure for which this Court itself is responsible. If the system that has been in place for 200 years (and remains widely approved) "shock[s]" the dissenters' consciences, * * * perhaps they should doubt the calibration of their consciences, or, better still, the usefulness of "conscience shocking" as a legal test.

I nonetheless join the entirety of the Court's opinion, including the final portion, * * * because there is no legal error in deciding a case by assuming, *arguendo*, that an asserted constitutional right exists, and because I can understand, or at least am accustomed to, the reluctance of the present Court to admit publicly that Our Perfect Constitution * * * lets stand any injustice, much less the execution of an innocent man who has received, though to no avail, all the process that our society has traditionally deemed adequate. With any luck, we shall avoid ever having to face this embarrassing question again, since it is improbable that evidence of innocence as convincing as today's opinion requires would fail to produce an executive pardon.

* * *

JUSTICE WHITE, concurring in the judgment.

In voting to affirm, I assume that a persuasive showing of "actual innocence" made after trial, even though made after the expiration of the time provided by law for the presentation of newly discovered evidence, would render unconstitutional the execution of petitioner in this case. To be entitled to relief, however, petitioner would at the very least be required to show that based on proffered newly discovered evidence and the entire record before the jury that convicted him, "no rational trier of fact could [find] proof of guilt beyond a reasonable doubt." * * * For the reasons stated in the Court's opinion, petitioner's showing falls far short of satisfying even that standard, and I therefore concur in the judgment.

JUSTICE BLACKMUN, with whom JUSTICE STEVENS and JUSTICE SOUTER join with respect to Parts I–IV, dissenting.

Nothing could be more contrary to contemporary standards of decency * * * than to execute a person who is actually innocent.

I therefore must disagree with the long and general discussion that precedes the Court's disposition of this case. * * * That discussion, of course, is dictum because the Court assumes, "for the sake of argument in deciding this case, that in a capital case a truly persuasive demonstration of 'actual innocence' made after trial would render the execution of a defendant unconstitutional." * * * Without articulating the standard it is applying, however, the Court then decides that this petitioner has not made a sufficiently persuasive case. Because I believe that in the first instance the District Court should decide whether petitioner is entitled to a hearing and whether he is entitled to relief on the merits of his claim, I would reverse the order of the Court of Appeals and remand this case for further proceedings in the District Court.

I

The Court's enumeration * * * of the constitutional rights of criminal defendants surely is entirely beside the point. These protections sometimes fail. * * * We really are being asked to decide whether the Constitution forbids the execution of a person who has been validly convicted and sentenced but who, nonetheless, can prove his innocence with newly discovered evidence. Despite the State of Texas' astonishing protestation to the contrary, * * I do not see how the answer can be anything but "yes."

A

The Eighth Amendment prohibits "cruel and unusual punishments." This proscription is not static but rather reflects evolving standards of decency. * * *I think it is crystal clear that the execution of an innocent person is "at odds with contemporary standards of fairness and decency." * * * Indeed, it is at odds with any standard of decency that I can imagine.

This Court has ruled that punishment is excessive and unconstitutional if it is "nothing more than the purposeless and needless imposition of pain and suffering," or if it is "grossly out of proportion to the severity of the crime." * * * It has held that death is an excessive punishment for rape, *Coker v. Georgia*, 433 U.S. [584], 592 [(1977)], and for mere participation in a robbery during which a killing takes place. * ** If it is violative of the Eighth Amendment to execute someone who is guilty of those crimes, then it plainly is violative of the Eighth Amendment to execute a person who is actually innocent. Executing an innocent person epitomizes "the purposeless and needless imposition of pain and suffering." * * *

* * *

I believe it contrary to any standard of decency to execute someone who is actually innocent. Because the Eighth Amendment applies to questions of guilt or innocence * * * and to persons upon whom a valid sentence of death has been imposed, * * * I also believe that petitioner may raise an Eighth Amendment challenge to his punishment on the ground that he is actually innocent.

B

Execution of the innocent is equally offensive to the Due Process Clause of the Fourteenth Amendment. The majority's discussion misinterprets petitioner's Fourteenth Amendment claim as raising a procedural, rather than a substantive, due process challenge. * * *

* * *

II

The majority's discussion of petitioner's constitutional claims is even more perverse when viewed in the light of this Court's recent habeas jurisprudence. Beginning with a trio of decisions in 1986, this Court shifted the focus of federal habeas review of successive, abusive, or defaulted claims away from the preservation of constitutional rights to a fact-based inquiry into the habeas petitioner's guilt or innocence. * * * The Court sought to strike a balance between the State's interest in the finality of its criminal judgments and the prisoner's interest in access to a forum to test the basic justice of his sentence. * * *

* * *

* * * In other words, even a prisoner who appears to have had a *constitutionally perfect* trial "retains a powerful and legitimate interest in obtaining his release from custody if he is innocent of the charge for which he was incarcerated." It is obvious that this reasoning extends beyond the context of successive, abusive, or defaulted claims to substantive claims of actual innocence. * * *

* * *

III

The Eighth and Fourteenth Amendments, of course, are binding on the States, and one would normally expect the States to adopt procedures to consider claims of actual innocence based on newly discovered evidence. * * * The majority's disposition of this case, however, leaves the States uncertain of their constitutional obligations.

A

Whatever procedures a State might adopt to hear actual-innocence claims, one thing is certain: The possibility of executive clemency is *not* sufficient to satisfy the requirements of the Eighth and Fourteenth Amendments. The majority correctly points out: "'A pardon is an act of grace.'" * ** The vindication of rights guaranteed by the Constitution has never been made to turn on the unreviewable discretion of an executive official or administrative tribunal. * * *

* * *

C

* * *

I think the standard for relief on the merits of an actual-innocence claim must be higher than the threshold standard for merely reaching that claim or any other claim that has been procedurally defaulted or is successive or abusive. I would hold that, to obtain relief on a claim of actual innocence, the petitioner must show that he probably is innocent. This standard is supported by several considerations. First, new evidence of innocence may be discovered long after the defendant's conviction. Given the passage of time, it may be difficult for the State to retry a defendant who obtains relief from his conviction or sentence on an actual-innocence claim. The actual-innocence proceeding thus may constitute the final word on whether the defendant may be punished. In light of this fact, an otherwise constitutionally valid conviction or sentence should not be set aside lightly. Second, conviction after a constitutionally adequate trial strips the defendant of the presumption of innocence. The government bears the burden of proving the defendant's guilt beyond a reasonable doubt, * * * but once the government has done so, the burden of proving innocence must shift to the convicted defendant. The actual-innocence inquiry is therefore distinguishable from review for sufficiency of the evidence, where the question is not whether the defendant is innocent but whether the government has met its constitutional burden of proving the defendant's guilt beyond a reasonable doubt. When a defendant seeks to challenge the determination of guilt after he has been validly convicted and sentenced, it is fair to place on him the burden of proving his innocence, not just raising doubt about his guilt.

* * *

V

I have voiced disappointment over this Court's obvious eagerness to do away with any restriction on the States' power to execute whomever and however they please. * * * I have also expressed doubts about whether, in the absence of such restrictions, capital punishment remains constitutional at all. * * * Of one thing, however, I am certain. Just as an execution without adequate safeguards is unacceptable, so too is an execution when the condemned prisoner can prove that he is innocent. The execution of a person who can show that he is innocent comes perilously close to simple murder.

Notes

1. Subsequent case history

Leonel Herrera was executed on May 12, 1993.

2. The role of habeas review

According to *Herrera*, the rule that "the existence merely of newly discovered evidence relevant to guilt of a state prisoner is not a ground for relief in federal habeas corpus" is "grounded in the principle that federal habeas courts sit to ensure that individuals are not imprisoned in violation of the Constitution—not to correct errors of fact." 506 U.S. at 400. The Court then parenthetically cites *Moore v. Dempsey*, 261 U.S. 86, 87–88 (1923), for the proposition that "what we have to deal with [on habeas review] is not the petitioners' innocence or guilt but solely the question whether their constitutional rights have been preserved." 506 U.S. at 400.

Do you agree that the proper role of habeas review is to ensure that constitutional rights have been preserved, rather than to address questions of innocence? If the general public perception is that courts exist to correct errors of fact, how does one explain the Court's position in *Herrera* to the general public?

3. "*For the sake of argument*"

The opinions reveal a wide range of approaches to the question of whether execution of a validly convicted but actually innocent person is in and of itself unconstitutional, as well as what the standard for evaluating post-conviction claims of actual innocence should be.

Justice Rehnquist "assumes," "for the sake of argument," that in a capital case "a truly persuasive demonstration of 'actual innocence' after trial would render the execution of an innocent defendant unconstitutional, and warrant federal habeas relief if there were no state avenue open to process such a claim." Justice Rehnquist asserts that the "threshold showing for making such a claim would necessarily be 'extraordinarily high.'" In her concurrence, Justice O'Connor writes that the "execution of a legally and factually innocent person would be a constitutionally intolerable event." Justice O'Connor emphasizes that *Herrera* does not answer the question whether a federal court may consider "convincing" free-standing claims of actual innocence and expresses hope that constitutional procedural protections and pardon and clemency safeguards may preclude the Court's ever deciding that question. In contrast, Justice Scalia (joined by Justice Thomas) believes the Court should have answered the question and found no constitutional entitlement to judicial consideration of post-conviction claims of newly discovered evidence of innocence. Justice White, in a separate concurrence, "assumes" that the execution of one who made a "persuasive showing" of actual innocence would be unconstitutional. Justice White proposes that to be entitled to relief, a petitioner would have to show that, based on the newly discovered evidence combined with the trial evidence, no rational trier of fact could find guilt beyond a reasonable doubt.

Why do you think the Justices who voted to affirm avoid deciding whether the Constitution requires recognition of a free-standing claim of innocence? In light of her agreement with the dissent that execution of an innocent person would be unconstitutional, why does Justice O'Connor vote with the majority?

Justice Blackmun, joined by Justices Souter and Stevens, states affirmatively that execution of a person who can prove his innocence violates "any standard of decency," and thus violates the Eighth Amendment prohibition against cruel and unusual punishment. Noting that constitutional protections sometimes fail to protect the innocent, Blackmun would not make judicial review of newly discovered evidence of innocence dependent upon a showing of a constitutional violation in the determination of guilt. Blackmun proposes that a petitioner seeking relief on the merits of an actual innocence claim be required to show that he is probably innocent, a higher standard than what is required to reach a claim that is successive, abusive, or procedurally defaulted.

Do you agree with the standard Justice Blackmun proposes for a free-standing claim of innocence? Why or why not?

4. *Clemency*

The term clemency is used to refer to a range of executive powers: pardon; commutation of a sentence (from a death sentence to life, from life to a term of years, from a longer to a shorter sentence); and restoration of civil rights after the sentence has been served.

Who has clemency power and how it may be exercised depends upon the jurisdiction. In the federal system, the Attorney General investigates an application for clemency and makes a non-binding recommendation to the President. The clemency process varies from state to state. In some states the governor makes clemency decisions, while other states rely on a board of advisors or on a combination of both the governor and a board. Some commentators call for a citizens' selection board, comprised of unpaid citizens which would then appoint the commutation authority.

What is your assessment of the pros and cons of each type of authority?

A. "*A matter of grace*"

Is there a constitutional right to be considered for clemency or commutation? Are there any constitutional implications for the clemency process?

In *Ohio Adult Parole Authority v. Woodard,* 523 U.S. 272 (1998), the Court decided the question of whether an inmate sentenced to death has a protected life interest in clemency proceedings. Following its earlier decisions in *Greenholtz v. Nebraska Penal Inmates,* 442 U.S. 1 (1979)(rejecting inmates' claim that the state statutes and the Board's procedures denied them procedural due process and finding no constitutional right of conditional release before the expiration of a valid sentence), and *Connecticut Bd. Of Pardons v. Dumschat,* 452 U. S. 458, 465 (1981)(holding that an inmate has "no constitutional or inherent right" to commutation of his sentence and describing an expectation of commutation as "simply a unilateral hope"), the Court first rejected the argument that the inmate has a life interest in clemency broader in scope than the original life interest adjudicated at the trial and sentencing phase. The Court stated that "[t]he process respondent seeks would be inconsistent with the heart of executive clemency, which is to grant clemency as a matter of grace." *Id.* at 280–281. The Court found no difference, in the clemency context, between capital and non-capital cases because the nature of the benefit sought is the same in both cases: "A death row inmate's petition for clemency is also a 'unilateral hope.'" *Id.* at 282. "The mandatory procedures [of Ohio's clemency process] do not create a substantive expectation of clemency, given the broad discretion retained by the governor, the ultimate decisionmaker."

The Court rejected the petitioner's additional argument, based on *Evitts v. Lucey,* 469 U.S. 387, 393 (1985), that he was entitled to due process protections in the clemency proceedings because they are "an integral part of the ... system for finally adjudicating the guilt or innocence of a defendant." The Court held that *Evitts* did not create a new "strand" of due process when it held there is a constitutional right to effective assistance of counsel on a first appeal as of right, nor did it rest on the idea of a continuum of due process rights. In contrast to a first appeal as of right, the clemency process is not part of an adjudicatory process and it is not intended primarily to enhance the reliability of the trial process. Given that "[p]rocedures mandated under the Due Process Clause should be consistent with the nature of the governmental power being invoked," the state's clemency procedures do not violate due process. "[T]he executive's clemency authority would cease to be a matter of grace committed to the executive authority if it were constrained by the sort of procedural requirements that respondent urges. Respondent is already under a sentence of death, determined to have been lawfully imposed. If clemency is granted, he obtains a benefit; if it is denied, he is no worse off than he was before." *Id.* at 285.

B. *Clemency as a "fail safe" for the actually innocent*

The Supreme Court relies upon clemency as a fail safe for otherwise unreachable miscarriages of justice. In *Herrera*, the Court asserted that executive clemency has historically provided the "fail safe" in the criminal justice system, citing a 1932 study of 65 wrongful convictions, in which the author found that most had been pardoned and the remainder had been acquitted in a new trial. Justice Scalia expressed doubt that executive clemency would ever fail to afford relief to a person who presents the quality of evidence of innocence required by the Court to obtain relief in a habeas proceeding. In his dissent, Blackmun asserted that executive clemency does not satisfy the requirements of the Eighth and Fourteenth Amendments and that vindication of constitutional rights should not depend upon "the unreviewable discretion of an executive official or administrative tribunal." Which view is the most persuasive? In the decades since *Herrera*, how have the Justices' assumptions (about the exceptionalism of the truly innocent and the availability of clemency to correct those wrongful convictions) been borne out?

Many commentators have documented a decrease in clemency actions in the last several decades at both the federal and state levels.[2] One commentator notes that federal pardon policy "became part and parcel of a tough-on-crime agenda ... [that] served primarily to ratify the results achieved by prosecutors, not to provide any real possibility of revising them."[3] On the state level, exercise of the gubernatorial pardon power varies widely across the country. A prisoner's chances of obtaining clemency may depend less on the merits of his petition for clemency than on the personal politics and convictions of the governor, the tradition of granting clemency in his state, the size of the prison population and the level of overcrowding, and the prevailing politics of the time.[4]

Since *Herrera*, four governors have granted clemency to all or to a majority of death row inmates in their states based on systemic concerns about the state's criminal justice system. Governor George Ryan's 2003 commutations or pardons of all 172 inmates on Illinois' death row in 2003 account for the vast majority of these acts of clemency.[5] Apart from clemency given by these four governors, only 55 commutations have been given to death row inmates since 1976. This number represents an average of less than two commutations of death row inmates each year since 1976.[6] In contrast, the number of inmates on death row has ranged from 420 in 1976 to 3,207 in 2008.[7]

---

2. U.S. Department of Justice, Presidential Clemency Actions by Administration, 1945 to Present, http://www.justice.gov/pardon/actions_administration.htm; Rachel E. Barkow, *The Politics of Forgivenss: Reconceptualizing Clemency*, 21 Fed. Sent'g. Rep. 153 (2009); Margaret Colgate Love, *The Twilight of the Pardon Power*, 100 J. Crim. L. & Criminology ___ (2010) (providing an extensive review of the exercise of presidential pardon power since 1789).

3. Love, *supra* note 3. Love also notes that even as the granting of pardons declined, clemency petitions to the President increased because of federal sentencing guidelines, the severity of mandatory prison terms, the limited ability of federal courts to individualize or revise sentences once imposed, and the repeal or disuse of post-conviction early release mechanisms. *Id.* at 40.

4. *See* Margaret Colgate Love, Relief from the Collateral Consequences of a Criminal Conviction; A State-By-State Resource Guide (William S. Hein, 2006). For examples of the possible role of politics in clemency decisions, see Adam Liptak, *Governor Rebuffs Clemency Board in Murder Case*, N.Y. Times, June 14, 2010 (reporting speculation that the governor of Arizona's election campaign influenced her decision to deny clemency to William Macumber, without any explanation, even after the five members of the Arizona Board of Executive Clemency unanimously recommended to the governor that he be released after 35 years in prison "to correct a miscarriage of justice."); *Texas state board says arson investigators used flawed science*, CNN Justice, http://www.cnnnews/2010/CRIME/07/23/texas.execution.probe/(reporting the findings of a state Forensics Science Commission that the prosecution used flawed forensic evidence to convict Todd Willingham of the murders of his children by arson in 1991. The article notes charges by critics of Governor Rick Perry—who had replaced the chairman of the board a few days before it was to hear from an independent arson expert—that he was trying to curtail review of the case because of upcoming elections. Willingham maintained his innocence until he was executed in 2004. Prior to his execution, Governor Perry denied his petition for clemency.).

5. The other three are Gov. Toney Anaya in New Mexico in 1986 (all inmates); Gov. Richard Celeste in Ohio in 1991 (8 inmates); and Jon Corzine in New Jersey in 2007 (all inmates). http://www.deathpenaltyinfo.org/clemency.

6. Descriptions of these 248 commutations can be found at http://www.deathpenaltyinfo.org/clemency.

7. A table listing the number of inmates on death row from 1953 to 2008 is available on the Bureau of Justice Statistics website at http://bjs.ojp.usdoj.gov/content/glance/tables/drtab.cfm.

In light of these considerations, is it reasonable for the Court to rely on executive clemency as a "fail safe" to pardon wrongfully convicted persons who claim that newly discovered evidence establishes their innocence?

Schlup v. Delo

513 U.S. 298 (1995)

JUSTICE STEVENS delivered the opinion of the Court.

Petitioner Lloyd E. Schlup, Jr., a Missouri prisoner currently under a sentence of death, filed a second federal habeas corpus petition alleging that constitutional error deprived the jury of critical evidence that would have established his innocence. The District Court, without conducting an evidentiary hearing, declined to reach the merits of the petition, holding that petitioner could not satisfy the threshold showing of "actual innocence" required by *Sawyer v. Whitley*, 505 U.S. 333 (1992). Under *Sawyer*, the petitioner must show "by clear and convincing evidence that, but for a constitutional error, no reasonable juror would have found the petitioner" guilty. * * * The Court of Appeals affirmed. We granted certiorari to consider whether the *Sawyer* standard provides adequate protection against the kind of miscarriage of justice that would result from the execution of a person who is actually innocent.

I

On February 3, 1984, on Walk 1 of the high security area of the Missouri State Penitentiary, a black inmate named Arthur Dade was stabbed to death. Three white inmates from Walk 2, including petitioner, were charged in connection with Dade's murder.

At petitioner's trial in December 1985, the State's evidence consisted principally of the testimony of two corrections officers who had witnessed the killing. On the day of the murder, Sergeant Roger Flowers was on duty on Walk 1 and Walk 2, the two walks on the lower floor of the prison's high security area. Flowers testified that he first released the inmates on Walk 2 for their noon meal and relocked their cells. After unlocking the cells to release the inmates on Walk 1, Flowers noticed an inmate named Rodnie Stewart moving against the flow of traffic carrying a container of steaming liquid. Flowers watched as Stewart threw the liquid in Dade's face. According to Flowers, Schlup then jumped on Dade's back, and Robert O'Neal joined in the attack. Flowers shouted for help, entered the walk, and grabbed Stewart as the two other assailants fled.

Officer John Maylee witnessed the attack from Walk 7, which is three levels and some 40–50 feet above Walks 1 and 2. * * * Maylee first noticed Schlup, Stewart, and O'Neal as they were running from Walk 2 to Walk 1 against the flow of traffic. According to Maylee's testimony, Stewart threw a container of liquid at Dade's face, and then Schlup jumped on Dade's back. O'Neal then stabbed Dade several times in the chest, ran down the walk, and threw the weapon out a window. Maylee did not see what happened to Schlup or Stewart after the stabbing.

The State produced no physical evidence connecting Schlup to the killing, and no witness other than Flowers and Maylee testified to Schlup's involvement in the murder. * * *

Schlup's defense was that the State had the wrong man. * * * He relied heavily on a videotape from a camera in the prisoners' dining room. The tape showed that Schlup was the first inmate to walk into the dining room for the noon meal, and that he went through the line and got his food. Approximately 65 seconds after Schlup's entrance, several guards ran out of the dining room in apparent response to a distress call. Twenty-six seconds later, O'Neal ran into the dining room, dripping blood. * * * Shortly thereafter, Schlup and O'Neal were taken into custody.

Schlup contended that the videotape, when considered in conjunction with testimony that he had walked at a normal pace from his cell to the dining room, * * * demonstrated that he could not have participated in the assault. Because the videotape showed conclusively that Schlup was in the dining room 65 seconds before the guards responded to the distress call, a critical element of Schlup's defense was determining when the distress call went out. Had the distress call sounded shortly after the murder, Schlup would not have had time to get from the prison floor to the dining room, and thus he could not have participated in the murder. Conversely, had there been a delay of several minutes between the murder and the distress call, Schlup might have had sufficient time to participate in the murder and still get to the dining room over a minute before the distress call went out. * * *

The prosecutor adduced evidence tending to establish that such a delay had in fact occurred. First, Flowers testified that none of the officers on the prison floor had radios, thus implying that neither he nor any of the other officers on the floor was able to radio for help when the stabbing occurred. Second, Flowers testified that after he shouted for help, it took him "a couple [of] minutes" to subdue Stewart. * * * Flowers then brought Stewart downstairs, encountered Captain James Eberle, and told Eberle that there had been a "disturbance." * * * Eberle testified that he went upstairs to the prison floor, and then radioed for assistance. Eberle estimated that the elapsed time from when he first saw Flowers until he radioed for help was "approximately a minute." *** The prosecution also offered testimony from a prison investigator who testified that he was able to run from the scene of the crime to the dining room in 33 seconds and to walk the distance at a normal pace in a minute and 37 seconds.

After deliberating overnight, the jury returned a verdict of guilty. Following the penalty phase, at which the victim of one of Schlup's prior offenses testified extensively about the sordid details of that offense, * * * the jury sentenced Schlup to death. The Missouri Supreme Court affirmed Schlup's conviction and death sentence, * * * and this Court denied certiorari. * * *

II

On January 5, 1989, after exhausting his state collateral remedies, * * * Schlup filed a *pro se* petition for a federal writ of habeas corpus, asserting the claim, among others, that his trial counsel was ineffective for failing to interview and to call witnesses who could establish Schlup's innocence. * * * The District Court concluded that Schlup's ineffectiveness claim was procedurally barred, and it denied relief on that claim without conducting an evidentiary hearing. * * * The Court of Appeals affirmed, though it did not rely on the alleged procedural bar. * * * Instead, based on its own examination of the record, the Court found that trial counsel's performance had not been constitutionally ineffective, both because counsel had reviewed statements that Schlup's potential witnesses had given to prison investigators, and because the testimony of those witnesses "would be repetitive of the testimony to be presented at trial." * * * The Court of Appeals denied a petition for rehearing and suggestion for rehearing en banc, * * * and we denied a petition for certiorari. * * *

On March 11, 1992, represented by new counsel, Schlup filed a second federal habeas corpus petition. That petition raised a number of claims, including that (1) Schlup was actually innocent of Dade's murder, and that his execution would therefore violate the Eighth and Fourteenth Amendments; * * * (2) trial counsel was ineffective for failing to interview alibi witnesses; and (3) the State had failed to disclose critical exculpatory evidence. The petition was supported by numerous affidavits from inmates attesting to Schlup's innocence.

The State filed a response arguing that various procedural bars precluded the District Court from reaching the merits of Schlup's claims and that the claims were in any event meritless. Attached to the State's response were transcripts of inmate interviews conducted by prison investigators just five days after the murder. One of the transcripts contained an interview with John Green, an inmate who at the time was the clerk for the housing unit. In his interview, Green stated that he had been in his office at the end of the walks when the murder occurred. Green stated that Flowers had told him to call for help, and that Green had notified base of the disturbance shortly after it began. * * *

Schlup immediately filed a traverse arguing that Green's affidavit provided conclusive proof of Schlup's innocence. Schlup contended that Green's statement demonstrated that a call for help had gone out shortly after the incident. Because the videotape showed that Schlup was in the dining room some 65 seconds before the guards received the distress call, Schlup argued that he could not have been involved in Dade's murder. Schlup emphasized that Green's statement was not likely to have been fabricated, because at the time of Green's interview, neither he nor anyone else would have realized the significance of Green's call to base. Schlup tried to buttress his claim of innocence with affidavits from inmates who stated that they had witnessed the event and that Schlup had not been present. * * * Two of those affidavits suggested that Randy Jordan—who occupied the cell between O'Neal and Stewart in Walk 2, and who, as noted above, * * * is shown on the videotape arriving at lunch with O'Neal—was the third assailant.

On August 23, 1993, without holding a hearing, the District Court dismissed Schlup's second habeas petition and vacated the stay of execution that was then in effect. The District Court concluded that Schlup's various filings did not provide adequate cause for failing to raise his new claims more promptly. Moreover, the court concluded that Schlup had failed to meet the *Sawyer v. Whitley, supra*, standard for showing that a refusal to entertain those claims would result in a fundamental miscarriage of justice. In its discussion of the evidence, the court made no separate comment on the significance of Green's statement. * * *

On September 7, 1993, petitioner filed a motion to set aside the order of dismissal, again calling the court's attention to Green's statement. Two days later, Schlup filed a supplemental motion stating that his counsel had located John Green * * * and had obtained an affidavit from him. That affidavit confirmed Green's postincident statement that he had called base shortly after the assault. Green's affidavit also identified Jordan rather than Schlup as the third assailant. * * * The District Court denied the motion and the supplemental motion without opinion.

* * *

On November 17, 1993, the Court of Appeals denied a suggestion for rehearing en banc. Dissenting from that denial, three judges joined an opinion describing the question whether the majority should have applied the standard announced in *Sawyer v. Whitley, supra*, rather than the *Kuhlmann* standard as "a question of great importance in habeas corpus jurisprudence." * * * We granted certiorari to consider that question. * * *

III

As a preliminary matter, it is important to explain the difference between Schlup's claim of actual innocence and the claim of actual innocence asserted in *Herrera v. Collins*, 506 U.S. 390 (1993). In *Herrera*, the petitioner advanced his claim of innocence to support a novel substantive constitutional claim, namely, that the execution of an innocent person would violate the Eighth Amendment. * * * Under petitioner's theory in *Herrera*, even if the proceedings that had resulted in his conviction and sentence were entirely fair and error free, his innocence would render his execution a "constitutionally intolerable event." * * *

Schlup's claim of innocence, on the other hand, is procedural, rather than substantive. His constitutional claims are based not on his innocence, but rather on his contention that the ineffectiveness of his counsel, * * * and the withholding of evidence by the prosecution, *see Brady v. Maryland*, 373 U.S. 83 (1963), denied him the full panoply of protections afforded to criminal defendants by the Constitution. Schlup, however, faces procedural obstacles that he must overcome before a federal court may address the merits of those constitutional claims. Because Schlup has been unable to establish "cause and prejudice" sufficient to excuse his failure to present his evidence in support of his first federal petition, * * * Schlup may obtain review of his constitutional claims only if he falls within the "narrow class of cases ... implicating a fundamental miscarriage of justice." * * * Schlup's claim of innocence is offered only to bring him within this "narrow class of cases."

Schlup's claim thus differs in at least two important ways from that presented in *Herrera*. First, Schlup's claim of innocence does not by itself provide a basis for relief. Instead, his claim for relief depends critically on the validity of his *Strickland* and *Brady* claims. * * * Schlup's claim of innocence is thus "not itself a constitutional claim, but instead a gateway through which a habeas petitioner must pass to have his otherwise barred constitutional claim considered on the merits." * * *

* * *

* * * Without any new evidence of innocence, even the existence of a concededly meritorious constitutional violation is not in itself sufficient to establish a miscarriage of justice that would allow a habeas court to reach the merits of a barred claim. However, if a petitioner such as Schlup presents evidence of innocence so strong that a court cannot have confidence in the outcome of the trial unless the court is also satisfied that the trial was free of nonharmless constitutional error, the petitioner should be allowed to pass through the gateway and argue the merits of his underlying claims.

Consequently, Schlup's evidence of innocence need carry less of a burden. In *Herrera* (on the assumption that petitioner's claim was, in principle, legally well founded), the evidence of innocence would have had to be strong enough to make his execution "constitutionally intolerable" *even if* his conviction was the product of a fair trial. For Schlup, the evidence must establish sufficient doubt about his guilt to justify the conclusion that his execution would be a miscarriage of justice *unless* his conviction was the product of a fair trial.

Our rather full statement of the facts illustrates the foregoing distinction between a substantive *Herrera* claim and Schlup's procedural claim. Three items of evidence are particularly relevant: the affidavit of black inmates attesting to the innocence of a white defendant in a racially motivated killing; the affidavit of Green describing his prompt call for assistance; and the affidavit of Lieutenant Faherty describing Schlup's unhurried walk to the dining room. If there were no question about the fairness of the criminal trial, a *Herrera*-type claim would have to fail unless the federal habeas court is itself convinced that those new facts unquestionably establish Schlup's innocence. On the other hand, if the habeas court were merely convinced that those new facts raised sufficient doubt about Schlup's guilt to undermine confidence in the result of the trial without the assurance that that trial was untainted by constitutional error, Schlup's threshold showing of innocence would justify a review of the merits of the constitutional claims.

IV

* * *

To ensure that the fundamental miscarriage of justice exception would remain "rare" and would only be applied in the "extraordinary case," while at the same time ensuring that the exception would extend relief to those who were truly deserving, this Court explicitly tied the miscarriage of justice exception to the petitioner's innocence. * * *

* * *

V

* * *

As we have stated, the fundamental miscarriage of justice exception seeks to balance the societal interests in finality, comity, and conservation of scarce judicial resources with the individual interest in justice that arises in the extraordinary case. We conclude that *Carrier*, rather than *Sawyer*, properly strikes that balance when the claimed injustice is that constitutional error has resulted in the conviction of one who is actually innocent of the crime.

Claims of actual innocence pose less of a threat to scarce judicial resources and to principles of finality and comity than do claims that focus solely on the erroneous imposition of the death penalty. Though challenges to the propriety of imposing a sentence of death are routinely asserted in capital cases, experience has taught us that a substantial claim that constitutional error has caused the conviction of an innocent person is extremely rare. * * * To be credible, such a claim requires petitioner to support his allegations of constitutional error with new reliable evidence—whether it be exculpatory scientific evidence, trustworthy eyewitness accounts, or critical physical evidence—that was not presented at trial. Because such evidence is obviously unavailable in the vast majority of cases, claims of actual innocence are rarely successful. Even under the pre-*Sawyer* regime, "in virtually every case, the allegation of actual innocence has been summarily rejected." * * * The threat to judicial resources, finality, and comity posed by claims of actual innocence is thus significantly less than that posed by claims relating only to sentencing.

Of greater importance, the individual interest in avoiding injustice is most compelling in the context of actual innocence. The quintessential miscarriage of justice is the execution of a person who is entirely innocent. * * * Indeed, concern about the injustice that results from the conviction of an innocent person has long been at the core of our criminal justice system. That concern is reflected, for example, in the "fundamental value determination of our society that it is far worse to convict an innocent man than to let a guilty man go free." * * *

The overriding importance of this greater individual interest merits protection by imposing a somewhat less exacting standard of proof on a habeas petitioner alleging a fundamental miscarriage of justice than on one alleging that his sentence is too severe. * * *

* * *

[W]e hold that the *Carrier* "probably resulted" standard rather than the more stringent *Sawyer* standard must govern the miscarriage of justice inquiry when a petitioner who has been sentenced to death raises a claim of actual innocence to avoid a procedural bar to the consideration of the merits of his constitutional claims.

VI

The *Carrier* standard requires the habeas petitioner to show that "a constitutional violation has probably resulted in the conviction of one who is actually innocent." * * *To establish the requisite probability, the petitioner must show that it is more likely than not that no reasonable juror would have convicted him in the light of the new evidence. The petitioner thus is required to make a stronger showing than that needed to establish prejudice. * * * At the same time, the showing of "more likely than not" imposes a lower burden of proof than the "clear and convincing" standard required under *Sawyer*. The *Carrier* standard thus ensures that petitioner's case is truly "extraordinary," * * * while still providing petitioner a meaningful avenue by which to avoid a manifest injustice.

Carrier requires a petitioner to show that he is "actually innocent." As used in *Carrier*, actual innocence is closely related to the definition set forth by this Court in *Sawyer*. To satisfy the *Carrier* gateway standard, a petitioner must show that it is more likely than not that no reasonable juror would have found petitioner guilty beyond a reasonable doubt.

Several observations about this standard are in order. The *Carrier* standard is intended to focus the inquiry on actual innocence. In assessing the adequacy of petitioner's showing, therefore, the district court is not bound by the rules of admissibility that would govern at trial. Instead, the emphasis on "actual innocence" allows the reviewing tribunal also to consider the probative force of relevant evidence that was either excluded or unavailable at trial. Indeed, with respect to this aspect of the *Carrier* standard, we believe that Judge Friendly's description of the inquiry is appropriate: The habeas court must make its determination concerning the petitioner's innocence "in light of all the evidence, including that alleged to have been illegally admitted (but with due regard to any unreliability of it) and evidence tenably claimed to have been wrongly excluded or to have become available only after the trial." * * *

* * *

We note finally that the *Carrier* standard requires a petitioner to show that it is more likely than not that "no reasonable juror" would have convicted him. The word "reasonable" in that formulation is not without meaning. It must be presumed that a reasonable juror would consider fairly all of the evidence presented. It must also be presumed that such a juror would conscientiously obey the instructions of the trial court requiring proof beyond a reasonable doubt. * * *

Though the *Carrier* standard requires a substantial showing, it is by no means equivalent to the standard of *Jackson v. Virginia*, 443 U.S. 307 (1979), that governs review of claims of insufficient evidence. The *Jackson* standard, which focuses on whether any rational juror could have convicted, looks to whether there is sufficient evidence which, if credited, could support the conviction. The *Jackson* standard thus differs in at least two important ways from the *Carrier* standard. First, under *Jackson*, the assessment of the credibility of witnesses is generally beyond the scope of review. In contrast, under the gateway standard we describe today, the newly presented evidence may indeed call into question the credibility of the witnesses presented at trial. In such a case, the habeas court may have to make some credibility assessments. Second, and more fundamentally, the focus of the inquiry is different under *Jackson* from under *Carrier*. Under *Jackson*, the use of the word "could" focuses the inquiry on the power of the trier of fact to reach its conclusion. Under *Carrier*, the use of the word "would" focuses the inquiry on the likely behavior of the trier of fact.

Indeed, our adoption of the phrase "more likely than not" reflects this distinction. Under *Jackson*, the question whether the trier of fact has power to make a finding of guilt requires a binary response: Either the trier of fact has power as a matter of law or it does not. Under *Carrier*, in contrast, the habeas court must consider what reasonable triers of fact are likely to do. Under this probabilistic inquiry, it makes sense to have a probabilistic standard such as "more likely than not." * * * Thus, though under *Jackson* the mere existence of sufficient evidence to convict would be determinative of petitioner's claim, that is not true under *Carrier*.

* * *

Because both the Court of Appeals and the District Court evaluated the record under an improper standard, further proceedings are necessary. The fact-intensive nature of the inquiry, together with the District Court's ability to take testimony from the few key witnesses if it deems that course advisable, convinces us that the most expeditious procedure is to order that the decision of the Court of Appeals be vacated and that the case be remanded to the Court of Appeals with instructions to remand to the District Court for further proceedings consistent with this opinion.

It is so ordered.

JUSTICE O'CONNOR, concurring.

I write to explain, in light of the dissenting opinions, what I understand the Court to decide and what it does not.

The Court holds that, in order to have an abusive or successive habeas claim heard on the merits, a petitioner who cannot demonstrate cause and prejudice "must show that it is more likely than not that no reasonable juror would have convicted him" in light of newly discovered evidence of innocence. * * * This standard is higher than that required for prejudice, which requires only "a reasonable probability that, absent the errors, the factfinder would have had a reasonable doubt respecting guilt." * * * The Court today does not sow confusion in the law. Rather, it properly balances the dictates of justice with the need to ensure that the actual innocence exception remains only a "'safety valve' for the 'extraordinary case.'" * * *

* * *

CHIEF JUSTICE REHNQUIST, with whom JUSTICE KENNEDY and JUSTICE THOMAS join, dissenting.

The Court decides that the threshold standard for a showing of "actual innocence" in a successive or abusive habeas petition is that set forth in *Murray v. Carrier*, 477 U.S. 478 (1986), rather than that set forth in *Sawyer v. Whitley*, 505 U.S. 333 (1992). For reasons which I later set out, I believe the *Sawyer* standard should be applied to claims of guilt or innocence as well as to challenges to a petitioner's sentence. But, more importantly, I believe the Court's exegesis of the *Carrier* standard both waters down the standard suggested in that case, and will inevitably create confusion in the lower courts. * * *

The Court fails to acknowledge expressly the similarities between the standard it has adopted and the *Jackson* standard. A habeas court reviewing a claim of actual innocence does not write on a clean slate. * * * Therefore, as the Court acknowledges, a petitioner making a claim of actual innocence under *Carrier* falls short of satisfying his burden if the reviewing court determines that *any* juror reasonably would have found petitioner guilty of the crime. * * *

* * *

JUSTICE SCALIA, with whom JUSTICE THOMAS joins, dissenting.

A federal statute entitled "Finality of Determination"—to be found at § 2244 of Title 28 of the United States Code—specifically addresses the problem of second and subsequent petitions for the writ of habeas corpus. The reader of today's opinion will be unencumbered with knowledge of this law, since it is not there discussed or quoted, and indeed is only cited *en passant*. * * * Rather than asking what the statute says, or even what we have said the statute says, the Court asks only what is the fairest standard to apply, and answers that question by looking to the various semi-consistent standards articulated in our most recent decisions—minutely parsing phrases, and seeking shades of meaning in the interstices of sentences and words, as though a discursive judicial opinion were a statute. I would proceed differently. Within the very broad limits set by the Suspension Clause, U.S. Const., Art. I, § 9, cl. 2, the federal writ of habeas corpus is governed by statute. Section 2244 controls this case; the disposition it announces is plain enough, and our decisions contain nothing that would justify departure from that plain meaning.

Section 2244(b) provides:

> When after an evidentiary hearing on the merits of a material factual issue, or after a hearing on the merits of an issue of law, a person in custody pursuant to the judgment of a State court has been denied by a court of the United States or a justice or judge of the United States release from custody or other remedy on an application for a writ of habeas corpus, a subsequent application for a writ of habeas corpus in behalf of such person need not be entertained by a court of the United States or a justice or judge of the United States unless the application alleges and is predicated on a factual or other ground not adjudicated on the hearing of the earlier application for the writ, and unless the court, justice, or judge is satisfied that the applicant has not on the earlier application deliberately withheld the newly asserted ground or otherwise abused the writ.

A long sentence, but not a difficult one. A federal district court that receives a second or subsequent petition for the writ of habeas corpus, when a prior petition has been denied on the merits, "need not … entertain" (*i.e.*, may dismiss) the petition unless it is neither (to use our shorthand terminology) successive nor abusive. * * * Today, however, the Court obliquely but unmistakably pronounces that a successive or abusive petition *must* be entertained and may *not* be dismissed so long as the petitioner makes a sufficiently persuasive showing that a "fundamental miscarriage of justice" has occurred. * * * ("If a petitioner such as Schlup presents [adequate] evidence of innocence … the petitioner should be allowed to pass through the gateway and argue the merits"). * * * That conclusion flatly contradicts the statute, and is not required by our precedent.

* * *

Notes

1. *Subsequent case history*

Lloyd Schlup's conviction was vacated by a federal district court. After the state refiled, he pleaded guilty and received a life sentence, which he is currently serving. Assuming Schlup was in fact innocent, what could have been some of the reasons why he chose to plead guilty?

2. *Equitable remedy*

In what ways did the concept of the writ of habeas corpus as an equitable remedy inform the Court's decision? Does the decision in *Schlup* have a constitutional basis?

3. *Sawyer v. Whitley*

In *Schlup*, the Court affirmed its holding in *Sawyer v. Whitley*, 505 U.S. 333 (1992), but adopted a less restrictive ("probably innocent") standard for actual innocence claims that would otherwise be procedurally barred. In *Sawyer*, the Court decided what standard should be applied in a case of a defaulted, abusive, or successive petition where the petitioner alleged he was innocent of the death penalty rather than of the crime.

Sawyer, convicted of murder, acknowledged at trial that he had committed murder, but raised a "toxic psychosis" defense. At the sentencing phase he testified he was intoxicated at the time of the murder, and his sister testified to his character and background. The jury found three aggravating factors and no mitigating factors and sentenced him to death. Sawyer lost in his direct appeal, in state post-conviction proceedings, and in his first habeas action, where the district court denied all of his eighteen claims on the merits. Sawyer filed a second habeas petition, which alleged the jury did not hear evidence relating to his role in the offense because of *Brady* violations and did not hear mental health evidence due to ineffective assistance of counsel during the sentencing phase. The district court denied one of his claims on the merits and found the other claims barred as successive or abusive. The Court of Appeals refused to consider his second habeas petition on the merits on the ground that he had not shown cause for his failure to raise his claims in his first habeas petition and that he had not shown that he was actually innocent of the crime or of the death penalty imposed.

The Court made clear that the miscarriage of justice exception, or "actual innocence," may include innocence of the death penalty as well as actual innocence of the crime. The Court defined what innocent of death means in the context of actual innocence jurisprudence: "that there [were] no aggravating circumstances or that some other condition of eligibility [for the death penalty] ha[s] not been met." *Id.* at 345. The Court specifically declined to include additional evidence of mitigating circumstances as potentially establishing innocence of the death penalty.

The Court affirmed the lower court, holding that "to show 'actual innocence' one must show by clear and convincing evidence that, but for constitutional error at his sentencing hearing, no reasonable juror would have found him eligible for the death penalty under the [state] ... law." Applying this standard to Sawyer's claims, the Court concluded that Sawyer's new evidence did not meet this standard.

4. *The "gateway"*

The Court adopts the *Carrier* gateway standard for Schlup's case, maintaining that a petitioner such as Schlup must show that it is more likely than not that no reasonable juror would have found petitioner guilty beyond a reasonable doubt. Why did the Court reject the *Sawyer* standard for the *Carrier* standard in this case?

After *Schlup*, how clear is the Court's standard for passing through the "gate"?

What direction does the Court give to reviewing courts for application of the *Schlup* standard? To petitioners seeking to raise otherwise procedurally barred claims of innocence? How does the *Schlup* standard differ from the *Jackson v. Virginia* standard for sufficiency of the evidence? What is the difference between what a reasonable juror *could do* and *would do*? How does it differ from the *Herrera* standard?

5. *Innocent of death and actual innocence*

The Court adopts a different standard for judicial review of defaulted, successive, or abusive claims of erroneous imposition of the death penalty (*Sawyer*) and claims of actual innocence of the crime (*Schlup*). How does the Court justify different standards?

6. *Is there an actual innocence exception to AEDPA's one-year statute of limitations?*

The Court has not decided if *Schlup's* gateway standard for successive or defaulted petitions can also serve to override the one-year statute of limitations for original habeas petitions. The Ninth Circuit considered this issue in *Lee v. Lampert*, 610 F.3d 1125 (9th Cir. 2010), in which a petitioner alleging ineffective assistance of trial counsel filed his first habeas petition after the one-year statute of limitations had expired. Lee's petition was initially dismissed as untimely. He then filed an amended petition, and the district court held several evidentiary hearings. The district court found that Lee had established both ineffective assistance of counsel and actual innocence under the *Schlup* standard and granted the writ. On appeal, Lee acknowledged he had not filed his petition within the one-year time limit and that none of the other statutory start-dates for the one-year applied to his case. Instead, he argued that a showing of actual innocence pursuant to *Schlup* entitled him to have his habeas petition decided on the merits. Distinguishing *Holland v. Florida, supra*, Chapter 3, the Ninth Circuit found there is no presumption that non-jurisdictional statutes of limitations are subject to an actual innocence exception. The Ninth Circuit pointed out that there is no actual innocence exception enumerated in the exceptions listed in § 2244(d), in contrast to the exceptions in § 2244(b)(2)(B) (governing successive and abusive petitions). The Ninth Circuit noted that at the time of its enactment, Congress was aware of the *Schlup* exception and did not include it in the statute of limitations exceptions. The Ninth Circuit declined to add a "judge-made" exception.

House v. Bell

547 U.S. 518 (2006)

JUSTICE KENNEDY delivered the opinion of the Court.

Some 20 years ago in rural Tennessee, Carolyn Muncey was murdered. A jury convicted petitioner Paul Gregory House of the crime and sentenced him to death, but new revelations cast doubt on the jury's verdict. House, protesting his innocence, seeks access to federal court to pursue habeas corpus relief based on constitutional claims that are procedurally barred under state law. Out of respect for the finality of state-court judgments federal habeas courts, as a general rule, are closed to claims that state courts would consider defaulted. In certain exceptional cases involving a compelling claim of actual innocence, however, the state procedural default rule is not a bar to a federal habeas corpus petition. *See Schlup v. Delo*. After careful review of the full record, we conclude that House has made the stringent showing required by this exception; and we hold that his federal habeas action may proceed.

I

We begin with the facts surrounding Mrs. Muncey's disappearance, the discovery of her body, and House's arrest. Around 3 p.m. on Sunday, July 14, 1985, two local residents found her body concealed amid brush and tree branches on an embankment roughly 100 yards up the road from her driveway. Mrs. Muncey had been seen last on the evening before, when, around 8 p.m., she and her two children—Lora Muncey, age 10, and Matthew Muncey, age 8—visited their neighbor, Pam Luttrell. According to Luttrell, Mrs. Muncey mentioned her husband, William Hubert Muncey, Jr., known in the community as "Little Hube" and to his family as "Bubbie." As Luttrell recounted Mrs. Muncey's comment, Mr. Muncey "had gone to dig a grave, and he hadn't come back, but that was all right, because [Mrs. Muncey] was going to make him take her fishing the next day." Mrs. Muncey returned home, and some time later, before 11:00 p.m. at the latest, Luttrell "heard a car rev its motor as it went down the road," something Mr. Muncey customarily did when he drove by on his way home. Luttrell then went to bed.

Around 1 a.m., Lora and Matthew returned to Luttrell's home, this time with their father, Mr. Muncey, who said his wife was missing. Muncey asked Luttrell to watch the children while he searched for his wife. After he left, Luttrell talked with Lora. According to Luttrell:

> [Lora] said she heard a horn blow, she thought she heard a horn blow, and somebody asked if Bubbie was home, and her mama, you know, told them—no. And then she said she didn't know if she went back to sleep or not, but then she heard her mama going down the steps crying and I am not sure if that is when she told me that she heard her mama say—oh God, no, not me, or if she told me that the next day, but I do know that she said she heard her mother going down the steps crying.

While Lora was talking, Luttrell recalled, "Matt kept butting in, you know, on us talking, and he said—sister they said daddy had a wreck, they said daddy had a wreck."

At House's trial, Lora repeated her account of the night's events, this time referring to the "wreck" her brother had mentioned. * * * [I]it should be noted that Mrs. Muncey's father-in-law * * * was sometimes called "Big Hube." Lora and her brother called him "Paw Paw." We refer to him as Mr. Muncey, Sr. According to Lora, Mr. Muncey, Sr. had a deep voice, as does petitioner House.

Lora testified that after leaving Luttrell's house with her mother, she and her brother "went to bed." Later, she heard someone, or perhaps two different people, ask for her mother. Lora's account of the events after she went to bed was as follows:

> "Q Laura [sic], at some point after you got back home and you went to bed, did anything happen that caused your mother to be upset or did you hear anything?
>
> "A Well, it sounded like PawPaw said—where's daddy at, and she said digging a grave.
>
> "Q Okay. Do you know if it was PawPaw or not, or did it sound like PawPaw?
>
> "A It just sounded like PawPaw.
>
> "Q And your mother told him what?
>
> "A That he was digging a grave.
>
> "Q Had you ever heard that voice before that said that?
>
> "A I don't remember.
>
> "Q After that, at some point later, did you hear anything else that caused your mother to be upset?
>
> "A Well, they said that daddy had a wreck down the road and she started crying—next to the creek.
>
> "Q Your mother started crying. What was it that they said?
>
> "A That daddy had a wreck.
>
> "Q Did they say where?
>
> "A Down there next to the creek."

Lora did not describe hearing any struggle. Some time later, Lora and her brother left the house to look for their mother * * * . After the children returned home, according to Lora, her father came home and "fixed him a bologna sandwich and he took a bit of it and he says—sissy, where is mommy at, and I said—she ain't been here for a little while." Lora recalled that Mr. Muncey went outside and, not seeing his wife, returned to take Lora and Matthew to the Luttrells' so that he could look further.

The next afternoon Billy Ray Hensley, the victim's first cousin, heard of Mrs. Muncey's disappearance and went to look for Mr. Muncey. As he approached the Munceys' street, Hensley allegedly "saw Mr. House come out from under a bank, wiping his hands on a black rag." Just when and where Hensley saw House, and how well he could have observed him, were disputed at House's trial. Hensley admitted on cross-examination that he could not have seen House "walking up or climbing up" the embankment; rather, he saw House, in "[j]ust a glance," "appear out of nowhere," "next to the embankment." On the Munceys' street, opposite the area where Hensley said he saw House, a white Plymouth was parked near a sawmill. Another witness, Billy Hankins, whom the defense called, claimed that around the same time he saw a "boy" walking down the street away from the parked Plymouth and toward the Munceys' home. This witness, however, put the "boy" on the side of the street with the parked car and the Munceys' driveway, not the side with the embankment.

Hensley, after turning onto the Munceys' street, continued down the road and turned into their driveway. "I pulled up in the driveway where I could see up toward Little Hube's house," Hensley testified, "and I seen Little Hube's car wasn't there, and I backed out in the road, and come back [the other way]." As he traveled up the road, Hensley saw House traveling in the opposite direction in the white Plymouth. House "flagged [Hensley] down" through his windshield * * * According to Hensley, House said he had heard Mrs. Muncey was missing and was looking for her husband. Though House had only recently moved to the area, he was acquainted with the Munceys, had attended a dance with them, and had visited their home. He later told law enforcement officials he considered both of the Munceys his friends. According to Hensley, House said he had heard that Mrs. Muncey's husband, who was an alcoholic, was elsewhere "getting drunk."

As Hensley drove off, he "got to thinking to [him]self—he's hunting Little Hube, and Little Hube drunk—what would he be doing off that bank...." His suspicion aroused, Hensley later returned to the Munceys' street with a friend named Jack Adkins. The two checked different spots on the embankment, and though Hensley saw nothing where he looked, Adkins found Mrs. Muncey. Her body lay across from the sawmill near the corner where House's car had been parked, dumped in the woods a short way down the bank leading toward a creek.

Around midnight, Dr. Alex Carabia, a practicing pathologist and county medical examiner, performed an autopsy. Dr. Carabia put the time of death between 9 and 11 p.m. Mrs. Muncey had a black eye, both her hands were bloodstained up to the wrists, and she had bruises on her legs and neck. Dr. Carabia described the bruises as consistent with a "traumatic origin," *i.e.*, a fight or a fall on hard objects. Based on the neck bruises and other injuries, he concluded Mrs. Muncey had been choked, but he ruled this out as the cause of death. The cause of death, in Dr. Carabia's view, was a severe blow to the left forehead that inflicted both a laceration penetrating to the bone and, inside the skull, a severe right-side hemorrhage, likely caused by Mrs. Muncey's brain slamming into the skull opposite the impact. Dr. Carabia described this head injury as consistent either with receiving a blow from a fist or other instrument or with striking some object.

The county sheriff, informed about Hensley's earlier encounter with House, questioned House shortly after the body was found. That evening, House answered further questions during a voluntary interview at the local jail. Special Agent Ray Presnell of the Tennessee Bureau of Investigation (TBI) prepared a statement of House's answers, which House signed. Asked to describe his whereabouts on the previous evening, House claimed—falsely, as it turned out—that he spent the entire evening with his girlfriend, Donna Turner, at her trailer. Asked whether he was wearing the same pants he had worn the night before, House replied—again, falsely—that he was. House was on probation at the time, having recently been released on parole following a sentence of five years to life for aggravated sexual assault in Utah. House had scratches on his arms and hands, and a knuckle on his right ring finger was bruised. He attributed the scratches to Turner's cats and the finger injury to recent construction work tearing down a shed. The next day House gave a similar statement to a different TBI agent, Charles Scott.

In fact House had not been at Turner's home. After initially supporting House's alibi, Turner informed authorities that House left her trailer around 10:30 or 10:45 p.m. to go for a walk. According to Turner's trial testimony, House returned later—she was not sure when—hot and panting, missing his shirt and his shoes. House, Turner testified, told her that while he was walking on the road near her home, a vehicle pulled up beside him, and somebody inside "called him some names and then they told him he didn't belong here anymore." House said he tried to ignore the taunts and keep walking, but the vehicle pulled in behind him, and "one of them got out and grabbed him by the shoulder ... and [House] swung around with his right hand" and "hit something." According to Turner, House said "he took off down the bank and started running and he said that he—he said it seemed forever where he was running. And he said they fired two shots at him while he took off down the bank...." House claimed the assailants "grabbed ahold of his shirt," which Turner remembered as "a blue tank top, trimmed in yellow," and "they tore it to where it wouldn't stay on him and he said—I just throwed it off when I was running." Turner, noticing House's bruised knuckle, asked how he hurt it, and House told her "that's where he hit." Turner testified that she "thought maybe my ex-husband had something to do with it."

Although the white Plymouth House drove the next day belonged to Turner, Turner insisted House had not used the car that night. No forensic evidence connected the car to the crime; law enforcement officials inspected a white towel covering the driver seat and concluded it was clean. Turner's trailer was located just under two miles by road, through hilly terrain, from the Muncey residence.

Law enforcement officers also questioned the victim's husband. Though Mrs. Muncey's comments to Luttrell gave no indication she knew this, Mr. Muncey had spent the evening at a weekly dance at a recreation center roughly a mile and a half from his home. In his statement to law enforcement—a statement House's trial counsel claims he never saw—Muncey admitted leaving the dance early, but said it was only for a brief trip to the package store to buy beer. He also stated that he and his wife had had sexual relations Saturday morning.

Late in the evening on Monday, July 15—two days after the murder—law enforcement officers visited Turner's trailer. With Turner's consent, Agent Scott seized the pants House was wearing the night Mrs. Muncey disappeared. The heavily soiled pants were sitting in a laundry hamper; years later, Agent Scott recalled noticing "reddish brown stains" he "suspected" were blood. Around 4 p.m. the next day, two local law enforcement officers set out for the Federal Bureau of Investigation in Washington, D.C., with House's pants, blood samples from the autopsy, and other evidence packed together in a box. They arrived at 2:00 a.m. the next morning. On July 17, after initial FBI testing revealed human blood on the pants, House was arrested.

II

The State of Tennessee charged House with capital murder. At House's trial, the State presented testimony by Luttrell, Hensley, Adkins, Lora Muncey, Dr. Carabia, the sheriff, and other law enforcement officials. Through TBI Agents Presnell and Scott, the jury learned of House's false statements. Central to the State's case, however, was what the FBI testing showed—that semen consistent (or so it seemed) with House's was present on Mrs. Muncey's nightgown and panties, and that small bloodstains consistent with Mrs. Muncey's blood but not House's appeared on the jeans belonging to House.

Regarding the semen, FBI Special Agent Paul Bigbee, a serologist, testified that the source was a "secretor," meaning someone who "secrete[s] the ABO blood group substances in other body fluids, such as semen and saliva"—a characteristic shared by 80 percent of the population, including House. Agent Bigbee further testified that the source of semen on the gown was blood-type A, House's own blood type. As to the semen on the panties, Agent Bigbee found only the H blood-group substance, which A and B blood-type secretors secrete along with substances A and B, and which O-type secretors secrete exclusively. Agent Bigbee explained, however—using science an *amicus* here sharply disputes—that House's A antigens could have "degraded" into H. Agent Bigbee thus concluded that both semen deposits could have come from House, though he acknowledged that the H antigen could have come from Mrs. Muncey herself if she was a secretor—something he "was not able to determine,"—and that, while Mr. Muncey was himself blood-type A (as was his wife), Agent Bigbee was again "not able to determine his secretor status." Agent Bigbee acknowledged on cross-examination that "a saliva sample" would have sufficed to determine whether Mr. Muncey was a secretor; the State did not provide such a sample, though it did provide samples of Mr. Muncey's blood.

As for the blood, Agent Bigbee explained that "spots of blood" appeared "on the left outside leg, the right bottom cuff, on the left thigh and in the right inside pocket and on the lower pocket on the outside." Agent Bigbee determined that the blood's source was type A (the type shared by House, the victim, and Mr. Muncey). He also successfully tested for the enzyme phosphoglucomutase and the blood serum haptoglobin, both of which "are found in all humans" and carry "slight chemical differences" that vary genetically and "can be grouped to differentiate between two individuals if those types are different." Based on these chemical traces and on the A blood type, Agent Bigbee determined that only some 6.75 percent of the population carry similar blood, that the blood was "consistent" with Mrs. Muncey's (as determined by testing autopsy samples), and that it was "impossible" that the blood came from House.

A different FBI expert, Special Agent Chester Blythe, testified about fiber analysis performed on Mrs. Muncey's clothes and on House's pants. Although Agent Blythe found blue jean fibers on Mrs. Muncey's nightgown, brassier, housecoat, and panties, and in fingernail scrapings taken from her body (scrapings that also contained trace, unidentifiable amounts of blood), he acknowledged that, as the prosecutor put it in questioning the witness, "blue jean material is common material," so "this doesn't mean that the fibers that were all over the victim's clothing were necessarily from [House's] pair of blue jeans." On House's pants, though cotton garments both transfer and retain fibers readily, Agent Blythe found neither hair nor fiber consistent with the victim's hair or clothing.

In the defense case House called Hankins, Clinton, and Turner, as well as House's mother, who testified that House had talked to her by telephone around 9:30 p.m. on the night of the murder and that he had not used her car that evening. House also called the victim's brother, Ricky Green, as a witness. Green testified that on July 2, roughly two weeks before the murder, Mrs. Muncey called him and "said her and Little Hube had been into it and she said she was wanting to leave Little Hube, she said she was wanting to get out—out of it, and she was scared." Green recalled that at Christmastime in 1982 he had seen Mr. Muncey strike Mrs. Muncey after returning home drunk.

As Turner informed the jury, House's shoes were found several months after the crime in a field near her home. Turner delivered them to authorities. Though the jury did not learn of this fact (and House's counsel claims he did not either), the State tested the shoes for blood and found none. House's shirt was not found.

The State's closing argument suggested that on the night of her murder, Mrs. Muncey "was deceived.... She had been told [her husband] had had an accident." The prosecutor emphasized the FBI's blood analysis, noting that "after running many, many, many tests," Agent Bigbee:

> "was able to tell you that the blood on the defendant's blue jeans was not his own blood, could not be his own blood. He told you that the blood on the blue jeans was consistent with every characteristic in every respect of the deceased's, Carolyn Muncey's, and that ninety-three (93%) percent of the white population would not have that blood type.... He can't tell you one hundred (100%) percent for certain that it was her blood. But folks, he can sure give you a pretty good—a pretty good indication."

In the State's rebuttal, after defense counsel questioned House's motive "to go over and kill a woman that he barely knew[,][w]ho was still dressed, still clad in her clothes," the prosecutor referred obliquely to the semen stains. While explaining that legally "it does not make any difference under God's heaven, what the motive was," the prosecutor told the jury, "you may have an idea why he did it":

> "The evidence at the scene which seemed to suggest that he was subjecting this lady to some kind of indignity, why would you get a lady out of her house, late at night, in her night clothes, under the trick that her husband has had a wreck down by the creek? ... Well, it is because either you don't want her to tell what indignities you have subjected her to, or she is unwilling and fights against you, against being subjected to those indignities. In other words, it is either to keep her from telling what you have done to her, or it is that you are trying to get her to do something that she nor any mother on that road would want to do with Mr. House, under those conditions, and you kill her because of her resistance. That is what the evidence at the scene suggests about motive."

In addition the government suggested the black rag Hensley said he saw in House's hands was in fact the missing blue tank top, retrieved by House from the crime scene. And the prosecution reiterated the importance of the blood. "[D]efense counsel," he said, "does not start out discussing the fact that his client had blood on his jeans on the night that Carolyn Muncey was killed.... He doesn't start with the fact that nothing that the defense has introduced in this case explains what blood is doing on his jeans, all over his jeans, that is scientifically, completely different from his blood." The jury found House guilty of murder in the first degree.

The trial advanced to the sentencing phase. As aggravating factors to support a capital sentence, the State sought to prove: (1) that House had previously been convicted of a felony involving the use or threat of violence; (2) that the homicide was especially heinous, atrocious, or cruel in that it involved torture or depravity of mind; and (3) that the murder was committed while House was committing, attempting to commit, or fleeing from the commission of, rape or kidnapping. After presenting evidence of House's parole status and aggravated sexual assault conviction, the State rested. As mitigation, the defense offered testimony from House's father and mother, as well as evidence, presented through House's mother, that House attempted suicide after the guilt-phase verdict. Before the attempt House wrote his mother a letter professing his innocence.

In closing the State urged the jury to find all three aggravating factors and impose death. As to the kidnapping or rape factor, the prosecution suggested Mrs. Muncey was "decoy[ed] or entic[ed] ... away from her family, and confin [ed] her against her will because you know that as she was being beaten to death." "We also think," the prosecutor added, "the proof shows strong evidence of attempted sexual molestation of the victim to accompany the taking away and murdering her." Later the prosecutor argued, "I think the proof shows in the record that it is more likely than not that having been through the process before and having been convicted of a crime involving the threat of violence, or violence to another person, aggravated sexual assault, that the defendant cannot benefit from the type of rehabilitation that correction departments can provide." The jury unanimously found all three aggravating factors and concluded "there are no mitigating circumstances sufficiently substantial to outweigh the statutory aggravating circumstance or circumstances." The jury recommended a death sentence, which the trial judge imposed.

III

The Tennessee Supreme Court affirmed House's conviction and sentence, describing the evidence against House as "circumstantial" but "quite strong." * * * House filed a *pro se* petition for postconviction relief, arguing he received ineffective assistance of counsel at trial. The court appointed counsel, who amended the petition to raise other issues, including a challenge to certain jury instructions. At a hearing before the same judge who conducted the trial, House's counsel offered no proof beyond the trial transcript. The trial court dismissed the petition, deeming House's trial counsel adequate and overruling House's other objections. On appeal House's attorney renewed only the jury-instructions argument. * * * [T]he Tennessee Court of Criminal Appeals affirmed, and both the Tennessee Supreme Court and this Court denied review.

House filed a second postconviction petition in state court reasserting his ineffective-assistance claim and seeking investigative and/or expert assistance. * * * [T]he Tennessee Supreme Court held that House's claims were barred under a state statute providing that claims not raised in prior postconviction proceedings are presumptively waived, and that courts may not consider grounds for relief "which the court finds should be excluded because they have been waived or previously determined." * * * This Court denied certiorari.

House next sought federal habeas relief, asserting numerous claims of ineffective assistance of counsel and prosecutorial misconduct. The United States District Court for the Eastern District of Tennessee, though deeming House's claims procedurally defaulted and granting summary judgment to the State on the majority of House's claims, held an evidentiary hearing to determine whether House fell within the "actual innocence" exception to procedural default that this Court recognized as to substantive offenses in *Schlup* and as to death sentences in *Sawyer v. Whitley*. Presenting evidence we describe in greater detail below, House attacked the semen and blood evidence used at his trial and presented other evidence, including a putative confession, suggesting that Mr. Muncey, not House, committed the murder. The District Court nevertheless denied relief, holding that House had neither demonstrated actual innocence of the murder under *Schlup* nor established that he was ineligible for the death penalty under *Sawyer*.

The Court of Appeals for the Sixth Circuit granted a certificate of appealability under 28 U.S.C. § 2253(c) as to all claims in the habeas petition. On the merits a divided panel affirmed, but its opinion was withdrawn and the case taken en banc. A divided en banc court certified state-law questions to the Tennessee Supreme Court. Concluding that House had made a compelling showing of actual innocence, and recognizing that in *Herrera v. Collins*, this Court assumed without deciding that "in a capital case a truly persuasive demonstration of 'actual innocence' made after trial would render the execution of a defendant unconstitutional, and warrant federal habeas relief if there were no state avenue open to process such a claim," the six-judge majority certified questions to the

State Supreme Court. The questions sought "to ascertain whether there remains a 'state avenue open to process such a claim' in this case." Four dissenting judges argued the court should have reached the merits, rather than certifying questions to the state court; these judges asserted that House could not obtain relief under *Schlup,* let alone *Sawyer* and *Herrera.* A fifth dissenter explained that while he agreed with the majority that House "presents a strong claim for habeas relief, at least at the sentencing phase of the case," he objected to the certification of questions to the Tennessee high court. This Court denied certiorari.

The State urged the Tennessee Supreme Court not to answer the Court of Appeals' certified questions, and the state court did not do so. The case returned to the United States Court of Appeals for the Sixth Circuit. This time an eight-judge majority affirmed the District Court's denial of habeas relief. Six dissenters argued that House not only had met the actual innocence standard for overcoming procedural default but also was entitled to immediate release under *Herrera.* A seventh dissenter (the same judge who wrote separately in the previous en banc decision) described the case as "a real-life murder mystery, an authentic 'who-done-it' where the wrong man may be executed." He concluded such grave uncertainty necessitated relief in the form of a new trial for House.

We granted certiorari, and now reverse.

IV

As a general rule, claims forfeited under state law may support federal habeas relief only if the prisoner demonstrates cause for the default and prejudice from the asserted error. *See Murray v. Carrier*; *Engle v. Isaac*; *Wainwright v. Sykes.* The rule is based on the comity and respect that must be accorded to state-court judgments. The bar is not, however, unqualified. In an effort to "balance the societal interests in finality, comity, and conservation of scarce judicial resources with the individual interest in justice that arises in the extraordinary case," *Schlup,* the Court has recognized a miscarriage-of-justice exception. "'[I]n appropriate cases,'" the Court has said, "the principles of comity and finality that inform the concepts of cause and prejudice 'must yield to the imperative of correcting a fundamentally unjust incarceration,'" *Carrier.*

In *Schlup,* the Court adopted a specific rule to implement this general principle. It held that prisoners asserting innocence as a gateway to defaulted claims must establish that, in light of new evidence, "it is more likely than not that no reasonable juror would have found petitioner guilty beyond a reasonable doubt." * * *

For purposes of this case several features of the *Schlup* standard bear emphasis. First, although "[t]o be credible" a gateway claim requires "new reliable evidence—whether it be exculpatory scientific evidence, trustworthy eyewitness accounts, or critical physical evidence—that was not presented at trial," the habeas court's analysis is not limited to such evidence. There is no dispute in this case that House has presented some new reliable evidence; the State has conceded as much. In addition, because the District Court held an evidentiary hearing in this case, and because the State does not challenge the court's decision to do so, we have no occasion to elaborate on *Schlup's* observation that when considering an actual-innocence claim in the context of a request for an evidentiary hearing, the District Court need not "test the new evidence by a standard appropriate for deciding a motion for summary judgment," but rather may "consider how the timing of the submission and the likely credibility of the affiants bear on the probable reliability of that evidence." Our review in this case addresses the merits of the *Schlup* inquiry, based on a fully developed record, and with respect to that inquiry *Schlup* makes plain that the habeas court must consider "'all the evidence,'" old and new, incriminating and exculpatory, without regard to whether it would necessarily be admitted under "rules of admissibility that would govern at trial." Based on this total record, the court must make "a probabilistic determination about what reasonable, properly instructed jurors would do." *[Schlup]*. The court's function is not to make an independent factual determination about what likely occurred, but rather to assess the likely impact of the evidence on reasonable jurors.

Second, it bears repeating that the *Schlup* standard is demanding and permits review only in the "'extraordinary'" case. At the same time, though, the *Schlup* standard does not require absolute certainty about the petitioner's guilt or innocence. A petitioner's burden at the gateway stage is to demonstrate that more likely than not, in light of the new evidence, no reasonable juror would find him guilty beyond a reasonable doubt—or, to remove the double negative, that more likely than not any reasonable juror would have reasonable doubt.

Finally, as the *Schlup* decision explains, the gateway actual-innocence standard is "by no means equivalent to the standard of *Jackson v. Virginia,*" which governs claims of insufficient evidence. When confronted with a challenge based on trial evidence, courts presume the jury resolved evidentiary disputes reasonably so long as sufficient evidence supports the verdict. Because a *Schlup* claim involves evidence the trial jury did not have before it, the inquiry requires the federal court to assess how reasonable jurors would react to the overall, newly supplemented record. If new evidence so requires, this may include consideration of "the credibility of the witnesses presented at trial."

As an initial matter, the State argues that the Antiterrorism and Effective Death Penalty Act of 1996 (AEDPA), has replaced the *Schlup* standard with a stricter test based on *Sawyer,* which permits consideration of successive, abusive, or defaulted sentencing-related claims only if the petitioner "show[s] by clear and convincing evidence that, but for a constitutional error, no reasonable juror would have found the petitioner eligible for the death penalty under the applicable state law." One AEDPA provision establishes a similar standard for second or successive petitions involving no retroactively applicable new law; another sets it as a threshold for obtaining an evidentiary hearing on claims the petitioner failed to develop in state court. Neither provision addresses the type of petition at issue here—a first federal habeas petition seeking consideration of defaulted claims based on a showing of actual innocence. Thus, the standard of review in these provisions is inapplicable. * * *

The State also argues that the District Court's findings in this case tie our hands, precluding a ruling in House's favor absent a showing of clear error as to the District Court's specific determinations. This view overstates the effect of the District Court's ruling. Deference is given to a trial court's assessment of evidence presented to it in the first instance. Yet the *Schlup* inquiry, we repeat, requires a holistic judgment about "'all the evidence,'" and its likely effect on reasonable jurors applying the reasonable-doubt standard. As a general rule, the inquiry does not turn on discrete findings regarding disputed points of fact, and "[i]t is not the district court's independent judgment as to whether reasonable doubt exists that the standard addresses." Here, although the District Court attentively managed complex proceedings, carefully reviewed the extensive record, and drew certain conclusions about the evidence, the court did not clearly apply *Schlup's* predictive standard regarding whether reasonable jurors would have reasonable doubt. As we shall explain, moreover, we are uncertain about the basis for some of the District Court's conclusions—a consideration that weakens our reliance on its determinations.

With this background in mind we turn to the evidence developed in House's federal habeas proceedings.

DNA Evidence

First, in direct contradiction of evidence presented at trial, DNA testing has established that the semen on Mrs. Muncey's nightgown and panties came from her husband, Mr. Muncey, not from House. The State, though conceding this point, insists this new evidence is immaterial. At the guilt phase at least, neither sexual contact nor motive were elements of the offense, so in the State's view the evidence, or lack of evidence, of sexual assault or sexual advance is of no consequence. We disagree. In fact we consider the new disclosure of central importance.

From beginning to end the case is about who committed the crime. When identity is in question, motive is key. The point, indeed, was not lost on the prosecution, for it introduced the evidence and relied on it in the final guilt-phase closing argument. Referring to "evidence at the scene," the prosecutor suggested that House committed, or attempted to commit, some "indignity" on Mrs. Muncey that neither she "nor any mother on that road would want to do with Mr. House." Particularly in a case like this where the proof was, as the State Supreme Court observed, circumstantial, we think a jury would have given this evidence great weight. Quite apart from providing proof of motive, it was the only forensic evidence at the scene that would link House to the murder.

Law and society, as they ought to do, demand accountability when a sexual offense has been committed, so not only did this evidence link House to the crime; it likely was a factor in persuading the jury not to let him go free. At sentencing, moreover, the jury came to the unanimous conclusion, beyond a reasonable doubt, that the murder was committed in the course of a rape or kidnapping. The alleged sexual motivation relates to both those determinations. This is particularly so given that, at the sentencing phase, the jury was advised that House had a previous conviction for sexual assault.

A jury informed that fluids on Mrs. Muncey's garments could have come from House might have found that House trekked the nearly two miles to the victim's home and lured her away in order to commit a sexual offense. By contrast a jury acting without the assumption that the semen could have come from House would have found it necessary to establish some different motive, or, if the same motive, an intent far more speculative. When the only direct evidence of sexual assault drops out of the case, so, too, does a central theme in the State's narrative linking House to the crime. In that light, furthermore, House's odd evening walk and his false statements to authorities, while still potentially incriminating, might appear less suspicious.

Bloodstains

The other relevant forensic evidence is the blood on House's pants, which appears in small, even minute, stains in scattered places. As the prosecutor told the jury, they were stains that, due to their small size, "you or I might not detect[,] [m]ight not see, but which the FBI lab was able to find on [House's] jeans." The stains appear inside the right pocket, outside that pocket, near the inside button, on the left thigh and outside leg, on the seat of the pants, and on the right bottom cuff, including inside the pants. * * * At trial, the government argued "nothing that the defense has introduced in this case explains what blood is doing on his jeans, all over [House's] jeans, that is scientifically, completely different from his blood." House, though not disputing at this point that the blood is Mrs. Muncey's, now presents an alternative explanation that, if credited, would undermine the probative value of the blood evidence.

During House's habeas proceedings, Dr. Cleland Blake, an Assistant Chief Medical Examiner for the State of Tennessee and a consultant in forensic pathology to the TBI for

22 years, testified that the blood on House's pants was chemically too degraded, and too similar to blood collected during the autopsy, to have come from Mrs. Muncey's body on the night of the crime. The blood samples collected during the autopsy were placed in test tubes without preservative. Under such conditions, according to Dr. Blake, "you will have enzyme degradation. You will have different blood group degradation, blood marker degradation." The problem of decay, moreover, would have been compounded by the body's long exposure to the elements, sitting outside for the better part of a summer day. In contrast, if blood is preserved on cloth, "it will stay there for years" * * * The blood on House's pants, judging by Agent Bigbee's tests, showed "similar deterioration, breakdown of certain of the named numbered enzymes" as in the autopsy samples. "[I]f the victim's blood had spilled on the jeans while the victim was alive and this blood had dried," Dr. Blake stated, "the deterioration would not have occurred," *ibid.*, and "you would expect [the blood on the jeans] to be different than what was in the tube." Dr. Blake thus concluded the blood on the jeans came from the autopsy samples, not from Mrs. Muncey's live (or recently killed) body.

Other evidence confirms that blood did in fact spill from the vials. * * * The blood was contained in four vials, evidently with neither preservative nor a proper seal. The vials, in turn, were stored in a styrofoam box, but nothing indicates the box was kept cool. Rather, in what an evidence protocol expert at the habeas hearing described as a violation of proper procedure, the styrofoam box was packed in the same cardboard box as other evidence including House's pants (apparently in a paper bag) and other clothing (in separate bags). The cardboard box was then carried in the officers' car while they made the 10-hour journey from Tennessee to the FBI lab. Dr. Blake stated that blood vials in hot conditions (such as a car trunk in the summer) could blow open; and in fact, by the time the blood reached the FBI it had hemolyzed, or spoiled, due to heat exposure. By the time the blood passed from the FBI to a defense expert, roughly a vial and a half were empty, though Agent Bigbee testified he used at most a quarter of one vial. Blood, moreover, had seeped onto one corner of the styrofoam box and onto packing gauze inside the box below the vials.

In addition, although the pants apparently were packaged initially in a paper bag and FBI records suggest they arrived at the FBI in one, the record does not contain the paper bag but does contain a plastic bag with a label listing the pants and Agent Scott's name—and the plastic bag has blood on it. The blood appears in a forked streak roughly five inches long and two inches wide running down the bag's outside front. Though testing by House's expert confirmed the stain was blood, the expert could not determine the blood's source. Speculations about when and how the blood got there add to the confusion regarding the origins of the stains on House's pants.

Faced with these indications of, at best, poor evidence control, the State attempted to establish at the habeas hearing that all blood spillage occurred after Agent Bigbee examined the pants. Were that the case, of course, then blood would have been detected on the pants before any spill—which would tend to undermine Dr. Blake's analysis and support using the bloodstains to infer House's guilt. In support of this theory the State put on testimony by a blood spatter expert who believed the "majority" of the stains were "transfer stains," that is, stains resulting from "wip[ing] across the surface of the pants" rather than seeping or spillage. Regarding the spillage in the styrofoam box, the expert noted that yellow "Tennessee Crime Laboratory" tape running around the box and down all four sides did not line up when the bloodstains on the box's corner were aligned. The inference was that the FBI received the box from Tennessee authorities, opened it, and resealed it before the spillage occurred. Reinforcing this theory, Agent Bigbee testified that he observed no blood spillage in the styrofoam box and that had he detected such signs of evidence contamination, FBI policy would have required immediate return of the evidence.

In response House argued that even assuming the tape alignment showed spillage occurring after FBI testing, spillage on one or more earlier occasions was likely. In fact even the State's spatter expert declined to suggest the blood in the box and on the packing gauze accounted for the full vial and a quarter missing. And when the defense expert opened the box and discovered the spills, the bulk of the blood-caked gauze was located around and underneath the half-full vial, which was also located near the stained corner. No gauze immediately surrounding the completely empty vial was stained. The tape, moreover, circled the box in two layers, one underneath the other, and in one spot the underlying layer stops cleanly at the lid's edge, as if cut with a razor, and does not continue onto the body of the box below. In House's view this clean cut suggests the double layers could not have resulted simply from wrapping the tape around twice, as the spatter expert claimed; rather, someone possessing Tennessee Crime Lab tape—perhaps the officers transporting the blood and pants—must have cut the box open and resealed it, possibly creating an opportunity for spillage. Supporting the same inference, a label on the box's lid lists both blood and vaginal secretions as the box's contents, though Agent Bigbee's records show the vaginal fluids arrived at the FBI in a separate envelope. Finally, cross-examination revealed that Agent Bigbee's practice did not always match the letter of FBI policy. Although Mrs. Muncey's bra and housecoat were packed together in a single bag, creating, according to Agent Bigbee, a risk of "cross contamination," he did not return them; nor did he note the discrepancy between the "[b]lood and [v]aginal secretions" label and the styrofoam box's actual contents, though he insisted his customary practice was to match labels with contents immediately upon opening an evidence box.

The State challenged Dr. Blake's scientific conclusions * * * Agent Bigbee defended the testimony he had given at the trial. * * * Agent Bigbee further asserted that, whereas Dr. Blake (in Bigbee's view) construed the results to mean the enzyme was not present at all, in fact the results indicated only that Bigbee could not identify the marker type on whatever enzymes were present. Yet the State did not cross-examine Dr. Blake on this point, nor did the District Court resolve the dispute one way or the other, so on this record it seems possible that Dr. Blake meant only to suggest the blood was too degraded to permit conclusive typing. The State, moreover, does not ask us to question Dr. Blake's basic premise about the durability of blood chemicals deposited on cotton—a premise Agent Bigbee appeared to accept as a general matter. Given the record as it stands, then, we cannot say Dr. Blake's conclusions have been discredited * * * At the least, the record before us contains credible testimony suggesting that the missing enzyme markers are generally better preserved on cloth than in poorly kept test tubes, and that principle could support House's spillage theory for the blood's origin.

In this Court, as a further attack on House's showing, the State suggests that, given the spatter expert's testimony, House's theory would require a jury to surmise that Tennessee officials donned the pants and deliberately spread blood over them. We disagree. This should be a matter for the trier of fact to consider in the first instance, but we can note a line of argument that could refute the State's position. It is correct that the State's spatter expert opined that the stains resulted from wiping or smearing rather than direct spillage; and she further stated that the distribution of stains in some spots suggests the pants were "folded in some manner or creased in some manner" when the transfers occurred. While the expert described this pattern, at least with respect to stains on the lap of the pants, as "consistent" with the pants being worn at the time of the staining, her testimony, as we understand it, does not refute the hypothesis that the packaging of the pants for transport was what caused them to be folded or creased. It seems permissible, moreover, to conclude that the small size and wide distribution of stains—inside the right pocket, outside that pocket, near the inside button, on the left thigh and outside leg, on the seat of the pants, and on the right bottom cuff, including inside the pants—fits as well with spillage in transport as with wiping and smearing from bloody objects at the crime scene, as the State proposes. (As has been noted, no blood was found on House's shoes.)

The District Court discounted Dr. Blake's opinion * * * based on testimony from Agent Scott indicating he saw, as the District Court put it, "what appeared to be bloodstains on Mr. House's blue jeans when the jeans were removed from the laundry hamper at Ms. Turner's trailer." This inference seems at least open to question, however. Agent Scott stated only that he "saw reddish brownish stains [he] suspected to be blood"; he admitted that he "didn't thoroughly examine the blue jeans at that time." The pants were in fact extensively soiled with mud and reddish stains, only small portions of which are blood.

In sum, considering "'all the evidence,'" *Schlup,* on this issue, we think the evidentiary disarray surrounding the blood, taken together with Dr. Blake's testimony and the limited rebuttal of it in the present record, would prevent reasonable jurors from placing significant reliance on the blood evidence. We now know, though the trial jury did not, that an Assistant Chief Medical Examiner believes the blood on House's jeans must have come from autopsy samples; that a vial and a quarter of autopsy blood is unaccounted for; that the blood was transported to the FBI together with the pants in conditions that could have caused vials to spill; that the blood did indeed spill at least once during its journey from Tennessee authorities through FBI hands to a defense expert; that the pants were stored in a plastic bag bearing both a large blood stain and a label with TBI Agent Scott's name; and that the styrofoam box containing the blood samples may well have been opened before it arrived at the FBI lab. Thus, whereas the bloodstains, emphasized by the prosecution, seemed strong evidence of House's guilt at trial, the record now raises substantial questions about the blood's origin.

A Different Suspect

Were House's challenge to the State's case limited to the questions he has raised about the blood and semen, the other evidence favoring the prosecution might well suffice to bar relief. There is, however, more; for in the post-trial proceedings House presented troubling evidence that Mr. Muncey, the victim's husband, himself could have been the murderer.

At trial * * * the jury heard that roughly two weeks before the murder Mrs. Muncey's brother received a frightened phone call from his sister indicating that she and Mr. Muncey had been fighting, that she was scared, and that she wanted to leave him. The jury also learned that the brother once saw Mr. Muncey "smac[k]" the victim. House now has produced evidence from multiple sources suggesting that Mr. Muncey regularly abused his wife. For example, one witness—Kathy Parker, a lifelong area resident who denied any animosity towards Mr. Muncey—recalled that Mrs. Muncey "was constantly with black eyes and busted mouth." In addition Hazel Miller, who is Kathy Parker's mother and a lifelong acquaintance of Mr. Muncey, testified at the habeas hearing that two or three months before the victim's death Mr. Muncey came to Miller's home and "tried to get my daughter [Parker] to go out with him," * * * According to Miller, Muncey said "[h]e was upset with his wife, that they had had an argument and he said he was going to get rid of that woman one way or the other."

Another witness—Mary Atkins, also an area native who "grew up" with Mr. Muncey and professed no hard feelings—claims she saw Mr. Muncey "backhan[d]" Mrs. Muncey on the very night of the murder. Atkins recalled that during a break in the recreation center dance, she saw Mr. Muncey and his wife arguing in the parking lot. Mr. Muncey "grabbed her and he just backhanded her." After that, Mrs. Muncey "left walking." There was also testimony from Atkins' mother, named Artie Lawson. A self-described "good friend" of Mr. Muncey, Lawson said Mr. Muncey visited her the morning after the murder, before the body was found. According to Lawson, Mr. Muncey asked her to tell anyone who inquired not only that she had been at the dance the evening before and had seen him, but also that he had breakfasted at her home at 6 o'clock that morning. Lawson had not in fact been at the dance, nor had Mr. Muncey been with her so early.

Of most importance is the testimony of Kathy Parker and her sister Penny Letner. They testified at the habeas hearing that, around the time of House's trial, Mr. Muncey had confessed to the crime. Parker recalled that she and "some family members and some friends [were] sitting around drinking" at Parker's trailer when Mr. Muncey "just walked in and sit down." Muncey, who had evidently been drinking heavily, began "rambling off ... [t]alking about what happened to his wife and how it happened and he didn't mean to do it." According to Parker, Mr. Muncey "said they had been into [an] argument and he slapped her and she fell and hit her head and it killed her and he didn't mean for it to happen." Parker said she "freaked out and run him off."

Letner similarly recalled that at some point either "during [House's] trial or just before," Mr. Muncey intruded on a gathering at Parker's home. Appearing "pretty well blistered," Muncey "went to crying and was talking about his wife and her death and he was saying that he didn't mean to do it." "[D]idn't mean to do what[?]," Letner asked, at which point Mr. Muncey explained:

> [S]he was 'bitching him out' because he didn't take her fishing that night, that he went to the dance instead. He said when he come home that she was still on him pretty heavily 'bitching him out' again and that he smacked her and that she fell and hit her head. He said I didn't mean to do it, but I had to get rid of her, because I didn't want to be charged with murder.

Letner, who was then 19 years old with a small child, said Mr. Muncey's statement "scared [her] quite badly," so she "got out of there immediately." Asked whether she reported the incident to the authorities, Letner stated, "I was frightened, you know.... I figured me being 19 year old they wouldn't listen to anything I had to say." Parker, on the other hand, claimed she (Parker) in fact went to the Sherriff's Department, but no one would listen:

> "I tried to speak to the Sheriff but he was real busy. He sent me to a deputy. The deputy told me to go upstairs to the courtroom and talk to this guy, I can't remember his name. I never did really get to talk to anybody."

Parker said she did not discuss the matter further because "[t]hey had it all signed, sealed and delivered. We didn't know anything to do until we heard that they reopened [House's] trial." Parker's mother, Hazel Miller, confirmed she had driven Parker to the courthouse, where Parker "went to talk to some of the people about this case."

Other testimony suggests Mr. Muncey had the opportunity to commit the crime. According to Dennis Wallace, a local law enforcement official who provided security at the dance on the night of the murder, Mr. Muncey left the dance "around 10:00, 10:30, 9:30 to 10:30." Although Mr. Muncey told law enforcement officials just after the murder that he left the dance only briefly and returned, Wallace could not recall seeing him back there again. Later that evening, Wallace responded to Mr. Muncey's report that his wife was missing. Muncey denied he and his wife had been "a fussing or a fighting"; he claimed his wife had been "kidnapped." Wallace did not recall seeing any blood, disarray, or knocked-over furniture, although he admitted he "didn't pay too much attention" to whether the floor appeared especially clean. According to Wallace, Mr. Muncey said " let's search for her" and then led Wallace out to search "in the weeds" around the home and the driveway (not out on the road where the body was found).

In the habeas proceedings, then, two different witnesses (Parker and Letner) described a confession by Mr. Muncey; two more (Atkins and Lawson) described suspicious behavior (a fight and an attempt to construct a false alibi) around the time of the crime; and still other witnesses described a history of abuse.

As to Parker and Letner, the District Court noted that it was "not impressed with the allegations of individuals who wait over ten years to come forward with their evidence," especially considering that "there was no physical evidence in the Munceys' kitchen to corroborate [Mr. Muncey's] alleged confession that he killed [his wife] there." Parker and Letner, however, did attempt to explain their delay coming forward, and the record indicates no reason why these two women, both lifelong acquaintances of Mr. Muncey, would have wanted either to frame him or to help House. Furthermore, the record includes at least some independent support for the statements Parker and Letner attributed to Mr. Muncey. The supposed explanation for the fatal fight—that his wife was complaining about going fishing—fits with Mrs. Muncey's statement to Luttrell earlier that evening that her husband's absence was "all right, because she was going to make him take her fishing the next day." And Dr. Blake testified, in only partial contradiction of Dr. Carabia, that Mrs. Muncey's head injury resulted from "a surface with an edge" or "a hard surface with a corner," not from a fist.

Mr. Muncey testified at the habeas hearing, and the District Court did not question his credibility. Though Mr. Muncey said he seemed to remember visiting Lawson the day after the murder, he denied either killing his wife or confessing to doing so. Yet Mr. Muncey also claimed, contrary to Constable Wallace's testimony and to his own prior statement, that he left the dance on the night of the crime only when it ended at midnight. Mr. Muncey, moreover, denied ever hitting Mrs. Muncey; the State itself had to impeach him with a prior statement on this point.

It bears emphasis, finally, that Parker's and Letner's testimony is not comparable to the sort of eleventh-hour affidavit vouching for a defendant and incriminating a conveniently absent suspect that Justice O'Connor described in her concurring opinion in *Herrera* as "unfortunate" and "not uncommon" in capital cases; nor was the confession Parker and Letner described induced under pressure of interrogation. The confession evidence here involves an alleged spontaneous statement recounted by two eyewitnesses with no evident motive to lie. For this reason it has more probative value than, for example, incriminating testimony from inmates, suspects, or friends or relations of the accused.

The evidence pointing to Mr. Muncey is by no means conclusive. If considered in isolation, a reasonable jury might well disregard it. In combination, however, with the challenges to the blood evidence and the lack of motive with respect to House, the evidence pointing to Mr. Muncey likely would reinforce other doubts as to House's guilt.

Other Evidence

Certain other details were presented at the habeas hearing. First, Dr. Blake, in addition to testifying about the blood evidence and the victim's head injury, examined photographs of House's bruises and scratches and concluded, based on 35 years' experience monitoring the development and healing of bruises, that they were too old to have resulted from the crime. In addition Dr. Blake claimed that the injury on House's right knuckle was indicative of "[g]etting mashed"; it was not consistent with striking someone. (That of course would also eliminate the explanation that the injury came from the blow House supposedly told Turner he gave to his unidentified assailant.)

The victim's daughter, Lora Muncey (now Lora Tharp), also testified at the habeas hearing. She repeated her recollection of hearing a man with a deep voice like her grandfather's and a statement that her father had had a wreck down by the creek. She also denied seeing any signs of struggle or hearing a fight between her parents, though she also said she could not recall her parents ever fighting physically. The District Court found her credible, and this testimony certainly cuts in favor of the State.

Finally, House himself testified at the habeas proceedings. He essentially repeated the story he allegedly told Turner about getting attacked on the road. The District Court found, however, based on House's demeanor, that he "was not a credible witness."

Conclusion

This is not a case of conclusive exoneration. Some aspects of the State's evidence—Lora Muncey's memory of a deep voice, House's bizarre evening walk, his lie to law enforcement, his appearance near the body, and the blood on his pants—still support an inference of guilt. Yet the central forensic proof connecting House to the crime—the blood and the semen—has been called into question, and House has put forward substantial evidence pointing to a different suspect. Accordingly, and although the issue is close, we conclude that this is the rare case where—had the jury heard all the conflicting testimony—it is more likely than not that no reasonable juror viewing the record as a whole would lack reasonable doubt.

V

In addition to his gateway claim under *Schlup,* House argues that he has shown freestanding innocence and that as a result his imprisonment and planned execution are unconstitutional. In *Herrera,* decided three years before *Schlup,* the Court assumed without deciding that "in a capital case a truly persuasive demonstration of 'actual innocence' made after trial would render the execution of a defendant unconstitutional, and warrant federal habeas relief if there were no state avenue open to process such a claim." "[T]he threshold showing for such an assumed right would necessarily be extraordinarily high," the Court explained, and petitioner's evidence there fell "far short of that which would have to be made in order to trigger the sort of constitutional claim which we have assumed, *arguendo,* to exist." House urges the Court to answer the question left open in *Herrera* and hold not only that freestanding innocence claims are possible but also that he has established one.

We decline to resolve this issue. We conclude here, much as in *Herrera,* that whatever burden a hypothetical freestanding innocence claim would require, this petitioner has not satisfied it. To be sure, House has cast considerable doubt on his guilt—doubt sufficient to satisfy *Schlup's* gateway standard for obtaining federal review despite a state procedural default. In *Herrera,* however, the Court described the threshold for any hypothetical freestanding innocence claim as "extraordinarily high." The sequence of the Court's decisions in *Herrera* and *Schlup*—first leaving unresolved the status of freestanding claims and then establishing the gateway standard—implies at the least that *Herrera* requires more convincing proof of innocence than *Schlup*. It follows, given the closeness of the *Schlup* question here, that House's showing falls short of the threshold implied in *Herrera*.

House has satisfied the gateway standard set forth in *Schlup* and may proceed on remand with procedurally defaulted constitutional claims. The judgment of the Court of Appeals is reversed, and the case is remanded for further proceedings consistent with this opinion.

It is so ordered.

CHIEF JUSTICE ROBERTS, with whom JUSTICE SCALIA and JUSTICE THOMAS join, concurring in the judgment in part and dissenting in part.

To overcome the procedural hurdle that Paul House created by failing to properly present his constitutional claims to a Tennessee court, he must demonstrate that the constitutional violations he alleges "ha[ve] probably resulted in the conviction of one who is actually innocent," such that a federal court's refusal to hear the defaulted claims would be a "miscarriage of justice." *Schlup v. Delo*. To make the requisite showing of actual innocence, House must produce "new *reliable* evidence" and "must show that it is more likely than not that no reasonable juror would have convicted him in the light of the new evidence." The question is not whether House was prejudiced at his trial because the jurors were not aware of the new evidence, but whether all the evidence, considered together, proves that House was actually innocent, so that no reasonable juror would vote to convict him. Considering all the evidence, and giving due regard to the District Court's findings on whether House's new evidence was reliable, I do not find it probable that no reasonable juror would vote to convict him, and accordingly I dissent.

Because I do not think that House has satisfied the actual innocence standard set forth in *Schlup,* I do not believe that he has met the higher threshold for a freestanding innocence claim, assuming such a claim exists. *See Herrera v. Collins*. I therefore concur in the judgment with respect to the Court's disposition of that separate claim.

* * *

The majority essentially disregards the District Court's role in assessing the reliability of House's new evidence. With regard to the sisters' testimony, the majority casts aside the District Court's determination that their statements came too late and were too inconsistent with credible record evidence to be reliable, instead observing that the women had no obvious reason to lie, that a few aspects of their testimony have record support, and that they recounted an uncoerced confession. As for the District Court's express finding that the autopsy blood spilled after the FBI tested House's jeans, the majority points to Dr. Blake's testimony that blood enzymes "are generally better preserved on cloth," and even conjures up its own theory in an attempt to refute Ms. Sutton's expert testimony that the pattern of some bloodstains was consistent with blood being transferred while the pants were being worn.

The majority's assessment of House's new evidence is precisely the summary judgment-type inquiry *Schlup* said was inappropriate. By casting aside the District Court's factual determinations made after a comprehensive evidentiary hearing, the majority has done little more than reiterate the factual disputes presented below. * * *[I]t is not our role to make credibility findings and construct theories of the possible ways in which Mrs. Muncey's blood could have been spattered and wiped on House's jeans. The District Court did not painstakingly conduct an evidentiary hearing to compile a record for us to sort through * * * assessing for ourselves the reliability of what we see. *Schlup* made abundantly clear that reliability determinations were essential, but were for the district court to make. We are to defer to the better situated District Court on reliability, unless we determine that its findings are clearly erroneous. We are not concerned with "the district court's independent judgment as to whether reasonable doubt exists," but the District Court here made basic factual findings about the reliability of House's new evidence; it did not offer its personal opinion about whether it doubted House's guilt. *Schlup* makes clear that those findings are controlling unless clearly erroneous.

I have found no clear error in the District Court's reliability findings. * * * I would defer to the District Court's determination that [Parker and Leitner] are not credible, and the evidence in the record undermining the tale of an accidental killing during a fight in the Muncey home convinces me that this credibility finding is not clearly erroneous. Dr. Alex Carabia, who performed the autopsy, testified to injuries far more severe than a bump on the head * * * ; [Mrs/ Muncey's] injuries were consistent with a struggle and traumatic strangulation. And, of course, Lora Tharp has consistently recalled a deep-voiced visitor arriving late at night to tell Mrs. Muncey that her husband was in a wreck near the creek.

* * *

II

With due regard to the District Court's reliability findings, this case invites a straightforward application of the legal standard adopted in *Schlup*. A petitioner does not pass through the *Schlup* gateway if it is "more likely than not that there is *any* juror who, acting reasonably, would have found the petitioner guilty beyond a reasonable doubt." (O'Connor, J., concurring).

The majority states that if House had presented just one of his three key pieces of evidence—or even two of the three—he would not pass through the *Schlup* gateway. According to the majority, House has picked the trifecta of evidence that places conviction outside the realm of choices *any* juror, acting reasonably, would make. Because the case against House remains substantially unaltered from the case presented to the jury, I disagree.

At trial, the State presented its story about what happened on the night of Mrs. Muncey's murder. The Munceys' daughter heard a deep-voiced perpetrator arrive at the Muncey home late at night and tell Mrs. Muncey that her husband had been in a wreck near the creek. Ms. Tharp relayed her testimony again at the evidentiary hearing, and the District Court determined that she was a "very credible witness."

When police questioned House after witnesses reported seeing him emerge from the embankment near Mrs. Muncey's body shortly before it was discovered, he told two different officers that he never left Donna Turner's trailer the previous evening, even recounting the series of television programs he watched before going to bed. He had worked to concoct an alibi we now know was a lie. On the day Mrs. Muncey's body was found, Bill Breeding, a criminal investigator at the Union County Sheriff's Office, observed House at the local jail and noticed that he had abrasions "across his knuckles and about his hands," two or three bruises on his right arm, scratches on his chest, and his right ring finger was red and swollen. The interviewing officers noticed similar injuries. House told them that his finger was swollen because he fell off a porch, and the scratches and bruises were from tearing down a building, and from a cat. Ms. Turner initially confirmed House's alibi, but she changed her story when police warned her that covering up a homicide was a serious offense. Ms. Turner then told police that House had in fact left her house that night between 10:30 and 10:45 p.m. He came back some time later panting and sweating, shirtless and shoeless, and with various injuries.

Also on the day the body was found, Sheriff Earl Loy asked House if he was wearing the same clothes he wore the night before. House "hesitated," then stated that he had changed his shirt, *but not his jeans*. In other words, he specifically tried to conceal from the police that he had worn other jeans the night before, for reasons that were to become clear. Ms. Turner revealed that House's statement that he had not changed his jeans was a lie, and police retrieved House's dirty jeans from Ms. Turner's hamper. Of course, FBI testing revealed that House's jeans were stained with Mrs. Muncey's blood, and the District Court determined that House's new evidence of blood spillage did not undermine those test results. If in fact Mrs. Muncey's blood only got on House's jeans from later evidentiary spillage, House would have had no reason to lie to try to keep the existence of the concealed jeans from the police.

Through Ms. Turner's testimony at trial, the jury also heard House's story about what happened that night. He left Ms. Turner's trailer late at night to go for a walk. When he returned some time later—panting, sweating, and missing his shirt and shoes—he told her that some men in a truck tried to kill him. When Ms. Turner asked House about his injuries, he attributed them to fighting with his assailants. House retold this story to the District Court, saying that he initially lied to police because he was on parole and did not want to draw attention to himself. In other words, having nothing to hide and facing a murder charge, House lied—and when he was caught in the lie, he said he lied not to escape the murder charge, but solely to avoid unexplained difficulties with his parole officer. The jury rejected House's story about the night's events, and the District Court "considered Mr. House's demeanor and found that he was not a credible witness."

The jury also heard House's attempt to implicate Mr. Muncey in his wife's murder by calling Mrs. Muncey's brother, Ricky Green, as a witness. Mr. Green testified that two weeks before the murder, his sister called him to say that she and Mr. Muncey had been fighting, that she wanted to leave him, and that she was scared. Mr. Green also testified that the Munceys had marital problems, and that he had previously seen Mr. Muncey hit his wife. The jury rejected House's attempt to implicate Mr. Muncey, and the District Court was not persuaded by House's attempt to supplement this evidence at the evidentiary hearing, finding that his new witnesses were not credible.

Noticeably absent from the State's story about what happened to Mrs. Muncey on the night of her death was much mention of the semen found on Mrs. Muncey's clothing. House's single victory at the evidentiary hearing was new DNA evidence proving that the semen was deposited by Mr. Muncey. The majority identifies the semen evidence as "[c]entral to the State's case" against House, but House's jury would probably be quite surprised by this characterization. At trial, Agent Bigbee testified that from the semen stains on Mrs. Muncey's clothing, he could determine that the man who deposited the semen had type A blood, and was a secretor. Agent Bigbee also testified that House and Mr. Muncey both have type A blood, that House is a secretor, and that "[t]here is an *eighty (80%) percent* chance that [Mr. Muncey] is a secretor." Moreover, Agent Bigbee informed the jury that because 40 percent of people have type A blood, and 80 percent of those people are secretors, the semen on Mrs. Muncey's clothing could have been deposited by roughly one out of every three males. The jury was also informed several times by the defense that Mrs. Muncey's body was found fully clothed.

The majority describes House's sexual motive as "a central theme in the State's narrative linking House to the crime," and states that without the semen evidence, "a jury ... would have found it necessary to establish some different motive, or, if the same motive, an intent far more speculative." The State, however, consistently directed the jury's attention *away* from motive, and sexual motive was far from a "central theme" of the State's case—presumably because of the highly ambiguous nature of the semen evidence recounted above. The Tennessee Supreme Court did not mention that evidence in cataloging the "[p]particularly incriminating" or "[d]amaging" evidence against House. The State did not mention the semen evidence in its opening statement to the jury, instead focusing on premeditation. The defense used its opening statement to expose lack of motive as a weakness in the State's case. After the State's equivocal presentation of the semen evidence through Agent Bigbee's testimony at trial, the State again made no reference to the semen evidence or to a motive in its closing argument, prompting the defense to again highlight this omission.

In rebuttal, the State disclaimed any responsibility to prove motive, again shifting the jury's focus to premeditation:

> The law says that if you take another person's life, you beat them, you strangle them, and then you don't succeed, and then you kill them by giving them multiple blows to the head, and one massive blow to the head, and that that causes their brains to crash against the other side of their skull, and caused such severe bleeding inside the skull itself, that you die—that it does not make any difference under God's heaven, what the motive was. That is what the law is. The law is that if motive is shown, it can be considered by the jury as evidence of guilt. But the law is that if you prove that a killing was done, beyond a reasonable doubt, by a person, and that he premeditated it, he planned it, it is not necessary for the jury to conclude why he did it.

As a follow-up to this explanation, when the trial was almost over and only in response to the defense's consistent prodding, the State made its first and only reference to a possible motive, followed immediately by another disclaimer:

> Now, you may have an idea why he did it. The evidence at the scene which seemed to suggest that he was subjecting this lady to some kind of indignity, why would you get a lady out of her house, late at night, in her night clothes, under the trick that her husband has had a wreck down by the creek? ... Why is it that you choke her? Why is it that you repeatedly beat her? Why is it that she has scrapes all over her body? Well, it is because either you don't want her to tell what indignities you have subjected her to, or she is unwilling and fights against you, against being subjected to those indignities.... That is what the evidence at the scene suggests about motive. But motive is not an element of the crime. It is something that you can consider, or ignore. Whatever you prefer. The issue is not motive. The issue is premeditation.

It is on this "obliqu[e]" reference to the semen evidence during the State's closing argument that the majority bases its assertion that House's sexual motive was a "central theme in the State's narrative." Although it is possible that one or even some jurors might have entertained doubt about House's guilt absent the clearest evidence of motive, I do not find it more likely than not that *every* juror would have done so, and that is the legal standard under *Schlup*. The majority aphoristically states that "[w]hen identity is in question, motive is key." Not at all. Sometimes, when identity is in question, alibi is key. Here, House came up with one—and it fell apart, later admitted to be fabricated when his girlfriend would not lie to protect him. Scratches from a cat, indeed. Surely a reasonable juror would give the fact that an alibi had been made up and discredited significant weight. People facing a murder charge, who are innocent, do not make up a story out of concern that the truth might somehow disturb their parole officer. And people do not lie to the police about which jeans they were wearing the night of a murder, if they have no reason to believe the jeans would be stained with the blood shed by the victim in her last desperate struggle to live.

In *Schlup*, we made clear that the standard we adopted requires a "stronger showing than that needed to establish prejudice." In other words, House must show more than just a "reasonable probability that ... the factfinder would have had a reasonable doubt respecting guilt." *Strickland v. Washington*. House must present such compelling evidence of innocence that it becomes more likely than not that no single juror, acting reasonably, would vote to convict him. *Schlup*. The majority's conclusion is that given the sisters' testimony (if believed), and Dr. Blake's rebutted testimony about how to interpret Agent Bigbee's enzyme marker analysis summary (if accepted), combined with the revelation that the semen on Mrs. Muncey's clothing was deposited by her husband (which the jurors knew was just as likely as the semen having been deposited by House), no reasonable juror would vote to convict House. Given the District Court's reliability findings about the first two pieces of evidence, the evidence before us now is not substantially different from that considered by House's jury. I therefore find it more likely than not that in light of this new evidence, at least one juror, acting reasonably, would vote to convict House. The evidence as a whole certainly does not establish that House is actually innocent of the crime of murdering Carolyn Muncey, and accordingly I dissent.

Notes

1. *Subsequent case history*

Three years of additional litigation followed the Court's decision. In December 2007, the district court granted a conditional writ of habeas corpus, giving the state 180 days to retry House. The State appealed and the district court then stayed the conditional writ during pendency of the appeal. The Sixth Circuit, in an expedited appeal, affirmed the conditional writ of habeas corpus in May 2008. The district court then granted House's motion for release from custody pending retrial (which the state opposed) and House was released from prison on July 2, 2008, to live with his mother under house arrest and on electronic monitoring. The retrial was postponed for additional DNA testing, which revealed that DNA found on hair in Muncey's hands, on fingernail scrapings, and on cigarette butts found near her body did not come from either House or Muncey. On May 12, 2009, a few weeks before the trial date, the District Attorney requested dismissal of the charges, informing the court that "new evidence raises a reasonable doubt that [House] acted alone." He continued to maintain that House had some role during or after the murder. James Satterfield, *Prosecutor drops charges; House's family on 'Cloud Nine,'* Knoxville News Sentinel, May 12, 2009, available at http://www.knoxnews.com/news/2009/may/12/prosecutor-moves-drop-charges-against-ex.

2. *The impact and import of one vote*

The Sixth Circuit denied House's habeas petition by one vote—8 to 7—before the case reached the Supreme Court. Of the seven dissenters, six believed House had proven his innocence and should be freed, and the seventh thought he was at least entitled to a new trial. Adam Liptak, *Execution May Occur Despite Votes of 7 Judges*, N.Y. Times, October 7, 2004. In the Supreme Court, five justices reversed the Court of Appeals, while three dissented and one did not participate. If the case had tied 4–4, House would have faced execution. The additional DNA testing described in the previous note likely would not have been performed.

What do the justices' vastly divergent views of the evidence—and thus their conclusions about whether House was eligible for habeas review—say about legal guilt?

3. *Proof of actual innocence*

What guidance does the majority provide regarding the difference between the "extraordinary" case sufficient to meet the *Schlup* standard of proof of actual innocence and the "extraordinarily high" standard of a hypothetical freestanding innocence claim?

4. *Finality*

The continuing advances in DNA testing turns conventional wisdom on its head—that evidence necessarily grows increasingly stale and less reliable as time passes. As the District Attorney told the court in requesting dismissal of the charges against Paul House,

"[T]echnology exists today that we didn't have 24 years ago. And it clearly shows other people were involved in this crime." David G. Savage, *Murder charges dropped because of DNA evidence*, Los Angeles Times, May 13, 2009. What impact might evolving forensic technology have on notions of "finality"?

District Attorney's Office for the Third Judicial District v. Osborne

129 S.Ct. 2308 (2009)

CHIEF JUSTICE ROBERTS delivered the opinion of the Court.

DNA testing has an unparalleled ability both to exonerate the wrongly convicted and to identify the guilty. It has the potential to significantly improve both the criminal justice system and police investigative practices. The Federal Government and the States have recognized this, and have developed special approaches to ensure that this evidentiary tool can be effectively incorporated into established criminal procedure—usually but not always through legislation.

Against this prompt and considered response, the respondent, William Osborne, proposes a different approach: the recognition of a freestanding and far-reaching constitutional right of access to this new type of evidence. The nature of what he seeks is confirmed by his decision to file this lawsuit in federal court under *42 U.S.C. § 1983*, not within the state criminal justice system. This approach would take the development of rules and procedures in this area out of the hands of legislatures and state courts shaping policy in a focused manner and turn it over to federal courts applying the broad parameters of the *Due Process Clause*. There is no reason to constitutionalize the issue in this way. Because the decision below would do just that, we reverse.

I

A

This lawsuit arose out of a violent crime committed 16 years ago, which has resulted in a long string of litigation in the state and federal courts. On the evening of March 22, 1993, two men driving through Anchorage, Alaska, solicited sex from a female prostitute, K. G. She agreed to perform fellatio on both men for $100 and got in their car. The three spent some time looking for a place to stop and ended up in a deserted area near Earthquake Park. When K. G. demanded payment in advance, the two men pulled out a gun and forced her to perform fellatio on the driver while the passenger penetrated her vaginally, using a blue condom she had brought. The passenger then ordered K. G. out of the car and told her to lie face-down in the snow. Fearing for her life, she refused, and the two men choked her and beat her with the gun. When K. G. tried to flee, the passenger beat her with a wooden axe handle and shot her in the head while she lay on the ground. They kicked some snow on top of her and left her for dead.

K. G. did not die; the bullet had only grazed her head. Once the two men left, she found her way back to the road, and flagged down a passing car to take her home. Ultimately, she received medical care and spoke to the police. At the scene of the crime, the police recovered a spent shell casing, the axe handle, some of K. G.'s clothing stained with blood, and the blue condom.

Six days later, two military police officers at Fort Richardson pulled over Dexter Jackson for flashing his headlights at another vehicle. In his car they discovered a gun (which matched the shell casing), as well as several items K. G. had been carrying the night of the attack. The car also matched the description K. G. had given to the police. Jackson admitted that he had been the driver during the rape and assault, and told the police that William

Osborne had been his passenger. Other evidence also implicated Osborne. K. G. picked out his photograph (with some uncertainty) and at trial she identified Osborne as her attacker. Other witnesses testified that shortly before the crime, Osborne had called Jackson from an arcade, and then driven off with him. An axe handle similar to the one at the scene of the crime was found in Osborne's room on the military base where he lived.

The State also performed DQ Alpha testing on sperm found in the blue condom. DQ Alpha testing is a relatively inexact form of DNA testing that can clear some wrongly accused individuals, but generally cannot narrow the perpetrator down to less than 5% of the population. The semen found on the condom had a genotype that matched a blood sample taken from Osborne, but not ones from Jackson, K. G., or a third suspect named James Hunter. Osborne is black, and approximately 16% of black individuals have such a genotype. In other words, the testing ruled out Jackson and Hunter as possible sources of the semen, and also ruled out over 80% of other black individuals. The State also examined some pubic hairs found at the scene of the crime, which were not susceptible to DQ Alpha testing, but which state witnesses attested to be similar to Osborne's.

B

Osborne and Jackson were convicted by an Alaska jury of kidnapping, assault, and sexual assault. They were acquitted of an additional count of sexual assault and of attempted murder. Finding it "'nearly miraculous'" that K. G. had survived, the trial judge sentenced Osborne to 26 years in prison, with 5 suspended. His conviction and sentence were affirmed on appeal.

Osborne then sought postconviction relief in Alaska state court. He claimed that he had asked his attorney, Sidney Billingslea, to seek more discriminating restriction-fragment-length-polymorphism (RFLP) DNA testing during trial, and argued that she was constitutionally ineffective for not doing so. Billingslea testified that after investigation, she had concluded that further testing would do more harm than good. She planned to mount a defense of mistaken identity, and thought that the imprecision of the DQ Alpha test gave her "'very good numbers in a mistaken identity, cross-racial identification case, where the victim was in the dark and had bad eyesight.'" Because she believed Osborne was guilty, "'insisting on a more advanced ... DNA test would have served to prove that Osborne committed the alleged crimes.'" The Alaska Court of Appeals concluded that Billingslea's decision had been strategic and rejected Osborne's claim.

In this proceeding, Osborne also sought the DNA testing that Billingslea had failed to perform, relying on an Alaska postconviction statute, Alaska Stat. § 12.72 (2008), and the State and Federal Constitutions. In two decisions, the Alaska Court of Appeals concluded that Osborne had no right to the RFLP test. According to the court, § 12.72 "apparently" did not apply to DNA testing that had been available at trial. The court found no basis in our precedents for recognizing a federal constitutional right to DNA evidence. After a remand for further findings, the Alaska Court of Appeals concluded that Osborne could not claim a state constitutional right either, because the other evidence of his guilt was too strong and RFLP testing was not likely to be conclusive. Two of the three judges wrote separately to say that "[i]f Osborne could show that he were in fact innocent, it would be unconscionable to punish him," and that doing so might violate the Alaska Constitution.

The court relied heavily on the fact that Osborne had confessed to some of his crimes in a 2004 application for parole—in which it is a crime to lie. In this statement, Osborne acknowledged forcing K. G. to have sex at gunpoint, as well as beating her and covering her with snow. He repeated this confession before the parole board. Despite this acceptance of responsibility, the board did not grant him discretionary parole. In 2007, he was released on mandatory parole, but he has since been rearrested for another offense, and the State has petitioned to revoke this parole.

Meanwhile, Osborne had also been active in federal court, suing state officials under *42 U.S.C. § 1983*. He claimed that the *Due Process Clause* and other constitutional provisions gave him a constitutional right to access the DNA evidence for what is known as short-tandem-repeat (STR) testing (at his own expense). This form of testing is more discriminating than the DQ Alpha or RFLP methods available at the time of Osborne's trial. The District Court first dismissed the claim under *Heck v. Humphrey*, 512 U.S. 477, (1994), holding it "inescapable" that Osborne sought to "set the stage" for an attack on his conviction, and therefore "must proceed through a writ of habeas corpus." The United States Court of Appeals for the Ninth Circuit reversed, concluding that § 1983 was the proper vehicle for Osborne's claims, while "express[ing] no opinion as to whether Osborne ha[d] been deprived of a federally protected right."

On cross-motions for summary judgment after remand, the District Court concluded that "there *does* exist, *under the unique and specific facts presented*, a very limited constitutional right to the testing sought." The court relied on several factors: that the testing Osborne sought had been unavailable at trial, that the testing could be accomplished at almost no cost to the State, and that the results were likely to be material. It therefore granted summary judgment in favor of Osborne.

The Court of Appeals affirmed, relying on the prosecutorial duty to disclose exculpatory evidence recognized in *Pennsylvania v. Ritchie*, 480 U.S. 39 (1987), and *Brady v. Maryland*. While acknowledging that our precedents "involved only the right to *pre-trial* disclosure," the court concluded that the *Due Process Clause* also "extends the government's duty to disclose (or the defendant's right of access) to *post-conviction* proceedings." Although Osborne's trial and appeals were over, the court noted that he had a "potentially viable" state constitutional claim of "actual innocence," and relied on the "well-established assumption" that a similar claim arose under the Federal Constitution; cf. *Herrera v. Collins*. The court held that these potential claims extended some of the State's *Brady* obligations to the postconviction context.

The court declined to decide the details of what showing must be made to access the evidence because it found "Osborne's case for disclosure ... so strong on the facts" that "[w]herever the bar is, he crosses it." While acknowledging that Osborne's prior confessions were "certainly relevant," the court concluded that they did not "necessarily trum[p] ... the right to obtain post-conviction access to evidence" in light of the "emerging reality of wrongful convictions based on false confessions."

We granted certiorari to decide whether Osborne's claims could be pursued using § 1983, and whether he has a right under the Due Process Clause to obtain postconviction access to the State's evidence for DNA testing. We now reverse on the latter ground.

II

Modern DNA testing can provide powerful new evidence unlike anything known before. Since its first use in criminal investigations in the mid-1980s, there have been several major advances in DNA technology, culminating in STR technology. It is now often possible to determine whether a biological tissue matches a suspect with near certainty. While of course many criminal trials proceed without any forensic and scientific testing at all, there is no technology comparable to DNA testing for matching tissues when such evidence is at issue. DNA testing has exonerated wrongly convicted people, and has confirmed the convictions of many others.

At the same time, DNA testing alone does not always resolve a case. Where there is enough other incriminating evidence and an explanation for the DNA result, science alone cannot prove a prisoner innocent. See *House v. Bell.* The availability of technologies not available at trial cannot mean that every criminal conviction, or even every criminal conviction involving biological evidence, is suddenly in doubt. The dilemma is how to harness DNA's power to prove innocence without unnecessarily overthrowing the established system of criminal justice.

That task belongs primarily to the legislature. "[T]he States are currently engaged in serious, thoughtful examinations," of how to ensure the fair and effective use of this testing within the existing criminal justice framework. Forty-six States have already enacted statutes dealing specifically with access to DNA evidence. The State of Alaska itself is considering joining them. The Federal Government has also passed the Innocence Protection Act of 2004, § 411, 118 Stat. 2278, codified in part at 18 U.S.C. § 3600, which allows federal prisoners to move for court-ordered DNA testing under certain specified conditions. That Act also grants money to States that enact comparable statutes and as a consequence has served as a model for some state legislation. At oral argument, Osborne agreed that the federal statute is a model for how States ought to handle the issue.

These laws recognize the value of DNA evidence but also the need for certain conditions on access to the State's evidence. A requirement of demonstrating materiality is common, *e.g.*, 18 U.S.C. § 3600(a)(8), but it is not the only one. The federal statute, for example, requires a sworn statement that the applicant is innocent. This requirement is replicated in several state statutes. States also impose a range of diligence requirements. Several require the requested testing to "have been technologically impossible at trial." Others deny testing to those who declined testing at trial for tactical reasons.

Alaska is one of a handful of States yet to enact legislation specifically addressing the issue of evidence requested for DNA testing. But that does not mean that such evidence is unavailable for those seeking to prove their innocence. Instead, Alaska courts are addressing how to apply existing laws for discovery and postconviction relief to this novel technology. The same is true with respect to other States that do not have DNA-specific statutes.

First, access to evidence is available under Alaska law for those who seek to subject it to newly available DNA testing that will prove them to be actually innocent. Under the State's general postconviction relief statute, a prisoner may challenge his conviction when "there exists evidence of material facts, not previously presented and heard by the court, that requires vacation of the conviction or sentence in the interest of justice." Such a claim is exempt from otherwise applicable time limits if "newly discovered evidence," pursued with due diligence, "establishes by clear and convincing evidence that the applicant is innocent."

Both parties agree that under these provisions of § 12.72, "a defendant is entitled to post-conviction relief if the defendant presents newly discovered evidence that establishes by clear and convincing evidence that the defendant is innocent." If such a claim is brought, state law permits general discovery. See Alaska Rule Crim. Proc. 35.1(g). Alaska courts have explained that these procedures are available to request DNA evidence for newly available testing to establish actual innocence.

In addition to this statutory procedure, the Alaska Court of Appeals has invoked a widely accepted three-part test to govern additional rights to DNA access under the State Constitution. Drawing on the experience with DNA evidence of State Supreme Courts around the country, the Court of Appeals explained that it was "reluctant to hold that

Alaska law offers no remedy to defendants who could prove their factual innocence." It was "prepared to hold, however, that a defendant who seeks post-conviction DNA testing ... must show (1) that the conviction rested primarily on eyewitness identification evidence, (2) that there was a demonstrable doubt concerning the defendant's identification as the perpetrator, and (3) that scientific testing would likely be conclusive on this issue." Thus, the Alaska courts have suggested that even those who do not get discovery under the State's criminal rules have available to them a safety valve under the State Constitution.

This is the background against which the Federal Court of Appeals ordered the State to turn over the DNA evidence in its possession, and it is our starting point in analyzing Osborne's constitutional claims.

III

The parties dispute whether Osborne has invoked the proper federal statute in bringing his claim. He sued under the federal civil rights statute, 42 U.S.C. § 1983, which gives a cause of action to those who challenge a State's "deprivation of any rights ... secured by the Constitution." The State insists that Osborne's claim must be brought under *28 U.S.C. § 2254*, which allows a prisoner to seek "a writ of habeas corpus ... on the ground that he is in custody in violation of the Constitution."

While Osborne's claim falls within the literal terms of § 1983, we have also recognized that *§ 1983* must be read in harmony with the habeas statute. "Stripped to its essence," the State says, "Osborne's *§ 1983* action is nothing more than a request for evidence to support a hypothetical claim that he is actually innocent.... [T]his hypothetical claim sounds at the core of habeas corpus."

Osborne responds that his claim does not sound in habeas at all. Although invalidating his conviction is of course his ultimate goal, giving him the evidence he seeks "would not necessarily imply the invalidity of [his] confinement." If he prevails, he would receive only *access* to the DNA, and even if DNA testing exonerates him, his conviction is not automatically invalidated. He must bring an entirely separate suit or a petition for clemency to invalidate his conviction. If he were proved innocent, the State might also release him on its own initiative, avoiding any need to pursue habeas at all.

Osborne also invokes our recent decision in *Wilkinson v. Dotson*, 544 U.S. 74 (2005). There, we held that prisoners who sought new hearings for parole eligibility and suitability need not proceed in habeas. We acknowledged that the two plaintiffs "hope[d]" their suits would "help bring about earlier release," *id.*, at 78, but concluded that the § 1983 suit would not accomplish that without further proceedings. "Because neither prisoner's claim would necessarily spell speedier release, neither l[ay] at the core of habeas corpus." *Id.* at 82. Every Court of Appeals to consider the question since *Dotson* has decided that because access to DNA evidence similarly does not "necessarily spell speedier release," *ibid.*, it can be sought under § 1983. On the other hand, the State argues that Dotson is distinguishable because the challenged procedures in that case did not affect the ultimate "exercise of discretion by the parole board." It also maintains that *Dotson* does not set forth "the *exclusive* test for whether a prisoner may proceed under § 1983."

While we granted certiorari on this question, our resolution of Osborne's claims does not require us to resolve this difficult issue. Accordingly, we will assume without deciding that the Court of Appeals was correct that *Heck* does not bar Osborne's § 1983 claim. Even under this assumption, it was wrong to find a due process violation.

IV

A

"No State shall ... deprive any person of life, liberty, or property, without due process of law." U.S. Const., Amdt. 14, § 1; accord Amdt. 5. This Clause imposes procedural limitations on a State's power to take away protected entitlements. Osborne argues that access to the State's evidence is a "process" needed to vindicate his right to prove himself innocent and get out of jail. Process is not an end in itself, so a necessary premise of this argument is that he has an entitlement (what our precedents call a "liberty interest") to prove his innocence even after a fair trial has proved otherwise. We must first examine this asserted liberty interest to determine what process (if any) is due.

In identifying his potential liberty interest, Osborne first attempts to rely on the Governor's constitutional authority to "grant pardons, commutations, and reprieves." That claim can be readily disposed of. We have held that noncapital defendants do not have a liberty interest in traditional state executive clemency, to which no particular claimant is *entitled* as a matter of state law. *Connecticut Bd. of Pardons v. Dumschat,* 452 U.S. 458, 464, (1981). Osborne therefore cannot challenge the constitutionality of any procedures available to vindicate an interest in state clemency.

Osborne does, however, have a liberty interest in demonstrating his innocence with new evidence under state law. As explained, Alaska law provides that those who use "newly discovered evidence" to "establis[h] by clear and convincing evidence that [they are] innocent" may obtain "vacation of [their] conviction or sentence in the interest of justice." This "state-created right can, in some circumstances, beget yet other rights to procedures essential to the realization of the parent right." *Dumschat, supra, at 463. See also Wolff v. McDonnell,* 418 U.S. 539, 556–558(1974).

The Court of Appeals went too far, however, in concluding that the Due Process Clause requires that certain familiar preconviction trial rights be extended to protect Osborne's postconviction liberty interest. After identifying Osborne's possible liberty interests, the court concluded that the State had an obligation to comply with the principles of *Brady v. Maryland.* In that case, we held that due process requires a prosecutor to disclose material exculpatory evidence to the defendant before trial. The Court of Appeals acknowledged that nothing in our precedents suggested that this disclosure obligation continued after the defendant was convicted and the case was closed, but it relied on prior Ninth Circuit precedent applying "*Brady* as a post-conviction right." Osborne does not claim that *Brady* controls this case, and with good reason.

A criminal defendant proved guilty after a fair trial does not have the same liberty interests as a free man. At trial, the defendant is presumed innocent and may demand that the government prove its case beyond reasonable doubt. But "[o]nce a defendant has been afforded a fair trial and convicted of the offense for which he was charged, the presumption of innocence disappears." *Herrera v. Collins.* "Given a valid conviction, the criminal defendant has been constitutionally deprived of his liberty." *Dumschat, supra,* at 464.

The State accordingly has more flexibility in deciding what procedures are needed in the context of postconviction relief. "[W]hen a State chooses to offer help to those seeking relief from convictions," due process does not "dictat[e] the exact form such assistance must assume." Osborne's right to due process is not parallel to a trial right, but rather must be analyzed in light of the fact that he has already been found guilty at a fair trial, and has only a limited interest in postconviction relief. *Brady* is the wrong framework.

Instead, the question is whether consideration of Osborne's claim within the framework of the State's procedures for postconviction relief "offends some principle of justice so rooted in the traditions and conscience of our people as to be ranked as fundamental," or "transgresses any recognized principle of fundamental fairness in operation." See *Herrera, supra,* at 407–408. Federal courts may upset a State's postconviction relief procedures only if they are fundamentally inadequate to vindicate the substantive rights provided.

We see nothing inadequate about the procedures Alaska has provided to vindicate its state right to postconviction relief in general, and nothing inadequate about how those procedures apply to those who seek access to DNA evidence. Alaska provides a substantive right to be released on a sufficiently compelling showing of new evidence that establishes innocence. It exempts such claims from otherwise applicable time limits. The State provides for discovery in postconviction proceedings, and has—through judicial decision—specified that this discovery procedure is available to those seeking access to DNA evidence. These procedures are not without limits. The evidence must indeed be newly available to qualify under Alaska's statute, must have been diligently pursued, and must also be sufficiently material. These procedures are similar to those provided for DNA evidence by federal law and the law of other States, and they are not inconsistent with the "traditions and conscience of our people" or with "any recognized principle of fundamental fairness."

And there is more. While the Alaska courts have not had occasion to conclusively decide the question, the Alaska Court of Appeals has suggested that the State Constitution provides an additional right of access to DNA. In expressing its "reluctan[ce] to hold that Alaska law offers no remedy" to those who belatedly seek DNA testing, and in invoking the three-part test used by other state courts, the court indicated that in an appropriate case the State Constitution may provide a failsafe even for those who cannot satisfy the statutory requirements under general postconviction procedures.

To the degree there is some uncertainty in the details of Alaska's newly developing procedures for obtaining postconviction access to DNA, we can hardly fault the State for that. Osborne has brought this § 1983 action without ever using these procedures in filing a state or federal habeas claim relying on actual innocence. In other words, he has not tried to use the process provided to him by the State or attempted to vindicate the liberty interest that is now the centerpiece of his claim. When Osborne *did* request DNA testing in state court, he sought RFLP testing that had been available at trial, not the STR testing he now seeks, and the state court relied on that fact in denying him testing under Alaska law.

His attempt to sidestep state process through a new federal lawsuit puts Osborne in a very awkward position. If he simply seeks the DNA through the State's discovery procedures, he might well get it. If he does not, it may be for a perfectly adequate reason, just as the federal statute and all state statutes impose conditions and limits on access to DNA evidence. It is difficult to criticize the State's procedures when Osborne has not invoked them. This is not to say that Osborne must exhaust state-law remedies. But it is Osborne's burden to demonstrate the inadequacy of the state-law procedures available to him in state postconviction relief. These procedures are adequate on their face, and without trying them, Osborne can hardly complain that they do not work in practice.

As a fallback, Osborne also obliquely relies on an asserted federal constitutional right to be released upon proof of "actual innocence." Whether such a federal right exists is an open question. We have struggled with it over the years, in some cases assuming, *arguendo*, that it exists while also noting the difficult questions such a right would pose and the high standard any claimant would have to meet. *House, Herrera.* In this case too we can assume without deciding that such a claim exists, because even if so there is no due process Osborne does not dispute that a federal actual innocence claim (as opposed to a DNA access claim) would be brought in habeas. If such a habeas claim is viable, federal procedural rules permit discovery "for good cause." Just as with state law, Osborne cannot show that available discovery is facially inadequate, and cannot show that it would be arbitrarily denied to him.

B

The Court of Appeals below relied only on procedural due process, but Osborne seeks to defend the judgment on the basis of substantive due process as well. He asks that we recognize a freestanding right to DNA evidence untethered from the liberty interests he hopes to vindicate with it. We reject the invitation and conclude, in the circumstances of this case, that there is no such substantive due process right. "As a general matter, the Court has always been reluctant to expand the concept of substantive due process because guideposts for responsible decisionmaking in this unchartered area are scarce and open-ended." Osborne seeks access to state evidence so that he can apply new DNA-testing technology that might prove him innocent. There is no long history of such a right, and "[t]he mere novelty of such a claim is reason enough to doubt that 'substantive due process' sustains it."

And there are further reasons to doubt. The elected governments of the States are actively confronting the challenges DNA technology poses to our criminal justice systems and our traditional notions of finality, as well as the opportunities it affords. To suddenly constitutionalize this area would short-circuit what looks to be a prompt and considered legislative response. The first DNA testing statutes were passed in 1994 and 1997. In the past decade, 44 States and the Federal Government have followed suit, reflecting the increased availability of DNA testing. As noted, Alaska itself is considering such legislation. "By extending constitutional protection to an asserted right or liberty interest, we, to a great extent, place the matter outside the arena of public debate and legislative action. We must therefore exercise the utmost care whenever we are asked to break new ground in this field." "[J]udicial imposition of a categorical remedy ... might pretermit other responsible solutions being considered in Congress and state legislatures." If we extended substantive due process to this area, we would cast these statutes into constitutional doubt and be forced to take over the issue of DNA access ourselves. We are reluctant to enlist the Federal Judiciary in creating a new constitutional code of rules for handling DNA.

Establishing a freestanding right to access DNA evidence for testing would force us to act as policymakers, and our substantive-due-process rulemaking authority would not only have to cover the right of access but a myriad of other issues. We would soon have to decide if there is a constitutional obligation to preserve forensic evidence that might later be tested. If so, for how long? Would it be different for different types of evidence? Would the State also have some obligation to gather such evidence in the first place? How much, and when? No doubt there would be a miscellany of other minor directives.

In this case, the evidence has already been gathered and preserved, but if we extend substantive due process to this area, these questions would be before us in short order, and it is hard to imagine what tools federal courts would use to answer them. At the end of the day, there is no reason to suppose that their answers to these questions would be any better than those of state courts and legislatures, and good reason to suspect the opposite.

* * *

DNA evidence will undoubtedly lead to changes in the criminal justice system. It has done so already. The question is whether further change will primarily be made by legislative revision and judicial interpretation of the existing system, or whether the Federal Judiciary must leap ahead—revising (or even discarding) the system by creating a new constitutional right and taking over responsibility for refining it.

Federal courts should not presume that state criminal procedures will be inadequate to deal with technological change. The criminal justice system has historically accommodated new types of evidence, and is a time-tested means of carrying out society's interest in convicting the guilty while respecting individual rights. That system, like any human endeavor, cannot be perfect. DNA evidence shows that it has not been. But there is no basis for Osborne's approach of assuming that because DNA has shown that these procedures are not flawless, DNA evidence must be treated as categorically outside the process, rather than within it. That is precisely what his *§ 1983* suit seeks to do, and that is the contention we reject.

The judgment of the Court of Appeals is reversed, and the case is remanded for further proceedings consistent with this opinion.

It is so ordered.

JUSTICE STEVENS, with whom JUSTICE GINSBURG AND BREYER join, and with whom JUSTICE SOUTER joins as to Part I, dissenting.

The State of Alaska possesses physical evidence that, if tested, will conclusively establish whether respondent William Osborne committed rape and attempted murder. If he did, justice has been served by his conviction and sentence. If not, Osborne has needlessly spent decades behind bars while the true culprit has not been brought to justice. The DNA test Osborne seeks is a simple one, its cost modest, and its results uniquely precise. Yet for reasons the State has been unable or unwilling to articulate, it refuses to allow Osborne to test the evidence at his own expense and to thereby ascertain the truth once and for all.

On two equally problematic grounds, the Court today blesses the State's arbitrary denial of the evidence Osborne seeks. First, while acknowledging that Osborne may have a due process right to access the evidence under Alaska's postconviction procedures, the Court concludes that Osborne has not yet availed himself of all possible avenues for relief in state court. As both a legal and factual matter, that conclusion is highly suspect. More troubling still, based on a fundamental mischaracterization of the right to liberty that Osborne seeks to vindicate, the Court refuses to acknowledge "in the circumstances of this case" any right to access the evidence that is grounded in the Due Process Clause itself. Because I am convinced that Osborne has a constitutional right of access to the evidence he wishes to test and that, on the facts of this case, he has made a sufficient showing of entitlement to that evidence, I would affirm the decision of the Court of Appeals.

I

The Fourteenth Amendment provides that "[n]o State shall ... deprive any person of life, liberty, or property, without due process of law." § 1. Our cases have frequently recognized that protected liberty interests may arise "from the Constitution itself, by reason of guarantees implicit in the word 'liberty,'... or it may arise from an expectation or interest created by state laws or policies." Osborne contends that he possesses a right to access DNA evidence arising from both these sources.

Osborne first anchors his due process right in Alaska Stat. § 12.72.010(4) (2008). Under that provision, a person who has been "convicted of, or sentenced for, a crime may institute a proceeding for post-conviction relief if the person claims ... that there exists evidence of material facts, not previously presented and heard by the court, that requires vacation of the conviction or sentence in the interest of justice." Osborne asserts that exculpatory DNA test results obtained using state-of-the-art Short Tandem Repeat (STR) and Mitochondrial (mtDNA) analysis would qualify as newly discovered evidence entitling him to relief under the state statute. The problem is that the newly discovered evidence he wishes to present cannot be generated unless he is first able to access the State's evidence—something he cannot do without the State's consent or a court order.

Although States are under no obligation to provide mechanisms for postconviction relief, when they choose to do so, the procedures they employ must comport with the demands of the Due Process Clause, see *Evitts v. Lucey*, 469 U.S. 387, 393(1985), by providing litigants with fair opportunity to assert their state-created rights. Osborne contends that by denying him an opportunity to access the physical evidence, the State has denied him meaningful access to state postconviction relief, thereby violating his right to due process.

Although the majority readily agrees that Osborne has a protected liberty interest in demonstrating his innocence with new evidence under Alaska Stat. § 12.72.010(4), it rejects the Ninth Circuit's conclusion that Osborne is constitutionally entitled to access the State's evidence. The Court concludes that the adequacy of the process afforded to Osborne must be assessed under the standard set forth in *Medina v. California*, 505 U.S. 437 (1992). Under that standard, Alaska's procedures for bringing a claim will not be found to violate due process unless they "'offen[d] some principle of justice so rooted in the traditions and conscience of our people as to be ranked as fundamental,' or 'transgres[s] any recognized principle of fundamental fairness in operation.'" After conducting a cursory review of the relevant statutory text, the Court concludes that Alaska's procedures are constitutional on their face.

While I agree that the statute is not facially deficient, the state courts' application of § 12.72.010(4) raises serious questions whether the State's procedures are fundamentally unfair in their operation. As an initial matter, it is not clear that Alaskan courts ordinarily permit litigants to utilize the state postconviction statute to obtain new evidence in the form of DNA tests. The majority assumes that such discovery is possible based on a single, unpublished, nonprecedential decision from the Alaska Court of Appeals but the State concedes that no litigant yet has obtained evidence for such testing under the statute.

Of even greater concern is the manner in which the state courts applied § 12.72.010(4) to the facts of this case. In determining that Osborne was not entitled to relief under the postconviction statute, the Alaska Court of Appeals concluded that the DNA testing Osborne wished to obtain could not qualify as "newly discovered" because it was available at the time of trial. In his arguments before the state trial court and his briefs to the Alaska Court of Appeals, however, Osborne had plainly requested STR DNA testing, a form of DNA testing not yet in use at the time of his trial. The state appellate court's conclusion that the requested testing had been available at the time of trial was therefore clearly erroneous. Given these facts, the majority's assertion that Osborne "attempt[ed] to sidestep state process" by failing "to use the process provided to him by the State" is unwarranted.

The same holds true with respect to the majority's suggestion that the Alaska Constitution might provide additional protections to Osborne above and beyond those afforded under § 12.72.010(4). In Osborne's state postconviction proceedings, the Alaska Court of Appeals held out the possibility that even when evidence does not meet the requirements of § 12.72.010(4), the State Constitution might offer relief to a defendant who is able to make certain threshold showings. On remand from that decision, however, the state trial court denied Osborne relief on the ground that he failed to show that (1) his conviction rested primarily on eyewitness identification; (2) there was a demonstrable doubt concerning his identity as the perpetrator; and (3) scientific testing would like be conclusive on this issue. The first two reasons reduce to an evaluation of the strength of the prosecution's original case—a consideration that carries little weight when balanced against evidence as powerfully dispositive as an exculpatory DNA test. The final reason offered by the state court—that further testing would not be conclusive on the issue of Osborne's guilt or innocence—is surely a relevant factor in deciding whether to release evidence for DNA testing. Nevertheless, the state court's conclusion that such testing would not be conclusive in this case is indefensible, as evidenced by the State's recent concession on that point.

Osborne made full use of available state procedures in his efforts to secure access to evidence for DNA testing so that he might avail himself of the postconviction relief afforded by the State of Alaska. He was rebuffed at every turn. The manner in which the Alaska courts applied state law in this case leaves me in grave doubt about the adequacy of the procedural protections afforded to litigants under Alaska Stat. § 12.72.010(4), and provides strong reason to doubt the majority's flippant assertion that if Osborne were "simply [to] see[k] the DNA through the State's discovery procedures, he might well get it." However, even if the Court were correct in its assumption that Osborne might be given the evidence he seeks were he to present his claim in state court a second time, there should be no need for him to do so.

II

Wholly apart from his state-created interest in obtaining postconviction relief under Alaska Stat. § 12.72.010(4), Osborne asserts a right to access the State's evidence that derives from the Due Process Clause itself. Whether framed as a "substantive liberty interest ... protected through a procedural due process right" to have evidence made available for testing, or as a substantive due process right to be free of arbitrary government action, the result is the same: On the record now before us, Osborne has established his entitlement to test the State's evidence.

The liberty protected by the Due Process Clause is not a creation of the Bill of Rights. Indeed, our Nation has long recognized that the liberty safeguarded by the Constitution has far deeper roots. The "most elemental" of the liberties protected by the Due Process Clause is "the interest in being free from physical detention by one's own government." *Hamdi v. Rumsfeld,* 542 U.S. 507, 529, (2004) (plurality opinion).

Although a valid criminal conviction justifies punitive detention, it does not entirely eliminate the liberty interests of convicted persons. For while a prisoner's "rights may be diminished by the needs and exigencies of the institutional environment[,] ... [t]here is no iron curtain drawn between the Constitution and the prisons of this country." Our cases have recognized protected interests in a variety of postconviction contexts, extending substantive constitutional protections to state prisoners on the premise that the *Due* Process Clause of the Fourteenth Amendment requires States to respect certain fundamental liberties in the postconviction context. It is therefore far too late in the day to question the basic proposition that convicted persons such as Osborne retain a constitutionally protected measure of interest in liberty, including the fundamental liberty of freedom from physical restraint.

Recognition of this right draws strength from the fact that 46 States and the Federal Government have passed statutes providing access to evidence for DNA testing, and 3 additional states (including Alaska) provide similar access through court-made rules alone. These legislative developments are consistent with recent trends in legal ethics recognizing that prosecutors are obliged to disclose all forms of exculpatory evidence that come into their possession following conviction. See, *e.g.*, ABA Model Rules of Professional Conduct 3.8(g)–(h) (2008); see also *Imbler v. Pachtman,* 424 U.S. 409, 427, n.25, (1976). The fact that nearly all the States have now recognized some postconviction right to DNA evidence makes it more, not less, appropriate to recognize a limited federal right to such evidence in cases where litigants are unfairly barred from obtaining relief in state court.

Insofar as it is process Osborne seeks, he is surely entitled to less than "the full panoply of rights," that would be due a criminal defendant prior to conviction; see *Morrissey v. Brewer,* 408 U.S. 471, 480, 484 (1972). That does not mean, however, that our pretrial due process cases have no relevance in the postconviction context. In *Brady v. Maryland,* we held that the State violates due process when it suppresses "evidence favorable to an accused" that is "material either to guilt or to punishment, irrespective of the good faith or bad faith of the prosecution." Although *Brady* does not directly provide for a postconviction right to such evidence, the concerns with fundamental fairness that motivated our decision in that case are equally present when convicted persons such as Osborne seek access to dispositive DNA evidence following conviction.

Recent scientific advances in DNA analysis have made "it literally possible to confirm guilt or innocence beyond any question whatsoever, at least in some categories of cases." As the Court recognizes today, the powerful new evidence that modern DNA testing can provide is "unlike anything known before." Discussing these important forensic developments in his oft-cited opinion in *Harvey* [*v. Horan,* 285 F.3d 298, 318–319 (4th Cir. 2002)], Judge Luttig explained that although "no one would contend that fairness, in the constitutional sense, requires a post-conviction right of access or a right to disclosure anything approaching in scope that which is required pre-trial," in cases "where the government holds previously-produced forensic evidence, the testing of which concededly could prove beyond any doubt that the defendant did not commit the crime for which he was convicted, the very same principle of elemental fairness that dictates pre-trial production of all potentially exculpatory evidence dictates post-trial production of this infinitely narrower category of evidence." It does so "out of recognition of the same systemic interests in fairness and ultimate truth." *Ibid.*

Observing that the DNA evidence in this case would be so probative of Osborne's guilt or innocence that it exceeds the materiality standard that governs the disclosure of evidence under *Brady,* the Ninth Circuit granted Osborne's request for access to the State's evidence. In doing so, the Court of Appeals recognized that Osborne possesses a narrow right of postconviction access to biological evidence for DNA testing "where [such] evidence was used to secure his conviction, the DNA testing is to be conducted using methods that were unavailable at the time of trial and are far more precise than the methods that were then available, such methods are capable of conclusively determining whether Osborne is the source of the genetic material, the testing can be conducted without cost or prejudice to the State, and the evidence is material to available forms of post-conviction relief." That conclusion does not merit reversal.

If the right Osborne seeks to vindicate is framed as purely substantive, the proper result is no less clear. The touchstone of due process is protection of the individual against arbitrary action of government. When government action is so lacking in justification that it "can properly be characterized as arbitrary, or conscience shocking, in a constitutional sense," it violates the *Due Process Clause*. In my view, the State's refusal to provide Osborne with access to evidence for DNA testing qualifies as arbitrary.

Throughout the course of state and federal litigation, the State has failed to provide any concrete reason for denying Osborne the DNA testing he seeks, and none is apparent. Because Osborne has offered to pay for the tests, cost is not a factor. And as the State now concedes, there is no reason to doubt that such testing would provide conclusive confirmation of Osborne's guilt or revelation of his innocence. In the courts below, the State refused to provide an explanation for its refusal to permit testing of the evidence, and in this Court, its explanation has been, at best, unclear. Insofar as the State has articulated any reason at all, it appears to be a generalized interest in protecting the finality of the judgment of conviction from any possible future attacks.

While we have long recognized that States have an interest in securing the finality of their judgments, finality is not a stand-alone value that trumps a State's overriding interest in ensuring that justice is done in its courts and secured to its citizens. Indeed, when absolute proof of innocence is readily at hand, a State should not shrink from the possibility that error may have occurred. Rather, our system of justice is strengthened by "recogniz[ing] the need for, and imperative of, a safety valve in those rare instances where objective proof that the convicted actually did not commit the offense later becomes available through the progress of science." DNA evidence has led to an extraordinary series of exonerations, not only in cases where the trial evidence was weak, but also in cases where the convicted parties confessed their guilt and where the trial evidence against them appeared overwhelming. The examples provided by *amici* of the power of DNA testing serve to convince me that the fact of conviction is not sufficient to justify a State's refusal to perform a test that will conclusively establish innocence or guilt.

This conclusion draws strength from the powerful state interests that offset the State's purported interest in finality *per se*. When a person is convicted for a crime he did not commit, the true culprit escapes punishment. DNA testing may lead to his identification. See Brief for Current and Former Prosecutors as *Amici Curiae* 16 (noting that in more than one-third of all exonerations DNA testing identified the actual offender). Crime victims, the law enforcement profession, and society at large share a strong interest in identifying and apprehending the actual perpetrators of vicious crimes, such as the rape and [attempted murder that gave rise to this case.

The arbitrariness of the State's conduct is highlighted by comparison to the private interests it denies. It seems to me obvious that if a wrongly convicted person were to produce proof of his actual innocence, no state interest would be sufficient to justify his continued punitive detention. If such proof can be readily obtained without imposing a significant burden on the State, a refusal to provide access to such evidence is wholly unjustified.

In sum, an individual's interest in his physical liberty is one of constitutional significance. That interest would be vindicated by providing postconviction access to DNA evidence, as would the State's interest in ensuring that it punishes the true perpetrator of a crime. In this case, the State has suggested no countervailing interest that justifies its refusal to allow Osborne to test the evidence in its possession and has not provided any other nonarbitrary explanation for its conduct. Consequently, I am left to conclude that the State's failure to provide Osborne access to the evidence constitutes arbitrary action that offends basic principles of due process. On that basis, I would affirm the judgment of the Ninth Circuit.

III

The majority denies that Osborne possesses a cognizable substantive due process right "under the circumstances of this case," and offers two meager reasons for its decision. First, citing a general reluctance to "'expand the concept of substantive due process,'" the

Court observes that there is no long history of postconviction access to DNA evidence. "'The mere novelty of such a claim,'" the Court asserts, "'is reason enough to doubt that 'substantive due process' sustains it.'" The flaw is in the framing. Of course courts have not historically granted convicted persons access to physical evidence for STR and mtDNA testing. But, as discussed above, courts have recognized a residual substantive interest in both physical liberty and in freedom from arbitrary government action. It is Osborne's interest in those well-established liberties that justifies the Court of Appeals' decision to grant him access to the State's evidence for purposes of previously unavailable DNA testing.

* * *

IV

Osborne has demonstrated a constitutionally protected right to due process which the State of Alaska thus far has not vindicated and which this Court is both empowered and obliged to safeguard. On the record before us, there is no reason to deny access to the evidence and there are many reasons to provide it, not least of which is a fundamental concern in ensuring that justice has been done in this case. I would affirm the judgment of the Court of Appeals, and respectfully dissent from the Court's refusal to do so.

JUSTICE SOUTER, dissenting.

I respectfully dissent on the ground that Alaska has failed to provide the effective procedure required by the Fourteenth Amendment for vindicating the liberty interest in demonstrating innocence that the state law recognizes. I therefore join Part I of Justice Stevens's dissenting opinion.

I would not decide Osborne's broad claim that the Fourteenth Amendment's guarantee of due process requires our recognition at this time of a substantive right of access to biological evidence for DNA analysis and comparison. I would reserve judgment on the issue simply because there is no need to reach it; at a general level Alaska does not deny a right to postconviction testing to prove innocence, and in any event, Osborne's claim can be resolved by resort to the procedural due process requirement of an effective way to vindicate a liberty interest already recognized in state law, see *Evitts v. Lucey*, 469 U.S. 387, 393 (1985). My choice to decide this case on that procedural ground should not, therefore, be taken either as expressing skepticism that a new substantive right to test should be cognizable in some circumstances, or as implying agreement with the Court that it would necessarily be premature for the Judicial Branch to decide whether such a general right should be recognized.

There is no denying that the Court is correct when it notes that a claim of right to DNA testing, post-trial at that, is a novel one, but that only reflects the relative novelty of testing DNA, and in any event is not a sufficient reason alone to reject the right asserted. Tradition is of course one serious consideration in judging whether a challenged rule or practice, or the failure to provide a new one, should be seen as violating the guarantee of substantive due process as being arbitrary, or as falling wholly outside the realm of reasonable governmental action. We recognize the value and lessons of continuity with the past, but as Justice Harlan pointed out, society finds reasons to modify some of its traditional practices and the accumulation of new empirical knowledge can turn yesterday's reasonable range of the government's options into a due process anomaly over time.

* * *

Changes in societal understanding of the fundamental reasonableness of government actions work out in much the same way that individuals reconsider issues of fundamental belief. We can change our own inherited views just so fast, and a person is not labeled a stick-in-the-mud for refusing to endorse a new moral claim without having some time to work through it intellectually and emotionally. Just as attachment to the familiar and the limits of experience affect the capacity of an individual to see the potential legitimacy of a moral position, the broader society needs the chance to take part in the dialectic of public and political back and forth about a new liberty claim before it makes sense to declare unsympathetic state or national laws arbitrary to the point of being unconstitutional. The time required is a matter for judgment depending on the issue involved, but the need for some time to pass before a court entertains a substantive due process claim on the subject is not merely the requirement of judicial restraint as a general approach, but a doctrinal demand to be satisfied before an allegedly lagging legal regime can be held to lie beyond the discretion of reasonable political judgment.

Despite my agreement with the Court on this importance of timing, though, I do not think that the doctrinal requirement necessarily stands in the way of any substantive due process consideration of a postconviction right to DNA testing, even as a right that is freestanding. Given the pace at which DNA testing has come to be recognized as potentially dispositive in many cases with biological evidence, there is no obvious argument that considering DNA testing at a general level would subject wholly intransigent legal systems to substantive due process review prematurely. But, as I said, there is no such issue before us, for Alaska does not flatly deny access to evidence for DNA testing in postconviction cases.

In effect, Alaska argues against finding any right to relief in a federal *§ 1983* action because the procedure the State provides is reasonable and adequate to vindicate the posttrial liberty interest in testing evidence that the State has chosen to recognize. When I first considered the State's position I thought Alaska's two strongest points were these: (1) that in Osborne's state litigation he failed to request access for the purpose of a variety of postconviction testing that could not have been done at time of trial (and thus sought no new evidence by his state-court petition); and (2) that he failed to aver actual innocence (and thus failed to place his oath behind the assertion that the evidence sought would be material to his postconviction claim). Denying him any relief under these circumstances, the argument ran, did not indicate any inadequacy in the state procedure that would justify resort to *§ 1983* for providing due process.

Yet the record shows that Osborne has been denied access to the evidence even though he satisfied each of these conditions. As for the requirement to claim testing by a method not available at trial, Osborne's state-court appellate brief specifically mentioned his intent to conduct short tandem repeat (STR) analysis, and the State points to no pleading, brief, or evidence that Osborne ever changed this request.

Standing alone, the inadequacy of each of the State's reasons for denying Osborne access to the DNA evidence he seeks would not make out a due process violation.4 But taken as a whole the record convinces me that, while Alaska has created an entitlement of access to DNA evidence under conditions that are facially reasonable, the State has demonstrated a combination of inattentiveness and intransigence in applying those conditions that add up to procedural unfairness that violates the *Due Process Clause.*

Notes

1. *Subsequent case history*

William G. Osborne remains in the custody of the Alaska Department of Corrections. www.vinelink.com (last visited June 23, 2010).

2. *Concurrence by Justice Alito*

In a concurring opinion not included in the text, Justice Alito asserted two additional reasons for denying Osborne's claim. In Part I, joined by Justice Kennedy, Justice Alito explained why he would hold that a state prisoner asserting a federal constitutional right to perform DNA testing must proceed through habeas and not under § 1983. In addition to emphasizing the principles of federalism and comity, Justice Alito expressed concern about state prisoners trying to "bypass state courts with their discovery requests," about opportunities for "sandbagging by defense lawyers," and avoidance of AEDPA's exhaustion requirements and limits on discovery "through artful pleading." *Osborne*, 129 S.Ct. at 2324–25.

Do you think these concerns are legitimate? In light of the record to which Justices Stevens and Souter point, do these descriptions fit the facts of *Osborne*?

In Part II of his concurrence (joined by Justices Kennedy and Thomas), Justice Alito would deny Osborne's claim on the merits for an additional and independent reason: that a defendant who made a strategic decision to not have DNA testing at trial has no constitutional right to DNA testing after conviction. Again, Justice Alito expressed concern that a defendant will "game the system" and asserted that Osborne tried to do just that. Even if Osborne had in fact objected to his attorney's tactical choice to not pursue DNA testing for trial, "it is a well-accepted principle that ... a criminal defendant is bound by his attorney's tactical decisions unless the attorney provided constitutionally ineffective assistance." *Osborne*, 129 S.Ct. at 2330.

Given the unique value of DNA testing, do you agree that this should be the standard for a state inmate who did not have DNA testing for trial? Why or why not?

3. *Due process*

The lower court granted relief to Osborne after applying a *Brady v. Maryland* analysis. What are the Due Process analyses relied upon by Justices Stevens and Souter in their dissents? How do they compare with the majority's view of Due Process in this case? Which do you find most persuasive?

4. Heck v. Humphrey *and* Wilkerson v. Dotson

The Court declined to decide whether *Heck v. Humphrey* barred Osborne from pursuing access to evidence for DNA testing in a § 1983 action—an issue on which the lower courts are in conflict. In *Heck*, a prisoner sought monetary damages in a § 1983 suit that alleged malicious prosecution, illegal identification procedures, and destruction of exculpatory evidence. The Court set a standard to distinguish claims that can be brought under § 1983 and those that can be brought under federal habeas statutes:

> [T]he district court must consider whether a judgment in favor of the plaintiff would necessarily imply the invalidity of his conviction or sentence; if it would, the complaint must be dismissed unless the plaintiff can demonstrate that the conviction or sentence has already been invalidated. But if the district court determines that the plaintiff's action, even if successful, will not demonstrate the invalidity of any outstanding criminal judgment against the plaintiff, the action should be allowed to proceed in the absence of some other bar to the suit.

Heck v. Humphrey, 512 U.S. 477, 487 (1994). Applying this rule to Heck's claims, the Court affirmed dismissal of his § 1983 suit, finding that his suit for damages was a challenge to his conviction.

In *Wilkerson v. Dotson*, 544 U.S. 74 (2005), two state prisoners alleged in § 1983 suits that state parole procedures were unconstitutional and sought declaratory and injunctive relief that would render invalid the procedures used to deny them parole. The Court held that the *Heck* doctrine did not bar a prisoner from bringing a § 1983 claim even when success on that claim is a first step in achieving a reduction of sentence.

In light of *Heck* and *Dotson,* what are the most persuasive arguments a prisoner might make to maintain a § 1983 action to secure post-conviction access to evidence for testing?

5. *Habeas v. § 1983*

What might be the implications for a state prisoner of foreclosing access to DNA testing through a § 1983 action? What might be the implications of recognizing a freestanding right to access the State's DNA evidence?

6. *Recent Supreme Court action*

On May 24, 2010, the Supreme Court granted certiorari in *Skinner v. Switzer*, 130 S. Ct. 3323 (2010), a case that might resolve the question of whether a prisoner seeking access to post-conviction DNA testing can assert this claim in a civil rights action under § 1983 or whether the claim can be made only in a habeas action—the same issue the Court granted certiorari on, but did not decide, in *Osborne.*

Henry Skinner was convicted of capital murder and sentenced to death for the murder of his girlfriend and her two sons in 1995. His convictions and sentence were affirmed on direct appeal. Skinner filed a § 1983 action, claiming that the prosecutor's refusal to allow him access to evidence to conduct DNA testing violated his Fourteenth Amendment right to Due Process and his Eighth Amendment right to be free from cruel and unusual punishment. Skinner's due process claim rests on the argument that he has a state-created, constitutionally protected liberty and life interest in seeking state habeas relief or clemency with exculpatory evidence. The evidence he seeks access to—including vaginal swabs, fingernail clippings, and weapons found at the scene—was available at Skinner's capital murder trial but was not tested. At trial, defense counsel argued that the state's failure to test this evidence created a reasonable doubt.

Skinner first sought post-conviction DNA testing by making requests to the prosecutor, and then by filing two successive motions for access pursuant to Texas's DNA testing statutes, enacted after his convictions. In the first motion for access to testing, the trial court determined that Skinner had not met his burden under Texas's DNA statute to establish by a preponderance of evidence that a reasonable probability exists that he would not have been prosecuted or convicted if exculpatory results had been obtained through DNA testing. The state appellate court affirmed, finding that even if the items to be tested were exculpatory, they would not constitute affirmative evidence of innocence because previous testing of other evidence had been inculpatory. Thus, Skinner had not demonstrated a reasonable probability that an exculpatory DNA test would prove his innocence. *Skinner v. Texas*, 122 S.W.3d 808 (Tex. Crim. App. 2003). Skinner then filed both state and federal habeas claims. His federal habeas claims included due process, Sixth Amendment, and ineffective assistance of counsel claims. His claims were not addressed on the merits in the state proceedings because of the pendency of the federal habeas action. The federal district court, after an evidentiary hearing, found that trial counsel had a reasonable strategy for not pursuing DNA testing at trial—that he feared it would be inculpatory—and denied Skinner's petition. Skinner's second motion in state court for DNA testing was also denied, in part because he could not show ineffective assistance of trial counsel for not seeking testing at trial. Thus, as the appellate court noted in affirming the second denial, Skinner was not able to meet the statutory requirement that failure to test was not his fault. *Skinner v. Texas*, 293 S.W.3d 196 (Tex. Crim. App. 2009).

Skinner then filed his § 1983 suit alleging violations of his rights under the Fourteenth and Eighth Amendments. The district court granted a motion to dismiss Skinner's action for failure to state a claim, based on Fifth Circuit precedent interpreting *Heck v. Humphrey* to mean that Skinner's claims are cognizable only in habeas. The Fifth Circuit affirmed on the same basis.

7. *The prosecutor as a "minister of justice"*

In *United States v. Agurs*, 427 U.S. 97, 110–11 (1976), the Court recognized the dual role of a prosecutor: "For though the attorney for the sovereign must prosecute the accused with earnestness and vigor, he must always be faithful to his client's overriding interest that 'justice be done.'"

In *Osborne*, the Court held that the due process principles of *Brady* do not apply to evidence sought to be discovered after conviction. What if a prosecutor obtains evidence favorable to the accused after the conviction? In either circumstance, how do you think a prosecutor should fulfill her role as "a minister of justice"?

The Court emphasizes that most states and the federal government have passed legislation allowing access to DNA testing in some circumstances. Should there be special ethical rules for prosecutors relating to post-conviction access to DNA testing?

8. *How well do courts judge innocence?*

Two recent scholarly reviews of the first 200 DNA exonerations suggest that courts do not have great success in separating the innocent from the guilty.

Professor Brandon L. Garrett conducted a comprehensive review of the cases of the first 200 DNA exonerees, primarily focusing on the claims raised on appeal and in post-conviction proceedings of the 133 among this group for whom he could locate written decisions. Garrett compared the characteristics of the innocence group with a matched comparison group with similar cases but without DNA testing. Garrett found that the reversal rates for the comparison group were virtually identical with the known innocent group: 14% of the entire group and only 9% of the non-capital defendants among them. Brandon L. Garrett, *Judging Innocence*, 108 Colum. L. Rev. 55, 109 (2008).

Professor Keith Findley, after reviewing the empirical data in Professor Garrett's study as well as data from 1,000 felony cases in Wisconsin,[8] wrote:

> If protecting against mistaken conviction of the innocent is indeed a primary objective in criminal appeals, it is fair to ask how well the system serves that function. Unfortunately, judging by the recent evidence, especially the empirical evidence from cases in which postconviction testing has proved that an innocent person was wrongly convicted, the appellate process in criminal cases is largely a failure on this most important score * * * Substantive doctrine, procedural barriers, cognitive biases, institutional pressures, and a demand for extreme deference to trial-level factual determinations conspire to prevent courts from directly guarding against erroneous judgments of guilt. Appellate courts by design focus on procedural justice, rather than substantive justice."

Keith A. Findley, *Innocence Protection in the Appellate Process*, 93 Marq. L. Rev. 591 (2009).

---

8. Wisconsin is the only state that provides a means, available as of right in every case, for defendants to bring postconviction motions in the trial court after conviction and sentencing, but before direct appeal. The postconviction motion proceedings are then part of the direct review process. Wis. Stat. § 809.30(2)(h)(2007–08).

Justice Stevens refers to one of Professor Garrett's findings in a footnote in *Osborne*, omitted from the text, that "in 50% of cases in which DNA evidence exonerated a convicted person, reviewing courts had commented on the exoneree's likely guilt and in 10% of the cases had described the evidence supporting conviction as 'overwhelming.'" *Osborne*, 129 S.Ct. at 2337 n.9 (Stevens, J. dissenting). Indeed, Justice Stevens had made just such a comment in *Arizona v. Youngblood*, 488 U.S. 51 (1988), in which Larry Youngblood was convicted of the abduction and rape of a young boy. The Arizona Court of Appeals dismissed the case on appeal as a sanction for the prosecution's failure to preserve critical evidence. The Supreme Court of Arizona denied review and the State petitioned the Supreme Court for a writ of certiorari. The Supreme Court reversed, finding the prosecutor had not acted in bad faith. In a concurring opinion, Stevens concluded that the jury's rejection of counsel's argument about the lost evidence indicated that "the evidence was so overwhelming that it was highly improbable that the lost evidence was exculpatory." *Youngblood*, 488 U.S. at 60. Seventeen years after the offense, Youngblood was exonerated following DNA testing. The testing identified another man as the assailant.

What reforms in the appellate process, legal standards, or legal doctrine might improve the reliability of appellate outcomes?

In re Troy Anthony Davis

557 U. S. (2009)

JUSTICES ROBERTS, STEVENS, KENNEDY, GINSBERG, and BREYER ordered the following:

The motion of NAACP, et al. for leave to file a brief as *amici curiae* is granted. The motion of Bob Barr, et al. for leave to file a brief as *amici curiae* is granted. The petition for a writ of habeas corpus is transferred to the United States District Court for the Southern District of Georgia for hearing and determination. The District Court should receive testimony and make findings of fact as to whether evidence that could not have been obtained at the time of trial clearly establishes petitioner's innocence.

JUSTICE STEVENS, with whom JUSTICE GINSBURG and JUSTICE BREYER join, concurring.

JUSTICE SCALIA's dissent is wrong in two respects. First, he assumes as a matter of fact that petitioner Davis is guilty of the murder of Officer MacPhail. He does this even though seven of the State's key witnesses have recanted their trial testimony; several individuals have implicated the State's principal witness as the shooter; and "*no* court," state or federal, "has ever conducted a hearing to assess the reliability of the score of [post-conviction] affidavits that, if reliable, would satisfy the threshold showing for a truly persuasive demonstration of actual innocence." The substantial risk of putting an innocent man to death clearly provides an adequate justification for holding an evidentiary hearing. Simply put, the case is sufficiently "exceptional" to warrant utilization of this Court's Rule 20.4(a), 28 U.S.C. § 2241(b), and our original habeas jurisdiction. See *Byrnes v. Walker,* 371 U.S. 937 (1962); *Chaapel v. Cochran,* 369 U.S. 869 (1962).

Second, JUSTICE SCALIA assumes as a matter of law that, "[e]ven if the District Court were to be persuaded by Davis's affidavits, it would have no power to grant relief" in light of 28 U.S.C. § 2254(d)(1). For several reasons, however, this transfer is by no means "a fool's errand." The District Court may conclude that § 2254(d)(1) does not apply, or does not apply with the same rigidity, to an original habeas petition such as this. See *Felker v. Turpin*, 518 U.S. 651, 663 (1996) (expressly leaving open the question whether and to what extent the Antiterrorism and Effective Death Penalty Act of 1996 (AEDPA) applies to original petitions). The court may also find it relevant to the AEDPA analysis that Davis is bringing an "actual innocence" claim. Even if the court finds that §2254(d)(1) applies in full, it is arguably unconstitutional to the extent it bars relief for a death row inmate who has established his innocence. Alternatively, the court may find in such a case that the statute's text is satisfied, because decisions of this Court clearly support the proposition that it "would be an atrocious violation of our Constitution and the principles upon which it is based" to execute an innocent person.

JUSTICE SCALIA would pretermit all of these unresolved legal questions on the theory that we must treat even the most robust showing of actual innocence identically on habeas review to an accusation of minor procedural error. Without briefing or argument, he concludes that Congress chose to foreclose relief and that the Constitution permits this. But imagine a petitioner in Davis's situation who possesses new evidence conclusively and definitively proving, beyond any scintilla of doubt, that he is an innocent man. The dissent's reasoning would allow such a petitioner to be put to death nonetheless. The Court correctly refuses to endorse such reasoning.

JUSTICE SCALIA, with whom JUSTICE THOMAS joins, dissenting.

Today this Court takes the extraordinary step—one not taken in nearly 50 years—of instructing a district court to adjudicate a state prisoner's petition for an original writ of habeas corpus. The Court proceeds down this path even though every judicial and executive body that has examined petitioner's stale claim of innocence has been unpersuaded, and (to make matters worst) even though it would be impossible for the District Court to grant any relief. Far from demonstrating, as this Court's *Rule 20.4(a)* requires, "exceptional circumstances" that "warrant the exercise of the Court's discretionary powers," petitioner's claim is a sure loser. Transferring his petition to the District Court is a confusing exercise that can serve no purpose except to delay the State's execution of its lawful criminal judgment. I respectfully dissent.

Eighteen years ago, after a trial untainted by constitutional defect, a unanimous jury found petitioner Troy Anthony Davis guilty of the murder of Mark Allen MacPhail. The evidence showed that MacPhail, an off-duty police officer, was shot multiple times after responding to the beating of a homeless man in a restaurant parking lot. Davis admits that he was present during the beating of the homeless man, but he maintains that it was one of his companions who shot Officer MacPhail. It is this claim of "actual innocence"—the same defense Davis raised at trial but now allegedly supported by new corroborating affidavits—that Davis raises as grounds for relief. And (presumably) it is this claim that the Court wants the District Court to adjudicate once the petition is transferred.

Even if the District Court were to be persuaded by Davis's affidavits, it would have no power to grant relief. Federal courts may order the release of convicted state prisoners only in accordance with the restrictions imposed by the Antiterrorism and Effective Death Penalty Act of 1996. See *Felker v. Turpin*, 518 U.S. 651, 662 (1996). Insofar as it applies to the present case, that statute bars the issuance of a writ of habeas corpus "with respect to any claim that was adjudicated on the merits in State court proceedings unless the adjudication of the claim ... resulted in a decision that was contrary to, or involved an unreasonable application of, clearly established Federal law, as determined by the Supreme Court of the United States." 28 U.S.C. §2254(d)(1).

The Georgia Supreme Court rejected petitioner's "actual-innocence" claim on the merits, denying his extraordinary motion for a new trial. Davis can obtain relief only if that determination was contrary to, or an unreasonable application of, "clearly established Federal law, as determined by the Supreme Court of the United States." It most assuredly was not. This Court has *never* held that the Constitution forbids the execution of a convicted defendant who has had a full and fair trial but is later able to convince a habeas court that he is "actually" innocent. Quite to the contrary, we have repeatedly left that question unresolved, while expressing considerable doubt that any claim based on alleged "actual innocence" is constitutionally cognizable. See *Herrera v. Collins; House v. Bell; District Attorney's Office for Third Judicial Dist. v. Osborne.* A state court cannot possibly have contravened, or even unreasonably applied, "clearly established Federal law, as determined by the Supreme Court of the United States," by rejecting a type of claim that the Supreme Court has not once accepted as valid.

JUSTICE STEVENS says that we need not be deterred by the limitations that Congress has placed on federal courts' authority to issue the writ, because we cannot rule out the possibility that the District Court might find those limitations unconstitutional as applied to actual-innocence claims. (This is not a possibility that Davis has raised, but one that JUSTICE STEVENS has imagined.) But acknowledging that possibility would make a nullity of § 2254(d)(1). There is no sound basis for distinguishing an actual-innocence claim from any other claim that is alleged to have produced a wrongful conviction. If the District Court here can ignore § 2254(d)(1) on the theory that otherwise Davis's actual-innocence claim would (unconstitutionally) go unaddressed, the same possibility would exist for *any* claim going beyond "clearly established Federal law."

The existence of that possibility is incompatible with the many cases in which we have reversed lower courts for their failure to apply § 2254(d)(1), with no consideration of constitutional entitlement. We have done so because the argument that the Constitution requires federal-court screening of all state convictions for constitutional violations is frivolous. For much of our history, federal habeas review was not available even for those state convictions claimed to be in violation of clearly established federal law. It seems to me improper to grant the extraordinary relief of habeas corpus on the possibility that we have approved—indeed, directed—the disregard of constitutional imperatives in the past. If we have new-found doubts regarding the constitutionality of § 2254(d)(1), we should hear Davis's application and resolve that question (if necessary) ourselves.

Transferring this case to a court that has no power to grant relief is strange enough. It becomes stranger still when one realizes that the allegedly new evidence we shunt off to be examined by the District Court has already been considered (and rejected) multiple times. Davis's postconviction "actual-innocence" claim is not new. Most of the evidence on which it is based is almost a decade old. A State Supreme Court, a State Board of Pardons and Paroles, and a Federal Court of Appeals have all considered the evidence Davis now presents and found it lacking. (I do not rely upon the similar conclusion of the Georgia trial court, since unlike the others that court relied substantially upon Georgia evidentiary rules rather than the unpersuasiveness of the evidence Davis brought forward.)

The Georgia Supreme Court "look[ed] beyond bare legal principles that might otherwise be controlling to the core question of whether a jury presented with Davis's allegedly-new testimony would probably find him not guilty or give him a sentence other than death." After analyzing each of Davis's proffered affidavits and comparing them with the evidence adduced at trial, it concluded that it was not probable that they would produce a different result.

When Davis sought clemency before the Georgia Board of Pardons and Paroles, that tribunal stayed his execution and "spent more than a year studying and considering [his] case." It "gave Davis'sattorneys an opportunity to present every witness they desired to support their allegation that there is doubt as to Davis's guilt"; it "heard each of these witnesses and questioned them closely." It "studied the voluminous trial transcript, the police investigation report and the initial statements of the witnesses," and "had certain physical evidence retested and Davis interviewed." After an exhaustive review of all available information regarding the Troy Davis case and after considering all possible reasons for granting clemency, "the Board ... determined that clemency is not warranted."

After reviewing the record, the Eleventh Circuit came to a conclusion "wholly consonant with the repeated conclusions of the state courts and the State Board of Pardons and Paroles." "When we view all of this evidence as a whole, we cannot honestly say that Davis can establish by clear and convincing evidence that a jury would not have found him guilty of Officer MacPhail's murder." Today, without explanation and without any meaningful guidance, this Court sends the District Court for the Southern District of Georgia on a fool's errand. That court is directed to consider evidence of actual innocence which has been reviewed and rejected at least three times, and which, even if adequate to persuade the District Court, cannot (as far as anyone knows) form the basis for any relief. I truly do not see how the District Court can discern what is expected of it. If this Court thinks it possible that capital convictions obtained in full compliance with law can never be final, but are always subject to being set aside by federal courts for the reason of "actual innocence," it should set this case on our own docket so that we can (if necessary) resolve that question. Sending it to a district court that "might" be authorized to provide relief, but then again "might" be reversed if it did so, is not a sensible way to proceed.

Notes

1. *Subsequent case history*

The district court held an evidentiary hearing in June, 2010. Defense counsel presented nine witnesses, some of whom recanted their trial testimony. The defense did not call Sylvester Coles (or Davis) to testify, leading to a warning by the judge that he might not credit the testimony of two witnesses to whom Coles allegedly confessed. After the hearing, the court asked counsel to brief several legal questions: (1) Does AEDPA bar relief; and 2) Assuming Davis received a fair trial, would Davis's execution violate the Eighth Amendment? Bill Rankin, *Judge must decide whether Troy Davis proved innocence in cop killing*, ATLANTA JOURNAL-CONSTITUTION, June 24, 2010, available at http://www.ajc.com/ news/atlanta/judge-must-decide-whether-556708.html; Russ Bynum, *Troy Davis case full of murky legal questions*, ATLANTA JOURNAL-CONSTITUTION, July 5, 2010, available at http:// www.ajc.com/news/troy-davis-case-full-564707.html. On August 24, 2010, the district court denied Davis's petition. Although it decided that a freestanding claim of innocence is cognizable, it held that Davis failed to make a showing of actual innocence that would entitle him to habeas relief in federal court. In re Troy Anthony Davis, CV409-130 (S.D. Ga., Aug. 24, 2010).

2. *Prior case history*

The Eleventh Circuit opinion denying Davis's application for a second and successive habeas petition contains a detailed procedural history of the numerous appeals and post-conviction proceedings in state and federal court since Davis's conviction in 1991. *In Re: Troy Anthony Davis*, 565 F.3d 810 (2009). In his first federal habeas petition, Davis raised actual innocence under *Schlup v. Delo* (to reach constitutional claims alleging *Brady* and *Giglio* violations as well as ineffective assistance of counsel). In his application to file a second habeas petition, Davis raised a free-standing claim of actual innocence. As Justice Stevens points out in his concurrence, the decisions resulting from post-conviction proceedings in which Davis raised actual innocence have not rested on evidentiary hearings and fact-finding, but rather on affidavits Davis submitted. As the Court of Appeals explained, the newly discovered evidence Davis submitted included: "(1) seven affidavits containing recantations of eyewitnesses who testified at trial; (2) three affidavits averring post-trial confessions to the murder by another man, Sylvester 'Red' Coles (a chief prosecution witness at trial); (3) several affidavits of persons who had not previously testified who were either present at the scene of the murder of in the general area immediately following the crime; (4) two expert affidavits addressing ballistic evidence and eyewitness identifications; (5) affidavits of jurors; and (6) a general cache of additional affidavits." *Id.* at 817.

Davis's execution has been stayed three times. As a result of the post-conviction litigation, all of his claims—except free-standing actual innocence—had been resolved before the recent federal evidentiary hearing in the southern district of Georgia.

3. *Original habeas jurisdiction*

As the opinion notes, the Supreme Court has not exercised original habeas jurisdiction since 1962, when it did so in two cases. In *Chaapel v. Cochran,* in response to a motion for leave to file an application for a writ of habeas corpus, the Court transferred the motion "for hearing and determination" to the United States District Court for the Southern District of Florida. The Court, without comment, cited 28 U.S.C. §2241(b); Rule 31(5), Revised Rules of The Supreme Court of the United States (1954), and *Ex parte Abernathy,* 320 U.S. 219 (1943). Within the year, the Court transferred a similar application to the United States District Court of the Eastern District of Louisiana—again for "hearing and determination," and again without comment. *Ex parte Abernathy* involved multiple applicants, and the Court refused to issue a writ to any of them. The Court stated: "That jurisdiction [to issue writs in aid of the Court's appellate jurisdiction] is discretionary, and this Court does not, save in exceptional circumstances, exercise it in a case where an adequate remedy may be had in a lower federal court, or, if the relief sought is from the judgment of a state court, where the petitioner has not exhausted his remedies in the state Courts."

Why do you think the Court did not deny Davis's application?

4. *Actual vs. legal innocence*

Justice Scalia asserts that there "is no sound basis for distinguishing an actual-innocence claim from any other claim that is alleged to have produced a wrongful conviction." Do you agree with Justice Scalia? Why or why not?

Is Innocence Irrelevant? Collateral Attack on Criminal Judgments

Henry J. Friendly 38 U. Chi. L. Rev. 142 (1970)

Legal history has many instances where a remedy initially serving a felt need has expanded bit by bit, without much thought being given to any single step, until it has assumed an aspect so different from its origin as to demand reappraisal—agonizing or not. That, in my view, is what has happened with respect to collateral attack on criminal convictions. After trial, conviction, sentence, appeal, affirmance, and denial of certiorari by the Supreme Court, in proceedings where the defendant had the assistance of counsel at every step, the criminal process, in Winston Churchill's phrase, has not reached the end, or even the beginning of the end, but only the end of the beginning. Any murmur of dissatisfaction with this situation provokes immediate incantation of the Great Writ, with the inevitable initial capitals, often accompanied by a suggestion that the objector is the sort of person who would cheerfully desecrate the Ark of the Covenant. My thesis is that, with a few important exceptions, convictions should be subject to collateral attack only when the prisoner supplements his constitutional plea with a colorable claim of innocence.

* * *

I believe, with qualifications I will elaborate, that this position ought to be the law and that legislation can and should make it so. When I speak of legislation, I am thinking mainly of federal habeas corpus for state prisoners and its equivalent for federal prisoners, since no other course seems realistic in light of Supreme Court opinions. In many states it may still be possible to reach the proper result by judicial decision. Although, if past experience is any guide, I am sure I will be accused of proposing to abolish habeas corpus, my aim is rather to restore the Great Writ to its deservedly high estate and rescue it from the disrepute invited by current excesses.

Seventeen years ago, in his concurring opinion in *Brown v. Allen*, 344 U.S. 443 (1953), Mr. Justice Jackson expressed deep concern over the "floods of stale, frivolous and repetitious petitions [for federal habeas corpus by state prisoners which] inundate the docket of the lower courts and swell our own." * * * These "comprise the largest single element in the civil caseload of the district courts" and "accounted for more than one-sixth of the civil filings." * * *There has been a corresponding increase in the load imposed by post-conviction petitions upon the federal courts of appeals. Despite the safeguard intended to be afforded by the requirement of a certificate of probable cause, * * * there were over twice as many *appeals* by state prisoners in 1969 as there were *petitions* in 1952. * * * A similar explosion of collateral attack has occurred in the courts of many of the states. * * *

The proverbial man from Mars would surely think we must consider our system of criminal justice terribly bad if we are willing to tolerate such efforts at undoing judgments of conviction. He would be surprised, I should suppose, to be told both that it never was really bad and that it has been steadily improving, particularly because of the Supreme Court's decision that an accused, whatever his financial means, is entitled to the assistance of counsel at every critical stage. * * * His astonishment would grow when we told him that the one thing almost never suggested on collateral attack is that the prisoner was innocent of the crime. * * * His surprise would mount when he learned that collateral attack on a criminal conviction by a court of general jurisdiction is almost unknown in the country that gave us the writ of habeas corpus and has been long admired for its fair treatment of accused persons. * * * With all this, and with the American Bar Association having proposed standards relating to post-conviction remedies * * * which, despite some kind words about finality, in effect largely repudiate it, the time is ripe for reflection on the right road for the future.

I wish to emphasize at the outset that my chief concern is about the basic principle of collateral attack, rather than with the special problem of federal relief for state prisoners which has absorbed so much attention since *Brown v. Allen*. I must therefore make my main analysis in the context of a unitary system. My model will be designed for our only pure example of a unitary structure, the federal system when dealing with federal convictions. Later I shall advocate adoption of the same model by the states for their much larger number of prisoners and of corresponding changes with respect to federal habeas for state prisoners. I shall conclude by showing that these proposals are wholly consistent with the Constitution.

I

For many reasons, collateral attack on criminal convictions carries a serious burden of justification.

First, as Professor Bator has written, "it is essential to the educational and deterrent functions of the criminal law that we be able to say that one violating the law will swiftly and certainly become subject to punishment, just punishment." * * * Unbounded willingness to entertain attacks on convictions must interfere with at least one aim of punishment—"a realization by the convict that he is justly subject to sanction, that he stands in need of rehabilitation." * * *

A second set of difficulties arises from the fact that under our present system collateral attack may be long delayed—in *habeas corpus* as long as the custody endures, is in federal *coram nobis* forever. * * * The longer the delay, the less the reliability of the determination of any factual issue giving rise to the attack. * * * It is chimerical to suppose that police officers can remember what warnings they gave a particular suspect ten years ago, although the prisoner will claim to remember very well. Moreover, although successful attack usually entitles the prisoner only to a retrial, a long delay makes this a matter of theory only. * * * Inability to try the prisoner is even more likely in the case of collateral attack on convictions after guilty pleas, since there will be no transcript of testimony of witnesses who are no longer available. * * * Although the longer the attack has been postponed, the larger the proportion of the sentence that will have been served, we must assume that the entire sentence was warranted. * * *The argument against this, that only a handful of prisoners gain release, whether absolute or conditional, by post-conviction remedies, is essentially self-defeating, * * * even if it is factually correct. To such extent as accurate figures might indicate the problem of release to have been exaggerated, they would also show what a gigantic waste of effort a collateral attack has come to be. A remedy that produces no result in the overwhelming majority of cases, apparently well over ninety percent, an unjust one to the state in much of the exceedingly small minority, and a truly good one only rarely, would seem to need reconsideration with a view to caring for the unusual case of the innocent man without being burdened by so much dross in the process.

Indeed, the most serious single evil with today's proliferation of collateral attack is its drain upon the resources of the community—judges, prosecutors, and attorneys appointed to aid the accused, and even of that oft overlooked necessity, courtrooms. Today of all times we should be conscious of the falsity of the bland assumption that these are in endless supply. * * * Everyone concerned with the criminal process, whether his interest is with the prosecution, with the defense, or with neither, agrees that our greatest single problem is the long delay in bringing accused persons to trial. * * *

A fourth consideration is Justice Jackson's never refuted observation that "[i]t must prejudice the occasional meritorious application to be buried in a flood of worthless ones." * * * The thought may be distasteful but no judge can honestly deny it is real.

Finally, there is the point which, as Professor Bator says, is "difficult to formulate because so easily twisted into an expression of mere complacency." * * * This is the human desire that things must sometime come to an end. Mr. Justice Harlan has put it as well as anyone:

> Both the individual criminal defendant and society have an interest in insuring that there will at some point be the certainty that comes with an end to litigation, and that attention will ultimately be focused not on whether a conviction was free from error but rather on whether the prisoner can be restored to a useful place in the community. * * *

Beyond this, it is difficult to urge public respect for judgments of criminal courts in one breath and to countenance free reopening of them in the next. I say "free" because, as I will later show, the limitation of collateral attack to "constitutional" grounds has become almost meaningless.

These five objections are not all answered by the Supreme Court's conclusory pronouncement: "Conventional notions of finality of litigation have no place where life or liberty is at stake and infringement of constitutional rights is alleged." * * * Why do they have *no* place? One will readily agree that "where life or liberty is at stake," different rules should govern the determination of guilt than when only property is at issue: The prosecution must establish guilt beyond a reasonable doubt, the jury must be unanimous, the defendant need not testify, and so on. The defendant must also have a full and fair opportunity to show an infringement of constitutional rights by the prosecution even though his guilt is clear. I would agree that even when he has had all this at trial and on appeal, "[t]he policy against incarcerating or executing an innocent man ... should far outweigh the desired termination of litigation." * * * But this shows only that "conventional notions of finality" should not have *as much* place in criminal as in civil litigation, not that they should have *none*. A statement like that just quoted, entirely sound with respect to a man who is or may be innocent, is readily metamorphosed into broader ones, such as the Supreme Court's pronouncement mentioned above, * * * expansive enough to cover a man steeped in guilt who attacks his conviction years later because of some technical error by the police that was or could have been considered at his trial.

Admittedly, reforms such as I am about to propose might not immediately meet some of these points. Aside from the most drastic measures, * * * changes that would narrow the grounds available for collateral attack would not necessarily discourage prisoners from trying; they have everything to gain and nothing to lose. Indeed, collateral attack may have become so much a way of prison life as to have created its own self-generating force: it may now be considered merely something done as a matter of course during long incarceration. Today's growing number of prisoner petitions despite the minute percentage granted points that way. * * * Furthermore, a requirement that, with certain exceptions, an applicant for habeas corpus must make a colorable showing of innocence would enable courts of first instance to screen out rather rapidly a great multitude of applications not deserving their attention and devote their time to those few where injustice may have been done, and would affect an even greater reduction in the burden on appellate courts. In any event, if we are dissatisfied with the present efflorescence of collateral attack on criminal convictions and yet are as unwilling as I am to outlaw it and rely as in England, solely on executive clemency, * * * it is important to consider reform. If mine is not the best mousetrap, perhaps it may lead others to develop a better one.

II

Broadly speaking, the original sphere for collateral attack on a conviction was where the tribunal lacked jurisdiction either in the usual sense * * * or because the statute under which the defendant had been prosecuted was unconstitutional * * * or because the sentence was one the court could not lawfully impose. * * *

* * * In such cases the criminal process itself has broken down; the defendant has not had the kind of trial the Constitution guarantees. * * * ... [I]n these cases where the attack concerns the very basis of the criminal process, few would object to allowing collateral attack regardless of the defendant's probable guilt. These cases would include all those in which the defendant claims he was without counsel to whom he was constitutionally entitled. * * *

Another area in which collateral attack is readily justified irrespective of any question of innocence is where a denial of constitutional rights is claimed on the basis of facts which "are *dehors* the record and their effect on the judgment was not open to consideration and review on appeal." * * * The original judgment is claimed to have been perverted, and collateral attack is the only avenue for the defendant to vindicate his rights. Examples are convictions on pleas of guilty obtained by improper means, * * *or on evidence known to the prosecution to be perjured, * * * or where it later appears that the defendant was incompetent to stand trial. * * *

A third justifiable area for collateral attack irrespective of innocence is where the state has failed to provide proper procedure for making a defense at trial and on appeal. The paradigm is *Jackson v. Denno*, 378 U.S. 368 (1964), allowing collateral attack by federal habeas corpus on all New York convictions where the voluntariness of a confession had been submitted to the jury without a proper determination by the judge..* * * ... [O]ne can hardly quarrel with the proposition that if a state does not afford a proper way of raising a constitutional defense at trial, it must be afforded one thereafter, and this without a colorable showing of innocence by the defendant.

New constitutional developments relating to criminal procedure are another special case. * * * But here the Supreme Court itself has given us the lead. In only a few instances has it determined that its decisions shall be fully retroactive—the right to counsel, *Jackson v. Denno*, equal protections claims, * * * the sixth amendment right to confrontation, * * * and double jeopardy. * * * In most cases the Court has ruled that its new constitutional decisions concerning criminal procedure need not be made available for collateral attack on earlier convictions. These include the extension to the states of the exclusionary rule with respect to illegally seized evidence, * * * the prohibition of comment on a defendant's failure to take the stand, * * * the rules concerning interrogation of persons in custody, * * * the right to a jury trial in state criminal cases, * * * the requirement of counsel at line-ups, * * * and the application of the fourth amendment to non-trespassory wiretapping. * * * While neither a state nor the United States is bound to limit collateral attack on the basis of a new constitutional rule of criminal procedure to what the Supreme Court holds to be demanded, I see no occasion to be holier than the pope.

None of these four important but limited lines of decision supports the broad proposition that collateral attack should always be open for the asserted denial of a "constitutional" right, even though this was or could have been litigated in the criminal trial and on appeal. The belief that it should stems mainly from the Supreme Court's construction of the Habeas Corpus Act of 1867 * * * and its successors, * * * providing that the writ may issue "in all cases where any person may be restrained of his or her liberty in violation of the constitution, or any other treaty or law of the United States." Despite this language no one supposes that a person who is confined after a proper trial, may mount a collateral attack because the court has misinterpreted a law of the United States; * * * indeed the Supreme Court has explicitly decided the contrary even where the error was as apparent as could be. * * * In such instances we are content that "conventional notions of finality" should keep an innocent man in prison unless, as one would hope, executive clemency releases him.

As a matter of ordinary reading of language, it is hard to see how the result can be different when a constitutional claim has been rejected, allegedly in error, after thoroughly constitutional proceedings, and the history does not suggest that the statute was so intended. * * * The reason why the Supreme Court did so construe the Act in *Brown v. Allen* * * * was, I believe, its consciousness that, with the growth of the country and the attendant increase in the Court's business, it could no longer perform its historic function of correcting constitutional error in criminal cases by review of judgments of state courts and had to summon the inferior federal judges to its aid. * * * Once it was held that state prisoners could maintain proceedings in the federal courts to attack convictions for constitutional error after full and fair proceedings in the state courts, it was hard to read the same statutory words as meaning less for federal prisoners, even though the policy considerations were quite different. * * * And once all this was decided, it was easy to slide into the belief that the states should, or even must, similarly expand their own procedures for collateral attack.

With a commentator's ability to consider policy free from imprisonment by statutory language, I perceive no general principle mandating a second round of attacks simply because the alleged error is a "constitutional" one. We have been conclusorily told there is "an institutional need for separate proceeding—one insulated from inquiry into the guilt or innocence of the defendant and designed specifically to protect constitutional rights." * * * No empirical data is cited to support this, and so far as concerns proceeding within the same system, it seems fanciful. The supposition that the judge who has overlooked or disparaged constitutional contentions presented on pre-trial motions to suppress evidence or in the course of trial will avidly entertain claims of his own error after completion of the trial and a guilty verdict defies common sense. * * *

The dimensions of the problem of collateral attack today are a consequence of two developments. * * * One has been the Supreme Court's imposition of the rules of the fourth, fifth, sixth, and eighth amendments concerning unreasonable searches and seizures, double jeopardy, speedy trial, compulsory self-incrimination, jury trial in criminal cases, confrontation of adverse witnesses, assistance of counsel, and cruel and unusual punishments, upon state criminal trials. The other has been a tendency to read these provisions with ever increasing breadth. The Bill of Rights, as I warned in 1965, has become a detailed Code of Criminal Procedure, * * * to which a new chapter is added every year. The result of these two developments has been a vast expansion of the claims of error in criminal cases for which a resourceful defense lawyer can find a constitutional basis. * * * Today it is the rare criminal appeal that does *not* involve a "constitutional" claim.

I am not now concerned with the merits of these decisions which, whether right or wrong, have become part of our way of life. What I do challenge is the assumption that simply because a claim can be characterized as "constitutional," it should necessarily constitute a basis for collateral attack when there has been fair opportunity to litigate it at trial and on appeal. Whatever may have been true when the Bill of Rights was read to protect a state criminal defendant only if the state had acted in a manner "repugnant to the conscience of mankind," * * * the rule prevailing when *Brown v. Allen* was decided, the "constitutional" label no longer assists in appraising how far society should go in permitting relitigation of criminal convictions.

It defies good sense to say that after government has afforded a defendant every means to avoid conviction, not only on the merits but by preventing the prosecution from utilizing probative evidence obtained in violation of his constitutional rights, he is entitled to repeat engagements directed to issues of the latter type even though his guilt is patent. A rule recognizing this would go a long way toward halting the "inundation;" it would permit the speedy elimination of most of the petitions that are hopeless on the facts and the law, themselves a great preponderance of the total, and of others, where, because of previous opportunity to litigate the point, release of a guilty man is not required in the interest of justice even though he might have escaped deserved punishment in the first instance with a brighter lawyer or a different judge.

* * *

IV

Before going further I should clarify what I mean by a colorable showing of innocence. I can begin with a negative. A defendant would not bring himself within this criterion by showing that he might not, or even would not, have been convicted in the absence of evidence claimed to have been unconstitutionally obtained. * * * Perhaps as good a formulation of the criterion as any is that the petitioner for collateral attack must show a fair probability that, in light of all the evidence, including that alleged to have been illegally admitted (but with due regard to any unreliability of it) and evidence tenably claimed to have been wrongly excluded or to have become available only after the trial, the trier of the facts would have entertained a reasonable doubt of his guilt. * * *

As indicated, my proposal would almost always preclude collateral attack on claims of illegal search and seizure. * * *

* * *

Another type of claim, certain to be a prodigious litigation breeder, concerning which I would forbid collateral attack in the absence of a colorable showing of innocence, consists of cases arising under *Miranda v. Arizona*, 384 U.S. 436 (1966). * * * This is generally not "the kind of constitutional claim that casts some shadow of doubt" upon the defendant's guilt. * * * The mere failure to administer *Miranda* warnings in on-the-scene questioning creates little risk of unreliability, and the deterrent value of permitting collateral attack goes beyond the point of diminishing returns. * * * I would take the same view on collateral attack based on claims of lack of full warnings or voluntary waiver with respect to station-house questioning where there is no indication of the use of methods that might cast doubt on the reliability of the answers.

The confession involuntary in the pre-*Miranda* sense helps to illustrate where I would draw the line. In a case where the prosecution had no other substantial evidence, as, for example, when identification testimony was weak or conflicting and there was nothing else, I would allow collateral attack regardless of what happened in the original proceedings. Such a case fits the formula that considerations of finality should not keep a possibly innocent man in jail. I would take a contrary view where the state had so much other evidence, even though some of this was obtained as a result of the confession, * * * as to eliminate any reasonable doubt of guilt.

Neither your patience nor mine would tolerate similar examination of the application of my proposal to all constitutional claims. Such soundings as I have taken convince me that in other contexts as well the proposal would fully protect the innocent, while relieving the courts of most of the collateral challenges with which they are now unnecessarily burdened.

V

Assuming that collateral attack by federal prisoners should be restricted as I have suggested, what should be done with respect to the far more numerous prisoners held by the states, in whose hands the maintenance of public order largely rests? * * * The subject has two aspects: The first is whether any changes should be made with respect to federal habeas corpus for state prisoners. The second is whether, in formulating their own procedures, the states should do what they would deem appropriate in the absence of the likelihood of a federal proceeding or should allow collateral attack in every case where the eyes of the federal big brother may penetrate.

At first blush it might seem that to whatever extent collateral attack on criminal judgments should be restricted within a unitary system, it ought to be even more so when one system operates on the judgments of another. The case to the contrary rests primarily on the practical inability of the Supreme Court to correct "constitutional" errors in state criminal proceedings through the appellate process. * * * There is, of course, no such impediment when the issue is an important rule of criminal procedure as contrasted to its application in a particular case. * * * Almost all the Court's most important decisions on criminal procedure, for example, those relating to equal protection for indigent defendants, * * * comment on a defendant's failure to testify, * * * the extension to the states of the exclusionary rule with respect to illegally seized evidence, * * * confrontation, * * *and custodial interrogation, * * * have been made on direct review of state judgments. * * *

The argument for federal habeas corpus with respect to prisoners who have had a full and fair hearing and determination of their constitutional claims in the state courts thus must relate to two other categories of constitutional claims—disputed determinations of fact and the application of legal standards. The contention is that only federal judges, with the protections of life tenure and supposedly greater knowledge of and sympathy for the Supreme Court's interpretations of the Constitution, can be trusted with the "final say" in such matters, although great deference to state factual determinations is required. * * *

Assuming the final federal say is here to stay, is there any way to accelerate it and thereby avoid the upsetting of a conviction by a federal court when the state can no longer conduct a retrial? One way would be to route appeals from state criminal decisions, whether on direct or on collateral attack, to a federal appellate tribunal—either the appropriate court of appeals or a newly created court * * *—and preclude federal habeas corpus as to issues for which that remedy is available. Although a number of different models could be visualized, one possibility would be this: After a state rule but upon a state fact-finding or application of a federal constitutional rule, a petition for review would lie not to the Supreme Court but to the federal appellate court. * * * The standard for granting such review would be quite different from the Supreme Court's on certiorari. It would be more like what the courts of appeals now apply with respect to certificates of probable cause in state prisoner cases—not whether the issue was important to the law but whether the appeal raised a substantial claim of violation of constitutional rights. The criterion for such *appellate* review would thus be considerably more liberal than I have proposed with respect to *collateral attack* within a unitary system. When a prisoner had failed to seek such review, or the appellate court had declined to grant it or had decided adversely federal habeas corpus with respect to any issue that could have been so presented would be foreclosed, except for those cases where I would preserve collateral attack within a unitary system, and for them only if the state had not provided means for collateral attack in its own courts. Where it did, the prisoner must use it, and final state decisions would be reviewable in the same manner as proposed for state decisions on direct appeal.

Such a scheme would preserve the original understanding that judgments of the highest courts of the states are to be re-examined only by a federal appellate court rather than at nisi prius. * * * More important, it would force the prisoner to use his federal remedy while the record is reasonably fresh and a retrial is practical. While the proposal depends on the state court's having made an adequate record and findings, the court of appeals could remand where it had not. * * *

Whether there is merit in this proposal or not, I would subject federal habeas for state prisoners to the same limitations that I have proposed for federal prisoners. With the four exceptions noted at the outset, I see no sufficient reason for federal intervention on behalf of a state prisoner who raised or had an opportunity to raise his constitutional claim in the state courts, in the absence of a colorable showing of innocence. It is sufficient if the benefit of fact-finding and the application of constitutional standards by a federal judge is available in cases of that sort.

Assuming that nothing happens on the federal scene, whether through congressional inertia or otherwise, what should the states do with respect to their own systems for collateral attack on convictions? In my view, if a state considers that its system of post-conviction remedies should take the lines I have proposed, it should feel no obligation to go further simply because this will leave some cases where the only postconviction review will be in a federal court.

I realize this may seem to run counter to what has become the received wisdom, even among many state judges and prosecutors. One part of the angry reaction of the Conference of State Chief Justices to *Brown v. Allen* * * * was the recommendation that:

> State statutes should provide a postconviction process at least as broad in scope as existing Federal statutes under which claims of violation of constitutional right asserted by State prisoners are determined in Federal courts under Federal habeas corpus statutes. * * *

The recommendation for broadening state post-conviction remedies was doubtless salutary in 1954 when many states had few or none. * * *As my remarks have made evident, I recognize a considerable area for collateral attack; indeed, I think there are circumstances, such as post-trial discovery of the knowing use of material perjured evidence by the prosecutor or claims of coercion to plead guilty, where failure to provide this would deny due process of law. * * * My submission here is simply that when a state has done what it considers right and has met due process standards, it should not feel obliged to do more *merely* because federal habeas may be available in some cases where it declines to allow state collateral attack.

* * * It is, of course, somewhat ironic that after federal habeas has been justified in part on the basis of the superiority of fact determinations by the federal judge, the states should be urged to elaborate their post-conviction remedies so as to enable him to avoid the task. Moreover, conflict is even more acrid when a federal judge rejects not simply a state determination after trial and appeal but also its denial of post-conviction relief. * * * It should be remembered also that my proposal contemplates state post-conviction record making when there is new evidence that was not available at trial, and that the state trial or pre-trial proceedings will contain a record whenever the point was then raised. The problem areas would thus largely be cases where the point could have been but was not raised at state trial. * * * Be all this as it may, such considerations are for the state to weigh against what it may well consider an excessive expenditure of effort in dealing with collateral attack. While the immediate result of a state's failure to provide the full panoply of post-conviction remedies now available in federal habeas would be an increase in the burdens on the federal courts, this might afford the impetus necessary to prod Congress into action.

VI

* * *

My submission, therefore, is that innocence should not be irrelevant on collateral attack even though it may continue to be largely so on direct appeal. To such extent as we have gone beyond this, and it is an enormous extent, the system needs revision to prevent abuse by prisoners, a waste of the precious and limited resources available for the criminal process, and public disrespect for the judgments of criminal courts.

Notes

1. *Overuse of the writ?*

Judge Friendly is highly critical of what he perceives to be the overuse of the writ of habeas corpus within the judicial system. He says that labeling an error one of constitutional dimension as a road into the federal courts does nothing to limit the availability of federal review. Is the judge right?

2. *Do Justice Friendly's comments still resonate?*

Do you think the amendments to the habeas statutes and Supreme Court decisions over the past 40 years address Justice Friendly's concerns? Why or why not?

PART III
Access to Federal Courts

Chapter 8

Exhaustion of State Remedies

Violations of state law are never cognizable in federal habeas proceedings. Only claims asserting violations of federal rights may be litigated. Moreover, a violation of a federal right will not be remedied on federal review if the claim was not first fairly presented to the state court. This fair presentation rule is known as the exhaustion requirement. Exhaustion of a claim through state remedies is a prerequisite to federal consideration of the issues.

The Court has justified the exhaustion rule as a necessary component of comity in our state-federal system and as an important sign of respect for state courts in their role as interpreters of federal law. Exhaustion, then, is best understood as "an accommodation of our federal system designed to give the State an initial opportunity to pass upon and correct alleged violations of its prisoners' federal rights." *Wilwording v. Swenson*, 404 U.S. 249, 250 (1971) (citation omitted). Notably, as a principle of comity and a practical reflection of the desire to give states the first opportunity to "right the wrong," the exhaustion requirement is a purely prudential, and not a jurisdictional, requirement. As a prudential doctrine, federal courts are not absolutely barred from reviewing an unexhausted claim. Federal statutes, however, do impose a rigid bar to federal review in such circumstances.

Under 28 U.S.C. § 2254(b)-(c),

> (b) An application for a writ of habeas corpus on behalf of a person in custody pursuant to the judgment of a State court shall not be granted unless it appears that ... the applicant has exhausted the remedies available in the courts of the State; or ... there is an absence of available State corrective process, or circumstances exist that render such process ineffective to protect the rights of the applicant. [Moreover,] ... [a] State shall not be deemed to have waived the exhaustion requirement or be estopped from reliance upon the requirement unless the State, through counsel, expressly waives the requirement.
>
> (c) An applicant shall not be deemed to have exhausted the remedies available in the courts of the State, within the meaning of this section, if he has the right under the law of the State to raise, by any available procedure, the question presented.

The cases and notes in this chapter further define the concept of exhaustion and explore its application in a variety of contexts. In *Fay v. Noia*, the Supreme Court reviewed the historical context of the writ, then evaluated Noia's right to a hearing in federal court by examining whether he had exhausted his claims in state court and, if not, whether he deliberately bypassed the state court proceedings. *Rose v. Lundy* examined the question of what to do with a petition for a writ of habeas corpus that is "mixed," which means that it contains both exhausted and unexhausted claims. The third case in this chapter, *Granberry v. Greer*, examined the practical implications of the fact that exhaustion is a prudential—that is, non-jurisdictional—rule and held that a state may waive the exhaustion rule by failing to raise it in federal court. In other words, *Granberry* leaves open the possibility that un-exhausted claims could be addressed by a federal court.

Fay v. Noia

372 U.S. 391 (1963)

JUSTICE BRENNAN delivered the opinion of the Court.

This case presents important questions touching the federal habeas corpus jurisdiction, 28 U.S.C. § 2241, in its relation to state criminal justice. The narrow question is whether the respondent Noia may be granted federal habeas corpus relief from imprisonment under a New York conviction now admitted by the State to rest upon a confession obtained from him in violation of the Fourteenth Amendment, after he was denied state post-conviction relief because the coerced confession claim had been decided against him at the trial and Noia had allowed the time for a direct appeal to lapse without seeking review by a state appellate court.

Noia was convicted in 1942 with Santo Caminito and Frank Bonino in the County Court of Kings County, New York, of a felony murder in the shooting and killing of one Hammeroff during the commission of a robbery. The sole evidence against each defendant was his signed confession. Caminito and Bonino, but not Noia, appealed their convictions to the Appellate Division of the New York Supreme Court. These appeals were unsuccessful, but subsequent legal proceedings resulted in the releases of Caminito and Bonino on findings that their confessions had been coerced and their convictions therefore procured in violation of the Fourteenth Amendment. Although it has been stipulated that the coercive nature of Noia's confession was also established, the United States District Court for the Southern District of New York held in Noia's federal habeas corpus proceeding that because of his failure to appeal he must be denied relief under the provision of 28 U.S.C. § 2254 whereby "An application for a writ of habeas corpus in behalf of a person in custody pursuant to the judgment of a State court shall not be granted unless it appears that the applicant has exhausted the remedies available in the courts of the State." The Court of Appeals for the Second Circuit reversed, one judge dissenting, and ordered that Noia's conviction be set aside and that he be discharged from custody unless given a new trial forthwith. The Court of Appeals questioned whether § 2254 barred relief on federal habeas corpus where the applicant had failed to exhaust state remedies no longer available to him at the time the habeas proceeding was commenced (here a direct appeal from the conviction), but held that in any event exceptional circumstances were present which excused compliance with the section. The court also rejected other arguments advanced in support of the proposition that the federal remedy was unavailable to Noia. * * *

We granted certiorari. We affirm the judgment of the Court of Appeals but reach that court's result by a different course of reasoning. We hold: (1) Federal courts have power under the federal habeas statute to grant relief despite the applicant's failure to have pursued a state remedy not available to him at the time he applies; the doctrine under which state procedural defaults are held to constitute an adequate and independent state law ground barring direct Supreme Court review is not to be extended to limit the power granted the federal courts under the federal habeas statute. (2) Noia's failure to appeal was not a failure to exhaust "the remedies available in the courts of the State" as required by § 2254; that requirement refers only to a failure to exhaust state remedies still open to the applicant at the time he files his application for habeas corpus in the federal court. (3) Noia's failure to appeal cannot under the circumstances be deemed an intelligent and understanding waiver of his right to appeal such as to justify the withholding of federal habeas corpus relief.

I

The question has been much mooted under what circumstances, if any, the failure of a state prisoner to comply with a state procedural requirement, as a result of which the state courts decline to pass on the merits of his federal defense, bars subsequent resort to the federal courts for relief on habeas corpus. Plainly it is a question that has important implications for federal-state relations in the area of the administration of criminal justice. It cannot be answered without a preliminary inquiry into the historical development of the writ of habeas corpus.

[The Court then outlined the historical development of the writ. A similar discussion of the history of the writ is included in the introduction to Chapter 1.]

* * * Although in form the Great Writ is simply a mode of procedure, its history is inextricably intertwined with the growth of fundamental rights of personal liberty. For its function has been to provide a prompt and efficacious remedy for whatever society deems to be intolerable restraints. Its root principle is that in a civilized society, government must always be accountable to the judiciary for a man's imprisonment: if the imprisonment cannot be shown to conform with the fundamental requirements of law, the individual is entitled to his immediate release. Thus there is nothing novel in the fact that today habeas corpus in the federal courts provides a mode for the redress of denials of due process of law. * * *

* * *

The course of decisions of this Court from *Lange* and *Siebold* to the present makes plain that restraints contrary to our fundamental law, the Constitution, may be challenged on federal habeas corpus even though imposed pursuant to the conviction of a federal court of competent jurisdiction.

[The Court continued by explaining more of the historical context of the development of habeas corpus law. Throughout its opinion, the Court also referenced a case from the 1670's known as "Bushell's Case." Bushell was one of the jurors in the trial of William Penn and William Mead, who were charged with tumultuous assembly and other crimes. The trial was held before the Court of Oyer and Terminer at the Old Bailey. When the jury found the defendants "not guilty," the court ordered the jurors committed for contempt. Bushell sought habeas corpus, and the Court of Common Pleas ordered him discharged from custody.]

And so, although almost 300 years have elapsed since *Bushell's Case*, changed conceptions of the kind of criminal proceedings so fundamentally defective as to make imprisonment pursuant to them constitutionally intolerable should not be allowed to obscure the basic continuity in the conception of the writ as the remedy for such imprisonments.

It now remains to consider this principle in the application to the present case. * * * Under the conditions of modern society, Noia's imprisonment, under a conviction procured by a confession held by the Court of Appeals in *Caminito v. Murphy* to have been coerced, and which the State here concedes was obtained in violation of the Fourteenth Amendment, is no less intolerable than was Bushell's under the conditions of a very different society; and habeas corpus is no less the appropriate remedy.

II

But, it is argued, a different result is compelled by the exigencies of federalism, which played no role in *Bushell's Case*. We can appraise this argument only in light of the historical accommodation that has been worked out between the state and federal courts respecting the administration of federal habeas corpus. Our starting point is the Judiciary Act of February 5, 1867, c. 28, § 1, 14 Stat. 385-386, which first extended federal habeas corpus to state prisoners generally, and which survives, except for some changes in wording, in the present statutory codification. * * * Although the Act of 1867, like its English and American predecessors, nowhere defines habeas corpus, its expansive language and imperative tone, viewed against the background of post-Civil War efforts in Congress to deal severely with the States of the former Confederacy, would seem to make inescapable the conclusion that Congress was enlarging the habeas remedy as previously understood, not only in extending its coverage to state prisoners, but also in making its procedures more efficacious. In 1867, Congress was anticipating resistance to its Reconstruction measures and planning the implementation of the post-war constitutional Amendments. Debated and enacted at the very peak of the Radical Republicans' power, the measure that became the Act of 1867 seems plainly to have been designed to furnish a method additional to and independent of direct Supreme Court review of state court decisions for the vindication of the new constitutional guarantees. Congress seems to have had no thought, thus, that a state prisoner should abide state court determination of his constitutional defense—the necessary predicate of direct review by this Court—before resorting to federal habeas corpus. Rather, a remedy almost in the nature of removal from the state to the federal courts of state prisoners' constitutional contentions seems to have been envisaged. * * *

The elaborate provisions in the Act for taking testimony and trying the facts anew in habeas hearings lend support to this conclusion, as does the legislative history of House bill No. 605, which became, with slight changes, the Act of February 5, 1867. The bill was introduced in response to a resolution of the House on December 19, 1865, asking the Judiciary Committee to determine "what legislation is necessary to enable the courts of the United States to enforce the freedom of the wives and children of soldiers of the United States ... and also to enforce the liberty of all persons under the operation of the constitutional amendment abolishing slavery." Cong. Globe, 39th Cong., 1st Sess. 87. The terms in which it was described by its proponent, Representative Lawrence of Ohio, leave little doubt of the breadth of its intended scope: "the effect of ... (bill no. 605) is to enlarge the privilege of the writ of hobeas (sic) corpus, and make the jurisdiction of the courts and judges of the United States coextensive with all the powers that can be conferred upon them. It is a bill of the largest liberty." Cong. Globe, 39th Cong., 1st Sess. 4151 (1866). This Court, shortly after the passage of the Act, described it in equally broad terms: "This legislation is of the most comprehensive character. It brings within the habeas corpus jurisdiction of every court and of every judge every possible case of privation of liberty contrary to the National Constitution, treaties, or laws. It is impossible to widen this jurisdiction." *Ex parte McCardle*, 6 Wall. 318, 325-326 (1867).

In thus extending the habeas corpus power of the federal courts evidently to what was conceived to be its constitutional limit, the Act of February 5, 1867, clearly enough portended difficult problems concerning the relationship of the state and federal courts in the area of criminal administration. * * *

* * *

[The Court's prior] decisions fashioned a doctrine of abstention, whereby full play would be allowed the States in the administration of their criminal justice without prejudice to federal rights enwoven in the state proceedings. Thus the Court has frequently held that application for a writ of habeas corpus should have been denied "without prejudice to a renewal of the same after the accused had availed himself of such remedies as the laws of the state afforded...." *Minnesota v. Brundage*, 180 U.S. 499, 500-501 (1901). With refinements, this doctrine requiring the exhaustion of state remedies is now codified in 28 U.S.C. § 2254. But its rationale has not changed: "it would be unseemly in our dual system of government for a federal district court to upset a state court conviction without an opportunity to the state courts to correct a constitutional violation.... Solution was found in the doctrine of comity between courts, a doctrine which teaches that one court should defer action on causes properly within its jurisdiction until the courts of another sovereignty with concurrent powers, and already cognizant of the litigation, have had an opportunity to pass upon the matter." *Darr v. Burford*, 339 U.S. 200, 204 (1950). The rule of exhaustion "is not one defining power but one which relates to the appropriate exercise of power." *Bowen v. Johnston*, 306 U.S. 19, 27 (1939).

* * *

[The Court next explained how it had not deviated from the general position that after the state courts had decided a federal question on the merits against a habeas petitioner, he could return to the federal court on habeas and there relitigate the question.]

* * * Thus, we have left the weight to be given a particular state court adjudication of a federal claim later pressed on habeas substantially in the discretion of the Federal District Court: "the state adjudication carries the weight that federal practice gives to the conclusion of a court ... of another jurisdiction on federal constitutional issues. It is not res judicata." *Brown v. Allen*, *supra*, 344 U.S. at 458 (opinion of Justice Reed). " ... No binding weight is to be attached to the State determination. The congressional requirement is greater. The State court cannot have the last say when it, though on fair consideration and what procedurally may be deemed fairness, may have misconceived a federal constitutional right." [*Id.*] at 508 (opinion of Justice Frankfurter). Even if the state court adjudication turns wholly on primary, historical facts, the Federal District Court has a broad power on habeas to hold an evidentiary hearing and determine the facts. *See Brown v. Allen*, 344 U.S. at 478 (opinion of Reed, J.), 506 (opinion of Frankfurter, J.).

The breadth of the federal courts' power of independent adjudication on habeas corpus stems from the very nature of the writ, and conforms with the classic English practice. * * * So also, the traditional characterization of the writ of habeas corpus as an original (save perhaps when issued by this Court) civil remedy for the enforcement of the right to personal liberty, rather than as a stage of the state criminal proceedings or as an appeal therefrom, emphasizes the independence of the federal habeas proceedings from what has gone before. This is not to say that a state criminal judgment resting on a constitutional error is void for all purposes. But conventional notions of finality in criminal litigation cannot be permitted to defeat the manifest federal policy that federal constitutional rights of personal liberty shall not be denied without the fullest opportunity for plenary federal judicial review.

Despite the Court's refusal to give binding weight to state court determinations of the merits in habeas, it has not infrequently suggested that where the state court declines to reach the merits because of a procedural default, the federal courts may be foreclosed from granting the relief sought on habeas corpus. But the Court's practice in this area has been far from uniform, and even greater divergency has characterized the practice of the lower federal courts.

For the present, however, it suffices to note that rarely, if ever, has the Court predicated its deference to state procedural rules on a want of power to entertain a habeas application where a procedural default was committed by the defendant in the state courts. Typically, the Court, like the District Court in the instant case, has approached the problem as an aspect of the rule requiring exhaustion of state remedies, which is not a rule distributing power as between the state and federal courts. * * * The point is that the Court, by relying upon a rule of discretion, avowedly flexible, *Frisbie v. Collins*, 342 U.S. 519, yielding always to "exceptional circumstances," *Bowen v. Johnston*, 306 U.S. 19, 27, has refused to concede jurisdictional significance to the abortive state court proceeding.

III

We have reviewed the development of habeas corpus at some length because the question of the instant case has obvious importance to the proper accommodation of a great constitutional privilege and the requirements of the federal system. Our survey discloses nothing to suggest that the Federal District Court lacked the power to order Noia discharged because of a procedural forfeiture he may have incurred under state law. On the contrary, the nature of the writ at common law, the language and purpose of the Act of February 5, 1867, and the course of decisions in this Court extending over nearly a century are wholly irreconcilable with such a limitation. At the time the privilege of the writ was written into the Federal Constitution it was settled that the writ lay to test any restraint contrary to fundamental law, which in England stemmed ultimately from Magna Charta but in this country was embodied in the written Constitution. Congress in 1867 sought to provide a federal forum for state prisoners having constitutional defenses by extending the habeas corpus powers of the federal courts to their constitutional maximum. Obedient to this purpose, we have consistently held that federal court jurisdiction is conferred by the allegation of an unconstitutional restraint and is not defeated by anything that may occur in the state court proceedings. State procedural rules plainly must yield to this overriding federal policy.

A number of arguments are advanced against this conclusion. One, which concedes the breadth of federal habeas power, is that a state prisoner who forfeits his opportunity to vindicate federal defenses in the state court has been given all the process that is constitutionally due him, and hence is not restrained contrary to the Constitution. But this wholly misconceives the scope of due process of law, which comprehends not only the right to be heard but also a number of explicit procedural rights—for example, the right not to be convicted upon evidence which includes one's coerced confession—drawn from the Bill of Rights. * * *

* * * A defendant by committing a procedural default may be debarred from challenging his conviction in the state courts even on federal constitutional grounds. But a forfeiture of remedies does not legitimize the unconstitutional conduct by which his conviction was procured. Would Noia's failure to appeal have precluded him from bringing an action under the Civil Rights Acts against his inquisitors? The Act of February 5, 1867, like the Civil Rights Acts, was intended to furnish an independent, collateral remedy for certain privations of liberty. * * * The very question we face is how completely federal remedies fall with the state remedies; when we have answered this, we shall know in what sense custody may be rendered lawful by a supervening procedural default.

It is a familiar principle that this Court will decline to review state court judgments which rest on independent and adequate state grounds, notwithstanding the co-presence of federal grounds. *See, e.g.*, *N.A.A.C.P. v. Alabama ex rel. Patterson*, 357 U.S. 449 (1958); *Fox Film Corp. v. Muller*, 296 U.S. 207 (1935). * * * Thus, a default such as Noia's, if deemed adequate and independent (a question on which we intimate no view), would cut off review by this Court of the state *coram nobis* proceeding in which the New York Court of Appeals refused him relief. It is contended that it follows from this that the remedy of federal habeas corpus is likewise cut off.

The fatal weakness of this contention is its failure to recognize that the adequate state-ground rule is a function of the limitations of appellate review. Most of the opinion in the *Murdock* case is devoted to demonstrating the Court's lack of jurisdiction on direct review to decide questions of state law in cases also raising federal questions. It followed from this holding that if the state question was dispositive of the case, the Court could not decide the federal question. The federal question was moot; nothing turned on its resolution. And so we have held that the adequate state-ground rule is a consequence of the Court's obligation to refrain from rendering advisory opinions or passing upon moot questions.

But while our appellate function is concerned only with the judgments or decrees of state courts, the habeas corpus jurisdiction of the lower federal courts is not so confined. The jurisdictional prerequisite is not the judgment of a state court but detention *simpliciter*. The entire course of decisions in this Court elaborating the rule of exhaustion of state remedies is wholly incompatible with the proposition that a state court judgment is required to confer federal habeas jurisdiction. And the broad power of the federal courts under 28 U.S.C. § 2243 summarily to hear the application and to "determine the facts, and dispose of the matter as law and justice require," is hardly characteristic of an appellate jurisdiction. Habeas lies to enforce the right of personal liberty; when that right is denied and a person confined, the federal court has the power to release him. Indeed, it has no other power; it cannot revise the state court judgment; it can act only on the body of the petitioner. *In re Medley, Petitioner*, 134 U.S. 160, 173 (1890). To be sure, this may not be the entire answer to the contention that the adequate state-ground principle should apply to the federal courts on habeas corpus as well as to the Supreme Court on direct review of state judgments. * * * For the federal courts to refuse to give effect in habeas proceedings to state procedural defaults might conceivably have some effect upon the States' regulation of their criminal procedures. * * * In Noia's case the only relevant substantive law is federal—the Fourteenth Amendment. State law appears only in the procedural framework for adjudicating the substantive federal question. The paramount interest is federal. That is not to say that the States have not a substantial interest in exacting compliance with their procedural rules from criminal defendants asserting federal defenses. Of course orderly criminal procedure is a desideratum, and of course there must be sanctions for the flouting of such procedure. But that state interest "competes ... against an ideal ... [the] ideal of fair procedure." Schaefer, *Federalism and State Criminal Procedure*, 70 HARV. L. REV. 1, 5 (1956). And the only concrete impact the assumption of federal habeas jurisdiction in the face of a procedural default has on the state interest we have described, is that it prevents the State from closing off the convicted defendant's last opportunity to vindicate his constitutional rights, thereby punishing him for his default and deterring others who might commit similar defaults in the future.

* * *

* * * That the Court nevertheless ordinarily gives effect to state procedural grounds may be attributed to considerations which are peculiar to the Court's role and function and have no relevance to habeas corpus proceedings in the Federal District Courts: the unfamiliarity of members of this Court with the minutiae of 50 States' procedures; the inappropriateness of crowding our docket with questions turning wholly on particular state procedures; the web of rules and statutes that circumscribes our appellate jurisdiction; and the inherent and historical limitations of such a jurisdiction.

A practical appraisal of the state interest here involved plainly does not justify the federal courts' enforcing on habeas corpus a doctrine of forfeitures under the guise of applying the adequate state-ground rule. We fully grant, *infra*, that the exigencies of federalism warrant a limitation whereby the federal judge has the discretion to deny relief to one who has deliberately sought to subvert or evade the orderly adjudication of his federal defenses in the state courts. Surely no stricter rule is a realistic necessity. A man under conviction for crime has an obvious inducement to do his very best to keep his state remedies open, and not stake his all on the outcome of a federal habeas proceeding which, in many respects, may be less advantageous to him than a state court proceeding. And if because of inadvertence or neglect he runs afoul of a state procedural requirement, and thereby forfeits his state remedies, appellate and collateral, as well as direct review thereof in this Court, those consequences should be sufficient to vindicate the State's valid interest in orderly procedure. Whatever residuum of state interest there may be under such circumstances is manifestly insufficient in the face of the federal policy, drawn from the ancient principles of the writ of habeas corpus, embodied both in the Federal Constitution and in the habeas corpus provisions of the Judicial Code, and consistently upheld by this Court, of affording an effective remedy for restraints contrary to the Constitution. For these several reasons we reject as unsound in principle, as well as not supported by authority, the suggestion that the federal courts are without power to grant habeas relief to an applicant whose federal claims would not be heard on direct review in this Court because of a procedural default furnishing an adequate and independent ground of state decision.

* * * Very little support can be found in the long course of previous decisions by this Court elaborating the rule of exhaustion for the proposition that it was regarded at the time of the revision of the Judicial Code as jurisdictional rather than merely as a rule ordering the state and federal proceedings so as to eliminate unnecessary federal-state friction. There is thus no warrant for attributing to Congress, in the teeth of the language of § 2254, intent to work a radical innovation in the law of habeas corpus. We hold that § 2254 is limited in its application to failure to exhaust state remedies still open to the habeas applicant at the time he files his application in federal court. * * *

IV

Noia timely sought and was denied certiorari here from the adverse decision of the New York Court of Appeals.... * * *

* * * The writ of certiorari, which today provides the usual mode of invoking this Court's appellate jurisdiction of state criminal judgments, "is not a matter of right, but of sound judicial discretion, and will be granted only where there are special and important reasons therefore." Supreme Court Rule 19(1). Review on certiorari therefore does not provide a normal appellate channel in any sense comparable to the writ of error.

* * *

* * * The goal of prompt and fair criminal justice has been impeded because in the overwhelming number of cases the applications for certiorari have been denied for failure to meet the standard of Rule 19. And the demands upon our time in the examination and decision of the large volume of petitions which fail to meet that test have unwarrantably taxed the resources of this Court. Indeed, it has happened that counsel on oral argument has confessed that the record was insufficient to justify our consideration of the case but that he had felt compelled to make the futile time-consuming application in order to qualify for proceeding in a Federal District Court on habeas corpus to make a proper record. *Bullock v. South Carolina*, 365 U.S. 292 (1961). And so in a number of cases the Court has apparently excused compliance with the requirement. The same practice has sometimes been followed in the Federal District Courts.

Moreover, comity does not demand that such a price in squandered judicial resources be paid; the needs of comity are adequately served in other ways. The requirement that the habeas petitioner exhaust state court remedies available to him when he applies for federal habeas corpus relief gives state courts the opportunity to pass upon and correct errors of federal law in the state prisoner's conviction. And the availability to the States of eventual review on certiorari of such decisions of lower federal courts as may grant relief is always open. Our function of making the ultimate accommodation between state criminal law enforcement and state prisoners' constitutional rights becomes more meaningful when grounded in the full and complete record which the lower federal courts on habeas corpus are in a position to provide.

V

Although we hold that the jurisdiction of the federal courts on habeas corpus is not affected by procedural defaults incurred by the applicant during the state court proceedings, we recognize a limited discretion in the federal judge to deny relief to an applicant under certain circumstances. Discretion is implicit in the statutory command that the judge, after granting the writ and holding a hearing of appropriate scope, "dispose of the matter as law and justice require," 28 U.S.C. § 2243; and discretion was the flexible concept employed by the federal courts in developing the exhaustion rule. Furthermore, habeas corpus has traditionally been regarded as governed by equitable principles. *United States ex rel. Smith. v. Baldi*, 344 U.S. 561, 573 (dissenting opinion) (1953). Among them is the principle that a suitor's conduct in relation to the matter at hand may disentitle him to the relief he seeks. Narrowly circumscribed, in conformity to the historical role of the writ of habeas corpus as an effective and imperative remedy for detentions contrary to fundamental law, the principle is unexceptionable. We therefore hold that the federal habeas judge may in his discretion deny relief to an applicant who has deliberately bypassed the orderly procedure of the state courts and in so doing has forfeited his state court remedies.

But we wish to make very clear that this grant of discretion is not to be interpreted as a permission to introduce legal fictions into federal habeas corpus. The classic definition of waiver enunciated in *Johnson v. Zerbst*, 304 U.S. 458, 464 (1938)—"an intentional relinquishment or abandonment of a known right or privilege"—furnishes the controlling standard. If a habeas applicant, after consultation with competent counsel or otherwise, understandingly and knowingly forewent the privilege of seeking to vindicate his federal claims in the state courts, whether for strategic, tactical, or any other reasons that can fairly be described as the deliberate by-passing of state procedures, then it is open to the federal court on habeas to deny him all relief if the state courts refused to entertain his federal claims on the merits—though of course only after the federal court has satisfied itself, by holding a hearing or by some other means, of the facts bearing upon the applicant's default. *Cf. Price v. Johnston*, 334 U.S. 266, 291 (1948). At all events we wish it clearly understood that the standard here put forth depends on the considered choice of the petitioner. A choice made by counsel not participated in by the petitioner does not automatically bar relief. Nor does a state court's finding of waiver bar independent determination of the question by the federal courts on habeas, for waiver affecting federal rights is a federal question. *E.g., Rice v. Olson*, 324 U.S. 786 (1945).

The application of the standard we have adumbrated to the facts of the instant case is not difficult. Under no reasonable view can the State's version of Noia's reason for not appealing support an inference of deliberate by-passing of the state court system. For Noia to have appealed in 1942 would have been to run a substantial risk of electrocution. His was the grisly choice whether to sit content with life imprisonment or to travel the uncertain avenue of appeal which, if successful, might well have led to a retrial and death sentence. *See, e.g., Palko v. Connecticut*, 302 U.S. 319 (1937). He declined to play Russian roulette in this fashion. This was a choice by Noia not to appeal, but under the circumstances it cannot realistically be deemed a merely tactical or strategic litigation step, or in any way a deliberate circumvention of state procedures. This is not to say that in every case where a heavier penalty, even the death penalty, is a risk incurred by taking an appeal or otherwise foregoing a procedural right, waiver as we have defined it cannot be found. Each case must stand on its facts. In the instant case, the language of the judge in sentencing Noia made the risk that Noia, if reconvicted, would be sentenced to death, palpable and indeed unusually acute.

VI

It should be unnecessary to repeat what so often has been said and what so plainly is the case: that the availability of the Great Writ of habeas corpus in the federal courts for persons in the custody of the States offends no legitimate state interest in the enforcement of criminal justice or procedure. Our decision today swings open no prison gates. Today as always few indeed is the number of state prisoners who eventually win their freedom by means of federal habeas corpus. Those few who are ultimately successful are persons whom society has grievously wronged and for whom belated liberation is little enough compensation. Surely no fair-minded person will contend that those who have been deprived of their liberty without due process of law ought nevertheless to languish in prison. Noia, no less than his codefendants Caminito and Bonino, is conceded to have been the victim of unconstitutional state action. Noia's case stands on its own; but surely no just and humane legal system can tolerate a result whereby a Caminito and a Bonino are at liberty because their confessions were found to have been coerced yet a Noia, whose confession was also coerced, remains in jail for life. For such anomalies, such affronts to the conscience of a civilized society, habeas corpus is predestined by its historical role in the struggle for personal liberty to be the ultimate remedy. If the States withhold effective remedy, the federal courts have the power and the duty to provide it. Habeas corpus is one of the precious heritages of Anglo-American civilization. We do no more today than confirm its continuing efficacy.

Affirmed.

* * *

[Dissenting opinion written by JUSTICE HARLAN, joined by JUSTICE CLARK and JUSTICE STEWART, omitted. Dissenting opinion written by JUSTICE CLARK also omitted.]

Notes

1. *Subsequent case history*

Charles Noia was originally convicted in 1942 in Kings County, New York. The Supreme Court granted his writ in 1963 through this case.

2. *Dissenting opinion of Justice Clark*

In his dissent, Justice Clark stated the following:

> Beyond question the federal courts until today have had no power to release a prisoner in respondent Noia's predicament, there being no basis for such power in either the Constitution or the statute. But the Court today in releasing Noia makes an "abrupt break" not only with the Constitution and the statute but also with its past decisions, disrupting the delicate balance of federalism so foremost in the minds of the Founding Fathers and so uniquely important in the field of law enforcement. The short of it is that Noia's incarceration rests entirely on an adequate and independent state ground—namely, that he knowingly failed to perfect any appeal from his conviction of murder. While it may be that the Court's "decision today swings open no prison gates," the Court must admit in all candor that it effectively swings closed the doors of justice in the face of the State, since it certainly cannot prove its case 20 years after the fact.

Do you agree with Justice Clark's assessment that in this decision, the Court makes an "abrupt break" with the Constitution, the statute, and with its past decisions? Why or why not?

3. *Coram nobis*

Coram nobis is an old writ, authorized by the All-Writs Acts (28 U.S.C. § 1651), whereby federal convicts could advance the same claims they would otherwise have advanced in § 2255 motions. *Coram nobis* relief differs from habeas relief in that it is available to petitioners when they are not in custody, and as such it typically is used by former inmates after they have served their sentences in order to remove the stigma of conviction or to change some condition of parole. A federal court's power to entertain an application for a writ of *coram nobis* rests on the federal court's original jurisdiction in the criminal prosecution about which the applicant is complaining. Convicts challenging state convictions thus cannot seek *coram nobis* relief but only can pursue a writ of habeas corpus. Larry Yackle, Federal Courts: Habeas Corpus 144-45 (2003).

4. *Deliberate by-pass*

In articulating the deliberate by-pass standard, Justice Brennan underscored the importance of the petitioner's participation in deciding whether to bypass filing federal claims in state court: "At all events we wish it clearly understood that the standard here put forth depends on the considered choice of the petitioner. A choice made by counsel not participated in by the petitioner does not automatically bar relief." On a practical level, how would a federal court decide whether a petitioner had knowingly decided to bypass filing his federal claims in state court and/or whether the petitioner was merely "sandbagging" those claims in the event his first petition failed? On the other hand, do we want to bar claims that were simply missed by counsel or to which the client did not consent?

5. *The overlap of "exhaustion" and "right to a hearing"*

How is the concept of "exhaustion" intertwined with the concept of "right to a hearing"? How must a petitioner develop any factual issues in state court before they can be brought before a federal district court in a habeas proceeding? In considering this, keep in mind 28 U.S.C. § 2254(e):

> (1) In a proceeding instituted by an application for a writ of habeas corpus by a person in custody pursuant to the judgment of a State court, a determination of a factual issue made by a State court shall be presumed to be correct. The applicant shall have the burden of rebutting the presumption of correctness by clear and convincing evidence.
>
> (2) If the applicant has failed to develop the factual basis of a claim in State court proceedings, the court shall not hold an evidentiary hearing on the claim unless the applicant shows that—
>
> (A) the claim relies on—
>
> (i) a new rule of constitutional law, made retroactive to cases on collateral review by the Supreme Court, that was previously unavailable; or
>
> (ii) a factual predicate that could not have been previously discovered through the exercise of due diligence; and
>
> (B) the facts underlying the claim would be sufficient to establish by clear and convincing evidence that but for constitutional error, no reasonable factfinder would have found the applicant guilty of the underlying offense.

6. *The Court comments on* Fay

Nearly thirty years after *Fay v. Noia*, the Court observed the following in *Coleman v. Thompson*, 501 U.S. 722, 750 (1991): "The *Fay* standard was based on a conception of federal/state relations that undervalued the important interest in finality served by state procedural rules and the significant harm to the States that results from the failure of the federal courts to respect them." What is your assessment of this statement?

Rose v. Lundy

455 U.S. 509 (1982)

JUSTICE O'CONNOR delivered the opinion of the Court, except as to Part III-C.

In this case we consider whether the exhaustion rule in 28 U.S.C. §§ 2254(b), (c) requires a federal district court to dismiss a petition for a writ of habeas corpus containing any claims that have not been exhausted in the state courts. Because a rule requiring exhaustion of all claims furthers the purposes underlying the habeas statute, we hold that a district court must dismiss such "mixed petitions," leaving the prisoner with the choice of returning to state court to exhaust his claims or of amending or resubmitting the habeas petition to present only exhausted claims to the district court.

I

Following a jury trial, respondent Noah Lundy was convicted on charges of rape and crime against nature, and sentenced to the Tennessee State Penitentiary. After the Tennessee Court of Criminal Appeals affirmed the convictions and the Tennessee Supreme Court denied review, the respondent filed an unsuccessful petition for post-conviction relief in the Knox County Criminal Court.

The respondent subsequently filed a petition in Federal District Court for a writ of habeas corpus under 28 U.S.C. § 2254, alleging four grounds for relief: (1) that he had been denied the right to confrontation because the trial court limited the defense counsel's questioning of the victim; (2) that he had been denied the right to a fair trial because the prosecuting attorney stated that the respondent had a violent character; (3) that he had been denied the right to a fair trial because the prosecutor improperly remarked in his closing argument that the State's evidence was uncontradicted; and (4) that the trial judge improperly instructed the jury that every witness is presumed to swear the truth. After reviewing the state-court records, however, the District Court concluded that it could not consider claims three and four "in the constitutional framework" because the respondent had not exhausted his state remedies for those grounds. The court nevertheless stated that "in assessing the atmosphere of the cause taken as a whole these items may be referred to collaterally."

Apparently in an effort to assess the "atmosphere" of the trial, the District Court reviewed the state trial transcript and identified 10 instances of prosecutorial misconduct, only five of which the respondent had raised before the state courts. In addition, although purportedly not ruling on the respondent's fourth ground for relief—that the state trial judge improperly charged that "every witness is presumed to swear the truth"—the court nonetheless held that the jury instruction, coupled with both the restriction of counsel's cross-examination of the victim and the prosecutor's "personal testimony" on the weight of the State's evidence violated the respondent's right to a fair trial. * * * In short, the District Court considered several instances of prosecutorial misconduct never challenged in the state trial or appellate courts, or even raised in the respondent's habeas petition.

The Sixth Circuit affirmed the judgment of the District Court, concluding in an unreported order that the court properly found that the respondent's constitutional rights had been "seriously impaired by the improper limitation of his counsel's cross-examination of the prosecutrix and by the prosecutorial misconduct." The court specifically rejected the State's argument that the District Court should have dismissed the petition because it included both exhausted and unexhausted claims.

II

The petitioner urges this Court to apply a "total exhaustion" rule requiring district courts to dismiss every habeas corpus petition that contains both exhausted and unexhausted claims. The petitioner argues at length that such a rule furthers the policy of comity underlying the exhaustion doctrine because it gives the state courts the first opportunity to correct federal constitutional errors and minimizes federal interference and disruption of state judicial proceedings. The petitioner also believes that uniform adherence to a total exhaustion rule reduces the amount of piecemeal habeas litigation.

Under the petitioner's approach, a district court would dismiss a petition containing both exhausted and unexhausted claims, giving the prisoner the choice of returning to state court to litigate his unexhausted claims, or of proceeding with only his exhausted claims in federal court. The petitioner believes that a prisoner would be reluctant to choose the latter route since a district court could, in appropriate circumstances under Habeas Corpus Rule 9(b), dismiss subsequent federal habeas petitions as an abuse of the writ. [Rule 9(b) provides that "[a] second or successive petition may be dismissed if the judge finds that it fails to allege new or different grounds for relief and the prior determination was on the merits or, if new and different grounds are alleged, the judge finds that the failure of the petitioner to assert those grounds in a prior petition constituted an abuse of the writ."] In other words, if the prisoner amended the petition to delete the unexhausted claims or immediately refiled in federal court a petition alleging only his exhausted claims, he could lose the opportunity to litigate his presently unexhausted claims in federal court. This argument is addressed in Part III-C of this opinion.

In order to evaluate the merits of the petitioner's arguments, we turn to the habeas statute, its legislative history, and the policies underlying the exhaustion doctrine.

III

A

The exhaustion doctrine existed long before its codification by Congress in 1948. In *Ex parte Royall*, 117 U.S. 241, 251 (1886), this Court wrote that as a matter of comity, federal courts should not consider a claim in a habeas corpus petition until after the state courts have had an opportunity to act. * * *

Subsequent cases refined the principle that state remedies must be exhausted except in unusual circumstances. *See, e.g.*, *United States ex rel. Kennedy v. Tyler*, 269 U.S. 13, 17-19 (1925) (holding that the lower court should have dismissed the petition because none of the questions had been raised in the state courts. * * *). In *Ex parte Hawk*, 321 U.S. 114, 117 (1944), this Court reiterated that comity was the basis for the exhaustion doctrine. * * *

In 1948, Congress codified the exhaustion doctrine in 28 U.S.C. § 2254, citing *Ex parte Hawk* as correctly stating the principle of exhaustion. * * * Because the legislative history of § 2254, as well as the pre-1948 cases, contains no reference to the problem of mixed petitions, in all likelihood Congress never thought of the problem. Consequently, we must analyze the policies underlying the statutory provision to determine its proper scope.

B

The exhaustion doctrine is principally designed to protect the state courts' role in the enforcement of federal law and prevent disruption of state judicial proceedings. Under our federal system, the federal and state "courts [are] equally bound to guard and protect rights secured by the Constitution." *Ex parte Royall.* Because "it would be unseemly in our dual system of government for a federal district court to upset a state court conviction without an opportunity to the state courts to correct a constitutional violation," federal courts apply the doctrine of comity, which "teaches that one court should defer action on causes properly within its jurisdiction until the courts of another sovereignty with concurrent powers, and already cognizant of the litigation, have had an opportunity to pass upon the matter." *Darr v. Burford*, 339 U.S. 200, 204 (1950).

A rigorously enforced total exhaustion rule will encourage state prisoners to seek full relief first from the state courts, thus giving those courts the first opportunity to review all claims of constitutional error. As the number of prisoners who exhaust all of their federal claims increases, state courts may become increasingly familiar with and hospitable toward federal constitutional issues. Equally as important, federal claims that have been fully exhausted in state courts will more often be accompanied by a complete factual record to aid the federal courts in their review.

The facts of the present case underscore the need for a rule encouraging exhaustion of all federal claims. In his opinion, the District Court Judge wrote that "there is such mixture of violations that one cannot be separated from and considered independently of the others." Because the two unexhausted claims for relief were intertwined with the exhausted ones, the judge apparently considered all of the claims in ruling on the petition. Requiring dismissal of petitions containing both exhausted and unexhausted claims will relieve the district courts of the difficult if not impossible task of deciding when claims are related, and will reduce the temptation to consider unexhausted claims.

* * *

* * * [O]ur interpretation of §§ 2254(b), (c) provides a simple and clear instruction to potential litigants: before you bring any claims to federal court, be sure that you first have taken each one to state court. Just as *pro se* petitioners have managed to use the federal habeas machinery, so too should they be able to master this straightforward exhaustion requirement. Those prisoners who misunderstand this requirement and submit mixed petitions nevertheless are entitled to resubmit a petition with only exhausted claims or to exhaust the remainder of their claims.

Rather than increasing the burden on federal courts, strict enforcement of the exhaustion requirement will encourage habeas petitioners to exhaust all of their claims in state court and to present the federal court with a single habeas petition. To the extent that the exhaustion requirement reduces piecemeal litigation, both the courts and the prisoners should benefit, for as a result the district court will be more likely to review all of the prisoner's claims in a single proceeding, thus providing for a more focused and thorough review.

C

The prisoner's principal interest, of course, is in obtaining speedy federal relief on his claims. A total exhaustion rule will not impair that interest since he can always amend the petition to delete the unexhausted claims, rather than returning to state court to exhaust all of his claims. By invoking this procedure, however, the prisoner would risk forfeiting consideration of his unexhausted claims in federal court. Under 28 U.S.C. § 2254 Rule 9(b), a district court may dismiss subsequent petitions if it finds that "the failure of the petitioner to assert those [new] grounds in a prior petition constituted an abuse of the writ." * * * [A] prisoner who decides to proceed only with his exhausted claims and deliberately sets aside his unexhausted claims risks dismissal of subsequent federal petitions.

IV

In sum, because a total exhaustion rule promotes comity and does not unreasonably impair the prisoner's right to relief, we hold that a district court must dismiss habeas petitions containing both exhausted and unexhausted claims. Accordingly, the judgment of the Court of Appeals is reversed, and the case is remanded for proceedings consistent with this opinion.

It is so ordered.

JUSTICE BLACKMUN, concurring in the judgment.

* * *

I do not dispute the value of comity when it is applicable and productive of harmony between state and federal courts, nor do I deny the principle of exhaustion that §§ 2254(b) and (c) so clearly embrace. What troubles me is that the "total exhaustion" rule, now adopted by this Court, can be read into the statute, as the Court concedes, only by sheer force; that it operates as a trap for the uneducated and indigent pro se prisoner-applicant; that it delays the resolution of claims that are not frivolous; and that it tends to increase, rather than to alleviate, the caseload burdens on both state and federal courts. To use the old expression, the Court's ruling seems to me to "throw the baby out with the bath water."

* * *

* * * As the Court notes, the District Court erred in considering both exhausted and unexhausted claims when ruling on Lundy's § 2254 petition. * * *

* * *

I therefore would remand the case, directing that the courts below dismiss respondent's unexhausted claims and examine those that have been properly presented to the state courts in order to determine whether they are interrelated with the unexhausted grounds and, if not, whether they warrant collateral relief.

* * *

JUSTICE BRENNAN, with whom JUSTICE MARSHALL joins, concurring in part and dissenting in part.

I join the opinion of the Court (Parts I, II, III-A, III-B, and IV), but I do not join in the opinion of the plurality (Part III-C). I agree with the Court's holding that the exhaustion requirement of 28 U.S.C. §§ 2254(b), (c) obliges a federal district court to dismiss, without consideration on the merits, a habeas corpus petition from a state prisoner when that petition contains claims that have not been exhausted in the state courts, "leaving the prisoner with the choice of returning to state court to exhaust his claims or of amending or resubmitting the habeas petition to present only exhausted claims to the district court." But I disagree with the plurality's view, in Part III-C, that a habeas petitioner must "risk forfeiting consideration of his unexhausted claims in federal court" if he "decides to proceed only with his exhausted claims and deliberately sets aside his unexhausted claims" in the face of the district court's refusal to consider his "mixed" petition. The issue of Rule 9(b)'s proper application to successive petitions brought as the result of our decision today is not before us—it was not among the questions presented by petitioner, nor was it briefed and argued by the parties. Therefore, the issue should not be addressed until we have a case presenting it. In any event, I disagree with the plurality's proposed disposition of the issue. In my view, Rule 9(b) cannot be read to permit dismissal of a subsequent petition under the circumstances described in the plurality's opinion.

* * *

IV

I conclude that when a prisoner's original, "mixed" habeas petition is dismissed without any examination of its claims on the merits, and when the prisoner later brings a second petition based on the previously unexhausted claims that had earlier been refused a hearing, then the remedy of dismissal for "abuse of the writ" cannot be employed against that second petition, absent unusual factual circumstances truly suggesting abuse. This conclusion is to my mind inescapably compelled not only by *Sanders* [*v. United States*, 373 U.S. 1 (1963)], but also by the Advisory Committee explanation of the Rule, and by Congress' subsequent incorporation of the higher, "abusive" standard into the Rule. The plurality's conclusion, in contrast, has no support whatever from any of these sources. Nor, of course, does it have the support of a majority of the Court.

[JUSTICE WHITE rejected the plurality's conclusion in Part III-C, as did JUSTICE BLACKMUN. JUSTICE STEVENS did not reach this issue.]

JUSTICE WHITE, concurring in part and dissenting in part.

I agree with most of JUSTICE BRENNAN's opinion; but like JUSTICE BLACKMUN, I would not require a "mixed" petition to be dismissed in its entirety, with leave to resubmit the exhausted claims. The trial judge cannot rule on the unexhausted issues and should dismiss them. But he should rule on the exhausted claims unless they are intertwined with those he must dismiss or unless the habeas petitioner prefers to have his entire petition dismissed. In any event, if the judge rules on those issues that are ripe and dismisses those that are not, I would not tax the petitioner with abuse of the writ if he returns with the latter claims after seeking state relief.

JUSTICE STEVENS, dissenting.

This case raises important questions about the authority of federal judges. In my opinion the District Judge properly exercised his statutory duty to consider the merits of the claims advanced by respondent that previously had been rejected by the Tennessee courts. The District Judge exceeded, however, what I regard as proper restraints on the scope of collateral review of state-court judgments. Ironically, instead of correcting his error, the Court today fashions a new rule of law that will merely delay the final disposition of this case and, as JUSTICE BLACKMUN demonstrates, impose unnecessary burdens on both state and federal judges.

* * *

In my opinion claims of constitutional error are not fungible. There are at least four types. The one most frequently encountered is a claim that attaches a constitutional label to a set of facts that does not disclose a violation of any constitutional right. In my opinion, each of the four claims asserted in this case falls in that category. The second class includes constitutional violations that are not of sufficient import in a particular case to justify reversal even on direct appeal, when the evidence is still fresh and a fair retrial could be promptly conducted. A third category includes errors that are important enough to require reversal on direct appeal but do not reveal the kind of fundamental unfairness to the accused that will support a collateral attack on a final judgment. *See, e.g.*, *Stone v. Powell*, 428 U.S. 465 [(1976)]. The fourth category includes those errors that are so fundamental that they infect the validity of the underlying judgment itself, or the integrity of the process by which that judgment was obtained. This category cannot be defined precisely; concepts of "fundamental fairness" are not frozen in time. But the kind of error that falls in this category is best illustrated by recalling the classic grounds for the issuance of a writ of habeas corpus—that the proceeding was dominated by mob violence; that the prosecutor knowingly made use of perjured testimony; or that the conviction was based on a confession extorted from the defendant by brutal methods. Errors of this kind justify collateral relief no matter how long a judgment may have been final and even though they may not have been preserved properly in the original trial.

* * *

If my appraisal of respondent's exhausted claims is incorrect—if the trial actually was fundamentally unfair to the respondent—postponing relief until another round of review in the state and federal judicial systems has been completed is truly outrageous. The unnecessary delay will make it more difficult for the prosecutor to obtain a conviction on retrial if respondent is in fact guilty; if he is innocent, requiring him to languish in jail because he made a pleading error is callous indeed.

There are some situations in which a district judge should refuse to entertain a mixed petition until all of the prisoner's claims have been exhausted. If the unexhausted claim appears to involve error of the most serious kind and if it is reasonably clear that the exhausted claims do not, addressing the merits of the exhausted claims will merely delay the ultimate disposition of the case. Or if an evidentiary hearing is necessary to decide the merits of both the exhausted and unexhausted claims, a procedure that enables all fact questions to be resolved in the same hearing should be followed. I therefore would allow district judges to exercise discretion to determine whether the presence of an unexhausted claim in a habeas corpus application makes it inappropriate to consider the merits of a properly pleaded exhausted claim. The inflexible, mechanical rule the Court adopts today arbitrarily denies district judges the kind of authority they need to administer their calendars effectively.

II

In recent years federal judges at times have lost sight of the true office of the great writ of habeas corpus. * * * The writ of habeas corpus is a fundamental guarantee of liberty.

The fact that federal judges have at times construed their power to issue writs of habeas corpus as though it were tantamount to the authority of an appellate court considering a direct appeal from a trial court judgment has had two unfortunate consequences. First, it has encouraged prisoners to file an ever-increasing volume of federal applications that often amount to little more than a request for further review of asserted grounds for reversal that already have been adequately considered and rejected on direct review. Second, it has led this Court into the business of creating special procedural rules for dealing with this floodgate of litigation. The doctrine of nonretroactivity, the emerging "cause and prejudice" doctrine, and today's "total exhaustion" rule are examples of judicial lawmaking that might well have been avoided by confining the availability of habeas corpus relief to cases that truly involve fundamental unfairness.

When that high standard is met, there should be no question about the retroactivity of the constitutional rule being enforced. Nor do I believe there is any need to fashion definitions of "cause" and "prejudice" to determine whether an error that was not preserved at trial or on direct appeal is subject to review in a collateral federal proceeding.

The availability of habeas corpus relief should depend primarily on the character of the alleged constitutional violation and not on the procedural history underlying the claim.

The "total exhaustion" rule the Court crafts today demeans the high office of the great writ. Perhaps a rule of this kind would be an appropriate response to a flood of litigation requesting review of minor disputes. An assumption that most of these petitions are groundless might be thought to justify technical pleading requirements that would provide a mechanism for reducing the sheer number of cases in which the merits must be considered. But the Court's experience has taught us not only that most of these petitions lack merit, but also that there are cases in which serious injustice must be corrected by the issuance of the writ. In such cases, the statutory requirement that adequate state remedies be exhausted must, of course, be honored. When a person's liberty is at stake, however, there surely is no justification for the creation of needless procedural hurdles.

Procedural regularity is a matter of fundamental importance in the administration of justice. But procedural niceties that merely complicate and delay the resolution of disputes are another matter. In my opinion the federal habeas corpus statute should be construed to protect the former and, whenever possible, to avoid the latter.

I respectfully dissent.

Notes

1. *Subsequent case history*

As noted in the Court's decision, Noah Lundy was sentenced to consecutive terms of 120 years on the rape charge and from 5 to 15 years on the crime against nature charge. *Rose v. Lundy*, 455 U.S. 509, 510 n.1 (1982).

2. *AEDPA statute of limitations*

At the time that *Rose v. Lundy* was decided, there was no federal statute of limitations for filing a federal habeas petition. How does the rule announced in *Rose v. Lundy* interact with the one-year limitation on the filing of a federal petition imposed by AEDPA, § 2244(d)?

"The combined effect of *Rose* and [the] limitations period is that if a petitioner comes to federal court with a mixed petition toward the end of the limitations period, a dismissal of his mixed petition could result in the loss of all of his claims—including those already exhausted—because the limitations period could expire during the time a petitioner returns to state court to exhaust his unexhausted claims." *Pliler v. Ford*, 542 U.S. 225, 230 (2004). In *Rhines v. Weber*, 544 U.S. 269 (2005), the Court developed a "stay and abeyance" procedure in order to reconcile *Rose*'s "total exhaustion" rule with AEDPA's one-year statute of limitations. As Justice O'Connor explained in *Rhines*:

> As a result of the interplay between AEDPA's 1-year statute of limitations and *Lundy*'s dismissal requirement, petitioners who come to federal court with "mixed" petitions run the risk of forever losing their opportunity for any federal review of their unexhausted claims. If a petitioner files a timely but mixed petition in federal district court, and the district court dismisses it under *Lundy* after the limitations period has expired, this will likely mean the termination of any federal review. [Remember that the AEDPA's 1-year statute of limitations is not tolled during a federal district court's consideration of a petition for habeas corpus.] * * * Similarly, if a district court dismisses a mixed petition close to the end of the 1-year period, the petitioner's chances of exhausting his claims in state

> court and refiling his petition in federal court before the limitations period runs are slim. The problem is not limited to petitioners who file close to the AEDPA deadline. Even a petitioner who files early will have no way of controlling when the district court will resolve the question of exhaustion. Thus, whether a petitioner ever receives federal review of his claims may turn on which district court happens to hear his case.
>
> [S]ome district courts have adopted a version of the "stay-and-abeyance" procedure employed by the District Court below. Under this procedure, rather than dismiss the mixed petition pursuant to *Lundy*, a district court might stay the petition and hold it in abeyance while the petitioner returns to state court to exhaust his previously unexhausted claims. Once the petitioner exhausts his state remedies, the district court will lift the stay and allow the petitioner to proceed in federal court.

544 U.S. at 275-76.

The Court in *Rhines* also pointed out that AEDPA's 1-year statute of limitations has the twin aims of (1) creating more finality in state criminal decisions and (2) helping to "streamline" federal habeas proceedings. *Rhines*, 544 U.S. at 276-77. Considering this, the Court held: "Staying a federal habeas petition frustrates AEDPA's objective of encouraging finality by allowing a petitioner to delay the resolution of the federal proceedings. It also undermines AEDPA's goal of streamlining federal habeas proceedings by decreasing a petitioner's incentive to exhaust all his claims in state court prior to filing his federal petition." *Id.* at 277.

Accordingly, the Court held that a stay and abeyance should not always be granted: "Because granting a stay effectively excuses a petitioner's failure to present his claims first to the state courts, stay and abeyance is only appropriate when the district court determines there was good cause for the petitioner's failure to exhaust his claims first in state court. Moreover, even if a petitioner had good cause for that failure, the district court would abuse its discretion if it were to grant him a stay when his unexhausted claims are plainly meritless." *Id.*

3. *Required to permit exhaustion*

What if the district court determines that a claim is both unexhausted and facially meritless? Must the district court provide a *Rhines* stay so as to allow the claim to be exhausted?

Under § 2254(b), the answer is no. "An application for a writ of habeas corpus may be denied on the merits, notwithstanding the failure of the applicant to exhaust the remedies available in the courts of the State." *See also supra* note 2.

4. *Good Cause*

What do you think counts as "good cause" for a failure to exhaust such that the petitioner is entitled to a *Rhines* stay?

5. *Timeliness*

AEDPA's principal goal is to streamline habeas appeals. How long do you think a prisoner should have to exhaust his claims during a valid *Rhines* stay? Many courts have suggested that it is appropriate to require the prisoner to file the unexhausted claims within 30 days of the stay and that it is likewise appropriate to require the prisoner to re-commence the federal proceedings within 30 days of the adjudication of the claims by the state. *See Rhines*, 544 U.S. at 277-78.

6. *Delaying final disposition and burdening judges*

In his dissenting opinion, Justice Stevens stated that the "Court today fashions a new rule of law that will merely delay the final disposition of this case and ... impose unnecessary burdens on both state and federal judges." Has Justice Stevens's prediction come true? How is his concern addressed by the discussion in *Rhines* concerning the twin aims of AEDPA?

7. *Finality*

One of the complaints about federal habeas review of state convictions is the lack of finality and the length of time the case remains "open." How might the *Rose v. Lundy* decision impact these concerns? How are they further affected by the decision in *Rhines*?

Granberry v. Greer

481 U.S. 129 (1987)

JUSTICE STEVENS delivered the opinion of the Court.

Petitioner, a state prisoner, applied to the District Court for the Southern District of Illinois for a writ of habeas corpus pursuant to 28 U.S.C. § 2254. The Magistrate to whom the District Court referred the case ordered the State of Illinois to file an answer; the State instead filed a motion to dismiss under Rule 12(b)(6) of the Federal Rules of Civil Procedure, arguing that the petition failed to state a claim upon which relief could be granted. The District Court adopted the Magistrate's recommendation and dismissed the petition on the merits. When petitioner appealed to the Court of Appeals for the Seventh Circuit, respondent for the first time interposed the defense that petitioner had not exhausted his state remedies. In response, petitioner contended that the State had waived that defense by failing to raise it in the District Court. The Court of Appeals rejected the waiver argument and remanded the cause to the District Court with instructions to dismiss without prejudice. Because the Courts of Appeals have given different answers to the question whether the State's failure to raise nonexhaustion in the district court constitutes a waiver of that defense in the court of appeals, we granted certiorari. How an appellate court ought to handle a nonexhausted habeas petition when the State has not raised this objection in the district court is a question that might be answered in three different ways. We might treat the State's silence on the matter as a procedural default precluding the State from raising the issue on appeal. At the other extreme, we might treat nonexhaustion as an inflexible bar to consideration of the merits of the petition by the federal court, and therefore require that a petition be dismissed when it appears that there has been a failure to exhaust. Or, third, we might adopt an intermediate approach and direct the courts of appeals to exercise discretion in each case to decide whether the administration of justice would be better served by insisting on exhaustion or by reaching the merits of the petition forthwith.

We have already decided that the failure to exhaust state remedies does not deprive an appellate court of jurisdiction to consider the merits of a habeas corpus application. *See Strickland v. Washington*, 466 U.S. 668 (1984). As the *Strickland* case demonstrates, there are some cases in which it is appropriate for an appellate court to address the merits of a habeas corpus petition notwithstanding the lack of complete exhaustion.[1] Although there

1. *Eds.* The unexhausted claim in *Strickland* alleged that the trial judge had taken a psychiatric report not available to defendant's counsel into consideration when sentencing the defendant to death. *Washington v. Strickland*, 673 F.2d 879, 889 n.5 (5th Cir. Unit B 1982). If the judge had done so, it would have been in violation of the Supreme Court's holding in *Gardner v. Florida*, 430 U.S. 349 (1977). However the district court decided, affirmed by the appellate court, that the claim had no merit and that it fell into one of the exceptions to the exhaustion rule. *Washington v. Strickland*, 693

is a strong presumption in favor of requiring the prisoner to pursue his available state remedies, his failure to do so is not an absolute bar to appellate consideration of his claims.

We have also expressed our reluctance to adopt rules that allow a party to withhold raising a defense until after the "main event"—in this case, the proceeding in the District Court—is over. *See Wainwright v. Sykes*. Although the record indicates that the State's failure to raise the nonexhaustion defense in this case was the result of inadvertence, rather than a matter of tactics, it seems unwise to adopt a rule that would permit, and might even encourage, the State to seek a favorable ruling on the merits in the district court while holding the exhaustion defense in reserve for use on appeal if necessary. If the habeas petition is meritorious, such a rule would prolong the prisoner's confinement for no other reason than the State's postponement of the exhaustion defense to the appellate level. Moreover, if the court of appeals is convinced that the petition has no merit, a belated application of the exhaustion rule might simply require useless litigation in the state courts.

We are not persuaded by either of the extreme positions. The appellate court is not required to dismiss for nonexhaustion notwithstanding the State's failure to raise it, and the court is not obligated to regard the State's omission as an absolute waiver of the claim. Instead, we think the history of the exhaustion doctrine, as recently reviewed in *Rose v. Lundy*, 455 U.S. 509 (1982), points in the direction of a middle course. * * *

When the State answers a habeas corpus petition, it has a duty to advise the district court whether the prisoner has, in fact, exhausted all available state remedies. As this case demonstrates, however, there are exceptional cases in which the State fails, whether inadvertently or otherwise, to raise an arguably meritorious nonexhaustion defense. The State's omission in such a case makes it appropriate for the court of appeals to take a fresh look at the issue. The court should determine whether the interests of comity and federalism will be better served by addressing the merits forthwith or by requiring a series of additional state and district court proceedings before reviewing the merits of the petitioner's claim.

If, for example, the case presents an issue on which an unresolved question of fact or of state law might have an important bearing, both comity and judicial efficiency may make it appropriate for the court to insist on complete exhaustion to make sure that it may ultimately review the issue on a fully informed basis. On the other hand, if it is perfectly clear that the applicant does not raise even a colorable federal claim, the interests of the petitioner, the warden, the state attorney general, the state courts, and the federal courts will all be well served even if the State fails to raise the exhaustion defense, the district court denies the habeas petition, and the court of appeals affirms the judgment of the district court forthwith.

Conversely, if a full trial has been held in the district court and it is evident that a miscarriage of justice has occurred, it may also be appropriate for the court of appeals to hold that the nonexhaustion defense has been waived in order to avoid unnecessary delay in granting relief that is plainly warranted. * * *

In this case the Court of Appeals simply held that the nonexhaustion defense could not be waived, and made no attempt to determine whether the interests of justice would be better served by addressing the merits of the habeas petition or by requiring additional

---

F.2d 1243, 1248 n.7 (Former 5th Cir. 1982) (citing *Galtieri v. Wainwright*, 582 F.2d 348, 355 (5th Cir. 1978) (describing the exceptions to the exhaustion rule)). The Supreme Court agreed with the appellate court and held that the district court was correct to continue the habeas proceeding despite the fact that it was technically a mixed claim. *Strickland*, 466 U.S. at 679.

state proceedings before doing so. Accordingly, we vacate the judgment of the Court of Appeals and remand the case for further proceedings consistent with this opinion.

It is so ordered.

Notes

1. *Subsequent case history*

Waldo Granberry is serving a sentence of life in prison without the possibility of parole. See Inmate Search at www.idoc.state.il.us.

2. *Reasons to require exhaustion*

In *Granberry v. Greer*, the Court discusses the reasons to require exhaustion of claims. What is the importance of those reasons? What if one of the claims is that there was no court before which to bring the non-exhausted claims? For example, in Virginia, a defendant has only 21 days after conviction to present newly discovered evidence to the state courts. If *Brady* material is discovered later than 21 days after conviction, how can the defendant exhaust his or her claims?

3. *The effect of bedrock constitutional violations on exhaustion*

Should exhaustion be unnecessary when there is a bedrock constitutional violation, such as denial of counsel? What would be the advantages and disadvantages of such an exception?

4. *Effect of AEDPA*

Refer to the text of § 2254(b) &(c) (included earlier in this chapter). How does AEDPA alter the *Granberry* rule?

In a recent capital case the Court explained, "We note in this regard that, while AEDPA forbids a finding that exhaustion has been waived unless the State expressly waives the requirement, 28 U.S.C. § 2254(b)(3), under pre-AEDPA law, exhaustion and procedural default defenses could be waived based on the State's litigation conduct (referencing *Granberry v. Greer*)." *Banks v. Dretke*, 540 U.S. 668, 705 (2004).

What do you suppose an "express waiver" would look like? Must the State use the magic word "waiver"? Could a failure by the government to assert the exhaustion defense ever satisfy the waiver requirement? *Pike v. Guarino*, 492 F.3d 61, 72 (1st Cir. 2007) ("It is hornbook law that waivers of exhaustion will not lightly be inferred but, rather, must be clear and explicit.").

Chapter 9

Procedural Default

In the cases in this chapter, the Supreme Court explains how a state court's adherence to state procedural rules as a basis for denying relief interacts with the availability of federal habeas corpus review.

In *Brown v. Allen*, 344 U.S. 443 (1953) (*see* Chapter 1), the Court concluded that a state prisoner's challenge to the trial court's resolution of dispositive federal issues can be heard in federal habeas. Then in *Fay v. Noia*, 372 U.S. 391 (1963) (*see* Chapter 8), the Court said that "the doctrine under which state procedural defaults are held to constitute an adequate and independent state law ground barring direct Supreme Court review is not to be extended to limit the power granted the federal courts under the federal habeas statute." In so doing, the Court articulated a "deliberate bypass" standard whereby a federal judge had discretion to deny relief to an applicant who had deliberately bypassed the orderly procedure of the state courts and thus forfeited his state court remedies.

In the first case in this chapter, *Wainwright v. Sykes*, the "deliberate bypass standard" from *Fay* gave way to a "cause and prejudice" requirement. The Court held that an "adequate and independent" finding of procedural default bars federal habeas review of a federal claim unless the habeas petitioner can show "cause" and "prejudice." Then in *Coleman v. Thompson*, the Supreme Court acknowledged that its decision in *Sykes* had left open the question of whether *Fay*'s deliberate bypass standard would continue to apply in a case in which a state prisoner defaulted his entire appeal. *Coleman* answered that question by finding that in all cases in which a state prisoner has defaulted his federal claims in state court pursuant to an independent and adequate state procedural rule, federal habeas review of the claims is barred unless the prisoner can demonstrate either (1) cause and prejudice or (2) that failure to consider the claims will result in a fundamental miscarriage of justice.

Wainwright v. Sykes

433 U.S. 72 (1977)

JUSTICE REHNQUIST delivered the opinion of the Court

We granted certiorari to consider the availability of federal habeas corpus to review a state convict's claim that testimony was admitted at his trial in violation of his rights under *Miranda v. Arizona*, 384 U.S. 436 (1966), a claim which the Florida courts have previously refused to consider on the merits because of noncompliance with a state contemporaneous-objection rule. Petitioner Wainwright, on behalf of the State of Florida, here challenges a decision of the Court of Appeals for the Fifth Circuit ordering a hearing in state court on the merits of respondent's contention.

Respondent Sykes was convicted of third-degree murder after a jury trial in the Circuit Court of DeSoto County. He testified at trial that on the evening of January 8, 1972, he told his wife to summon the police because he had just shot Willie Gilbert. Other evidence indicated that when the police arrived at respondent's trailer home, they found Gilbert dead of a shotgun wound, lying a few feet from the front porch. Shortly after their arrival, respondent came from across the road and volunteered that he had shot Gilbert, and a few minutes later respondent's wife approached the police and told them the same thing. Sykes was immediately arrested and taken to the police station.

Once there, it is conceded that he was read his *Miranda* rights, and that he declined to seek the aid of counsel and indicated a desire to talk. He then made a statement, which was admitted into evidence at trial through the testimony of the two officers who heard it, to the effect that he had shot Gilbert from the front porch of his trailer home. There were several references during the trial to respondent's consumption of alcohol during the preceding day and to his apparent state of intoxication, facts which were acknowledged by the officers who arrived at the scene. At no time during the trial, however, was the admissibility of any of respondent's statements challenged by his counsel on the ground that respondent had not understood the *Miranda* warnings. Nor did the trial judge question their admissibility on his own motion or hold a factfinding hearing bearing on that issue.

Respondent appealed his conviction, but apparently did not challenge the admissibility of the inculpatory statements. He later filed in the trial court a motion to vacate the conviction and, in the State District Court of Appeals and Supreme Court, petitions for habeas corpus. These filings, apparently for the first time, challenged the statements made to police on grounds of involuntariness. In all of these efforts respondent was unsuccessful.

Having failed in the Florida courts, respondent initiated the present action under 28 U.S.C. § 2254, asserting the inadmissibility of his statements by reason of his lack of understanding of the *Miranda* warnings. The United States District Court for the Middle District of Florida ruled that *Jackson v. Denno*, 378 U.S. 368 (1964), requires a hearing in a state criminal trial prior to the admission of an inculpatory out-of-court statement by the defendant. It held further that respondent had not lost his right to assert such a claim by failing to object at trial or on direct appeal, since only "exceptional circumstances" of "strategic decisions at trial" can create such a bar to raising federal constitutional claims in a federal habeas action. The court stayed issuance of the writ to allow the state court to hold a hearing on the "voluntariness" of the statements.

Petitioner warden then appealed this decision to the United States Court of Appeals for the Fifth Circuit. That court first considered the nature of the right to exclusion of statements made without a knowing waiver of the right to counsel and the right not to incriminate oneself. It noted that *Jackson v. Denno*, 378 U.S. 368 (1964), guarantees a right to a hearing on whether a defendant has knowingly waived his rights as described to him in the Miranda warnings, and stated that under Florida law "[t]he burden is on the State to secure [a] prima facie determination of voluntariness, not upon the defendant to demand it."

The court then directed its attention to the effect on respondent's right of Florida Rule Crim. Proc. 3.190(i), which it described as "a contemporaneous objection rule" applying to motions to suppress a defendant's inculpatory statements * * * and concluded that the failure to comply with the rule requiring objection at the trial would only bar review of the suppression claim where the right to object was deliberately bypassed for reasons relating to trial tactics. * * * It found that prejudice is "inherent" in any situation, like the present one, where the admissibility of an incriminating statement is concerned. Concluding that "[t]he failure to object in this case cannot be dismissed as a trial tactic, and thus a deliberate bypass," the court affirmed the District Court order that the State hold a hearing on whether respondent knowingly waived his *Miranda* rights at the time he made the statements.

The simple legal question before the Court calls for a construction of the language of 28 U.S.C. § 2254(a), which provides that the federal courts shall entertain an application for a writ of habeas corpus "in behalf of a person in custody pursuant to the judgment of a state court only on the ground that he is in custody in violation of the Constitution or laws or treaties of the United States." But, to put it mildly, we do not write on a clean slate in construing this statutory provision. Its earliest counterpart, applicable only to prisoners detained by federal authority, is found in the Judiciary Act of 1789. Construing that statute for the Court in *Ex parte Watkins*, 28 U.S. 193, 202 (1830), Chief Justice Marshall said:

> An imprisonment under a judgment cannot be unlawful, unless that judgment be an absolute nullity; and it is not a nullity if the Court has general jurisdiction of the subject, although it should be erroneous.

See Ex parte Kearney, [20 U.S. 38] (1822).

In 1867, Congress expanded the statutory language so as to make the writ available to one held in state as well as federal custody. For more than a century since the 1867 amendment, this Court has grappled with the relationship between the classical common-law writ of habeas corpus and the remedy provided in 28 U.S.C. § 2254. Sharp division within the Court has been manifested on more than one aspect of the perplexing problems which have been litigated in this connection. Where the habeas petitioner challenges a final judgment of conviction rendered by a state court, this Court has been called upon to decide no fewer than four different questions, all to a degree interrelated with one another: (1) What types of federal claims may a federal habeas court properly consider? (2) Where a federal claim is cognizable by a federal habeas court, to what extent must that court defer to a resolution of the claim in prior state proceedings? (3) To what extent must the petitioner who seeks federal habeas exhaust state remedies before resorting to the federal court? (4) In what instances will an adequate and independent state ground bar consideration of otherwise cognizable federal issues on federal habeas review?

Each of these four issues has spawned its share of litigation. With respect to the first, the rule laid down in *Ex parte Watkins*, [28 U.S. 193], was gradually changed by judicial decisions expanding the availability of habeas relief beyond attacks focused narrowly on the jurisdiction of the sentencing court. *Ex parte Siebold*, 100 U.S. 371 (1880), authorized use of the writ to challenge a conviction under a federal statute where the statute was claimed to violate the United States Constitution. *Frank v. Mangum*, 237 U.S. 309 (1915), and *Moore v. Dempsey*, 261 U.S. 86 (1923), though in large part inconsistent with one another, together broadened the concept of jurisdiction to allow review of a claim of "mob domination" of what was in all other respects a trial in a court of competent jurisdiction.

In *Johnson v. Zerbst*, 304 U.S. 458 (1938), an indigent federal prisoner's claim that he was denied the right to counsel at his trial was held to state a contention going to the "power and authority" of the trial court, which might be reviewed on habeas. Finally, in *Waley v. Johnston*, 316 U.S. 101 (1942), the Court openly discarded the concept of jurisdiction—by then more a fiction than anything else—as a touchstone of the availability of federal habeas review, and acknowledged that such review is available for claims of "disregard of the constitutional rights of the accused, and where the writ is the only effective means of preserving his rights." *Id.* In *Brown v. Allen*, 344 U.S. 443 (1953), it was made explicit that a state prisoner's challenge to the trial court's resolution of dispositive federal issues is always fair game on federal habeas. * * *

The degree of deference to be given to a state court's resolution of a federal-law issue was elaborately canvassed in the Court's opinion in *Brown v. Allen*, *supra*. Speaking for the

Court, Justice Reed stated: "[Such] state adjudication carries the weight that federal practice gives to the conclusion of a court of last resort of another jurisdiction on federal constitutional issues. It is not *res judicata*." * * *

The exhaustion-of-state-remedies requirement was first articulated by this Court in the case of *Ex parte Royall*, 117 U.S. 241 (1886). There, a state defendant sought habeas in advance of trial on a claim that he had been indicted under an unconstitutional statute. The writ was dismissed by the District Court, and this Court affirmed, stating that while there was power in the federal courts to entertain such petitions, as a matter of comity they should usually stay their hand pending consideration of the issue in the normal course of the state trial. * * *

* * *

* * * The application of this principle in the context of a federal habeas proceeding has therefore excluded from consideration any questions of state *substantive* law, and thus effectively barred federal habeas review where questions of that sort are either the only ones raised by a petitioner or are in themselves dispositive of his case. The area of controversy which has developed has concerned the reviewability of federal claims which the state court has declined to pass on because not presented in the manner prescribed by its procedural rules. The adequacy of such an independent state procedural ground to prevent federal habeas review of the underlying federal issue has been treated very differently than where the state-law ground is substantive. The pertinent decisions marking the Court's somewhat tortuous efforts to deal with this problem are: *Ex parte Spencer*, 228 U.S. 652 (1913); *Brown v. Allen*, 344 U.S. 443 (1953); *Fay v. Noia*, [372 U.S. 391 (1963)]; *Davis v. United States*, 411 U.S. 233 (1973); and *Francis v. Henderson*, 425 U.S. 536 (1976).

In *Brown*, petitioner Daniels' lawyer had failed to mail the appeal papers to the State Supreme Court on the last day provided by law for filing, and hand delivered them one day after that date. Citing the state rule requiring timely filing, the Supreme Court of North Carolina refused to hear the appeal. This Court, relying in part on its earlier decision in *Ex parte Spencer*, held that federal habeas was not available to review a constitutional claim which could not have been reviewed on direct appeal here because it rested on an independent and adequate state procedural ground.

In *Fay v. Noia*, respondent Noia sought federal habeas to review a claim that his state-court conviction had resulted from the introduction of a coerced confession in violation of the Fifth Amendment to the United States Constitution. While the convictions of his two co-defendants were reversed on that ground in collateral proceedings following their appeals, Noia did not appeal and the New York courts ruled that his subsequent *coram nobis* action was barred on account of that failure. This Court held that petitioner was nonetheless entitled to raise the claim in federal habeas, and thereby overruled its decision 10 years earlier in *Brown v. Allen*:

> [T]he doctrine under which state procedural defaults are held to constitute an adequate and independent state law ground barring direct Supreme Court review is not to be extended to limit the power granted the federal courts under the federal habeas statute.

As a matter of comity but not of federal power, the Court acknowledged "a limited discretion in the federal judge to deny relief ... to an applicant who had deliberately bypassed the orderly procedure of the state courts and in so doing has forfeited his state court remedies." *Id.* In so stating, the Court made clear that the waiver must be knowing and actual—"'an intentional relinquishment or abandonment of a known right or privilege.'" *Id.* (*quoting Johnson v. Zerbst*). Noting petitioner's "grisly choice" between acceptance of his life sentence and pursuit of an appeal which might culminate in a sentence of death, the Court concluded that there had been no deliberate bypass of the right to have the federal issues reviewed through a state appeal.

A decade later we decided *Davis v. United States*, in which a federal prisoner's application under 28 U.S.C. § 2255 sought for the first time to challenge the makeup of the grand jury which indicted him. The Government contended that he was barred by the requirement of Fed. Rule Crim. Proc. 12(b)(2) providing that such challenges must be raised "by motion before trial." The Rule further provides that failure to so object constitutes a waiver of the objection, but that "the court for cause shown may grant relief from the waiver." We noted that the Rule "promulgated by this Court and, pursuant to 18 U.S.C. § 3771, 'adopted' by Congress, governs by its terms the manner in which the claims of defects in the institution of criminal proceedings may be waived" and held that this standard contained in the Rule, rather than the *Fay v. Noia* concept of waiver, should pertain in federal habeas as on direct review. Referring to previous constructions of Rule 12(b)(2), we concluded that review of the claim should be barred on habeas, as on direct appeal, absent a showing of cause for the noncompliance and some showing of actual prejudice resulting from the alleged constitutional violation.

* * *

To the extent that the dicta of *Fay v. Noia* may be thought to have laid down an all-inclusive rule rendering state contemporaneous-objection rules ineffective to bar review of underlying federal claims in federal habeas proceedings—absent a "knowing waiver" or a "deliberate bypass" of the right to so object—its effect was limited by *Francis*, which applied a different rule and barred a habeas challenge to the makeup of a grand jury. Petitioner Wainwright in this case urges that we further confine its effect by applying the principle enunciated in *Francis* to a claimed error in the admission of a defendant's confession.

Respondent first contends that any discussion as to the effect that noncompliance with a state procedural rule should have on the availability of federal habeas is quite unnecessary because in his view Florida did not actually have a contemporaneous-objection rule. He would have us interpret Florida Rule Crim. Proc. 3.190(i), which petitioner asserts is a traditional "contemporaneous objection rule," to place the burden on the trial judge to raise on his own motion the question of the admissibility of any inculpatory statement. Respondent's approach is, to say the least, difficult to square with the language of the Rule, which in unmistakable terms and with specified exceptions requires that the motion to suppress be raised before trial. Since all of the Florida appellate courts refused to review petitioner's federal claim on the merits after his trial, and since their action in so doing is quite consistent with a line of Florida authorities interpreting the rule in question as requiring a contemporaneous objection, we accept the State's position on this point.

Respondent also urges that a defendant has a right under *Jackson v. Denno*, 378 U.S. 368 (1964), to a hearing as to the voluntariness of a confession, even though the defendant does not object to its admission. But we do not read *Jackson* as creating any such requirement. In that case the defendant's objection to the use of his confession was brought to the attention of the trial court, and nothing in the Court's opinion suggests that a hearing would have been required even if it had not been. To the contrary, the Court prefaced its entire discussion of the merits of the case with a statement of the constitutional rule that was to prove dispositive—that a defendant has a "right at some stage in the proceedings to object to the use of the confession and to have a fair hearing and a reliable determination on the issue of voluntariness...." Language in subsequent decisions of this Court has reaffirmed the view that the Constitution does not require a voluntariness hearing absent some contemporaneous challenge to the use of the confession.

We therefore conclude that Florida procedure did, consistently with the United States Constitution, require that respondent's confession be challenged at trial or not at all, and thus his failure to timely object to its admission amounted to an independent and adequate state procedural ground which would have prevented direct review here. *See Henry v. Mississippi*, 379 U.S. 443 (1965). We thus come to the crux of this case. Shall the rule of *Francis v. Henderson*, *supra*, barring federal habeas review absent a showing of "cause" and "prejudice" attendant to a state procedural waiver, be applied to a waived objection to the admission of a confession at trial? We answer that question in the affirmative.

As earlier noted in the opinion, since *Brown v. Allen*, 344 U.S. 443 (1953), it has been the rule that the federal habeas petitioner who claims he is detained pursuant to a final judgment of a state court in violation of the United States Constitution is entitled to have the federal habeas court make its own independent determination of his federal claim, without being bound by the determination on the merits of that claim reached in the state proceedings. This rule of *Brown v. Allen* is in no way changed by our holding today. Rather, we deal only with contentions of federal law which were *not* resolved on the merits in the state proceeding due to respondent's failure to raise them there as required by state procedure. We leave open for resolution in future decisions the precise definition of the "cause"-and-"prejudice" standard, and note here only that it is narrower than the standard set forth in dicta in *Fay v. Noia*, which would make federal habeas review generally available to state convicts absent a knowing and deliberate waiver of the federal constitutional contention. It is the sweeping language of *Fay v. Noia*, going far beyond the facts of the case eliciting it, which we today reject.

The reasons for our rejection of it are several. The contemporaneous-objection rule itself is by no means peculiar to Florida, and deserves greater respect than *Fay* gives it, both for the fact that it is employed by a coordinate jurisdiction within the federal system and for the many interests which it serves in its own right. A contemporaneous objection enables the record to be made with respect to the constitutional claim when the recollections of witnesses are freshest, not years later in a federal habeas proceeding. It enables the judge who observed the demeanor of those witnesses to make the factual determinations necessary for properly deciding the federal constitutional question. While the 1966 amendment to § 2254 requires deference to be given to such determinations made by state courts, the determinations themselves are less apt to be made in the first instance if there is no contemporaneous objection to the admission of the evidence on federal constitutional grounds.

* * *

The failure of the federal habeas courts generally to require compliance with a contemporaneous-objection rule tends to detract from the perception of the trial of a criminal case in state court as a decisive and portentous event. A defendant has been accused of a serious crime, and this is the time and place set for him to be tried by a jury of his peers and found either guilty or not guilty by that jury. To the greatest extent possible all issues which bear on this charge should be determined in this proceeding: the accused is in the courtroom, the jury is in the box, the judge is on the bench, and the witnesses, having been subpoenaed and duly sworn, await their turn to testify. Society's resources have been concentrated at that time and place in order to decide, within the limits of human fallibility, the question of guilt or innocence of one of its citizens. Any procedural rule which encourages the result that those proceedings be as free of error as possible is thoroughly desirable, and the contemporaneous-objection rule surely falls within this classification.

We believe the adoption of the *Francis* rule in this situation will have the salutary effect of making the state trial on the merits the "main event," so to speak, rather than a "tryout on the road" for what will later be the determinative federal habeas hearing. There is nothing in the Constitution or in the language of § 2254 which requires that the state trial on the issue of guilt or innocence be devoted largely to the testimony of fact witnesses directed to the elements of the state crime, while only later will there occur in a federal habeas hearing a full airing of the federal constitutional claims which were not raised in the state proceedings. If a criminal defendant thinks that an action of the state trial court is about to deprive him of a federal constitutional right there is every reason for his following state procedure in making known his objection.

The "cause"-and-"prejudice" exception of the *Francis* rule will afford an adequate guarantee, we think, that the rule will not prevent a federal habeas court from adjudicating for the first time the federal constitutional claim of a defendant who in the absence of such an adjudication will be the victim of a miscarriage of justice. Whatever precise content may be given those terms by later cases, we feel confident in holding without further elaboration that they do not exist here. Respondent has advanced no explanation whatever for his failure to object at trial, and, as the proceeding unfolded, the trial judge is certainly not to be faulted for failing to question the admission of the confession himself. The other evidence of guilt presented at trial, moreover, was substantial to a degree that would negate any possibility of actual prejudice resulting to the respondent from the admission of his inculpatory statement.

We accordingly conclude that the judgment of the Court of Appeals for the Fifth Circuit must be reversed, and the cause remanded to the United States District Court for the Middle District of Florida with instructions to dismiss respondent's petition for a writ of habeas corpus.

It is so ordered.

[Concurring opinions by CHIEF JUSTICE BURGER, JUSTICE STEVENS, and JUSTICE WHITE, omitted.]

JUSTICE BRENNAN, with whom JUSTICE MARSHALL joins, dissenting.

Over the course of the last decade, the deliberate-bypass standard announced in *Fay v. Noia* has played a central role in efforts by the federal judiciary to accommodate the constitutional rights of the individual with the States' interests in the integrity of their judicial procedural regimes. The Court today decides that this standard should no longer apply with respect to procedural defaults occurring during the trial of a criminal defendant. In its place, the Court adopts the two-part "cause"-and-"prejudice" test originally developed in *Davis v. United States*, 411 U.S. 233 (1973), and *Francis v. Henderson*, 425 U.S. 536 (1976). As was true with these earlier cases, however, today's decision makes no effort to provide concrete guidance as to the content of those terms. More particularly, left unanswered is the thorny question that must be recognized to be central to a realistic rationalization of this area of law: How should the federal habeas court treat a procedural default in a state court that is attributable purely and simply to the error or negligence of a defendant's trial counsel? Because this key issue remains unresolved, I shall attempt in this opinion a re-examination of the policies that should inform—and in *Fay* did inform—the selection of the standard governing the availability of federal habeas corpus jurisdiction in the face of an intervening procedural default in the state court.

I

I begin with the threshold question: What is the meaning and import of a procedural default? If it could be assumed that a procedural default more often than not is the product of a defendant's conscious refusal to abide by the duly constituted, legitimate processes of the state courts, then I might agree that a regime of collateral review weighted in favor of a State's procedural rules would be warranted. *Fay*, however, recognized that such rarely is the case; and therein lies *Fay*'s basic unwillingness to embrace a view of habeas jurisdiction that results in "an airtight system of [procedural] forfeitures."

This, of course, is not to deny that there are times when the failure to heed a state procedural requirement stems from an intentional decision to avoid the presentation of constitutional claims to the state forum. *Fay* was not insensitive to this possibility. Indeed, the very purpose of its bypass test is to detect and enforce such intentional procedural forfeitures of outstanding constitutionally based claims. * * * For this reason, the Court's assertion that it "think[s]" that the *Fay* rule encourages intentional "sandbagging" on the part of the defense lawyers is without basis, *ante*; certainly the Court points to no cases or commentary arising during the past 15 years of actual use of the *Fay* test to support this criticism. Rather, a consistent reading of case law demonstrates that the bypass formula has provided a workable vehicle for protecting the integrity of state rules in those instances when such protection would be both meaningful and just.

But having created the bypass exception to the availability of collateral review, *Fay* recognized that intentional, tactical forfeitures are not the norm upon which to build a rational system of federal habeas jurisdiction. In the ordinary case, litigants simply have no incentive to slight the state tribunal, since constitutional adjudication on the state and federal levels are not mutually exclusive. *Brown v. Allen*. Under the regime of collateral review recognized since the days of *Brown v. Allen*, and enforced by the *Fay* bypass test, no rational lawyer would risk the "sandbagging" feared by the Court. If a constitutional challenge is not properly raised on the state level, the explanation generally will be found elsewhere than in an intentional tactical decision.

* * *

Fay's answer thus is plain: the bypass test simply refuses to credit what is essentially a lawyer's mistake as a forfeiture of constitutional rights. I persist in the belief that the interests of Sykes and the State of Florida are best rationalized by adherence to this test, and by declining to react to inadvertent defaults through the creation of an "airtight system of forfeitures."

II

What are the interests that Sykes can assert in preserving the availability of federal collateral relief in the face of his inadvertent state procedural default? Two are paramount.

As is true with any federal habeas applicant, Sykes seeks access to the federal court for the determination of the validity of his federal constitutional claim. Since at least *Brown v. Allen*, it has been recognized that the "fair effect [of] the habeas corpus jurisdiction as enacted by Congress" entitles a state prisoner to such federal review. 344 U.S. at 500 (opinion of Frankfurter, J.). While some of my Brethren may feel uncomfortable with this congressional choice of policy, *see, e.g.*, *Stone v. Powell*, 428 U.S. 465 (1976), the Legislative Branch nonetheless remains entirely free to determine that the constitutional rights of an individual subject to state custody, like those of the civil rights plaintiff suing under 42 U.S.C. § 1983, are best preserved by "interpos[ing] the federal courts between the States and the people, as guardians of the people's federal rights...." *Mitchum v. Foster*, 407 U.S. 225 (1972).

* * *

Thus, I remain concerned that undue deference to local procedure can only serve to undermine the ready access to a federal court to which a state defendant otherwise is entitled. But federal review is not the full measure of Sykes' interest, for there is another of even greater immediacy: assuring that his constitutional claims can be addressed to *some* court. For the obvious consequence of barring Sykes from the federal courthouse is to insulate Florida's alleged constitutional violation from any and all judicial review because of a lawyer's mistake. From the standpoint of the habeas petitioner, it is a harsh rule indeed that denies him "any review at all where the state has granted none," *Brown v. Allen* (Black, J., dissenting), particularly when he would have enjoyed both state and federal consideration had his attorney not erred.

* * *

In sum, I believe that *Fay*'s commitment to enforcing intentional but not inadvertent procedural defaults offers a realistic measure of protection for the habeas corpus petitioner seeking federal review of federal claims that were not litigated before the State. The threatened creation of a more "airtight system of forfeitures" would effectively deprive habeas petitioners of the opportunity for litigating their constitutional claims before any forum and would disparage the paramount importance of constitutional rights in our system of government. Such a restriction of habeas corpus jurisdiction should be countenanced, I submit, only if it fairly can be concluded that *Fay*'s focus on knowing and voluntary forfeitures unduly interferes with the legitimate interests of state courts or institutions. The majority offers no suggestion that actual experience has shown that *Fay*'s bypass test can be criticized on this score. And, as I now hope to demonstrate, any such criticism would be unfounded.

* * *

IV

* * *

One final consideration deserves mention. Although the standards recently have been relaxed in various jurisdictions, it is accurate to assert that most courts, this one included, traditionally have resisted any realistic inquiry into the competency of trial counsel. There is nothing unreasonable, however, in adhering to the proposition that it is the responsibility of a trial lawyer who takes on the defense of another to be aware of his client's basic legal rights and of the legitimate rules of the forum in which he practices his profession. If he should unreasonably permit such rules to bar the assertion of the colorable constitutional claims of his client, then his conduct may well fall below the level of competence that can fairly be expected of him. For almost 40 years it has been established that inadequacy of counsel undercuts the very competence and jurisdiction of the trial court and is always open to collateral review. *Johnson v. Zerbst*, 304 U.S. 458 (1938). Obviously, as a practical matter, a trial counsel cannot procedurally waive his own inadequacy. If the scope of habeas jurisdiction previously governed by *Fay v. Noia* is to be redefined so as to enforce the errors and neglect of lawyers with unnecessary and unjust rigor, the time may come when conscientious and fairminded federal and state courts, in adhering to the teaching of *Johnson v. Zerbst*, will have to reconsider whether they can continue to indulge the comfortable fiction that all lawyers are skilled or even competent craftsmen in representing the fundamental rights of their clients.

Notes

1. *Concurring opinion by Chief Justice Burger*

In his concurring opinion, Chief Justice Burger wrote separately to emphasize that in his view, "the 'deliberate bypass' standard enunciated in *Fay v. Noia* was never designed for, and is inapplicable to, errors—even of constitutional dimension—alleged to have been committed during trial." He explained:

> In *Fay v. Noia*, the Court applied the "deliberate bypass" standard to a case where the critical procedural decision—whether to take a criminal appeal—was entrusted to a convicted defendant. Although Noia, the habeas petitioner, was represented by counsel, he himself had to make the decision whether to appeal or not; the role of the attorney was limited to giving advice and counsel. In giving content to the new deliberate-bypass standard, *Fay* looked to the Court's decision in *Johnson v. Zerbst*, a case where the defendant had been called upon to make the decision whether to request representation by counsel in his federal criminal trial. Because in both *Fay* and *Zerbst*, important rights hung in the balance of the defendant's own decision, the Court required that a waiver impairing such rights be a knowing and intelligent decision by the defendant himself.
>
> * * *

Since trial decisions are of necessity entrusted to the accused's attorney, the *Fay-Zerbst* standard of "knowing and intelligent waiver" is simply inapplicable. The dissent in this case, written by the author of *Fay v. Noia*, implicitly recognizes as much. According to the dissent, *Fay* imposes the knowing-and-intelligent-waiver standard "where possible" during the course of the trial. In an extraordinary modification of *Fay*, Justice Brennan would now require "that the lawyer actually exercis[e] his expertise and judgment in his client's service, and with his client's knowing and intelligent participation *where possible*"; he does not intimate what guidelines would be used to decide when or under what circumstances this would actually be "possible."

Should the standard of a "knowing and intelligent waiver" be inapplicable because trial decisions are necessarily entrusted to the accused's attorney?

Chief Justice Burger criticized Justice Brennan's dissent for not explaining what guidelines would be used to decide the circumstances under which it would be possible for a lawyer to exercise his expertise and judgment in his client's service and with his client's knowing and intelligent participation. What guidelines might make such an assessment possible?

2. *Concurring opinion by Justice Stevens*

In his concurrence, Justice Stevens explained that "[a]lthough the Court's decision today may be read as a significant departure from the 'deliberate bypass' standard announced in *Fay v. Noia*," he was "persuaded that the holding is consistent with the way other federal courts have actually been applying *Fay*." Because "[m]atters such as the competence of counsel, the procedural context in which the asserted waiver occurred, the character of the constitutional right at stake, and the overall fairness of the entire proceeding, may be more significant than the language of the test the Court purports to apply," Justice Stevens believed the Court had "wisely refrained from attempting to give precise content to its 'cause' and 'prejudice' exception."

In what ways did the Court refrain from giving precise content to its cause-and-prejudice exception? Was Justice Stevens correct that such ambiguity was wise?

After *Wainwright v. Sykes*, a conflict emerged among the Courts of Appeals over the standard for determining whether a state court's ambiguous invocation of a procedural default barred federal habeas review. The Court resolved this conflict in *Harris v. Reed*, 489 U.S. 255, 260 (1989). In *Harris*, the Court articulated a "plain statement" rule for determining whether a state court has relied on adequate and independent state grounds: "a procedural default does not bar consideration of a federal claim on either direct or habeas review unless the last state court rendering a judgment in the case 'clearly and expressly' states that its judgment rests on a state procedural bar." 489 U.S. at 263.

After articulating this bright-line rule, the Court clarified what it meant by "clearly and expressly" in *Ylst v. Nunnemaker*, 501 U.S. 797 (1991), and *Coleman v. Thompson* (discussed *infra*).

Nunnemaker was tried in California state court for murder and raised the defense of diminished capacity. In response, the State introduced—without objection from defense counsel—statements Nunnemaker had made to a psychiatrist who had interviewed him. After the jury found him guilty, Nunnemaker appealed by claiming for the first time that the State's psychiatric testimony was inadmissible because Nunnemaker had not been given a *Miranda* warning before his interview with the State psychiatrist. The California Court of Appeals affirmed the conviction on the basis of a state procedural rule that "an objection based upon a *Miranda* violation cannot be raised for the first time on appeal." *Id.* at 799.

After the California Supreme Court denied discretionary review, Nunnemaker filed various petitions for collateral relief, state habeas corpus, and a petition for writ of federal habeas corpus that either were denied or were dismissed without prejudice. It was not until Nunnemaker filed his second petition for habeas relief in federal court that the Ninth Circuit held that because the California Supreme Court did not "'clearly and expressly state its reliance on Nunnemaker's procedural default,'" the federal court could not say that the Supreme Court's order "'was based on a procedural default rather than on the underlying merits of Nunnemaker's claims.'" *Id.* at 801.

Reversing the judgment of the Court of Appeals, the Court held that "[w]here there has been one reasoned state judgment rejecting a federal claim, later unexplained orders upholding that judgment or rejecting the same claim rest upon the same ground." This means that if the "last reasoned opinion on the claim explicitly imposes a procedural default, [the Court] will presume that a later decision rejecting the claim did not silently disregard that bar and consider the merits." Thus, the respondent could only overcome the procedural bar by establishing "cause and prejudice" for the default.

Although the Court issued *Ylst* and *Coleman* on the same day, most of the Court's reasoning is found in *Coleman*.

Coleman v. Thompson

501 U.S. 722 (1991)

JUSTICE O'CONNOR delivered the opinion of the Court.

This is a case about federalism. It concerns the respect that federal courts owe the States and the States' procedural rules when reviewing the claims of state prisoners in federal habeas corpus.

I

A Buchanan County, Virginia, jury convicted Roger Keith Coleman of rape and capital murder and fixed the sentence at death for the murder. The trial court imposed the death sentence, and the Virginia Supreme Court affirmed both the convictions and the sentence. This Court denied certiorari.

Coleman then filed a petition for a writ of habeas corpus in the Circuit Court for Buchanan County, raising numerous federal constitutional claims that he had not raised on direct appeal. After a 2-day evidentiary hearing, the Circuit Court ruled against Coleman on all claims. The court entered its final judgment on September 4, 1986.

Coleman filed his notice of appeal with the Circuit Court on October 7, 1986, 33 days after the entry of final judgment. Coleman subsequently filed a petition for appeal in the Virginia Supreme Court. The Commonwealth of Virginia, as appellee, filed a motion to dismiss the appeal. The sole ground for dismissal urged in the motion was that Coleman's notice of appeal had been filed late. Virginia Supreme Court Rule 5:9(a) provides that no appeal shall be allowed unless a notice of appeal is filed with the trial court within 30 days of final judgment.

The Virginia Supreme Court did not act immediately on the Commonwealth's motion, and both parties filed several briefs on the subject of the motion to dismiss and on the merits of the claims in Coleman's petition. On May 19, 1987, the Virginia Supreme Court issued the following order, dismissing Coleman's appeal:

> On December 4, 1986 came the appellant, by counsel, and filed a petition for appeal in the above-styled case.
>
> Thereupon came the appellee, by the Attorney General of Virginia, and filed a motion to dismiss the petition for appeal; on December 19, 1986 the appellant filed a memorandum in opposition to the motion to dismiss; on December 19, 1986 the appellee filed a reply to the appellant's memorandum; on December 23, 1986 the appellee filed a brief in opposition to the petition for appeal; on December 23, 1986 the appellant filed a surreply in opposition to the appellee's motion to dismiss; and on January 6, 1987 the appellant filed a reply brief.
>
> Upon consideration whereof, the motion to dismiss is granted and the petition for appeal is dismissed.

This Court again denied certiorari.

Coleman next filed a petition for writ of habeas corpus in the United States District Court for the Western District of Virginia. In his petition, Coleman presented four federal constitutional claims he had raised on direct appeal in the Virginia Supreme Court and seven claims he had raised for the first time in state habeas. The District Court concluded that, by virtue of the dismissal of his appeal by the Virginia Supreme Court in state habeas, Coleman had procedurally defaulted the seven claims. The District Court nonetheless went on to address the merits of all 11 of Coleman's claims. The court ruled against Coleman on all of the claims and denied the petition.

The United States Court of Appeals for the Fourth Circuit affirmed. The court held that Coleman had defaulted all of the claims that he had presented for the first time in state habeas. Coleman argued that the Virginia Supreme Court had not "clearly and expressly" stated that its decision in state habeas was based on a procedural default, and therefore the federal courts could not treat it as such under the rule of *Harris v. Reed*, 489 U.S. 255 (1989). The Fourth Circuit disagreed. It concluded that the Virginia Supreme Court had met the "plain statement" requirement of *Harris* by granting a motion to dismiss that was based solely on procedural grounds. The Fourth Circuit held that the Virginia Supreme Court's decision rested on independent and adequate state grounds and that Coleman had not shown cause to excuse the default. As a consequence, federal review of the claims Coleman presented only in the state habeas proceeding was barred. We granted certiorari to resolve several issues concerning the relationship between state procedural defaults and federal habeas review, and now affirm.

II

A

This Court will not review a question of federal law decided by a state court if the decision of that court rests on a state law ground that is independent of the federal question and adequate to support the judgment. *See, e. g., Fox Film Corp. v. Muller*, 296 U.S. 207 (1935). This rule applies whether the state law ground is substantive or procedural. In the context of direct review of a state court judgment, the independent and adequate state ground doctrine is jurisdictional. Because this Court has no power to review a state law determination that is sufficient to support the judgment, resolution of any independent federal ground for the decision could not affect the judgment and would therefore be advisory.

We have applied the independent and adequate state ground doctrine not only in our own review of state court judgments, but in deciding whether federal district courts should address the claims of state prisoners in habeas corpus actions. The doctrine applies to bar federal habeas when a state court declined to address a prisoner's federal claims because the prisoner had failed to meet a state procedural requirement. In these cases, the state judgment rests on independent and adequate state procedural grounds. *See Wainwright v. Sykes*, 433 U.S. 72 (1977).

The basis for application of the independent and adequate state ground doctrine in federal habeas is somewhat different than on direct review by this Court. When this Court reviews a state court decision on direct review pursuant to 28 U.S.C. § 1257, it is reviewing the *judgment*; if resolution of a federal question cannot affect the judgment, there is nothing for the Court to do. This is not the case in habeas. When a federal district court reviews a state prisoner's habeas corpus petition pursuant to 28 U.S.C. § 2254, it must decide whether the petitioner is "in custody in violation of the Constitution or laws or treaties of the United States." The court does not review a judgment, but the lawfulness of the petitioner's custody *simpliciter*. *See Fay v. Noia*, 372 U.S. 391 (1963).

Nonetheless, a state prisoner is in custody *pursuant* to a judgment. When a federal habeas court releases a prisoner held pursuant to a state court judgment that rests on an independent and adequate state ground, it renders ineffective the state rule just as completely as if this Court had reversed the state judgment on direct review. *See id.* (Harlan, J., dissenting). In such a case, the habeas court ignores the State's legitimate reasons for holding the prisoner.

In the habeas context, the application of the independent and adequate state ground doctrine is grounded in concerns of comity and federalism. Without the rule, a federal district court would be able to do in habeas what this Court could not do on direct review; habeas would offer state prisoners whose custody was supported by independent and adequate state grounds an end run around the limits of this Court's jurisdiction and a means to undermine the State's interest in enforcing its laws.

When the independent and adequate state ground supporting a habeas petitioner's custody is a state procedural default, an additional concern comes into play. This Court has long held that a state prisoner's federal habeas petition should be dismissed if the prisoner has not exhausted available state remedies as to any of his federal claims. *See Ex parte Royall*, 117 U.S. 241 (1886). *See also Rose v. Lundy*, 455 U.S. 509 (1989); 28 U.S.C. § 2254(b) (codifying the rule). This exhaustion requirement is also grounded in principles of comity; in a federal system, the States should have the first opportunity to address and correct alleged violations of state prisoner's federal rights. As we explained in *Rose*:

> The exhaustion doctrine is principally designed to protect the state courts' role in the enforcement of federal law and prevent disruption of state judicial proceedings.

> Under our federal system, the federal and state "courts [are] equally bound to guard and protect rights secured by the Constitution." *Ex parte Royall*, 117 U.S. at 251 (1886). Because "it would be unseemly in our dual system of government for a federal district court to upset a state court conviction without an opportunity to the state courts to correct a constitutional violation," federal courts apply the doctrine of comity, which "teaches that one court should defer action on causes properly within its jurisdiction until the courts of another sovereignty with concurrent powers, and already cognizant of the litigation, have had an opportunity to pass upon the matter."

These same concerns apply to federal claims that have been procedurally defaulted in state court. Just as in those cases in which a state prisoner fails to exhaust state remedies, a habeas petitioner who has failed to meet the State's procedural requirements for presenting his federal claims has deprived the state courts of an opportunity to address those claims in the first instance. A habeas petitioner who has defaulted his federal claims in state court meets the technical requirements for exhaustion; there are no state remedies any longer "available" to him. *See* 28 U.S.C. § 2254(b). In the absence of the independent and adequate state ground doctrine in federal habeas, habeas petitioners would be able to avoid the exhaustion requirement by defaulting their federal claims in state court. The independent and adequate state ground doctrine ensures that the States' interest in correcting their own mistakes is respected in all federal habeas cases.

B

It is not always easy for a federal court to apply the independent and adequate state ground doctrine. State court opinions will, at times, discuss federal questions at length and mention a state law basis for decision only briefly. In such cases, it is often difficult to determine if the state law discussion is truly an independent basis for decision or merely a passing reference. In other cases, state opinions purporting to apply state constitutional law will derive principles by reference to federal constitutional decisions from this Court. Again, it is unclear from such opinions whether the state law decision is independent of federal law.

[The Court then discusses two previous cases, *Michigan v. Long*, 463 U.S. 1032 (1983), and *Caldwell v. Mississippi*, 472 U.S. 320 (1985). In *Long*, the Court partially solved this problem by presuming that a state court's decision is dependent on federal law if it "fairly appears" to rest upon or be interwoven with federal law and when the adequacy and independence of any state ground is unclear. A state court still could "clearly and expressly" state that its decision is based on adequate and independent grounds to avoid this presumption. In *Caldwell*, the Mississippi Supreme Court raised the issue of procedural default *sua sponte*, and the Supreme Court applied the *Long* presumption despite the State then claiming this as adequate and independent state ground.]

Long and *Caldwell* were direct review cases. We first considered the problem of ambiguous state court decisions in the application of the independent and adequate state ground doctrine in a federal habeas case in *Harris v. Reed*, 489 U.S. 255 (1989). Harris, a state prisoner, filed a petition for state postconviction relief, alleging that his trial counsel had rendered ineffective assistance. The state trial court dismissed the petition, and the Appellate Court of Illinois affirmed. In its order, the Appellate Court referred to the Illinois rule that "'those [issues] which could have been presented [on direct appeal], but were not, are considered waived.'" *Id.* The court concluded that Harris could have raised his ineffective assistance claims on direct review. Nonetheless, the court considered and rejected Harris' claims on the merits. Harris then petitioned for federal habeas.

The situation presented to this Court was nearly identical to that in *Long* and *Caldwell*: a state court decision that fairly appeared to rest primarily on federal law in a context in which a federal court has an obligation to determine if the state court decision rested on an independent and adequate state ground. "Faced with a common problem, we adopted a common solution." *Harris*. *Harris* applied in federal habeas the presumption this Court adopted in *Long* for direct review cases. Because the Illinois Appellate Court did not "clearly and expressly" rely on waiver as a ground for rejecting Harris' ineffective assistance of counsel claims, the *Long* presumption applied and Harris was not barred from federal habeas. *Harris*.

After *Harris*, federal courts on habeas corpus review of state prisoner claims, like this Court on direct review of state court judgments, will presume that there is no independent and adequate state ground for a state court decision when the decision "fairly appears to rest primarily on federal law, or to be interwoven with the federal law, and when the adequacy and independence of any possible state law ground is not clear from the face of the opinion." *Long*. In habeas, if the decision of the last state court to which the petitioner presented his federal claims fairly appeared to rest primarily on resolution of those claims, or to be interwoven with those claims, and did not clearly and expressly rely on an independent and adequate state ground, a federal court may address the petition.

III

A

Coleman contends that the presumption of *Long* and *Harris* applies in this case and precludes a bar to habeas because the Virginia Supreme Court's order dismissing Coleman's appeal did not "clearly and expressly" state that it was based on state procedural grounds. Coleman reads *Harris* too broadly. A predicate to the application of the *Harris* presumption is that the decision of the last state court to which the petitioner presented his federal claims must fairly appear to rest primarily on federal law or to be interwoven with federal law.

Coleman relies on other language in *Harris*. That opinion announces that "a procedural default does not bar consideration of a federal claim on either direct or habeas review unless the last state court rendering a judgment in the case clearly and expressly states that its judgment rests on a state procedural bar." *Harris*. Coleman contends that this rule, by its terms, applies to all state court judgments, not just those that fairly appear to rest primarily on federal law.

Coleman has read the rule out of context. It is unmistakably clear that *Harris* applies the same presumption in habeas that *Long* and *Caldwell* adopted in direct review cases in this Court. Indeed, the quoted passage purports to state the rule "on either direct or habeas review." *Harris*, being a federal habeas case, could not change the rule for direct review; the reference to both direct and habeas review makes plain that *Harris* applies precisely the same rule as *Long*. *Harris* describes the *Long* presumption, and hence its own, as applying only in those cases in which "'it fairly appears that the state court rested its decision primarily on federal law.'" *Harris* (*quoting Long*). That in one particular exposition of its rule *Harris* does not mention the predicate to application of the presumption does not change the holding of the opinion.

Coleman urges a broader rule: that the presumption applies in all cases in which a habeas petitioner presented his federal claims to the state court. This rule makes little sense. In direct review cases, "it is ... 'incumbent upon this Court ... to ascertain for itself ... whether the asserted non-federal ground independently and adequately supports the [state court] judgment.'" *Long*. Similarly, federal habeas courts must ascertain for themselves if the petitioner is in custody pursuant to a state court judgment that rests on independent and adequate state grounds. In cases in which the *Long* and *Harris* presumption applies, federal courts will conclude that the relevant state court judgment does not rest on an independent and adequate state ground. The presumption, like all conclusive presumptions, is designed to avoid the costs of excessive inquiry where a *per se* rule will achieve the correct result in almost all cases. * * *

Per se rules should not be applied, however, in situations where the generalization is incorrect as an empirical matter; the justification for a conclusive presumption disappears when application of the presumption will not reach the correct result most of the time. * * *

* * *

* * * We decline to so expand the *Harris* presumption.

B

The *Harris* presumption does not apply here. Coleman does not argue, nor could he, that it "fairly appears" that the Virginia Supreme Court's decision rested primarily on federal law or was interwoven with such law. The Virginia Supreme Court stated plainly that it was granting the Commonwealth's motion to dismiss the petition for appeal. That motion was based solely on Coleman's failure to meet the Supreme Court's time requirements. There is no mention of federal law in the Virginia Supreme Court's three-sentence dismissal order. It "fairly appears" to rest primarily on state law.

Coleman concedes that the Virginia Supreme Court dismissed his state habeas appeal as untimely, applying a state procedural rule. He argues instead that the court's application of this procedural rule was not independent of federal law.

Virginia Supreme Court Rule 5:5(a) declares that the 30-day requirement for filing a notice of appeal is "mandatory." The Virginia Supreme Court has reiterated the unwaivable nature of this requirement. Despite these forthright pronouncements, Coleman contends that in this case the Virginia Supreme Court did not automatically apply its time requirement. Rather, Coleman asserts, the court first considered the merits of his federal claims and applied the procedural bar only after determining that doing so would not abridge one of Coleman's constitutional rights. In *Ake v. Oklahoma*, 470 U.S. 68 (1985), this Court held that a similar Oklahoma rule, excusing procedural default in cases of "fundamental trial error," was not independent of federal law so as to bar direct review because "the State had made application of the procedural bar depend on an antecedent ruling on federal law." *Id.* For the same reason, Coleman argues, the Virginia Supreme Court's time requirement is not independent of federal law.

Ake was a direct review case. We have never applied its rule regarding independent state grounds in federal habeas. But even if *Ake* applies here, it does Coleman no good because the Virginia Supreme Court relied on an independent state procedural rule.

* * *

* * * [T]he notice of appeal is a document filed *with the trial court* that notifies that court and the Virginia Supreme Court, as well as the parties, that there will be an appeal; it is a purely ministerial document. The notice of the appeal must be filed within 30 days of the final judgment of the trial court. Coleman has cited no authority indicating that the Virginia Supreme Court has recognized an exception to the time requirement for filing a notice of appeal.

* * *

Coleman contends also that the procedural bar was not adequate to support the judgment. Coleman did not petition for certiorari on this question, and we therefore accept the Court of Appeals' conclusion that the bar was adequate.

IV

In *Daniels v. Allen*, the companion case to *Brown v. Allen*, 344 U.S. 443 (1953), we confronted a situation nearly identical to that here. Petitioners were convicted in a North Carolina trial court and then were one day late in filing their appeal as of right in the North Carolina Supreme Court. That court rejected the appeals as procedurally barred. We held that federal habeas was also barred unless petitioners could prove that they were "detained without opportunity to appeal because of lack of counsel, incapacity, or some interference by officials." *Id.*

Fay v. Noia, 372 U.S. 391 (1963), overruled this holding. Noia failed to appeal at all in state court his state conviction, and then sought federal habeas review of his claim that his confession had been coerced. This Court held that such a procedural default in state court does not bar federal habeas review unless the petitioner has deliberately bypassed state procedures by intentionally forgoing an opportunity for state review. *Id. Fay* thus created a presumption in favor of federal habeas review of claims procedurally defaulted in state court. The Court based this holding on its conclusion that a State's interest in orderly procedure is sufficiently vindicated by the prisoner's forfeiture of his state remedies. "Whatever residuum of state interest there may be under such circumstances is manifestly insufficient in the face of the federal policy ... of affording an effective remedy for restraints contrary to the Constitution." *Id.*

Our cases after *Fay* that have considered the effect of state procedural default on federal habeas review have taken a markedly different view of the important interests served by state procedural rules. *Francis v. Henderson*, 425 U.S. 536 (1976), involved a Louisiana prisoner challenging in federal habeas the composition of the grand jury that had indicted him. Louisiana law provided that any such challenge must be made in advance of trial or it would be deemed waived. Because Francis had not raised a timely objection, the Louisiana courts refused to hear his claim. In deciding whether this state procedural default would also bar review in federal habeas, we looked to our decision in *Davis v. United States*, 411 U.S. 233 (1973). Davis, a federal prisoner, had defaulted an identical federal claim pursuant to Federal Rule of Criminal Procedure 12(b)(2). We held that a federal court on collateral review could not hear the claim unless Davis could show "cause" for his failure to challenge the composition of the grand jury before trial and actual prejudice as a result of the alleged constitutional violations. *Id.*

The *Francis* Court noted the important interests served by the pretrial objection requirement of Rule 12(b)(2) and the parallel state rule: the possible avoidance of an unnecessary trial or of a retrial, the difficulty of making factual determinations concerning grand juries long after the indictment has been handed down and the grand jury disbanded, and the potential disruption to numerous convictions of finding a defect in a grand jury only after the jury has handed down indictments in many cases. *Francis*. These concerns led us in *Davis* to enforce Rule 12(b)(2) in collateral review. We concluded in *Francis* that a proper respect for the States required that federal courts give to the state procedural rule the same effect they give to the federal rule:

> If, as *Davis* held, the federal courts must give effect to these important and legitimate concerns in § 2255 proceedings, then surely considerations of comity and federalism require that they give no less effect to the same clear interests when asked to overturn state criminal convictions. These considerations require that recog-

> nition be given "to the legitimate interests of both State and National Governments, and ... [that] the National Government, anxious though it may be to vindicate and protect federal rights and federal interests, always [endeavor] to do so in ways that will not unduly interfere with the legitimate activities of the States." *Younger v. Harris*, 401 U.S. 37 (1971). "Plainly the interest in finality is the same with regard to both federal and state prisoners.... There is no reason to ... give greater preclusive effect to procedural defaults by federal defendants than to similar defaults by state defendants. To hold otherwise would reflect an anomalous and erroneous view of federal-state relations.' *Kaufman v. United States*, 394 U.S. 217 (1969)." *Francis*.

We held that Francis' claim was barred in federal habeas unless he could establish cause and prejudice. *Id.*

Wainwright v. Sykes, 433 U.S. 72 (1977), applied the cause and prejudice standard more broadly. Sykes did not object at trial to the introduction of certain inculpatory statements he had earlier made to the police. Under Florida law, this failure barred state courts from hearing the claim on either direct appeal or state collateral review. We recognized that this contemporaneous objection rule served strong state interests in the finality of its criminal litigation. *Id.* To protect these interests, we adopted the same presumption against federal habeas review of claims defaulted in state court for failure to object at trial that *Francis* had adopted in the grand jury context: the cause and prejudice standard. "We believe the adoption of the *Francis* rule in this situation will have the salutary effect of making the state trial on the merits the 'main event,' so to speak, rather than a 'tryout on the road' for what will later be the determinative federal habeas hearing." *Id.*

In so holding, *Sykes* limited *Fay* to its facts. The cause and prejudice standard in federal habeas evinces far greater respect for state procedural rules than does the deliberate bypass standard of *Fay*. These incompatible rules are based on very different conceptions of comity and of the importance of finality in state criminal litigation. In *Sykes*, we left open the question whether the deliberate bypass standard still applied to a situation like that in *Fay*, where a petitioner has surrendered entirely his right to appeal his state conviction. We rejected explicitly, however, "the sweeping language of *Fay v. Noia*, going far beyond the facts of the case eliciting it."

Our cases since *Sykes* have been unanimous in applying the cause and prejudice standard. *Engle v. Isaac*, 456 U.S. 107 (1982), held that the standard applies even in cases in which the alleged constitutional error impaired the truthfinding function of the trial. Respondents had failed to object at trial to jury instructions that placed on them the burden of proving self-defense. Ohio's contemporaneous objection rule barred respondents' claim on appeal that the burden should have been on the State. We held that this independent and adequate state ground barred federal habeas as well, absent a showing of cause and prejudice.

Recognizing that the writ of habeas corpus "is a bulwark against convictions that violate fundamental fairness," we also acknowledged that "the Great Writ entails significant costs." *Id.* The most significant of these is the cost to finality in criminal litigation that federal collateral review of state convictions entails....

* * *

In *Carrier*, as in *Sykes*, we left open the question whether *Fay*'s deliberate bypass standard continued to apply under the facts of that case, where a state prisoner has defaulted his entire appeal. *See* [*Murray v.*] *Carrier*, [477 U.S. 478] (1986) [("[w]here a constitutional violation has probably resulted in the conviction of one who is actually innocent, a federal habeas court may grant the writ even in the absence of a showing of cause for the procedural default")]. We are now required to answer this question. By filing late, Coleman defaulted his entire state collateral appeal. This was no doubt an inadvertent error, and respondent concedes that Coleman did not "understandingly and knowingly" forgo the privilege of state collateral appeal. *See Fay*. Therefore, if the *Fay* deliberate by-pass standard still applies, Coleman's state procedural default will not bar federal habeas.

In *Harris*, we described in broad terms the application of the cause and prejudice standard, hinting strongly that *Fay* had been superseded....

* * *

We now make it explicit: In all cases in which a state prisoner has defaulted his federal claims in state court pursuant to an independent and adequate state procedural rule, federal habeas review of the claims is barred unless the prisoner can demonstrate cause for the default and actual prejudice as a result of the alleged violation of federal law, or demonstrate that failure to consider the claims will result in a fundamental miscarriage of justice. *Fay* was based on a conception of federal/state relations that undervalued the importance of state procedural rules. The several cases after *Fay* that applied the cause and prejudice standard to a variety of state procedural defaults represent a different view. We now recognize the important interest in finality served by state procedural rules, and the significant harm to the States that results from the failure of federal courts to respect them.

Carrier applied the cause and prejudice standard to the failure to raise a particular claim on appeal. There is no reason that the same standard should not apply to a failure to appeal at all. All of the State's interests—in channeling the resolution of claims to the most appropriate forum, in finality, and in having an opportunity to correct its own errors—are implicated whether a prisoner defaults one claim or all of them. A federal court generally should not interfere in either case. By applying the cause and prejudice standard uniformly to all independent and adequate state procedural defaults, we eliminate the irrational distinction between *Fay* and the rule of cases like *Francis*, *Sykes*, *Engle*, and *Carrier*.

We also eliminate inconsistency between the respect federal courts show for state procedural rules and the respect they show for their own. This Court has long understood the vital interest served by *federal* procedural rules, even when they serve to bar federal review of constitutional claims. * * *

* * *

No less respect should be given to state rules of procedure.

V

A

Coleman maintains that there was cause for his default. The late filing was, he contends, the result of attorney error of sufficient magnitude to excuse the default in federal habeas.

Murray v. Carrier considered the circumstances under which attorney error constitutes cause. Carrier argued that his attorney's inadvertence in failing to raise certain claims in his state appeal constituted cause for the default sufficient to allow federal habeas review. We rejected this claim, explaining that the costs associated with an ignorant or inadvertent procedural default are no less than where the failure to raise a claim is a deliberate strategy: It deprives the state courts of the opportunity to review trial errors. When a federal habeas court hears such a claim, it undercuts the State's ability to enforce its procedural rules just as surely as when the default was deliberate. We concluded: "So long as a defendant is represented by counsel whose performance is not constitutionally ineffective under the standard established in *Strickland v. Washington*, 466 U.S. 668 (1984), we discern no inequity in requiring him to bear the risk of attorney error that results in a procedural default." *Id.*

Applying the *Carrier* rule as stated, this case is at an end. There is no constitutional right to an attorney in state post-conviction proceedings. *Pennsylvania v. Finley*, 481 U.S. 551 (1987). Consequently, a petitioner cannot claim constitutionally ineffective assistance of counsel in such proceedings. *See Wainwright v. Torna*, 455 U.S. 586 (1982) (where there is no constitutional right to counsel there can be no deprivation of effective assistance). Coleman contends that it was his attorney's error that led to the late filing of his state habeas appeal. This error cannot be constitutionally ineffective; therefore Coleman must "bear the risk of attorney error that results in a procedural default."

Coleman attempts to avoid this reasoning by arguing that *Carrier* does not stand for such a broad proposition. He contends that *Carrier* applies by its terms only in those situations where it is possible to state a claim for ineffective assistance of counsel. Where there is no constitutional right to counsel, Coleman argues, it is enough that a petitioner demonstrate that his attorney's conduct would meet the *Strickland* standard, even though no independent Sixth Amendment claim is possible.

This argument is inconsistent not only with the language of *Carrier*, but with the logic of that opinion as well. We explained clearly that "cause" under the cause and prejudice test must be something *external* to the petitioner, something that cannot fairly be attributed to him: "We think that the existence of cause for a procedural default must ordinarily turn on whether the prisoner can show that some objective factor external to the defense impeded counsel's efforts to comply with the State's procedural rule." For example, "a showing that the factual or legal basis for a claim was not reasonably available to counsel, ... or that 'some interference by officials'... made compliance impracticable, would constitute cause under this standard." *See also id.* ("Cause for a procedural default on appeal ordinarily requires a showing of some external impediment preventing counsel from constructing or raising the claim").

Attorney ignorance or inadvertence is not "cause" because the attorney is the petitioner's agent when acting, or failing to act, in furtherance of the litigation, and the petitioner must "bear the risk of attorney error." *Id.* Attorney error that constitutes ineffective assistance of counsel is cause, however. This is not because, as Coleman contends, the error is so bad that "the lawyer ceases to be an agent of the petitioner." In a case such as this, where the alleged attorney error is inadvertence in failing to file a timely notice, such a rule would be contrary to well-settled principles of agency law. Rather, as *Carrier* explains, "if the procedural default is the result of ineffective assistance of counsel, the Sixth Amendment itself requires that responsibility for the default be imputed to the State." In other words, it is not the gravity of the attorney's error that matters, but that it constitutes a violation of petitioner's right to counsel, so that the error must be seen as an external factor, *i.e.*, "imputed to the State."

Where a petitioner defaults a claim as a result of the denial of the right to effective assistance of counsel, the State, which is responsible for the denial as a constitutional matter, must bear the cost of any resulting default and the harm to state interests that federal habeas review entails. A different allocation of costs is appropriate in those circumstances where the State has no responsibility to ensure that the petitioner was represented by competent counsel. As between the State and the petitioner, it is the petitioner who must bear the burden of a failure to follow state procedural rules. In the absence of a constitutional violation, the petitioner bears the risk in federal habeas for all attorney errors made in the course of the representation, as *Carrier* says explicitly.

B

Among the claims Coleman brought in state habeas, and then again in federal habeas, is ineffective assistance of counsel during trial, sentencing, and appeal. Coleman contends that, at least as to these claims, attorney error in state habeas must constitute cause. This is because, under Virginia law at the time of Coleman's trial and direct appeal, ineffective assistance of counsel claims related to counsel's conduct during trial or appeal could be brought only in state habeas. Coleman argues that attorney error in failing to file timely in the first forum in which a federal claim can be raised is cause.

We reiterate that counsel's ineffectiveness will constitute cause only if it is an independent constitutional violation. *Finley* and [*Murray v.*] *Giarratano* established that there is no right to counsel in state collateral proceedings. For Coleman to prevail, therefore, there must be an exception to the rule of *Finley* and *Giarratano* in those cases where state collateral review is the first place a prisoner can present a challenge to his conviction. We need not answer this question broadly, however, for one state court has addressed Coleman's claims: the state habeas trial court. The effectiveness of Coleman's counsel before that court is not at issue here. Coleman contends that it was the ineffectiveness of his counsel during the appeal from that determination that constitutes cause to excuse his default. We thus need to decide only whether Coleman had a constitutional right to counsel on appeal from the state habeas trial court judgment. We conclude that he did not.

Douglas v. California, 372 U.S. 353 (1963), established that an indigent criminal defendant has a right to appointed counsel in his first appeal as of right in state court. *Evitts v. Lucey* held that this right encompasses a right to effective assistance of counsel for all criminal defendants in their first appeal as of right. We based our holding in *Douglas* on that "equality demanded by the Fourteenth Amendment." Recognizing that "absolute equality is not required," we nonetheless held that "where the merits of *the one and only appeal* an indigent has as of right are decided without benefit of counsel, we think an unconstitutional line has been drawn between rich and poor." *Id.*

Coleman has had his "one and only appeal," if that is what a state collateral proceeding may be considered; the Buchanan County Circuit Court, after a 2-day evidentiary hearing, addressed Coleman's claims of trial error, including his ineffective assistance of counsel claims. What Coleman requires here is a right to counsel on appeal from *that* determination. Our case law will not support it.

In *Ross v. Moffitt*, 417 U.S. 600 (1974), and *Pennsylvania v. Finley*, 481 U.S. 551 (1987), we declined to extend the right to counsel beyond the first appeal of a criminal conviction. We held in *Ross* that neither the fundamental fairness required by the Due Process Clause nor the Fourteenth Amendment's equal protection guarantee necessitated that States provide counsel in state discretionary appeals where defendants already had one appeal as of right. "The duty of the State under our cases is not to duplicate the legal arsenal that may be privately retained by a criminal defendant in a continuing effort to reverse his conviction, but only to assure the indigent defendant an adequate opportunity to present his claims fairly in the context of the State's appellate process." Similarly, in *Finley* we held that there is no right to counsel in state collateral proceedings after exhaustion of direct appellate review.

These cases dictate the answer here. Given that a criminal defendant has no right to counsel beyond his first appeal in pursuing state discretionary or collateral review, it would defy logic for us to hold that Coleman had a right to counsel to appeal a state collateral determination of his claims of trial error.

Because Coleman had no right to counsel to pursue his appeal in state habeas, any attorney error that led to the default of Coleman's claims in state court cannot constitute cause to excuse the default in federal habeas. As Coleman does not argue in this Court that federal review of his claims is necessary to prevent a fundamental miscarriage of justice, he is barred from bringing these claims in federal habeas. Accordingly, the judgment of the Court of Appeals is

Affirmed.

[Concurring opinion by JUSTICE WHITE omitted.]

JUSTICE BLACKMUN, with whom JUSTICE MARSHALL and JUSTICE STEVENS join, dissenting.

Federalism; comity; state sovereignty; preservation of state resources; certainty: The majority methodically inventories these multifarious state interests before concluding that the plain-statement rule of *Michigan v. Long*, 463 U.S. 1032 (1983), does not apply to a summary order. One searches the majority's opinion in vain, however, for any mention of petitioner Coleman's right to a criminal proceeding free from constitutional defect or his interest in finding a forum for his constitutional challenge to his conviction and sentence of death. Nor does the majority even allude to the "important need for uniformity in federal law," which justified this Court's adoption of the plain-statement rule in the first place. Rather, displaying obvious exasperation with the breadth of substantive federal habeas doctrine and the expansive protection afforded by the Fourteenth Amendment's guarantee of fundamental fairness in state criminal proceedings, the Court today continues its crusade to erect petty procedural barriers in the path of any state prisoner seeking review of his federal constitutional claims. Because I believe that the Court is creating a Byzantine morass of arbitrary, unnecessary, and unjustifiable impediments to the vindication of federal rights, I dissent.

I

The Court cavalierly claims that "this is a case about federalism" and proceeds without explanation to assume that the purposes of federalism are advanced whenever a federal court refrains from reviewing an ambiguous state-court judgment. Federalism, however, has no inherent normative value: It does not, as the majority appears to assume, blindly protect the States from any incursion by the federal courts. Rather, federalism secures to citizens the liberties that derive from the diffusion of sovereign power. * * * In this context, it cannot lightly be assumed that the interests of federalism are fostered by a rule that impedes federal review of federal constitutional claims.

Moreover, the form of federalism embraced by today's majority bears little resemblance to that adopted by the Framers of the Constitution and ratified by the original States. The majority proceeds as if the sovereign interests of the States and the Federal Government were coequal. Ours, however, is a federal republic, conceived on the principle of a supreme federal power and constituted first and foremost of citizens, not of sovereign States. * * *

Federal habeas review of state-court judgments, respectfully employed to safeguard federal rights, is no invasion of state sovereignty. * * * Thus, the considered exercise by federal courts—in vindication of fundamental constitutional rights—of the habeas jurisdiction conferred on them by Congress exemplifies the full expression of this Nation's federalism.

* * *

II

* * *

B

* * * In its attempt to justify a blind abdication of responsibility by the federal courts, the majority's opinion marks the nadir of the Court's recent habeas jurisprudence, where the discourse of rights is routinely replaced with the functional dialect of interests. The Court's habeas jurisprudence now routinely, and without evident reflection, subordinates fundamental constitutional rights to mere utilitarian interests. *See, e.g., McCleskey v. Zant*, 499 U.S. 467 (1991). Such unreflective cost-benefit analysis is inconsistent with the very idea of rights. The Bill of Rights is not, after all, a collection of technical interests, and "surely it is an abuse to deal too casually and too lightly with rights guaranteed" therein. *Brown v. Allen*, 344 U.S. at 498 (opinion of Frankfurter, J.).

It is well settled that the existence of a state procedural default does not divest a federal court of jurisdiction on collateral review. *See Wainwright v. Sykes*, 433 U.S. 72 (1977). Rather, the important office of the federal courts in vindicating federal rights gives way to the States' enforcement of their procedural rules to protect the States' interest in being an equal partner in safeguarding federal rights. This accommodation furthers the values underlying federalism in two ways. First, encouraging a defendant to assert his federal rights in the appropriate state forum makes it possible for transgressions to be arrested sooner and before they influence an erroneous deprivation of liberty. Second, thorough examination of a prisoner's federal claims in state court permits more effective review of those claims in federal court, honing the accuracy of the writ as an implement to eradicate unlawful detention. *See Rose v. Lundy*, 455 U.S. 509 (1982); *Brown v. Allen* (opinion of Frankfurter, J.). The majority ignores these purposes in concluding that a State need not bear the burden of making clear its intent to rely on such a rule. When it is uncertain whether a state-court judgment denying relief from federal claims rests on a procedural bar, it is inconsistent with federalism principles for a federal court to exercise discretion to decline to review those federal claims.

* * *

Even if the majority correctly attributed the relevant state interests, they are, nonetheless, misconceived. The majority appears most concerned with the financial burden that a retrial places on the States. Of course, if the initial trial conformed to the mandate of the Federal Constitution, not even the most probing federal review would necessitate a retrial. Thus, to the extent the State must "pay the price" of retrying a state prisoner, that price is incurred as a direct result of the State's failure scrupulously to honor his federal rights, not as a consequence of unwelcome federal review.

* * *

C

* * *

The Court's decisions in this case and in *Ylst v. Nunnemaker*, [501 U.S.] 797 (1991), well reveal the illogic of the ad hoc approach. In this case, to determine whether the admittedly ambiguous state-court judgment rests on an adequate and independent state ground, the Court looks to the "nature of the disposition" and the "surrounding circumstances" that "indicate" that the basis [of the decision] was procedural default. *Ylst*. This method of searching for "clues" to the meaning of a facially ambiguous order is inherently indeterminate. Tellingly, both the majority and concurring opinions in this case concede that it remains uncertain whether the state court relied on a procedural default. The plain-statement rule effectively and equitably eliminates this unacceptable uncertainty. I cannot condone the abandonment of such a rule when the result is to foreclose federal habeas review of federal claims based on conjecture as to the "meaning" of an unexplained order.

The Court's decision in *Ylst* demonstrates that we are destined to relive the period where we struggled to develop principles to guide the interpretation of ambiguous state-court orders. In *Ylst*, the last state court to render a judgment on Nunnemaker's federal claims was the California Supreme Court. Nunnemaker had filed a petition for habeas corpus in that court, invoking its original jurisdiction. Accordingly, the court was not sitting to review the judgment of another state court, but to entertain, as an original matter, Nunnemaker's collateral challenge to his conviction. The court's order denying relief was rendered without explanation or citation. Rejecting the methodology employed just today by the *Coleman* majority, the *Ylst* Court does not look to the pleadings filed in the original action to determine the "meaning" of the unexplained order. Rather, the Court adopts a broad *per se* presumption that "where there has been one reasoned state judgment rejecting a federal claim, later unexplained orders upholding that judgment or rejecting the same claim rest upon the same ground." *Ylst*. This presumption does not purport to distinguish between unexplained judgments that are entered on review of the reasoned opinion and those that are independent thereof.

The *Ylst* Court demonstrates the employment of the presumption by simply ignoring the judgment of the highest court of California, and by looking back to an intermediate court judgment rendered 12 years earlier to conclude that Nunnemaker's federal claims have been procedurally defaulted. In so concluding, the Court determines that an intervening order by the California Supreme Court, which, with citations to two state-court decisions, denied Nunnemaker's earlier petition invoking the court's original jurisdiction, is not "informative with respect to the question" whether a state court has considered the merits of Nunnemaker's claims since the procedural default was recognized. Thus, the Court dismisses two determinations of the California Supreme Court, rendered not in review of an earlier state-court judgment but as an exercise of its original jurisdiction, because it finds those determinations not "informative." While the Court may comfort itself by labeling this exercise "looking through," it cannot be disputed that the practice represents disrespect for the State's determination of how best to structure its mechanisms for seeking postconviction relief.

Moreover, the presumption adopted by the *Ylst* Court further complicates the efforts of state courts to understand and accommodate this Court's federal habeas jurisprudence. Under *Long*, a state court need only recognize that it must clearly express its intent to rely on a state procedural default in order to preclude federal habeas review in most cases. After today, however, a state court that does not intend to rely on a procedural default but wishes to deny a meritless petition in a summary order must now remember that its unexplained order will be ignored by the federal habeas court. Thus, the state court must review the procedural history of the petitioner's claim and determine which state-court judgment a federal habeas court is likely to recognize. It then must determine whether that judgment expresses the substance that the court wishes to convey in its summary order, and react accordingly. If the previous reasoned judgment rests on a procedural default, and the subsequent court wishes to forgive that default, it now must clearly and expressly indicate that its judgment *does not* rest on a state procedural default. I see no benefit in abandoning a clear rule to create chaos.

III

* * *

The majority's conclusion that Coleman's allegations of ineffective assistance of counsel, if true, would not excuse a procedural default that occurred in the state postconviction proceeding is particularly disturbing because, at the time of Coleman's appeal, state law precluded defendants from raising certain claims on direct appeal. As the majority acknowledges, under state law as it existed at the time of Coleman's trial and appeal, Coleman could raise his ineffective-assistance-of-counsel claim with respect to counsel's conduct during trial and appeal only in state habeas. This Court has made clear that the Fourteenth Amendment obligates a State "'to assure the indigent defendant an adequate opportunity to present his claims fairly in the context of the State's appellate process,'" *Pennsylvania v. Finley*, 481 U.S. [551 (1987)], and "require[s] that the state appellate system be 'free from unreasoned distinctions.'" While the State may have wide latitude to structure its appellate process as it deems most effective, it cannot, consistent with the Fourteenth Amendment, structure it in such a way as to deny indigent defendants meaningful access. Accordingly, if a State desires to remove from the process of direct appellate review a claim or category of claims, the Fourteenth Amendment binds the State to ensure that the defendant has effective assistance of counsel for the entirety of the procedure where the removed claims may be raised. Similarly, fundamental fairness dictates that the State, having removed certain claims from the process of direct review, bear the burden of ineffective assistance of counsel in the proceeding to which the claim has been removed.

Ultimately, the Court's determination that ineffective assistance of counsel cannot constitute cause of a procedural default in a state postconviction proceeding is patently unfair. In concluding that it was not inequitable to apply the cause and prejudice standard to procedural defaults that occur on appeal, the *Murray* Court took comfort in the "additional safeguard against miscarriages of justice in criminal cases": the right to effective assistance of counsel. [*Murray v. Carrier*, 477 U.S. 478 (1986).] The Court reasoned: "The presence of such a safeguard may properly inform this Court's judgment in determining 'what standards should govern the exercise of the habeas court's equitable discretion' with respect to procedurally defaulted claims." "Fundamental fairness is the central concern of the writ of habeas corpus." *Strickland v. Washington*, 466 U.S. 668 (1984). It is the quintessence of inequity that the Court today abandons that safeguard while continuing to embrace the cause and prejudice standard.

I dissent.

Notes

1. *Subsequent case history*

Roger Coleman was executed on May 20, 1992, by electric chair in Virginia. For an extensive analysis of the facts and history behind Roger Coleman's case, see John C. Tucker's *May God Have Mercy: A True Story of Crime and Punishment* (1998). Even though Roger Coleman was executed in 1992, the debate continued over the possibility of using DNA testing to prove his guilt or innocence. The issue was finally resolved in 2006, when testing demonstrated that Coleman was almost certainly guilty. See Warren Fiske, *Roger Keith Coleman Case: DNA Proves Executed Man Raped, Killed Sister-in-Law*, The Virginian-Pilot, Jan. 13, 2006, at A1.

2. *Concurring opinion*

Justice White noted in his concurring opinion that if it were true that "on occasion" the Virginia Supreme Court waived the untimeliness rule, then "the rule would not be an adequate and independent state ground barring direct or habeas review." At the same time, Justice White stated that he was not "convinced that there is a practice of waiving the rule when constitutional issues are at stake, even fundamental ones. The evidence is too scanty to permit a conclusion that the rule is no longer an adequate and independent state ground barring federal review."

What kind of evidence would help to prove whether a procedural rule a state court invoked to deny relief was a rule that the court waived "on occasion"? How many times would a court have to waive the rule to constitute waiving it "on occasion"?

3. *Subsequent decision*

In *Lee v. Kemna*, 534 U.S. 362 (2002), the Supreme Court recognized that while violation of "'firmly established and regularly followed'" state rules ordinarily is adequate to foreclose review of a federal claim, "[t]here are, however, exceptional cases in which exorbitant application of a generally sound rule renders the state ground inadequate to stop consideration of a federal question." Lee asserted an alibi defense to the charge of first-degree murder and a related crime, but when it came time to present his alibi defense, his witnesses—who were all family—had inexplicably left the courthouse. Defense counsel moved for an overnight continuance to find his witnesses, but the trial court denied his motion and the jury found Lee guilty. The Missouri Court of Appeals relied on two state procedural rules to bar him relief: (1) A state supreme court rule requiring such applications be written and accompanied by an affidavit, and (2) a state supreme court rule stating that a denial of a motion to continue based on a "deficient application" does not constitute an abuse of discretion. These procedural oversights were first raised more than two and half years after Lee's trial.

The Court recognized three considerations that, in combination, led the Court to conclude that the asserted state grounds were inadequate to block adjudication of a federal claim. First, the trial judge who denied Lee's motion to continue did not state he was denying his motion because it was not in writing. Instead, he said that he would not be available the next day because his daughter was in the hospital and that he could not continue Lee's trial until the next business day because he already had scheduled another trial to begin then. Second, "no published Missouri decision direct[ed] flawless compliance with [the state procedural rules relied upon to deny him relief] in the unique circumstances this case present[ed]—the sudden, unanticipated, and at the time unexplained disappearance of critical, subpoenaed witnesses on what became the trial's last day. Lee's predicament * * * was one Missouri courts had not confronted before." Third, and most important according to the Court, "given 'the realities of trial,' Lee substantially complied with Missouri's key Rule."

Is the Court's decision in *Lee v. Kemna* consistent with its decision in *Coleman*?

Chapter 10

Successive Petitions

One of the complaints about habeas litigation is that it seems to "never end." The question of when, how, or whether a successive petition may be filed has been answered differently by the courts at different times. In *Sanders v. United States*, the Court interpreted the section of 28 U.S.C. § 2255 (a writ by a federal prisoner) that reads "[t]he sentencing court shall not be required to entertain a second or successive motion for similar relief on behalf of the same prisoner." In *Kuhlmann v. Wilson*, the Court described the circumstances under which federal courts can entertain a state prisoner's petition for a writ of habeas corpus that raises previously rejected claims. In *McClesky v. Zant*, the Court defined what it means to abuse the writ through successive petitions, adopting the same cause and prejudice standard used in procedural default cases.

Five years after *McClesky* was decided, on April 24, 1996, President Clinton signed the Antiterrorism and Effective Death Penalty Act into law (AEDPA). Because the Act contained several amendments affecting federal habeas corpus law, the Supreme Court soon was asked to decide whether those amendments were constitutional. *Felker v. Turpin* was decided on June 28, 1996, a mere two months after the law was enacted. The issue in *Felker* was whether the provisions in the Act, concerning second or successive habeas petitions, unconstitutionally restrict the jurisdiction of the Court. The Court examined the amendment in AEDPA that created a "gatekeeping" mechanism for second or successive applications. Under that amendment, a habeas petitioner must ask a three-judge panel from a federal court of appeals for leave to file a second or successive habeas petition in the district court. Because the new amendment also held that the panel's decision—either granting or denying permission to file a second or successive application—is not appealable, and shall not be the subject of a petition for rehearing or for a writ of certiorari, the Court considered whether such a restriction is constitutional. Ultimately, the Court found that it is.

Sanders v. United States

373 U.S. 1 (1963)

JUSTICE BRENNAN delivered the opinion of the Court.

We consider here the standards which should guide a federal court in deciding whether to grant a hearing on a motion of a federal prisoner under 28 U.S.C. § 2255. Under that statute, a federal prisoner who claims that his sentence was imposed in violation of the Constitution or laws of the United States may seek relief from the sentence by filing a motion in the sentencing court stating the facts supporting his claim. "[A] prompt hearing" on the motion is required "[u]nless the motion and the files and records of the case conclusively show that the prisoner is entitled to no relief...." The section further provides that "[t]he sentencing court shall not be required to entertain a second or successive motion for similar relief on behalf of the same prisoner."

The petitioner is serving a 15-year sentence for robbery of a federally insured bank in violation of 18 U.S.C. §2113(a). He filed two motions under §2255. The first alleged no facts but only bare conclusions in support of his claim. The second, filed eight months after the first, alleged facts which, if true, might entitle him to relief. Both motions were denied, without hearing, by the District Court for the Northern District of California. On appeal from the denial of the second motion, the Court of Appeals for the Ninth Circuit affirmed. We granted leave to proceed *in forma pauperis* and certiorari.

On January 19, 1959, petitioner was brought before the United States District Court for the Northern District of California, and was handed a copy of a proposed information charging him with the robbery. He appeared without counsel. In response to inquiries of the trial judge, petitioner stated that he wished to waive assistance of counsel and to proceed by information rather than indictment; he signed a waiver of indictment, and then pleaded guilty to the charge in the information. On February 10 he was sentenced. Before sentence was pronounced, petitioner said to the judge: "If possible, your Honor, I would like to go to Springfield or Lexington for addiction cure. I have been using narcotics off and on for quite a while." The judge replied that he was "willing to recommend that."

On January 4, 1960, petitioner, appearing *pro se*, filed his first motion. He alleged no facts but merely the conclusions that (1) the "Indictment" was invalid, (2) "Appellant was denied adequate assistance of Counsel as guaranteed by the Sixth Amendment," and (3) the sentencing court had "allowed the Appellant to be intimidated and coerced into intering [sic] a plea without Counsel, and any knowledge of the charges lodged against the Appellant." He filed with the motion an application for a writ of habeas corpus *ad testificandum* requiring the prison authorities to produce him before the court to testify in support of his motion. On February 3 the District Court denied both the motion and the application. In a memorandum accompanying the denial, the court explained that the motion, "although replete with conclusions, sets forth no facts upon which such conclusions can be founded. For this reason alone, this motion may be denied without a hearing." Nevertheless, the court stated further that the motion "sets forth nothing but unsupported charges, which are completely refuted by the files and records of this case. Since the motion and the files and records of the case conclusively show that the prisoner is entitled to no relief, no hearing on the motion is necessary." No appeal was taken by the petitioner from this denial.

On September 8 petitioner, again appearing *pro se*, filed his second motion. This time he alleged that at the time of his trial and sentence he was mentally incompetent as a result of narcotics administered to him while he was held in the Sacramento County Jail pending trial. He stated in a supporting affidavit that he had been confined in the jail from on or about January 16, 1959, to February 18, 1959; that during this period and during the period of his "trial" he had been intermittently under the influence of narcotics; and that the narcotics had been administered to him by the medical authorities in attendance at the jail because of his being a known addict. The District Court denied the motion without hearing, stating: "As there is no reason given, or apparent to this Court, why petitioner could not, and should not, have raised the issue of mental incompetency at the time of his first motion, the Court will refuse, in the exercise of its statutory discretion, to entertain the present petition." The court also stated that "petitioner's complaints are without merit in fact." On appeal from the order denying this motion, the Court of Appeals for the Ninth Circuit affirmed. The Court of Appeals said in a *per curiam* opinion: "Where, as here, it is apparent from the record that at the time of filing the first motion the movant knew the facts on which the second motion is based, yet in the second motion set forth no reason why he was previously unable to assert the new ground and did not allege that he had previously been unaware of the significance of the relevant facts, the district court, may, in its discretion, decline to entertain the second motion."

We reverse. We hold that the sentencing court should have granted a hearing on the second motion.

I

The statute in terms requires that a prisoner shall be granted a hearing on a motion which alleges sufficient facts to support a claim for relief unless the motion and the files and records of the case "conclusively show" that the claim is without merit. This is the first case in which we have been called upon to determine what significance, in deciding whether to grant a hearing, the sentencing court should attach to any record of proceedings on prior motions for relief which may be among the files and records of the case, in light of the provision that: "The sentencing court shall not be required to entertain a second or successive motion for similar relief on behalf of the same prisoner." * * *

At common law, the denial by a court or judge of an application for habeas corpus was not *res judicata*. * * *

It has been suggested that this principle derives from the fact that at common law habeas corpus judgments were not appealable. But its roots would seem to go deeper. Conventional notions of finality of litigation have no place where life or liberty is at stake and infringement of constitutional rights is alleged. If "government [is] always [to] be accountable to the judiciary for a man's imprisonment," *Fay v. Noia*, access to the courts on habeas must not be thus impeded. The inapplicability of *res judicata* to habeas, then, is inherent in the very role and function of the writ.

* * *

Very shortly after the *Price* [*v. Johnston*, 334 U.S. 266 (1948)] decision, as part of the 1948 revision of the Judicial Code, the Court's statement in *Salinger* [*v. Loisel*, 265 U.S. 224 (1924)] of the governing principle in the treatment of a successive application was given statutory form. 28 U.S.C. § 2244. There are several things to be observed about this codification.

First, it plainly was not intended to change the law as judicially evolved. Not only does the Reviser's Note disclaim any such intention, but language in the original bill which would have injected *res judicata* into federal habeas corpus was deliberately eliminated from the Act as finally passed. * * *

Second, even with respect to successive applications on which hearings may be denied because the ground asserted was previously heard and decided, as in *Salinger*, § 2244 is faithful to the Court's phrasing of the principle in *Salinger*, and does not enact a rigid rule. The judge is permitted, not compelled, to decline to entertain such an application, and then only if he "is satisfied that the ends of justice will not be served" by inquiring into the merits.

Third, § 2244 is addressed only to the problem of successive applications based on grounds previously heard and decided. It does not cover a second or successive application containing a ground "not theretofore presented and determined," and so does not touch the problem of abuse of the writ. * * *

* * *

II

We think the judicial and statutory evolution of the principles governing successive applications for federal habeas corpus and motions under § 2255 has reached the point at which the formulation of basic rules to guide the lower federal courts is both feasible and desirable. Since the motion procedure is the substantial equivalent of federal habeas corpus, we see no need to differentiate the two for present purposes. It should be noted that these rules are not operative in cases where the second or successive application is shown, on the basis of the application, files, and records of the case alone, conclusively to be without merit. In such a case the application should be denied without a hearing.

A. Successive Motions on Grounds Previously Heard and Determined.

Controlling weight may be given to denial of a prior application for federal habeas corpus or § 2255 relief only if (1) the same ground presented in the subsequent application was determined adversely to the applicant on the prior application, (2) the prior determination was on the merits, and (3) the ends of justice would not be served by reaching the merits of the subsequent application.

(1) By "ground," we mean simply a sufficient legal basis for granting the relief sought by the applicant. For example, the contention that an involuntary confession was admitted in evidence against him is a distinct ground for federal collateral relief. But a claim of involuntary confession predicated on alleged psychological coercion does not raise a different "ground" than does one predicated on alleged physical coercion. In other words, identical grounds may often be proved by different factual allegations. So also, identical grounds may often be supported by different legal arguments, or be couched in different language, or vary in material respects. Should doubts arise in particular cases as to whether two grounds are different or the same, they should be resolved in favor of the applicant.

(2) The prior denial must have rested on an adjudication of the merits of the ground presented in the subsequent application. This means that if factual issues were raised in the prior application, and it was not denied on the basis that the files and records conclusively resolved these issues, an evidentiary hearing was held.

(3) Even if the same ground was rejected on the merits on a prior application, it is open to the applicant to show that the ends of justice would be served by permitting the redetermination of the ground. If factual issues are involved, the applicant is entitled to a new hearing upon showing that the evidentiary hearing on the prior application was not full and fair; we canvassed the criteria of a full and fair evidentiary hearing recently in *Townsend v. Sain*, and that discussion need not be repeated here. If purely legal questions are involved, the applicant may be entitled to a new hearing upon showing an intervening change in the law or some other justification for having failed to raise a crucial point or argument in the prior application. Two further points should be noted. First, the foregoing enumeration is not intended to be exhaustive; the test is "the ends of justice" and it cannot be too finely particularized. Second, the burden is on the applicant to show that, although the ground of the new application was determined against him on the merits on a prior application, the ends of justice would be served by a redetermination of the ground.

B. The Successive Application Claimed to be an Abuse of Remedy.

* * *

To say that it is open to the respondent to show that a second or successive application is abusive is simply to recognize that "habeas corpus has traditionally been regarded as governed by equitable principles. Among them is the principle that a suitor's conduct in relation to the matter at hand may disentitle him to the relief he seeks. Narrowly circumscribed, in conformity to the historical role of the writ of habeas corpus as an effective and imperative remedy for detentions contrary to fundamental law, the principle is unexceptionable." *Fay v. Noia*. Thus, for example, if a prisoner deliberately withholds one of two grounds for federal collateral relief at the time of filing his first application, in the hope of being granted two hearings rather than one or for some other such reason, he may be deemed to have waived his right to a hearing on a second application presenting the withheld ground. The same may be true if * * * the prisoner deliberately abandons one of his grounds at the first hearing. Nothing in the traditions of habeas corpus requires the federal courts to tolerate needless piecemeal litigation, or to entertain collateral proceedings whose only purpose is to vex, harass, or delay.

* * *

* * * The principles governing both justifications for denial of a hearing on a successive application are addressed to the sound discretion of the federal trial judges. Theirs is the major responsibility for the just and sound administration of the federal collateral remedies, and theirs must be the judgment as to whether a second or successive application shall be denied without consideration of the merits. Even as to such an application, the federal judge clearly has the power—and, if the ends of justice demand, the duty—to reach the merits. We are confident that this power will be soundly applied.

III

* * *

On remand, a hearing will be required. This is not to say, however, that it will automatically become necessary to produce petitioner at the hearing to enable him to testify. Not every colorable allegation entitles a federal prisoner to a trip to the sentencing court. Congress, recognizing the administrative burden involved in the transportation of prisoners to and from a hearing in the sentencing court, provided in § 2255 that the application may be entertained and determined "without requiring the production of the prisoner at the hearing." This does not mean that a prisoner can be prevented from testifying in support of a substantial claim where his testimony would be material. However, we think it clear that the sentencing court has discretion to ascertain whether the claim is substantial before granting a full evidentiary hearing. In this connection, the sentencing court might find it useful to appoint counsel to represent the applicant. * * *

* * *

The need for great care in criminal collateral procedure is well evidenced by the instant case. Petitioner was adjudged guilty of a crime carrying a heavy penalty in a summary proceeding at which he was not represented by counsel. Very possibly, the proceeding was constitutionally adequate. But by its summary nature, and because defendant was unrepresented by counsel, a presumption of adequacy is obviously less compelling than it would be had there been a full criminal trial. Moreover, the nature of the proceeding was such as to preclude direct appellate review. In such a case it is imperative that a fair opportunity for collateral relief be afforded. An applicant for such relief ought not to be held to the niceties of lawyers' pleadings or be cursorily dismissed because his claim seems unlikely to prove meritorious. That his application is vexatious or repetitious, or that his claim lacks any substance, must be fairly demonstrated.

Finally, we remark that the imaginative handling of a prisoner's first motion would in general do much to anticipate and avoid the problem of a hearing on a second or successive motion. The judge is not required to limit his decision on the first motion to the grounds narrowly alleged, or to deny the motion out of hand because the allegations are vague, conclusional, or inartistically expressed. He is free to adopt any appropriate means for inquiry into the legality of the prisoner's detention in order to ascertain all possible grounds upon which the prisoner might claim to be entitled to relief. Certainly such an inquiry should be made if the judge grants a hearing on the first motion and allows the prisoner to be present. The disposition of all grounds for relief ascertained in this way may then be spread on the files and records of the case. Of course, to the extent the files and records "conclusively show" that the prisoner is entitled to no relief on any such grounds, no hearing on a second or successive motion, to the extent of such grounds, would be necessary.

The judgment of the Court of Appeals is reversed and the case is remanded to the District Court for a hearing consistent with this opinion.

It is so ordered.

[A dissenting opinion by JUSTICE HARLAN, joined by JUSTICE CLARK, is omitted.]

Notes

1. *Subsequent case history*

Charles Edward Sanders originally was sentenced to fifteen years in prison in February of 1959. After the Supreme Court's reversal, the district court set aside the original proceeding, and the State once again indicted Sanders. After a jury convicted him, the district court sentenced Sanders to twenty years in prison. 272 F. Supp. 245 (E.D. Cal. 1967). Sanders unsuccessfully challenged the increase in sentence.

2. *Dissenting opinion by Justice Harlan*

> JUSTICE HARLAN, whom JUSTICE CLARK joins, dissenting:
>
> * * * The present case involves successive § 2255 applications (and similar habeas corpus proceedings under § 2244, which the Court finds sets the pattern for § 2255) arising out of federal convictions.
>
> The over-all effect of this trilogy of pronouncements is to relegate to a back seat, as it affects state and federal criminal cases finding their way into federal post-conviction proceedings, the principle that there must be some end to litigation.
>
> * * *
>
> III
>
> * * *
>
> I seriously doubt the wisdom of these "guideline" decisions. They suffer the danger of pitfalls that usually go with judging in a vacuum. However carefully written, they are apt in their application to carry unintended consequences which once accomplished are not always easy to repair. Rules respecting matters daily arising in the federal courts are ultimately likely to find more solid formulation if left to focused adjudication on a case-by-case basis, or to the normal rule-making processes of the Judicial Conference, rather than to *ex cathedra* pronouncements by this Court, which is remote from the arena.
>
> In dealing with cases of this type, I think we do better to confine ourselves to the particular issues presented, and on that basis I would affirm the judgment of the Court of Appeals.

Is the dissent's concern with finality a legitimate concern? Why or why not?

3. *Expanding the reach of habeas corpus?*

Does it seem that the Court expanded the reach of habeas in this case? What are the political ramifications of its decision?

Kuhlmann v. Wilson

477 U.S. 436 (1986)

JUSTICE POWELL announced the judgment of the Court and delivered the opinion of the Court with respect to Parts I, IV, and V, and an opinion with respect to Parts II and III in which THE CHIEF JUSTICE, JUSTICE REHNQUIST, and JUSTICE O'CONNOR join.

This case requires us to define the circumstances under which federal courts should entertain a state prisoner's petition for writ of habeas corpus that raises claims rejected on a prior petition for the same relief.

I

In the early morning of July 4, 1970, respondent and two confederates robbed the Star Taxicab Garage in the Bronx, New York, and fatally shot the night dispatcher. Shortly before, employees of the garage had observed respondent, a former employee there, on the premises conversing with two other men. They also witnessed respondent fleeing after the robbery, carrying loose money in his arms. After eluding the police for four days, respondent turned himself in. Respondent admitted that he had been present when the crimes took place, claimed that he had witnessed the robbery, gave the police a description of the robbers, but denied knowing them. Respondent also denied any involvement in the robbery or murder, claiming that he had fled because he was afraid of being blamed for the crimes.

After his arraignment, respondent was confined in the Bronx House of Detention, where he was placed in a cell with a prisoner named Benny Lee. Unknown to respondent, Lee had agreed to act as a police informant. Respondent made incriminating statements that Lee reported to the police. Prior to trial, respondent moved to suppress the statements on the ground that they were obtained in violation of his right to counsel. The trial court held an evidentiary hearing on the suppression motion, which revealed that the statements were made under the following circumstances.

Before respondent arrived in the jail, Lee had entered into an arrangement with Detective Cullen, according to which Lee agreed to listen to respondent's conversations and report his remarks to Cullen. Since the police had positive evidence of respondent's participation, the purpose of placing Lee in the cell was to determine the identities of respondent's confederates. Cullen instructed Lee not to ask respondent any questions, but simply to "keep his ears open" for the names of the other perpetrators. Respondent first spoke to Lee about the crimes after he looked out the cellblock window at the Star Taxicab Garage, where the crimes had occurred. Respondent said, "someone's messing with me," and began talking to Lee about the robbery, narrating the same story that he had given the police at the time of his arrest. Lee advised respondent that this explanation "didn't sound too good," but respondent did not alter his story. Over the next few days, however, respondent changed details of his original account. Respondent then received a visit from his brother, who mentioned that members of his family were upset because they believed that respondent had murdered the dispatcher. After the visit, respondent again described the crimes to Lee. Respondent now admitted that he and two other men, whom he never identified, had planned and carried out the robbery, and had murdered the dispatcher. Lee informed Cullen of respondent's statements and furnished Cullen with notes that he had written surreptitiously while sharing the cell with respondent.

After hearing the testimony of Cullen and Lee, the trial court found that Cullen had instructed Lee "to ask no questions of [respondent] about the crime but merely to listen as to what [respondent] might say in his presence." The court determined that Lee obeyed these instructions, that he "at no time asked any questions with respect to the crime," and that he "only listened to [respondent] and made notes regarding what [respondent] had to say." The trial court also found that respondent's statements to Lee were "spontaneous" and "unsolicited." Under state precedent, a defendant's volunteered statements to a police agent were admissible in evidence because the police were not required to prevent talkative defendants from making incriminating statements. The trial court accordingly denied the suppression motion.

The jury convicted respondent of common-law murder and felonious possession of a weapon. On May 18, 1972, the trial court sentenced him to a term of 20 years to life on the murder count and to a concurrent term of up to 7 years on the weapons count. The Appellate Division affirmed without opinion, and the New York Court of Appeals denied respondent leave to appeal.

On December 7, 1973, respondent filed a petition for federal habeas corpus relief. Respondent argued, among other things, that his statements to Lee were obtained pursuant to police investigative methods that violated his constitutional rights. After considering *Massiah v. United States*, 377 U.S. 201 (1964), the District Court for the Southern District of New York denied the writ on January 7, 1977. The [judge found that the] record demonstrated "no interrogation whatsoever" by Lee and "only spontaneous statements" from respondent. In the District Court's view, these "fact[s] preclude[d] any Sixth Amendment violation."

A divided panel of the Court of Appeals for the Second Circuit affirmed. The court noted that a defendant is denied his Sixth Amendment rights when the trial court admits in evidence incriminating statements that state agents "'had deliberately elicited from him after he had been indicted and in the absence of counsel'" (quoting *Massiah*). Relying in part on *Brewer v. Williams*, 430 U.S. 387 (1977), the court reasoned that the "deliberately elicited" test of *Massiah* requires something more than incriminating statements uttered in the absence of counsel. On the facts found by the state trial court, which were entitled to a presumption of correctness under 28 U.S.C. §2254(d), the court held that respondent had not established a violation of his Sixth Amendment rights. We denied a petition for a writ of certiorari.

Following this Court's decision in *United States v. Henry*, 447 U.S. 264 (1980), which applied the *Massiah* test to suppress statements made to a paid jailhouse informant, respondent decided to relitigate his Sixth Amendment claim. On September 11, 1981, he filed in state trial court a motion to vacate his conviction. The judge denied the motion, on the grounds that *Henry* was factually distinguishable from this case, and that under state precedent *Henry* was not to be given retroactive effect. The Appellate Division denied respondent leave to appeal.

On July 6, 1982, respondent returned to the District Court for the Southern District of New York on a habeas petition, again arguing that admission in evidence of his incriminating statements to Lee violated his Sixth Amendment rights. Respondent contended that the decision in *Henry* constituted a new rule of law that should be applied retroactively to this case. The District Court found it unnecessary to consider retroactivity because it decided that *Henry* did not undermine the Court of Appeals' prior disposition of respondent's Sixth Amendment claim. Noting that *Henry* reserved the question whether the Constitution forbade admission in evidence of an accused's statements to an informant who made "no effort to stimulate conversations about the crime charged," the District Court believed that this case presented that open question and that the question must be answered negatively. The District Court noted that the trial court's findings were presumptively correct and were fully supported by the record. The court concluded that these findings were "fatal" to respondent's claim under *Henry* since they showed that Lee made no "affirmative effort" of any kind "to elicit information" from respondent.

A different, and again divided, panel of the Court of Appeals reversed. As an initial matter, the court stated that, under *Sanders v. United States*, the "ends of justice" required consideration of this petition, notwithstanding the fact that the prior panel had determined the merits adversely to respondent. The court then reasoned that the circumstances under which respondent made his incriminating statements to Lee were indistinguishable from the facts of *Henry*. Finally, the court decided that *Henry* was fully applicable here because it did not announce a new constitutional rule, but merely applied settled principles to new facts. Therefore, the court concluded that all of the judges who had considered and rejected respondent's claim had erred, and remanded the case to the District Court with instructions to order respondent's release from prison unless the State elected to retry him.

We granted certiorari to consider the Court of Appeals' decision that the "ends of justice" required consideration of this successive habeas corpus petition and that court's application of our decision in *Henry* to the facts of this case. We now reverse.

II

A

In concluding that it was appropriate to entertain respondent's successive habeas corpus petition, the Court of Appeals relied upon *Sanders v. United States*, which announced guidelines for the federal courts to follow when presented with habeas petitions or their equivalent claimed to be "successive" or an "abuse of the writ." The narrow question in *Sanders* was whether a federal prisoner's motion under 28 U.S.C. § 2255 was properly denied without a hearing on the ground that the motion constituted a successive application. The Court undertook not only to answer that question, but also to explore the standard that should govern district courts' consideration of successive petitions. *Sanders* framed the inquiry in terms of the requirements of the "ends of justice," advising district courts to dismiss habeas petitions or their equivalent raising claims determined adversely to the prisoner on a prior petition if "the ends of justice would not be served by reaching the merits of the subsequent application." While making clear that the burden of proof on this issue rests on the prisoner, the Court in *Sanders* provided little specific guidance as to the kind of proof that a prisoner must offer to establish that the "ends of justice" would be served by relitigation of the claims previously decided against him.

The Court of Appeals' decision in this case demonstrates the need for this Court to provide that guidance. The opinion of the Court of Appeals sheds no light on this important threshold question, merely declaring that the "ends of justice" required successive federal habeas corpus review. Failure to provide clear guidance leaves district judges "at large in disposing of applications for a writ of habeas corpus," creating the danger that they will engage in "the exercise not of law but of arbitrariness." This Court therefore must now define the considerations that should govern federal courts' disposition of successive petitions for habeas corpus.

B

Since 1867, when Congress first authorized the federal courts to issue the writ on behalf of persons in state custody, this Court often has been called upon to interpret the language of the statutes defining the scope of that jurisdiction. It may be helpful to review our cases construing these frequently used statutes before we answer the specific question before us today.

Until the early years of this century, the substantive scope of the federal habeas corpus statutes was defined by reference to the scope of the writ at common law, where the courts' inquiry on habeas was limited exclusively "to the jurisdiction of the sentencing tribunal." *Stone v. Powell. See Wainwright v. Sykes*. Thus, the finality of the judgment of a committing court of competent jurisdiction was accorded absolute respect on habeas review. During this century, the Court gradually expanded the grounds on which habeas corpus relief was available, authorizing use of the writ to challenge convictions where the prisoner claimed a violation of certain constitutional rights. *See Wainwright v. Sykes*; *Stone v. Powell*. The Court initially accomplished this expansion while purporting to adhere to the inquiry into the sentencing court's jurisdiction. *Wainwright v. Sykes*. Ultimately, the Court abandoned the concept of jurisdiction and acknowledged that habeas "review is available for claims of 'disregard of the constitutional rights of the accused, and where the writ is the only effective means of preserving his rights.'"

Our decisions have not been limited to expanding the scope of the writ. Significantly, in *Stone v. Powell*, we removed from the reach of the federal habeas statutes a state prisoner's claim that "evidence obtained in an unconstitutional search or seizure was introduced at his trial" unless the prisoner could show that the State had failed to provide him "an opportunity for full and fair litigation" of his Fourth Amendment claim. Although the Court previously had accepted jurisdiction of search and seizure claims, we were persuaded that any "advance of the legitimate goal of furthering Fourth Amendment rights" through application of the judicially created exclusionary rule on federal habeas was "outweighed by the acknowledged costs to other values vital to a rational system of criminal justice." Among those costs were diversion of the attention of the participants at a criminal trial "from the ultimate question of guilt or innocence," and exclusion of reliable evidence that was "often the most probative information bearing on the guilt or innocence of the defendant." Our decision to except this category of claims from habeas corpus review created no danger that we were denying a "safeguard against compelling an innocent man to suffer an unconstitutional loss of liberty." Rather, a convicted defendant who pressed a search and seizure claim on collateral attack was "usually asking society to redetermine an issue that ha[d] no bearing on the basic justice of his incarceration."

In decisions of the past two or three decades construing the reach of the habeas statutes, whether reading those statutes broadly or narrowly, the Court has reaffirmed that "habeas corpus has traditionally been regarded as governed by equitable principles." *Fay v. Noia*. The Court uniformly has been guided by the proposition that the writ should be available to afford relief to those "persons whom society has grievously wronged" in light of modern concepts of justice. *Fay v. Noia*. Just as notions of justice prevailing at the inception of habeas corpus were offended when a conviction was issued by a court that lacked jurisdiction, so the modern conscience found intolerable convictions obtained in violation of certain constitutional commands. But the Court never has defined the scope of the writ simply by reference to a perceived need to assure that an individual accused of crime is afforded a trial free of constitutional error. Rather, the Court has performed its statutory task through a sensitive weighing of the interests implicated by federal habeas corpus adjudication of constitutional claims determined adversely to the prisoner by the state courts.

III

A

The Court in *Sanders* drew the phrase "ends of justice" directly from the version of 28 U.S.C. § 2244 in effect in 1963. The provision, which then governed petitions filed by both federal and state prisoners, stated in relevant part that no federal judge "shall be required to entertain an application for a writ of habeas corpus to inquire into the detention of a person..., if it appears that the legality of such detention has been determined" by a federal court "on a prior application for a writ of habeas corpus and the petition presents no new ground not theretofore presented and determined, and the judge ... is satisfied that the *ends of justice will not be served by such inquiry.*" 28 U.S.C. § 2244 (1964 ed.) (emphasis added). Accordingly, in describing guidelines for successive petitions, *Sanders* did little more than quote the language of the then-pertinent statute, leaving for another day the task of giving that language substantive content.

In 1966, Congress carefully reviewed the habeas corpus statutes and amended their provisions, including § 2244. Section 2244(b), which we construe today, governs successive petitions filed by state prisoners. The section makes no reference to the "ends of justice," and provides that the federal courts "need not" entertain "subsequent applications" from state prisoners "unless the application alleges and is predicated on a factual or other ground not adjudicated on" the prior application "and unless the court ... is satisfied that the applicant has not on the earlier application deliberately withheld the newly asserted ground or otherwise abused the writ." In construing this language, we are cognizant that Congress adopted the section in light of the need—often recognized by this Court—to weigh the interests of the individual prisoner against the sometimes contrary interests of the State in administering a fair and rational system of criminal laws.

The legislative history demonstrates that Congress intended the 1966 amendments, including those to § 2244(b), to introduce "a greater degree of finality of judgments in habeas corpus proceedings." * * * The House also expressed concern that the increasing number of habeas applications from state prisoners "greatly interfered with the procedures and processes of the State courts by delaying, in many cases, the proper enforcement of their judgments."

Based on the 1966 amendments and their legislative history, petitioner argues that federal courts no longer must consider the "ends of justice" before dismissing a successive petition. We reject this argument. It is clear that Congress intended for district courts, as the general rule, to give preclusive effect to a judgment denying on the merits a habeas petition alleging grounds identical in substance to those raised in the subsequent petition. But the permissive language of § 2244(b) gives federal courts discretion to entertain successive petitions under some circumstances. Moreover, Rule 9(b) of the Rules Governing Section 2254 Cases in the United States District Courts, which was amended in 1976, contains similar permissive language, providing that the district court "may" dismiss a "second or successive petition" that does not "allege new or different grounds for relief." Consistent with Congress' intent in enacting § 2244(b), however, the Advisory Committee Note to Rule 9(b), 28 U.S.C., p. 358, states that federal courts should entertain successive petitions only in "rare instances." Unless those "rare instances" are to be identified by whim or caprice, district judges must be given guidance for determining when to exercise the limited discretion granted them by § 2244(b). Accordingly, as a means of identifying the rare case in which federal courts should exercise their discretion to hear a successive petition, we continue to rely on the reference in *Sanders* to the "ends of justice." Our task is to provide a definition of the "ends of justice" that will accommodate Congress' intent to give finality to federal habeas judgments with the historic function of habeas corpus to provide relief from unjust incarceration.

B

We now consider the limited circumstances under which the interests of the prisoner in relitigating constitutional claims held meritless on a prior petition may outweigh the countervailing interests served by according finality to the prior judgment. We turn first to the interests of the prisoner.

The prisoner may have a vital interest in having a second chance to test the fundamental justice of his incarceration. Even where, as here, the many judges who have reviewed the prisoner's claims in several proceedings provided by the State and on his first petition for federal habeas corpus have determined that his trial was free from constitutional error, a prisoner retains a powerful and legitimate interest in obtaining his release from custody if he is innocent of the charge for which he was incarcerated. That interest does not extend, however, to prisoners whose guilt is conceded or plain. * * *

Balanced against the prisoner's interest in access to a forum to test the basic justice of his confinement are the interests of the State in administration of its criminal statutes. Finality serves many of those important interests. Availability of unlimited federal collateral review to guilty defendants frustrates the State's legitimate interest in deterring crime, since the deterrent force of penal laws is diminished to the extent that persons contemplating criminal activity believe there is a possibility that they will escape punishment through repetitive collateral attacks. Similarly, finality serves the State's goal of rehabilitating those who commit crimes because "[r]ehabilitation demands that the convicted defendant realize that 'he is justly subject to sanction, that he stands in need of rehabilitation.'" Finality also serves the State's legitimate punitive interests. When a prisoner is freed on a successive petition, often many years after his crime, the State may be unable successfully to retry him. This result is unacceptable if the State must forgo conviction of a guilty defendant through the "erosion of memory" and "dispersion of witnesses" that occur with the passage of time that invariably attends collateral attack.

In the light of the historic purpose of habeas corpus and the interests implicated by successive petitions for federal habeas relief from a state conviction, we conclude that the "ends of justice" require federal courts to entertain such petitions only where the prisoner supplements his constitutional claim with a colorable showing of factual innocence. * * * We adopt this standard now to effectuate the clear intent of Congress that successive federal habeas review should be granted only in rare cases, but that it should be available when the ends of justice so require. The prisoner may make the requisite showing by establishing that under the probative evidence he has a colorable claim of factual innocence. The prisoner must make his evidentiary showing even though—as argued in this case—the evidence of guilt may have been unlawfully admitted.

C

Applying the foregoing standard in this case, we hold that the Court of Appeals erred in concluding that the "ends of justice" would be served by consideration of respondent's successive petition. The court conceded that the evidence of respondent's guilt "was nearly overwhelming." The constitutional claim argued by respondent does not itself raise any question as to his guilt or innocence. The District Court and the Court of Appeals should have dismissed this successive petition under § 2244(b) on the ground that the prior judgment denying relief on this identical claim was final.

IV

Even if the Court of Appeals had correctly decided to entertain this successive habeas petition, we conclude that it erred in holding that respondent was entitled to relief under

United States v. Henry, 447 U.S. 264 (1980). As the District Court observed, *Henry* left open the question whether the Sixth Amendment forbids admission in evidence of an accused's statements to a jailhouse informant who was "placed in close proximity but [made] no effort to stimulate conversations about the crime charged." Our review of the line of cases beginning with *Massiah v. United States* shows that this question must, as the District Court properly decided, be answered negatively.

A

The decision in *Massiah* had its roots in two concurring opinions written in *Spano v. New York*, 360 U.S. 315 (1959). Following his indictment for first-degree murder, the defendant in *Spano* retained a lawyer and surrendered to the authorities. Before leaving the defendant in police custody, counsel cautioned him not to respond to interrogation. The prosecutor and police questioned the defendant, persisting in the face of his repeated refusal to answer and his repeated request to speak with his lawyer. The lengthy interrogation involved improper police tactics, and the defendant ultimately confessed. Following a trial at which his confession was admitted in evidence, the defendant was convicted and sentenced to death. Agreeing with the Court that the confession was involuntary and thus improperly admitted in evidence under the Fourteenth Amendment, the concurring Justices also took the position that the defendant's right to counsel was violated by the secret interrogation. As Justice Stewart observed, an indicted person has the right to assistance of counsel throughout the proceedings against him. The defendant was denied that right when he was subjected to an "all-night inquisition," during which police ignored his repeated requests for his lawyer.

The Court in *Massiah* adopted the reasoning of the concurring opinions in *Spano* and held that, once a defendant's Sixth Amendment right to counsel has attached, he is denied that right when federal agents "deliberately elicit" incriminating statements from him in the absence of his lawyer. The Court adopted this test, rather than one that turned simply on whether the statements were obtained in an "interrogation," to protect accused persons from "'indirect and surreptitious interrogations as well as those conducted in the jailhouse. In this case, Massiah was more seriously imposed upon ... because he did not even know that he was under interrogation by a government agent.'" Thus, the Court made clear that it was concerned with interrogation or investigative techniques that were equivalent to interrogation, and that it so viewed the technique in issue in *Massiah*.

In *United States v. Henry*, the Court applied the *Massiah* test to incriminating statements made to a jailhouse informant. The Court of Appeals in that case found a violation of *Massiah* because the informant had engaged the defendant in conversations and "had developed a relationship of trust and confidence with [the defendant] such that [the defendant] revealed incriminating information." This Court affirmed, holding that the Court of Appeals reasonably concluded that the Government informant "deliberately used his position to secure incriminating information from [the defendant] when counsel was not present." Although the informant had not questioned the defendant, the informant had "stimulated" conversations with the defendant in order to "elicit" incriminating information. The Court emphasized that those facts, like the facts of *Massiah*, amounted to "'indirect and surreptitious interrogation[]'" of the defendant.

Earlier this Term, we applied the *Massiah* standard in a case involving incriminating statements made under circumstances substantially similar to the facts of *Massiah* itself. In *Maine v. Moulton*, 474 U.S. 159 (1985), the defendant made incriminating statements in a meeting with his accomplice, who had agreed to cooperate with the police. During that meeting, the accomplice, who wore a wire transmitter to record the conversation, discussed with the defendant the charges pending against him, repeatedly asked the defendant to remind him of the details of the crime, and encouraged the defendant to describe his plan for killing witnesses. The Court concluded that these investigatory techniques denied the defendant his right to counsel on the pending charges. Significantly, the Court emphasized that, because of the relationship between the defendant and the informant, the informant's engaging the defendant "in active conversation about their upcoming trial was certain to elicit" incriminating statements from the defendant. Thus, the informant's participation "in this conversation was 'the functional equivalent of interrogation.'"

As our recent examination of this Sixth Amendment issue in *Moulton* makes clear, the primary concern of the *Massiah* line of decisions is secret interrogation by investigatory techniques that are the equivalent of direct police interrogation. Since "the Sixth Amendment is not violated whenever—by luck or happenstance—the State obtains incriminating statements from the accused after the right to counsel has attached," a defendant does not make out a violation of that right simply by showing that an informant, either through prior arrangement or voluntarily, reported his incriminating statements to the police. Rather, the defendant must demonstrate that the police and their informant took some action, beyond merely listening, that was designed deliberately to elicit incriminating remarks.

B

It is thus apparent that the Court of Appeals erred in concluding that respondent's right to counsel was violated under the circumstances of this case. Its error did not stem from any disagreement with the District Court over appropriate resolution of the question reserved in *Henry*, but rather from its implicit conclusion that this case did not present that open question. That conclusion was based on a fundamental mistake, namely, the Court of Appeals' failure to accord to the state trial court's factual findings the presumption of correctness expressly required by 28 U.S.C. § 2254(d).

The state court found that Officer Cullen had instructed Lee only to listen to respondent for the purpose of determining the identities of the other participants in the robbery and murder. The police already had solid evidence of respondent's participation. The court further found that Lee followed those instructions, that he "at no time asked any questions" of respondent concerning the pending charges, and that he "only listened" to respondent's "spontaneous" and "unsolicited" statements. The only remark made by Lee that has any support in this record was his comment that respondent's initial version of his participation in the crimes "didn't sound too good." Without holding that any of the state court's findings were not entitled to the presumption of correctness under § 2254(d), the Court of Appeals focused on that one remark and gave a description of Lee's interaction with respondent that is completely at odds with the facts found by the trial court. In the Court of Appeals' view, "[s]ubtly and slowly, but surely, Lee's ongoing verbal intercourse with [respondent] served to exacerbate [respondent's] already troubled state of mind." After thus revising some of the trial court's findings, and ignoring other more relevant findings, the Court of Appeals concluded that the police "deliberately elicited" respondent's incriminating statements. This conclusion conflicts with the decision of every other state and federal judge who reviewed this record, and is clear error in light of the provisions and intent of § 2254(d).

V

The judgment of the Court of Appeals is reversed, and the case is remanded for further proceedings consistent with this opinion.

It is so ordered.

[Dissenting opinion by JUSTICE BRENNAN, joined by JUSTICE MARSHALL, is omitted. A concurrence by CHIEF JUSTICE BURGER and a dissent by JUSTICE STEVENS also are omitted.]

Notes

1. *Subsequent case history*

Joseph Allan Wilson was paroled on August 29, 1990, after serving eighteen years in prison. *See* http://nysdocslookup.docs.state.ny.us/kinqw00.

2. *What the "ends of justice" require*

At the end of section III(B), Justice Powell writes:

> In the light of the historic purpose of habeas corpus and the interests implicated by successive petitions for federal habeas relief from a state conviction, we conclude that the "ends of justice" require federal courts to entertain such petitions only where the prisoner supplements his constitutional claim with a colorable showing of factual innocence. * * * We adopt this standard now to effectuate the clear intent of Congress that successive federal habeas review should be granted only in rare cases, but that it should be available when the ends of justice so require. The prisoner may make the requisite showing by establishing that under the probative evidence he has a colorable claim of factual innocence. The prisoner must make his evidentiary showing even though—as argued in this case—the evidence of guilt may have been unlawfully admitted.

Why did the Supreme Court choose to differentiate between constitutional violations that stand on their own and those that are connected to "colorable claims of innocence"?

3. *Drawing distinctions*

Chief Justice Burger's concurrence made the following observation: "There is a vast difference between placing an 'ear' in the suspect's cell and placing a voice in the cell to encourage conversation for the 'ear' to record." Do you agree?

4. *Dissenting opinion by Justice Stevens*

In Justice Stevens's dissent, he stated:

> When a district court is confronted with the question whether the "ends of justice" would be served by entertaining a state prisoner's petition for habeas corpus raising a claim that has been rejected on a prior federal petition for the same relief, one of the facts that may properly be considered is whether the petitioner has advanced a "colorable claim of innocence." But I agree with JUSTICE BRENNAN that this is not an essential element of every just disposition of a successive petition. More specifically, I believe that the District Court did not abuse its discretion in entertaining the petition in this case, although I would also conclude that this is one of those close cases in which the District Court could have properly decided that a second review of the same contention was not required despite the intervening decision in *United States v Henry*.

Why do you think Justice Stevens dissented, given that he finds the "colorable claim of innocence" standard to be reasonably considered?

McCleskey v. Zant

499 U.S. 467 (1991)

JUSTICE KENNEDY delivered the opinion of the Court.

The doctrine of abuse of the writ defines the circumstances in which federal courts decline to entertain a claim presented for the first time in a second or subsequent petition for a writ of habeas corpus. Petitioner Warren McCleskey in a second federal habeas petition presented a claim under *Massiah v. United States* that he failed to include in his first federal petition. The Court of Appeals for the Eleventh Circuit held that assertion of the *Massiah* claim in this manner abused the writ. Though our analysis differs from that of the Court of Appeals, we agree that the petitioner here abused the writ, and we affirm the judgment.

I

McCleskey and three other men, all armed, robbed a Georgia furniture store in 1978. One of the robbers shot and killed an off duty policeman who entered the store in the midst of the crime. McCleskey confessed to the police that he participated in the robbery. When on trial for both the robbery and the murder, however, McCleskey renounced his confession after taking the stand with an alibi denying all involvement. To rebut McCleskey's testimony, the prosecution called Offie Evans, who had occupied a jail cell next to McCleskey's. Evans testified that McCleskey admitted shooting the officer during the robbery and boasted that he would have shot his way out of the store even in the face of a dozen policemen.

Although no one witnessed the shooting, further direct and circumstantial evidence supported McCleskey's guilt of the murder. An eyewitness testified that someone ran from the store carrying a pearl-handled pistol soon after the robbery. Other witnesses testified that McCleskey earlier had stolen a pearl-handled pistol of the same caliber as the bullet that killed the officer. Ben Wright, one of McCleskey's accomplices, confirmed that during the crime McCleskey carried a white-handled handgun matching the caliber of the fatal bullet. Wright also testified that McCleskey admitted shooting the officer. Finally, the prosecutor introduced McCleskey's confession of participation in the robbery.

In December 1978, the jury convicted McCleskey of murder and sentenced him to death. Since his conviction, McCleskey has pursued direct and collateral remedies for more than a decade. We describe this procedural history in detail, both for a proper understanding of the case and as an illustration of the context in which allegations of abuse of the writ arise.

On direct appeal to the Supreme Court of Georgia, McCleskey raised six grounds of error. * * * The portion of the appeal relevant for our purposes involves McCleskey's attack on Evans' rebuttal testimony. McCleskey contended that the trial court "erred in allowing evidence of [McCleskey's] oral statement admitting the murder made to [Evans] in the next cell, because the prosecutor had deliberately withheld such statement" in violation of *Brady v. Maryland*, 373 U.S. 83 (1963). A unanimous Georgia Supreme Court acknowledged that the prosecutor did not furnish Evans' statement to the defense, but ruled that because the undisclosed evidence was not exculpatory, McCleskey suffered no material prejudice and was not denied a fair trial under *Brady*. The court noted, moreover, that the evidence McCleskey wanted to inspect was "introduced to the jury in its entirety" through Evans' testimony, and that McCleskey's argument that "the evidence was needed in order to prepare a proper defense or impeach other witnesses ha[d] no merit because the evidence requested was statements made by [McCleskey] himself." The court rejected McCleskey's other contentions and affirmed his conviction and sentence. We denied certiorari.

McCleskey then initiated postconviction proceedings. In January 1981, he filed a petition for state habeas corpus relief. The amended petition raised 23 challenges to his murder conviction and death sentence. Three of the claims concerned Evans' testimony. First, McCleskey contended that the State violated his due process rights under *Giglio v. United States*, 405 U.S. 150 (1972), by its failure to disclose an agreement to drop pending escape charges against Evans in return for his cooperation and testimony. Second, McCleskey reasserted his *Brady* claim that the State violated his due process rights by the deliberate withholding of the statement he made to Evans while in jail. Third, McCleskey alleged that admission of Evans' testimony violated the Sixth Amendment right to counsel as construed in *Massiah v. United States, supra*. On this theory, "[t]he introduction into evidence of [his] statements to [Evans], elicited in a situation created to induce [McCleskey] to make incriminating statements without the assistance of counsel, violated [McCleskey's] right to counsel under the Sixth Amendment to the Constitution of the United States."

At the state habeas corpus hearing, Evans testified that one of the detectives investigating the murder agreed to speak a word on his behalf to the federal authorities about certain federal charges pending against him. The state habeas court ruled that the *ex parte* recommendation did not implicate *Giglio*, and it denied relief on all other claims. The Supreme Court of Georgia denied McCleskey's application for a certificate of probable cause, and we denied his second petition for a writ of certiorari.

In December, 1981, McCleskey filed his first federal habeas corpus petition in the United States District Court for the Northern District of Georgia, asserting 18 grounds for relief. The petition failed to allege the *Massiah* claim, but it did reassert the *Giglio* and *Brady* claims. Following extensive hearings in August and October 1983, the District Court held that the detective's statement to Evans was a promise of favorable treatment, and that failure to disclose the promise violated *Giglio*. The District Court further held that Evans' trial testimony may have affected the jury's verdict on the charge of malice murder. On these premises it granted relief.

The Court of Appeals reversed the District Court's grant of the writ. The court held that the State had not made a promise to Evans of the kind contemplated by *Giglio*, and that in any event the *Giglio* error would be harmless. The court affirmed the District Court on all other grounds. We granted certiorari limited to the question whether Georgia's capital sentencing procedures were constitutional, and denied relief.

McCleskey continued his postconviction attacks by filing a second state habeas corpus action in 1987 which, as amended, contained five claims for relief. One of the claims again centered on Evans' testimony, alleging that the State had an agreement with Evans that it had failed to disclose. The state trial court held a hearing and dismissed the petition. The Supreme Court of Georgia denied McCleskey's application for a certificate of probable cause.

In July 1987, McCleskey filed a second federal habeas action, the one we now review. In the District Court, McCleskey asserted seven claims, including a *Massiah* challenge to the introduction of Evans' testimony. McCleskey had presented a *Massiah* claim, it will be recalled, in his first state habeas action when he alleged that the conversation recounted by Evans at trial had been "elicited in a situation created to induce" him to make an incriminating statement without the assistance of counsel. The first federal petition did not present a *Massiah* claim. The proffered basis for the *Massiah* claim in the second federal petition was a 21-page signed statement that Evans made to the Atlanta Police Department on August 1, 1978, two weeks before the trial began. The department furnished the document to McCleskey one month before he filed his second federal petition.

The statement related pretrial jailhouse conversations that Evans had with McCleskey and that Evans overheard between McCleskey and Bernard Dupree. By the statement's own terms, McCleskey participated in all the reported jail-cell conversations. Consistent with Evans' testimony at trial, the statement reports McCleskey admitting and boasting about the murder. It also recounts that Evans posed as Ben Wright's uncle and told McCleskey he had talked with Wright about the robbery and the murder.

In his second federal habeas petition, McCleskey asserted that the statement proved Evans "was acting in direct concert with State officials" during the incriminating conversations with McCleskey, and that the authorities "deliberately elicited" inculpatory admissions in violation of McCleskey's Sixth Amendment right to counsel. Among other responses, the State of Georgia contended that McCleskey's presentation of a *Massiah* claim for the first time in the second federal petition was an abuse of the writ.

The District Court held extensive hearings in July and August, 1987, focusing on the arrangement the jailers had made for Evans' cell assignment in 1978. Several witnesses denied that Evans had been placed next to McCleskey by design or instructed to overhear conversations or obtain statements from McCleskey. McCleskey's key witness was Ulysses Worthy, a jailer at the Fulton County Jail during the summer of 1978. McCleskey's lawyers contacted Worthy after a detective testified that the 1978 Evans statement was taken in Worthy's office. The District Court characterized Worthy's testimony as "often confused and self-contradictory." Worthy testified that someone at some time requested permission to move Evans near McCleskey's cell. He contradicted himself, however, concerning when, why, and by whom Evans was moved, and about whether he overheard investigators urging Evans to engage McCleskey in conversation.

On December 23, 1987, the District Court granted McCleskey relief based upon a violation of *Massiah*. The court stated that the Evans statement "contains strong indication of an *ab initio* relationship between Evans and the authorities." In addition, the court credited Worthy's testimony suggesting that the police had used Evans to obtain incriminating information from McCleskey. Based on the Evans statement and portions of Worthy's testimony, the District Court found that the jail authorities had placed Evans in the cell adjoining McCleskey's "for the purpose of gathering incriminating information"; that "Evans was probably coached in how to approach McCleskey and given critical facts unknown to the general public"; that Evans talked with McCleskey and eavesdropped on McCleskey's conversations with others; and that Evans reported what he had heard to the authorities. These findings, in the District Court's view, established a *Massiah* violation.

In granting habeas relief, the District Court rejected the State's argument that McCleskey's assertion of the *Massiah* claim for the first time in the second federal petition constituted an abuse of the writ. The court ruled that McCleskey did not deliberately abandon the claim after raising it in his first state habeas petition. "This is not a case," the District Court reasoned, "where petitioner has reserved his proof or deliberately withheld his claim for a second petition." The District Court also determined that when McCleskey filed his first federal petition, he did not know about either the 21-page Evans document or the identity of Worthy, and that the failure to discover the evidence for the first federal petition "was not due to [McCleskey's] inexcusable neglect."

The Eleventh Circuit reversed, holding that the District Court abused its discretion by failing to dismiss McCleskey's *Massiah* claim as an abuse of the writ. The Court of Appeals agreed with the District Court that the petitioner must "show that he did not deliberately abandon the claim and that his failure to raise it [in the first federal habeas proceeding] was not due to inexcusable neglect." Accepting the District Court's findings that at the first petition stage McCleskey knew neither the existence of the Evans statement nor the identity of Worthy, the court held that the District Court "misconstru[ed] the meaning of deliberate abandonment." Because McCleskey included a *Massiah* claim in his first state petition, dropped it in his first federal petition, and then reasserted it in his second federal petition, he "made a knowing choice not to pursue the claim after having raised it previously" that constituted a prima facie showing of "deliberate abandonment." The court further found the State's alleged concealment of the Evans statement irrelevant because it "was simply the catalyst that caused counsel to pursue the *Massiah* claim more vigorously" and did not itself "demonstrate the existence of a *Massiah* violation." The court concluded that McCleskey had presented no reason why counsel could not have discovered Worthy earlier. Finally, the court ruled that McCleskey's claim did not fall within the ends of justice exception to the abuse-of-the-writ doctrine because any *Massiah* violation that may have been committed would have been harmless error.

McCleskey petitioned this Court for a writ of certiorari, alleging numerous errors in the Eleventh Circuit's abuse-of-the-writ analysis. In our order granting the petition, we requested the parties to address the following additional question: "Must the State demonstrate that a claim was deliberately abandoned in an earlier petition for a writ of habeas corpus in order to establish that inclusion of that claim in a subsequent habeas petition constitutes abuse of the writ?"

II

The parties agree that the government has the burden of pleading abuse of the writ, and that once the government makes a proper submission, the petitioner must show that he has not abused the writ in seeking habeas relief. Much confusion exists though, on the standard for determining when a petitioner abuses the writ. Although the standard is central to the proper determination of many federal habeas corpus actions, we have had little occasion to define it. Indeed, there is truth to the observation that we have defined abuse of the writ in an oblique way, through dicta and denials of certiorari petitions or stay applications. Today we give the subject our careful consideration. * * *

[The Court then discusses the history of the writ of habeas corpus.]

* * *

III

Our discussion demonstrates that the doctrine of abuse of the writ refers to a complex and evolving body of equitable principles informed and controlled by historical usage, statutory developments, and judicial decisions. Because of historical changes and the complexity of the subject, the Court has not "always followed an unwavering line in its conclusions as to the availability of the Great Writ." *Fay v. Noia*. Today we attempt to define the doctrine of abuse of the writ with more precision.

Although our decisions on the subject do not all admit of ready synthesis, one point emerges with clarity: Abuse of the writ is not confined to instances of deliberate abandonment. *Sanders* mentioned deliberate abandonment as but one example of conduct that disentitled a petitioner to relief. *Sanders* cited a passage in *Townsend v. Sain*, which applied the principle of inexcusable neglect, and noted that this principle also governs in the abuse-of-the-writ context.

As *Sanders*' reference to *Townsend* demonstrates, as many Courts of Appeals recognize, and as McCleskey concedes, a petitioner may abuse the writ by failing to raise a claim through inexcusable neglect. Our recent decisions confirm that a petitioner can abuse the writ by raising a claim in a subsequent petition that he could have raised in his first, regardless of whether the failure to raise it earlier stemmed from a deliberate choice.

The inexcusable neglect standard demands more from a petitioner than the standard of deliberate abandonment. But we have not given the former term the content necessary to guide district courts in the ordered consideration of allegedly abusive habeas corpus petitions. For reasons we explain below, a review of our habeas corpus precedents leads us to decide that the same standard used to determine whether to excuse state procedural defaults should govern the determination of inexcusable neglect in the abuse-of-the-writ context.

The prohibition against adjudication in federal habeas corpus of claims defaulted in state court is similar in purpose and design to the abuse-of-the-writ doctrine, which in general prohibits subsequent habeas consideration of claims not raised, and thus defaulted, in the first federal habeas proceeding. The terms "abuse of the writ" and "inexcusable neglect," on the one hand, and "procedural default," on the other, imply a background norm of procedural regularity binding on the petitioner. This explains the presumption against habeas adjudication both of claims defaulted in state court and of claims defaulted in the first round of federal habeas. A federal habeas court's power to excuse these types of defaulted claims derives from the court's equitable discretion. *See Reed v. Ross*, 468 U.S. 1, 9 (1984) (procedural default); *Sanders v. United States* (abuse of writ). In habeas, equity recognizes that "a suitor's conduct in relation to the matter at hand may disentitle him to the relief he seeks." For these reasons, both the abuse-of-the-writ doctrine and our procedural default jurisprudence concentrate on a petitioner's acts to determine whether he has a legitimate excuse for failing to raise a claim at the appropriate time.

The doctrines of procedural default and abuse of the writ implicate nearly identical concerns flowing from the significant costs of federal habeas corpus review. To begin with, the writ strikes at finality. One of the law's very objects is the finality of its judgments. Neither innocence nor just punishment can be vindicated until the final judgment is known. "Without finality, the criminal law is deprived of much of its deterrent effect." *Teague v. Lane*. And when a habeas petitioner succeeds in obtaining a new trial, the "'erosion of memory' and 'dispersion of witnesses' that occur with the passage of time" prejudice the government and diminish the chances of a reliable criminal adjudication. Though *Fay v. Noia* may have cast doubt upon these propositions, since *Fay* we have taken care in our habeas corpus decisions to reconfirm the importance of finality.

Finality has special importance in the context of a federal attack on a state conviction. Reexamination of state convictions on federal habeas "frustrate[s] ...'both the States' sovereign power to punish offenders and their good-faith attempts to honor constitutional rights.'" *Murray v. Carrier*, [447 U.S. 478,] 487. Our federal system recognizes the independent power of a State to articulate societal norms through criminal law; but the power of a State to pass laws means little if the State cannot enforce them.

Habeas review extracts further costs. Federal collateral litigation places a heavy burden on scarce federal judicial resources, and threatens the capacity of the system to resolve primary disputes. *Schneckloth v. Bustamonte*, 412 U.S. 218, 260 (1970) (Powell, J., concurring). Finally, habeas corpus review may give litigants incentives to withhold claims for manipulative purposes and may establish disincentives to present claims when evidence is fresh. *Reed v. Ross, supra*; *Wainwright v. Sykes*.

Far more severe are the disruptions when a claim is presented for the first time in a second or subsequent federal habeas petition. If "[c]ollateral review of a conviction extends the ordeal of trial for both society and the accused," the ordeal worsens during subsequent collateral proceedings. Perpetual disrespect for the finality of convictions disparages the entire criminal justice system. * * *

If reexamination of a conviction in the first round of federal habeas stretches resources, examination of new claims raised in a second or subsequent petition spreads them thinner still. These later petitions deplete the resources needed for federal litigants in the first instance, including litigants commencing their first federal habeas action. * * *

The federal writ of habeas corpus overrides all these considerations, essential as they are to the rule of law, when a petitioner raises a meritorious constitutional claim in a proper manner in a habeas petition. Our procedural default jurisprudence and abuse-of-the-writ jurisprudence help define this dimension of procedural regularity. Both doctrines impose on petitioners a burden of reasonable compliance with procedures designed to discourage baseless claims and to keep the system open for valid ones; both recognize the law's interest in finality; and both invoke equitable principles to define the court's discretion to excuse pleading and procedural requirements for petitioners who could not comply with them in the exercise of reasonable care and diligence. It is true that a habeas court's concern to honor state procedural default rules rests in part on respect for the integrity of procedures "employed by a coordinate jurisdiction within the federal system," *Wainright v. Sykes*, and that such respect is not implicated when a petitioner defaults a claim by failing to raise it in the first round of federal habeas review. Nonetheless, the doctrines of procedural default and abuse of the writ are both designed to lessen the injury to a State that results through reexamination of a state conviction on a ground that the State did not have the opportunity to address at a prior, appropriate time; and both doctrines seek to vindicate the State's interest in the finality of its criminal judgments.

We conclude from the unity of structure and purpose in the jurisprudence of state procedural defaults and abuse of the writ that the standard for excusing a failure to raise a claim at the appropriate time should be the same in both contexts. We have held that a procedural default will be excused upon a showing of cause and prejudice. *Wainright v. Sykes.* We now hold that the same standard applies to determine if there has been an abuse of the writ through inexcusable neglect.

In procedural default cases, the cause standard requires the petitioner to show that "some objective factor external to the defense impeded counsel's efforts" to raise the claim in state court. *Murray v. Carrier.* Objective factors that constitute cause include "'interference by officials'" that makes compliance with the State's procedural rule impracticable, and "a showing that the factual or legal basis for a claim was not reasonably available to counsel." In addition, constitutionally "[i]neffective assistance of counsel ... is cause." Attorney error short of ineffective assistance of counsel, however, does not constitute cause and will not excuse a procedural default. Once the petitioner has established cause, he must show "'actual prejudice' resulting from the errors of which he complains."

Federal courts retain the authority to issue the writ of habeas corpus in a further, narrow class of cases despite a petitioner's failure to show cause for a procedural default. These are extraordinary instances when a constitutional violation probably has caused the conviction of one innocent of the crime. We have described this class of cases as implicating a fundamental miscarriage of justice. *Murray v. Carrier.*

The cause and prejudice analysis we have adopted for cases of procedural default applies to an abuse-of-the-writ inquiry in the following manner. When a prisoner files a second or subsequent application, the government bears the burden of pleading abuse of the writ. The government satisfies this burden if, with clarity and particularity, it notes petitioner's prior writ history, identifies the claims that appear for the first time, and alleges that petitioner has abused the writ. The burden to disprove abuse then becomes petitioner's. To excuse his failure to raise the claim earlier, he must show cause for failing to raise it and prejudice therefrom as those concepts have been defined in our procedural default decisions. The petitioner's opportunity to meet the burden of cause and prejudice will not include an evidentiary hearing if the district court determines as a matter of law that petitioner cannot satisfy the standard. If petitioner cannot show cause, the failure to raise the claim in an earlier petition may nonetheless be excused if he or she can show that a fundamental miscarriage of justice would result from a failure to entertain the claim. Application of the cause and prejudice standard in the abuse-of-the-writ context does not mitigate the force of *Teague v. Lane*, which prohibits, with certain exceptions, the retroactive application of new law to claims raised in federal habeas. Nor does it imply that there is a constitutional right to counsel in federal habeas corpus.

* * *

We now apply these principles to the case before us.

IV

McCleskey based the *Massiah* claim in his second federal petition on the 21-page Evans document alone. Worthy's identity did not come to light until the hearing. The District Court found, based on the document's revelation of the tactics used by Evans in engaging McCleskey in conversation (such as his pretending to be Ben Wright's uncle and his claim that he was supposed to participate in the robbery), that the document established an *ab initio* relationship between Evans and the authorities. It relied on the finding and on Worthy's later testimony to conclude that the State committed a *Massiah* violation.

This ruling on the merits cannot come before us or any federal court if it is premised on a claim that constitutes an abuse of the writ. We must consider, therefore, the preliminary question whether McCleskey had cause for failing to raise the *Massiah* claim in his first federal petition. The District Court found that neither the 21-page document nor Worthy were known or discoverable before filing the first federal petition. Relying on these findings, McCleskey argues that his failure to raise the *Massiah* claim in the first petition should be excused. For reasons set forth below, we disagree.

That McCleskey did not possess, or could not reasonably have obtained, certain evidence fails to establish cause if other known or discoverable evidence could have supported the claim in any event. "[C]ause ... requires a showing of some external impediment *preventing* counsel from constructing or raising the claim." *Murray v. Carrier*. For cause to exist, the external impediment, whether it be government interference or the reasonable unavailability of the factual basis for the claim, must have prevented petitioner from raising the claim. Abuse of the writ doctrine examines petitioner's conduct: the question is whether petitioner possessed, or by reasonable means could have obtained, a sufficient basis to allege a claim in the first petition and pursue the matter through the habeas process. The requirement of cause in the abuse-of-the-writ context is based on the principle that petitioner must conduct a reasonable and diligent investigation aimed at including all relevant claims and grounds for relief in the first federal habeas petition. If what petitioner knows or could discover upon reasonable investigation supports a claim for relief in a federal habeas petition, what he does not know is irrelevant. Omission of the claim will not be excused merely because evidence discovered later might also have supported or strengthened the claim.

In applying these principles, we turn first to the 21-page signed statement. It is essential at the outset to distinguish between two issues: (1) Whether petitioner knew about or could have discovered the 21-page document; and (2) whether he knew about or could have discovered the evidence the document recounted, namely, the jail-cell conversations. The District Court's error lies in its conflation of the two inquiries, an error petitioner would have us perpetuate here.

The 21-page document unavailable to McCleskey at the time of the first petition does not establish that McCleskey had cause for failing to raise the *Massiah* claim at the outset. Based on testimony and questioning at trial, McCleskey knew that he had confessed the murder during jail-cell conversations with Evans, knew that Evans claimed to be a relative of Ben Wright during the conversations, and knew that Evans told the police about the conversations. Knowledge of these facts alone would put McCleskey on notice to pursue the *Massiah* claim in his first federal habeas petition as he had done in the first state habeas petition.

But there was more. The District Court's finding that the 21-page document established an *ab initio* relationship between Evans and the authorities rested in its entirety on conversations in which McCleskey himself participated. Though at trial McCleskey denied the inculpatory conversations, his current arguments presuppose them. Quite apart from the inequity in McCleskey's reliance on that which he earlier denied under oath, the more fundamental point remains that because McCleskey participated in the conversations reported by Evans, he knew everything in the document that the District Court relied upon to establish the *ab initio* connection between Evans and the police. McCleskey has had at least constructive knowledge all along of the facts he now claims to have learned only from the 21-page document. The unavailability of the document did not prevent McCleskey from raising the *Massiah* claim in the first federal petition and is not cause for his failure to do so. And of course, McCleskey cannot contend that his false representations at trial constitute cause for the omission of a claim from the first federal petition.

The District Court's determination that jailer Worthy's identity and testimony could not have been known prior to the first federal petition does not alter our conclusion. It must be remembered that the 21-page statement was the only new evidence McCleskey had when he filed the *Massiah* claim in the second federal petition in 1987. Under McCleskey's own theory, nothing was known about Worthy even then. If McCleskey did not need to know about Worthy and his testimony to press the *Massiah* claim in the second petition, neither did he need to know about him to assert it in the first. Ignorance about Worthy did not prevent McCleskey from raising the *Massiah* claim in the first federal petition and will not excuse his failure to do so.

* * *

We do address whether the Court should nonetheless exercise its equitable discretion to correct a miscarriage of justice. That narrow exception is of no avail to McCleskey. The *Massiah* violation, if it be one, resulted in the admission at trial of truthful inculpatory evidence which did not affect the reliability of the guilt determination. The very statement McCleskey now seeks to embrace confirms his guilt. As the District Court observed:

> After having read [the Evans statement], the court has concluded that nobody short of William Faulkner could have contrived that statement, and as a consequence finds the testimony of Offie Evans absolutely to be true, and the court states on the record that it entertains absolutely no doubt as to the guilt of Mr. McCleskey.

We agree with this conclusion. McCleskey cannot demonstrate that the alleged *Massiah* violation caused the conviction of an innocent person.

The history of the proceedings in this case, and the burden upon the State in defending against allegations made for the first time in federal court some nine years after the trial, reveal the necessity for the abuse-of-the-writ doctrine. The cause and prejudice standard we adopt today leaves ample room for consideration of constitutional errors in a first federal habeas petition and in a later petition under appropriate circumstances. Petitioner has not satisfied this standard for excusing the omission of the *Massiah* claim from his first petition. The judgment of the Court of Appeals is

Affirmed.

[Appendix to Opinion of the Court is omitted.]

JUSTICE MARSHALL, with whom JUSTICE BLACKMUN and JUSTICE STEVENS join, dissenting.

Today's decision departs drastically from the norms that inform the proper judicial function. Without even the most casual admission that it is discarding longstanding legal principles, the Court radically redefines the content of the "abuse of the writ" doctrine, substituting the strict-liability "cause and prejudice" standard of *Wainwright v. Sykes* for the good-faith "deliberate abandonment" standard of *Sanders v. United States*. This doctrinal innovation, which repudiates a line of judicial decisions codified by Congress in the governing statute and procedural rules, was by no means foreseeable when the petitioner in this case filed his first federal habeas application. Indeed, the new rule announced and applied today was not even *requested* by respondent at any point in this litigation. Finally, rather than remand this case for reconsideration in light of its new standard, the majority performs an independent reconstruction of the record, disregarding the factual findings of the District Court and applying its new rule in a manner that encourages state officials to *conceal* evidence that would likely prompt a petitioner to raise a particular claim on habeas. Because I cannot acquiesce in this unjustifiable assault on the Great Writ, I dissent.

* * *

II

The real question posed by the majority's analysis is not *whether* the cause-and-prejudice test departs from the principles of *Sanders*—for it clearly does—but whether the majority has succeeded in *justifying* this departure as an exercise of this Court's common-lawmaking discretion. In my view, the majority does not come close to justifying its new standard.

* * *

B

Even if the fusion of cause-and-prejudice into the abuse-of-the-writ doctrine were not foreclosed by the will of Congress, the majority fails to demonstrate that such a rule would be a wise or just exercise of the Court's common-lawmaking discretion. In fact, the majority's abrupt change in law subverts the policies underlying § 2244(b) and unfairly prejudices the petitioner in this case.

The majority premises adoption of the cause-and-prejudice test almost entirely on the importance of "finality." At best, this is an insufficiently developed justification for cause-and-prejudice or any other possible conception of the abuse-of-the-writ doctrine. For the very essence of the Great Writ is our criminal justice system's commitment to suspending "[c]onventional notions of finality of litigation ... where life or liberty is at stake and infringement of constitutional rights is alleged." To recognize this principle is not to make the straw-man claim that the writ must be accompanied by "'[a] procedural system which permits an endless repetition of inquiry into facts and law in a vain search for ultimate certitude.'" Rather, it is only to point out the plain fact that we may not, "[u]nder the guise of fashioning a procedural rule, ... wip[e] out the practical efficacy of a jurisdiction conferred by Congress on the District Courts."

* * *

This injustice is compounded by the Court's activism in fashioning its new rule. The applicability of *Sykes'* cause-and-prejudice test was not litigated in either the District Court or the Court of Appeals. The additional question that we requested the parties to address reasonably could have been read to relate merely to the burden of proof under the abuse-of-the-writ doctrine; it evidently did not put the parties on notice that this Court was contemplating a change in the governing legal standard, since respondent did not even mention *Sykes* or cause-and-prejudice in his brief or at oral argument, much less request the Court to adopt this standard. In this respect, too, today's decision departs from norms that inform the proper judicial function. It cannot be said that McCleskey had a fair opportunity to challenge the reasoning that the majority today invokes to strip him of his *Massiah* claim.

III

The manner in which the majority applies its new rule is as objectionable as the manner in which the majority creates that rule. As even the majority acknowledges, the standard that it announces today is not the one employed by the Court of Appeals, which purported to rely on *Sanders*. Where, as here, application of a different standard from the one applied by the lower court requires an in-depth review of the record, the ordinary course is to remand so that the parties have a fair opportunity to address, and the lower court to consider, all of the relevant issues.

* * *

To appreciate the hollowness—and the dangerousness—of this reasoning, it is necessary to recall the District Court's central finding: that the State *did* covertly plant Evans in an adjoining cell for the purpose of eliciting incriminating statements that could be used against McCleskey at trial. Once this finding is credited, it follows that the State affirmatively misled McCleskey and his counsel throughout their unsuccessful pursuit of the *Massiah* claim in state collateral proceedings and their investigation of that claim in preparing for McCleskey's first federal habeas proceeding. McCleskey's counsel deposed or interviewed the assistant district attorney, various jailers, and other government officials responsible for Evans' confinement, all of whom denied any knowledge of an agreement between Evans and the State.

Against this background of deceit, the State's withholding of Evans' 21-page statement assumes critical importance. The majority overstates McCleskey's and his counsel's awareness of the statement's contents. For example, the statement relates that state officials were present when Evans made a phone call at McCleskey's request to McCleskey's girlfriend, a fact that McCleskey and his counsel had no reason to know and that strongly supports the District Court's finding of an *ab initio* relationship between Evans and the State. But in any event, the importance of the statement lay much less in what the statement said than in its simple *existence*. Without the statement, McCleskey's counsel had nothing more than his client's testimony to back up counsel's own suspicion of a possible *Massiah* violation; given the state officials' adamant denials of any arrangement with Evans, and given the state habeas court's rejection of the *Massiah* claim, counsel quite reasonably concluded that raising this claim in McCleskey's first habeas petition would be futile. All this changed once counsel finally obtained the statement, for at that point, there was credible, independent corroboration of counsel's suspicion. This additional evidence not only gave counsel the reasonable expectation of success that had previously been lacking, but also gave him a basis for conducting further investigation into the underlying claim. Indeed, it was by piecing together the circumstances under which the statement had been transcribed that McCleskey's counsel was able to find Worthy, a state official who was finally willing to admit that Evans had been planted in the cell adjoining McCleskey's.

* * *

IV

Ironically, the majority seeks to defend its doctrinal innovation on the ground that it will promote respect for the "rule of law." Obviously, respect for the rule of law must start with those who are responsible for *pronouncing* the law. The majority's invocation of "'the orderly administration of justice'" rings hollow when the majority itself tosses aside established precedents without explanation, disregards the will of Congress, fashions rules that defy the reasonable expectations of the persons who must conform their conduct to the law's dictates, and applies those rules in a way that rewards state misconduct and deceit. Whatever "abuse of the writ" today's decision is designed to avert pales in comparison with the majority's own abuse of the norms that inform the proper judicial function.

I dissent.

Notes

1. *Subsequent case history*

Warren McCleskey was executed on September 25, 1991, by electrocution. *See* http://deathpenaltyinfo.org/executions.

2. *The reach of* McCleskey

When a United States District Court re-characterizes a *pro se* federal prisoner's first post conviction motion as a habeas petition under 28 U.S.C. § 2255, does such re-characterization place the prisoner's subsequent attempt to file a "second or successive petition" within the purview of AEDPA?

3. *Public policy concerns*

Justice Marshall's dissent discussed the public policy concerns engendered by the concealment of evidence by police. How does the majority opinion confront this problem?

The following case, *Felker v. Turpin*, 518 U.S. 651 (1996), was decided soon after President Clinton signed the Antiterrorism and Effective Death Penalty Act into law. The Act, among other things, proscribed the situations that allowed an inmate to file successive petitions for habeas relief, and the Court considered whether these proscriptions were constitutional.

28 U.S.C. 2244 reads in part:

> **(b)(1)** A claim presented in a second or successive habeas corpus application under section 2254 that was presented in a prior application shall be dismissed.
>
> (2) A claim presented in a second or successive habeas corpus application under section 2254 that was not presented in a prior application shall be dismissed unless—

(A) the applicant shows that the claim relies on a new rule of constitutional law, made retroactive to cases on collateral review by the Supreme Court, that was previously unavailable; or

(B)(i) the factual predicate for the claim could not have been discovered previously through the exercise of due diligence; and

(ii) the facts underlying the claim, if proven and viewed in light of the evidence as a whole, would be sufficient to establish by clear and convincing evidence that, but for constitutional error, no reasonable factfinder would have found the applicant guilty of the underlying offense.

(3)(A) Before a second or successive application permitted by this section is filed in the district court, the applicant shall move in the appropriate court of appeals for an order authorizing the district court to consider the application.

(B) A motion in the court of appeals for an order authorizing the district court to consider a second or successive application shall be determined by a three-judge panel of the court of appeals.

(C) The court of appeals may authorize the filing of a second or successive application only if it determines that the application makes a prima facie showing that the application satisfies the requirements of this subsection.

* * *

(E) The grant or denial of an authorization by a court of appeals to file a second or successive application shall not be appealable and shall not be the subject of a petition for rehearing or for a writ of certiorari.

Felker v. Turpin

518 U.S. 651 (1996)

CHIEF JUSTICE REHNQUIST delivered the opinion of the Court.

Title I of the Antiterrorism and Effective Death Penalty Act of 1996 (Act) works substantial changes to chapter 153 of Title 28 of the United States Code, which authorizes federal courts to grant the writ of habeas corpus. We hold that the Act does not preclude this Court from entertaining an application for habeas corpus relief, although it does affect the standards governing the granting of such relief. We also conclude that the availability of such relief in this Court obviates any claim by petitioner under the Exceptions Clause of Article III, § 2, of the Constitution, and that the operative provisions of the Act do not violate the Suspension Clause of the Constitution, Art. I, § 9.

I

On a night in 1976, petitioner approached Jane W. in his car as she got out of hers. Claiming to be lost and looking for a party nearby, he used a series of deceptions to induce Jane to accompany him to his trailer home in town. Petitioner forcibly subdued her, raped her, and sodomized her. Jane pleaded with petitioner to let her go, but he said he could not because she would notify the police. She escaped later, when petitioner fell asleep. Jane notified the police, and petitioner was eventually convicted of aggravated sodomy and sentenced to 12 years imprisonment.

Petitioner was paroled four years later. On November 23, 1981, he met Joy Ludlam, a cocktail waitress, at the lounge where she worked. She was interested in changing jobs, and petitioner used a series of deceptions involving offering her a job at "The Leather

Shoppe," a business he owned, to induce her to visit him the next day. The last time Joy was seen alive was the evening of the next day. Her dead body was discovered two weeks later in a creek. Forensic analysis established that she had been beaten, raped, and sodomized, and that she had been strangled to death before being left in the creek. Investigators discovered hair resembling petitioner's on Joy's body and clothes, hair resembling Joy's in petitioner's bedroom, and clothing fibers like those in Joy's coat in the hatchback of petitioner's car. One of petitioner's neighbors reported seeing Joy's car at petitioner's house the day she disappeared.

A jury convicted petitioner of murder, rape, aggravated sodomy, and false imprisonment. Petitioner was sentenced to death on the murder charge. The Georgia Supreme Court affirmed petitioner's conviction and death sentence, and we denied certiorari. A state trial court denied collateral relief, the Georgia Supreme Court declined to issue a certificate of probable cause to appeal the denial, and we again denied certiorari.

Petitioner then filed a petition for a writ of habeas corpus in the United States District Court for the Middle District of Georgia, alleging that (1) the State's evidence was insufficient to convict him; (2) the State withheld exculpatory evidence, in violation of *Brady v. Maryland*, 373 U.S. 83 (1963); (3) petitioner's counsel rendered ineffective assistance at sentencing; (4) the State improperly used hypnosis to refresh a witness' memory; and (5) the State violated double jeopardy and collateral estoppel principles by using petitioner's crime against Jane W. as evidence at petitioner's trial for crimes against Joy Ludlam. The District Court denied the petition. The United States Court of Appeals for the Eleventh Circuit affirmed, extended on denial of petition for rehearing, and we denied certiorari.

The State scheduled petitioner's execution for the period May 2–9, 1996. On April 29, 1996, petitioner filed a second petition for state collateral relief. The state trial court denied this petition on May 1, and the Georgia Supreme Court denied certiorari on May 2.

On April 24, 1996, the President signed [AEDPA] into law. Title I of this Act contained a series of amendments to existing federal habeas corpus law. The provisions of the Act pertinent to this case concern second or successive habeas corpus applications by state prisoners. Section 106(b) specifies the conditions under which claims in second or successive applications must be dismissed, amending 28 U.S.C. § 2244(b) to read:

> (1) A claim presented in a second or successive habeas corpus application under section 2254 that was presented in a prior application shall be dismissed.
>
> (2) A claim presented in a second or successive habeas corpus application under section 2254 that was not presented in a prior application shall be dismissed unless—
>
> (A) the applicant shows that the claim relies on a new rule of constitutional law, made retroactive to cases on collateral review by the Supreme Court, that was previously unavailable; or
>
> (B)(i) the factual predicate for the claim could not have been discovered previously through the exercise of due diligence; and
>
> (ii) the facts underlying the claim, if proven and viewed in light of the evidence as a whole, would be sufficient to establish by clear and convincing evidence that, but for constitutional error, no reasonable fact-finder would have found the applicant guilty of the underlying offense.

Title 28 U.S.C.A. § 2244(b)(3) creates a "gatekeeping" mechanism for the consideration of second or successive applications in district court. The prospective applicant must file in the court of appeals a motion for leave to file a second or successive habeas application in the district court. A three-judge panel has 30 days to determine whether "the application makes a prima facie showing that the application satisfies the requirements of" § 2244(b). Section 2244(b)(3)(E) specifies that "the grant or denial of an authorization by a court of appeals to file a second or successive application shall not be appealable and shall not be the subject of a petition for rehearing or for a writ of certiorari."

On May 2, 1996, petitioner filed in the United States Court of Appeals for the Eleventh Circuit a motion for stay of execution and a motion for leave to file a second or successive federal habeas corpus petition under § 2254. Petitioner sought to raise two claims in his second petition, the first being that the state trial court violated due process by equating guilt "beyond a reasonable doubt" with "moral certainty" of guilt in voir dire and jury instructions. *See Cage v. Louisiana*, 498 U.S. 39 (1990) (*per curiam*). He also alleged that qualified experts, reviewing the forensic evidence after his conviction, had established that Joy must have died during a period when petitioner was under police surveillance for Joy's disappearance and thus had a valid alibi. He claimed that the testimony of the State's forensic expert at trial was suspect because he is not a licensed physician, and that the new expert testimony so discredited the State's testimony at trial that petitioner had a colorable claim of factual innocence.

The Court of Appeals denied both motions the day they were filed, concluding that petitioner's claims had not been presented in his first habeas petition, that they did not meet the standards of § 2244(b)(2), and that they would not have satisfied pre-[AEDPA] standards for obtaining review on the merits of second or successive claims. Petitioner filed in this Court a pleading styled a "Petition for Writ of Habeas Corpus, for Appellate or Certiorari Review of the Decision of the United States Circuit Court for the Eleventh Circuit, and for Stay of Execution." On May 3, we granted petitioner's stay application and petition for certiorari. We ordered briefing on the extent to which the provisions of Title I of the Act apply to a petition for habeas corpus filed in this Court, whether application of the Act suspended the writ of habeas corpus in this case, and whether Title I of the Act, especially the provision to be codified at § 2244(b)(3)(E), constitutes an unconstitutional restriction on the jurisdiction of this Court.

II

We first consider to what extent the provisions of Title I of the Act apply to petitions for habeas corpus filed as original matters in this Court pursuant to 28 U.S.C. §§ 2241 and 2254. We conclude that although the Act does impose new conditions on our authority to grant relief, it does not deprive this Court of jurisdiction to entertain original habeas petitions.

A

Section 2244(b)(3)(E) prevents this Court from reviewing a court of appeals order denying leave to file a second habeas petition by appeal or by writ of certiorari. More than a century ago, we considered whether a statute barring review by appeal of the judgment of a circuit court in a habeas case also deprived this Court of power to entertain an original habeas petition. *Ex parte Yerger*, 75 U.S. 85 (1869). We consider the same question here with respect to § 2244(b)(3)(E).

Yerger's holding is best understood in the light of the availability of habeas corpus review at that time. Section 14 of the Judiciary Act of 1789 authorized all federal courts, including this Court, to grant the writ of habeas corpus when prisoners were "in custody, under or by colour of the authority of the United States, or [were] committed for trial before some court of the same." Congress greatly expanded the scope of federal habeas corpus in 1867, authorizing federal courts to grant the writ, "in addition to the authority already conferred by law," "in all cases where any person may be restrained of his or her liberty in violation of the constitution, or of any treaty or law of the United States." Before the Act of 1867, the only instances in which a federal court could issue the writ to produce a state prisoner were if the prisoner was "necessary to be brought into court to testify," was "committed ... for any act done ... in pursuance of a law of the United States," or was a "subject or citizen of a foreign State, and domiciled therein," and held under state law.

The Act of 1867 also expanded our statutory appellate jurisdiction to authorize appeals to this Court from the final decision of any circuit court on a habeas petition. This enactment changed the result of *Barry v. Mercein*, 46 U.S. 103 (1847), in which we had held that the Judiciary Act of 1789 did not authorize this Court to conduct appellate review of circuit court habeas decisions. However, in 1868, Congress revoked the appellate jurisdiction it had given in 1867, repealing "so much of the [Act of 1867] as authorizes an appeal from the judgment of the circuit court to the Supreme Court of the United States."

In *Yerger*, we considered whether the Act of 1868 deprived us not only of power to hear an appeal from a[n] inferior court's decision on a habeas petition, but also of power to entertain a habeas petition to this Court under § 14 of the Act of 1789. We concluded that the 1868 Act did not affect our power to entertain such habeas petitions. We explained that the 1868 Act's text addressed only jurisdiction over appeals conferred under the Act of 1867, not habeas jurisdiction conferred under the Acts of 1789 and 1867. We rejected the suggestion that the Act of 1867 had repealed our habeas power by implication. Repeals by implication are not favored, we said, and the continued exercise of original habeas jurisdiction was not "repugnant" to a prohibition on review by appeal of circuit court habeas judgments.

Turning to the present case, we conclude that Title I of the Act has not repealed our authority to entertain original habeas petitions, for reasons similar to those stated in *Yerger*. No provision of Title I mentions our authority to entertain original habeas petitions; in contrast, § 103 amends the Federal Rules of Appellate Procedure to bar consideration of original habeas petitions in the courts of appeals. Although § 2244(b)(3)(E) precludes us from reviewing, by appeal or petition for certiorari, a judgment on an application for leave to file a second habeas petition in district court, it makes no mention of our authority to hear habeas petitions filed as original matters in this Court. As we declined to find a repeal of § 14 of the Judiciary Act of 1789 as applied to this Court by implication then, we decline to find a similar repeal of § 2241 of Title 28—its descendant—by implication now.

This conclusion obviates one of the constitutional challenges raised. The critical language of Article III, § 2, of the Constitution provides that, apart from several classes of cases specifically enumerated in this Court's original jurisdiction, "[i]n all the other Cases ... the [S]upreme Court shall have appellate Jurisdiction, both as to Law and Fact, with such Exceptions, and under such Regulations as the Congress shall make." Previous decisions construing this clause have said that while our appellate powers "are given by the constitution," "they are limited and regulated by the [Judiciary Act of 1789], and by such other acts as have been passed on the subject." *Durousseau v. United States*, 10 U.S. 307 (1810); *see also United States v. More*, 7 U.S. 159 (1805). The Act does remove our authority to entertain an appeal or a petition for a writ of certiorari to review a decision of a court of appeals exercising its "gatekeeping" function over a second petition. But since it does not repeal our authority to entertain a petition for habeas corpus, there can be no plausible argument that the Act has deprived this Court of appellate jurisdiction in violation of Article III, § 2.

B

We consider next how Title I affects the requirements a state prisoner must satisfy to show he is entitled to a writ of habeas corpus from this Court. Title I of the Act has changed the standards governing our consideration of habeas petitions by imposing new requirements for the granting of relief to state prisoners. Our authority to grant habeas relief to state prisoners is limited by § 2254, which specifies the conditions under which such relief may be granted to "a person in custody pursuant to the judgment of a State court." § 2254(a). Several sections of the Act impose new requirements for the granting of relief under this section, and they therefore inform our authority to grant such relief as well.

Section 2244(b) addresses second or successive habeas petitions. Section 2244(b)(3)'s "gatekeeping" system for second petitions does not apply to our consideration of habeas petitions because it applies to applications "filed in the district court." There is no such limitation, however, on the restrictions on repetitive and new claims imposed by §§ 2244(b)(1) and (2). These restrictions apply without qualification to any "second or successive habeas corpus application under section 2254." Whether or not we are bound by these restrictions, they certainly inform our consideration of original habeas petitions.

III

Next, we consider whether the Act suspends the writ of habeas corpus in violation of Article I, § 9, clause 2, of the Constitution. This clause provides that "[t]he Privilege of the Writ of Habeas Corpus shall not be suspended, unless when in Cases of Rebellion or Invasion the public Safety may require it." The writ of habeas corpus known to the Framers was quite different from that which exists today. As we explained previously, the first Congress made the writ of habeas corpus available only to prisoners confined under the authority of the United States, not under state authority. The class of judicial actions reviewable by the writ was more restricted as well. In *Ex parte Watkins*, 3 Pet. 193 (1830), we denied a petition for a writ of habeas corpus from a prisoner "detained in prison by virtue of the judgment of a court, which court possesses general and final jurisdiction in criminal cases." Reviewing the English common law which informed American courts' understanding of the scope of the writ, we held that "the judgment of the circuit court in a criminal case is of itself evidence of its own legality," and that we could not "usurp that power by the instrumentality of the writ of habeas corpus."

It was not until 1867 that Congress made the writ generally available in "all cases where any person may be restrained of his or her liberty in violation of the constitution, or of any treaty or law of the United States." And it was not until well into this century that this Court interpreted that provision to allow a final judgment of conviction in a state court to be collaterally attacked on habeas. *See, e.g.*, *Waley v. Johnston*, 316 U.S. 101 (1942) (per curiam); *Brown v. Allen*, 344 U.S. 443 (1953). But we assume, for purposes of decision here, that the Suspension Clause of the Constitution refers to the writ as it exists today, rather than as it existed in 1789. *See Swain v. Pressley*, 430 U.S. 372 (1977).

The Act requires a habeas petitioner to obtain leave from the court of appeals before filing a second habeas petition in the district court. But this requirement simply transfers from the district court to the court of appeals a screening function which would previously have been performed by the district court as required by 28 U.S.C. § 2254 Rule 9(b). The Act also codifies some of the pre-existing limits on successive petitions, and further restricts the availability of relief to habeas petitioners. But we have long recognized that "the power to award the writ by any of the courts of the United States, must be given by written law," *Ex parte Bollman*, 8 U.S. 75 (1807), and we have likewise recognized that judgments about the proper scope of the writ are "normally for Congress to make." *Lonchar v. Thomas*, 517 U.S. 314 (1996).

The new restrictions on successive petitions constitute a modified *res judicata* rule, a restraint on what is called in habeas corpus practice "abuse of the writ." In *McCleskey v. Zant*, we said that "the doctrine of abuse of the writ refers to a complex and evolving body of equitable principles informed and controlled by historical usage, statutory developments, and judicial decisions." The added restrictions which the Act places on second habeas petitions are well within the compass of this evolutionary process, and we hold that they do not amount to a "suspension" of the writ contrary to Article I, § 9.

IV

We have answered the questions presented by the petition for certiorari in this case, and we now dispose of the petition for an original writ of habeas corpus. Our Rule 20.4(a) delineates the standards under which we grant such writs:

> A petition seeking the issuance of a writ of habeas corpus shall comply with the requirements of 28 U.S.C. §§ 2241 and 2242, and in particular with the provision in the last paragraph of § 2242 requiring a statement of the "reasons for not making application to the district court of the district in which the applicant is held." If the relief sought is from the judgment of a state court, the petition shall set forth specifically how and wherein the petitioner has exhausted available remedies in the state courts or otherwise comes within the provisions of 28 U.S.C. § 2254(b). To justify the granting of a writ of habeas corpus, the petitioner must show exceptional circumstances warranting the exercise of the Court's discretionary powers and must show that adequate relief cannot be obtained in any other form or from any other court. These writs are rarely granted.

Reviewing petitioner's claims here, they do not materially differ from numerous other claims made by successive habeas petitioners which we have had occasion to review on stay applications to this Court. Neither of them satisfies the requirements of the relevant provisions of the Act, let alone the requirement that there be "exceptional circumstances" justifying the issuance of the writ.

* * *

The petition for writ of certiorari is dismissed for want of jurisdiction. The petition for an original writ of habeas corpus is denied.

It is so ordered.

JUSTICE STEVENS, with whom JUSTICE SOUTER and JUSTICE BREYER join, concurring.

While I join the Court's opinion, I believe its response to the argument that the Act has deprived this Court of appellate jurisdiction in violation of Article III, § 2, is incomplete. I therefore add this brief comment.

As the Court correctly concludes, the Act does not divest this Court of jurisdiction to grant petitioner relief by issuing a writ of habeas corpus. It does, however, except the category of orders entered by the courts of appeals pursuant to 28 U.S.C.A. § 2244(b)(3) from this Court's statutory jurisdiction to review cases in the courts of appeals pursuant to 28 U.S.C. § 1254(1). The Act does not purport to limit our jurisdiction under that section to review interlocutory orders in such cases, to limit our jurisdiction under § 1254(2), or to limit our jurisdiction under the All Writs Act, 28 U.S.C. § 1651.

Accordingly, there are at least three reasons for rejecting petitioner's argument that the limited exception violates Article III, § 2. First, if we retain jurisdiction to review the gatekeeping orders pursuant to the All Writs Act—and petitioner has not suggested otherwise—such orders are not immune from direct review. Second, by entering an appropriate interlocutory order, a court of appeals may provide this Court with an opportunity to review its proposed disposition of a motion for leave to file a second or successive habeas application. Third, in the exercise of our habeas corpus jurisdiction, we may consider earlier gatekeeping orders entered by the court of appeals to inform our judgments and provide the parties with the functional equivalent of direct review. In this case the Court correctly denies the writ of habeas corpus because petitioner's claims do not satisfy the requirements of our pre-Act jurisprudence or the requirements of the Act, including the standards governing the court of appeals' gatekeeping function.

JUSTICE SOUTER, with whom JUSTICE STEVENS and JUSTICE BREYER join, concurring.

I join the Court's opinion. The Court holds today that the Antiterrorism and Effective Death Penalty Act of 1996 precludes our review, by "certiorari" or by "appeal," over the courts of appeals' "gatekeeper" determinations. The statute's text does not necessarily foreclose all of our appellate jurisdiction, nor has Congress repealed our authority to entertain original petitions for writs of habeas corpus. Because petitioner sought only a writ of certiorari (which Congress has foreclosed) and a writ of habeas corpus (which, even applying the traditional criteria, we would choose to deny), I have no difficulty with the conclusion that the statute is not on its face, or as applied here, unconstitutional. I write only to add that if it should later turn out that statutory avenues other than certiorari for reviewing a gatekeeping determination were closed, the question whether the statute exceeded Congress's Exceptions Clause power would be open. The question could arise if the courts of appeals adopted divergent interpretations of the gatekeeper standard.

Notes

1. *Subsequent case history*

After this decision, there remained controversy about this case. An autopsy performed by an untrained technician determined that Ludlum had been dead for five days when found. Realizing that this finding would eliminate Felker as a suspect due to his surveillance, the findings were changed. Later study of the autopsy notes by independent analysis showed that Ludlum had been dead no more than three days when found. In September 1996, as a result of an Open Records Act lawsuit, Felker's attorneys received boxes of evidence that had been unlawfully withheld by the prosecution. This included possible DNA samples of the perpetrator and a signed confession made by another suspect who was mentally retarded. The District Attorney denied under oath that such evidence existed and the presiding judge at one of Felker's hearings stated that Felker's right to a fair trial had been severely compromised. Nonetheless, the Georgia Supreme Court declined to order a new trial or even grant a stay long enough to sort through the mountains of paperwork that had been withheld in the case. The court's decision was premised on the fact that he had been on death row for some time and had not appealed any of the evidence until a death warrant was issued. Felker originally was scheduled to be executed in May 1996, but a stay was granted and the execution was delayed during the summer Olympics that were being held in Atlanta. He was eventually executed on November 15, 1996, at the age of 48. *See* Rhonda Cook, *DNA testing ordered in case of man already executed*, The Atlanta Journal Constitution, *available at* http://www.truthinjustice.org/felker.htm.

In 2000, several news organizations obtained an order for DNA testing, but subsequent analysis of fingernail scrapings was inconclusive because there was too little DNA to either identify or exclude Felker as the source of the DNA. *Tests shed no light on Georgia execution*, United Press International, December 12, 2000.

2. *"New conditions" on the Court's authority to grant relief*

In his analysis, Justice Rehnquist observed that "although the Act does impose new conditions on our authority to grant relief, it does not deprive this Court of jurisdiction to entertain original habeas petitions." What are the "new conditions" to which Justice Rehnquist is referring? Do you agree that these "new conditions" do not deprive the Court of its original jurisdiction over habeas petitions?

3. *Souter's concurrence*

In his concurrence, Justice Souter observed that "if it should later turn out that statutory avenues other than certiorari for reviewing a gatekeeping determination were closed, the question whether the statute exceeded Congress's Exceptions Clause power would be open. The question could arise if the courts of appeals adopted divergent interpretations of the gatekeeper standard." What kind of divergent interpretations of the "gatekeeper" standard could the courts of appeals adopt?

4. *Problem*

Counsel for a state prisoner filed a petition for a writ of habeas corpus in federal district court, and after hearing, but before a decision was made, the petitioner filed a *pro se* petition, raising some of the same claims but others as well. The state then filed a motion to dismiss the *pro se* petition as successive. How should the district court rule?

PART IV
Federal Habeas Procedure

Chapter 11

Litigating Questions of Fact

Up to this point, the materials in this book have placed federal habeas corpus in a historical context to better understand the consequences of AEDPA, introduced some of the key claims that are cognizable on federal habeas review, explained AEDPA provisions governing substantive deference, and examined the procedural barriers to a prisoner hoping to pursue federal habeas (such as exhaustion and procedural default). Another critical piece of the federal habeas puzzle relates to the procedural aspects of the actual federal adjudication of a state prisoner's constitutional claims. The materials in Chapters 11 and 12 provide an introduction to two of the most contentious questions of federal habeas litigation: (A) The discovery and admissibility of "new" evidence during federal habeas proceedings; and (B) The applicability of AEDPA's deferential scheme.

As set forth in Chapter 1, habeas corpus proceedings are considered collateral civil proceedings because they do not constitute a direct appeal of the trial court's determination of guilt (or its sentence). As a collateral proceeding, the outcome of the habeas adjudication does not involve the relitigation of the evidence presented at trial; instead, most federal habeas litigation hinges on the court's review of "new" evidence that is extrinsic to the trial record. Stated more simply, federal habeas corpus litigation is fact-intensive litigation and the relevant facts in dispute are not those that were presented, tested by a jury, or appealed during direct appeal proceedings. As one commentator has observed

> One constant among the many judicially and legislatively created variables is that the availability of habeas relief will hinge, more than anything else, on how the fact finder has appraised the relevant facts. The questions regarding what facts may be considered by a federal court and how much deference the court must afford to certain facts are typically dispositive as to whether the prisoner will obtain relief. Procedural victories regarding the ability to develop particular factual evidence will, in many cases, be dispositive as to the ultimate result.[1]

Given the high stakes for both the prisoner and the prosecution, it should come as no surprise that much of habeas corpus litigation involves technical battles over discovery and evidentiary development.

A. The Habeas Rules

In *Harris v. Nelson*, the Court confronted the difficult question of when the Rules of Civil Procedure ought to apply to habeas petitions and concluded that, as a general mat-

1. Justin F. Marceau, *Deference and Doubt: The Interaction of AEDPA §§ 2254(d)(2) and (e)(1)*, 82 Tul. L. Rev. 385, 391 (2007).

ter, the Rules of Civil Procedure are ill-suited for federal habeas litigation. Nonetheless, the Court held that federal district courts have the inherent power to fashion discovery procedures as needed for the fair resolution of any particular habeas case.

Harris v. Nelson

394 U.S. 286 (1969)

JUSTICE FORTAS delivered the opinion of the Court.

This case presents the question whether state prisoners who have commenced habeas corpus proceedings in a federal district court may, in proper circumstances, utilize the instrument of interrogatories for discovery purposes.

I

Petitioner is the Chief Judge of the United States District Court for the Northern District of California. Respondent is the warden of the California State Prison at San Quentin. The proceeding was initiated by Alfred Walker who had been convicted in the California courts of the crime of possession of marihuana. After exhausting state remedies, he filed a petition for habeas corpus in the Federal District Court, alleging that evidence seized in the search incident to his arrest was improperly admitted at his trial. The basis for this claim was his allegation that the arrest and incidental search were based solely on the statement of an informant who, according to Walker's sworn statement, was not shown to have been reliable; who, in fact, was unreliable; and whose statements were accepted by the police without proper precautionary procedures.

The District Court issued an order to show cause and respondent made return. Thereafter, Walker filed a motion for an evidentiary hearing, which the District Court granted. Two months later, Walker served upon the respondent warden a series of interrogatories, pursuant to Rule 33 of the Federal Rules of Civil Procedure, seeking discovery of certain facts directed to proof of the informant's unreliability. Respondent filed objections to the interrogatories, alleging the absence of authority for their issuance. The District Judge, without stating his reasons, disallowed the objections and directed that the interrogatories be answered. Respondent applied to the Court of Appeals for the Ninth Circuit for a writ of mandamus or prohibition. The Ninth Circuit vacated the order of the District Court. It held that the discovery provisions of the Federal Rules of Civil Procedure were not applicable to habeas corpus proceedings and that 28 U.S.C. § 2246, the statutory provision specifically relating to the use of interrogatories in habeas corpus proceedings, did not authorize their use for discovery. *Wilson v. Harris*, 378 F.2d 141 (1967).

Because of the importance of the questions presented and the diversity of views among the district and appellate courts that have considered the problem, we granted certiorari. We agree with the Ninth Circuit that Rule 33 of the Federal Rules of Civil Procedure is not applicable to habeas corpus proceedings and that 28 U.S.C. § 2246 does not authorize interrogatories except in limited circumstances not applicable to this case; but we conclude that, in appropriate circumstances, a district court, confronted by a petition for habeas corpus which establishes a prima facie case for relief, may use or authorize the use of suitable discovery procedures, including interrogatories, reasonably fashioned to elicit facts necessary to help the court to 'dispose of the matter as law and justice require.' Accordingly, we reverse and remand the case in order that the District Court may reconsider the matter before it in light of our opinion and judgment.

II

The writ of habeas corpus is the fundamental instrument for safeguarding individual freedom against arbitrary and lawless state action. Its pre-eminent role is recognized by the admonition in the Constitution that: "The Privilege of the Writ of Habeas Corpus shall not be suspended...." U.S. Const., Art. I, § 9, cl. 2. The scope and flexibility of the writ—its capacity to reach all manner of illegal detention—its ability to cut through barriers of form and procedural mazes—have always been emphasized and jealously guarded by courts and lawmakers. The very nature of the writ demands that it be administered with the initiative and flexibility essential to insure that miscarriages of justice within its reach are surfaced and corrected.

* * *

In the present case, we are confronted with a procedural problem which tests the reality of these great principles. We are asked by Walker to establish the existence of rights for those in custody to discover facts which may aid their petitions for release. We are asked to do this by declaring that the provisions of the Federal Rules of Civil Procedure granting such rights to litigants in civil causes are available to Walker; or if we refuse so to conclude, to affirm the existence of power in the District Court to authorize discovery by written interrogatories. We address ourselves to those issues.

III

Rule 1 of the Federal Rules of Civil Procedure provides that: "These rules govern the procedure in the United States district courts in all suits of a civil nature ... with the exceptions stated in Rule 81" At the time of the decision below Rule 81(a)(2) provided, in relevant part, that the Rules were not applicable in habeas corpus "except to the extent that the practice in such proceedings is not set forth in statutes of the United States and has heretofore conformed to the practice in actions at law or suits in equity."

The Court of Appeals for the Ninth Circuit held that the second requirement—"conformity" with practice—made it necessary to show that "prior to September 16, 1938, discovery was actually being used in habeas proceedings, and that such use conformed to the then discovery practice in actions at law or suits in equity." No such showing was made and it is not here contended that it can be made. Walker contends, however, that the rule requires only a showing that habeas proceedings conformed generally to pre-existing practice in law and equity, and he contends that this general requirement is met.

We need not consider this contention that the Court of Appeals took an unnecessarily restricted view of the thrust of the "conformity" requirement, because for other reasons we conclude that the intended scope of the Federal Rules of Civil Procedure and the history of habeas corpus procedure, make it clear that Rule 81(a)(2) must be read to exclude the application of Rule 33 in habeas corpus proceedings.

It is, of course, true that habeas corpus proceedings are characterized as "civil." But the label is gross and inexact. Essentially, the proceeding is unique. Habeas corpus practice in the federal courts has conformed with civil practice only in a general sense. There is no indication that with respect to pretrial proceedings for the development of evidence, habeas corpus practice had conformed to the practice at law or in equity "to the extent" that the application of rules newly developed in 1938 to govern discovery in "civil" cases should apply in order to avoid a divergence in practice which had theretofore been substantially uniform. Although there is little direct evidence, relevant to the present problem, of the purpose of the "conformity" provision of Rule 81(a)(2), the concern of the draftsmen, as a general matter, seems to have been to provide for the continuing applicability of the "civil" rules in their new form to those areas of practice in habeas corpus and other enumerated proceedings in which the "specified" proceedings had theretofore utilized the modes of civil practice. Otherwise, those proceedings were to be considered outside of the scope of the rules without prejudice, of course, to the use of particular rules by analogy or otherwise, where appropriate.

Such specific evidence as there is with respect to the intent of the draftsmen of the rules indicates nothing more than a general and nonspecific understanding that the rules would have very limited application to habeas corpus proceedings. At the very least, it is clear that there was no intention to extend to habeas corpus, as a matter of right, the broad discovery provisions which, even in ordinary civil litigation, were "one of the most significant innovations" of the new rules. *Hickman v. Taylor*, 329 U.S. 495, 500 (1947). Walker does not claim that there was any general discovery practice in habeas corpus proceedings prior to adoption of the Federal Rules of Civil Procedure.

In considering the intended application of the new rules to habeas corpus, it is illuminating to note that in 1938 the expansion of federal habeas corpus to its present scope was only in its early stages. *Mooney v. Holohan*, 294 U.S. 103 (1935); *Johnson v. Zerbst*, 304 U.S. 458 (1938); *Waley v. Johnston*, 316 U.S. 101 (1942). It was not until many years later that the federal courts considering a habeas corpus petition were held to be required in many cases to make an independent determination of the factual basis of claims that state convictions had violated the petitioner's federal constitutional rights. *Brown v. Allen*, 344 U.S. 443 (1953); *Townsend v. Sain*, 372 U.S. 293 (1963). In these circumstances it is readily understandable that, as indicated by the language and the scanty contemporary exegesis of Rule 81(a)(2) which is available, the draftsmen of the rule did not contemplate that the discovery provisions of the rules would be applicable to habeas corpus proceedings.

It is also of some relevance that in 1948, when Congress enacted 28 U.S.C. § 2246 expressly referring to the right of parties in habeas corpus proceedings to propound written interrogatories, its legislation was limited to interrogatories for the purpose of obtaining evidence from affiants where affidavits were admitted in evidence. Again, the restricted scope of this legislation indicates that the adoption in 1938 of the Federal Rules of Civil Procedure was not intended to make available in habeas corpus proceedings the discovery provisions of those rules.

Indeed, it is difficult to believe that the draftsmen of the Rules or Congress would have applied the discovery rules without modification to habeas corpus proceedings because their specific provisions are ill-suited to the special problems and character of such proceedings. For example, Rule 33, which Walker here invoked, provides for written interrogatories to be served by any party upon any "adverse party." As the present case illustrates, this would usually mean that the prisoner's interrogatories must be directed to the warden although the warden would be unable to answer from personal knowledge questions relating to petitioner's arrest and trial. Presumably the warden could solicit answers from the appropriate officials and reply "under oath," as the rule requires; but the warden is clearly not the kind of "adverse party" contemplated by the discovery rules, and the result of their literal application would be to invoke a procedure which is circuitous, burdensome, and time consuming.

The scope of interrogatories which may be served under Rule 33 also indicates the unsuitability of applying to habeas corpus provisions which were drafted without reference to its peculiar problems.

By reference to Rule 26(b), the rule would give the prisoner a right to inquire into "any matter, not privileged, which is relevant to the subject matter involved in the pending action," whether admissible at trial or not. This rule has been generously construed to provide a great deal of latitude for discovery. Such a broad-ranging preliminary inquiry is neither necessary nor appropriate in the context of a habeas corpus proceeding.

Except for interrogatories to be served by the "plaintiff" within 10 days after the commencement of "the action," Rule 33 provides that the interrogatories may be served without leave of court. The "adverse party" must then take the initiative to contest the interrogatories and a hearing in court on his objections is required. Unavoidably, unless there is a measure of responsibility in the originator of the proceeding, the "plaintiff" or petitioner, this procedure can be exceedingly burdensome and vexatious. The interrogatory procedure would be available to the prisoners themselves since most habeas petitions are prepared and filed by prisoners, generally without the guidance or restraint of members of the bar. For this reason, too, we conclude that the literal application of Rule 33 to habeas corpus proceedings would do violence to the efficient and effective administration of the Great Writ. The burden upon courts, prison officials, prosecutors, and police, which is necessarily and properly incident to the processing and adjudication of habeas corpus proceedings, would be vastly increased; and the benefit to prisoners would be counterbalanced by the delay which the elaborate discovery procedures would necessarily entail.

It is true that the availability of Rule 33 would provide prisoners with an instrument of discovery which could be activated on their own initiative, without prior court approval, and that this would be of considerable tactical advantage to them in the prosecution of their efforts to demonstrate such error in their trial as would result in their release. But despite the forceful and ingenious argument of Walker's counsel and *amici curiae*, this consideration cannot carry the day. It is a long march from this contention to a conclusion that the discovery provisions of the Federal Rules of Civil Procedure were intended to extend to habeas corpus proceedings. We have no power to rewrite the Rules by judicial interpretations. We have no power to decide that Rule 33 applies to habeas corpus proceedings unless, on conventional principles of statutory construction, we can properly conclude that the literal language or the intended effect of the Rules indicates that this was within the purpose of the draftsmen or the congressional understanding.

IV

To conclude that the Federal Rules' discovery provisions do not apply completely and automatically by virtue of Rule 81(a)(2) is not to say that there is no way in which a district court may, in an appropriate case, arrange for procedures which will allow development, for purposes of the hearing, of the facts relevant to disposition of a habeas corpus petition. Petitioners in habeas corpus proceedings are entitled to careful consideration and plenary processing of their claims including full opportunity for presentation of the relevant facts. * * *

Flexible provision is made for taking evidence by oral testimony, by deposition, or upon affidavit and written interrogatory. The court shall "summarily hear and determine the facts, and dispose of the matter as law and justice require." 28 U.S.C. § 2243. But with respect to methods for securing facts where necessary to accomplish the objective of the proceedings Congress has been largely silent. Clearly, in these circumstances, the habeas corpus jurisdiction and the duty to exercise it being present, the courts may fashion appropriate modes of procedure, by analogy to existing rules or otherwise in conformity with judicial usage. Where their duties require it, this is the inescapable obligation of the courts. Their authority is expressly confirmed in the All Writs Act, 28 U.S.C. § 1651. This statute has served since its inclusion, in substance, in the original Judiciary Act as a "legislatively approved source of procedural instruments designed to achieve 'the rational ends of law.'" *Price v. Johnston*, 334 U.S. 266 (1948). It has been recognized that the courts may rely upon this statute in issuing orders appropriate to assist them in conducting factual inquiries. In *Price v. Johnston*, this Court held explicitly that the purpose and function of the All Writs Act to supply the courts with the instruments needed to perform their duty, as prescribed by the Congress and the Constitution, provided only that such instruments are "agreeable" to the usages and principles of law, extend to habeas corpus proceedings.

* * *

We do not assume that courts in the exercise of their discretion will pursue or authorize pursuit of all allegations presented to them. We are aware that confinement sometimes induces fantasy which has its basis in the paranoia of prison rather than in fact. But where specific allegations before the court show reason to believe that the petitioner may, if the facts are fully developed, be able to demonstrate that he is confined illegally and is therefore entitled to relief, it is the duty of the court to provide the necessary facilities and procedures for an adequate inquiry. Obviously, in exercising this power, the court may utilize familiar procedures, as appropriate, whether these are found in the civil or criminal rules or elsewhere in the "usages and principles of law."

Accordingly, we reverse the judgment of the Court of Appeals for the Ninth Circuit and remand the case for further proceedings in accordance with this opinion.

Reversed and remanded.

Notes

1. *"[T]he label is gross and inexact"*

Why does the Court call the characterization of federal habeas review as a civil proceeding gross and inexact? When do you suppose the Rules of Civil Procedure apply to a habeas case?

2. *The All Writs Act*

If the Rules of Civil Procedure do not apply so as to provide the district court with the authority to permit discovery, why doesn't the Court simply dismiss the case instead of remanding it?

3. *Discretionary or mandatory discovery?*

Does the *Harris* Court consider discovery a matter of discretion that is vested in the district court or a right to which the prisoner is entitled in appropriate circumstances?

4. *The rule-making machinery*

In a footnote at the end of *Harris*, the Court recommended that "the rule-making machinery ... be invoked to formulate rules of practice with respect to federal habeas corpus ... proceedings." In 1976, the Court followed the lead of the *Harris* footnote and promulgated, and Congress adopted, the Rules Governing § 2254 Cases. Three of the Habeas Rules that are particularly relevant to the study of factual development are Rules 6, 7, and 8 (provided immediately below). Notably, the Advisory Committee Reports refer to *Harris v. Nelson* and the case continues to be at the center of discovery-related litigation in the federal habeas context.

Rule 6. Discovery

(a) Leave of Court Required. A judge may, for good cause, authorize a party to conduct discovery under the Federal Rules of Civil Procedure and may limit the extent of discovery. If necessary for effective discovery, the judge must appoint an attorney for a petitioner who qualifies to have counsel appointed under 18 U.S.C. § 3006A.

(b) Requesting Discovery. A party requesting discovery must provide reasons for the request. The request must also include any proposed interrogatories and requests for admission, and must specify any requested documents.

(c) Deposition Expenses. If the respondent is granted leave to take a deposition, the judge may require the respondent to pay the travel expenses, subsistence expenses, and fees of the petitioner's attorney to attend the deposition.

Rule 7. Expanding the Record

(a) In General. If the petition is not dismissed, the judge may direct the parties to expand the record by submitting additional materials relating to the petition. The judge may require that these materials be authenticated.

(b) Types of Materials. The materials that may be required include letters predating the filing of the petition, documents, exhibits, and answers under oath to written interrogatories propounded by the judge. Affidavits may also be submitted and considered as part of the record.

(c) Review by the Opposing Party. The judge must give the party against whom the additional materials are offered an opportunity to admit or deny their correctness.

Rule 8. Evidentiary Hearing

(a) Determining Whether to Hold a Hearing. If the petition is not dismissed, the judge must review the answer, any transcripts and records of state-court proceedings, and any materials submitted under Rule 7 to determine whether an evidentiary hearing is warranted.

5. *Rule 6 of the discovery rules governing § 2254*

After reading Rule 6, in what way does it attempt to balance a restricted, yet flexible, view of habeas corpus?

B. The Right to a Federal Hearing

The federal evidentiary hearing is the most important vehicle through which prisoners demonstrate that their constitutional rights were violated during the state court process. Evidentiary hearings in habeas cases are extraordinarily rare, but habeas relief in the absence of such a hearing is virtually non-existent.[1] Consequently, the grant or denial of an evidentiary hearing is the best proxy for assessing the likelihood of a prisoner's success on the merits in any particular case.

Despite the practical significance of assessing a prisoner's right to a federal hearing, restrictions imposed by AEDPA and recent cases have complicated what was historically a relatively straightforward area of the law. Presently, there is considerable confusion among federal

1. 1 Randy Hertz & James S. Liebman, Federal Habeas Corpus Practice and Procedure § 2.4b n.26 (5th ed. 2005) (citing a study finding that hearings are held in only 1.17% of all habeas corpus cases).

courts regarding the extent to which pre-AEDPA law continues to govern evidentiary hearing determinations. This section surveys the landmark developments in this area of the law.

At least since the enactment of the Habeas Corpus Act of 1867, the lower federal courts had express authority to "hear and determine facts and dispose of the matter as law and justice require." 28 U.S.C. § 2243. Grounding its decision in implicit requirements of due process and the express mandates of the habeas statute, in 1963, the Court handed down the landmark habeas decision *Townsend v. Sain*. To this day, the meaning and continued applicability of *Townsend* dominates litigation regarding a prisoner's access to a federal hearing.

Townsend v. Sain

372 U.S. 293 (1963)

CHIEF JUSTICE WARREN delivered the opinion of the Court.

This case, in its present posture raising questions as to the right to a plenary hearing in federal habeas corpus, comes to us once again after a tangle of prior proceedings. In 1955 the petitioner, Charles Townsend, was tried before a jury for murder in the Criminal Court of Cook County, Illinois. At his trial petitioner, through his court-appointed counsel, the public defender, objected to the introduction of his confession on the ground that it was the product of coercion. A hearing was held outside the presence of the jury, and the trial judge denied the motion to suppress. He later admitted the confession into evidence. Further evidence relating to the issue of voluntariness was introduced before the jury. The charge permitted them to disregard the confession if they found that it was involuntary. Under Illinois law the admissibility of the confession is determined solely by the trial judge, but the question of voluntariness, because it bears on the issue of credibility, may also be presented to the jury. The jury found petitioner guilty and affixed the death penalty to its verdict. The Supreme Court of Illinois affirmed the conviction, two justices dissenting. This Court denied a writ of certiorari.

Petitioner next sought post-conviction collateral relief in the Illinois State courts. The Cook County Criminal Court dismissed his petition without holding an evidentiary hearing. The Supreme Court of Illinois by order affirmed, holding that the issue of coercion was *res judicata*, and this Court again denied certiorari. The issue of coercion was pressed at all stages of these proceedings.

Having thoroughly exhausted his state remedies, Townsend petitioned for habeas corpus in the United States District Court for the Northern District of Illinois. That court, considering only the pleadings filed in the course of that proceeding and the opinion of the Illinois Supreme Court rendered on direct appeal, denied the writ. The Court of Appeals for the Seventh Circuit dismissed an appeal. However, this Court granted a petition for certiorari, vacated the judgment and remanded for a decision as to whether, in the light of the state-court record, a plenary hearing was required.

On the remand, the District Court held no hearing and dismissed the petition, finding only that "Justice would not be served by ordering a full hearing or by awarding any or all of [the] relief sought by Petitioner." The judge stated that he was satisfied from the state-court records before him that the decision of the state courts holding the challenged confession to have been freely and voluntarily given by petitioner was correct, and that there had been no denial of federal due process of law. On appeal the Court of Appeals concluded that "[o]n habeas corpus, the district court's inquiry is limited to a study of the undisputed portions of the record" and that the undisputed portions of this record showed no deprivation of constitutional rights. We granted certiorari to determine whether the courts below had correctly determined and applied the standards governing hearings in federal habeas corpus. The case was first argued during the October Term 1961. Two of the Justices were unable to participate in a decision, and we subsequently ordered it reargued. We now have it before us for decision.

The undisputed evidence adduced at the trial-court hearing on the motion to suppress showed the following. Petitioner was arrested by Chicago police shortly before or after 2 a.m. on New Year's Day 1954. They had received information from one Campbell, then in their custody for robbery, that petitioner was connected with the robbery and murder of Jack Boone, a Chicago steelworker and the victim in this case. Townsend was 19 years old at the time, a confirmed heroin addict and a user of narcotics since age 15. He was under the influence of a dose of heroin administered approximately one and one-half hours before his arrest. It was his practice to take injections three to five hours apart. At about 2:30 a.m. petitioner was taken to the second district police station and, shortly after his arrival, was questioned for a period variously fixed from one-half to two hours. During this period, he denied committing any crimes. Thereafter at about 5 a.m. he was taken to the 19th district station where he remained, without being questioned, until about 8:15 p.m. that evening. At that time he was returned to the second district station and placed in a line-up with several other men so that he could be viewed by one Anagnost, the victim of another robbery. When Anagnost identified another man, rather than petitioner, as his assailant, a scuffle ensued, the details of which were disputed by petitioner and the police. Following this incident petitioner was again subjected to questioning. He was interrogated more or less regularly from about 8:45 until 9:30 by police officers. At that time an Assistant State's Attorney arrived. Some time shortly before or after nine o'clock, but before the arrival of the State's attorney, petitioner complained to Officer Cagney that he had pains in his stomach, that he was suffering from other withdrawal symptoms, that he wanted a doctor, and that he was in need of a dose of narcotics. Petitioner clutched convulsively at his stomach a number of times. Cagney, aware that petitioner was a narcotic addict, telephoned for a police physician. There was some dispute between him and the State's Attorney, both prosecution witnesses, as to whether the questioning continued until the doctor arrived. Cagney testified that it did and the State's Attorney to the contrary. In any event, after the withdrawal symptoms commenced it appears that petitioner was unresponsive to questioning. The doctor appeared at 9:45. In the presence of Officer Cagney he gave Townsend a combined dosage by injection of 1/8-grain of phenobarbital and 1/230-grain of hyoscine. Hyoscine is the same as scopolamine and is claimed by petitioner in this proceeding to have the properties of a "truth serum." The doctor also left petitioner four or five 1/4-grain tablets of phenobarbital. Townsend was told to take two of these that evening and the remainder the following day. The doctor testified that these medications were given to petitioner for the purpose of alleviating the withdrawal symptoms; the police officers and the State's Attorney testified that they did not know what the doctor had given petitioner. The doctor departed between 10 and 10:30. The medication alleviated the discomfort of the withdrawal symptoms, and petitioner promptly responded to questioning.

As to events succeeding this point in time on January 1, the testimony of the prosecution witnesses and of the petitioner irreconcilably conflicts. However, for the purposes of this proceeding both sides agree that the following occurred. After the doctor left, Officer Fitzgerald and the Assistant State's Attorney joined Officer Cagney in the room with the petitioner, where he was questioned for about 25 minutes. They all then went to another room; a court reporter there took down petitioner's statements. The State's Attorney turned the questioning to the Boone case about 11:15. In less than nine minutes a full confession was transcribed. At about 11:45 the questioning was terminated, and petitioner was returned to his cell.

The following day, Saturday, January 2, at about 1 p.m. petitioner was taken to the office of the prosecutor where the Assistant State's Attorney read, and petitioner signed, transcriptions of the statements which he had made the night before. When Townsend again experienced discomfort on Sunday evening, the doctor was summoned. He gave petitioner more 1/4-grain tablets of phenobarbital. On Monday, January 4, Townsend was taken to a coroner's inquest where he was called to the witness stand by the State and, after being advised of his right not to testify, again confessed. At the time of the inquest petitioner was without counsel. The public defender was not appointed to represent him until his arraignment on January 12.

Petitioner testified at the motion to suppress to the following version of his detention. He was initially questioned at the second district police station for a period in excess of two hours. Upon his return from the 19th district and after Anagnost, the robbery victim who had viewed the line-up, had identified another person as the assailant, Officer Cagney accompanied Anagnost into the hall and told him that he had identified the wrong person. Another officer then entered the room, hit the petitioner in the stomach and stated that petitioner knew that he had robbed Anagnost. Petitioner fell to the floor and vomited water and a little blood. Officer Cagney spoke to Townsend 5 or 10 minutes later, Townsend told him that he was sick from the use of drugs, and Cagney offered to call a doctor if petitioner would "cooperate" and tell the truth about the Boone murder. Five minutes later the officer had changed his tack; he told petitioner that he thought him innocent and that he would call the doctor, implying that the doctor would give him a narcotic. The doctor gave petitioner an injection in the arm and five pills. Townsend took three of these immediately. Although he felt better, he felt dizzy and sleepy and his distance vision was impaired. Anagnost was then brought into the room, and petitioner was asked by someone to tell Anagnost that he had robbed him. Petitioner then admitted the robbery, and the next thing he knew was that he was sitting at a desk. He fell asleep but was awakened and handed a pen; he signed his name believing that he was going to be released on bond. Townsend was taken to his cell but was later taken back to the room in which he had been before. He could see "a lot of lights flickering," and someone told him to hold his head up. This went on for a minute or so, and petitioner was then again taken back to his cell. The next morning petitioner's head was much clearer, although he could not really remember what had occurred following the injection on the previous evening. An officer then told petitioner that he had confessed. Townsend was taken into a room and asked about a number of robberies and murders. "I believe I said yes to all of them." He could not hear very well and felt sleepy. That afternoon, after he had taken the remainder of the phenobarbital pills, he was taken to the office of the State's Attorney. Half asleep he signed another paper although not aware of its contents. The doctor gave him six or seven pills of a different color on Sunday evening. He took some of these immediately. They kept him awake all night. The following Monday morning he took more of these pills. Later that day he was taken to a coroner's inquest. He testified at the inquest because the officers had told him to do so.

Essentially the prosecution witnesses contradicted all of the above. They testified that petitioner had been questioned initially for only one-half hour, that he had scuffled with the man identified by Anagnost, and not an officer, and that he had not vomited. The officers and the Assistant State's Attorney also testified that petitioner had appeared to be awake and coherent throughout the evening of the 1st of January and at all relevant times thereafter, and that he had not taken the pills given to him by the doctor on the evening of the 1st. They stated that the petitioner had appeared to follow the statement which he signed and which was read to him at the State's Attorney's office. Finally they denied that any threats or promises of any sort had been made or that Townsend had been told to testify at the coroner's inquest. As stated above counsel was not provided for him at this inquest.

There was considerable testimony at the motion to suppress concerning the probable effects of hyoscine and phenobarbital. Dr. Mansfield, who had prescribed for petitioner on the evening when he had first confessed, testified for the prosecution. He stated that a full therapeutic dose of hyoscine was 1/100 of a grain; that he gave Townsend 1/230 of a grain; that "Phenobarbital ... reacts very well combined with [hyoscine when] ... you want to quiet" a person; that the combination will "pacify" because "it has an effect on the mind"; but that the dosage administered would not put a person to sleep and would not cause amnesia or impairment of eyesight or of mental condition. The doctor denied that he had administered any "truth serum." However, he did not disclose that hyoscine is the same as scopolamine or that the latter is familiarly known as "truth serum." Petitioner's expert was a doctor of physiology, pharmacology and toxicology. He was formerly the senior toxicological chemist of Cook County and at the time of trial was a professor of pharmacology, chemotherapy and toxicology at the Loyola University School of Medicine. He testified to the effect of the injection upon a hypothetical subject, obviously the petitioner. The expert stated that the effect of the prescribed dosage of hyoscine upon the subject, assumed to be a narcotic addict, "would be of such a nature that it could range between absolute sleep ... and drowsiness, as one extreme, and the other extreme ... would incorporate complete disorientation and excitation...." And, assuming that the subject took 1/8-grain phenobarbital by injection and 1/2-grain orally at the same time, the expert stated that the depressive effect would be accentuated. The expert testified that the subject would suffer partial or total amnesia for five to eight hours and loss of near vision for four to six hours.

The trial judge summarily denied the motion to suppress and later admitted the court reporter's transcription of the confession into evidence. He made no findings of fact and wrote no opinion stating the grounds of his decision. Thereafter, for the purpose of testing the credibility of the confession, the evidence relating to coercion was placed before the jury. At that time additional noteworthy testimony was elicited. The identity of hyoscine and scopolamine was established (but no mention of the drug's properties as a "truth serum" was made). An expert witness called by the prosecution testified that Townsend had such a low intelligence that he was a near mental defective and "just a little above moron." Townsend testified that the officers had slapped him on several occasions and had threatened to shoot him. Finally, Officer Corcoran testified that about 9 p.m., Friday evening before the doctor's arrival, Townsend had confessed to the Boone assault and robbery in response to a question propounded by Officer Cagney in the presence of Officers Fitzgerald, Martin and himself. But although Corcoran, Cagney and Martin had testified extensively at the motion to suppress, none had mentioned any such confession. Furthermore, both Townsend and Officer Fitzgerald at the motion to suppress had flatly said that no statement had been made before the doctor arrived. Although the other three officers testified at the trial, not one of them was asked to corroborate this phase of Corcoran's testimony.

It was established that the homicide occurred at about 6 p.m. on December 18, 1953. Essentially the only evidence which connected petitioner with the crime, other than his confession, was the testimony of Campbell, then on probation for robbery, and of the pathologist who performed the autopsy on Boone. Campbell testified that about the "middle" of December at about 8:30 p.m. he had seen Townsend walking down a street in the vicinity of the murder with a brick in his hand. He was unable to fix the exact date, did not know of the Boone murder at the time and, so far as his testimony revealed, had no reason to suspect that Townsend had done anything unlawful previous to their meeting.

The pathologist testified that death was caused by a "severe blow to the top of his [Boone's] head...." Contrary to the statement in the opinion of the Illinois Supreme Court on direct appeal there was no testimony that the wounds were "located in such a manner as to have been inflicted by a blow with a house brick...." In any event, that court characterized the evidence as meagre and noted that "it was brought out by cross-examination that Campbell had informed on the defendant to obtain his own release from custody." Prior to petitioner's trial Campbell was placed on probation for robbery. Justice Schaefer, joined by Chief Justice Klingbiel in dissent, found Campbell's testimony "inherently incredible."

The theory of petitioner's application for habeas corpus did not rest upon allegations of physical coercion. Rather, it relied upon the hitherto undisputed testimony and alleged: (1) that petitioner vomited water and blood at the police station when he became ill from the withdrawal of narcotics; (2) that scopolamine is a "truth serum" and that this fact was not brought out at the motion to suppress or at the trial; (3) that scopolamine "either alone or combined with Phenobarbital, is not the proper medication for a narcotic addict [and that] ... [t]he effect of the intravenous injection of hyoscine and Phenobarbital ... is to produce a physiological and psychological condition adversely affecting the mind and will ... [and] a psychic effect which removes the subject thus injected from the scope of reality; so that the person so treated is removed from contact with his environment, he is not able to see and feel properly, he loses proper use of his eye-sight, his hearing and his sense of perception and his ability to withstand interrogation"; (4) that the police doctor willfully suppressed this information and information of the identity of hyoscine and scopolamine, of his knowledge of these things, and of his intention to inject the hyoscine for the purpose of producing in Townsend "a physiological and psychological state ... susceptible to interrogation resulting in ... confessions ..."; (5) that the injection caused Townsend to confess; (6) that on the evening of January 1, immediately after the injection of scopolamine, petitioner confessed to three murders and one robbery other than the murder of Boone and the robbery of Anagnost. Although there was some mention of other confessions at the trial, only the confession to the Anagnost robbery was specifically testified to.

* * *

I

Numerous decisions of this Court have established the standards governing the admissibility of confessions into evidence. If an individual's "will was overborne" or if his confession was not "the product of a rational intellect and a free will," his confession is inadmissible because coerced. These standards are applicable whether a confession is the product of physical intimidation or psychological pressure and, of course, are equally applicable to a drug-induced statement. It is difficult to imagine a situation in which a confession would be less the product of a free intellect, less voluntary, than when brought about by a drug having the effect of a "truth serum." It is not significant that the drug may have been administered and the questions asked by persons unfamiliar with hyoscine's properties as a "truth serum," if these properties exist. Any questioning by police officers which in fact produces a confession which is not the product of a free intellect renders that confession inadmissible. * * *

Thus we conclude that the petition for habeas corpus alleged a deprivation of constitutional rights. The remaining question before us then is whether the District Court was required to hold a hearing to ascertain the facts which are a necessary predicate to a decision of the ultimate constitutional question.

The problem of the power and duty of federal judges, on habeas corpus, to hold evidentiary hearings—that is, to try issues of fact anew—is a recurring one. The Court last dealt at length with it in *Brown v. Allen*, 344 U.S. 443 (1953), in opinions by Justices Reed and Frankfurter, both speaking for a majority of the Court. Since then, we have but touched upon it. We granted certiorari in the 1959 Term to consider the question, but ultimately disposed of the case on a more immediate ground. *Rogers v. Richmond*, 365 U.S. 534, 540 (1961). It has become apparent that [our] opinions do not provide answers for all aspects of the hearing problem for the lower federal courts, which have reached widely divergent, in fact often irreconcilable, results. We mean to express no opinion on the correctness of particular decisions. But we think that it is appropriate at this time to elaborate the considerations which ought properly to govern the grant or denial of evidentiary hearings in federal habeas corpus proceedings.

II

The broad considerations bearing upon the proper interpretation of the power of the federal courts on habeas corpus are reviewed at length in the Court's opinion in *Fay v. Noia*, 372 U.S. 391 (1963), and need not be repeated here. We pointed out there that the historic conception of the writ, anchored in the ancient common law and in our Constitution as an efficacious and imperative remedy for detentions of fundamental illegality, has remained constant to the present day. We pointed out, too, that the Act of February 5, 1867, which in extending the federal writ to state prisoners described the power of the federal courts to take testimony and determine the facts *de novo* in the largest terms, restated what apparently was the common-law understanding. *Fay v. Noia*. The hearing provisions of the 1867 Act remain substantially unchanged in the present codification. In construing the mandate of Congress, so plainly designed to afford a trial-type proceeding in federal court for state prisoners aggrieved by unconstitutional detentions, this Court has consistently upheld the power of the federal courts on habeas corpus to take evidence relevant to claims of such detention. "Since *Frank v. Mangum*, this Court has recognized that habeas corpus in the federal courts by one convicted of a criminal offense is a proper procedure 'to safeguard the liberty of all persons within the jurisdiction of the United States against infringement through any violation of the Constitution,' even though the events which were alleged to infringe did not appear upon the face of the record of his conviction." *Hawk v. Olson*, 326 U.S. 271, 274 (1945). *Brown v. Allen* and numerous other cases have recognized this.

The rule could not be otherwise. The whole history of the writ—its unique development—refutes a construction of the federal courts' habeas corpus powers that would assimilate their task to that of courts of appellate review. The function on habeas is different. It is to test by way of an original civil proceeding, independent of the normal channels of review of criminal judgments, the very gravest allegations. State prisoners are entitled to relief on federal habeas corpus only upon proving that their detention violates the fundamental liberties of the person, safeguarded against state action by the Federal Constitution. Simply because detention so obtained is intolerable, the opportunity for redress, which presupposes the opportunity to be heard, to argue and present evidence, must never be totally foreclosed. It is the typical, not the rare, case in which constitutional claims turn upon the resolution of contested factual issues. Thus a narrow view of the hearing power would totally subvert Congress' specific aim in passing the Act of February 5, 1867, of affording state prisoners a forum in the federal trial courts for the determination of claims of detention in violation of the Constitution. The language of Congress, the history of the writ, the decisions of this Court, all make clear that the power of inquiry on federal habeas corpus is plenary. Therefore, where an applicant for a writ of habeas corpus alleges facts which, if proved, would entitle him to relief, the federal court to which the application is made has the power to receive evidence and try the facts anew.

III

We turn now to the considerations which in certain cases may make exercise of that power mandatory. The appropriate standard—which must be considered to supersede, to the extent of any inconsistencies, the opinions in *Brown v. Allen*—is this: Where the facts are in dispute, the federal court in habeas corpus must hold an evidentiary hearing if the habeas applicant did not receive a full and fair evidentiary hearing in a state court, either at the time of the trial or in a collateral proceeding. In other words a federal evidentiary hearing is required unless the state-court trier of fact has after a full hearing reliably found the relevant facts.

It would be unwise to overly particularize this test. The federal district judges are more intimately familiar with state criminal justice, and with the trial of fact, than are we, and to their sound discretion must be left in very large part the administration of federal habeas corpus. But experience proves that a too general standard—the "exceptional circumstances" and "vital flaw" tests of the opinions in *Brown v. Allen*—does not serve adequately to explain the controlling criteria for the guidance of the federal habeas corpus courts. Some particularization may therefore be useful. We hold that a federal court must grant an evidentiary hearing to a habeas applicant under the following circumstances: If (1) the merits of the factual dispute were not resolved in the state hearing; (2) the state factual determination is not fairly supported by the record as a whole; (3) the fact-finding procedure employed by the state court was not adequate to afford a full and fair hearing; (4) there is a substantial allegation of newly discovered evidence; (5) the material facts were not adequately developed at the state-court hearing; or (6) for any reason it appears that the state trier of fact did not afford the habeas applicant a full and fair fact hearing.

(1) There cannot even be the semblance of a full and fair hearing unless the state court actually reached and decided the issues of fact tendered by the defendant. Thus, if no express findings of fact have been made by the state court, the District Court must initially determine whether the state court has impliedly found material facts. No relevant findings have been made unless the state court decided the constitutional claim tendered by the defendant on the merits. If relief has been denied in prior state collateral proceedings after a hearing but without opinion, it is often likely that the decision is based upon a procedural issue—that the claim is not collaterally cognizable—and not on the merits. On the other hand, if the prior state hearing occurred in the course of the original trial—for example, on a motion to suppress allegedly unlawful evidence, as in the instant case—it will usually be proper to assume that the claim was rejected on the merits.

If the state court has decided the merits of the claim but has made no express findings, it may still be possible for the District Court to reconstruct the findings of the state trier of fact, either because his view of the facts is plain from his opinion or because of other indicia. In some cases this will be impossible, and the Federal District Court will be compelled to hold a hearing.

Reconstruction is not possible if it is unclear whether the state finder applied correct constitutional standards in disposing of the claim. Under such circumstances the District Court cannot ascertain whether the state court found the law or the facts adversely to the petitioner's contentions. Since the decision of the state trier of fact may rest upon an error of law rather than an adverse determination of the facts, a hearing is compelled to ascertain the facts. Of course, the possibility of legal error may be eliminated in many situations if the fact finder has articulated the constitutional standards which he has applied. Furthermore, the coequal responsibilities of state and federal judges in the administration of federal constitutional law are such that we think the district judge may, in the ordinary case in which there has been no articulation, properly assume that the state trier of fact applied correct standards of federal law to the facts, in the absence of evidence, such as was present in *Rogers v. Richmond*, that there is reason to suspect that an incorrect standard was in fact applied. Thus, if third-degree methods of obtaining a confession are alleged and the state court refused to exclude the confession from evidence, the district judge may assume that the state trier found the facts against the petitioner, the law being, of course, that third-degree methods necessarily produce a coerced confession.

In any event, even if it is clear that the state trier of fact utilized the proper standard, a hearing is sometimes required if his decision presents a situation in which the "so-called facts and their constitutional significance [are] ... so blended that they cannot be severed in consideration." *Rogers v. Richmond*. *See Frank v. Mangum* (Holmes, J., dissenting). Unless the district judge can be reasonably certain that the state trier would have granted relief if he had believed petitioner's allegations, he cannot be sure that the state trier in denying relief disbelieved these allegations. If any combination of the facts alleged would prove a violation of constitutional rights and the issue of law on those facts presents a difficult or novel problem for decision, any hypothesis as to the relevant factual determinations of the state trier involves the purest speculation. The federal court cannot exclude the possibility that the trial judge believed facts which showed a deprivation of constitutional rights and yet (erroneously) concluded that relief should be denied. Under these circumstances it is impossible for the federal court to reconstruct the facts, and a hearing must be held.

(2) This Court has consistently held that state factual determinations not fairly supported by the record cannot be conclusive of federal rights. *Fiske v. Kansas*, 274 U.S. 380, 385 (1927); *Blackburn v. Alabama*, 361 U.S. 199, 208–209 (1960). Where the fundamental liberties of the person are claimed to have been infringed, we carefully scrutinize the state-court record. *See, e.g.*, *Blackburn v. Alabama*; *Moore v. Michigan*, 355 U.S. 155 (1957). The duty of the Federal District Court on habeas is no less exacting.

(3) However, the obligation of the Federal District Court to scrutinize the state-court findings of fact goes farther than this. Even if all the relevant facts were presented in the state-court hearing, it may be that the fact-finding procedure there employed was not adequate for reaching reasonably correct results. If the state trial judge has made serious procedural errors (respecting the claim pressed in federal habeas) in such things as the burden of proof, a federal hearing is required. Even where the procedure employed does not violate the Constitution, if it appears to be seriously inadequate for the ascertainment of the truth, it is the federal judge's duty to disregard the state findings and take evidence anew. Of course, there are procedural errors so grave as to require an appropriate order directing the habeas applicant's release unless the State grants a new trial forthwith. Our present concern is with errors which, although less serious, are nevertheless grave enough to deprive the state evidentiary hearing of its adequacy as a means of finally determining facts upon which constitutional rights depend.

(4) Where newly discovered evidence is alleged in a habeas application, evidence which could not reasonably have been presented to the state trier of facts, the federal court must grant an evidentiary hearing. Of course, such evidence must bear upon the constitutionality of the applicant's detention; the existence merely of newly discovered evidence relevant to the guilt of a state prisoner is not a ground for relief on federal habeas corpus. Also, the district judge is under no obligation to grant a hearing upon a frivolous or incredible allegation of newly discovered evidence.

(5) The conventional notion of the kind of newly discovered evidence which will permit the reopening of a judgment is, however, in some respects too limited to provide com-

plete guidance to the federal district judge on habeas. If, for any reason not attributable to the inexcusable neglect of petitioner, *see Fay v. Noia*, evidence crucial to the adequate consideration of the constitutional claim was not developed at the state hearing, a federal hearing is compelled. The standard of inexcusable default set down in *Fay v. Noia* adequately protects the legitimate state interest in orderly criminal procedure, for it does not sanction needless piecemeal presentation of constitutional claims in the form of deliberate by-passing of state procedures. *Compare Price v. Johnston*: "The primary purpose of a habeas corpus proceeding is to make certain that a man is not unjustly imprisoned. And if for some justifiable reason he was previously unable to assert his rights or was unaware of the significance of relevant facts, it is neither necessary nor reasonable to deny him all opportunity of obtaining judicial relief."

(6) Our final category is intentionally open-ended because we cannot here anticipate all the situations wherein a hearing is demanded. It is the province of the district judges first to determine such necessities in accordance with the general rules. The duty to try the facts anew exists in every case in which the state court has not after a full hearing reliably found the relevant facts.

IV

It is appropriate to add a few observations concerning the proper application of the test we have outlined.

First. The purpose of the test is to indicate the situations in which the holding of an evidentiary hearing is mandatory. In all other cases where the material facts are in dispute, the holding of such a hearing is in the discretion of the district judge. If he concludes that the habeas applicant was afforded a full and fair hearing by the state court resulting in reliable findings, he may, and ordinarily should, accept the facts as found in the hearing. But he need not. In every case he has the power, constrained only by his sound discretion, to receive evidence bearing upon the applicant's constitutional claim. There is every reason to be confident that federal district judges, mindful of their delicate role in the maintenance of proper federal-state relations, will not abuse that discretion. We have no fear that the hearing power will be used to subvert the integrity of state criminal justice or to waste the time of the federal courts in the trial of frivolous claims.

Second. Although the district judge may, where the state court has reliably found the relevant facts, defer to the state court's findings of fact, he may not defer to its findings of law. It is the district judge's duty to apply the applicable federal law to the state court fact findings independently. The state conclusions of law may not be given binding weight on habeas. That was settled in *Brown v. Allen* (opinion of Mr. Justice Frankfurter).

Third. A District Court sitting in habeas corpus clearly has the power to compel production of the complete state-court record. Ordinarily such a record—including the transcript of testimony (or if unavailable some adequate substitute, such as a narrative record), the pleadings, court opinions, and other pertinent documents—is indispensable to determining whether the habeas applicant received a full and fair state-court evidentiary hearing resulting in reliable findings. Of course, if because no record can be obtained the district judge has no way of determining whether a full and fair hearing which resulted in findings of relevant fact was vouchsafed, he must hold one. So also, there may be cases in which it is more convenient for the district judge to hold an evidentiary hearing forthwith rather than compel production of the record. It is clear that he has the power to do so.

Fourth. It rests largely with the federal district judges to give practical form to the principles announced today. We are aware that the too promiscuous grant of evidentiary hearings on habeas could both swamp the dockets of the District Courts and cause acute and unnecessary friction with state organs of criminal justice, while the too limited use of such hearings would allow many grave constitutional errors to go forever uncorrected. The accommodation of these competing factors must be made on the front line, by the district judges who are conscious of their paramount responsibility in this area.

V

Application of the foregoing principles to the particular litigation before us is not difficult. Townsend received an evidentiary hearing at his original trial, where his confession was held to be voluntary. Having exhausted his state remedies without receiving any further such hearing, he turned to the Federal District Court. Twice now, habeas corpus relief has been denied without an evidentiary hearing. On appeal from the second denial, the Court of Appeals held that "[o]n habeas corpus, the district court's inquiry is limited to a study of the undisputed portions of the record." That formulation was error. And we believe that on this record it was also error to refuse Townsend an evidentiary hearing in the District Court. The state trial judge rendered neither an opinion, conclusions of law, nor findings of fact. He made no charge to the jury setting forth the constitutional standards governing the admissibility of confessions. In short, there are no indicia which would indicate whether the trial judge applied the proper standard of federal law in ruling upon the admissibility of the confession. The Illinois Supreme Court opinion rendered at the time of direct appeal contains statements which might indicate that the court thought the confession was admissible if it satisfied the "coherency" standard. Under that test the confession would be admissible "[s]o long as the accused [was] ... capable of making a narrative of past events or of stating his own participation in the crime...." As we have indicated in Part I of this opinion, this test is not the proper one. Possibly the state trial judge believed that the admissibility of allegedly drug-induced confessions was to be judged by the "coherency" standard. However, even if this possibility could be eliminated, and it could be ascertained that correct standards of law were applied, it is still unclear whether the state trial judge would have excluded Townsend's confession as involuntary if he had believed the evidence which Townsend presented at the motion to suppress. The problem which the trial judge faced was novel and by no means without difficulty. We believe that the Federal District Court could not conclude that the state trial judge admitted the confession because he disbelieved the evidence which would show that it was involuntary. We believe that the findings of fact of the state trier could not be successfully reconstructed. We hold that, for this reason, an evidentiary hearing was compelled.

Furthermore, a crucial fact was not disclosed at the state-court hearing: that the substance injected into Townsend before he confessed has properties which may trigger statements in a legal sense involuntary. This fact was vital to whether his confession was the product of a free will and therefore admissible. To be sure, there was medical testimony as to the general properties of hyoscine, from which might have been inferred the conclusion that Townsend's power of resistance had been debilitated. But the crucially informative characterization of the drug, the characterization which would have enabled the judge and jury, mere laymen, intelligently to grasp the nature of the substance under inquiry, was inexplicably omitted from the medical experts' testimony. Under the circumstances, disclosure of the identity of hyoscine as a "truth serum" was indispensable to a fair, rounded, development of the material facts. And the medical experts' failure to testify fully cannot realistically be regarded as Townsend's inexcusable default. *See Fay v. Noia.*

On the remand it would not, of course, be sufficient for the District Court merely to hear new evidence and to read the state-court record. Where an unresolved factual dispute exists, demeanor evidence is a significant factor in adjudging credibility. And questions of credibility, of course, are basic to resolution of conflicts in testimony. To be sure, the state-court record is competent evidence, and either party may choose to rely solely upon the evidence contained in that record, but the petitioner, and the State, must be given the opportunity to present other testimonial and documentary evidence relevant to the disputed issues. This was not done here.

In deciding this case as we do, we do not mean to prejudge the truth of the allegations of the petition for habeas corpus. We decide only that on this record the federal district judge was obliged to hold a hearing.

Reversed and remanded.

[JUSTICE GOLDBERG wrote a concurring opinion, which is omitted. A dissenting opinion by JUSTICE STEWART, who was joined by JUSTICE CLARK, JUSTICE HARLAN, and JUSTICE WHITE, also is omitted.]

Notes

1. *Subsequent case history*

Charles Townsend was convicted and sentenced to death in Cook County, Illinois, in 1955. After several trips up and down the courts, the Seventh Circuit ultimately gave Illinois the option of resentencing Townsend, retrying him, or immediately releasing him. 452 F.2d 350, 363 (7th Cir. 1971).

Charles Townsend never was executed and is not incarcerated in Illinois presently. The Illinois Department of Corrections has no records that appear to match those of Charles Townsend, and the Cook County State's Attorney's Office has no further information on his case.

2. *Habeas v. appellate proceedings*

The majority expressly rejected the characterization of habeas corpus review as "appellate." Why? How is this relevant to the Court's emphasis that in habeas corpus the prisoner must be permitted to look behind the "face of the record of his conviction?"

3. *Relevance of innocence*

Assume that you represent a prisoner sentenced to life in prison. You are appointed at the completion of the state post-conviction process, and you hire an experienced investigator to look into the case in support of the federal habeas corpus petition you will be filing in the federal district court. Assume further that your investigator uncovers substantial evidence that your client was innocent. For example, she realizes that key fingerprints from the crime scene do not belong to your client and she quickly locates two credible alibi witnesses. Under *Townsend*, are you permitted a federal hearing in order to establish your client's innocence? What are your client's best options for success?

4. *Deliberate bypass*

Under *Townsend*, what constitutes a "deliberate bypass"? How does the Court evaluate whether a petitioner has deliberately bypassed state court proceedings?

5. *Mandatory hearings*

The *Townsend* decision unequivocally imposed a mandatory hearing system on lower federal courts. In essence, the decision dictated that material factual disputes must be resolved through a federal hearing. But the Court also recognized that it is not appropriate to hold a hearing in every case and noted that, to a certain extent, it was up to the "district judges to give practical form to the principles" announced in *Townsend*. Fourteen years later, in *Blackledge v. Allison*, 431 U.S. 63 (1977), the Court itself provided some guidance as to when a material question of fact actually exists—it is not the case that a prisoner simply may allege facts and earn an evidentiary hearing through which to prove them.

Assessing whether an evidentiary hearing was appropriate, the Court provided:

> This Court noted that the allegations, if proved, would entitle the defendant to relief, and that they raised an issue of fact that could not be resolved simply on the basis of an affidavit from the prosecutor denying the allegations. [Moreover, the] allegations "related primarily to purported occurrences outside the court-room and upon which the record could, therefore, cast no real light" and were not so "vague [or] conclusory" as to permit summary disposition.

Id. at 72–73.

The Court went on:

> The critical question is whether these allegations, when viewed against the record of the plea hearing, were so "palpably incredible," so "patently frivolous or false" as to warrant summary dismissal. In the light of the nature of the record of the proceeding at which the guilty plea was accepted, and of the ambiguous status of the process of plea bargaining at the time the guilty plea was made, we conclude that Allison's petition should not have been summarily dismissed.

Id. at 76.

The *Blackledge v. Allison* holding serves as an important gloss on the *Townsend* rule. Evidentiary hearings are required under *Townsend* when material questions of fact exist. However, when the questions of fact are so *patently frivolous* or *palpably incredible* as to be absurd, or when discovery renders the allegations of factual dispute a nullity, an evidentiary hearing should not be held.

Townsend represents the high-water mark for prisoners in terms of access to federal hearings. If an unencumbered *Townsend* continued to govern, then the law regarding the availability of federal hearings likely would be very well sorted out at this point. Presently, however, the law in this field is dominated by confusion over what aspects of *Townsend*, if any, continue to govern. The confusion regarding the continued viability of *Townsend* has come in two distinct waves: the first was judicial (*Keeney*), in 1992, and the second was legislative (AEDPA), in 1996. The retreat from *Townsend* started in *Keeney v. Tamayo-Reyes*.

Keeney v. Tamayo-Reyes

504 U.S. 1 (1992)

JUSTICE WHITE delivered the opinion of the Court.

Respondent is a Cuban immigrant with little education and almost no knowledge of English. In 1984, he was charged with murder arising from the stabbing death of a man who had allegedly attempted to intervene in a confrontation between respondent and his girlfriend in a bar.

Respondent was provided with a defense attorney and interpreter. The attorney recommended to respondent that he plead *nolo contendere* to first-degree manslaughter. Respondent signed a plea form that explained in English the rights he was waiving by entering the plea. The state court held a plea hearing, at which petitioner was represented by counsel and his interpreter. The judge asked the attorney and interpreter if they had explained to respondent the rights in the plea form and the consequences of his plea; they responded in the affirmative. The judge then explained to respondent, in English, the rights he would waive by his plea, and asked the interpreter to translate. Respondent indicated that he understood his rights and still wished to plead *nolo contendere*. The judge accepted his plea.

Later, respondent brought a collateral attack on the plea in a state-court proceeding. He alleged his plea had not been knowing and intelligent and therefore was invalid because his translator had not translated accurately and completely for him the *mens rea* element of manslaughter. He also contended that he did not understand the purposes of the plea form or the plea hearing. He contended that he did not know he was pleading no contest to manslaughter, but rather that he thought he was agreeing to be tried for manslaughter.

After a hearing, the state court dismissed respondent's petition, finding that respondent was properly served by his trial interpreter and that the interpreter correctly, fully, and accurately translated the communications between respondent and his attorney. The State Court of Appeals affirmed, and the State Supreme Court denied review.

Respondent then entered Federal District Court seeking a writ of habeas corpus. Respondent contended that the material facts concerning the translation were not adequately developed at the state-court hearing, implicating the fifth circumstance of *Townsend v. Sain*, 372 U.S. 293, 313 (1963), and sought a federal evidentiary hearing on whether his *nolo contendere* plea was unconstitutional. The District Court found that the failure to develop the critical facts relevant to his federal claim was attributable to inexcusable neglect and that no evidentiary hearing was required. Respondent appealed.

The Court of Appeals for the Ninth Circuit recognized that the alleged failure to translate the *mens rea* element of first-degree manslaughter, if proved, would be a basis for overturning respondent's plea and determined that material facts had not been adequately developed in the state postconviction court, apparently due to the negligence of postconviction counsel. The court held that *Townsend v. Sain* and *Fay v. Noia*, 372 U.S. 391 (1963), required an evidentiary hearing in the District Court unless respondent had deliberately bypassed the orderly procedure of the state courts. Because counsel's negligent failure to develop the facts did not constitute a deliberate bypass, the Court of Appeals ruled that respondent was entitled to an evidentiary hearing on the question whether the *mens rea* element of first-degree manslaughter was properly explained to him.

We granted certiorari to decide whether the deliberate bypass standard is the correct standard for excusing a habeas petitioner's failure to develop a material fact in state-court proceedings. We reverse.

Because the holding of *Townsend v. Sain* that *Fay v. Noia*'s deliberate bypass standard is applicable in a case like this had not been reversed, it is quite understandable that the Court of Appeals applied that standard in this case. However, in light of more recent decisions of this Court, *Townsend*'s holding in this respect must be overruled. *Fay v. Noia* was itself a case where the habeas petitioner had not taken advantage of state remedies by failing to appeal—a procedural default case. Since that time, however, this Court has rejected the deliberate bypass standard in state procedural default cases and has applied instead a standard of cause and prejudice.

* * *

The concerns that motivated the rejection of the deliberate bypass standard in *Wainwright*, *Coleman*, and other cases are equally applicable to this case. As in cases of state procedural default, application of the cause-and-prejudice standard to excuse a state prisoner's failure to develop material facts in state court will appropriately accommodate concerns of finality, comity, judicial economy, and channeling the resolution of claims into the most appropriate forum.

Applying the cause-and-prejudice standard in cases like this will obviously contribute to the finality of convictions, for requiring a federal evidentiary hearing solely on the basis of a habeas petitioner's negligent failure to develop facts in state-court proceedings dramatically increases the opportunities to relitigate a conviction.

Similarly, encouraging the full factual development in state court of a claim that state courts committed constitutional error advances comity by allowing a coordinate jurisdiction to correct its own errors in the first instance. It reduces the "inevitable friction" that results when a federal habeas court "overturn[s] either the factual or legal conclusions reached by the state-court system." *Sumner v. Mata*, 449 U.S. 539, 550 (1981).

Also, by ensuring that full factual development takes place in the earlier, state-court proceedings, the cause-and-prejudice standard plainly serves the interest of judicial economy. It is hardly a good use of scarce judicial resources to duplicate factfinding in federal court merely because a petitioner has negligently failed to take advantage of opportunities in state-court proceedings.

Furthermore, ensuring that full factual development of a claim takes place in state court channels the resolution of the claim to the most appropriate forum. The state court is the appropriate forum for resolution of factual issues in the first instance, and creating incentives for the deferral of factfinding to later federal-court proceedings can only degrade the accuracy and efficiency of judicial proceedings. This is fully consistent with, and gives meaning to, the requirement of exhaustion. The Court has long held that state prisoners must exhaust state remedies before obtaining federal habeas relief. *Ex parte Royall*, 117 U.S. 241 (1886). The requirement that state prisoners exhaust state remedies before a writ of habeas corpus is granted by a federal court is now incorporated in the federal habeas statute. Exhaustion means more than notice. In requiring exhaustion of a federal claim in state court, Congress surely meant that exhaustion be serious and meaningful.

The purpose of exhaustion is not to create a procedural hurdle on the path to federal habeas court, but to channel claims into an appropriate forum, where meritorious claims may be vindicated and unfounded litigation obviated before resort to federal court. Comity concerns dictate that the requirement of exhaustion is not satisfied by the mere statement of a federal claim in state court. Just as the State must afford the petitioner a full and fair hearing on his federal claim, so must the petitioner afford the State a full and fair opportunity to address and resolve the claim on the merits.

Finally, it is worth noting that applying the cause-and-prejudice standard in this case also advances uniformity in the law of habeas corpus. There is no good reason to maintain in one area of habeas law a standard that has been rejected in the area in which it was principally enunciated. And little can be said for holding a habeas petitioner to one standard for failing to bring a claim in state court and excusing the petitioner under another, lower standard for failing to develop the factual basis of that claim in the same forum. A different rule could mean that a habeas petitioner would not be excused for negligent failure to object to the introduction of the prosecution's evidence, but nonetheless would be excused for negligent failure to introduce any evidence of his own to support a constitutional claim.

Respondent Tamayo-Reyes is entitled to an evidentiary hearing if he can show cause for his failure to develop the facts in state-court proceedings and actual prejudice resulting from that failure. We also adopt the narrow exception to the cause-and-prejudice requirement: A habeas petitioner's failure to develop a claim in state-court proceedings will be excused and a hearing mandated if he can show that a fundamental miscarriage of justice would result from failure to hold a federal evidentiary hearing. *Cf. McCleskey v. Zant*, 499 U.S. at 494.

The State concedes that a remand to the District Court is appropriate in order to afford respondent the opportunity to bring forward evidence establishing cause and prejudice, and we agree that respondent should have that opportunity. Accordingly, the decision of the Court of Appeals is reversed, and the cause is remanded to the District Court for further proceedings consistent with this opinion.

So ordered.

JUSTICE O'CONNOR, with whom JUSTICE BLACKMUN, JUSTICE STEVENS, and JUSTICE KENNEDY join, dissenting.

Under the guise of overruling "a remnant of a decision" and achieving "uniformity in the law," the Court has changed the law of habeas corpus in a fundamental way by effectively overruling cases decided long before *Townsend v. Sain*. I do not think this change is supported by the line of our recent procedural default cases upon which the Court relies: In my view, the balance of state and federal interests regarding whether a federal court will consider a claim raised on habeas cannot be simply lifted and transposed to the different question whether, once the court will consider the claim, it should hold an evidentiary hearing. Moreover, I do not think the Court's decision can be reconciled with 28 U.S.C. § 2254(d), a statute Congress enacted three years after *Townsend*.

I

Jose Tamayo-Reyes' habeas petition stated that because he does not speak English he pleaded *nolo contendere* to manslaughter without any understanding of what "manslaughter" means. If this assertion is true, his conviction was unconstitutionally obtained, and Tamayo-Reyes would be entitled to a writ of habeas corpus. Despite the Court's attempt to characterize his allegation as a technical quibble—"his translator had not translated accurately and completely for him the *mens rea* element of manslaughter"—this much is not in dispute. Tamayo-Reyes has alleged a fact that, if true, would entitle him to the relief he seeks.

Tamayo-Reyes initially, and properly, challenged the voluntariness of his plea in a petition for postconviction relief in state court. The court held a hearing, after which it found that "[p]etitioner's plea of guilty was knowingly and voluntarily entered." Yet the record of the postconviction hearing hardly inspires confidence in the accuracy of this determination. Tamayo-Reyes was the only witness to testify, but his attorney did not ask him whether his interpreter had translated "manslaughter" for him. Counsel instead introduced the deposition testimony of the interpreter, who admitted that he had translated "manslaughter" only as "less than murder." No witnesses capable of assessing the interpreter's performance were called; the attorney instead tried to direct the court's attention to various sections of the interpreter's deposition and attempted to point out where the interpreter had erred. When the prosecutor objected to this discussion on the ground that counsel was not qualified as an expert witness, his "presentation of the issue quickly disintegrated." The state court had no other relevant evidence before it when it determined that Tamayo-Reyes actually understood the charge to which he was pleading.

Contrary to the impression conveyed by this Court's opinion, the question whether a federal court should defer to this sort of dubious "factfinding" in addressing a habeas corpus petition is one with a long history behind it, a history that did not begin with *Townsend v. Sain*.

II

A

The availability and scope of habeas corpus have changed over the writ's long history, but one thing has remained constant: Habeas corpus is not an appellate proceeding, but rather an original civil action in a federal court. *See, e.g., Browder v. Director, Dept. of Corrections of Ill.*, 434 U.S. 257, 269 (1978). It was settled over a hundred years ago that "[t]he prosecution against [a criminal defendant] is a criminal prosecution, but the writ of habeas corpus ... is not a proceeding in that prosecution. On the contrary, it is a new suit brought by him to enforce a civil right." *Ex parte Tom Tong*, 108 U.S. 556, 559–60 (1883). Any possible doubt about this point has been removed by the statutory procedure Congress has provided for the disposition of habeas corpus petitions, a procedure including such nonappellate functions as the allegation of facts, 28 U.S.C. § 2242, the taking of depositions and the propounding of interrogatories, § 2246, the introduction of documentary evidence, § 2247, and, of course, the determination of facts at evidentiary hearings, § 2254(d).

To be sure, habeas corpus has its own peculiar set of hurdles a petitioner must clear before his claim is properly presented to the district court. The petitioner must, in general, exhaust available state remedies, § 2254(b), avoid procedural default, *Coleman v. Thompson*, 501 U.S. 722 (1991), not abuse the writ, *McCleskey v. Zant*, 499 U.S. 467 (1991), and not seek retroactive application of a new rule of law, *Teague v. Lane*, 489 U.S. 288 (1989). For much of our history, the hurdles were even higher. *See, e.g., Ex parte Watkins*, 28 U.S. (3 Pet.) 193, 203 (1830) (habeas corpus available only to challenge jurisdiction of trial court). But once they have been surmounted—once the claim is properly before the district court—a habeas petitioner, like any civil litigant, has had a right to a hearing where one is necessary to prove the facts supporting his claim. Thus when we observed in *Townsend v. Sain* that "the opportunity for redress ... presupposes the opportunity to be heard, to argue and present evidence," we were saying nothing new. We were merely restating what had long been our understanding of the method by which contested factual issues raised on habeas should be resolved.

Habeas corpus has always differed from ordinary civil litigation, however, in one important respect: The doctrine of res judicata has never been thought to apply. *See, e.g., Brown v. Allen*, 344 U.S. 443 (1953). A state prisoner is not precluded from raising a federal claim on habeas that has already been rejected by the state courts. This is not to say that state court factfinding is entitled to no weight, or that every state prisoner has the opportunity to relitigate facts found against him by the state courts. Concerns of federalism and comity have pushed us from this extreme just as the importance of the writ has repelled us from the opposite extreme, represented by the strict application of res judicata. Instead, we have consistently occupied the middle ground. Even before *Townsend*, federal courts deferred to state court findings of fact where the federal district judge was satisfied that the state court had fairly considered the issues and the evidence and had reached a satisfactory result. *See, e.g., Brown*. But where such was not the case, the federal court entertaining the habeas petition would examine the facts anew. *See, e.g., Ex parte Hawk*. In *Brown*, we explained that a hearing may be dispensed with only "[w]here the record of the application affords an adequate opportunity to weigh the sufficiency of the allegations and the evidence, and no unusual circumstances calling for a hearing are presented."

Townsend "did not launch the Court in any new directions," Weisselberg, Evidentiary Hearings in Federal Habeas Corpus Cases, 1990 BYU L. Rev. 131, 150, but it clarified how the district court should measure the adequacy of the state court proceeding. *Townsend* specified six circumstances in which one could not be confident that "the state-court trier of fact has after a full hearing reliably found the relevant facts." * * *

That these principles marked no significant departure from our prior understanding of the writ is evident from the view expressed by the four dissenters, who had "no quarrel with the Court's statement of the basic governing principle which should determine whether a hearing is to be had in a federal habeas corpus proceeding," but disagreed only with the Court's attempt "to erect detailed hearing standards for the myriad situations presented by federal habeas corpus applications." *Townsend* thus did not alter the federal courts' practice of holding an evidentiary hearing unless the state court had fairly considered the relevant evidence.

The Court expressed concern in *Townsend* that a petitioner might abuse the fifth circumstance described in the opinion, by deliberately withholding evidence from the state factfinder in the hope of finding a more receptive forum in a federal court. To discourage this sort of disrespect for state proceedings, the Court held that such a petitioner would not be entitled to a hearing. The *Townsend* opinion did not need to address this concern in much detail, because a similar issue was discussed at greater length in another case decided the same day, *Fay v. Noia*. The *Townsend* opinion thus merely referred the reader to the discussion in *Fay*, where a similar exception was held to bar a state prisoner from habeas relief where the prisoner had intentionally committed a procedural default in state court. *See Townsend*, 372 U.S. at 317.

Nearly 30 years later, the Court implies that *Fay* and *Townsend* must stand or fall together. But this is not so: The *Townsend* Court did not suggest that the issues in *Townsend* and *Fay* were identical, or that they were so similar that logic required an identical answer to each. *Townsend* did not purport to rely on *Fay* as authority; it merely referred to *Fay*'s discussion as a shorthand device to avoid repeating similar analysis. Indeed, reliance on *Fay* as authority would have been unnecessary. *Townsend* was essentially an elaboration of our prior cases regarding the holding of hearings in federal habeas cases; *Fay* represented an overruling of our prior cases regarding procedural defaults. *See Coleman v. Thompson*, 501 U.S. at 744–47; *Wainwright v. Sykes*, 433 U.S. 72, 82 (1977).

As the Court recognizes, we have applied *Townsend*'s analysis ever since. But we have not, in my view, been unjustifiably clinging to a poorly reasoned precedent. While we properly abandoned *Fay* because it was inconsistent with prior cases that represented a better-reasoned balance of state and federal interests, the same cannot be said of *Townsend*.

The Court today holds that even when the reliability of state factfinding is doubtful because crucial evidence was not presented to the state trier of fact, a habeas petitioner is ordinarily not entitled to an opportunity to prove the facts necessary to his claim. This holding, of course, directly overrules a portion of *Townsend*, but more than that, I think it departs significantly from the pre-*Townsend* law of habeas corpus. Even before *Townsend*, when a habeas petitioner's claim was properly before a federal court, and when the accurate resolution of that claim depended on proof of facts that had been resolved against the petitioner in an unreliable state proceeding, the petitioner was entitled to his day in federal court. As Justice Holmes wrote for the Court, in a case where the state courts had rejected—under somewhat suspicious circumstances—the petitioner's allegation that his trial had been dominated by an angry mob: "[I]t does not seem to us sufficient to allow a Judge of the United States to escape the duty of examining the facts for himself when if true as alleged they make the trial absolutely void." *Moore*. The class of petitioners eligible to present claims on habeas may have been narrower in days gone by, and the class of claims one might present may have been smaller, but once the claim was properly before the court, the right to a hearing was not construed as narrowly as the Court construes it today.

B

Instead of looking to the history of the right to an evidentiary hearing, the Court simply borrows the cause and prejudice standard from a series of our recent habeas corpus cases. *Ante*. All but one of these cases address the question of when a habeas claim is properly before a federal court despite the petitioner's procedural default. The remaining case addresses the issue of a petitioner's abuse of the writ. *See McCleskey v. Zant*, 499 U.S. 467 (1991). These cases all concern the question whether the federal court will consider the merits of the claim, that is, whether the court has the authority to upset a judgment affirmed on direct appeal. So far as this threshold inquiry is concerned, our respect for state procedural rules and the need to discourage abuse of the writ provide the justification for the cause and prejudice standard. As we have said in the former context: "[T]he Great Writ imposes special costs on our federal system. The States possess primary authority for defining and enforcing the criminal law. In criminal trials they also hold the initial responsibility for vindicating constitutional rights. Federal intrusions into state criminal trials frustrate both the States' sovereign power to punish offenders and their good-faith attempts to honor constitutional rights." *Engle* [*v. Isaac*, 456 U.S. 107] at 128 (1982).

The question we are considering here is quite different. Here, the Federal District Court has already determined that it will consider the claimed constitutional violation; the only question is how the court will go about it. When it comes to determining whether a hearing is to be held to resolve a claim that is already properly before a federal court, the federalism concerns underlying our procedural default cases are diminished somewhat. By this point, our concern is less with encroaching on the territory of the state courts than it is with managing the territory of the federal courts in a manner that will best implement their responsibility to consider habeas petitions. Our adoption of a cause and prejudice standard to resolve the first concern should not cause us reflexively to adopt the same standard to resolve the second. Federalism, comity, and finality are all advanced by declining to permit relitigation of claims in federal court in certain circumstances; these interests are less significantly advanced, once relitigation properly occurs, by permitting district courts to resolve claims based on an incomplete record.

III

The Court's decision today cannot be reconciled with subsection (d) of 28 U.S.C. § 2254, which Congress enacted only three years after we decided *Townsend*. Subsection (d) provides that state court factfinding "shall be presumed to be correct, unless the applicant shall establish" one of eight listed circumstances. Most of these circumstances are taken word for word from *Townsend*, including the one at issue here; § 2254(d)(3) renders the presumption of correctness inapplicable where "the material facts were not adequately developed at the State court hearing." The effect of the presumption is to augment the habeas petitioner's burden of proof. Where state factfinding is presumed correct, the petitioner must establish the state court's error "by convincing evidence"; where state factfinding is not presumed correct, the petitioner must prove the facts necessary to support his claim by only a preponderance of the evidence. *Sumner v. Mata*, 449 U.S. 539, 551 (1981).

Section 2254(d) is not, in the strict sense, a codification of our holding in *Townsend*. The listed circumstances in *Townsend* are those in which a hearing must be held; the nearly identical listed circumstances in § 2254(d) are those in which facts found by a state court are not presumed correct. But the two are obviously intertwined. If a habeas petitioner fulfills one of the *Townsend* requirements he will be entitled to a hearing, and by virtue of fulfilling a *Townsend* requirement he will necessarily have also fulfilled one of the § 2254(d) requirements, so that at his hearing the presumption of correctness will not apply. On the other hand, if the petitioner has not fulfilled one of the *Townsend* requirements he will generally not have fulfilled the corresponding § 2254(d) requirement either, so he will be entitled neither to a hearing nor to an exception from the presumption of correctness. *Townsend* and § 2254(d) work hand in hand: Where a petitioner has a right to a hearing he must prove facts by a preponderance of the evidence, but where he has no right to a hearing he must prove facts by the higher standard of convincing evidence. Without the opportunity for a hearing, it is safe to assume that this higher standard will be unattainable for most petitioners.

In enacting a statute that so closely parallels *Townsend*, Congress established a procedural framework that relies upon *Townsend*'s continuing validity. In general, therefore, overruling *Townsend* would frustrate the evident intent of Congress that the question of when a hearing is to be held should be governed by the same standards as the question of when a federal court should defer to state court factfinding. In particular, the Court's adoption of a "cause and prejudice" standard for determining whether the material facts were adequately developed in state proceedings will frustrate Congress' intent with respect to that *Townsend* circumstance's statutory analog.

For a case to fit within this *Townsend* circumstance but none of *Townsend*'s other circumstances, the case will very likely be like this one, where the material facts were not developed because of attorney error. Any other reason the material facts might not have been developed, such as that they were unknown at the time or that the State denied a full and fair opportunity to develop them, will almost certainly be covered by one of *Townsend*'s other circumstances. *See Townsend*, 372 U.S. at 313. We have already held that attorney error short of constitutionally ineffective assistance of counsel does not amount to "cause." *See Murray v. Carrier*, 477 U.S. at 488. As a result, the practical effect of the Court's ruling today will be that for a case to fall within *Townsend*'s fifth circumstance but no other—for a petitioner to be entitled to a hearing on the ground that the material facts were not adequately developed in state court but on no other ground—the petitioner's attorney must have rendered constitutionally ineffective assistance in presenting facts to the state factfinder.

This effect is more than a little ironic. Where the state factfinding occurs at the trial itself, counsel's ineffectiveness will not just entitle the petitioner to a hearing—it will entitle the petitioner to a new trial. Where, as in this case, the state factfinding occurs at a postconviction proceeding, the petitioner has no constitutional right to the effective assistance of counsel, so counsel's poor performance can never constitute "cause" under the cause and prejudice standard. *Coleman v. Thompson*, 501 U.S. at 752. After today's decision, the only petitioners entitled to a hearing under *Townsend*'s fifth circumstance are the very people who do not need one, because they will have already obtained a new trial or because they will already be entitled to a hearing under one of the other circumstances. The Court has thus rendered unusable the portion of *Townsend* requiring hearings where the material facts were not adequately developed in state court.

As noted above, the fact that § 2254(d)(3) uses language identical to the language we used in *Townsend* strongly suggests that Congress presumed the continued existence of this portion of *Townsend*. Moreover, the Court's application of a cause and prejudice standard creates a conundrum regarding how to interpret § 2254(d)(3). If a cause and prejudice standard applies to § 2254(d)(3) as well as *Townsend*'s fifth circumstance, then the Court has rendered § 2254(d)(3) superfluous for the same reason this part of *Townsend* has become superfluous. While we may deprive portions of our own prior decisions of any effect, we generally may not, of course, do the same with portions of statutes. On the other hand, if a cause and prejudice standard does not apply to § 2254(d)(3), we will have uncoupled the statute from the case it was intended to follow, and there will likely be instances where a petitioner will be entitled to an exception from the presumption of correctness but will not be entitled to a hearing. This result does not accord with the evident intent of Congress that the first inquiry track the second. Reconciliation of these two questions is now left to the district courts, who still possess the discretion, which has not been removed by today's opinion, to hold hearings even where they are not mandatory. *See Townsend.*

For these reasons, I think § 2254(d) presumes the continuing validity of our decision in *Townsend*, including the portion of the decision that recognized a "deliberate bypass" exception to a petitioner's right to a hearing where the material facts were not adequately developed in the state court.

Jose Tamayo-Reyes alleges that he pleaded *nolo contendere* to a crime he did not understand. He has exhausted state remedies, has committed no procedural default, has properly presented his claim to a Federal District Court in his first petition for a writ of habeas corpus, and would be entitled to a hearing under the standard set forth in *Townsend.* Given that his claim is properly before the District Court, I would not cut off his right to prove his claim at a hearing. I respectfully dissent.

JUSTICE KENNEDY, dissenting.

By definition, the cases within the ambit of the Court's holding are confined to those in which the factual record developed in the state-court proceedings is inadequate to resolve the legal question. I should think those cases will be few in number. *Townsend v. Sain* has been the law for almost 30 years and there is no clear evidence that this particular classification of habeas proceedings has burdened the dockets of the federal courts. And in my view, the concept of factual inadequacy comprehends only those petitions with respect to which there is a realistic possibility that an evidentiary hearing will make a difference in the outcome. This serves to narrow the number of cases in a further respect and to ensure that they are the ones, as JUSTICE O'CONNOR points out, in which we have valid concerns with constitutional error.

Our recent decisions in *Coleman v. Thompson*, *McCleskey v. Zant*, and *Teague v. Lane* serve to protect the integrity of the writ, curbing its abuse and ensuring that the legal questions presented are ones which, if resolved against the State, can invalidate a final judgment. So we consider today only those habeas actions which present questions federal courts are bound to decide in order to protect constitutional rights. We ought not to take steps which diminish the likelihood that those courts will base their legal decision on an accurate assessment of the facts. For these reasons and all those set forth by JUSTICE O'CONNOR, I dissent from the opinion and judgment of the Court.

Notes

1. *Subsequent case history*

Jose Tamayo-Reyes was discharged from custody in November 1993.

2. *Replacing "deliberate bypass" with "cause-and-prejudice"*

In her dissent, Justice O'Connor stated that "[u]nder the guise of overruling 'a remnant of a decision' and achieving 'uniformity in the law,' the Court has changed the law of habeas corpus in a fundamental way by effectively overruling cases decided long before

Townsend v. Sain." In your analysis, what concerns appear to have influenced the Court's decision to replace *Fay* and *Townsend*'s deliberate bypass standard with a cause-and-prejudice analysis?

3. *Discretionary hearings after Keeney*

Does the *Keeney* decision limit a federal district court's ability to order a discretionary hearing?

C. AEDPA's Role in Limiting Evidentiary Hearings and Requiring Deference to State Court Findings of Fact

There are three principle provisions of AEDPA addressing the degree and type of deference owed to state court factual findings: § 2254(d)(2), § 2254(e)(1), and § 2254(e)(2)). In *Michael Williams v. Taylor*, the Court attempted to make sense of some aspects of these new statutory limitations. In particular, *Williams* addressed the impact of AEDPA's statutory regime (below) on the right to a hearing under *Townsend v. Sain*.

§ 2254(d)(2)

(d) An application for a writ of habeas corpus on behalf of a person in custody pursuant to the judgment of a State court shall not be granted with respect to any claim that was adjudicated on the merits in State court proceedings unless the adjudication of the claim—

(1) resulted in a decision that was contrary to, or involved an unreasonable application of, clearly established Federal law, as determined by the Supreme Court of the United States; or

(2) resulted in a decision that was based on an unreasonable determination of the facts in light of the evidence presented in the State court proceeding.

2254(e)(1)–(2)

(e)(1) In a proceeding instituted by an application for a writ of habeas corpus by a person in custody pursuant to the judgment of a State court, a determination of a factual issue made by a State court shall be presumed to be correct. The applicant shall have the burden of rebutting the presumption of correctness by clear and convincing evidence.

(2) If the applicant has failed to develop the factual basis of a claim in State court proceedings, the court shall not hold an evidentiary hearing on the claim unless the applicant shows that—

(A) the claim relies on—

(i) a new rule of constitutional law, made retroactive to cases on collateral review by the Supreme Court, that was previously unavailable; or

(ii) a factual predicate that could not have been previously discovered through the exercise of due diligence; and

(B) the facts underlying the claim would be sufficient to establish by clear and convincing evidence that but for constitutional error, no reasonable factfinder would have found the applicant guilty of the underlying offense.

Michael Williams v. Taylor

529 U.S. 420 (2000)

JUSTICE KENNEDY delivered the opinion of the Court.

Petitioner Michael Wayne Williams received a capital sentence for the murders of Morris Keller, Jr., and Keller's wife, Mary Elizabeth. Petitioner later sought a writ of habeas corpus in federal court. Accompanying his petition was a request for an evidentiary hearing on constitutional claims which, he alleged, he had been unable to develop in state-court proceedings. The question in this case is whether 28 U.S.C. § 2254(e)(2), as amended by the Antiterrorism and Effective Death Penalty Act of 1996 (AEDPA), bars the evidentiary hearing petitioner seeks. If petitioner "has failed to develop the factual basis of [his] claim[s] in State court proceedings," his case is subject to § 2254(e)(2), and he may not receive a hearing because he concedes his inability to satisfy the statute's further stringent conditions for excusing the deficiency.

I

On the evening of February 27, 1993, Verena Lozano James dropped off petitioner and his friend Jeffrey Alan Cruse near a local store in a rural area of Cumberland County, Virginia. The pair planned to rob the store's employees and customers using a .357 revolver petitioner had stolen in the course of a quadruple murder and robbery he had committed two months earlier. Finding the store closed, petitioner and Cruse walked to the Kellers' home. Petitioner was familiar with the couple, having grown up down the road from where they lived. He told Cruse they would have "a couple thousand dollars." Cruse, who had been holding the .357, handed the gun to petitioner and knocked on the door. When Mr. Keller opened the door, petitioner pointed the gun at him as the two intruders forced their way inside. Petitioner and Cruse forced Mr. Keller to the kitchen, where they discovered Mrs. Keller. Petitioner ordered the captives to remove their clothing. While petitioner kept guard on the Kellers, Cruse searched the house for money and other valuables. He found a .38-caliber handgun and bullets. Upon Cruse's return to the kitchen, petitioner had Cruse tie their captives with telephone cords. The Kellers were confined to separate closets while the intruders continued ransacking the house.

When they gathered all they wanted, petitioner and Cruse decided to rape Mrs. Keller. With Mrs. Keller pleading with them not to hurt her or her husband, petitioner raped her. Cruse did the same. Petitioner then ordered the Kellers to shower and dress and "take a walk" with him and Cruse. As they were leaving, petitioner told Mrs. Keller he and Cruse were going to burn down the house. Mrs. Keller begged to be allowed to retrieve her marriage license, which she did, guarded by petitioner.

As the prosecution later presented the case, details of the murders were as follows. Petitioner, now carrying the .38, and Cruse, carrying the .357, took the Kellers to a thicket down a dirt road from the house. With petitioner standing behind Mr. Keller and Cruse behind Mrs. Keller, petitioner told Cruse, "We'll shoot at the count of three." At the third count, petitioner shot Mr. Keller in the head, and Mr. Keller collapsed to the ground. Cruse did not shoot Mrs. Keller at the same moment. Saying "he didn't want to leave no witnesses," petitioner urged Cruse to shoot Mrs. Keller. Cruse fired one shot into her head. Despite his wound, Mr. Keller stood up, but petitioner shot him a second time. To ensure the Kellers were dead, petitioner shot each of them two or three more times.

After returning to the house and loading the stolen property into the Kellers' jeep, petitioner and Cruse set fire to the house and drove the jeep to Fredericksburg, Virginia, where they sold some of the property. They threw the remaining property and the .357 revolver into the Rappahannock River and set fire to the jeep.

* * *

Petitioner was arrested and charged with robbery, abduction, rape, and the capital murders of the Kellers. At trial in January 1994, Cruse was the Commonwealth's main witness. He recounted the murders as we have just described. Cruse testified petitioner raped Mrs. Keller, shot Mr. Keller at least twice, and shot Mrs. Keller several times after she had been felled by Cruse's bullet. He also described petitioner as the mastermind of the murders. The circumstances of the first plea agreement between the Commonwealth and Cruse and its revocation were disclosed to the jury. Testifying on his own behalf, petitioner admitted he was the first to shoot Mr. Keller and it was his idea to rob the store and set fire to the house. He denied, however, raping or shooting Mrs. Keller, and claimed to have shot Mr. Keller only once. Petitioner blamed Cruse for the remaining shots and disputed some other parts of Cruse's testimony.

The jury convicted petitioner on all counts. After considering the aggravating and mitigating evidence presented during the sentencing phase, the jury found the aggravating circumstances of future dangerousness and vileness of the crimes and recommended a death sentence. The trial court imposed the recommended sentence. The Supreme Court of Virginia affirmed petitioner's convictions and sentence, and we denied certiorari. In a separate proceeding, Cruse pleaded guilty to the capital murder of Mrs. Keller and the first-degree murder of Mr. Keller. After the prosecution asked the sentencing court to spare his life because of his testimony against petitioner, Cruse was sentenced to life imprisonment.

Petitioner filed a habeas petition in state court alleging, in relevant part, that the Commonwealth failed to disclose a second agreement it had reached with Cruse after the first one was revoked. The new agreement, petitioner alleged, was an informal undertaking by the prosecution to recommend a life sentence in exchange for Cruse's testimony. Finding no merit to petitioner's claims, the Virginia Supreme Court dismissed the habeas petition, and we again denied certiorari.

Petitioner filed a habeas petition in the United States District Court for the Eastern District of Virginia on November 20, 1996. In addition to his claim regarding the alleged undisclosed agreement between the Commonwealth and Cruse, the petition raised three claims relevant to questions now before us. First, petitioner claimed the prosecution had violated *Brady v. Maryland*, 373 U.S. 83 (1963), in failing to disclose a report of a confidential pre-trial psychiatric examination of Cruse. Second, petitioner alleged his trial was rendered unfair by the seating of a juror who at *voir dire* had not revealed possible sources of bias. Finally, petitioner alleged one of the prosecutors committed misconduct in failing to reveal his knowledge of the juror's possible bias.

The District Court granted an evidentiary hearing on the undisclosed agreement and the allegations of juror bias and prosecutorial misconduct but denied a hearing on the psychiatric report. Before the evidentiary hearing could be held, the Commonwealth filed an application for an emergency stay and a petition for a writ of mandamus and prohibition in the Court of Appeals. The Commonwealth argued that petitioner's evidentiary hearing was prohibited by 28 U.S.C. § 2254(e)(2). A divided panel of the Court of Appeals granted the emergency stay and remanded for the District Court to apply the statute to petitioner's request for an evidentiary hearing. On remand, the District Court vacated its order granting an evidentiary hearing and dismissed the petition, having determined petitioner could not satisfy § 2254(e)(2)'s requirements.

The Court of Appeals affirmed. It first considered petitioner's argument that § 2254(e)(2) did not apply to his case because he had been diligent in attempting to develop his claims in state court. * * * The court held, however, that petitioner had not been diligent and so had "failed to develop" in state court the factual bases of his *Brady*, juror bias, and prosecutorial misconduct claims. The Court of Appeals concluded petitioner could not satisfy the statute's conditions for excusing his failure to develop the facts and held him barred from receiving an evidentiary hearing. The Court of Appeals ruled in the alternative that, even if § 2254(e)(2) did not apply, petitioner would be ineligible for an evidentiary hearing under the cause and prejudice standard of pre-AEDPA law.

Addressing petitioner's claim of an undisclosed informal agreement between the Commonwealth and Cruse, the Court of Appeals rejected it on the merits under 28 U.S.C. § 2254(d)(1) and, as a result, did not consider whether § 2254(e)(2) applied.

On October 18, 1999, petitioner filed an application for stay of execution and a petition for a writ of certiorari. On October 28, we stayed petitioner's execution and granted certiorari to decide whether § 2254(e)(2) precludes him from receiving an evidentiary hearing on his claims. We now affirm in part and reverse in part.

II

A

Petitioner filed his federal habeas petition after AEDPA's effective date, so the statute applies to his case. The Commonwealth argues AEDPA bars petitioner from receiving an evidentiary hearing on any claim whose factual basis was not developed in state court, absent narrow circumstances not applicable here. Petitioner did not develop, or raise, his claims of juror bias, prosecutorial misconduct, or the prosecution's alleged *Brady* violation regarding Cruse's psychiatric report until he filed his federal habeas petition. Petitioner explains he could not have developed the claims earlier because he was unaware, through no fault of his own, of the underlying facts. As a consequence, petitioner contends, AEDPA erects no barrier to an evidentiary hearing in federal court.

Section 2254(e)(2), the provision which controls whether petitioner may receive an evidentiary hearing in federal district court on the claims that were not developed in the Virginia courts, becomes the central point of our analysis. It provides as follows:

> If the applicant has failed to develop the factual basis of a claim in State court proceedings, the court shall not hold an evidentiary hearing on the claim unless the applicant shows that—
>
> (A) the claim relies on—
>
> > (i) a new rule of constitutional law, made retroactive to cases on collateral review by the Supreme Court, that was previously unavailable; or
> >
> > (ii) a factual predicate that could not have been previously discovered through the exercise of due diligence; and
>
> (B) the facts underlying the claim would be sufficient to establish by clear and convincing evidence that but for constitutional error, no reasonable factfinder would have found the applicant guilty of the underlying offense.

By the terms of its opening clause the statute applies only to prisoners who have "failed to develop the factual basis of a claim in State court proceedings." If the prisoner has failed to develop the facts, an evidentiary hearing cannot be granted unless the prisoner's case meets the other conditions of § 2254(e)(2). Here, petitioner concedes his case does not comply with § 2254(e)(2)(B), so he may receive an evidentiary hearing only if his claims fall outside the opening clause.

There was no hearing in state court on any of the claims for which petitioner now seeks an evidentiary hearing. That, says the Commonwealth, is the end of the matter. In its view petitioner, whether or not through his own fault or neglect, still "failed to develop the factual basis of a claim in State court proceedings." Petitioner, on the other hand, says the phrase "failed to develop" means lack of diligence in developing the claims, a defalcation he contends did not occur since he made adequate efforts during state-court proceedings to discover and present the underlying facts. The Court of Appeals agreed with petitioner's interpretation of § 2254(e)(2) but believed petitioner had not exercised enough diligence to avoid the statutory bar. We agree with petitioner and the Court of Appeals that "failed to develop" implies some lack of diligence; but unlike the Court of Appeals, we find no lack of diligence on petitioner's part with regard to two of his three claims.

B

We start, as always, with the language of the statute. Section 2254(e)(2) begins with a conditional clause, "[i]f the applicant has failed to develop the factual basis of a claim in State court proceedings," which directs attention to the prisoner's efforts in state court. We ask first whether the factual basis was indeed developed in state court, a question susceptible, in the normal course, of a simple yes or no answer. Here the answer is no.

The Commonwealth would have the analysis begin and end there. Under its no-fault reading of the statute, if there is no factual development in the state court, the federal habeas court may not inquire into the reasons for the default when determining whether the opening clause of § 2254(e)(2) applies. We do not agree with the Commonwealth's interpretation of the word "failed."

We do not deny "fail" is sometimes used in a neutral way, not importing fault or want of diligence. So the phrase "We fail to understand his argument" can mean simply "We cannot understand his argument." This is not the sense in which the word "failed" is used here, however.

We give the words of a statute their "'ordinary, contemporary, common meaning,'" absent an indication Congress intended them to bear some different import. In its customary and preferred sense, "fail" connotes some omission, fault, or negligence on the part of the person who has failed to do something. * * *

Under the opening clause of § 2254(e)(2), a failure to develop the factual basis of a claim is not established unless there is lack of diligence, or some greater fault, attributable to the prisoner or the prisoner's counsel. In this we agree with the Court of Appeals and with all other courts of appeals which have addressed the issue.

Our interpretation of § 2254(e)(2)'s opening clause has support in *Keeney v. Tamayo-Reyes*, 504 U.S. 1 (1992), a case decided four years before AEDPA's enactment. In *Keeney*, a prisoner with little knowledge of English sought an evidentiary hearing in federal court, alleging his *nolo contendere* plea to a manslaughter charge was not knowing and voluntary because of inaccuracies in the translation of the plea proceedings. The prisoner had not developed the facts of his claim in state collateral proceedings, an omission caused by the negligence of his state postconviction counsel. The Court characterized this as the "prisoner's failure to develop material facts in state court." We required the prisoner to demonstrate cause and prejudice excusing the default before he could receive a hearing on his claim, unless the prisoner could "show that a fundamental miscarriage of justice would result from failure to hold a federal evidentiary hearing."

Section 2254(e)(2)'s initial inquiry into whether "the applicant has failed to develop the factual basis of a claim in State court proceedings" echoes *Keeney*'s language regarding "the state prisoner's failure to develop material facts in state court." In *Keeney*, the Court borrowed the cause and prejudice standard applied to procedurally defaulted claims, deciding there was no reason "to distinguish between failing to properly assert a federal claim in state court and failing in state court to properly develop such a claim." As is evident from the similarity between the Court's phrasing in *Keeney* and the opening clause of § 2254(e)(2), Congress intended to preserve at least one aspect of *Keeney*'s holding: prisoners who are at fault for the deficiency in the state-court record must satisfy a heightened standard to obtain an evidentiary hearing. To be sure, in requiring that prisoners who have not been diligent satisfy § 2254(e)(2)'s provisions rather than show cause and prejudice, and in eliminating a freestanding "miscarriage of justice" exception, Congress raised the bar *Keeney* imposed on prisoners who were not diligent in state-court proceedings. Contrary to the Commonwealth's position, however, there is no basis in the text of § 2254(e)(2) to believe Congress used "fail" in a different sense than the Court did in *Keeney* or otherwise intended the statute's further, more stringent requirements to control the availability of an evidentiary hearing in a broader class of cases than were covered by *Keeney*'s cause and prejudice standard.

In sum, the opening clause of § 2254(e)(2) codifies *Keeney*'s threshold standard of diligence, so that prisoners who would have had to satisfy *Keeney*'s test for excusing the deficiency in the state-court record prior to AEDPA are now controlled by § 2254(e)(2). When the words of the Court are used in a later statute governing the same subject matter, it is respectful of Congress and of the Court's own processes to give the words the same meaning in the absence of specific direction to the contrary.

* * *

We are not persuaded by the Commonwealth's further argument that anything less than a no-fault understanding of the opening clause is contrary to AEDPA's purpose to further the principles of comity, finality, and federalism. There is no doubt Congress intended AEDPA to advance these doctrines. Federal habeas corpus principles must inform and shape the historic and still vital relation of mutual respect and common purpose existing between the States and the federal courts. In keeping this delicate balance we have been careful to limit the scope of federal intrusion into state criminal adjudications and to safeguard the States' interest in the integrity of their criminal and collateral proceedings.

It is consistent with these principles to give effect to Congress' intent to avoid unneeded evidentiary hearings in federal habeas corpus, while recognizing the statute does not equate prisoners who exercise diligence in pursuing their claims with those who do not. Principles of exhaustion are premised upon recognition by Congress and the Court that state judiciaries have the duty and competence to vindicate rights secured by the Constitution in state criminal proceedings. Diligence will require in the usual case that the prisoner, at a minimum, seek an evidentiary hearing in state court in the manner prescribed by state law. "Comity ... dictates that when a prisoner alleges that his continued confinement for a state court conviction violates federal law, the state courts should have the first opportunity to review this claim and provide any necessary relief." For state courts to have their rightful opportunity to adjudicate federal rights, the prisoner must be diligent in developing the record and presenting, if possible, all claims of constitutional error. If the prisoner fails to do so, himself or herself contributing to the absence of a full and fair adjudication in state court, § 2254(e)(2) prohibits an evidentiary hearing to develop the relevant claims in federal court, unless the statute's other stringent requirements are met. Federal courts sitting in habeas are not an alternative forum for trying facts and issues which a prisoner made insufficient effort to pursue in state proceedings. Yet comity is not served by saying a prisoner "has failed to develop the factual basis of a claim" where he was unable to develop his claim in state court despite diligent effort. In that circumstance, an evidentiary hearing is not barred by § 2254(e)(2).

III

Now we apply the statutory test. If there has been no lack of diligence at the relevant stages in the state proceedings, the prisoner has not "failed to develop" the facts under § 2254(e)(2)'s opening clause, and he will be excused from showing compliance with the balance of the subsection's requirements. We find lack of diligence as to one of the three claims but not as to the other two.

A

* * *

[The Court examined the claim that the State violated *Brady v. Maryland* by not disclosing Cruse's psychiatric report.]

As we hold there was a failure to develop the factual basis of this *Brady* claim in state court, we must determine if the requirements in the balance of § 2254(e)(2) are satisfied so that petitioner's failure is excused. Subparagraph (B) of § 2254(e)(2) conditions a hearing upon a showing, by clear and convincing evidence, that no reasonable factfinder would have found petitioner guilty of capital murder but for the alleged constitutional error. Petitioner concedes he cannot make this showing, and the case has been presented to us on that premise. For these reasons, we affirm the Court of Appeals' judgment barring an evidentiary hearing on this claim.

B

We conclude petitioner has met the burden of showing he was diligent in efforts to develop the facts supporting his juror bias and prosecutorial misconduct claims in collateral proceedings before the Virginia Supreme Court.

* * *

The Court of Appeals held state habeas counsel was not diligent because petitioner's investigator on federal habeas discovered the relationships upon interviewing two jurors who referred in passing to Stinnett [who later became the jury foreperson, and who had been divorced from the prosecution's first witness—Deputy Sheriff Claude Meinhard—in 1979] as "Bonnie Meinhard." The investigator later confirmed Stinnett's prior marriage to Meinhard by checking Cumberland County's public records. We should be surprised, to say the least, if a district court familiar with the standards of trial practice were to hold that in all cases diligent counsel must check public records containing personal information pertaining to each and every juror. Because of Stinnett and Woodson's silence [Woodson was one of the prosecutors, and he had represented Stinnett in her divorce from Meinhard], there was no basis for an investigation into Stinnett's marriage history. Section 2254(e)(2) does not apply to petitioner's related claims of juror bias and prosecutorial misconduct.

We further note the Commonwealth has not argued that petitioner could have sought relief in state court once he discovered the factual bases of these claims some time between appointment of federal habeas counsel on July 2, 1996, and the filing of his federal habeas petition on November 20, 1996. As an indigent, petitioner had 120 days following appointment of state habeas counsel to file a petition with the Virginia Supreme Court. State habeas counsel was appointed on August 10, 1995, about a year before petitioner's investigator on federal habeas uncovered the information regarding Stinnett and Woodson. As state postconviction relief was no longer available at the time the facts came to light, it would have been futile for petitioner to return to the Virginia courts. In these circumstances, though the state courts did not have an opportunity to consider the new claims, petitioner cannot be said to have failed to develop them in state court by reason of having neglected to pursue remedies available under Virginia law.

Our analysis should suffice to establish cause for any procedural default petitioner may have committed in not presenting these claims to the Virginia courts in the first instance. Questions regarding the standard for determining the prejudice that petitioner must establish to obtain relief on these claims can be addressed by the Court of Appeals or the District Court in the course of further proceedings. These courts, in light of cases such as *Smith* [*v. Phillips*, 455 U.S. 209] at 215 ("[T]he remedy for allegations of juror partiality is a hearing in which the defendant has the opportunity to prove actual bias"), will take due account of the District Court's earlier decision to grant an evidentiary hearing based in part on its belief that "Juror Stinnett deliberately failed to tell the truth on voir dire."

IV

Petitioner alleges the Commonwealth failed to disclose an informal plea agreement with Cruse. The Court of Appeals rejected this claim on the merits under § 2254(d)(1), so it is unnecessary to reach the question whether § 2254(e)(2) would permit a hearing on the claim.

The judgment of the Court of Appeals is affirmed in part and reversed in part. The case is remanded for further proceedings consistent with this opinion.

It is so ordered.

Notes

1. *Subsequent case history*

On August 22, 2003, Michael Williams was sentenced to life in prison.

2. *Definition of "fail"*

Why do you think the Court went to such lengths to define the word "fail" in *Michael Williams v. Taylor*?

What is the relationship between *Keeney* and § 2254(e)? Assume that Williams *had* "failed" to develop the evidence in state court. How does he demonstrate the right to a federal hearing under *Keeney*? Under AEDPA? Is there any practical difference between the (e)(2) standard and the *Keeney* standard?

3. *Evolution of the Great Writ*

Consider the evolution of the Writ as explained in both Chapter 1 and in *Fay v. Noia* in Chapter 8, then consider how that history impacted the Court's decision in Michael Williams' case. Did AEDPA interfere with the historical evolution of the Writ or simply move it along?

Although the decision in *Michael Williams* appears to provide some clarity as to the meaning of § 2254(e)(2), in practice the lower courts are badly fractured as to the application of the *Williams* holding. Under *Williams*, a "lack of diligence, or some greater fault attributable to the prisoner" will suffice to constitute a failure for purposes of (e)(2). But what if the prisoner requests an evidentiary hearing; is this alone sufficient for purposes of a diligence showing under (e)(2)?

Insyxiengmay v. Morgan

403 F.3d 657 (9th Cir. 2005)

Before: D.W. NELSON, REINHARDT, and THOMAS, Circuit Judges.

REINHARDT, Circuit Judge:

Oloth Insyxiengmay was convicted of two counts of murder in the first degree and two counts of assault in the first degree for an attack on four high school teens who egged his gang's hangout. Following his conviction and a series of appeals in the Washington state courts, Insyxiengmay petitioned the district court for a writ of habeas corpus. He now contends that the district court erred in dismissing three of the six claims on the ground that the claims were procedurally barred and denying his Sixth Amendment claim that he and his counsel were improperly excluded from an *in camera* hearing regarding a confidential informant. The three claims that the district court dismissed on procedural grounds are that the trial court failed to give a manslaughter instruction (claim 1), that a non-testifying co-defendant's statement inculpating Insyxiengmay should not have been received in evidence (claim 2), and that the prosecution's key witness's adverse polygraph examination results should have been admitted (claim 6). Because Insyxiengmay timely presented the claims to the Washington Supreme Court as federal issues, and because his allegations regarding his Sixth Amendment claim necessitated an evidentiary hearing in federal court, we reverse the district court's dismissal of his petition and remand for consideration of his claims.

I. FACTUAL AND PROCEDURAL BACKGROUND

A. The Crime

On August 24, 1994, four high school boys drove down a Tacoma, Washington street throwing eggs at houses. Some of those eggs splattered on "the snake house," a hangout for a local gang called the Original Loco Boyz. Oloth Insyxiengmay, Nga Ngoeung, and Soutthanom Misaengsay were associated with the gang. All three were juveniles in 1994; Insyxiengmay was fifteen years old.

Insyxiengmay, Ngoeung, and Misaengsay were outside the snake house during the egging. Believing that the attack was gang-related, Insyxiengmay entered the house and grabbed the owner's rifle. All three boys scrambled into a silver Buick and, with Ngoeung driving, proceeded to follow the other car. According to Misaengsay, it was Insyxiengmay who put the rifle out of the window and fired at the other boys' car. The driver and front seat passenger of that car were shot and killed.

The three returned to the snake house after the shootings. Insyxiengmay handed the rifle to Wendy West, the only person present in the house, and told her to get rid of it. Insyxiengmay said, "We shot them up. We shot them up. They threw eggs at us, the Rickets. We shot them up." West testified that Insyxiengmay was highly upset: "He's usually smiling and happy, and he was almost—he was real fearful. He was almost in a state of tears." Meanwhile, she said, Misaengsay was "smirking and almost laughing."

Insyxiengmay was arrested on September 1, 1994. After being advised of his rights, he agreed to make a statement. He admitted to being in the car during the shootings, but he denied being the shooter. He accused a fourth person, known as J-Rock, instead.

Ngoeung was arrested two days later on September 3, 1994, based upon information as to his whereabouts provided by a confidential informant. Ngoeung confessed to police that he drove the car during the shootings.

* * * Although Insyxiengmay was fifteen at the time and had no prior convictions, he was eventually tried along with Ngoeung as an adult.

B. Confidential Informant

During pretrial motion hearings, the prosecutor revealed to defense counsel that a confidential informant had provided information leading to Ngoeung's arrest and that the informant was a passenger in one of the two cars stopped on September 3rd when Ngoeung was arrested. The prosecutor further informed counsel that the arresting deputy's report regarding the arrest of Ngoeung falsely stated that he was on routine surveillance when he located Ngoeung's car. In truth, the deputy "got a phone call from one of the individuals that was in the car with these people traveling down the freeway." Because the prosecutor was not willing to reveal the identity of the informant, defense counsel moved for disclosure. The state judge subsequently held an *in camera* hearing to discuss the potential testimony of the confidential informant. The only witness who appeared at the *in camera* hearing was the deputy sheriff who arrested the defendants. The judge barred defense counsel from the hearing, refused to take his written questions so that they could be read to the witness by the court, did not compel the confidential informant to appear at the hearing, and issued a protective order prohibiting defense counsel from discussing the existence of the confidential informant with Insyxiengmay and his co-defendant.

Deputy Cassio, the only witness at the *in camera* hearing, was the arresting officer who had falsified his report of the arrest. He testified at the hearing that he received a phone call from Kong Prak, an informant, on the day of the arrest alerting him to Ngoeung's location. Cassio informed the court that, like the defendants, Prak was a member of the Original Loco Boyz and had regularly provided reliable information regarding the "activities of different members of th[e] gang." The trial court did not question Cassio about what information Prak had provided regarding the shootings or whether, to his knowledge, Prak had information that could be helpful to the defense. The court asked only whether, "to [Cassio's] knowledge, [Prak was] present at the snake house during the time surrounding the events when this murder occurred?" Following the *in camera* hearing, the court announced that it had determined that the confidential informant could not provide any information that would be of assistance or benefit to the defendants.

C. The Trial

The case against Insyxiengmay proceeded to trial. Insyxiengmay contends that during the trial, the judge erroneously admitted a statement by one of Insyxiengmay's co-defendants which implicated Insyxiengmay, refused to admit the adverse polygraph examination results of the state's key witness, Misaengsay, and failed to give a manslaughter instruction. Insyxiengmay did not testify in his own defense, having waived his right to do so, although he sought unsuccessfully to rescind the waiver at a later point in the trial.

The jury rejected the charges of premeditated murder against Insyxiengmay, but found him guilty of two counts of murder in the first degree, based upon the element of extreme indifference to human life, and two counts of first degree assault. Ngoeung was convicted of two counts of aggravated first degree murder and two counts of first degree assault. Insyxiengmay was sentenced to over 72 years in prison.

On August 18, 1998, Insyxiengmay timely appealed his conviction and sentence to the Washington Court of Appeals. The court of appeals affirmed the conviction and the Washington Supreme Court summarily denied further review on June 1, 1999. The mandate issued on June 17, 1999.

D. State Habeas Proceedings

On May 31, 2000, Insyxiengmay, acting *pro se*, initiated his first personal restraint petition ("PRP") in the Washington Court of Appeals. In that petition, he argued that (i) the trial judge improperly ordered him to serve his sentences consecutively; (ii) the trial judge gave the wrong burden of proof instruction; (iii) he had been denied his right to a speedy trial as a result of the joinder of his trial with his co-defendant's; (iv) he had been denied his constitutional right to a unanimous verdict; and (v) he had been denied his constitutional due process right to full discovery.

* * *

A few days later, the court of appeals dismissed the first PRP because "Insyxiengmay had not demonstrated any error that entitles him to relief." The court did not discuss any of the issues raised in the second PRP, nor did it discuss its dismissal of that PRP.

Insyxiengmay timely moved the Washington Supreme Court for discretionary review of the dismissal of his first PRP, but that motion was denied on April 11, 2001, on the ground that Insyxiengmay had not shown that the court of appeals erred in dismissing his first PRP.

E. Federal Habeas Proceedings

* * * Insyxiengmay, acting *pro se*, petitioned the district court for a writ of habeas corpus, pursuant to 28 U.S.C. § 2254. Insyxiengmay raised six issues in that petition. * * *

* * * Insyxiengmay argued in the amended [and resubmitted] petition that: (i) the trial court erred in failing to instruct the jury on the lesser included offense of manslaughter; (ii) the introduction of a non-testifying co-defendant's statement implicating Insyxiengmay violated the Confrontation Clause; (iii) the trial court violated his constitutional rights when it denied his motion to reopen to permit him to testify; (iv) his constitutional rights were violated when he and his counsel were excluded from a critical stage of trial (the *in camera* hearing), and when his counsel was barred from discussing the existence of the informant with him; (v) the testimony of the state's prime witness pursuant to a coercive plea agreement violated his right to a fair trial and due process; and (vi) his Sixth Amendment rights were violated when the polygraph evidence was excluded at trial. The district court adopted the magistrate's report and recommendation, and dismissed the petition with prejudice on the ground that claims 1, 2, and 6 were procedurally barred and claims 3 through 5 failed on the merits. The court dismissed the first claim on the ground that it was presented to the Washington Supreme Court as an issue of state law, not as a matter of federal law. The second and sixth claims were dismissed on the ground that they were not raised either on direct appeal or in the first PRP. The court made no mention of the second PRP. On the merits, the court rejected the third, fourth, and fifth claims on the ground that Insyxiengmay had not shown that the Washington Court of Appeals' ruling was contrary to, or involved an unreasonable application of, clearly established federal law, as determined by the United States Supreme Court, or resulted in a decision that was based on an unreasonable determination of the facts in light of the evidence presented to the state courts. Insyxiengmay appealed.

This Court granted a Certificate of Appealability on two questions: one, whether the district court erred in ruling that three of Insyxiengmay's claims were procedurally barred, and two, whether the *in camera* hearing violated Insyxiengmay's constitutional rights.

II. STANDARD OF REVIEW

Because Insyxiengmay's application for habeas relief was filed after the effective date of the Antiterrorism and Effective Death Penalty Act of 1996 ("AEDPA"), our review is governed by AEDPA. * * *

Subject to those limitations, we review *de novo* the district court's denial of a petition for habeas corpus. Additionally, "the district court's application of AEDPA, as well as its conclusion that the standards set forth in AEDPA are satisfied, is a mixed question of law and fact which we review *de novo*." Thus, the Court reviews *de novo* "a district court's decision to dismiss a habeas petition for procedural default."

III. DISCUSSION

* * *

[Section A. addresses the State's argument that the prisoner's claims are procedurally defaulted and rejects these arguments on the grounds that the there was no independent and adequate state grounds.]

[Section B. addresses and rejects the State's argument that the claims were unexhausted.]

C. In Camera Hearing

Insyxiengmay challenges the trial court's decision to exclude him and his attorney from an *in camera* hearing regarding his request to be advised of the identity of the confidential informant and of any information the informant possessed that might be relevant to his defense. A defendant has a right guaranteed by the Confrontation Clause of the Sixth Amendment and the Due Process Clause of the Fifth Amendment to be present at every critical stage of the proceedings.

Because the trial court permitted only the witness (the law enforcement officer to whom the confidential informant reported) and the prosecutors to be present at the hearing and did not allow defense counsel to submit questions for the witness, the Washington Court of Appeals concluded that "[f]ailing to notify the defendant of an in camera proceeding or to permit the defense counsel to submit questions to be asked of the informant is a violation of basic Sixth Amendment due process," citing *State v. Smith*. On this appeal, the State has not questioned the correctness of the state court of appeals' determination that Insyxiengmay's Sixth Amendment right was violated. Instead, it relies exclusively on that court's prejudice ruling.

No court that has reviewed this case has disagreed that the exclusion of the defense from the *in camera* hearing violated Insyxiengmay's Sixth Amendment rights. The district court dismissed Insyxiengmay's claim, however, "because petitioner [ ] failed to show [the confidential informant] had any information pertinent to petitioner's case." In doing so, the court failed to recognize that the facts in the record before it gave rise to the clear inference that the informant possessed material information. More important, it erroneously failed to afford Insyxiengmay an evidentiary hearing.

We have previously outlined the procedure for district courts to follow when determining whether an evidentiary hearing is warranted post-AEDPA:

> Under the amended statutory scheme, a district court presented with a request for an evidentiary hearing ... must determine whether a factual basis exists in the record to support the petitioner's claim. If it does not, and an evidentiary hearing might be appropriate, the court's first task in determining whether to grant an evidentiary hearing is to ascertain whether the petitioner has "failed to develop the factual basis of a claim in State court." If so, the court must deny a hearing unless the applicant establishes one of the two narrow exceptions set forth in section 2254(e)(2)(A) & (B). If, on the other hand, the applicant has not "failed to develop" the facts in state court, the district court may proceed to con-

> sider whether a hearing is appropriate, or required under *Townsend* [*v. Sain*, 372 U.S. 293 (1963)].

Baja v. Ducharme, 187 F.3d 1075, 1078 (9th Cir. 1999). In *Townsend*, the Supreme Court concluded that a defendant is entitled to a federal evidentiary hearing on his factual allegations if:

> (1) the merits of the factual dispute were not resolved in the state hearing; (2) the state factual determination is not fairly supported by the record as a whole; (3) the fact-finding procedure employed by the state court was not adequate to afford a full and fair hearing; (4) there is a substantial allegation of newly discovered evidence; (5) the material facts were not adequately developed at the state-court hearing; or (6) for any reason it appears that the state trier of fact did not afford the habeas applicant a full and fair fact hearing.

372 U.S. at 313. Assuming that the petitioner has not failed to develop his claim and can meet one of the *Townsend* factors, "[a]n evidentiary hearing on a habeas corpus petition is required whenever petitioner's allegations, if proved, would entitle him to relief." *Turner v. Marshall*, 63 F.3d 807, 815 (9th Cir. 1995) (citations omitted).

The petitioner's allegations need only amount to a colorable claim. *See Beaty v. Stewart*, 303 F.3d 975, 993 (9th Cir. 2002) (citing *Townsend*, 372 U.S. at 313); *see also*, *Phillips v. Woodford*, 267 F.3d 966, 973 (9th Cir. 2001) ("Where a petitioner raises a colorable claim [to relief], and where there has not been a state or federal hearing on this claim, we must remand to the district court for an evidentiary hearing."). In sum, for a post-AEDPA petitioner to receive an evidentiary hearing in federal court, he must first show that he has not failed to develop the factual basis of the claim in the state courts: if he has failed, he must meet one of the two narrow exceptions stated in the statute. Then he must meet one of the *Townsend* factors and make colorable allegations that, if proved at an evidentiary hearing, would entitle him to habeas relief.

Insyxiengmay did not "fail to develop" the factual basis for his Sixth Amendment claim in the state courts. Under AEDPA, "a failure to develop the factual basis of a claim is not established unless there is a lack of diligence, or some greater fault, attributable to the prisoner or the prisoner's counsel." *Williams v. Taylor*, 529 U.S. 420, 432 (2000). Fault cannot be attributed to Insyxiengmay because both he and his counsel were barred from the *in camera* hearing, and the court prohibited counsel from informing him of it, as well as of the existence of the confidential informant.

Fault also cannot be attributed to Insyxiengmay's counsel. Counsel attempted to obtain information regarding the State's confidential informant and his knowledge of the facts. The trial court precluded him from speaking with his client about the informant, excluded him from the hearing, and refused to allow him to submit questions for the court to ask the informant. Thus, neither Insyxiengmay nor his counsel failed to develop the factual basis for the claim. Because, through no fault of his own, Insyxiengmay was not afforded a full and fair hearing by the state court, he is entitled to an evidentiary hearing if he has presented a colorable claim that he was prejudiced by the Sixth Amendment violation found by the Washington courts. *See Baja*, 187 F.3d at 1078.

Insyxiengmay alleges that the informant possessed "information substantial to his defense." At the *in camera* hearing, Deputy Cassio described having a "working relationship" with informant Prak, who had provided information "with regards to the activities of different members of" the defendants' gang. Although it is unclear precisely what the extent of the relationship was between the informant and the deputy, and what information the informant may have contributed to the shootings investigation, apparently the relationship was close enough that the deputy felt compelled to falsify his police report to exclude any reference to Prak. It was evident from the *in camera* hearing that the informant had spent time with all of the defendants after the shootings and presumably had conveyed information from them regarding the criminal occurrence to Deputy Cassio. Indeed, the informant was with Insyxiengmay's co-defendant at the time of his arrest. Prak knew both Insyxiengmay and the others involved in the shootings well and may also have obtained information from other gang members regarding the criminal conduct at issue. In short, the confidential informant was an individual who was in a position to provide highly relevant information to the defense.

Given all the circumstances, it was unreasonable for the state courts to assume that the informant did not possess information that could have materially benefitted the defendant. The facts suggest otherwise. Insyxiengmay has alleged a colorable claim of prejudice—a claim that he was precluded from developing at the state-court hearing. He is entitled to an evidentiary hearing.

IV. CONCLUSION

With respect to the manslaughter instruction (claim 1), the admission of the guilty plea (claim 2), and the exclusion of the adverse polygraph evidence (claim 6), we reverse because the claims are exhausted and are not procedurally barred. We remand those claims to the district court for a resolution on the merits. We also remand the Sixth Amendment claim to the district court for an evidentiary hearing on the question of prejudice.

Reversed and remanded for further proceedings consistent with this decision.

Notes

1. *Subsequent case history*

After further court proceedings, it was determined that the state trial court's exclusion of Insyxiengmay and his counsel from the in camera hearing did not actually prejudice him. Accordingly, relief was denied and he is currently serving his sentence in the Washington State Penitentiary.

2. *Diligence requirement*

In what other contexts does AEDPA impose a requirement of diligence on a prisoner? Does diligence mean the same thing in those other contexts?

3. *The procedural default overlay*

Many lower federal courts rely on state procedural rules—e.g., a rule requiring that a request for hearing be supported with an affidavit—when assessing whether the petitioner was diligent for purposes of 2254(e)(2). There is some support for this approach in the Court's decision, which requires that the petitioner, at a minimum, "seek an evidentiary hearing in state court in the manner prescribed by state law." But should non-compliance with an opaque, non-enforced rule of procedure constitute a failure of diligence for purposes of *Williams*?

Beyond the interpretive difficulties associated with sorting out what the term "diligence" means as it is used in *Williams*, there remains fundamental discord among the circuits as to whether, under *Townsend*, there ever is a mandatory right to a hearing. The Court had an opportunity to resolve this question in *Schriro v. Landrigan*. Unfortunately, the *Landrigan* decision lacks a clear rationale, and lower courts are struggling to discern what, if anything, remains of the bedrock *Townsend* rule.

Schriro v. Landrigan

550 U.S. 465 (2007)

JUSTICE THOMAS delivered the opinion of the Court.

In cases where an applicant for federal habeas relief is not barred from obtaining an evidentiary hearing by 28 U.S.C. § 2254(e)(2), the decision to grant such a hearing rests in the discretion of the district court. Here, the District Court determined that respondent could not make out a colorable claim of ineffective assistance of counsel and therefore was not entitled to an evidentiary hearing. It did so after reviewing the state-court record and expanding the record to include additional evidence offered by the respondent. The Court of Appeals held that the District Court abused its discretion in refusing to grant the hearing. We hold that it did not.

I

Respondent Jeffrey Landrigan was convicted in Oklahoma of second-degree murder in 1982. In 1986, while in custody for that murder, Landrigan repeatedly stabbed another inmate and was subsequently convicted of assault and battery with a deadly weapon. Three years later, Landrigan escaped from prison and murdered Chester Dean Dyer in Arizona.

An Arizona jury found Landrigan guilty of theft, second-degree burglary, and felony murder for having caused the victim's death in the course of a burglary. At sentencing, Landrigan's counsel attempted to present the testimony of Landrigan's ex-wife and birth mother as mitigating evidence. But at Landrigan's request, both women refused to testify. When the trial judge asked why the witnesses refused, Landrigan's counsel responded that "it's at my client's wishes." Counsel explained that he had "advised [Landrigan] very strongly that I think it's very much against his interests to take that particular position." The court then questioned Landrigan:

> "THE COURT: Mr. Landrigan, have you instructed your lawyer that you do not wish for him to bring any mitigating circumstances to my attention?
>
> "THE DEFENDANT: Yeah.
>
> "THE COURT: Do you know what that means?
>
> "THE DEFENDANT: Yeah.
>
> "THE COURT: Mr. Landrigan, are there mitigating circumstances I should be aware of?
>
> "THE DEFENDANT: Not as far as I'm concerned."

Still not satisfied, the trial judge directly asked the witnesses to testify. Both refused. The judge then asked counsel to make a proffer of the witnesses' testimony. Counsel attempted to explain that the witnesses would testify that Landrigan's birth mother used drugs and alcohol (including while she was pregnant with Landrigan), that Landrigan abused drugs and alcohol, and that Landrigan had been a good father.

But Landrigan would have none of it. When counsel tried to explain that Landrigan had worked in a legitimate job to provide for his family, Landrigan interrupted and stated "[i]f I wanted this to be heard, I'd have my wife say it." Landrigan then explained that he was not only working but also "doing robberies supporting my family." When counsel characterized Landrigan's first murder as having elements of self-defense, Landrigan interrupted and clarified: "He didn't grab me. I stabbed him." Responding to counsel's statement implying that the prison stabbing involved self-defense because the assaulted inmate knew Landrigan's first murder victim, Landrigan interrupted to clarify that the inmate was not acquainted with his first victim, but just "a guy I got in an argument with. I stabbed him 14 times. It was lucky he lived."

At the conclusion of the sentencing hearing, the judge asked Landrigan if he had anything to say. Landrigan made a brief statement that concluded, "I think if you want to give me the death penalty, just bring it right on. I'm ready for it."

The trial judge found two statutory aggravating circumstances: that Landrigan murdered Dyer in expectation of pecuniary gain and that Landrigan was previously convicted of two felonies involving the use or threat of violence on another person. In addition, the judge found two nonstatutory mitigating circumstances: that Landrigan's family loved him and an absence of premeditation. Finally, the trial judge stated that she considered Landrigan "a person who has no scruples and no regard for human life and human beings." Based on these findings, the court sentenced Landrigan to death. On direct appeal, the Arizona Supreme Court unanimously affirmed Landrigan's sentence and conviction. In addressing an ineffective-assistance-of-counsel claim not relevant here, the court noted that Landrigan had stated his "desire not to have mitigating evidence presented in his behalf." *State v. Landrigan*, 859 P.2d 111, 118 (1993).

On January 31, 1995, Landrigan filed a petition for state postconviction relief and alleged his counsel's "fail[ure] to explore additional grounds for arguing mitigation evidence." Specifically, Landrigan maintained that his counsel should have investigated the "biological component" of his violent behavior by interviewing his biological father and other relatives. In addition, Landrigan stated that his biological father could confirm that his biological mother used drugs and alcohol while pregnant with Landrigan.

The Arizona postconviction court, presided over by the same judge who tried and sentenced Landrigan, rejected Landrigan's claim. The court found that "[Landrigan] instructed his attorney not to present any evidence at the sentencing hearing, [so] it is difficult to comprehend how [Landrigan] can claim counsel should have presented other evidence at sentencing." Noting Landrigan's contention that he "'would have cooperated'" had other mitigating evidence been presented, the court concluded that Landrigan's "statements at sentencing belie his new-found sense of cooperation." Describing Landrigan's claim as "frivolous," the court declined to hold an evidentiary hearing and dismissed Landrigan's petition. The Arizona Supreme Court denied Landrigan's petition for review on June 19, 1996.

Landrigan then filed a federal habeas application under § 2254. The District Court determined, after "expand[ing] the record to include ... evidence of [Landrigan's] troubled background, his history of drug and alcohol abuse, and his family's history of criminal behavior," that Landrigan could not demonstrate that he was prejudiced by any error his counsel may have made. Because Landrigan could not make out even a "colorable" ineffective-assistance-of-counsel claim, the District Court refused to grant him an evidentiary hearing.

On appeal, a unanimous panel of the Court of Appeals for the Ninth Circuit affirmed, but the full court granted rehearing en banc, *Landrigan v. Stewart*, 397 F.3d 1235 (2005), and reversed. The en banc Court of Appeals held that Landrigan was entitled to an evidentiary hearing because he raised a "colorable claim" that his counsel's performance fell below the standard required by *Strickland v. Washington*, 466 U.S. 668 (1984). With respect to counsel's performance, the Ninth Circuit found that he "did little to prepare for the sentencing aspect of the case," and that investigation would have revealed a wealth of mitigating evidence, including the family's history of drug and alcohol abuse and propensity for violence.

Turning to prejudice, the court held the Arizona postconviction court's determination that Landrigan refused to permit his counsel to present any mitigating evidence was "an 'unreasonable determination of the facts.'" The Court of Appeals found that when Landrigan stated that he did not want his counsel to present any mitigating evidence, he was clearly referring only to the evidence his attorney was about to introduce—that of his ex-wife and birth mother. The court further held that, even if Landrigan intended to forgo the presentation of all mitigation evidence, such a "last-minute decision cannot excuse his counsel's failure to conduct an adequate investigation prior to the sentencing." In conclusion, the court found "a reasonable probability that, if Landrigan's allegations are true, the sentencing judge would have reached a different conclusion." The court therefore remanded the case for an evidentiary hearing.

We granted certiorari and now reverse.

II

Prior to the Antiterrorism and Effective Death Penalty Act of 1996 (AEDPA), the decision to grant an evidentiary hearing was generally left to the sound discretion of district courts. *Brown v. Allen*, 344 U.S. 443, 463–64 (1953); *see also Townsend v. Sain*, 372 U.S. 293, 313 (1963). That basic rule has not changed. *See* 28 U.S.C. § 2254, Rule 8(a) ("[T]he judge must review the answer [and] any transcripts and records of state-court proceedings ... to determine whether an evidentiary hearing is warranted").

AEDPA, however, changed the standards for granting federal habeas relief.[a] Under AEDPA, Congress prohibited federal courts from granting habeas relief unless a state court's adjudication of a claim "resulted in a decision that was contrary to, or involved an unreasonable application of, clearly established Federal law, as determined by the Supreme Court of the United States," § 2254(d)(1), or the relevant state-court decision "was based on an unreasonable determination of the facts in light of the evidence presented in the State court proceeding." § 2254(d)(2). The question under AEDPA is not whether a federal court believes the state court's determination was incorrect but whether that determination was unreasonable—a substantially higher threshold. *See* [Michael] *Williams v. Taylor*, 529 U.S. 362, 410 (2000). AEDPA also requires federal habeas courts to presume the correctness of state courts' factual findings unless applicants rebut this presumption with "clear and convincing evidence." § 2254(e)(1).

In deciding whether to grant an evidentiary hearing, a federal court must consider whether such a hearing could enable an applicant to prove the petition's factual allegations, which, if true, would entitle the applicant to federal habeas relief. *See, e.g., Mayes v. Gibson*, 210 F.3d 1284, 1287 ([10th Cir.] 2000). Because the deferential standards prescribed by § 2254 control whether to grant habeas relief, a federal court must take into account those standards in deciding whether an evidentiary hearing is appropriate.

It follows that if the record refutes the applicant's factual allegations or otherwise precludes habeas relief, a district court is not required to hold an evidentiary hearing. The Ninth Circuit has recognized this point in other cases, holding that "an evidentiary hear-

a. Although not at issue here, AEDPA generally prohibits federal habeas courts from granting evidentiary hearings when applicants have failed to develop the factual bases for their claims in state courts. 28 U.S.C. § 2254(e)(2).

ing is not required on issues that can be resolved by reference to the state court record."
* * ** *

This principle accords with AEDPA's acknowledged purpose of "reduc[ing] delays in the execution of state and federal criminal sentences." If district courts were required to allow federal habeas applicants to develop even the most insubstantial factual allegations in evidentiary hearings, district courts would be forced to reopen factual disputes that were conclusively resolved in the state courts. With these standards in mind, we turn to the facts of this case.

III

For several reasons, the Court of Appeals believed that Landrigan might be entitled to federal habeas relief and that the District Court, therefore, abused its discretion by denying Landrigan an evidentiary hearing. To the contrary, the District Court was well within its discretion to determine that, even with the benefit of an evidentiary hearing, Landrigan could not develop a factual record that would entitle him to habeas relief.

A

The Court of Appeals first addressed the State's contention that Landrigan instructed his counsel not to offer any mitigating evidence. If Landrigan issued such an instruction, counsel's failure to investigate further could not have been prejudicial under *Strickland*. The Court of Appeals rejected the findings of "the Arizona Supreme Court (on direct appeal) and the Arizona Superior Court (on habeas review)" that Landrigan instructed his counsel not to introduce any mitigating evidence. According to the Ninth Circuit, those findings took Landrigan's colloquy with the sentencing court out of context in a manner that "amounts to an 'unreasonable determination of the facts.'"

Upon review of record material and the transcripts from the state courts, we disagree. As a threshold matter, the language of the colloquy plainly indicates that Landrigan informed his counsel not to present any mitigating evidence. When the Arizona trial judge asked Landrigan if he had instructed his lawyer not to present mitigating evidence, Landrigan responded affirmatively. Likewise, when asked if there was any relevant mitigating evidence, Landrigan answered, "Not as far as I'm concerned." These statements establish that the Arizona postconviction court's determination of the facts was reasonable. And it is worth noting, again, that the judge presiding on postconviction review was ideally situated to make this assessment because she is the same judge that sentenced Landrigan and discussed these issues with him.

Notwithstanding the plainness of these statements, the Court of Appeals concluded that they referred to only the specific testimony that counsel planned to offer—that of Landrigan's ex-wife and birth mother. The Court of Appeals further concluded that Landrigan, due to counsel's failure to investigate, could not have known about the mitigating evidence he now wants to explore. The record conclusively dispels that interpretation. First, Landrigan's birth mother would have offered testimony that overlaps with the evidence Landrigan now wants to present. For example, Landrigan wants to present evidence from his biological father that would "confirm [his biological mother's] alcohol and drug use during her pregnancy." But the record shows that counsel planned to call Landrigan's birth mother to testify about her "drug us[e] during her pregnancy" and the possible effects of such drug use. Second, Landrigan interrupted repeatedly when counsel tried to proffer anything that could have been considered mitigating. He even refused to allow his attorney to proffer that he had worked a regular job at one point. This behavior confirms what is plain from the transcript of the colloquy: that Landrigan would have undermined the presentation of any mitigating evidence that his attorney might have uncovered.

On the record before us, the Arizona court's determination that Landrigan refused to allow the presentation of any mitigating evidence was a reasonable determination of the facts. In this regard, we agree with the initial Court of Appeals panel that reviewed this case:

> In the constellation of refusals to have mitigating evidence presented ... this case is surely a bright star. No other case could illuminate the state of the client's mind and the nature of counsel's dilemma quite as brightly as this one. No flashes of insight could be more fulgurous than those which this record supplies. *Landrigan v. Stewart*, 272 F.3d 1221, 1226 ([9th Cir.] 2001).

Because the Arizona postconviction court reasonably determined that Landrigan "instructed his attorney not to bring any mitigation to the attention of the [sentencing] court," it was not an abuse of discretion for the District Court to conclude that Landrigan could not overcome § 2254(d)(2)'s bar to granting federal habeas relief. The District Court was entitled to conclude that regardless of what information counsel might have uncovered in his investigation, Landrigan would have interrupted and refused to allow his counsel to present any such evidence. Accordingly, the District Court could conclude that because of his established recalcitrance, Landrigan could not demonstrate prejudice under *Strickland* even if granted an evidentiary hearing.

B

The Court of Appeals offered two alternative reasons for holding that Landrigan's inability to make a showing of prejudice under Strickland did not bar any potential habeas relief and, thus, an evidentiary hearing.

1

The Court of Appeals held that, even if Landrigan did not want any mitigating evidence presented, the Arizona courts' determination that Landrigan's claims were "'frivolous' and 'meritless' was an unreasonable application of United States Supreme Court precedent." This holding was founded on the belief that "Landrigan's apparently last-minute decision cannot excuse his counsel's failure to conduct an adequate investigation prior to the sentencing."

* * *

* * * *Strickland* [does not] address[] a situation in which a client interferes with counsel's efforts to present mitigating evidence to a sentencing court. * * * In short, at the time of the Arizona postconviction court's decision, it was not objectively unreasonable for that court to conclude that a defendant who refused to allow the presentation of any mitigating evidence could not establish *Strickland* prejudice based on his counsel's failure to investigate further possible mitigating evidence.

2

The Court of Appeals also stated that the record does not indicate that Landrigan's decision not to present mitigating evidence was "informed and knowing" and that "[t]he trial court's dialogue with Landrigan tells us little about his understanding of the consequences of his decision." We have never imposed an "informed and knowing" requirement upon a defendant's decision not to introduce evidence. Even assuming, however, that an "informed and knowing" requirement exists in this case, Landrigan cannot benefit from it, for three reasons.

First, Landrigan never presented this claim to the Arizona courts. Rather, he argued that he would have complied had other evidence been offered. Thus, Landrigan failed to develop this claim properly before the Arizona courts, and § 2254(e)(2) therefore barred the District Court from granting an evidentiary hearing on that basis.

Second, in Landrigan's presence, his counsel told the sentencing court that he had carefully explained to Landrigan the importance of mitigating evidence, "especially concerning the fact that the State is seeking the death penalty." Counsel also told the court that he had explained to Landrigan that as counsel, he had a duty to disclose "any and all mitigating factors ... to th[e] [c]ourt for consideration regarding the sentencing." In light of Landrigan's demonstrated propensity for interjecting himself into the proceedings, it is doubtful that Landrigan would have sat idly by while his counsel lied about having previously discussed these issues with him. And as Landrigan's counsel conceded at oral argument before this Court, we have never required a specific colloquy to ensure that a defendant knowingly and intelligently refused to present mitigating evidence.

Third, the Court of Appeals overlooked Landrigan's final statement to the sentencing court: "I think if you want to give me the death penalty, just bring it right on. I'm ready for it." It is apparent from this statement that Landrigan clearly understood the consequences of telling the judge that, "as far as [he was] concerned," there were no mitigating circumstances of which she should be aware.

IV

Finally, the Court of Appeals erred in rejecting the District Court's finding that the poor quality of Landrigan's alleged mitigating evidence prevented him from making "a colorable claim" of prejudice. As summarized by the Court of Appeals, Landrigan wanted to introduce as mitigation evidence

> [that] he was exposed to alcohol and drugs in utero, which may have resulted in cognitive and behavioral deficiencies consistent with fetal alcohol syndrome. He was abandoned by his birth mother and suffered abandonment and attachment issues, as well as other behavioral problems throughout his childhood.
>
> His adoptive mother was also an alcoholic, and Landrigan's own alcohol and substance abuse began at an early age. Based on his biological family's history of violence, Landrigan claims he may also have been genetically predisposed to violence.

As explained above, all but the last sentence refer to information that Landrigan's birth mother and ex-wife could have offered if Landrigan had allowed them to testify. Indeed, the state postconviction court had much of this evidence before it by way of counsel's proffer. The District Court could reasonably conclude that any additional evidence would have made no difference in the sentencing.

In sum, the District Court did not abuse its discretion in finding that Landrigan could not establish prejudice based on his counsel's failure to present the evidence he now wishes to offer. Landrigan's mitigation evidence was weak, and the postconviction court was well acquainted with Landrigan's exceedingly violent past and had seen first hand his belligerent behavior. Again, it is difficult to improve upon the initial Court of Appeals panel's conclusion:

> The prospect was chilling; before he was 30 years of age, Landrigan had murdered one man, repeatedly stabbed another one, escaped from prison, and within two months murdered still another man. As the Arizona Supreme Court so aptly put it when dealing with one of Landrigan's other claims, "[i]n his comments [to the sentencing judge], defendant not only failed to show remorse or offer

mitigating evidence, but he flaunted his menacing behavior." On this record, assuring the court that genetics made him the way he is could not have been very helpful. There was no prejudice.

V

The Court of Appeals erred in holding that the District Court abused its discretion in declining to grant Landrigan an evidentiary hearing. Even assuming the truth of all the facts Landrigan sought to prove at the evidentiary hearing, he still could not be granted federal habeas relief because the state courts' factual determination that Landrigan would not have allowed counsel to present any mitigating evidence at sentencing is not an unreasonable determination of the facts under § 2254(d)(2) and the mitigating evidence he seeks to introduce would not have changed the result. In such circumstances, a District Court has discretion to deny an evidentiary hearing. The judgment of the Court of Appeals for the Ninth Circuit is reversed, and the case is remanded for further proceedings consistent with this opinion.

It is so ordered.

Notes

1. *Subsequent case history*

Jeffrey Landrigan remains on death row with a scheduled execution date of October 26, 2010. *Killer says politics will force his execution*, available at http://azcapitoltimes.com/strike-everything/tag/jeffrey-landrigan/.

2. *Would evidence at an evidentiary hearing have mattered?*

Justice Thomas, writing for a 5–4 majority, concluded that the "mitigating evidence he seeks to introduce would not have changed the result." In contrast, the trial judge has stated that if she had known about Landrigan's background and organic brain damage, she would not have sentenced him to death. *The State of Arizona should not execute Jeff Landrigan on October 26, 2010*, available at http://www.azdeathpenalty.org/landrigan.html.

3. "*[T]he decision to grant such a hearing rests in the discretion of the district court*"

(a) Justice Thomas begins the opinion by announcing that the denial of a federal hearing was not an abuse of discretion. What would be an abuse of discretion in this context?

(b) What is the relationship between the abuse of discretion rule applied in *Landrigan* and the *Townsend* standard, which holds that in certain instances a federal court *must* hold an evidentiary hearing?

Chapter 12

Litigating Questions of Deference: When AEDPA Doesn't Apply

The application of § 2254(d)(1)'s limitations on a federal court's ability to reject a state court's incorrect application of the constitution has substantially reshaped federal habeas litigation. When AEDPA applies, a prisoner with a constitutional claim that is properly before a federal court now devotes considerable effort to limiting the reach and meaning of § 2254(d)(1). For a prisoner, establishing that (d)(1) does not apply quite often is the dispositive question. Indeed, many lower courts dismiss federal habeas petitions without even deciding the merits of the question; instead the court will simply note that even if the prisoner has stated a valid claim of constitutional injury, he cannot satisfy the exacting limitations imposed by the "unreasonable application" or "contrary to" clauses of (d)(1). The materials that follow provide a framework for assessing the threshold question of modern federal habeas review: Are there situations in which federal courts are not required to apply the deference enshrined in § 2254? In other words, post-AEDPA, when is *de novo* review of the merits of a claim permitted?

A. *De Novo* Review of the Merits of a Claim Permitted When State Court Denial of Relief Does Not Amount to an Adjudication on the Merits

The prefatory language of § 2254(d) provides: "An application for a writ of habeas corpus on behalf of a person in custody pursuant to the judgment of a State court shall not be granted with respect to any claim that was *adjudicated on the merits* in State court proceedings unless the adjudication of the claim...."

A number of federal circuits have defined the phrase "adjudication on the merits," as it is used in § 2254(d)(1), as a term of art referring to cases that were decided on the merits. Under this view, when a case is decided on the merits, as opposed to being dismissed on procedural grounds (*see* procedural default materials, Chapter 9), the case is said to have been adjudicated on the merits such that the limitations on relief contained in § 2254(d) apply. When a case is dismissed on procedural grounds, (d)(1) does not apply.

Of course, this is not to say that a state court denial of relief on procedural grounds is a desirable outcome for a prisoner seeking federal review; quite the contrary. In the usual case, a denial of relief on procedural grounds will completely bar federal review of the claim unless the prisoner can prove cause and prejudice or a miscarriage of justice. *See, e.g., Wainwright v. Sykes, supra*, Chapter 9. There are, however, circumstances in which a denial of relief on procedural grounds by the state court works to the benefit of the prisoner on federal habeas review.

For example, if the state court denies the prisoner relief on the basis of a procedural bar that is not independent and adequate, then federal review of this claim would not be constrained by AEDPA. *See Coleman v. Thompson*, *supra*, Chapter 9. In *Coleman*, the Supreme court concluded when a state decision "fairly appear[s] to rest primarily on federal law, or to be interwoven with the federal law, and when the adequacy and independence of any possible state law ground is not clear from the face of the opinion," there is no adequate and independent state procedural bar supporting the judgment. In the absence of an adequate and independent state procedural bar, federal review is not precluded. And if federal review is not precluded by an adequate and independent procedural rule, then federal review is unconstrained by AEDPA.

Likewise, a state court may ambiguously assert a procedural bar as to one or more of a prisoner's claims, and a federal court's inability to decipher which claims, if any, are actually being denied on procedural grounds may work to the benefit of the prisoner. For example, in *DeBerry v. Portuondo*, 403 F.3d 57, 67 (2d Cir. 2005), the court noted that "in many cases it will be necessary to determine whether the state court has adjudicated a claim on the merits to determine the standard of review" and it found that in the case at hand the state appellate court had failed to explain its basis for affirming the trial court's denial of post-conviction relief, thus making it inappropriate for the federal court to conclude that the claim was adjudicated on the merits. *Id.* Likewise, when the state court simply notes that the claims are *either* defaulted or without substantive merit, the federal court will not assume that the claims were adjudicated on the merits. *See Miranda v. Bennett*, 322 F.3d 171, 179 (2d Cir. 2003) ("catch-all sentence stating that [petitioner's] 'remaining contentions are unpreserved for appellate review, without merit, or do not require reversal'" does not justify AEDPA deference). In sum, a state court denial of relief on exclusively procedural grounds is not an adjudication of the merits for purposes of triggering § 2254(d).

Similarly, when a state court simply overlooks, ignores, or refuses to rule on a particular claim, it cannot fairly be said that there has been an adjudication on the merits as required to trigger the limitations contained in § 2254(d). Illustrative of this principle is the bifurcated analysis of ineffective assistance of counsel mandated by *Strickland v. Washington*, 466 U.S. 668 (1984). In evaluating the scope of AEDPA deference in the context of a *Strickland* claim the Court noted, "[b]ecause the state courts found the representation adequate, they never reached the issue of prejudice, and so we examine this element of the *Strickland* claim *de novo*...."[1] *Rompilla v. Beard*, 545 U.S. 374, 390 (2005). Where the state court has expressly refused to address one of the prongs of the *Strickland* claim, that prong will be subject to *de novo* federal review. By analogy, the refusal of a state court to reach the merits of an entire claim may warrant unconstrained federal review. The Tenth Circuit applied the same reasoning in *Morris v. Burnett*, 319 F.3d 1254, 1267 (10th Cir. 2003), where the court held that "[w]hen the state court addresses the great bulk of the issues raised by the petitioner's brief in that court but omits to address a particular claim, we have inferred that the claim was not decided 'on the merits' in state court." *See also Weeks v. Angelone*, 176 F.3d 249, 263 (4th Cir. 1999) ("We ... conclude that the Supreme Court of Virginia failed to address his [the petitioner's] request for expert assistance in the fields of pathology and ballistics on the merits. Thus, we do not apply the standards of review set forth in 28 U.S.C.A. § 2254(d), which requires that a claim be 'adjudicated on the merits in State court proceedings.'"); *Sellan v. Kuhlman*, 261 F.3d 303, 311 (2d Cir. 2001)

1. Recall that under *Strickland v. Washington*, the ineffective assistance of counsel inquiry consists of two distinct inquiries—adequacy of the representation and prejudice. In *Rompilla*, the state court denied relief solely on the basis of its determination that counsel had performed adequately.

(noting that § 2254(d) does not apply when a claim has not been adjudicated on the merits, meaning resolved "with res judicata effect").

Finally, because procedural default rules are not jurisdictional in nature, it is possible that a procedurally defaulted claim might be reviewed *de novo* by the federal court if the prosecution waives, expressly or impliedly, the procedural default in federal court. In *Medley v. Runnels*, Judge Ikuta described a case that followed this course:

> In those rare circumstances where the state has waived the procedural bar, and we nevertheless decide to proceed to the merits, we have held that *de novo* review is the applicable standard. *See Chaker v. Crogan*, 428 F.3d 1215 (9th Cir. 2005). In *Chaker*, the petitioner raised a constitutional objection to his criminal conviction for the first time in his third state habeas petition. The petition was denied "and the order denying the petition cited California cases concerning procedural default." When Chaker later filed a federal habeas petition, the state did not raise the issue of procedural default, either in the district court or on appeal. We therefore deemed it waived. After declining to dismiss Chaker's petition *sua sponte*, we held that we were "not precluded from ruling on the merits of Chaker's claim due to his procedural default." However, because there was no state court decision on Chaker's constitutional claim, there was thus "no state decision to review to determine whether the decision was 'contrary to, or involved an unreasonable application of, clearly established federal law, as determined by the Supreme Court of the United States.'" We concluded that "[i]n such a circumstance, we review the district court's decision *de novo* without the deference usually accorded state courts under 28 U.S.C. § 2254(d)(1)."
>
> This reasoning is consistent with AEDPA, which precludes us from granting a state habeas petition "with respect to any claim that was adjudicated on the merits in State court proceedings" unless the state's adjudication of the claim meets certain criteria. 28 U.S.C. § 2254(d) (emphasis added). We have held that "a state has 'adjudicated' a petitioner's constitutional claim 'on the merits' for purposes of § 2254(d) when it has decided the petitioner's right to post conviction relief on the basis of the substance of the constitutional claim advanced, rather than denying the claim on the basis of a procedural or other rule precluding state court review of the merits."

Medley, 506 F.3d 857, 869–70 (9th Cir. 2007) (Ikuta, J, concurring in part and dissenting in part).

B. *De Novo* Review of the Merits of a Claim Permitted When the State Court System Summarily Denies the Constitutional Claim

The inapplicability of § 2254(d)'s limitations on relief when the state court has not addressed the claims, or when it has only decided the claim on procedural grounds, is relatively uncontroversial. There is, however, a significant split among the federal circuits as to the question of whether a denial of a prisoner's federal constitutional claims, that is unsupported by any explanation or reasoning, should constitute an adjudication on the merits worthy of deference. If the state court provides no reasoning, or no basis, upon which to assume that it adjudicated all of the claims, much less that it adjudicated them under the controlling federal precedent, should the deference enshrined in § 2254(d) be applicable? Are perverse incentives created when, per the proper application of the "contrary to clause" of (d)(1), state decisions which expressly apply federal law incorrectly are reviewed *de novo*, but state decisions with no supporting reasoning are shielded by AEDPA deference? If summary state dispositions are entitled to deference under (d)(1), then, in effect, a state court that provides reasoning and attempts to explain the resulting denial of post-conviction relief risks receiving less deference from the reviewing federal court than a court that disposes of the claims through a summary disposition. This procedural dilemma has yet to be squarely addressed by the Supreme Court. Below are some examples of the treatment this important issue has received in the federal courts—should an unexplained denial of relief be treated the same as a non-adjudication, or should the full deference of (d)(1) apply? Or is there a third way?

As you read the various approaches below, consider which solution is most consistent with the goals of AEDPA and state sovereignty. Which is most consistent with the structure of our federal system? With the rule of constitutional supremacy?

(1) There Need Be No Deference to Silent State Court Judgments

Washington v. Schriver

255 F.3d 45 (2d Cir. 2001)

CALABRESI, Circuit Judge, Concurring:

* * * I write separately ... to explain my view that, though correct in delaying a decision, we do State courts no favor by declining to determine, and as soon as possible, that the pre-AEDPA standard of review should indeed be applied in cases like this one—cases, that is, in which State courts have rejected a petitioner's federal constitutional claim without specifically addressing it (even if only by citing to federal case law or to State court decisions that apply federal law).

The AEDPA requires federal courts hearing habeas petitions brought by persons incarcerated "pursuant to the judgment of a State court" to give deference to the State court judgments they review. Specifically, the AEDPA mandates that "a writ of habeas corpus ... shall not be granted with respect to any claim that was adjudicated on the merits in State court proceedings unless the adjudication of the claim—(1) resulted in a decision that was contrary to, or involved an unreasonable application of, clearly established Federal law as determined by the Supreme Court of the United States." 28 U.S.C. § 2254(d)(1). Hence, where a habeas petitioner's claims have received an "adjudicat[ion] on the merits" and, as a result of that adjudication, have been rejected by a State court, the AEDPA commands that federal courts yield to the state court decision, and do so even in some instances where that decision is legally incorrect. Federal courts must do this rather than undertake an independent, *de novo* review of the claim's merits. *See Williams v. Taylor*, 529 U.S. 362 (2000).

One of the Congress's principal purposes in adopting this deferential standard of review was to recognize the independent stature of State courts and to accord State court adjudications respect. This purpose is clearly revealed both on the face of the AEDPA and in multiple statements made by the statute's congressional proponents. Thus Senator Hatch stated that the deferential standard of review imposed by the AEDPA

> simply ends the improper review of State court decisions. After all, State courts are required to uphold the Constitution and to faithfully apply Federal laws. There is simply no reason that Federal courts should have the ability to virtually retry cases that have been properly adjudicated by our State courts.

* * *

But in spite of these sympathetic purposes, the AEDPA runs the risk of imposing a heavy, and sometimes unwanted and unmanageable, burden on State courts. Specifically, if AEDPA deference were deemed automatically and universally to apply, then that law would require extremely busy State court judges to figure out what can be very complicated questions of federal law at the pain of having a defendant incorrectly stay in prison should the State court decision of these complex questions turn out to be mistaken (but not unreasonably so). Indeed, under such a reading of the AEDPA, the only alternative to this outcome would be the highly undesirable one of having federal courts reviewing State court decisions on habeas frequently declare such decisions to be not just mistaken but also unreasonable. Assuming, as we surely should, that federal courts will not do this, State courts would inevitably be led to do a lot of work on all federal questions, no matter how difficult, in order to avoid mistaken, but not unreasonable, decisions. And they would do so regardless of whether they wished to spend the time arriving at deeply thought out judgments on such hard federal questions.

In contrast, a reading of the AEDPA under which AEDPA deference does not apply where a State court has rejected a petitioner's claim without expressly mentioning its federal aspects allows State courts to avoid this burden. It enables State courts to choose whether or not they wish to take on the burden and be deferred to. It does this by giving them a simple form of words—for example a specific reference to the law governing a petitioner's federal constitutional claims—through which they can signal their choice. Under this interpretation, State courts that wish fully to evaluate federal claims need only indicate that they have done so, and their decisions will be deferred to. Conversely, State courts that believe that their energy and resources are better employed elsewhere can remain silent without having the AEDPA impose on them the burden (and all the consequences) of being treated as if they have given the in depth consideration that AEDPA deference implicates. And they can make this docket controlling choice on a case by case basis.

The rule that State court rejections of a petitioner's federal constitutional claims receive AEDPA deference only where they make specific reference to these claims is, therefore, no empty formalism. It can, instead, be a substantial and appropriate part of the solution to the problem of coordinating the activities of the two structures of independent courts that characterize our federal system. Nor does this rule at all infringe on the freedom of State courts by "impos[ing] on [them] the responsibility for using particular language in every case in which a state prisoner presents a federal claim." *Coleman v. Thompson*, 501 U.S. 722 (1991). Rather than "dictating to state courts that they must issue opinions explicitly addressing the issues presented or else face 'second guessing' by the federal courts," the rule that AEDPA deference applies only where State courts have signaled that they have considered a petitioner's federal constitutional claim presents State courts with a powerful linguistic device by means of which they can command deference concerning the issues they wish to decide, and pass on for *de novo* review the issues they prefer to avoid, or to treat less fully. In this way, it permits them to exercise that control over their judicial resources which a true respect for state sovereignty requires.

Of course, even though this rule comports with the spirit underlying the AEDPA, we would be powerless to adopt it if the text of the AEDPA mandated otherwise. We would have to reject this approach if the AEDPA required federal courts hearing habeas petitions to defer to State court decisions in all cases, regardless of whether the State courts that issued the decisions wished to be given such deference. But the approach to AEDPA deference laid out above has been adopted by the Third Circuit. And, as one view noted in the panel opinion points out, this approach is consistent with the text of the AEDPA itself, and also coheres with the views expressed by at least six justices in *Williams v. Taylor*, 529 U.S. 362 (2000). All this demonstrates that, at the very least, the AEDPA is ambiguous on this point, and where the text of a statute is ambiguous, courts interpreting the statute should adopt the construction that best comports with the intent of the Congress that enacted the statute. And in this situation that purpose is unambiguously effectuated by the construction of the AEDPA proposed above.

Note

1. *Rationale*

Judge Calabresi here indicated that not requiring deference to a state court on a federal claim makes sense if the state court decides not to squarely address the issue. It appears that the Judge is trying to make this about the convenience of the state court rather than what ought to happen (or not to happen) for the petitioner. Why do you think Judge Calabresi expressed himself this way?

Section 2254(d) of the Federal Habeas Statute: Is It Beyond Reason?

Evan Tsen Lee

56 Hastings L.J. 283 (2004)

The most obvious policy objection to my argument is that it will force already overworked state appellate courts to write opinions. I am well aware that an integral part of appellate courts' response to caseload pressures has been an increasing use of summary dispositions, including summary affirmances of denials of relief in state habeas proceedings. It is also true that this trend would trouble scholars in the Legal Process tradition, for the duty of reasoned elaboration was a large part of what separated legitimate judicial power from brute fiat. But federal habeas review for reasonableness of the process would not come close to requiring opinions in all state criminal appeals. Such a rule merely creates an incentive for state courts to write opinions in those cases where they feel deference from federal courts is most important. Where the state court has documented its analysis in an opinion, the federal court could grant relief only if it concludes that the state court's analytical process is objectively unreasonable. Where the state court has left its analysis undocumented, the federal court would not automatically remand the case to state court for an opinion—indeed, a federal habeas court has no authority for any such remand. The federal court would simply perform a *de novo* review of the decision.

So let it be clear that I would not require anything of state courts that is not already required of them. They are already required to follow federal law, but they are not required to write opinions justifying their decisions. The pending question is what sort of review a federal habeas court ought to perform if the state court chooses not to write. If the state court wishes to take advantage of the "unreasonable application" clause of

§2254(d)(1), it can write; if not, then not. Some may still complain that this is tantamount to requiring state courts to write because, it might be said, of course all judges want their decisions reviewed as deferentially as possible. I am unmoved by this argument. The statute establishes a sort of *quid pro quo*: if state courts want their law application reviewed deferentially, then they owe the reviewing court an explanation of what they did. In spirit, this is entirely reminiscent of the more famous *quid pro quo* in AEDPA—a fast track for death penalty cases if states step up to the plate with adequate appointment and compensation programs for trial counsel.

(2) Complete Deference to Silent State Court Judgments

Reid v. True

349 F.3d 788 (4th Cir. 2003)

WILKINS, Chief Judge:

* * *

Because this claim was adjudicated on the merits by the Virginia Supreme Court, our review is limited to determining whether the decision of that court "was contrary to, or involved an unreasonable application of, clearly established Federal law, as determined by the Supreme Court." 28 U.S.C.A. §2254(d)(1). * * *

Reid maintains that the decision of the Virginia Supreme Court on his ineffective assistance claim was contrary to Supreme Court precedent because it must be presumed that the state court applied its ruling in *Williams v. Warden* (*Williams I*). In *Williams I*, the Virginia Supreme Court held that a habeas petitioner cannot prevail on an ineffective assistance claim simply by making the showing required under *Strickland*; rather, the court held that the petitioner must additionally demonstrate that "'the result of the proceeding was fundamentally unfair or unreliable.'" The Supreme Court subsequently declared that this standard was contrary to the clearly established law of *Strickland*. *See Williams II* (opinion of O'Connor, J.) ("[T]he Virginia Supreme Court's decision was contrary to ... clearly established federal law....").

As noted above, the Virginia Supreme Court rejected Reid's ineffective assistance claim summarily, without providing any reasoning for the decision. Reid maintains that because this decision was made after the Virginia Supreme Court decided *Williams I*, but before the United States Supreme Court decided *Williams II*, it must be presumed that the state court applied an incorrect standard.

It is not at all clear that this is a tenable assumption. During the interim between *Williams I* and *Williams II*, the Virginia Supreme Court decided at least two published opinions regarding claims of ineffective assistance without [making the same error as in *Williams I*]. *But see Pender v. Angelone* (noting that the Court had also decided a case perpetuating this error in the interim between *Williams I* and *Williams II*).

In any event, Reid's position cannot be squared with the way this court applies the §2254(d)(1) standard when the state court has not articulated the rationale for its decision. "In such cases, we conduct an independent examination of the record and the clearly established Supreme Court law, but we must still confine our review to whether the court's determination resulted in a decision that was contrary to, or involved an unreasonable application of, clearly established Federal law...." In other words, when the state court does not articulate a rationale for its decision, our analysis focuses solely on the result reached, and application of the "contrary to" prong is necessarily limited to determining whether the state court decision is contrary to a decision reached by the Supreme Court on indistinguishable facts. *Cf. Early v. Packer*, 537 U.S. 3 (2002) (holding that failure to cite federal law does not mean that state court decision was contrary to established federal law; state court need not even be aware of Supreme Court precedents, "so long as neither the reasoning nor the result of the state-court decision contradicts them"). Reid does not contend that the state court rejection of his ineffective assistance claim is "contrary to" Supreme Court precedent in this way. Accordingly, we turn to the question of whether the denial of relief by the state court on this claim is consistent with a reasonable application of Supreme Court precedent.

[The remainder of the opinion applies the "unreasonable application" prong of (d)(1) and concludes that habeas relief is not warranted under this deferential review.]

Notes

1. *Mercadel v. Cain*, 179 F.3d 271 (5th Cir. 1999)

In *Mercadel*, the Court recognizes that AEDPA deference applies to the decision of state courts regardless of whether the state court cited to or examined the governing federal law. But the Court also noted that "we determine whether a state court's disposition of a petitioner's claim is on the merits [by assessing]: (1) what the state courts have done in similar cases; (2) whether the history of the case suggests that the state court was aware of any ground for not adjudicating the case on the merits; and (3) whether the state courts' opinions suggest reliance upon procedural grounds rather than a determination on the merits.

2. Does the Court in *Mercadel* assign federal judges the duty of surveying state precedent? Or does the petitioner bear that duty? What are the potential costs of such an analysis?

3. *Deference-lite for silent state court decisions:* Brown *&* Mirzayance

<u>*Brown v. Palmateer*, 379 F.3d 1089 (9th Cir. 2004)</u>

* * *

The last reasoned state court decision in Brown's case was the Oregon Court of Appeals' decision on a petition for reconsideration, in which it adhered to its original dismissal of Brown's state habeas petition. *[S]ee Robinson v. Ignacio*, 360 F.3d 1044 (9th Cir. 2004) ("[T]he federal court should review the 'last reasoned opinion' by a state court ..."). In rejecting Brown's *Ex Post Facto* arguments, the *Brown* court stated simply that "the record d[oes] not support petitioner's contention." The opinion to which the court adhered was an affirmance without opinion. Because the Oregon courts have provided no *ratio decidendi* to review, or to which we can give deference, we employ the "objectively reasonable" test. In this situation, federal habeas courts accord the state court decisions less deference than in standard habeas cases.

* * *

<u>*Knowles v. Mirzayance*, 129 S.Ct. 1411, 1419 n.2 (2009)</u>

Mirzayance did question whether the California Court of Appeal's denial of his claim should receive as much deference as the "prototypical" state-court adjudication "involv[ing] both a reasoned, written opinion and an adequate development of the factual record in support of the claims." *Id.*, at 33. Mirzayance thus contends that "the usual § 2254(d) deferential approach must be modified and adapted" in evaluating his claim. *Id.*, at 34. Nonetheless, because Mirzayance has not argued that § 2254(d) is entirely inapplicable to his claim or that the state court failed to reach an adjudication on the merits, we initially evaluate his claim through the deferential lens of § 2254(d).

C. Statutory Interpretation: Full and Fair Procedures

A highly contested issue regarding the applicability of AEDPA is whether the limitations on relief contained in § 2254(d)(1) apply when the state court process was procedurally unfair or unreliable. Does the plain language of § 2254(d) limit the application of the deference provisions such that only procedurally adequate state decisions will be insulated from federal review? And if there is some requirement of procedural regularity, from the text of § 2254(d) or elsewhere, what does it require? What if a state court judge appears hostile or combative toward the prisoner's claims? What if the state court fails to hold a hearing when there are obvious questions of fact that must be resolved? What if the state court does not even review the trial transcripts?

Considering the importance of procedure in a variety of contexts, Professor Fredric Bloom has observed:

> Imagine that the Supreme Court required all civil rights claims to be decided by flipping a coin. Or that all antitrust issues were to be resolved by consulting a "Delphic oracle." Or even that all copyright questions were to be answered by "studying the entrails of a dead fowl."
>
> Something about these instructions seems—even feels—wrong, if still curiously close to reality. But what about these instructions is so unacceptable? Nothing about the coin or the oracle or the entrails ensures that a court will reach the wrong result in any particular case, so what prohibits the Court from making such demands?
>
> The answer, of course, has to do with process—and the deep procedural flaws in these coin-flipping, oracle-consulting, and entrails-studying models. "Procedure" has never been easy to define. In some contexts, "procedure" is merely a collection of "decision rules," a set of baseline standards that shape the mechanics of adjudication; in others, it is an alternative to (or bar against) consideration of the merits of a case; in still others, it is whatever "substantive law" is not. All of these definitions prove somehow accurate, if only partially so.
>
> And all of these definitions imply something unremarkable: Procedure matters. It matters enough, in fact, that some procedural errors face real (if imperfect) doctrinal restraints.

Frederic M. Bloom, *Unconstitutional Courses*, 83 WASH. U. L.Q. 1679, 1687–88 (2005).

Procedure may matter, but how do we know when enough procedure has been provided? More importantly, what type of fair procedures, if any, are required in the context of applying the limitations on relief contained in § 2254(d)? In what legal terms should the answer to such a question be framed?

(1) No "Full and Fair" Requirement Implied by § 2254(d)(2)

Although most federal courts seem to infer from the text of AEDPA a *quid pro quo* spirit that requires fundamentally fair procedures before deference will be awarded, the Fifth Circuit has adopted a plain text reading of AEDPA that rejects the notion that AEDPA deference is contingent upon procedural fairness.

Valdez v. Cockrell

274 F.3d 941 (5th Cir. 2001)

EMILIO M. GARZA, Circuit Judge:

Janie Cockrell, Director of the Texas Department of Criminal Justice, Institutional Division ("the Director") appeals the district court's grant of the writ of habeas corpus to the petitioner, Alberto Valdez ("Valdez"). We hold that a full and fair hearing is not a prerequisite to the application of 28 U.S.C. § 2254's deferential scheme. Therefore, we vacate and remand to the district court for an assessment of Valdez's claims applying the standards set forth in § 2254(d) and (e)(1). With respect to the Director's appeal of the district court's evidentiary rulings, we affirm in part and vacate in part.

I

A Texas jury found Valdez guilty of the capital murder of Police Sergeant J.D. Bock in May 1988. Following the sentencing phase, the jury answered the two special issue questions in the affirmative, finding that the act had been deliberate and that Valdez posed a future danger to society. The court then imposed a sentence of death. Valdez's conviction and sentence were affirmed on direct appeal.

Valdez filed a state habeas petition, raising twenty-four legal issues. The state habeas court held a two-day hearing in November of 1990. At this hearing, Valdez presented evidence of his ineffective assistance of counsel claim. Valdez's theory was that if his trial counsel had investigated his background, they would have found significant evidence that Valdez was mentally retarded, suffered abuse as a child at the hands of his father, and had behaved as a model prisoner during his previous periods of incarceration. Valdez argued that had the jury heard such evidence there was a reasonable probability that the jury would have answered one of the special questions differently, sparing his life. After the presentation of witnesses, the hearing recessed to allow both parties to secure additional witnesses if necessary.

On a motion by the parties to close the proceeding, the state habeas court held a final hearing on the proposed findings. During that hearing, counsel for Valdez and the State presented lengthy arguments as to those findings. One month later, the state habeas court issued findings of fact and law denying Valdez relief.

The state habeas court held that Valdez's trial counsel was not deficient and that any deficiency did not prejudice Valdez. The habeas court found that the trial counsel's lack of investigation into Valdez's background was reasonable. School records, admitted into evidence during the hearing, indicated that Valdez had a full scale I.Q. of 73 and had been classified as educable mentally retarded. The court found that the fact that Valdez had dropped out of school did not put his counsel on notice to inquire into these school records because it found that it was common for Hispanic males in the Corpus Christi, Nueces County, Texas area to drop out of school. With regard to a conviction in Hockley County, trial counsel had received the penitentiary packet containing the conviction and judgment but had not requested the underlying pleadings. These pleadings contained a letter from his attorney in that case requesting a psychiatric evaluation of Valdez, and the resulting evaluation, which would have also shown that Valdez had a full scale I.Q. of 63 and was determined to be of borderline intelligence. The state habeas court concluded that the failure to request these pleadings did not fall beyond the professional standard of conduct for defense attorneys. Moreover, the state habeas court found that the defendant had knowledge of this psychological testing and had not made it known to his attorneys.

* * *

Based on these findings and conclusions, the Texas Court of Criminal Appeals affirmed the denial of habeas relief in a one-page order. * * *

Valdez then filed the instant § 2254 petition in the United States District Court for the Southern District of Texas and requested an evidentiary hearing. The district court granted Valdez an evidentiary hearing with regard to his ineffective assistance of counsel claim. It did so because it determined that Valdez had not received a full and fair hearing before the state habeas court. Because Valdez had not received such a hearing, the district court concluded that, under *Townsend v. Sain*, 372 U.S. 293 (1963), an evidentiary hearing was mandatory.

The district court determined that the state habeas court denied Valdez a full and fair hearing because the state habeas court lost the exhibits admitted into evidence during the hearing, and, as a result, excluded those exhibits from its resolution of Valdez's case. These lost exhibits included: (1) the results of intelligence tests conducted on Valdez at age thirteen by the Corpus Christi School District; (2) the results of intelligence tests conducted on Valdez at age eighteen by the Big Spring State Hospital, and the accompanying psychiatric evaluation issued by the hospital; and (3) the fee applications submitted by Carl Lewis and David Gutierrez, his trial counsel. The district court also found that "it appear[ed] that other crucial evidence was excluded from proceedings," namely, the trial transcript, as the state habeas judge informed the parties at the hearing on the proposed findings that he "had never read the record of the trial" and that he "did not intend to" as he did not "have the time." Consequently, according to the district court, "the [state habeas] judge denied Valdez's petition without seeing evidence which might have been favorable to Valdez, which the judge did not rule must be excluded, and which the judge even indicated had to be reviewed."

The court found that the "exclusion" of exhibits also resulted in a failure to develop the state factual record, which Valdez had not caused. Hence, the district court concluded that 28 U.S.C. § 2254(e)(2) did not bar an evidentiary hearing. Moreover, as discussed above, *Townsend* required an evidentiary hearing. Alternatively, the district court found it had the discretion to order an evidentiary hearing under Rule 8 of the Rules Governing § 2254 Cases.

After the evidentiary hearing, the district court granted habeas relief concluding that Valdez's attorneys were ineffective in their preparation for and presentation at sentencing. In reaching this conclusion, the district court reviewed Valdez's ineffective assistance of counsel claim *de novo*. The district court found that the deferential framework set forth at § 2254(d) and 2254(e)(1) "largely d[id] not apply" because it had held an evidentiary hearing to remedy the state's denial of a full and fair hearing. Therefore, it applied the presumption of correctness only to the state habeas court's specific findings of historical fact, namely: (1) "it is common in the Corpus Christi, Nueces County Texas area for Hispanic males to drop out of school"; (2) "[t]he fact that the applicant had dropped out of school did not put Carl Lewis on notice of any potential mental problem, if any"; and (3) "Carl Lewis's failure to request the entire court jacket regarding the applicant's burglary charge in Hockley County did not fall below the professional standard of conduct for defense attorneys." The district court then applied a preponderance of the evidence standard to the remainder of the evidence presented at the evidentiary hearing and assessed Valdez's ineffective assistance claim, a question of mixed law and fact, *de novo*.

The Director appeals the district court's grant of habeas relief on the grounds that (1) the district court erred in finding that the state court denied Valdez a full and fair hearing; (2) even if Valdez was denied a full and fair hearing, such a hearing is not a prerequisite to the operation of the deference required under § 2254; (3) even under *de novo* review, Valdez received effective assistance of counsel; and (4) the district court exceeded its remedial powers by directing the State to resentence Valdez or to impose a sentence of less than death. Additionally, the Director appeals the district court's exclusion of evidence offered by the Director at the evidentiary hearing.

II

In reviewing a grant of the writ of habeas corpus, we review the district court's findings of fact for clear error. We review *de novo* the district court's disposition of pure issues of law and mixed issues of law and fact.

The Director disputes the district court's finding that the state habeas court denied him a full and fair hearing, challenging both the legal conclusion and the conclusion's factual underpinning. We need not address that dispute because we find that even if the state habeas court denied Valdez such a hearing, a full and fair hearing is not a prerequisite to the operation of AEDPA's deferential scheme.

AEDPA limits the power of federal courts to grant writs of habeas corpus to those instances in which the state court's adjudication on the merits "resulted in a decision that was contrary to, or involved an unreasonable application of, clearly established federal law, as determined by the Supreme Court of the United States" or "resulted in a decision that was based upon an unreasonable determination of the facts in light of the evidence presented in the state court proceeding." 28 U.S.C. § 2254(d). Under AEDPA, clearly established federal law "refers to the holdings, as opposed to the dicta, of [the Supreme] Court's decisions as of the time of the relevant state-court decision." * * *

Section 2254(d)'s deference operates when the state court has adjudicated the petitioner's claim on the merits. An "adjudication on the merits" occurs when the state court resolves the case on substantive grounds, rather than procedural grounds.

* * *

[In *Terry Williams v. Taylor*] the Court stated:

> Under § 2254(d)(1)'s "unreasonable application" clause, then, a federal habeas court may not issue the writ simply because that court concludes in its independent judgment that the relevant state-court decision applied clearly established law erroneously or incorrectly. Rather, that application must also be unreasonable.

Thus, a state court application may be incorrect in our independent judgment and, yet, reasonable. In *Gardner v. Johnson*, 247 F.3d 551 (5th Cir. 2001), we explored the level of deference to be accorded a state court decision under this standard and found that "we must reverse when we conclude that the state court decision applies the correct legal rule to a given set of facts in a manner that is so patently incorrect as to be 'unreasonable.'"

Finally, AEDPA requires us to presume state court findings of fact to be correct unless the petitioner rebuts that presumption by clear and convincing evidence.

A

The district court found that the AEDPA standards of review "largely did not apply" because it "held an evidentiary hearing in order to consider evidence improperly excluded from consideration by the state habeas court." * * * Thus, the district court selectively applied the presumption of correctness, and did not apply § 2254(d)'s standards.

The Director asserts that while the district court had the discretion to hold an evidentiary hearing, the district court's finding of the denial of a full and fair hearing and holding of a plenary hearing does not permit the district court to avoid the application of deference to the state court's adjudication on the merits. In response, Valdez contends that a determination that a petitioner has received a full and fair hearing before the state court is a prerequisite to a finding that the state court reached an adjudication on the merits, and, thus, a prerequisite to the application of § 2254(d)'s deference as well as the presumption of correctness under § 2254(e)(1). We disagree with Valdez's contention and conclude that a full and fair hearing is not a prerequisite to the application of AEDPA's deferential framework.

Prior to the AEDPA amendments, § 2254(d) provided in relevant part:

> a determination ... made by a State court ... evidenced by a written finding ... or other reliable and written indicia, shall be presumed to be correct, unless the applicant shall establish or it shall otherwise appear, or the respondent shall admit—
>
> (2) that the factfinding procedure employed by the State court was not adequate to afford a full and fair hearing; ...
>
> (6) that the applicant did not receive a full, fair, and adequate hearing in the State court proceeding.

28 U.S.C. § 2254(d) (1994) (repealed 1996).

Once a petitioner established one of the situations set forth under § 2254(d)(1)–(7), such as the denial of a full and fair hearing, the presumption no longer operated; instead, the district court reviewed the claim *de novo* and reached its own independent factual determinations. *See* 28 U.S.C. § 2254(d) (1994) (repealed 1996) (providing where one of the situations in (d)(1)–(7) was not shown "the burden shall rest upon the applicant to establish by clear and convincing evidence that the factual determination by the State court was erroneous"). * * *

Apart from simply establishing a starting place, the pre-AEDPA presumption of correctness was of limited application and it was § 2254's only source of deference to state court adjudications. The presumption applied only to findings of fact. It did not apply to mixed questions of law and fact nor did it apply to pure questions of law. Under the now repealed version of § 2254, we reviewed such questions *de novo*, granting no deference to state court adjudications.

In 1996, Congress enacted AEDPA, amending § 2254. These amendments jettisoned all references to a "full and fair hearing" from the presumption of correctness accorded state court findings of fact, along with the other situations which previously swept aside the presumption. The presumption of correctness erected in its place at § 2254(e)(1), now simply provides that unless the petitioner can rebut the findings of fact through clear and convincing evidence, those findings of fact are presumed to be correct. To reintroduce a full and fair hearing requirement that would displace the application of § 2254(e)(1)'s presumption would have the untenable result of rendering the amendments enacted by Congress a nullity. *See, e.g., Am. Nat'l Red Cross v. S.G.*, 505 U.S. 247 (1992) (a "change in statutory language is to be read, if possible, to have some effect").

Furthermore, as discussed above, AEDPA put into place a deferential scheme, under which we must defer to a state court adjudication on the merits. *See* 28 U.S.C. § 2254(d). In the prefatory paragraph to (d)(1) and (d)(2), the statute provides that an application for a writ of habeas corpus "shall not be granted with respect to any claim that was adjudicated on the merits in State court proceedings." The word "shall" is mandatory in meaning. Thus, we lack discretion as to the operation of this section. The use of "any" makes clear that this section applies to all cases adjudicated on their merits in state court. The term "adjudication on the merits," like its predecessor "resolution on the merits," refers solely to whether the state court reached a conclusion as to the substantive matter of a claim, as opposed to disposing of the matter for procedural reasons. * * * This mandatory and all-encompassing language combined with the meaning of "adjudication on the merits" leaves no room for judicial imposition of a full and fair hearing prerequisite.

Moreover, casting aside AEDPA's standards of review in the fashion urged by Valdez has another untenable result. Valdez asks us to inject a full and fair hearing as a prerequisite to the new deferential scheme applied to conclusions of law and mixed law and fact, which Congress put in place of our *de novo* review. In asking us to read the statute in this manner, Valdez would have us ignore the fact that Congress has excised this prerequisite from § 2254's presumption of correctness, and apply it to a deferential scheme which did not exist prior to AEDPA. The plain meaning of the text simply will not bear such a reading. Therefore, we hold that a full and fair hearing is not a precondition to according § 2254(e)(1)'s presumption of correctness to state habeas court findings of fact nor to applying § 2254(d)'s standards of review.

In response, Valdez attempts to undercut this statutory interpretation with three contentions. First, Valdez contends that this reading of the statute renders an evidentiary hearing in cases like his a useless exercise. Second, Valdez asserts that this holding overrules our Circuit's precedent. Third, he urges us to adopt the approach taken by the Tenth Circuit.

First, Valdez asserts that our view of the statute renders impotent an evidentiary hearing held where the petitioner received an adjudication on the merits after a state hearing that was less than full and fair. We disagree. Where a district court elects, in instances not barred by § 2254(e)(2), to hold an evidentiary hearing, the hearing may assist the district court in ascertaining whether the state court reached an unreasonable determination under either § 2254(d)(1) or (d)(2). An evidentiary hearing is not an exercise in futility just because §§ 2254(d) and (e)(1) require deference.

Second, Valdez maintains that we have elsewhere held that a full and fair hearing is a prerequisite to a determination that a state court has adjudicated a habeas applicant's petition on the merits. * * * [The court then surveys the precedent relied on by Valdez in support of this argument.]

* * *

Apart from being dicta, these references also appear to conflate the adjudication on the merits requirement with a full and fair hearing requirement, referring to the adjudication on the merits as a "full and fair adjudication on the merits." Where we have conducted an examination of whether an "adjudication on the merits" occurred, we have looked at whether the state court reached the merits of the petitioner's claim rather than deciding it on procedural grounds. In short, we find that [the cases relied on by Valdez] give us no guidance as to whether a full and fair hearing is a precondition to the operation of the AEDPA standards of review.

* * *

Third, Valdez urges us to adopt the approach of the Tenth Circuit. In *Miller v. Champion*, 161 F.3d 1249 (10th Cir. 1998), the state habeas court denied the petitioner relief on the merits of his claim without an evidentiary hearing. Our sister circuit found that in the absence of a state hearing the petitioner was entitled to a federal evidentiary hearing. More importantly, the Tenth Circuit concluded that the district court should not afford AEDPA's deference to the state court's mixed law and fact conclusions. For this conclusion, the court rested solely on *Nguyen v. Reynolds*, 131 F.3d 1340 (10th Cir. 1997). The *Nguyen* court, however, did not apply AEDPA to the petitioner's claims because he had filed before the Act's effective date, rendering AEDPA's standards inapplicable. Thus, in reaching its conclusion, the Tenth Circuit did not ground its decision on a reading of the statute, but in reliance on a case applying pre-AEDPA § 2254. Because of the rather tenuous footing of the Tenth Circuit's decision, we decline to adopt its approach.

Instead, our interpretation is in step with the Fourth Circuit's view of AEDPA deference. In an *en banc* decision, the Fourth Circuit recently rejected its prior decision in *Cardwell v. Greene*, 152 F.3d 331 (1998), which had adopted an approach akin to *Miller*. In *Cardwell*, like *Miller*, the state court summarily denied the petitioner's request for relief without an evidentiary hearing. The Fourth Circuit found that the failure to develop the claim occurred through no fault of the petitioner, and, thus, § 2254(e)(2) did not bar an evidentiary hearing. While the summary disposition qualified as an adjudication on the merits, the court concluded that the absence of an articulated rationale rendered the difference "between *de novo* review and 'reasonableness' review [ ] insignificant." The Fourth Circuit rejected *Cardwell*'s treatment of AEDPA's standards of review "to the extent that *Cardwell* requires federal habeas courts to conduct a *de novo* or effectively *de novo* review of a summary state court decision, or to grant habeas relief based upon an independent determination that the state court has violated the constitutional rights of the petitioner." In reaching this conclusion, the Fourth Circuit relied on the Supreme Court's recent elucidation of the AEDPA standards in *Terry Williams* [*v. Taylor*, 529 U.S. 362 (2000)]. The court concluded that, in *Terry Williams*, "the Supreme Court has made it clear that *de novo*, independent, or plenary review of state court adjudications is no longer appropriate, that there are indeed important distinctions between the 'reasonableness' review called for by the AEDPA and the *de novo* review." *Bell* [*v. Jarvis*], 236 F.3d 149 (4th Cir. 2000).

Admittedly, the focus of the *Bell* court was the summary nature of the state court's disposition, not that the state court denied Bell an evidentiary hearing. Nevertheless, the absence of a hearing is precisely a situation under our pre-AEDPA law where we would have found that the state court denied the petitioner a full and fair hearing, potentially making a federal evidentiary hearing mandatory. *See, e.g., Austin v. McKaskle*, 724 F.2d 1153 (5th Cir. 1984) (finding the denial of a full and fair hearing where no state evidentiary hearing was held). Likewise, the Fourth Circuit, pre-AEDPA would have found this to be the denial of a full and fair hearing. *See, e.g., Bacon v. Lee*, 225 F.3d 470 (4th Cir. 2000) (applying pre-AEDPA law and finding that in the absence of hearing, the petitioner had not received a full and fair hearing). In spite of what pre-AEDPA would have been the denial of a full and fair hearing, the Fourth Circuit found that the AEDPA standards applied, implying that there is no full and fair hearing requirement under AEDPA. Moreover, the Fourth Circuit's reasoning is sweeping, finding that AEDPA standards of review apply whenever there has been an adjudication on the merits.

In sum, we conclude the district court erred in determining that, where there had been a denial of a full and fair hearing, AEDPA's deferential framework, as set out in § 2254(d) and (e), did not apply to a state court's adjudication on the merits.

* * *

C

Because we find that the district court erred in its failure to apply § 2254's deferential framework, we decline to address the merits of Valdez's claims for habeas relief. Instead, we vacate the district court's grant of the writ of habeas corpus and remand to the district court for assessment of Valdez's claims under standards set forth above. Furthermore, because we vacate the grant of the writ, we need not reach the Director's contentions regarding the proper scope of the writ.

* * *

IV

In sum, we hold that a full and fair hearing is not a prerequisite to the application of 28 U.S.C. § 2254's deferential scheme. Therefore, we VACATE and REMAND to the district court for an assessment of Valdez's claims applying the standards set forth in § 2254(d) and (e)(1). With respect to the district court's evidentiary rulings, we AFFIRM in part and VACATE in part.

DENNIS, Circuit Judge, dissenting:

Director Cockrell asserts that the plenary hearing held by the district court in response to its finding that the state habeas court denied Valdez a full and fair hearing did not excuse the application of AEDPA "deference" to the state court's adjudication on the merits. Under this view, which the majority opinion embraces, the absence of a full and fair hearing in state court would entitle a petitioner to an evidentiary hearing before the federal district court, but the district court would nevertheless be required, pursuant to the AEDPA, to extend deference to the suspect determinations of the state court. In his brief, Valdez responds as follows:

> [I]t would make little sense to require a federal district court to conduct its own evidentiary hearing because of material deficiencies in the state court proceeding, yet at the same time require the district court to disregard the fully developed evidence presented in its own court and instead defer to the decision of the state court made on an incomplete record....

The simple and compelling logic underlying this response finds ample support in Fifth Circuit and Supreme Court precedent, as well as in the writings of leading habeas corpus scholars. Therefore, I respectfully dissent.

I. *The State Court Denied Valdez a Full and Fair Hearing*

Concluding that he had not received a full and fair hearing at the state habeas level, the federal district court granted Valdez an evidentiary hearing on his ineffective assistance of counsel claim. The district court based its conclusion on both (1) a finding that the state habeas court lost, and therefore did not consider, certain exhibits admitted into evidence during the hearing, and (2) the state habeas court's failure to read the trial transcript. One need only examine the latter ground to determine that the state court did indeed deny Valdez a full and fair hearing.

* * *

II. *A Full and Fair Hearing Is a Prerequisite to AEDPA "Deference"*

The district court found that the AEDPA standards of review "largely do not apply since this Court has held an evidentiary hearing in order to consider evidence improperly excluded from consideration by the state habeas court." Thus, the district court addressed "the ultimate conclusion regarding ineffective assistance of counsel without the presumption that the state court's conclusion was correct." In support of the court's finding, Valdez asserts that pre-AEDPA law governs the consequences that arise when a federal evidentiary hearing is mandatory because the state court failed to conduct a full and fair hearing. * * *

* * *

* * * The majority asserts that the mandatory language of § 2254(d)(1) "combined with the meaning of 'adjudication on the merits' leaves no room for judicial imposition of a full and fair hearing prerequisite." * * *

* * *

In explaining its statutory interpretation, the majority complains that Valdez would have the court apply the full and fair hearing requirement to a deferential scheme as to conclusions of law and mixed questions of law and fact that did not exist prior to the AEDPA, thereby rendering null the amendments enacted by Congress. But Valdez merely asserts that the AEDPA does not address the precise issue presently before the court. Moreover, his argument suggests that the amendments should be interpreted in a manner that comports with traditional notions of constitutional due process. It is a "cardinal principle" that if it is "fairly possible" to construe an act of Congress to avoid a constitutional question, then the statute should be interpreted in that way. The majority holds that the AEDPA prohibits a federal court from examining the process by which the state court arrived at its decision. This holding raises serious constitutional questions. * * * [I]n *Terry Williams v. Taylor*, Justice Stevens found:

> A construction of AEDPA that would require the federal courts to cede th[e] authority [to interpret federal law] to the courts of the States would be inconsistent with the practice that federal judges have traditionally followed in discharging their duties under Article III of the Constitution. If Congress had intended to require such an important change in the exercise of our jurisdiction, we believe it would have spoken with much greater clarity than is found in the text of AEDPA.

* * *

Finally, the majority generally advocates the "sweeping" view of "AEDPA deference" championed by the Fourth Circuit. But in *Terry Williams*, Justice Stevens issued a reminder "that the word 'deference' does not appear in the text of the statute itself." * * *

* * *

III. Conclusion

My greatest disappointment with the majority opinion concerns my colleagues' apparent belief that silence in the text of the AEDPA signifies affirmative repudiation by Congress of the pre-existing body of habeas corpus law, including "general notions of procedural regularity and substantive accuracy." Although the majority's approach may constitute sound statutory construction in appropriate instances, in the present case it ignores the delicate balance struck by the Supreme Court among competing concerns of federalism, due process, Article III jurisdiction, faithfulness to Congressional enactments, and the importance of the Great Writ to our legal tradition. *Townsend v. Sain*, 372 U.S. 293 (1963), has life remaining and, in the present case, it supports the district court's determination that, where there had been a denial of a full and fair hearing before the state habeas court, the AEDPA's review provisions, as set forth in 28 U.S.C. §§ 2254(d) and (e), did not apply. Thus, for the foregoing reasons, I respectfully dissent.

Note

1. *Legislative intent*

The majority in *Valdez* appears to say that a petitioner who did not get a full and fair hearing never can. Is that what the majority is holding? Based on your reading of AEDPA was that what Congress intended?

(2) "Full and Fair" Requirement Implied by § 2254(d)(2)

In *Rice v. Collins*, 546 U.S. 333 (2006) the Supreme Court implicitly acknowledged that the question of whether deference is owed to unfair state proceedings is unresolved. Recognizing that the resolution of this issue may turn on an interpretation of the interaction between §§ 2254(d)(2) and (e)(1), the Court said only "[a]lthough the Ninth Circuit assumed § 2254(e)(1)'s presumption applied in this case, the parties disagree about whether and when it does. We need not address that question."

In *Taylor v. Maddox*, Judge Kozinski provided an interpretation of (d)(2), which unlike the *Valdez* opinion, requires that federal deference be conditioned upon some degree of procedural fairness on the part of the state courts. In essence, the court concluded that the requirements of reasonableness under (d)(2) are not satisfied when the state court procedures are not procedurally full and fair.

Taylor v. Maddox

366 F.3d 992 (9th Cir. 2004)

KOZINSKI, Circuit Judge:

Petitioner is serving a life sentence without the possibility of parole for a crime committed when he was sixteen years old. The conviction hinges on a full confession petitioner gave after he was arrested in his home late one night and interrogated by two police detectives past 3:00 a.m. Pursuant to the Anti-terrorism and Effective Death Penalty Act of 1996 ("AEDPA"), we consider whether the state courts were objectively unreasonable in finding that the confession was lawfully and voluntarily obtained.

Facts and Procedural History

On May 31, 1993, William Shadden was riding his bicycle through a beachside area in Long Beach, California, when two assailants attempted to take it from him. Shadden resisted and the assailants fled. Unwisely, Shadden gave chase and one of the assailants shot Shadden twice, killing him. Three months later, Detectives Craig Remine and William MacLyman, both of the Long Beach Police Department, came to suspect that Leif Taylor had been involved and obtained a search warrant for his apartment. Remine, MacLyman and at least two other law enforcement officers executed the search warrant and an arrest warrant for Taylor at roughly 11:30 p.m. on September 1, 1993.

They found Taylor sleeping on a couch in his living room; his mother, who was his only custodial parent, was apparently absent. Taylor was startled awake by four men with guns drawn and flashlights trained around the room. Taylor was permitted to dress; he was then handcuffed and driven to the police station. He arrived at the station ten minutes later, was escorted onto an elevator to the third floor and placed in a small interrogation room, where he sat alone for about thirty minutes.

By the time Remine and MacLyman entered and began to question Taylor, it was past midnight. For three hours, the detectives interrogated the boy, who "was considerably younger and physically smaller" than they. Taylor "was given no food, offered no rest break, and may or may not have been given any water." Neither Taylor's mother nor an attorney was present to advise him during questioning. Taylor denied involvement in the crime "[f]or in excess of two-and-a-half hours" before finally inculpating himself. At the detectives' behest, he then memorialized on audio tape his confession and a waiver of his rights under *Miranda v. Arizona*, 384 U.S. 436 (1966). Begun at 3:02 a.m. and completed at 3:13 a.m., the recording was just eleven minutes long; there is no record of the earlier two-and-a-half hours of questioning. This is so because Remine and MacLyman questioned Taylor without turning on the tape recorder eventually used to record his confession—or the hidden recording equipment installed in the interrogation room—until after he had inculpated himself. Remine took notes during the questioning but subsequently disposed of them. There is no videotape, so we cannot see whether Taylor was calm and cool or tearful and agitated; nor do we have the audio tape to listen to.[2] Indeed, there is no contemporaneous record at all of what happened during most of the time that Taylor spent in the interrogation room with Remine and MacLyman.

The tape of Taylor's confession was played for the jury during the prosecution's case-in-chief. The jury subsequently convicted Taylor of first-degree felony murder and second-degree robbery; he was sentenced to life without the possibility of parole. The California Court of Appeal (Second District) affirmed; the California Supreme Court denied his petition for review without comment or citation.

Discussion

The district court below denied Taylor's *pro se* petition for habeas relief, adopting the magistrate judge's report and recommendation without modification. We review the district court's denial of Taylor's habeas petition *de novo*.

* * *

Taylor's state-court lawyer moved to suppress his inculpatory statements and, the day before trial commenced, Judge Charles Sheldon of the Superior Court of Los Angeles County held an evidentiary hearing. * * * Immediately after hearing all testimony and closing arguments, the court denied the suppression motion from the bench:

> I am a fact finder first, and I have to decide and say who I believe. I conclude, in this case, that I clearly believe, beyond a reasonable doubt, Officer Ramine [sic] and not the testimony of the defendant in this case. Not only because it is the defendant in this case, but for other reasons, which were the nature of the facts that were developed by both sides. Leading me, in addition, to my feelings about who I should believe and who I really do believe, but also, why I should believe as a secondary or perhaps a primary, to look at with that crediting Officer Ramine's [sic] testimony. It now sheds light upon the decision.

---

2. In footnote 3 of the opinion the court stated: "Responding to our request for the tape-recording of Taylor's confession, the state advised that all trial exhibits, including the tape, had been destroyed on June 16, 1999, and that the Los Angeles County District Attorney's office does not possess any copies of the recording. Letter from Deborah J. Chuang, Deputy Attorney General, to Office of the Clerk, U.S. Court of Appeals 1 (Sept. 4, 2003)."

* * *

> * * * I decline to suppress the statements that were given by the defendant to the officers in this case.

* * *

Principles of comity and federalism counsel against substituting our judgment for that of the state courts, a deference that is embodied in the requirements of the federal habeas statute, as amended by AEDPA. When it comes to state-court factual findings, AEDPA has two separate provisions. First, section 2254(d)(2) authorizes federal courts to grant habeas relief in cases where the state-court decision "was based on an unreasonable determination of the facts in light of the evidence presented in the State court proceeding." Or, to put it conversely, a federal court may not second-guess a state court's fact-finding process unless, after review of the state-court record, it determines that the state court was not merely wrong, but actually unreasonable. Second, section 2254(e)(1) provides that "a determination of a factual issue made by a State court shall be presumed to be correct," and that this presumption of correctness may be rebutted only by "clear and convincing evidence."

We interpret these provisions sensibly, faithful to their text and consistent with the maxim that we must construe statutory language so as to avoid contradiction or redundancy. The first provision—the "unreasonable determination" clause—applies most readily to situations where petitioner challenges the state court's findings based entirely on the state record. Such a challenge may be based on the claim that the finding is unsupported by sufficient evidence, that the process employed by the state court is defective, or that no finding was made by the state court at all. What the "unreasonable determination" clause teaches us is that, in conducting this kind of intrinsic review of a state court's processes, we must be particularly deferential to our state-court colleagues. For example, in concluding that a state-court finding is unsupported by substantial evidence in the state-court record, it is not enough that we would reverse in similar circumstances if this were an appeal from a district court decision. Rather, we must be convinced that an appellate panel, applying the normal standards of appellate review, could not reasonably conclude that the finding is supported by the record. Similarly, before we can determine that the state-court factfinding process is defective in some material way, or perhaps nonexistent, we must more than merely doubt whether the process operated properly. Rather, we must be satisfied that any appellate court to whom the defect is pointed out would be unreasonable in holding that the state court's fact-finding process was adequate.

Once the state court's fact-finding process survives this intrinsic review—or in those cases where petitioner does not raise an intrinsic challenge to the facts as found by the state court—the state court's findings are dressed in a presumption of correctness, which then helps steel them against any challenge based on extrinsic evidence, *i.e.*, evidence presented for the first time in federal court. AEDPA spells out what this presumption means: State-court fact-finding may be overturned based on new evidence presented for the first time in federal court only if such new evidence amounts to clear and convincing proof that the state-court finding is in error. Significantly, the presumption of correctness and the clear-and-convincing standard of proof only come into play once the state court's fact-findings survive any intrinsic challenge; they do not apply to a challenge that is governed by the deference implicit in the "unreasonable determination" standard of section 2254(d)(2).

Petitioner here did not present any evidence in federal court. Instead, the district court rejected petitioner's claim at the initial, or intrinsic, stage of the review process. The appeal before us is therefore governed by the "unreasonable determination" standard of section 2254(d)(2). What we must determine is whether petitioner's conviction "was based on an unreasonable determination of the facts in light of the evidence presented in the State court proceeding." This is a daunting standard—one that will be satisfied in relatively few cases. Nevertheless, the standard is not impossible to meet; as the Supreme Court pointed out in *Miller-El v. Cockrell*, 537 U.S. 322 (2003), "Deference does not by definition preclude relief. A federal court can disagree with a state court's credibility determination and, when guided by AEDPA, conclude the decision was unreasonable." Indeed, the Supreme Court, our court and other circuits have all found the standard met.

As noted, intrinsic challenges to state-court findings pursuant to the "unreasonable determination" standard come in several flavors, each presenting its own peculiar set of considerations. No doubt the simplest is the situation where the state court should have made a finding of fact but neglected to do so. In that situation, the state-court factual determination is perforce unreasonable and there is nothing to which the presumption of correctness can attach. A somewhat different set of considerations applies where the state court does make factual findings, but does so under a misapprehension as to the correct legal standard. Obviously, where the state court's legal error infects the fact-finding process, the resulting factual determination will be unreasonable and no presumption of correctness can attach to it.

Closely related to cases where the state courts make factual findings infected by substantive legal error are those where the fact-finding process itself is defective. If, for example, a state court makes evidentiary findings without holding a hearing and giving petitioner an opportunity to present evidence, such findings clearly result in an "unreasonable determination" of the facts. Similarly, where the state courts plainly misapprehend or misstate the record in making their findings, and the misapprehension goes to a material factual issue that is central to petitioner's claim, that misapprehension can fatally undermine the fact-finding process, rendering the resulting factual finding unreasonable. And, as the Supreme Court noted in *Miller-El*, the state-court fact-finding process is undermined where the state court has before it, yet apparently ignores, evidence that supports petitioner's claim. *Miller-El* ("Our concerns are amplified by the fact that the state court also had before it, and apparently ignored, testimony demonstrating that the Dallas County District Attorney's Office had, by its own admission, used this process to manipulate the racial composition of the jury in the past.").

Petitioner here claims the latter kind of defect in the state-court fact-finding process—failure to consider and weigh relevant evidence that was properly presented to the state courts and made part of the state-court record. In considering this kind of claim, we are mindful that the state courts are not required to address every jot and tittle of proof suggested to them, nor need they "make detailed findings addressing all the evidence before [them]." *Miller-El*, 537 U.S. 347 (2004). To fatally undermine the state fact-finding process, and render the resulting finding unreasonable, the overlooked or ignored evidence must be highly probative and central to petitioner's claim. In other words, the evidence in question must be sufficient to support petitioner's claim when considered in the context of the full record bearing on the issue presented in the habeas petition. We therefore proceed by reciting the evidence presented at Taylor's suppression hearing.

In his testimony at the suppression hearing, Taylor gave a disturbing account of his interrogation. He recalled that he awoke to find a flashlight and a gun pointed at him, and his living room filled with men. As he was handcuffed and placed in a police car, he was not told why he was being arrested. Taylor asked the officer driving the car if he knew the reason for the arrest. The officer said Taylor would be told at the station. Taylor also asked the officer if he "could call ... [his] mom when ... [he] got there. [The officer] ... said that she would be notified for ... [him]."

* * *

[Describing the interrogation itself], Taylor never wavered in his assertion that he wanted to call a lawyer during his interrogation and asked for access to a phone in order to do so.

According to Taylor, the detectives denied his requests. Instead, MacLyman drew long and short lines on a piece of paper, explaining to Taylor that he could go to jail for the rest of his life (long line) or just until he was twenty-five (short line), depending on whether he cooperated with the detectives. MacLyman also coaxed Taylor, saying he knew Taylor didn't kill Shadden deliberately but had done so unintentionally. Although Taylor steadfastly denied involvement, the detectives persisted in the questioning and would not permit Taylor to make a phone call until he told them "the truth."

Taylor became desperate and upset. Concluding that he could clear up the matter later, Taylor decided to yield to the detectives' insistent demands that he confess in order to gain access to a phone. He then made the eleven-minute recording memorializing his Miranda waiver and confession. Explaining why he would give a false confession, Taylor said,

> I am getting tired, so I just started agreeing with everything so I can get out and make a phone call, because I was thinking, you know, well I didn't do it anyways, so why don't I just try to get out of the room to get my phone call and just tell them what they want to hear.

* * *

In evaluating the relative credibility of these two sharply differing accounts of the events inside the interrogation room, the state courts treated this as a swearing-contest between Taylor and Remine. The state trial judge simply said that he believed Remine, not Taylor. He purported to give reasons for disbelieving Taylor's account of the interrogation, but his explanation defies rational understanding:

> Not only because it is the defendant in this case, but for other reasons, which were the nature of the facts that were developed by both sides. Leading me, in addition, to my feelings about who I should believe and who I really do believe, but also, why I should believe as a secondary or perhaps a primary, to look at with that crediting Officer Ramine's [sic] testimony. It now sheds light upon the decision.[3]

The court of appeal found that Ramine's testimony constituted a sufficient basis in the record for the trial court's findings, and therefore affirmed. Remarkably, neither the state trial court nor the state appellate court acknowledged that another witness testified at the suppression hearing—attorney Arthur Close, who said he received a telephone call from Taylor in the early morning hours of September 2, 1993, shortly after Taylor had given his confession. As detailed below, Close's testimony strongly corroborates Taylor's account of the interrogation and stands entirely unrefuted. Neither the state trial court nor the

3. In footnote 7 of the opinion, the court stated: "We would normally attribute incoherence in the trial court's explanation to mistakes in the transcribing process. However, we have carefully read the record and have found no unusual problems with the transcript of the suppression hearing. Everyone else who spoke is perfectly understandable. Nor is the passage quoted in text the only one in the judge's ruling that is less than pellucid. Just two sentences later, we also find this muddled passage:

> I find it is voluntary under the case law, that has developed on this whole issue, hundreds and hundreds of cases, actually, on this issue just like search and seizure, so I find it is both not a violation of Miranda, voluntary, I decline to suppress the statements that were given by the defendant to the officers in this case."

state appellate court found that Close had fabricated his testimony, nor was there any basis in the record for such a finding. The state courts simply ignored Close. For the reasons explained at length below, the state courts' failure to consider, or even acknowledge, Close's highly probative testimony casts serious doubt on the state-court fact-finding process and compels the conclusion that the state-court decisions were based on an unreasonable determination of the facts.

Close testified that Taylor had called him at home, at "approximately four a.m." on September 2. Taylor told Close that he had just confessed to murder, that he had requested his mother and Close more than once, that he had been prevented from making a phone call until after he confessed, that he had confessed falsely in order to gain permission to make that phone call, and that one of the two detectives questioning Taylor had thrust a "187" ring in his face, and had drawn a diagram to illustrate the alternatives facing Taylor depending on whether or not he cooperated by confessing. Close explained that Taylor did not tell him the exact significance of the diagrammed alternatives, only what had transpired. In all of these respects, Close substantially corroborated Taylor's story. But Close's testimony also went beyond the scope of Taylor's, for Close testified that "[Taylor] said he requested, by name, to speak to me on the elevator in the police department, prior to the questioning." Close further testified that Taylor was crying and upset during the call and that Taylor provided these details without prompting from Close.

The state trial judge said nothing at all about Close's testimony. In reviewing the trial court's ruling at the suppression hearing, the court of appeal similarly failed to mention Close's testimony or to consider its remarkable congruence with Taylor's account of what had transpired during his interrogation. * * * Thus, the court of appeal was aware of Close's testimony, yet never considered or even acknowledged that it corroborated particularly unusual details in Taylor's story: that Taylor rode an elevator to the floor where the interrogation room was located (at which time he allegedly asked for counsel), that Taylor asked for his mother, that one of the detectives wore a ring inscribed with a "187" and brandished the ring in Taylor's face, and that the detective with the ring "mapped" out Taylor's possible fate by drawing "a diagram of two different routes of what would happen to him. One route if he cooperated and confessed, the other route that if he refused to do so, and what the consequences would be." Nor did the court of appeal consider that Close testified that Taylor had told Close his requests for counsel and his mother had been denied. In other words, the court of appeal, like the state trial court, ignored the detailed quality of Close's testimony and the fact that it matched Taylor's account of the events inside the interrogation room.

While Close's testimony is based on what Taylor told him during their telephone conversation following the end of the interrogation, it nevertheless corroborates Taylor's account in important respects. To begin with, the record discloses that Taylor called Close at the first available opportunity. Taylor's taped confession ended at 3:13 a.m., and he was thereafter booked— a process that was completed no earlier than 3:55 a.m. Close testified that he received Taylor's call at approximately 4:00 a.m. This confirms Taylor's claim that he wanted to get in touch with Close at the first available opportunity. Moreover, Taylor's call also confirms his claim that he could, in fact, get in touch with a lawyer, even in the middle of the night: He knew Close's home phone number and felt comfortable waking him. Perhaps most important, the details of Taylor's story, as related to Close during their telephone conversation, precisely matched Taylor's testimony at the suppression hearing, precluding the possibility that Taylor had fabricated those details during the eleven months between his confession and the hearing. Finally, Close testified that, during the telephone conversation, Taylor was "in tears and highly agitated." This contradicts

Remine's account that Taylor was calm during questioning and confirms Taylor's account of the interrogation as a coercive ordeal.

While Close's testimony is perhaps not conclusive, it is certainly highly probative. A rational fact-finder might discount it or, conceivably, find it incredible, but no rational fact-finder would simply ignore it. Yet this is precisely what the state courts did in Taylor's case. At the end of the suppression hearing, the state trial court, in a ruling that is difficult to follow, found Ramine credible and Taylor incredible, and that was that. The court said nothing at all about Close, not even so much as to acknowledge that he had testified just minutes earlier. The state appellate court was similarly laconic, utterly failing to discuss the significance, or even the existence, of Close as a witness at the suppression hearing, even though the importance of his testimony was vigorously argued in Taylor's brief. A decision on which turns whether a teenager will spend the rest of his days behind bars merits closer judicial attention from the state courts.

* * *

* * * In making findings, a judge must acknowledge significant portions of the record, particularly where they are inconsistent with the judge's findings. The process of explaining and reconciling seemingly inconsistent parts of the record lays bare the judicial thinking process, enabling a reviewing court to judge the rationality of the fact-finder's reasoning. On occasion, an effort to explain what turns out to be unexplainable will cause the finder of fact to change his mind. By contrast, failure to take into account and reconcile key parts of the record casts doubt on the process by which the finding was reached, and hence on the correctness of the finding.

* * *

Failure to consider key aspects of the record is a defect in the fact-finding process. How serious the defect, of course, depends on what bearing the omitted evidence has on the record as a whole. Here, Close's testimony was very significant, as it provided the only glimpse into the events on the night of the interrogation by someone who was not one of the contending parties. It is not as good a look as we could have had, if the officers had taped the entire interview, or had permitted Taylor to have his mother or a lawyer present during questioning—or even if they had kept the notes of the interrogation. But it is much better evidence than we usually have because the phone call to Close "locked" Taylor's story soon after the interrogation ended and just minutes after Taylor was booked, and thereby foreclosed the opportunity for Taylor to embellish or fabricate after reflection or based on advice he got from friends, relatives or fellow inmates. By making their findings without taking Close's testimony into account, the state courts made an "unreasonable determination of the facts." In passing section 2254(d)(2), Congress has reminded us that we may no more uphold such a factual determination than we may set aside reasonable state-court fact-finding. When we determine that state-court fact-finding is unreasonable, therefore, we have an obligation to set those findings aside and, if necessary, make new findings.

* * *

[The Court of Appeals went on to make its own findings of fact and found: "Taylor, during questioning, asked to speak with a lawyer and with his mother more than once before inculpating himself; that these requests went unheeded; that MacLyman brandished his ring in Taylor's face; and that MacLyman threateningly mapped the potential consequences for Taylor if he did not confess, in a disingenuous effort to persuade Taylor that persisting in his denials would cost him dearly, and the only way to avoid a life sentence would be for him to fess up."]

In light of our findings, it follows that the court of appeal's conclusion that Taylor's confession was obtained in a constitutionally acceptable manner, and thus was admissible at trial, was an objectively unreasonable application of Supreme Court precedent.

* * *

The magistrate's report and recommendation adopted by the district court concluded that Taylor did not rebut the presumption of correctness and did not demonstrate that the state courts' determinations were objectively unreasonable. Based on our independent review of the record, we conclude the district court erred. Taylor is entitled to habeas relief. We therefore REVERSE the decision of the district court and REMAND with instructions to GRANT a conditional writ of habeas corpus, ordering Taylor's release unless the state of California notifies the district court within thirty days of the issuance of this court's mandate that it intends to retry Taylor based on evidence other than the illegally-obtained confession, and actually commences Taylor's retrial within seventy days of issuance of the mandate.

Notes

1. *Subsequent case history*

A retrial ended in a mistrial in February, 2006. Taylor's third trial ended in a conviction of murder. Peter y. Hong, *Man Guilty in 3rd Trial for Murder,* LA Times, July 25, 2006, available at http://articles.latimes.com/2006/jul25/local/m3-longbeach25.

2. *The interaction of (d)(2) and (e)(1)*

Why does Judge Kozinski conclude that the deference provided in (e)(1) does not apply to the state court's findings of fact in this case? Is this a fair reading of § 2254?

Consider the following explanation regarding the proper interpretation of § 2254(d)(2) and (e)(1):

> [T]his Article concludes that the text, structure, and history of § 2254 dictate that (e)(1)'s presumption of correctness must be considered independent from the (d)(2) reasonableness analysis; in this way, no presumption of correctness applies to substantively or procedurally deficient state findings of fact, and reasonable findings of fact may be rebutted by clear and convincing evidence. * * *
>
> * * *
>
> Under the procedural fairness approach [advocated for by the author], whenever a state court's findings of fact are intrinsically unreasonable—i.e., unreasonable on the basis of the state court record alone—the AEDPA deference embodied in (e)(1) does not apply. Accordingly, this approach avoids the standard of review problem associated with the blurring of (d)(2) and (e)(1) that is commonplace among federal courts. To illustrate, consider [a] hypothetical petitioner ... who was denied a full and fair opportunity to develop his claim in state court. Under the procedural fairness approach, [such a] prisoner would not be forced to overcome the state court's findings of fact by clear and convincing evidence as required under (e)(1). Having been denied a procedurally fair opportunity to develop his claim [in state court], the petitioner in the hypothetical would not be saddled with the onerous burden of rebutting by clear and convincing evidence a state finding that was procedurally unfair. Instead, the petitioner would be entitled to relief if he could establish by a preponderance of the evidence the facts that were material to his claim.

> [In sum], [c]omity and federalism are not served by deferring to a state finding where the fact-finding process itself was defective. More precisely, a state finding of fact is "unreasonable" whenever the state court makes specific findings in the absence of a hearing or some other opportunity for the petitioner to present evidence and whenever a state court simply ignores evidence in support of the petitioner's claims.

Justin F. Marceau, *Deference and Doubt: The Interaction of AEDPA § 2254(d)(2) and (e)(1)*, 82 Tul. L. Rev. 385 (2007).

3. Subsections *(d)(2)* and *(d)(1)*

Note 2 provides a theory for understanding why, as a matter of textual interpretation, it makes sense to read § 2254(d)(2) as imposing a requirement of procedural regularity or fairness. That is to say, some courts and commentators have reasoned that it defies common sense and the plain text of the statute to treat a procedurally unfair adjudication of facts as a reasonable determination of the facts under (d)(2). But what is the relationship between satisfying the strictures of (d)(2) and the requirements of (d)(1)? Why does it matter whether, as the Court holds in *Taylor*, the limitations on relief contained in (d)(2) are satisfied when the state courts fail to provide the prisoner with a fair review of his federal constitutional claims?

4. *Beyond* de novo *review*

In addition to securing *de novo* review of the merits of a claim when the limitations on relief contained in (d)(2) are satisfied, are there any other benefits that might flow to a prisoner who successfully asserts that the state court review of his claims was not procedurally full and fair? Consider the other limitations on relief contained in (d)(1). In *Davis v. Grigas*, 443 F.3d 1155 (9th Cir. 2006), the Ninth Circuit squarely held that relief was unavailable under (d)(1) because the claim rested on an interpretation of the constitution that was not "clearly established." However, the Court held that relief was nonetheless available under (d)(2), which does not impose the clearly established law requirement. In other words, if (d)(2) is satisfied, then the clearly established law limitation on the relief is not applicable.

Is *Davis* wrongly decided? Should deference under (d)(1) apply regardless of improper fact-finding?

(3) "Full and Fair" Requirement and Adjudication on the Merits

Courts have identified a third justification for applying *de novo* review to a federal constitutional claim that has not been reviewed in a procedurally fair manner by the state court: the prefatory language of § 2254(d). Recall that the limitations contained in § 2254(d)(1) or (d)(2) only apply to claims that were "adjudicated on the merits in State court proceedings." 28 U.S.C. § 2254(d). Accordingly, when the state court fails to provide full and fair proceedings such that the material questions of fact could be developed, or when the prosecution fails to disclose material evidence relevant to a claim—*e.g., Brady v. Maryland*—some federal courts have essentially held that there has been no adjudication on the merits of the claim at issue. That is to say, when significant new evidence is admitted in federal court, then, in the view of some courts, the underlying claim has changed so fundamentally that it is fair to say that there has not been an adjudication on the merits of the precise claim now pending before the federal court. The Supreme Court, without endorsing or rejecting this approach, has acknowledged its application by lower federal courts. In *Holland v. Jackson*, 542 U.S. 649, 653 (2004), for example, the Court explained, "Where new evidence is admitted [in federal court], some Courts of Appeals have conducted *de novo* review on the theory that there is no relevant state-court determination to which one could defer."

The Fourth Circuit's decision in *Monroe v. Angelone* is one of the most commonly cited examples of this interpretation of § 2254(d).

Monroe v. Angelone

323 F.3d 286 (4th Cir. 2003)

* * * In its appeal, the Commonwealth maintains that the district court failed to give proper deference to the state court adjudications of Monroe's *Brady* claim, as required by the Antiterrorism and Effective Death Penalty Act of 1996 ("AEDPA"). Under AEDPA, a federal court must defer to a state court's resolution of a claim that has been "adjudicated on the merits." 28 U.S.C. § 2254(d). Conversely, where a state court has not considered a properly preserved claim on its merits, a federal court must assess the claim *de novo*. [*S*]*ee Cargle v. Mullin*, 317 F.3d 1196 (10th Cir. 2003) ("[AEDPA] applies only when there is an antecedent state court decision on the same matter.").

Pursuant to this doctrine, AEDPA's deference requirement does not apply when a claim made on federal habeas review is premised on *Brady* material that has surfaced for the first time during federal proceedings.

Here, certain items of suppressed, exculpatory material first came to light during Monroe's federal habeas proceedings. In particular, Monroe first obtained the following through discovery in federal court: (1) some evidentiary material on the Smith sentence deal (particularly Riley's deposition); (2) some evidentiary material on Smith's informant history (particularly information in Riley's notes); (3) Smith's inconsistent statements; (4) the Lundy information; (5) Samuels's personal problems statement; (6) Samuels's napping habits statement; (7) Corinna's male heir statement; and (8) the secretaries' notes.[4] By contrast, the state courts have previously considered: (1) the Smith gun deal; (2) some evidentiary material on the Smith sentence deal; (3) some evidentiary material on Smith's informant history; and (4) the Bronco witnesses. In these circumstances, we are obliged to give deference to decisions of the state courts that the Commonwealth's failure to disclose these last four items of Brady evidence did not constitute a Brady violation.

The prosecution's late disclosure of the other eight items of exculpatory material listed above, however, precluded the state courts from considering those items when they ruled on Monroe's *Brady* claim. Because no state court was ever presented with these eight items of exculpatory material, we are obliged to make an independent determination of whether they are favorable to Monroe, and whether they were suppressed. *See Boyette v. Lefevre*, 246 F.3d 76 (2d Cir. 2001) ("[B]ecause no state court determined whether some documents were *Brady* materials, we must exercise *de novo* review of this issue."). In addition, we must determine whether all of the non-defaulted materials—those presented in state

4. Footnote 17 in the Court's opinion states: "Because Monroe was entitled 'to rely on ... the presumption that the prosecutor would fully perform his duty to disclose all exculpatory materials,' she did not default her right to rely on the material first obtained in federal habeas discovery by failing to bring it to the attention of the state courts. Strickler [v. Greene], 527 U.S. [263] at 284 [1999]."

court and those presented for the first time in federal court—considered and weighed collectively, made a material difference to the outcome of Monroe's trial.

In making this "materiality" determination, the third step in any *Brady* analysis, we are unable to accord AEDPA deference on an item-by-item basis to the four items of exculpatory material considered in state court, because we are obliged to assess the materiality of exculpatory evidence "collectively, not item by item." [*S*]*ee also Cargle* (holding that AEDPA does not apply to cumulative error analysis when no state court has considered all the material considered by federal courts). In these circumstances, we have no way of deferring to an earlier state court adjudication on materiality because no state court considered all of the *Brady* material presented here. As a result, we must make an independent assessment of whether the suppression of exculpatory evidence—including the evidence previously presented to the state courts—materially affected Monroe's first-degree murder conviction.

* * *

Notes

1. *Subsequent case history*

In June of 2003, prosecutors announced that they would not retry Monroe. *See* Mid-Atlantic Innocence Project, Beverly Monroe, http://www.exonerate.org/case-profiles/beverly-monroe.

2. *Similar reasoning was applied by the Sixth Circuit in* Brown v. Smith:

> This circuit has held that, in the context of a *Brady* claim, when the petitioner's habeas claim involves *Brady* material that was uncovered only during the federal habeas proceedings, AEDPA deference does not apply to an earlier, state-court *Brady* adjudication involving a different mix of allegedly improperly withheld evidence. We think that the same principle applies generally whenever new, substantial evidence supporting a habeas claim comes to light during the proceedings in federal district court.
>
> To be sure, this rule presupposes that the threshold standard for admitting new evidence in the federal district court is met: (1) the petitioner must not be at fault for failing to develop the evidence in state court, or (2) if the petitioner is at fault, the narrow exceptions set forth in 28 U.S.C. § 2254(e)(2) apply.

Brown, 551 F.3d 424, 429 (6th Cir. 2008).

3. *Extending the reasoning of* Monroe *to other claims*

Does *Monroe* allow a state prisoner to argue that his Sixth Amendment claim was not adjudicated by the state courts for purposes of triggering (d)(1) and (d)(2) if, for example, the state court summarily denied the prisoner's claims without a hearing or any other meaningful procedural review of the claim? Is it really the "same" claim of ineffective assistance of counsel once the significant evidence supporting the claim is, once and for all, presented and developed in federal court?

4. *Is the* Monroe *rule fair to state courts?*

Doesn't *Monroe* undermine the limitations on relief contained in § 2254(d) by providing prisoners an incentive to withhold critical evidence from the state post-conviction courts in order to ensure *de novo* review in federal court? In other words, doesn't *Monroe* encourage sand-bagging by the clever state prisoner?

5. *Constitutional weight*

Can the rules of statutory construction from *Monroe* or *Taylor* be afforded constitutional weight? Is there some constitutional pedigree for the notion that every prisoner is entitled to at least one full and fair review of his federal constitutional claims? Consider Professor Bator's article excerpted in Chapter 1, and the reasoning of *Frank v. Mangum*. *See Wright v. West*, 505 U.S. 277, 299 (1992) (O'Connor, J.); *Townsend v. Sain*, 372 U.S. 293, 313 (1963) (recognizing that the constitution requires additional, otherwise, discretionary federal procedures and review—i.e., an evidentiary hearing—when the state court process is not procedurally "adequate").

Chapter 13

Harmless Error

> Errors are the insects in the world of law, traveling through it in swarms, often unnoticed in their endless procession. Many are plainly harmless; some appear ominously harmful. Some, for all the benign appearance of their spindly traces, mark the way for a plague of followers that deplete trials of fairness ... [A]n inquiry into what makes an error harmless, though one of philosophical tenor, is also an intensely practical inquiry into the health and sanitation of the law.[1]

Harmless error is one of the most controversial and important doctrines of modern criminal law. It is controversial because it allows trial errors, even constitutional defects in the trial, to go unremedied. As Judge Posner famously explained in a Seventh Circuit decision, "The expansive code of constitutional criminal procedure that the Supreme Court has created in the name of the Constitution is like the grapes of Tantalus, since the equally expansive harmless error rule in most cases prevents a criminal defendant from obtaining any benefit from the code."[2] Quite often an individual may have a constitutional right, but because of the harmless error doctrine his right lacks a remedy. The significance of harmless error to modern criminal and habeas litigation likewise is easy to appreciate. It has been said that the harmless error rules determine whether the prisoner will prevail in more cases than any other doctrine. Consequently, the process of determining whether an error is harmless is central to the resolution of most habeas corpus claims.

Until the mid-1960s the doctrine of harmless error was limited to non-constitutional trial errors. Under the Federal Rules of Criminal Procedure, Rule 52(a), reversal is forbidden for all *non-constitutional* errors unless the error affected "substantial rights" of the defendant. It was not until the seminal case, *Chapman v. California*, 386 U.S. 18 (1967), that the Court addressed "whether there can ever be harmless constitutional error." The Court recognized that some constitutional violations—the denial of the right to counsel or the right to an impartial judge were among the examples given—cannot be subject to harmless error review and instead require reversal. However, the Court explicitly refused to require automatic reversal for all constitutional errors when it held that "there may be some constitutional errors which in the setting of a particular case are so unimportant and insignificant that they may, consistent with the Federal Constitution, be deemed harmless, not requiring the automatic reversal of the conviction." The Court also held that as a matter of federal constitutional law, the harmless error review of constitutional errors must be much more exacting than the harmless error review permitted for non-constitutional errors. Under the still prevailing rule of *Chapman*, a constitutional error is harmless or undeserving of remedy unless the reviewing court finds "beyond a reasonable doubt ... that [the errors] did not contribute to petitioners' convictions."

The cases that follow trace the application and development of the harmless error doctrine in the context of constitutional errors. The first case, *Greer v. Miller*, illustrates the

1. Roger Traynor, The Riddle of Harmless Error, at ix (1970).
2. *United States v. Pallais*, 921 F.2d 684, 692 (7th Cir. 1990).

confusion surrounding the distinction between the merits of a constitutional claim and the question of whether an error is harmless under *Chapman*, and it foreshadows the development of an alternative to the *Chapman* standard. The next case, *Arizona v. Fulminante*, addresses the crucial question left open in *Chapman*: how does a court determine whether a constitutional error is subject to harmless error review. The third case, *Brecht v. Abrahamson*, considers whether the *Chapman* harmless-error analysis applies to habeas corpus proceedings. The final case, *Fry v. Pliler*, attempts to reconcile the *Brecht* and *Chapman* rules with Section 2254(d) of the Anti-Terrorism and Effective Death Penalty Act.

Greer v. Miller

483 U.S. 756 (1987)

JUSTICE POWELL delivered the opinion of the Court.

The question before us is whether a prosecutor's question at trial concerning a criminal defendant's post-arrest silence requires reversal of the defendant's conviction.

I

In 1980, Neil Gorsuch was kidnapped, robbed, and murdered after leaving a bar in Jacksonville, Illinois. Three men were charged with the crimes: Randy Williams, Clarence Armstrong, and the respondent, Charles Miller. Williams confessed, and later entered into a plea agreement under which most of the charges against him were dropped in return for his testimony at the separate trials of Armstrong and Miller.

At Miller's trial, Williams testified that he, his brother, and Armstrong had met Gorsuch in a tavern on the evening of February 8. Armstrong offered the victim a ride back to his hotel, and the four men left together at about 1:30 a.m. After Williams' brother was dropped off, Armstrong began beating Gorsuch in the back seat of the car. According to Williams' testimony, the group stopped briefly at Williams' parents' home to pick up a shotgun, and the men then drove to the trailer home where Miller was staying. Williams testified that Miller joined the group, and that they then traveled to a bridge on an isolated road. Williams stated that once there each of the three men shot Gorsuch in the head with the shotgun.

Respondent Miller took the stand on his own behalf and told a different story. On direct examination he testified that he had taken no part in the crime, but that Armstrong and Williams had come to the trailer home after the murder was committed seeking Miller's advice. Miller testified that Armstrong confessed that he and Williams had beaten and robbed Gorsuch, and that they had killed him to avoid being identified as the perpetrators.

The prosecutor began his cross-examination of Miller as follows:

Q: Mr. Miller, how old are you?

A: 23.

Q: Why didn't you tell this story to anybody when you got arrested?

Defense counsel immediately objected. Out of the hearing of the jury, Miller's lawyer requested a mistrial on the ground that the prosecutor's question violated Miller's right to remain silent after arrest. The trial judge denied the motion, but immediately sustained the objection and instructed the jury to "ignore [the] question, for the time being." The prosecutor did not pursue the issue further, nor did he mention it during his closing argument. At the conclusion of the presentation of evidence, defense counsel did not renew his objection or request an instruction concerning the prosecutor's question. Moreover, the judge specifically instructed the jury to "disregard questions ... to which objections were sustained." Miller was convicted of murder, aggravated kidnapping, and robbery, and sentenced to 80 years in prison.

On appeal the State argued that if the prosecutor's question about Miller's post-arrest silence was prohibited by this Court's decision in *Doyle v. Ohio*, 426 U.S. 610 (1976), the error was harmless under the standards of *Chapman v. California*, 386 U.S. 18 (1967). The Illinois Appellate Court rejected the argument and reversed the conviction, concluding that the evidence against Miller "was not so overwhelming as to preclude all reasonable doubts about the effect of the prosecutor's comment." The Supreme Court of Illinois disagreed and reinstated the trial court's decision. The court noted that the prosecutor's question was an isolated comment made in the course of a lengthy trial, that the jury had been instructed to disregard the question, and that the evidence properly admitted was sufficient to establish Miller's guilt beyond a reasonable doubt. It therefore held that the error did not require reversal of the conviction.

Miller then filed a petition for a writ of habeas corpus in the Federal District Court for the Central District of Illinois. The District Court denied the petition, finding "no possibility that the prosecutor's questioning on post-arrest silence could have contributed to the conviction." A divided panel of the Court of Appeals for the Seventh Circuit reversed the District Court's decision, as did the full court on reargument en banc. The en banc court found that because Miller had received *Miranda* warnings at the time of his arrest for the offenses in question, "[t]he prosecutor's reference to Miller's silence at the time of his arrest ... violated his constitutional right to a fair trial." The court further held that the error was not harmless beyond a reasonable doubt under *Chapman v. California* because "[t]he evidence against Miller was not overwhelming, his story was not implausible, and the trial court's cautionary instruction was insufficient to cure the error." Three judges dissented, concluding that under the harmless-error standard, "this fifteen-second colloquy, alleviated by the trial judge's immediately sustaining the defendant's objection and instructing the jury to ignore the prosecutor's improper question and by a threshold jury instruction to disregard questions to which objections were sustained, did not affect the verdict." Judge Easterbrook also dissented. In his view, the harmless-error standard of *Chapman* is too stringent to be applied to this case for a number of reasons: the rule of *Doyle* is prophylactic rather than innocence-protecting; the issue is presented on collateral, rather than on direct, review; the error in this case could have been cured more fully had defense counsel so requested at trial; and the violation should be viewed as prosecutorial misconduct that requires reversal only if it rendered the trial fundamentally unfair.

We granted certiorari to review the Court of Appeals' determination that the prosecutor's question about the criminal defendant's post-arrest silence requires reversal of the conviction in this case. * * * We disagree with the Court of Appeals and now reverse.

II

The starting point of our analysis is *Doyle v. Ohio*, 426 U.S. 610 (1976). The petitioners in *Doyle* were arrested for selling marijuana. They were given *Miranda* warnings and made no post-arrest statements about their involvement in the crime. They contended at trial that they had been framed by the government informant. As part of his cross-examination, the prosecutor repeatedly asked petitioners why, if they were innocent, they did not give the explanation that they proffered at their separate trials to the police at the time of their arrest. Defense counsel's timely objections to this line of questioning were overruled. Also over timely objections, the trial court allowed the prosecutor to argue petitioners' post-arrest silence to the jury. On review, this Court found that the *Miranda* decision "compel[led] rejection" of the contention that such questioning and argument are proper means of impeachment. The Court noted that post-arrest silence may not be particularly probative of guilt. We also found that because *Miranda* warnings contain an implicit assurance "that silence will carry no penalty," "'it does not comport with due process to permit the prosecution during the trial to call attention to [the defendant's] silence at the time of arrest and to insist that because he did not speak about the facts of the case at that time, as he was told he need not do, an unfavorable inference might be drawn as to the truth of his trial testimony,'" *id.* at 619. Accordingly the Court in *Doyle* held that "the use for impeachment purposes of petitioners' silence, at the time of arrest and after receiving *Miranda* warnings, violated the Due Process Clause of the Fourteenth Amendment."

This Court has applied the holding of *Doyle* in a number of subsequent cases. These later holdings confirm that "*Doyle* rests on 'the fundamental unfairness of implicitly assuring a suspect that his silence will not be used against him and then using his silence to impeach an explanation subsequently offered at trial.'" *Wainwright v. Greenfield*, 474 U.S. 284, 291 (1986) (quoting *South Dakota v. Neville*, 459 U.S. 553, 565 (1983)). Thus, "absen[t] the sort of affirmative assurances embodied in the *Miranda* warnings," the Constitution does not prohibit the use of a defendant's post-arrest silence to impeach him at trial. *Fletcher v. Weir*, 455 U.S. 603, 607 (1982).

There is no question that Miller received the "implicit assurance" of *Miranda* warnings in this case. Thus, this prerequisite of a *Doyle* violation was met. But the holding of *Doyle* is that the Due Process Clause bars "*the use* for impeachment purposes" of a defendant's post-arrest silence. The Court noted that "'it does not comport with due process *to permit* the prosecution during trial to call attention to [the defendant's] silence.'" It is significant that in each of the cases in which this Court has applied *Doyle*, the trial court has permitted specific inquiry or argument respecting the defendant's post-*Miranda* silence. *See Jenkins v. Anderson*, 447 U.S. at 233–34 (extended questioning and closing argument reference); *Anderson v. Charles*, 447 U.S. at 405–406 (questioning); *Fletcher v. Weir*, 455 U.S. at 603–604 (questioning); *South Dakota v. Neville*, 459 U.S. at 564 (admission of refusal to take blood-alcohol test); *Wainwright v. Greenfield*, 474 U.S. at 285, 287 (closing argument).

In contrast to these cases, the trial court in this case did not permit the inquiry that *Doyle* forbids. Instead, the court explicitly sustained an objection to the only question that touched upon Miller's post-arrest silence. No further questioning or argument with respect to Miller's silence occurred, and the court specifically advised the jury that it should disregard any questions to which an objection was sustained. Unlike the prosecutor in *Doyle*, the prosecutor in this case was not "allowed to undertake impeachment on," or "permit[ted] ... to call attention to," Miller's silence. The fact of Miller's post-arrest silence was not submitted to the jury as evidence from which it was allowed to draw any permissible inference, and thus no *Doyle* violation occurred in this case.

III

Although the prosecutor's question did not constitute a *Doyle* violation, the fact remains that the prosecutor attempted to violate the rule of *Doyle* by asking an improper question in the presence of the jury. This Court has recognized that prosecutorial misconduct may "so infec[t] the trial with unfairness as to make the resulting conviction a denial of due process." *Donnelly v. DeChristoforo*, 416 U.S. 637, 643 (1974). To constitute a due process violation, the prosecutorial misconduct must be "'of sufficient significance to result in the denial of the defendant's right to a fair trial.'" *United States v. Bagley*, 473 U.S. 667, 676 (1985) (quoting *United States v. Agurs*, 427 U.S. 97, 108 (1976)).

The Illinois Supreme Court, applying the analysis of *Chapman v. California*, 386 U.S. 18 (1967), found that the prosecutor's question was harmless beyond a reasonable doubt. We thus are convinced that it would find no due process violation under the facts of this case. When a defendant contends that a prosecutor's question rendered his trial fundamentally unfair, it is important "as an initial matter to place th[e] remar[k] in context." *Darden v. Wainwright*, 477 U.S. 168, 179 (1986). *See Donnelly v. DeChristoforo*, 416 U.S. at 639 (determining whether "remarks, in the context of the entire trial, were sufficiently prejudicial to violate respondent's due process rights"). The sequence of events in this case—a single question, an immediate objection, and two curative instructions—clearly indicates that the prosecutor's improper question did not violate Miller's due process rights. The Illinois Supreme Court's determination that the properly admitted evidence at trial "was sufficient to prove defendant's guilt beyond a reasonable doubt" further supports this result.

IV

We reverse the judgment of the Court of Appeals for the Seventh Circuit and remand for proceedings consistent with this opinion.

It is so ordered.

JUSTICE STEVENS, concurring in the judgment.

Having dissented in *Doyle v. Ohio*, 426 U.S. 610, 620–35 (1976), I can readily understand why the Court might want to overrule that case. But if there is to be a rule that prohibits a prosecutor's use of a defendant's post-*Miranda* silence, it should be a clearly defined rule. Whether the trial court sustains an objection to an impermissible question, or whether the prosecutor is allowed to refer to the defendant's silence in his or her closing arguments, are questions that are relevant to the harmless-error inquiry, or to deciding whether the error made the trial fundamentally unfair. But they play no role in deciding whether a prosecutor violated the implicit promise of *Miranda*—as understood in *Doyle*—that the defendant's silence will not be used against him.

I, therefore, agree with the 10 Illinois judges and 12 federal judges who have concluded that the rule of the *Doyle* case was violated when the prosecutor called the jury's attention to respondent's silence. Moreover, for the reasons stated by the Court of Appeals, I think the violation was serious enough to support that court's conclusion that the error was not harmless beyond a reasonable doubt. Were this case here on direct appeal, therefore, I would vote to reverse the conviction.

Nonetheless, I concur in the Court's judgment because I believe the question presented in the certiorari petition—whether a federal court should apply a different standard in reviewing *Doyle* errors *in a habeas corpus action*—should be answered in the affirmative. In *Rose v. Lundy*, 455 U.S. 509 (1982), I argued that there are at least four types of alleged constitutional errors.

> The one most frequently encountered is a claim that attaches a constitutional label to a set of facts that does not disclose a violation of any constitutional right.... The second class includes constitutional violations that are not of sufficient import in a particular case to justify reversal even on direct appeal, when the evidence is still fresh and a fair retrial could be promptly conducted. *Chapman v. California*, 386 U.S. 18, 22 (1967); *Harrington v. California*, 395 U.S. 250 (1969). A third category includes errors that are important enough to require reversal on direct appeal but do not reveal the kind of fundamental unfairness to the accused that will support a collateral attack on a final judgment. *See, e.g., Stone v. Powell*, 428 U.S. 465 (1976). The fourth category includes those errors that

are so fundamental that they infect the validity of the underlying judgment itself, or the integrity of the process by which that judgment was obtained. *Id.* at 543–44 (dissenting opinion).

In my view, *Doyle* violations which cannot be deemed harmless beyond a reasonable doubt typically fall within the third of these categories. On *direct review*, a conviction should be reversed if a defendant can demonstrate that a *Doyle* error occurred at trial, and the State cannot demonstrate that it is harmless beyond a reasonable doubt. But, in typical *collateral attacks*, such as today's, *Doyle* errors are not so fundamentally unfair that convictions must be reversed whenever the State cannot bear the heavy burden of proving that the error was harmless beyond a reasonable doubt. On the other hand, there may be extraordinary cases in which the *Doyle* error is so egregious, or is combined with other errors or incidents of prosecutorial misconduct, that the integrity of the process is called into question. In such an event, habeas corpus relief should be afforded.

In sum, although I agree with the Court's judgment, and the standard that it applies here, I would apply this standard only to *Doyle* violations being considered on collateral review. On direct appeal, a *Doyle* error should give rise to reversal of the conviction unless the State can prove that the error was harmless beyond a reasonable doubt.

JUSTICE BRENNAN, with whom JUSTICE MARSHALL and JUSTICE BLACKMUN join, dissenting.

Today the Court holds that a prosecutor may comment on a defendant's post-arrest silence in an attempt to impeach his credibility without thereby violating the rule of *Doyle v. Ohio*, 426 U.S. 610 (1976). The Court arrives at this surprising conclusion only by confusing the question whether a *Doyle* violation occurred with the question whether that violation was harmless beyond a reasonable doubt. The holding is remarkable not only because it radically departs from the settled practice of the lower courts, but also because it is founded on a point conceded below and not raised here.

Until today, the common understanding of "our opinion in *Doyle v. Ohio* ... [was that it] shields from *comment* by a prosecutor a defendant's silence after receiving *Miranda* warnings." *Wainwright v. Greenfield*, 474 U.S. 284, 96 (1986) (REHNQUIST, J., concurring in result) (emphasis added). Accordingly, a defendant has been able to establish a *Doyle* violation simply by showing that the prosecutor "'call[ed] attention to'" the defendant's post-arrest silence. *Doyle*, 426 U.S. at 619. "The standard is strict; virtually any description of a defendant's silence following arrest and a *Miranda* warning will constitute a *Doyle* violation." *United States v. Shaw*, 701 F.2d 367, 82 ([5th Cir.] 1983). In light of this authority and the prosecutor's "clear-cut" attempt to use the defendant's post-arrest silence to impeach his credibility, *United States ex rel. Miller v. Greer*, 789 F.2d 438, 47 ([7th Cir.] 1986), it is not surprising that the five other courts that examined this case found a *Doyle* violation.

To support its decision that no *Doyle* violation occurred in this case, the Court argues in effect that a single comment cannot be sufficient to constitute a *Doyle* violation. A single comment, the Court suggests, does not amount to the "use" of a defendant's silence for impeachment purposes, and is not equivalent to an "inquiry or argument respecting the defendant's post-*Miranda* silence." *Ante*. What the Court overlooks, however, is the fact that a single comment is all the prosecutor needs to notify the jury that the defendant did not "tell his story" promptly after his arrest. Although silence at the time of arrest is "insolubly ambiguous" and may be "consistent with ... an exculpatory explanation," *Doyle*, 426 U.S. at 617, 618, and n.8, nevertheless "the jury is likely to draw" a "strong negative inference" from the fact of a defendant's post-arrest silence. *United States v. Hale*, 422 U.S.

171, 180 (1975). Thus, as the lower courts have consistently found, a prosecutor may in a single comment effectively use a defendant's post-arrest silence to impeach his or her credibility.

The Court also notes that the trial court sustained defendant's objection to the prosecutor's improper question, and that the court later instructed the jury to disregard all questions to which an objection had been sustained. These actions minimized the harm this particular comment might have caused, the Court implies, and also distinguish this case from previous cases in which this Court has applied *Doyle*. In the case on which *Doyle* was squarely based, however, the Court reversed a conviction because of improper questioning regarding post-*Miranda* silence even though the jury was immediately instructed to disregard that questioning. *See United States v. Hale*, 422 U.S. at 175, n.3. Moreover, the lower courts have routinely addressed similar situations, and in no case in which the prosecutor has commented on the defendant's silence have these courts found contemporaneous objections or curative instructions sufficient *automatically* to preclude finding a *Doyle* violation. Instead, the Courts of Appeals have examined the comment in context, and considered it along with the weight of the evidence against the defendant and the importance of the defendant's credibility to the defense, in determining whether a *Doyle* violation was harmless beyond a reasonable doubt. * * *

The approach taken by the lower courts reflects both the serious impact of *Doyle* violations on the fairness of a trial, and the inherent difficulty in undoing the harm that they cause. With respect to their impact, more than one Circuit has recognized that "*Doyle* violations are rarely harmless." *Williams v. Zahradnick*, 632 F.2d 353, 364 ([2d Cir.] 1980)(citing practice in the Fifth Circuit with approval). This is because "questions of guilt and credibility [are often] inextricably bound together," *Morgan v. Hall*, and because comments upon a defendant's failure to tell his or her story promptly after arrest may significantly undermine the defendant's credibility in the jury's eyes. This case illustrates the potential for harm. The only testimony the State offered that linked the defendant to the crime was that of an alleged accomplice. Jurors often give accomplice testimony reduced weight, particularly when the accomplice has received in return a promise of significant leniency. Here the State's case depended entirely on whether the jury believed the defendant or the alleged accomplice. The prosecutor's second question on cross-examination— "Why didn't you tell this story to anybody when you got arrested?"—thus struck directly at the heart of Miller's defense: his credibility. If the rationale of *Doyle* is to have any force, defendants must be protected from such tactics.

Lower courts have also recognized that once the prosecutor calls attention to the defendant's silence, the resultant harm is not easily cured. First, the jury is made aware of the fact of post-arrest silence, and a foundation is laid for subsequent, more subtle attacks. Second, "curative" instructions themselves call attention to defendant's silence, and may in some cases serve to exacerbate the harm. In a related context, involving a prosecutor's statement calling attention to the defendant's decision not to testify at trial, JUSTICE STEVENS has argued that "[i]t is unrealistic to assume that instructions on the right to silence always have a benign effect." *Lakeside v. Oregon*, 435 U.S. 333, 347 (dissenting opinion).

* * *

Courts below have therefore considered prompt objections and curative instructions relevant to the question whether a comment on a defendant's silence is harmless error, but irrelevant to the question whether the comment violates *Doyle*. The Court today confuses the two inquiries, and thereby eliminates much of the protection afforded by *Doyle*.

Today's radical departure from established practice is particularly inappropriate because this ground for decision was not presented either to the courts below or to this Court. The State "concede[d]" in the Court of Appeals that "any comment referring to [defendant's] silence after that arrest [for murder] would be improper." It sought review in this Court not of the question whether a *Doyle* violation occurred, but whether, assuming the existence of a *Doyle* violation, the standard for appellate review should be more lenient than harmless error. The question decided today was therefore *not* "fairly included in the question presented for review." Moreover, the Court's contention that this question was argued in the briefs appears to me simply mistaken. The Court has overturned the judgment below, and upset the settled practice of the lower courts, on a point which the State conceded below and did not raise here, and on which respondent has had no opportunity to be heard.

Today's decision saps *Doyle* of much of its vitality. I would adhere to *Doyle*'s principles, and to the established practice of the lower courts. I dissent.

Notes

1. *Case history*

Charles Miller was sentenced to 80 years for murder, 30 years for aggravated kidnapping, and 7 years for robbery. *United States ex rel. Miller v. Greer*, 789 F.2d 438, 441. He remains in the custody of the Illinois Department of corrections. See Inmate Search at www.idoc.state/il.us. Although the accomplice, Randy Williams, admitted shooting the victim, in return for Williams's testimony, the State dropped charges of murder, aggravated kidnapping, and robbery and agreed to a sentence of two years probation. *Id.* at 440, 446 n.7 (7th Cir. 1986). The jury was aware that a "deal" between the State and Williams had been struck. 483 U.S. at 772 n.2 (Brennan, J., dissenting).

2. *The curative instruction given at Miller's trial*

Many practitioners do not believe that a curative instruction really can fix the problem when an improper matter is placed before the jury—in other words, that one cannot "unring the bell." What are the reasons to think that a curative instruction will fix the problem? What are the reasons to think that it won't?

Arizona v. Fulminante

499 U.S. 279 (1991)

JUSTICE WHITE delivered an opinion, Parts I, II, and IV of which are the opinion of the Court, and Part III of which is a dissenting opinion. [JUSTICE MARSHALL, JUSTICE BLACKMUN and JUSTICE STEVENS join this opinion in its entirety; JUSTICE SCALIA joins Parts I and II; and JUSTICE KENNEDY joins Parts I and IV.]

The Arizona Supreme Court ruled in this case that respondent Oreste Fulminante's confession, received in evidence at his trial for murder, had been coerced and that its use against him was barred by the Fifth and Fourteenth Amendments to the United States Constitution. The court also held that the harmless-error rule could not be used to save the conviction. We affirm the judgment of the Arizona court, although for different reasons than those upon which that court relied.

I

Early in the morning of September 14, 1982, Fulminante called the Mesa, Arizona, Police Department to report that his 11-year-old stepdaughter, Jeneane Michelle Hunt, was missing. He had been caring for Jeneane while his wife, Jeneane's mother, was in the hospital. Two days later, Jeneane's body was found in the desert east of Mesa. She had been shot twice in the head at close range with a large caliber weapon, and a ligature was around her neck. Because of the decomposed condition of the body, it was impossible to tell whether she had been sexually assaulted.

Fulminante's statements to police concerning Jeneane's disappearance and his relationship with her contained a number of inconsistencies, and he became a suspect in her killing. When no charges were filed against him, Fulminante left Arizona for New Jersey. Fulminante was later convicted in New Jersey on federal charges of possession of a firearm by a felon.

Fulminante was incarcerated in the Ray Brook Federal Correctional Institution in New York. There he became friends with another inmate, Anthony Sarivola, then serving a 60-day sentence for extortion. The two men came to spend several hours a day together. Sarivola, a former police officer, had been involved in loansharking for organized crime but then became a paid informant for the Federal Bureau of Investigation. While at Ray Brook, he masqueraded as an organized crime figure. After becoming friends with Fulminante, Sarivola heard a rumor that Fulminante was suspected of killing a child in Arizona. Sarivola then raised the subject with Fulminante in several conversations, but Fulminante repeatedly denied any involvement in Jeneane's death. During one conversation, he told Sarivola that Jeneane had been killed by bikers looking for drugs; on another occasion, he said he did not know what had happened. Sarivola passed this information on to an agent of the Federal Bureau of Investigation, who instructed Sarivola to find out more.

Sarivola learned more one evening in October 1983, as he and Fulminante walked together around the prison track. Sarivola said that he knew Fulminante was "starting to get some tough treatment and whatnot" from other inmates because of the rumor. Sarivola offered to protect Fulminante from his fellow inmates, but told him, "'You have to tell me about it,' you know. I mean, in other words, 'For me to give you any help.'" Fulminante then admitted to Sarivola that he had driven Jeneane to the desert on his motorcycle, where he choked her, sexually assaulted her, and made her beg for her life, before shooting her twice in the head.

Sarivola was released from prison in November 1983. Fulminante was released the following May, only to be arrested the next month for another weapons violation. On September 4, 1984, Fulminante was indicted in Arizona for the first-degree murder of Jeneane.

Prior to trial, Fulminante moved to suppress the statement he had given Sarivola in prison, as well as a second confession he had given to Donna Sarivola, then Anthony Sarivola's fiancée and later his wife, following his May 1984 release from prison. He asserted that the confession to Sarivola was coerced, and that the second confession was the "fruit" of the first. Following the hearing, the trial court denied the motion to suppress, specifically finding that, based on the stipulated facts, the confessions were voluntary. The State introduced both confessions as evidence at trial, and on December 19, 1985, Fulminante was convicted of Jeneane's murder. He was subsequently sentenced to death.

Fulminante appealed, arguing, among other things, that his confession to Sarivola was the product of coercion and that its admission at trial violated his rights to due process under the Fifth and Fourteenth Amendments to the United States Constitution. After considering the evidence at trial as well as the stipulated facts before the trial court on the motion to suppress, the Arizona Supreme Court held that the confession was coerced, but initially determined that the admission of the confession at trial was harmless error, because of the overwhelming nature of the evidence against Fulminante. Upon Fulminante's motion for reconsideration, however, the court ruled that this Court's precedent precluded the use of the harmless-error analysis in the case of a coerced confession. The court therefore reversed the conviction and ordered that Fulminante be retried without the use of the confession to Sarivola. Because of differing views in the state and federal courts over whether the admission at trial of a coerced confession is subject to a harmless-error analysis, we granted the State's petition for certiorari. Although a majority of this Court finds that such a confession is subject to a harmless-error analysis, for the reasons set forth below, we affirm the judgment of the Arizona court.

II

We deal first with the State's contention that the court below erred in holding Fulminante's confession to have been coerced. The State argues that it is the totality of the circumstances that determines whether Fulminante's confession was coerced, *cf. Schneckloth v. Bustamonte*, 412 U.S. 218, 226 (1973), but contends that rather than apply this standard, the Arizona court applied a "but for" test, under which the court found that but for the promise given by Sarivola, Fulminante would not have confessed. In support of this argument, the State points to the Arizona court's reference to *Bram v. United States*, 168 U.S. 532 (1897). Although the Court noted in *Bram* that a confession cannot be obtained by "'any direct or implied promises, however slight, nor by the exertion of any improper influence,'" *id.*, it is clear that this passage from *Bram*, which under current precedent does not state the standard for determining the voluntariness of a confession, was not relied on by the Arizona court in reaching its conclusion. Rather, the court cited this language as part of a longer quotation from an Arizona case which accurately described the State's burden of proof for establishing voluntariness. Indeed, the Arizona Supreme Court stated that a "determination regarding the voluntariness of a confession ... must be viewed in a totality of the circumstances" and under that standard plainly found that Fulminante's statement to Sarivola had been coerced.

In applying the totality of the circumstances test to determine that the confession to Sarivola was coerced, the Arizona Supreme Court focused on a number of relevant facts. First, the court noted that "because [Fulminante] was an alleged child murderer, he was in danger of physical harm at the hands of other inmates." In addition, Sarivola was aware that Fulminante had been receiving "'rough treatment from the guys.'" Using his knowledge of these threats, Sarivola offered to protect Fulminante in exchange for a confession to Jeneane's murder, and "[i]n response to Sarivola's offer of protection, [Fulminante] confessed." Agreeing with Fulminante that "Sarivola's promise was 'extremely coercive,'" the Arizona court declared: "[T]he confession was obtained as a direct result of extreme coercion and was tendered in the belief that the defendant's life was in jeopardy if he did not confess. This is a true coerced confession in every sense of the word."

We normally give great deference to the factual findings of the state court. *Davis v. North Carolina*, 384 U.S. 737, 741 (1966). Nevertheless, "the ultimate issue of 'voluntariness' is a legal question requiring independent federal determination." *Miller v. Fenton*, 474 U.S. 104, 110 (1985).

Although the question is a close one, we agree with the Arizona Supreme Court's conclusion that Fulminante's confession was coerced. The Arizona Supreme Court found a credible threat of physical violence unless Fulminante confessed. Our cases have made clear that a finding of coercion need not depend upon actual violence by a government agent; a credible threat is sufficient. As we have said, "coercion can be mental as well as physical, and ... the blood of the accused is not the only hallmark of an unconstitutional inquisition." *Blackburn v. Alabama*, 361 U.S. 199, 206 (1960). As in *Payne v. Arkansas*, 356

U.S. 560, 561 (1958), where the Court found that a confession was coerced because the interrogating police officer had promised that if the accused confessed, the officer would protect the accused from an angry mob outside the jailhouse door, so too here, the Arizona Supreme Court found that it was fear of physical violence, absent protection from his friend (and Government agent) Sarivola, which motivated Fulminante to confess. Accepting the Arizona court's finding, permissible on this record, that there was a credible threat of physical violence, we agree with its conclusion that Fulminante's will was overborne in such a way as to render his confession the product of coercion.

III

Four of us, Justices Marshall, Blackmun, Stevens, and myself, would affirm the judgment of the Arizona Supreme Court on the ground that the harmless-error rule is inapplicable to erroneously admitted coerced confessions. We thus disagree with the Justices who have a contrary view.

The majority today abandons what until now the Court has regarded as the "axiomatic [proposition] that a defendant in a criminal case is deprived of due process of law if his conviction is founded, in whole or in part, upon an involuntary confession, without regard for the truth or falsity of the confession, *Rogers v. Richmond*, 365 U.S. 534 (1961), and even though there is ample evidence aside from the confession to support the conviction." *Jackson v. Denno*, 378 U.S. 368, 376 (1964). The Court has repeatedly stressed that the view that the admission of a coerced confession can be harmless error because of the other evidence to support the verdict is "an impermissible doctrine," *Lynumn v. Illinois*, 372 U.S. 528, 537 (1963); for "the admission in evidence, over objection, of the coerced confession vitiates the judgment because it violates the Due Process Clause of the Fourteenth Amendment," *Payne*, 356 U.S. at 568. * * * [T]he rule was the same even when another confession of the defendant had been properly admitted into evidence. Today, a majority of the Court, without any justification, *cf. Arizona v. Rumsey*, 467 U.S. 203, 212 (1984), overrules this vast body of precedent without a word and in so doing dislodges one of the fundamental tenets of our criminal justice system.

In extending to coerced confessions the harmless-error rule of *Chapman v. California*, the majority declares that because the Court has applied that analysis to numerous other "trial errors," there is no reason that it should not apply to an error of this nature as well. The four of us remain convinced, however, that we should abide by our cases that have refused to apply the harmless-error rule to coerced confessions, for a coerced confession is fundamentally different from other types of erroneously admitted evidence to which the rule has been applied. Indeed, as the majority concedes, *Chapman* itself recognized that prior cases "have indicated that there are some constitutional rights so basic to a fair trial that their infraction can *never* be treated as harmless error," and it placed in that category the constitutional rule against using a defendant's coerced confession against him at his criminal trial. * * *

Chapman specifically noted three constitutional errors that could not be categorized as harmless error: using a coerced confession against a defendant in a criminal trial, depriving a defendant of counsel, and trying a defendant before a biased judge. The majority attempts to distinguish the use of a coerced confession from the other two errors listed in *Chapman* first by distorting the decision in *Payne*, and then by drawing a meaningless dichotomy between "trial errors" and "structural defects" in the trial process. Viewing *Payne* as merely rejecting a test whereby the admission of a coerced confession could stand if there were "sufficient evidence," other than the confession, to support the conviction, the majority suggests that the Court in *Payne* might have reached a different result had it been considering a harmless-error test. It is clear, though, that in *Payne* the Court recognized that *regardless* of the amount of other evidence, "the admission in evidence, over objection, of the coerced confession vitiates the judgment," because "where, as here, a coerced confession constitutes a part of the evidence before the jury and a general verdict is returned, no one can say what credit and weight the jury gave to the confession." The inability to assess its effect on a conviction causes the admission at trial of a coerced confession to "defy analysis by 'harmless-error' standards," just as certainly as do deprivation of counsel and trial before a biased judge.

The majority also attempts to distinguish "trial errors" which occur "during the presentation of the case to the jury," and which it deems susceptible to harmless-error analysis, from "structural defects in the constitution of the trial mechanism," which the majority concedes cannot be so analyzed. This effort fails, for our jurisprudence on harmless error has not classified so neatly the errors at issue. For example, we have held susceptible to harmless-error analysis the failure to instruct the jury on the presumption of innocence, *Kentucky v. Whorton*, 441 U.S. 786 (1979), while finding it impossible to analyze in terms of harmless error the failure to instruct a jury on the reasonable-doubt standard, *Jackson v. Virginia*, 443 U.S. 307, 320, n.14 (1979). These cases cannot be reconciled by labeling the former "trial error" and the latter not, for both concern the exact same stage in the trial proceedings. Rather, these cases can be reconciled only by considering the nature of the right at issue and the effect of an error upon the trial. A jury instruction on the presumption of innocence is not constitutionally required in every case to satisfy due process, because such an instruction merely offers an additional safeguard beyond that provided by the constitutionally required instruction on reasonable doubt. *See Whorton*, 441 U.S. at 789. While it may be possible to analyze as harmless the omission of a presumption of innocence instruction when the required reasonable-doubt instruction has been given, it is impossible to assess the effect on the jury of the omission of the more fundamental instruction on reasonable doubt. In addition, omission of a reasonable-doubt instruction, though a "trial error," distorts the very structure of the trial because it creates the risk that the jury will convict the defendant even if the State has not met its required burden of proof. *Cf. In re Winship*, 397 U.S. 358, 364 (1970).

These same concerns counsel against applying harmless-error analysis to the admission of a coerced confession. A defendant's confession is "probably the most probative and damaging evidence that can be admitted against him," *Cruz v. New York*, 481 U.S. 186, 195 (1987) (White, J., dissenting), so damaging that a jury should not be expected to ignore it even if told to do so, *Bruton v. United States*, 391 U.S. 123, 140 (1968) (White, J., dissenting), and because in any event it is impossible to know what credit and weight the jury gave to the confession. *Cf. Payne*, 356 U.S. at 568. Concededly, this reason is insufficient to justify a *per se* bar to the use of *any* confession. Thus, *Milton v. Wainwright*, 407 U.S. 371 (1972), applied harmless-error analysis to a confession obtained and introduced in circumstances that violated the defendant's Sixth Amendment right to counsel. Similarly, the Courts of Appeals have held that the introduction of incriminating statements taken from defendants in violation of *Miranda v. Arizona* is subject to treatment as harmless error.

Nevertheless, in declaring that it is "impossible to create a meaningful distinction between confessions elicited in violation of the Sixth Amendment and those in violation of the Fourteenth Amendment," the majority overlooks the obvious. Neither *Milton v. Wainwright* nor any of the other cases upon which the majority relies involved a defendant's *coerced* confession, nor were there present in these cases the distinctive reasons underlying the exclusion of coerced incriminating statements of the defendant. First, some coerced confessions may be untrustworthy. *Jackson v. Denno*, 378 U.S. at 385–86. Consequently, admission of coerced confessions may distort the truth-seeking function of the trial upon which the majority focuses. More importantly, however, the use of coerced confessions, "whether true or false," is forbidden "because the methods used to extract them offend an underlying principle in the enforcement of our criminal law: that ours is an accusatorial and not an inquisitorial system—a system in which the State must establish guilt by evidence independently and freely secured and may not by coercion prove its charge against an accused out of his own mouth," *Rogers v. Richmond*, 365 U.S. at 540–41. This reflects the "strongly felt attitude of our society that important human values are sacrificed where an agency of the government, in the course of securing a conviction, wrings a confession out of an accused against his will," *Blackburn v. Alabama*, 361 U.S. at 206–07, as well as "the deep-rooted feeling that the police must obey the law while enforcing the law; that in the end life and liberty can be as much endangered from illegal methods used to convict those thought to be criminals as from the actual criminals themselves," *Spano*, 360 U.S. at 320–21. Thus, permitting a coerced confession to be part of the evidence on which a jury is free to base its verdict of guilty is inconsistent with the thesis that ours is not an inquisitorial system of criminal justice. *Cf. Chambers v. Florida*, 309 U.S. at 235–38.

As the majority concedes, there are other constitutional errors that invalidate a conviction even though there may be no reasonable doubt that the defendant is guilty and would be convicted absent the trial error. For example, a judge in a criminal trial "is prohibited from entering a judgment of conviction or directing the jury to come forward with such a verdict, regardless of how overwhelmingly the evidence may point in that direction." *United States v. Martin Linen Supply Co.*, 430 U.S. 564, 572–73 (1977). A defendant is entitled to counsel at trial, *Gideon v. Wainwright*, 372 U.S. 335 (1963), and as *Chapman* recognized, violating this right can never be harmless error. *See also White v. Maryland*, 373 U.S. 59 (1963), where a conviction was set aside because the defendant had not had counsel at a preliminary hearing without regard to the showing of prejudice. In *Vasquez v. Hillery*, 474 U.S. 254 (1986), a defendant was found guilty beyond reasonable doubt, but the conviction had been set aside because of the unlawful exclusion of members of the defendant's race from the grand jury that indicted him, despite overwhelming evidence of his guilt. The error at the grand jury stage struck at fundamental values of our society and "undermine[d] the structural integrity of the criminal tribunal itself, and [was] not amenable to harmless-error review." *Id.* at 263–64. *Vasquez*, like *Chapman*, also noted that rule of automatic reversal when a defendant is tried before a judge with a financial interest in the outcome, *Turney v. Ohio*, 273 U.S. 510, 535 (1927), despite a lack of any indication that bias influenced the decision. *Waller v. Georgia*, 467 U.S. 39, 49 (1984), recognized that violation of the guarantee of a public trial required reversal without any showing of prejudice and even though the values of a public trial may be intangible and unprovable in any particular case.

The search for truth is indeed central to our system of justice, but "certain constitutional rights are not, and should not be, subject to harmless-error analysis because those rights protect important values that are unrelated to the truth-seeking function of the trial." *Rose v. Clark*, 478 U.S. at 587 (Stevens, J., concurring in judgment). The right of a defendant not to have his coerced confession used against him is among those rights, for using a coerced confession "abort[s] the basic trial process" and "render[s] a trial fundamentally unfair." *Id.* at 577, 578, n.6.

For the foregoing reasons the four of us would adhere to the consistent line of authority that has recognized as a basic tenet of our criminal justice system, before and after both *Miranda* and *Chapman*, the prohibition against using a defendant's coerced confession against him at his criminal trial. *Stare decisis* is "of fundamental importance to the rule of law," *Welch v. Texas Dept. of Highways and Public Transportation*, 483 U.S. 468, 494 (1987); the majority offers no convincing reason for overturning our long line of decisions requiring the exclusion of coerced confessions.

IV

Since five Justices have determined that harmless-error analysis applies to coerced confessions, it becomes necessary to evaluate under that ruling the admissibility of Fulminante's confession to Sarivola. *Chapman v. California*, 386 U.S. at 24, made clear that "before a federal constitutional error can be held harmless, the court must be able to declare a belief that it was harmless beyond a reasonable doubt." The Court has the power to review the record *de novo* in order to determine an error's harmlessness. *See ibid.* In so doing, it must be determined whether the State has met its burden of demonstrating that the admission of the confession to Sarivola did not contribute to Fulminante's conviction. *Chapman*, 386 U.S. at 26. Five of us are of the view that the State has not carried its burden and accordingly affirm the judgment of the court below reversing respondent's conviction.

A confession is like no other evidence. Indeed, "the defendant's own confession is probably the most probative and damaging evidence that can be admitted against him.... [T]he admissions of a defendant come from the actor himself, the most knowledgeable and unimpeachable source of information about his past conduct. Certainly, confessions have profound impact on the jury, so much so that we may justifiably doubt its ability to put them out of mind even if told to do so." *Bruton v. United States*, 391 U.S. at 139–40 (White, J., dissenting). While some statements by a defendant may concern isolated aspects of the crime or may be incriminating only when linked to other evidence, a full confession in which the defendant discloses the motive for and means of the crime may tempt the jury to rely upon that evidence alone in reaching its decision. In the case of a coerced confession such as that given by Fulminante to Sarivola, the risk that the confession is unreliable, coupled with the profound impact that the confession has upon the jury, requires a reviewing court to exercise extreme caution before determining that the admission of the confession at trial was harmless.

In the Arizona Supreme Court's initial opinion, in which it determined that harmless-error analysis could be applied to the confession, the court found that the admissible second confession to Donna Sarivola rendered the first confession to Anthony Sarivola cumulative. The court also noted that circumstantial physical evidence concerning the wounds, the ligature around Jeneane's neck, the location of the body, and the presence of motorcycle tracks at the scene corroborated the second confession. The court concluded that "due to the overwhelming evidence adduced from the second confession, if there had not been a first confession, the jury would still have had the same basic evidence to convict" Fulminante.

We have a quite different evaluation of the evidence. Our review of the record leads us to conclude that the State has failed to meet its burden of establishing, beyond a reasonable doubt, that the admission of Fulminante's confession to Anthony Sarivola was harmless error. Three considerations compel this result.

First, the transcript discloses that both the trial court and the State recognized that a successful prosecution depended on the jury believing the two confessions. Absent the confessions, it is unlikely that Fulminante would have been prosecuted at all, because the physical evidence from the scene and other circumstantial evidence would have been insufficient to convict. Indeed, no indictment was filed until nearly two years after the murder. Although the police had suspected Fulminante from the beginning, as the prosecutor acknowledged in his opening statement to the jury, "[W]hat brings us to Court, what makes this case fileable, and prosecutable and triable is that later, Mr. Fulminante confesses this crime to Anthony Sarivola and later, to Donna Sarivola, his wife." After trial began, during a renewed hearing on Fulminante's motion to suppress, the trial court opined, "You know, I think from what little I know about this trial, the character of this man [Sarivola] for truthfulness or untruthfulness and his credibility is the centerpiece of this case, is it not?" The prosecutor responded, "It's very important, there's no doubt." Finally, in his closing argument, the prosecutor prefaced his discussion of the two confessions by conceding: "[W]e have a lot of [circumstantial] evidence that indicates that this is our suspect, this is the fellow that did it, but it's a little short as far as saying that it's proof that he actually put the gun to the girl's head and killed her. So it's a little short of that. We recognize that."

Second, the jury's assessment of the confession to Donna Sarivola could easily have depended in large part on the presence of the confession to Anthony Sarivola. Absent the admission at trial of the first confession, the jurors might have found Donna Sarivola's story unbelievable. Fulminante's confession to Donna Sarivola allegedly occurred in May 1984, on the day he was released from Ray Brook, as she and Anthony Sarivola drove Fulminante from New York to Pennsylvania. Donna Sarivola testified that Fulminante, whom she had never before met, confessed in detail about Jeneane's brutal murder in response to her casual question concerning why he was going to visit friends in Pennsylvania instead of returning to his family in Arizona. Although she testified that she was "disgusted" by Fulminante's disclosures, she stated that she took no steps to notify authorities of what she had learned. In fact, she claimed that she barely discussed the matter with Anthony Sarivola, who was in the car and overheard Fulminante's entire conversation with Donna. Despite her disgust for Fulminante, Donna Sarivola later went on a second trip with him. Although Sarivola informed authorities that he had driven Fulminante to Pennsylvania, he did not mention Donna's presence in the car or her conversation with Fulminante. Only when questioned by authorities in June 1985 did Anthony Sarivola belatedly recall the confession to Donna more than a year before, and only then did he ask if she would be willing to discuss the matter with authorities.

Although some of the details in the confession to Donna Sarivola were corroborated by circumstantial evidence, many, including details that Jeneane was choked and sexually assaulted, were not. As to other aspects of the second confession, including Fulminante's motive and state of mind, the *only* corroborating evidence was the first confession to Anthony Sarivola. Thus, contrary to what the Arizona Supreme Court found, it is clear that the jury might have believed that the two confessions reinforced and corroborated each other. For this reason, one confession was *not* merely cumulative of the other. While in some cases two confessions, delivered on different occasions to different listeners, might be viewed as being independent of each other, *cf. Milton v. Wainwright*, 407 U.S. 371 (1972), it strains credulity to think that the jury so viewed the two confessions in this case, especially given the close relationship between Donna and Anthony Sarivola.

The jurors could also have believed that Donna Sarivola had a motive to lie about the confession in order to assist her husband. Anthony Sarivola received significant benefits from federal authorities, including payment for information, immunity from prosecution, and eventual placement in the federal Witness Protection Program. In addition, the jury might have found Donna motivated by her own desire for favorable treatment, for she, too, was ultimately placed in the Witness Protection Program.

Third, the admission of the first confession led to the admission of other evidence prejudicial to Fulminante. For example, the State introduced evidence that Fulminante knew of Sarivola's connections with organized crime in an attempt to explain why Fulminante would have been motivated to confess to Sarivola in seeking protection. Absent the confession, this evidence would have had no relevance and would have been inadmissible at trial. The Arizona Supreme Court found that the evidence of Sarivola's connections with organized crime reflected on Sarivola's character, not Fulminante's, and noted that the evidence could have been used to impeach Sarivola. This analysis overlooks the fact that had the confession not been admitted, there would have been no reason for Sarivola to testify and thus no need to impeach his testimony. Moreover, we cannot agree that the evidence did not reflect on Fulminante's character as well, for it depicted him as someone who willingly sought out the company of criminals. It is quite possible that this evidence led the jury to view Fulminante as capable of murder.

Finally, although our concern here is with the effect of the erroneous admission of the confession on Fulminante's conviction, it is clear that the presence of the confession also influenced the sentencing phase of the trial. Under Arizona law, the trial judge is the sentencer. At the sentencing hearing, the admissibility of information regarding aggravating circumstances is governed by the rules of evidence applicable to criminal trials. In this case, "based upon admissible evidence produced at the trial," the judge found that only one aggravating circumstance existed beyond a reasonable doubt, *i.e.,* that the murder was committed in "an *especially* heinous, cruel, and depraved manner." In reaching this conclusion, the judge relied heavily on evidence concerning the manner of the killing and Fulminante's motives and state of mind which could only be found in the two confessions. For example, in labeling the murder "cruel," the judge focused in part on Fulminante's alleged statements that he choked Jeneane and made her get on her knees and beg before killing her. Although the circumstantial evidence was not inconsistent with this determination, neither was it sufficient to make such a finding beyond a reasonable doubt. Indeed, the sentencing judge acknowledged that the confessions were only partly corroborated by other evidence.

In declaring that Fulminante "acted with an especially heinous and depraved state of mind," the sentencing judge relied solely on the two confessions. While the judge found that the statements in the confessions regarding the alleged sexual assault on Jeneane should not be considered on the issue of cruelty because they were not corroborated by other evidence, the judge determined that they were worthy of belief on the issue of Fulminante's state of mind. The judge then focused on Anthony Sarivola's statement that Fulminante had made vulgar references to Jeneane during the first confession, and on Donna Sarivola's statement that Fulminante had made similar comments to her. Finally, the judge stressed that Fulminante's alleged comments to the Sarivolas concerning torture, choking, and sexual assault, "whether they all occurred or not," depicted "a man who was bragging and relishing the crime he committed."

Although the sentencing judge might have reached the same conclusions even without the confession to Anthony Sarivola, it is impossible to say so beyond a reasonable doubt. Furthermore, the judge's assessment of Donna Sarivola's credibility, and hence the reliability of the second confession, might well have been influenced by the corroborative effect of the erroneously admitted first confession. Indeed, the fact that the sentencing judge focused on the similarities between the two confessions in determining that they were reliable suggests that either of the confessions alone, even when considered with all the other evidence, would have been insufficient to permit the judge to find an aggravating circumstance beyond a reasonable doubt as a requisite prelude to imposing the death penalty.

Because a majority of the Court has determined that Fulminante's confession to Anthony Sarivola was coerced and because a majority has determined that admitting this confession was not harmless beyond a reasonable doubt, we agree with the Arizona

Supreme Court's conclusion that Fulminante is entitled to a new trial at which the confession is not admitted. Accordingly the judgment of the Arizona Supreme Court is

Affirmed.

[Part I and Part III of CHIEF JUSTICE REHNQUIST's opinion are omitted, as is JUSTICE KENNEDY's concurrence. Part II of CHIEF JUSTICE REHNQUIST's opinion, which garnered five votes and thus serves as the majority opinion as to the applicability of the harmless error standard, is reproduced below.]

II

Since this Court's landmark decision in *Chapman v. California*, 386 U.S. 18 (1967), in which we adopted the general rule that a constitutional error does not automatically require reversal of a conviction, the Court has applied harmless-error analysis to a wide range of errors and has recognized that most constitutional errors can be harmless. *See, e.g., Clemons v. Mississippi*, 494 U.S. 738 (1990) (unconstitutionally overbroad jury instructions at the sentencing stage of a capital case); *Satterwhite v. Texas*, 486 U.S. 249 (1988) (admission of evidence at the sentencing stage of a capital case in violation of the Sixth Amendment Counsel Clause); *Carella v. California*, 491 U.S. 263, 266 (1989) (jury instruction containing an erroneous conclusive presumption); *Pope v. Illinois*, 481 U.S. 497 (1987) (jury instruction misstating an element of the offense); *Rose v. Clark*, 478 U.S. 570 (1986) (jury instruction containing an erroneous rebuttable presumption); *Crane v. Kentucky*, 476 U.S. 683, 691 (1986) (erroneous exclusion of defendant's testimony regarding the circumstances of his confession); *Delaware v. Van Arsdall*, 475 U.S. 673 (1986) (restriction on a defendant's right to cross-examine a witness for bias in violation of the Sixth Amendment Confrontation Clause); *Rushen v. Spain*, 464 U.S. 114, 117–118, and n. 2 (1983) (denial of a defendant's right to be present at trial); *United States v. Hasting*, 461 U.S. 499 (1983) (improper comment on defendant's silence at trial, in violation of the Fifth Amendment Self-Incrimination Clause); *Hopper v. Evans*, 456 U.S. 605 (1982) (statute improperly forbidding trial court's giving a jury instruction on a lesser included offense in a capital case in violation of the Due Process Clause); *Kentucky v. Whorton*, 441 U.S. 786 (1979) (failure to instruct the jury on the presumption of innocence); *Moore v. Illinois*, 434 U.S. 220, 232 (1977) (admission of identification evidence in violation of the Sixth Amendment Counsel Clause); *Brown v. United States*, 411 U.S. 223, 231–232 (1973) (admission of the out-of-court statement of a nontestifying codefendant in violation of the Sixth Amendment Counsel Clause); *Milton v. Wainwright*, 407 U.S. 371 (1972) (confession obtained in violation of *Massiah v. United States*, 377 U.S. 201 (1964)); *Chambers v. Maroney*, 399 U.S. 42, 52–53 (1970) (admission of evidence obtained in violation of the Fourth Amendment); *Coleman v. Alabama*, 399 U.S. 1, 10–11 (1970) (denial of counsel at a preliminary hearing in violation of the Sixth Amendment Counsel Clause).

* * *

The admission of an involuntary confession—a classic "trial error"—is markedly different from the other two constitutional violations referred to in the *Chapman* footnote [denial of impartial judge and denial of right to counsel] as not being subject to harmless-error analysis. One of those violations, involved in *Gideon v. Wainwright*, 372 U.S. 335 (1963), was the total deprivation of the right to counsel at trial. The other violation, involved in *Tumey v. Ohio*, 273 U.S. 510 (1927), was a judge who was not impartial. These are structural defects in the constitution of the trial mechanism, which defy analysis by "harmless-error" standards. The entire conduct of the trial from beginning to end is obviously affected by the absence of counsel for a criminal defendant, just as it is by the presence on the bench of a judge who is not impartial. Since our decision in *Chapman*, other cases have added to the category of constitutional errors which are not subject to harmless error the following: unlawful exclusion of members of the defendant's race from a grand jury, *Vasquez v. Hillery*, 474 U.S. 254 (1986); the right to self-representation at trial, *McKaskle v. Wiggins*, 465 U.S. 168, 177–178, n. 8 (1984); and the right to public trial, *Waller v. Georgia*, 467 U.S. 39, 49, n. 9 (1984). Each of these constitutional deprivations is a similar structural defect affecting the framework within which the trial proceeds, rather than simply an error in the trial process itself. "Without these basic protections, a criminal trial cannot reliably serve its function as a vehicle for determination of guilt or innocence, and no criminal punishment may be regarded as fundamentally fair." *Rose v. Clark*, 478 U.S. at 577–78 (citation omitted).

It is evident from a comparison of the constitutional violations which we have held subject to harmless error, and those which we have held not, that involuntary statements or confessions belong in the former category. The admission of an involuntary confession is a "trial error," similar in both degree and kind to the erroneous admission of other types of evidence. The evidentiary impact of an involuntary confession, and its effect upon the composition of the record, is indistinguishable from that of a confession obtained in violation of the Sixth Amendment—of evidence seized in violation of the Fourth Amendment—or of a prosecutor's improper comment on a defendant's silence at trial in violation of the Fifth Amendment. When reviewing the erroneous admission of an involuntary confession, the appellate court, as it does with the admission of other forms of improperly admitted evidence, simply reviews the remainder of the evidence against the defendant to determine whether the admission of the confession was harmless beyond a reasonable doubt.

Nor can it be said that the admission of an involuntary confession is the type of error which "transcends the criminal process." This Court has applied harmless-error analysis to the violation of other constitutional rights similar in magnitude and importance and involving the same level of police misconduct. For instance, we have previously held that the admission of a defendant's statements obtained in violation of the Sixth Amendment is subject to harmless-error analysis. In *Milton v. Wainwright*, 407 U.S. 371 (1972), the Court held the admission of a confession obtained in violation of *Massiah v. United States*, 377 U.S. 201 (1964), to be harmless beyond a reasonable doubt. We have also held that the admission of an out-of-court statement by a nontestifying codefendant is subject to harmless-error analysis. *Brown v. United States*, 411 U.S., at 231–32; *Schneble v. Florida*, 405 U.S. 427 (1972); *Harrington v. California*, 395 U.S. 250 (1969). The inconsistent treatment of statements elicited in violation of the Sixth and Fourteenth Amendments, respectively, can be supported neither by evidentiary or deterrence concerns nor by a belief that there is something more "fundamental" about involuntary confessions. This is especially true in a case such as this one where there are no allegations of physical violence on behalf of the police. A confession obtained in violation of the Sixth Amendment has the same evidentiary impact as does a confession obtained in violation of a defendant's due process rights. Government misconduct that results in violations of the Fourth and Sixth Amendments may be at least as reprehensible as conduct that results in an involuntary confession. For instance, the prisoner's confession to an inmate-informer at issue in *Milton*, which the Court characterized as implicating the Sixth Amendment right to counsel, is similar on its facts to the one we face today. Indeed, experience shows that law enforcement violations of these constitutional guarantees can involve conduct as egregious as police conduct used to elicit statements in violation of the Fourteenth Amendment. It is thus impossible to create a meaningful distinction between confessions elicited in violation of the Sixth Amendment and those in violation of the Fourteenth Amendment.

Of course an involuntary confession may have a more dramatic effect on the course of a trial than do other trial errors—in particular cases it may be devastating to a defendant—but this simply means that a reviewing court will conclude in such a case that its admission was not harmless error; it is not a reason for eschewing the harmless-error test entirely. The Supreme Court of Arizona, in its first opinion in the present case, concluded that the admission of Fulminante's confession was harmless error. That court concluded that a second and more explicit confession of the crime made by Fulminante after he was released from prison was not tainted by the first confession, and that the second confession, together with physical evidence from the wounds (the victim had been shot twice in the head with a large calibre weapon at close range and a ligature was found around her neck) and other evidence introduced at trial rendered the admission of the first confession harmless beyond a reasonable doubt.

Notes

1. *Subsequent case history*

At his new trial, Oreste Fulminante was once again convicted and sentenced to death; however, the Arizona Supreme Court again reversed the conviction and ordered a new trial. *Arizona v. Fulminante*, 975 P.2d 75 (Ariz. 1999). On September 8, 1999, Fulminante pled guilty to murder and kidnapping and was sentenced to thirty-three years in prison.

2. *Additional facts*

In footnote 2, the Court states:

> There are additional facts in the record, not relied upon by the Arizona Supreme Court, which also support a finding of coercion. Fulminante possesses low average to average intelligence; he dropped out of school in the fourth grade. He is short in stature and slight in build. Although he had been in prison before, he had not always adapted well to the stress of prison life. While incarcerated at the age of 26, he had "felt threatened by the [prison] population," and he therefore requested that he be placed in protective custody. Once there, however, he was unable to cope with the isolation and was admitted to a psychiatric hospital. * * *

The Court observed that it has previously recognized that factors such as the ones in this case are relevant in determining whether a defendant's will has been overborne. *See, e.g., Payne v. Arkansas*, 356 U.S. 560, 567 (1958) (lack of education); *Reck v. Pate*, 367 U.S. 433, 441 (1961) (low intelligence). *Cf. Schneckloth v. Bustamonte*, 412 U.S. 218, 226 (1973) (listing potential factors). To what degree did such factors influence the Court's ultimate decision in this case?

3. *Burden of proof*

Who bears the burden of proof as to the question of whether an error is harmless? *In Brecht v. Abrahamson* (below) the Court seemed to suggest that the burden fell on the habeas petitioner and not the state: "[Petitioners] are not entitled to habeas relief based on trial error unless they can establish that it resulted in "actual prejudice." Subsequently, the Supreme Court has repeatedly, albeit indirectly, suggested that the burden is on the State to establish harmless error. *See Fry v. Pliler*, 551 U.S. 112, 121 n.3 (2007) ("The question presented included one additional issue: "[I]f the *Brecht* standard applies, does the petitioner or the State bear the burden of persuasion on the question of prejudice?" We have previously held that, when a court is "in virtual equipoise as to the harmlessness of the error" under the *Brecht* standard, the court should "treat the error ... as if it affected the verdict...." *O'Neal v. McAninch*, 513 U.S. 432, 435 (1995) * * * Moreover, the State has conceded throughout this § 2254 proceeding that it bears the burden of persuasion." Likewise in Part IV of Justice White's opinion in *Fulminante*, the Court explains that the "State has failed to meet its burden of establishing, beyond a reasonable doubt, that [the error] ... was harmless." *See also O'Neal v. McAninch*, 513 U.S. 432 (1995)). What about waiver? If the state fails to argue harmless error in the district court, have they waived the application of the doctrine on appeal?

4. *Structural versus harmless error*

In *Chapman*, the court observed that "that there are some constitutional rights so basic to a fair trial that their infraction can never be treated as harmless error." Errors as to such basic or fundamental rights are called structural errors and reversal is automatic. The Court has subsequently explained,

> we [have] divided constitutional errors into two classes. The first we called "trial error," because the errors "occurred during presentation of the case to the jury" and their effect may "be quantitatively assessed in the context of other evidence presented in order to determine whether [they were] harmless beyond a reasonable doubt. These include "most constitutional errors." The second class of constitutional error we called "structural defects." These "defy analysis by 'harmless-error' standards" because they "affec[t] the framework within which the trial proceeds," and are not "simply an error in the trial process itself."

U.S. v. Gonzalez-Lopez, 548 U.S. 140, 148 (2006).

Does a *Batson* violation constitute structural error? Should a trial judge's erroneous denial of a preemptory challenge be subject to harmless error review? *Rivera v. Illinois*, 129 S.Ct. 1446, 1454 (2009) ("Because peremptory challenges are within the States' province to grant or withhold, the mistaken denial of a state-provided peremptory challenge does not, without more, violate the Federal Constitution.").

In the context of a breached plea deal by a prosecutor, the Court recently explained:

> [B]reach of a plea deal is not a "structural" error as we have used that term. We have never described it as such, and it shares no common features with errors we *have* held structural. A plea breach does not "necessarily render a criminal trial fundamentally unfair or an unreliable vehicle for determining guilt or innocence," *Neder v. United States*, 527 U.S. 1, 9, (1999); it does not "defy analysis by 'harmless-error' standards" by affecting the entire adjudicatory framework, *Fulminante*, at 309; and the "difficulty of assessing the effect of the error," *United States v. Gonzalez-Lopez*, is no greater with respect to plea breaches at sentencing than with respect to other procedural errors at sentencing, which are routinely subject to harmlessness review.

Puckett v. U.S., 129 S.Ct. 1423, 1432 (2009).

For a thoughtful discussion of these issues see Russell D. Covey, *The Unbearable Lightness of* Batson*: Mixed Motives and Discrimination in Jury Selection*, 66 Md. L. Rev. 279 (2007).

Brecht v. Abrahamson

507 U.S. 619 (1993)

CHIEF JUSTICE REHNQUIST delivered the opinion of the Court.

In *Chapman v. California*, 386 U.S. 18, 24 (1967), we held that the standard for determining whether a conviction must be set aside because of federal constitutional error is whether the error "was harmless beyond a reasonable doubt." In this case we must decide whether the *Chapman* harmless-error standard applies in determining whether the prosecution's use for impeachment purposes of petitioner's post-*Miranda* silence, in violation of due process under *Doyle v. Ohio*, 426 U.S. 610 (1976), entitles petitioner to habeas corpus relief. We hold that it does not. Instead, the standard for determining whether habeas relief must be granted is whether the *Doyle* error "had substantial and injurious effect or influence in determining the jury's verdict." *Kotteakos v. United States*, 328 U.S. 750, 776 (1946). The *Kotteakos* harmless-error standard is better tailored to the nature and purpose of collateral review than the *Chapman* standard, and application of a less onerous harmless-error standard on habeas promotes the considerations underlying our habeas jurisprudence. Applying this standard, we conclude that petitioner is not entitled to habeas relief.

Petitioner Todd A. Brecht was serving time in a Georgia prison for felony theft when his sister and her husband, Molly and Roger Hartman, paid the restitution for petitioner's crime and assumed temporary custody of him. The Hartmans brought petitioner home with them to Alma, Wisconsin, where he was to reside with them before entering a halfway house. This caused some tension in the Hartman household because Roger Hartman, a local district attorney, disapproved of petitioner's heavy drinking habits and homosexual orientation, not to mention his previous criminal exploits. To make the best of the situation, though, the Hartmans told petitioner, on more than one occasion, that he was not to drink alcohol or engage in homosexual activities in their home. Just one week after his arrival, however, petitioner violated this house rule.

While the Hartmans were away, petitioner broke into their liquor cabinet and began drinking. He then found a rifle in an upstairs room and began shooting cans in the backyard. When Roger Hartman returned home from work, petitioner shot him in the back and sped off in Mrs. Hartman's car. Hartman crawled to a neighbor's house to summon help. (The downstairs phone in the Hartmans' house was inoperable because petitioner had taken the receiver on the upstairs phone off the hook.) Help came, but Hartman's wound proved fatal. Meanwhile, petitioner had driven Mrs. Hartman's car into a ditch in a nearby town. When a police officer stopped to offer assistance, petitioner told him that his sister knew about his car mishap and had called a tow truck. Petitioner then hitched a ride to Winona, Minnesota, where he was stopped by police. At first he tried to conceal his identity, but he later identified himself and was arrested. When he was told that he was being held for the shooting, petitioner replied that "it was a big mistake" and asked to talk with "somebody that would understand [him]." Petitioner was returned to Wisconsin, and thereafter was given his *Miranda* warnings at an arraignment.

Then petitioner was charged with first-degree murder. At trial in the Circuit Court for Buffalo County, he took the stand and admitted shooting Hartman, but claimed it was an accident. According to petitioner, when he saw Hartman pulling into the driveway on the evening of the shooting, he ran to replace the gun in the upstairs room where he had found it. But as he was running toward the stairs in the downstairs hallway, he tripped, causing the rifle to discharge the fatal shot. After the shooting, Hartman disappeared, so petitioner drove off in Mrs. Hartman's car to find him. Upon spotting Hartman at his neighbor's door, however, petitioner panicked and drove away.

The State argued that petitioner's account was belied by the fact that he had failed to get help for Hartman, fled the Hartmans' home immediately after the shooting, and lied to the police officer who came upon him in the ditch about having called Mrs. Hartman. In addition, the State pointed out that petitioner had failed to mention anything about the shooting being an accident to the officer who found him in the ditch, the man who gave him a ride to Winona, or the officers who eventually arrested him. Over the objections of defense counsel, the State also asked petitioner during cross-examination whether he had told anyone at any time before trial that the shooting was an accident, to which petitioner replied "no," and made several references to petitioner's pretrial silence during closing argument. Finally, the State offered extrinsic evidence tending to contradict petitioner's story, including the path the bullet traveled through Mr. Hartman's body (horizontal to slightly downward) and the location where the rifle was found after the shooting (outside), as well as evidence of motive (petitioner's hostility toward Mr. Hartman because of his disapproval of petitioner's sexual orientation).

The jury returned a guilty verdict, and petitioner was sentenced to life imprisonment. The Wisconsin Court of Appeals set the conviction aside on the ground that the State's references to petitioner's post-*Miranda* silence violated due process under *Doyle v. Ohio*, 426 U.S. 610 (1976), and that this error was sufficiently "prejudicial" to require reversal. The Wisconsin Supreme Court reinstated the conviction. Although it agreed that the State's use of petitioner's post-*Miranda* silence was impermissible, the court determined that this error "'was harmless beyond a reasonable doubt.'" *State v. Brecht*, 143 Wis.2d 297, 317 (1988) (quoting *Chapman v. California*, 386 U.S. 18, 24 (1967)). In finding the *Doyle* violation harmless, the court noted that the State's "improper references to Brecht's silence were infrequent," in that they "comprised less than two pages of a 900 page transcript, or a few minutes in a four day trial in which twenty-five witnesses testified," and that the State's evidence of guilt was compelling.

Petitioner then sought a writ of habeas corpus under 28 U.S.C. § 2254, reasserting his *Doyle* claim. The District Court agreed that the State's use of petitioner's post-*Miranda* silence violated *Doyle*, but disagreed with the Wisconsin Supreme Court that this error was harmless beyond a reasonable doubt, and set aside the conviction. The District Court based its harmless-error determination on its view that the State's evidence of guilt was not "overwhelming," and that the State's references to petitioner's post-*Miranda* silence, though "not extensive," were "crucial" because petitioner's defense turned on his credibility. The Court of Appeals for the Seventh Circuit reversed. It, too, concluded that the State's references to petitioner's post-*Miranda* silence violated *Doyle*, but it disagreed with both the standard that the District Court had applied in conducting its harmless-error inquiry and the result it reached.

The Court of Appeals held that the *Chapman* harmless-error standard does not apply in reviewing *Doyle* error on federal habeas. Instead, because of the "prophylactic" nature of the *Doyle* rule, as well as the costs attendant to reversing state convictions on collateral review, the Court of Appeals held that the standard for determining whether petitioner was entitled to habeas relief was whether the *Doyle* violation "'had substantial and injurious effect or influence in determining the jury's verdict.'" Applying this standard, the Court of Appeals concluded that petitioner was not entitled to relief because, "given the many more, and entirely proper, references to [petitioner's] silence preceding arraignment," he could not contend with a "straight face" that the State's use of his post-*Miranda* silence had a "substantial and injurious effect" on the jury's verdict.

We granted certiorari to resolve a conflict between Courts of Appeals on the question whether the *Chapman* harmless-error standard applies on collateral review of *Doyle* violations and now affirm.

We are the sixth court to pass on the question whether the State's use for impeachment purposes of petitioner's post-*Miranda* silence requires reversal of his murder conviction. Petitioner urges us to even the count, and decide matters in his favor once and for all. He argues that the *Chapman* harmless-error standard applies with equal force on collateral review of *Doyle* error. According to petitioner, the need to prevent state courts from relaxing their standards on direct review of *Doyle* claims, and the confusion which would ensue were we to adopt the *Kotteakos* harmless-error standard on collateral review, require application of the *Chapman* standard here. Before considering these arguments, however, we must first characterize the nature of *Doyle* error itself.

In *Doyle v. Ohio*, 426 U.S. at 619, we held that "the use for impeachment purposes of [a defendant's] silence, at the time of arrest and after receiving *Miranda* warnings, violate[s] the Due Process Clause of the Fourteenth Amendment." This rule "rests on 'the fundamental unfairness of implicitly assuring a suspect that his silence will not be used against him and then using his silence to impeach an explanation subsequently offered at trial.'" *Wainwright v. Greenfield*, 474 U.S. 284, 291 (1986) (quoting *South Dakota v. Neville*, 459 U.S. 553, 565 (1983)). The "implicit assurance" upon which we have relied in our *Doyle* line of cases is the right-to-remain-silent component of *Miranda*. Thus, the Constitution does not prohibit the use for impeachment purposes of a defendant's silence prior to arrest, *Jenkins v. Anderson*, 447 U.S. 231, 239 (1980), or after arrest if no *Miranda* warnings are given, *Fletcher v. Weir*, 455 U.S. 603, 606–7 (1982) (*per curiam*). Such silence is probative and does not rest on any implied assurance by law enforcement authorities that it will carry no penalty.

This case illustrates the point well. The first time petitioner claimed that the shooting was an accident was when he took the stand at trial. It was entirely proper—and probative—for the State to impeach his testimony by pointing out that petitioner had failed to tell anyone before the time he received his *Miranda* warnings at his arraignment about the shooting being an accident. Indeed, if the shooting was an accident, petitioner had every reason—including to clear his name and preserve evidence supporting his version of the events—to offer his account immediately following the shooting. On the other hand, the State's references to petitioner's silence after that point in time, or more generally to petitioner's failure to come forward with his version of events at any time before trial, crossed the *Doyle* line. For it is conceivable that, once petitioner had been given his *Miranda* warnings, he decided to stand on his right to remain silent because he believed his silence would not be used against him at trial.

The Court of Appeals characterized *Doyle* as "a prophylactic rule." It reasoned that, since the need for *Doyle* stems from the implicit assurance that flows from *Miranda* warnings, and "the warnings required by *Miranda* are not themselves part of the Constitution," "*Doyle* is ... a prophylactic rule designed to protect another prophylactic rule from erosion or misuse." But *Doyle* was not simply a further extension of the *Miranda* prophylactic rule. Rather, as we have discussed, it is rooted in fundamental fairness and due process concerns. However real these concerns, *Doyle* does not "'overprotect[]'" them. *Duckworth v. Eagan*, 492 U.S. 195, 209 (1989) (O'CONNOR, J., concurring). Under the rationale of *Doyle*, due process is violated whenever the prosecution uses for impeachment purposes a defendant's post-*Miranda* silence. *Doyle* thus does not bear the hallmarks of a prophylactic rule.

Instead, we think *Doyle* error fits squarely into the category of constitutional violations which we have characterized as "'trial error.'" *See Arizona v. Fulminante*, 499 U.S. 279, 307 (1991). Trial error "occur[s] during the presentation of the case to the jury," and is amenable to harmless-error analysis because it "may ... be quantitatively assessed in the context of other evidence presented in order to determine [the effect it had on the trial]." *Id.* At the other end of the spectrum of constitutional errors lie "structural defects in the constitution of the trial mechanism, which defy analysis by 'harmless-error' standards." *Id.* The existence of such defects—deprivation of the right to counsel, for example—requires automatic reversal of the conviction because they infect the entire trial process. *See id.* at 309–10. Since our landmark decision in *Chapman v. California*, 386 U.S. 18 (1967), we have applied the harmless-beyond-a-reasonable-doubt standard in reviewing claims of constitutional error of the trial type.

In *Chapman*, we considered whether the prosecution's reference to the defendants' failure to testify at trial, in violation of the Fifth Amendment privilege against self-incrimination, required reversal of their convictions. We rejected the argument that the Constitution requires a blanket rule of automatic reversal in the case of constitutional error, and concluded instead that "there may be some constitutional errors which in the setting of a particular case are so unimportant and insignificant that they may, consistent with the Federal Constitution, be deemed harmless." *Id.* at 22. After examining existing harmless-error rules, including the federal rule (28 U.S.C. § 2111), we held that "before a federal constitutional error can be held harmless, the court must be able to declare a belief that it was harmless beyond a reasonable doubt." The State bears the burden of proving that an error passes muster under this standard.

Chapman reached this Court on direct review, as have most of the cases in which we have applied its harmless-error standard. Although we have applied the *Chapman* standard in a handful of federal habeas cases, *see, e.g., Yates v. Evatt*, 500 U.S. 391 (1991); *Rose v. Clark*, 478 U.S. 570 (1986); *Milton v. Wainwright*, 407 U.S. 371 (1972); we have yet squarely to address its applicability on collateral review. Petitioner contends that we are bound by these habeas cases, by way of *stare decisis*, from holding that the *Kotteakos* harmless-error standard applies on habeas review of *Doyle* error. But since we have never squarely addressed the issue, and have at most assumed the applicability of the *Chapman* standard on habeas, we are free to address the issue on the merits. *See Edelman v. Jordan*, 415 U.S. 651, 670–71 (1974).

The federal habeas corpus statute is silent on this point. It permits federal courts to entertain a habeas petition on behalf of a state prisoner "only on the ground that he is in custody in violation of the Constitution or laws or treaties of the United States," 28 U.S.C. § 2254(a), and directs simply that the court "dispose of the matter as law and justice require," § 2243. The statute says nothing about the standard for harmless-error review in habeas cases. Respondent urges us to fill this gap with the *Kotteakos* standard, under which an error requires reversal only if it "had substantial and injurious effect or influence in determining the jury's verdict." *Kotteakos v. United States*. This standard is grounded in the federal harmless-error statute. 28 U.S.C. § 2111 ("On the hearing of any appeal or writ of certiorari in any case, the court shall give judgment after an examination of the record without regard to errors or defects which do not affect the substantial rights of the parties"). On its face § 2111 might seem to address the situation at hand, but to date we have limited its application to claims of nonconstitutional error in federal criminal cases. *See, e.g., United States v. Lane*, 474 U.S. 438 (1986).

Petitioner asserts that Congress' failure to enact various proposals since *Chapman* was decided that would have limited the availability of habeas relief amounts to legislative disapproval of application of a less stringent harmless-error standard on collateral review of constitutional error. Only one of these proposals merits discussion here. In 1972, a bill was proposed that would have amended 28 U.S.C. § 2254 to require habeas petitioners to show that "'a different result would probably have obtained if such constitutional violation had not occurred.'" 118 Cong. Rec. 24,936 (1972) (*quoting* S. 3833, 92d Cong., 2d Sess. (1972)). In response, the Attorney General suggested that the above provision be modified to make habeas relief available only where the petitioner "'suffered a substantial deprivation of his constitutional rights at his trial.'" 118 Cong. Rec. 24,939 (1972) (*quoting* letter from Richard G. Kleindienst, Attorney General, to Emanuel Celler, Chairman of the House Committee on the Judiciary (June 21, 1972)). This language of course parallels the federal harmless-error rule. But neither the Attorney General's suggestion nor the proposed bill itself was ever enacted into law.

As a general matter, we are "reluctant to draw inferences from Congress' failure to act." *Schneidewind v. ANR Pipeline Co.*, 485 U.S. 293, 306 (1988). We find no reason to depart from this rule here. In the absence of any express statutory guidance from Congress, it remains for this Court to determine what harmless-error standard applies on collateral review of petitioner's *Doyle* claim. We have filled the gaps of the habeas corpus statute with respect to other matters, *see, e.g., McCleskey v. Zant*, 499 U.S. 467, 487; *Wainwright v. Sykes*, 433 U.S. 72, 81; *Sanders v. United States*, 373 U.S. 1, 15; *Townsend v. Sain*, 372 U.S. 293, 312–13 (1963), and find it necessary to do so here. As always, in defining the scope of the writ, we look first to the considerations underlying our habeas jurisprudence, and then determine whether the proposed rule would advance or inhibit these considerations by weighing the marginal costs and benefits of its application on collateral review.

The principle that collateral review is different from direct review resounds throughout our habeas jurisprudence. *See, e.g., Wright v. West*, 505 U.S. 277, 292–93; *Pennsylvania v. Finley*, 481 U.S. 551, 556–57 (1987). Direct review is the principal avenue for challenging a conviction. "When the process of direct review—which, if a federal question is involved, includes the right to petition this Court for a writ of certiorari—comes to an end, a presumption of finality and legality attaches to the conviction and sentence. The role of federal habeas proceedings, while important in assuring that constitutional rights are observed, is secondary and limited. Federal courts are not forums in which to relitigate state trials." *Barefoot v. Estelle*, 463 U.S. 880, 887 (1983).

In keeping with this distinction, the writ of habeas corpus has historically been regarded as an extraordinary remedy, "a bulwark against convictions that violate 'fundamental fairness.'" *Engle v. Isaac*, 456 U.S. 107, 126 (quoting *Wainwright v. Sykes*, 433 U.S. at 97 (STEVENS, J., concurring)). "Those few who are ultimately successful [in obtaining habeas relief] are persons whom society has grievously wronged and for whom belated liberation is little enough compensation." *Fay v. Noia*, 372 U.S. 391, 440–41; *see also Kuhlmann v. Wilson*, 477 U.S. 436, 447 (1986) (plurality opinion) ("The Court uniformly has been guided by the proposition that the writ should be available to afford relief to those 'persons whom society has grievously wronged' in light of modern concepts of justice") (*quoting Fay v. Noia*, 372 U.S. at 440–41); *Jackson v. Virginia*, 443 U.S. 307, 332, n.5 (STEVENS, J., concurring in judgment) (Habeas corpus "is designed to guard against extreme malfunctions in the state criminal justice systems"). Accordingly, it hardly bears repeating that "'an error that may justify reversal on direct appeal will not necessarily support a collateral attack on a final judgment.'" *United States v. Frady*, 456 U.S. 152, 165 (quoting *United States v. Addonizio*, 442 U.S. 178, 184 (1979)).

Recognizing the distinction between direct and collateral review, we have applied different standards on habeas than would be applied on direct review with respect to matters other than harmless-error analysis. Our recent retroactivity jurisprudence is a prime example. Although new rules always have retroactive application to criminal cases on direct review, *Griffith v. Kentucky*, 479 U.S. 314, 320–28 (1987), we have held that they seldom have retroactive application to criminal cases on federal habeas, *Teague v. Lane*, 489 U.S. at 305–10 (opinion of O'CONNOR, J.). Other examples abound throughout our habeas cases. *See, e.g., Pennsylvania v. Finley*, 481 U.S. 551, 555–56 (1987) (Although the Constitution guarantees the right to counsel on direct appeal, *Douglas v. California*, 372

U.S. 353, 355 (1963), there is no "right to counsel when mounting collateral attacks"); *United States v. Frady*, 456 U.S. at 162–69 (While the federal "plain error" rule applies in determining whether a defendant may raise a claim for the first time on direct appeal, the "cause and prejudice" standard applies in determining whether that same claim may be raised on habeas); *Stone v. Powell*, 428 U.S. 465, 489–96 (Claims under *Mapp v. Ohio*, 367 U.S. 643 (1961), are not cognizable on habeas as long as the state courts have provided a full and fair opportunity to litigate them at trial or on direct review).

The reason most frequently advanced in our cases for distinguishing between direct and collateral review is the State's interest in the finality of convictions that have survived direct review within the state court system. *See, e.g., McCleskey v. Zant*, 499 U.S. at 491; *Wainwright v. Sykes*, 433 U.S. at 90. We have also spoken of comity and federalism. "The States possess primary authority for defining and enforcing the criminal law. In criminal trials they also hold the initial responsibility for vindicating constitutional rights. Federal intrusions into state criminal trials frustrate both the States' sovereign power to punish offenders and their good-faith attempts to honor constitutional rights." *Engle v. Isaac*, 456 U.S. at 128. *See also Coleman v. Thompson*, 501 U.S. 722, 748 (1991); *McCleskey*, 499 U.S. at 491. Finally, we have recognized that "[l]iberal allowance of the writ ... degrades the prominence of the trial itself," *Engle*, 456 U.S. at 127, and at the same time encourages habeas petitioners to relitigate their claims on collateral review, *see Rose v. Lundy*, 455 U.S. 509, 547 (STEVENS, J., dissenting).

In light of these considerations, we must decide whether the same harmless-error standard that the state courts applied on direct review of petitioner's *Doyle* claim also applies in this habeas proceeding. We are the sixth court to pass on the question whether the State's use for impeachment purposes of petitioner's post-*Miranda* silence in this case requires reversal of his conviction. Each court that has reviewed the record has disagreed with the court before it as to whether the State's *Doyle* error was "harmless." State courts are fully qualified to identify constitutional error and evaluate its prejudicial effect on the trial process under *Chapman*, and state courts often occupy a superior vantage point from which to evaluate the effect of trial error. *See Rushen v. Spain*, 464 U.S. 114, 120 (1983) (per curiam). For these reasons, it scarcely seems logical to require federal habeas courts to engage in the identical approach to harmless-error review that *Chapman* requires state courts to engage in on direct review.

Petitioner argues that application of the *Chapman* harmless-error standard on collateral review is necessary to deter state courts from relaxing their own guard in reviewing constitutional error and to discourage prosecutors from committing error in the first place. Absent affirmative evidence that state-court judges are ignoring their oath, we discount petitioner's argument that courts will respond to our ruling by violating their Article VI duty to uphold the Constitution. Federalism, comity, and the constitutional obligation of state and federal courts all counsel against any presumption that a decision of this Court will "deter" lower federal or state courts from fully performing their sworn duty. In any event, we think the costs of applying the *Chapman* standard on federal habeas outweigh the additional deterrent effect, if any, that would be derived from its application on collateral review.

Overturning final and presumptively correct convictions on collateral review because the State cannot prove that an error is harmless under *Chapman* undermines the States' interest in finality and infringes upon their sovereignty over criminal matters. Moreover, granting habeas relief merely because there is a "'reasonable possibility'" that trial error contributed to the verdict, *see Chapman v. California*, 386 U.S. at 24 (quoting *Fahy v. Connecticut*, 375 U.S. 85, 86 (1963)), is at odds with the historic meaning of habeas corpus—

to afford relief to those whom society has "grievously wronged." Retrying defendants whose convictions are set aside also imposes significant "social costs," including the expenditure of additional time and resources for all the parties involved, the "erosion of memory" and "dispersion of witnesses" that accompany the passage of time and make obtaining convictions on retrial more difficult, and the frustration of "society's interest in the prompt administration of justice." *United States v. Mechanik*, 475 U.S. 66, 72 (1986) (internal quotation marks omitted). And since there is no statute of limitations governing federal habeas, and the only laches recognized is that which affects the State's ability to defend against the claims raised on habeas, retrials following the grant of habeas relief ordinarily take place much later than do retrials following reversal on direct review.

The imbalance of the costs and benefits of applying the *Chapman* harmless-error standard on collateral review counsels in favor of applying a less onerous standard on habeas review of constitutional error. The *Kotteakos* standard, we believe, fills the bill. The test under *Kotteakos* is whether the error "had substantial and injurious effect or influence in determining the jury's verdict." Under this standard, habeas petitioners may obtain plenary review of their constitutional claims, but they are not entitled to habeas relief based on trial error unless they can establish that it resulted in "actual prejudice." *See United States v. Lane*, 474 U.S. 438, 449 (1986). The *Kotteakos* standard is thus better tailored to the nature and purpose of collateral review and more likely to promote the considerations underlying our recent habeas cases. Moreover, because the *Kotteakos* standard is grounded in the federal harmless-error rule, 28 U.S.C. § 2111, federal courts may turn to an existing body of case law in applying it. Therefore, contrary to the assertion of petitioner, application of the *Kotteakos* standard on collateral review is unlikely to confuse matters for habeas courts.

For the foregoing reasons, then, we hold that the *Kotteakos* harmless-error standard applies in determining whether habeas relief must be granted because of constitutional error of the trial type. All that remains to be decided is whether petitioner is entitled to relief under this standard based on the State's *Doyle* error. Because the Court of Appeals applied the *Kotteakos* standard below, we proceed to this question ourselves rather than remand the case for a new harmless-error determination. At trial, petitioner admitted shooting Hartman, but claimed it was an accident. The principal question before the jury, therefore, was whether the State met its burden in proving beyond a reasonable doubt that the shooting was intentional. Our inquiry here is whether, in light of the record as a whole, the State's improper use for impeachment purposes of petitioner's post-*Miranda* silence "had substantial and injurious effect or influence in determining the jury's verdict." We think it clear that it did not.

The State's references to petitioner's post-*Miranda* silence were infrequent, comprising less than two pages of the 900-page trial transcript in this case. And in view of the State's extensive and permissible references to petitioner's pre-*Miranda* silence—*i.e.*, his failure to mention anything about the shooting being an accident to the officer who found him in the ditch, the man who gave him a ride to Winona, or the officers who eventually arrested him—its references to petitioner's post-*Miranda* silence were, in effect, cumulative. Moreover, the State's evidence of guilt was, if not overwhelming, certainly weighty. The path of the bullet through Mr. Hartman's body was inconsistent with petitioner's testimony that the rifle had discharged as he was falling. The police officers who searched the Hartmans' home found nothing in the downstairs hallway that could have caused petitioner to trip. The rifle was found outside the house (where Hartman was shot), not inside where petitioner claimed it had accidentally fired, and there was a live round rammed in the gun's chamber, suggesting that petitioner had tried to fire a second shot. Finally, other circumstantial evidence, including the motive proffered by the State, also pointed to petitioner's guilt.

In light of the foregoing, we conclude that the *Doyle* error that occurred at petitioner's trial did not "substantial[ly] ... influence" the jury's verdict. Petitioner is therefore not entitled to habeas relief, and the judgment of the Court of Appeals is

Affirmed.

[A concurring opinion by JUSTICE STEVENS, in which JUSTICES WHITE AND BLACKMUN join, and in which JUSTICE SOUTER joins in part and dissents in part, is omitted.]

Notes

1. *Subsequent case history*

Todd Brecht began serving a life sentence in 1986. He was eligible for parole in July 2004.

2. *Excerpt from Stevens's concurrence*

Justice Stevens's concurrence includes the following observation:

> We disagree, however, about whether the same form of harmless-error analysis should apply in a collateral attack as on a direct appeal, and, if not, what the collateral attack standard should be for an error of this kind. The answer to the first question follows from our long history of distinguishing between collateral and direct review and confining collateral relief to cases that involve fundamental defects or omissions inconsistent with the rudimentary demands of fair procedure. The Court answers the second question by endorsing Justice Rutledge's thoughtful opinion for the Court in *Kotteakos v. United States*, 328 U.S. 750 (1946). Because that standard accords with the statutory rule for reviewing other trial errors that affect substantial rights; places the burden on prosecutors to explain why those errors were harmless; requires a habeas court to review the entire record *de novo* in determining whether the error influenced the jury's deliberations; and leaves considerable latitude for the exercise of judgment by federal courts, I am convinced that our answer is correct. I write separately only to emphasize that the standard is appropriately demanding.

Why did Justice Stevens choose to write separately to note that the standard is "appropriately demanding"?

3. *State sovereignty*

If *Chapman* is a constitutionally grounded rule, then how can the nature and meaning of the constitutional rule vary depending on whether a claim arises on direct or collateral review?

A motivating rationale for the *Brecht* majority seems to be the importance of respecting state sovereignty and finality rather than merely re-litigating state trials in federal court. Should the *Brecht* or the *Chapman* standard apply to federal habeas review of a federal conviction under § 2255?

4. *Dissent by Justice White*

Justice White (joined by Justice Blackmun and, in part, Justice Souter) dissented. His dissent includes concerns about the remedy a petitioner would have if the state appellate courts erroneously analyzed an error of this magnitude.

> If, however, the state courts erroneously concluded that no violation had occurred or (as is the case here) that it was harmless beyond a reasonable doubt,

> and supposing further that certiorari was either not sought or not granted, the majority would foreclose relief on federal habeas review. As a result of today's decision, in short, the fate of one in state custody turns on whether the state courts properly applied the Federal Constitution as then interpreted by decisions of this Court, and on whether we choose to review his claim on certiorari.

Is Justice White's concern legitimate? Why or why not? How does Justice White's concern about the heightened role that direct review through certiorari plays after *Brecht* correspond to federal habeas review under § 2254(d)? In other words, how important is certiorari review on direct review to a state defendant under § 2254 and under *Brecht*?

Three years after the *Brecht* decision, Congress passed the Antiterrorism and Effective Death Penalty Act (AEDPA), 28 U.S.C. § 2254. Section 2254(d)(1) precludes habeas relief unless the state court's decision was either contrary to or involved an unreasonable application of federal law. In *Fry v. Pliler*, the Court addressed the interaction of AEDPA and *Brecht* when the state court had failed to properly apply the *Chapman* standard. In other words, does AEDPA or *Brecht* trump when the state court erroneously fails to apply the *Chapman* standard?

Fry v. Pliler

551 U.S. 112 (2007)

SCALIA, J., delivered the opinion.

We decide whether a federal habeas court must assess the prejudicial impact of constitutional error in a state-court criminal trial under the "substantial and injurious effect" standard set forth in *Brecht v. Abrahamson*, 507 U.S. 619 (1993), when the state appellate court failed to recognize the error and did not review it for harmlessness under the "harmless beyond a reasonable doubt" standard set forth in *Chapman v. California*, 386 U.S. 18 (1967).

I

After two mistrials on account of hung juries, a third jury convicted petitioner of the 1992 murders of James and Cynthia Bell. At trial, petitioner sought to attribute the murders to one or more other persons. To that end, he offered testimony of several witnesses who linked one Anthony Hurtz to the killings. But the trial court excluded the testimony of one additional witness, Pamela Maples, who was prepared to testify that she had heard Hurtz discussing homicides bearing some resemblance to the murder of the Bells. In the trial court's view, the defense had provided insufficient evidence to link the incidents described by Hurtz to the murders for which petitioner was charged.

Following his conviction, petitioner appealed to the California Court of Appeal, arguing (among other things) that the trial court's exclusion of Maples' testimony deprived him of a fair opportunity to defend himself, in violation of *Chambers v. Mississippi*, 410 U.S. 284 (1973) (holding that a combination of erroneous evidentiary rulings rose to the level of a due process violation). Without explicitly addressing petitioner's *Chambers* argument, the state appellate court held that the trial court had not abused its discretion in excluding Maples' testimony under California's evidentiary rules, adding that "no possible prejudice" could have resulted in light of the "merely cumulative" nature of the testimony. The court did not specify which harmless-error standard it was applying in concluding that petitioner suffered "no possible prejudice." The Supreme Court of California denied discretionary review, and petitioner did not then seek a writ of certiorari from this Court.

Petitioner next filed a petition for writ of habeas corpus in the United States District Court for the Eastern District of California, raising the aforementioned due process claim. * * * The case was initially assigned to a Magistrate Judge, who ultimately recommended denying relief. He found the state appellate court's failure to recognize error under *Chambers* to be "an unreasonable application of clearly established law as set forth by the Supreme Court," and disagreed with the state appellate court's finding of "no possible prejudice." But he nevertheless concluded that "there ha[d] been an insufficient showing that the improper exclusion of the testimony of Ms. Maples had a substantial and injurious effect on the jury's verdict" under the standard set forth in *Brecht*. The District Court adopted the Magistrate Judge's findings and recommendations in full, and a divided panel of the United States Court of Appeals for the Ninth Circuit affirmed. We granted certiorari.

II

In *Chapman*, a case that reached this Court on direct review of a state-court criminal judgment, we held that a federal constitutional error can be considered harmless only if a court is "able to declare a belief that it was harmless beyond a reasonable doubt." In *Brecht*, we considered whether the *Chapman* standard of review applies on collateral review of a state-court criminal judgment under 28 U.S.C. § 2254. Citing concerns about finality, comity, and federalism, we rejected the *Chapman* standard in favor of the more forgiving standard of review applied to nonconstitutional errors on direct appeal from federal convictions. *See Kotteakos v. United States*, 328 U.S. 750 (1946). Under that standard, an error is harmless unless it "had substantial and injurious effect or influence in determining the jury's verdict." *Brecht*. The question in this case is whether a federal court must assess the prejudicial impact of the unconstitutional exclusion of evidence during a state-court criminal trial under *Brecht* even if the state appellate court has not found, as the state appellate court in *Brecht* had found, that the error was harmless beyond a reasonable doubt under *Chapman*.

We begin with the Court's opinion in *Brecht*. The primary reasons it gave for adopting a less onerous standard on collateral review of state-court criminal judgments did not turn on whether the state court itself conducted *Chapman* review. The opinion explained that application of *Chapman* would "undermin[e] the States' interest in finality," would "infring[e] upon [the States'] sovereignty over criminal matters," would undercut the historic limitation of habeas relief to those "'grievously wronged,'" and would " impos[e] significant 'social costs.'" Since each of these concerns applies with equal force whether or not the state court reaches the *Chapman* question, it would be illogical to make the standard of review turn upon that contingency.

The opinion in *Brecht* clearly assumed that the *Kotteakos* standard would apply in virtually all § 2254 cases. It suggested an exception only for the "unusual case" in which "a deliberate and especially egregious error of the trial type, or one that is combined with a pattern of prosecutorial misconduct ... infect[s] the integrity of the proceeding." This, of course, has nothing to do with whether the state court conducted harmless-error review. The concurring and dissenting opinions shared the assumption that *Kotteakos* would almost always be the standard on collateral review. The former stated in categorical terms that the "*Kotteakos* standard" "will now apply on collateral review" of state convictions (STEVENS, J., concurring). Justice White's dissent complained that under the Court's opinion *Kotteakos* would apply even where (as in this case) the state court found that "no violation had occurred," and Justice O'Connor's dissent stated that *Chapman* would "no longer appl[y] to any trial error asserted on habeas." Later cases also assumed that *Brecht*'s applicability does not turn on whether the state appellate court recognized the constitutional error and reached the *Chapman* question. *See Penry v. Johnson*, 532 U.S. 782, 795 (2001); *Calderon v. Coleman*, 525 U.S. 141, 145 (1998) (per curiam).

Petitioner's contrary position misreads (or at least exaggerates the significance of) a lone passage from our *Brecht* opinion. In that passage, the Court explained:

> State courts are fully qualified to identify constitutional error and evaluate its prejudicial effect on the trial process under *Chapman*, and state courts often occupy a superior vantage point from which to evaluate the effect of trial error. For these reasons, it scarcely seems logical to require federal habeas courts to engage in the identical approach to harmless-error review that *Chapman* requires state courts to engage in on direct review.

But the quoted passage does little to advance petitioner's position. To say (a) that since state courts are required to evaluate constitutional error under *Chapman* it makes no sense to establish *Chapman* as the standard for federal habeas review is not at all to say (b) that whenever a state court fails in its responsibility to apply *Chapman* the federal habeas standard must change. It would be foolish to equate the two, in view of the other weighty reasons given in *Brecht* for applying a less onerous standard on collateral review—reasons having nothing to do with whether the state court actually applied *Chapman*.

Petitioner argues that, if *Brecht* applies whether or not the state appellate court conducted *Chapman* review, then *Brecht* would apply even if a State eliminated appellate review altogether. That is not necessarily so. The federal habeas review rule applied to the class of case in which state appellate review is available does not have to be the same rule applied to the class of case where it is not. We have no occasion to resolve that hypothetical (and highly unrealistic) question now. In the case before us petitioner did obtain appellate review of his constitutional claim; the state court simply found the underlying claim weak and therefore did not measure its prejudicial impact under *Chapman*. The attempted analogy—between (1) eliminating appellate review altogether and (2) providing appellate review but rejecting a constitutional claim without assessing its prejudicial impact under *Chapman*—is a false one.

Petitioner contends that, even if *Brecht* adopted a categorical rule, post-*Brecht* developments require a different standard of review. Three years after we decided *Brecht*, Congress passed, and the President signed, the Antiterrorism and Effective Death Penalty Act of 1996 (AEDPA), under which a habeas petition may not be granted unless the state court's adjudication "resulted in a decision that was contrary to, or involved an unreasonable application of, clearly established Federal law, as determined by the Supreme Court of the United States...." 28 U.S.C. § 2254(d)(1). In *Mitchell v. Esparza*, 540 U.S. 12 (2003) (per curiam), we held that, when a state court determines that a constitutional violation is harmless, a federal court may not award habeas relief under § 2254 unless the harmlessness determination itself was unreasonable. Petitioner contends that § 2254(d)(1), as interpreted in *Esparza*, eliminates the requirement that a petitioner also satisfy *Brecht*'s standard. We think not. That conclusion is not suggested by *Esparza*, which had no reason to decide the point. Nor is it suggested by the text of AEDPA, which sets forth a precondition to the grant of habeas relief ("a writ of habeas corpus ... shall not be granted" unless the conditions of § 2254(d) are met), not an entitlement to it. Given our frequent recognition that AEDPA limited rather than expanded the availability of habeas relief, *see, e.g., Williams v. Taylor*, 529 U.S. 362, 412 (2000), it is implausible that, without saying so, AEDPA replaced the *Brecht* standard of "actual prejudice," with the more liberal AEDPA/*Chapman* standard which requires only that the state court's harmless-beyond-a-reasonable-doubt determination be unreasonable. That said, it certainly makes no sense to require formal application of both tests (AEDPA/*Chapman* and *Brecht*) when the latter obviously subsumes the former. Accordingly, the Ninth Circuit was correct to apply the *Brecht* standard of review in assessing the prejudicial impact of federal constitutional error in a state-court criminal trial.

* * *

We hold that in § 2254 proceedings a court must assess the prejudicial impact of constitutional error in a state-court criminal trial under the "substantial and injurious effect" standard set forth in *Brecht* whether or not the state appellate court recognized the error and reviewed it for harmlessness under the "harmless beyond a reasonable doubt" standard set forth in *Chapman*. Since the Ninth Circuit correctly applied the *Brecht* standard rather than the *Chapman* standard, we affirm the judgment below.

It is so ordered.

Justice STEVENS, with whom Justice SOUTER and Justice GINSBURG join, and with whom Justice BREYER joins in part, concurring in part and dissenting in part.

While I join all of the Court's opinion * * * I am persuaded that we should also answer the question whether the constitutional error was harmless under the standard announced in *Brecht v. Abrahamson*, 507 U.S. 619 (1993). * * *

Both the history of this litigation and the nature of the constitutional error involved provide powerful support for the conclusion that if the jurors had heard the testimony of Pamela Maples, they would at least have had a reasonable doubt concerning petitioner's guilt. Petitioner was not found guilty until after he had been tried three times. The first trial ended in a mistrial with the jury deadlocked 6 to 6. The second trial also resulted in a mistrial due to a deadlocked jury, this time 7 to 5 in favor of conviction. In the third trial, after the jurors had been deliberating for 11 days, the foreperson advised the judge that they were split 7 to 5 and "hopelessly deadlocked." When the judge instructed the jury to continue its deliberations, the foreperson requested clarification on the definition of "reasonable doubt." The jury deliberated for an additional 23 days after that exchange—a total of five weeks—before finally returning a guilty verdict.

It is not surprising that some jurors harbored a reasonable doubt as to petitioner's guilt weeks into their deliberations. The only person to offer eyewitness testimony, a disinterested truck driver, described the killer as a man who was 5'7" to 5'8" tall, weighed about 140 pounds, and had a full head of hair. Petitioner is 6'2" tall, weighed 300 pounds at the time of the murder, and is bald. Seven different witnesses linked the killings to a man named Anthony Hurtz, some testifying that Hurtz had admitted to them that he was in fact the killer. Each of those witnesses, unlike the truck driver, was impeached by evidence of bias, either against Hurtz or for petitioner.

However, Pamela Maples, a cousin of Hurtz's who was in all other respects a disinterested witness, did not testify at either of petitioner's first two trials. During the third trial, she testified out of the presence of the jury that she had overheard statements by Hurtz that he had committed a double murder strikingly similar to that witnessed by the truck driver. As the Magistrate Judge found, the exclusion of Maples' testimony for lack of foundation was clear constitutional error under *Chambers v. Mississippi*, 410 U.S. 284 (1973), and the State does not argue otherwise.

Chambers error is by nature prejudicial. We have said that *Chambers* "does not stand for the proposition that the defendant is denied a fair opportunity to defend himself whenever a state or federal rule excludes favorable evidence." *United States v. Scheffer*, 523 U.S. 303, 316 (1998). Rather, due process considerations hold sway over state evidentiary rules only when the exclusion of evidence "undermine[s] fundamental elements of the defendant's defense." *Id.* Hence, as a matter of law and logical inference, it is well-nigh impossible for a reviewing court to conclude that such error "did not influence the jury, or had but very slight effect" on its verdict. *Kotteakos*; *see also O'Neal v. McAninch*, 513 U.S. 432, 445 (1995) ("[W]hen a habeas court is in grave doubt as to the harmlessness of an error that affects substantial rights, it should grant relief").

It is difficult to imagine a less appropriate case for an exception to that commonsense proposition. We found in *Parker v. Gladden*, 385 U.S. 363 (1966) (per curiam), that 26 hours of juror deliberations in a murder trial "indicat[ed] a difference among them as to the guilt of petitioner." Here, the jury was deprived of significant evidence of third-party guilt, and still we measure the length of deliberations by weeks, not hours. In light of the jurors' evident uncertainty, the prospect of rebutting the near-conclusive presumption that the *Chambers* error did substantial harm vanishes completely.

We have not been shy in emphasizing that federal habeas courts do not lightly find constitutional error. *See Carey v. Musladin*, 549 U.S. 70 (2006). It follows that when they do find an error, they may not lightly discount its significance. Rather, a harmlessness finding requires "fair assurance, after pondering all that happened without stripping the erroneous action from the whole, that the judgment was not substantially swayed by the error." *Kotteakos*. Given "all that happened" in this case, and given the nature of the error, I cannot agree with the Ninth Circuit's conclusion that the erroneous exclusion of Maples' testimony was harmless under that standard.

Accordingly, I would reverse the judgment of the Court of Appeals.

[Justice BREYER concurred in part and dissented in part. This opinion is omitted.]

Notes

1. *Subsequent Case History*

John Fry remains in the custody of the California Department of Corrections. See Inmate Locator at http://inmatelocator.cdcr.ca.gov/.

2. *Additional facts*

According to Justice Stevens, three days before the jury reached a verdict in Fry's non-capital case, the trial judge speculated that it was perhaps the longest deliberation in the history of Solano County.

3. *Unresolved issue of excluded witness testimony*

It is important to note that a 5–4 majority declined to decide whether the exclusion of the witness in Fry's trial was harmless error under the *Brecht* standard.

4. *AEDPA and* Brecht

After *Fry*, it is clear that *Brecht* has survived the enactment of AEDPA. In the routine habeas case, however, the interaction between *Brecht* and § 2254(d)(1) remains unresolved. Should *Fry* be read as requiring *both* the deference codified in § 2254(d) and *Brecht* to apply? Must every federal habeas case reviewing a state conviction be subjected to two tiers of deference: (1) was the state court's decision contrary to or an unreasonable application of federal law; and (2) was petitioner prejudiced by the error under *Brecht*? Stated another way, even if a state court decision was an unreasonable application of federal law, must the court *also* assess whether the constitutional error had a "substantial and injurious effect" on the verdict under *Brecht*? Many lower courts after *Fry* assume that both § 2254 and *Brecht* must be satisfied before habeas relief is warranted.

PART V

The Future of Habeas Corpus

Chapter 14

Guantánamo Bay

There is a history of tension between the writ of habeas corpus and presidential power. Three United States presidents either have suspended or substantially curtailed access to the writ of habeas corpus since the Constitution was ratified. The first, President Lincoln, suspended the writ during the Civil War in 1861. In the early 1870s, during Reconstruction, President Ulysses Grant suspended the writ in parts of South Carolina. In 2005 the Detainee Treatment Act was passed and signed into law by President George Bush. It suspended habeas corpus for non-citizens being held at Guantánamo Bay, Cuba.

To best understand the complicated relationship between the writ of habeas corpus and the detainees held at Guantánamo Bay, it perhaps is best to start at the beginning. One week after the attacks on September 11, 2001, Congress approved the Authorization for Use of Military Force, Pub. L. No. 197-40, 115 Stat. 224 (2001) (AUMF), which gave the President the power "to use all necessary and appropriate force against those nations, organizations, or persons he determines planned, authorized, committed, or aided the terrorist attacks that occurred on September 11, 2001 ... in order to prevent any future acts of international terrorism against the United States." *Id.* at § 2. In January of 2002, the first men to be incarcerated at Guantánamo Bay were brought there under the authority of the AUMF.

In 2002 the first petitions for habeas corpus relief by detainees at Guantánamo were filed. The district court dismissed the petitions for lack of jurisdiction, reasoning that Guantánamo was outside the sovereign territory of the United States. *Rasul v. Bush*, 215 F.Supp.2d 55 (D.D.C. 2002). The decision was affirmed on appeal, *Al Odah v. United States*, 321 F.3d 1134 (D.C. Cir. 2003), and the Supreme Court granted certiorari. The Court held in *Rasul v. Bush*, 542 U.S. 466 (2004), presented below, that 28 U.S.C. § 2241 did give the district courts power to entertain habeas petitions from non-citizen detainees at Guantánamo and remanded. Decided the same day as *Rasul*, the Court specifically held in *Hamdi v. Rumsfeld*, 542 U.S. 507 (2004), that due process required that United States citizens being held as enemy combatants be given a meaningful opportunity to contest the factual bases of their detentions at Guantánamo. Nine days after the Court's decision in *Hamdi*, the Pentagon established combatant status review tribunals (CSRTs) to try to accommodate the Court's decision. These tribunals were meant to determine whether detainees held in Guantánamo are properly considered "enemy combatants" and to give them a limited amount of process.

While appeals were pending from the decision of *Rasul* on remand, Congress passed the Detainee Treatment Act, Pub. L. No. 109-148, 119 Stat, 2680 (2005) (DTA), which amended § 2241 to provide specifically that the courts do not have jurisdiction to entertain writs of habeas corpus from non-citizens being held at Guantánamo. It also gave exclusive power of review of CSRT decisions to the Court of Appeals for the District of Columbia. *See Boumediene v. Bush*, 128 S.Ct. 2229, 2241 (2008). The Court then held that the DTA's suspension of habeas corpus did not apply to cases that already were pending when the DTA was enacted. *Hamdan v. Rumsfeld*, 548 U.S. 557, 576-77 (2006). Additionally, the Court in *Hamdan* held that the DTA did not expressly authorize military commissions, that the military commissions' procedures violated the Uniform Code of Military Justice, and that the military commissions did not satisfy the Geneva Conventions.

In the same year as *Hamdan* was decided, Congress passed the Military Commissions Act of 2006, Pub. L. No. 109-366, 120 Stat. 2600 (2006) (MCA), which again amended § 2241 to strip habeas jurisdiction from federal courts for non-citizen, Guantánamo detainees. The MCA also specified, in response to *Hamdan*, that the suspension of habeas is to apply to all pending cases. In *Boumediene v. Bush*, *infra*, the Supreme Court reviewed the constitutionality of the MCA and held that non-citizens detained at Guantánamo Bay are entitled to the right of habeas corpus.

The recent history and unique relationship between Guantánamo Bay and the writ of habeas corpus accordingly prompts the question of whether Guantánamo Bay jurisprudence is itself an island, or whether it has important lessons for habeas corpus jurisprudence in general.

Rasul v. Bush

542 U.S. 466 (2004)

Justice STEVENS delivered the opinion of the Court.

[This case presents] the narrow but important question whether United States courts lack jurisdiction to consider challenges to the legality of the detention of foreign nationals captured abroad in connection with hostilities and incarcerated at the Guantánamo Bay Naval Base, Cuba.

I

* * *

Petitioners in these cases are 2 Australian citizens and 12 Kuwaiti citizens who were captured abroad during hostilities between the United States and the Taliban. Since early 2002, the U.S. military has held them—along with, according to the Government's estimate, approximately 640 other non-Americans captured abroad—at the naval base at Guantánamo Bay. The United States occupies the base, which comprises 45 square miles of land and water along the southeast coast of Cuba, pursuant to a 1903 Lease Agreement executed with the newly independent Republic of Cuba in the aftermath of the Spanish-American War. Under the agreement, "the United States recognizes the continuance of the ultimate sovereignty of the Republic of Cuba over the [leased areas]," while "the Republic of Cuba consents that during the period of the occupation by the United States ... the United States shall exercise complete jurisdiction and control over and within said areas." In 1934, the parties entered into a treaty providing that, absent an agreement to modify or abrogate the lease, the lease would remain in effect "[s]o long as the United States of America shall not abandon the ... naval station of Guantánamo."

In 2002, petitioners, through relatives acting as their next friends, filed various actions in the U.S. District Court for the District of Columbia challenging the legality of their detention at the base. All alleged that none of the petitioners has ever been a combatant against the United States or has ever engaged in any terrorist acts. They also alleged that none has been charged with any wrongdoing, permitted to consult with counsel, or provided access to the courts or any other tribunal.

The two Australians, Mamdouh Habib and David Hicks, each filed a petition for writ of habeas corpus, seeking release from custody, access to counsel, freedom from interrogations, and other relief. Fawzi Khalid Abdullah Fahad Al Odah and the 11 other Kuwaiti detainees filed a complaint seeking to be informed of the charges against them, to be allowed to meet with their families and with counsel, and to have access to the courts or some other impartial tribunal. They claimed that denial of these rights violates the Constitution, international law, and treaties of the United States. Invoking the court's jurisdiction under 28 U.S.C. §§ 1331 and 1350, among other statutory bases, they asserted causes of action under the Administrative Procedure Act, 5 U.S.C. §§ 555, 702, 706; the Alien Tort Statute, 28 U.S.C. § 1350; and the general federal habeas corpus statute, §§ 2241-2243.

Construing all three actions as petitions for writs of habeas corpus, the District Court dismissed them for want of jurisdiction. The court held, in reliance on our opinion in *Johnson v. Eisentrager*, 339 U.S. 763 (1950), that "aliens detained outside the sovereign territory of the United States [may not] invok[e] a petition for a writ of habeas corpus." The Court of Appeals affirmed. Reading *Eisentrager* to hold that "'the privilege of litigation' does not extend to aliens in military custody who have no presence in 'any territory over which the United States is sovereign,'" it held that the District Court lacked jurisdiction over petitioners' habeas actions, as well as their remaining federal statutory claims that do not sound in habeas. We granted certiorari and now reverse.

II

Congress has granted federal district courts, "within their respective jurisdictions," the authority to hear applications for habeas corpus by any person who claims to be held "in custody in violation of the Constitution or laws or treaties of the United States." 28 U.S.C. §§ 2241(a), (c)(3). The statute traces its ancestry to the first grant of federal-court jurisdiction: Section 14 of the Judiciary Act of 1789 authorized federal courts to issue the writ of habeas corpus to prisoners who are "in custody, under or by colour of the authority of the United States, or are committed for trial before some court of the same." In 1867, Congress extended the protections of the writ to "all cases where any person may be restrained of his or her liberty in violation of the constitution, or of any treaty or law of the United States."

Habeas corpus is, however, "a writ antecedent to statute, ... throwing its root deep into the genius of our common law." *Williams v. Kaiser*, 323 U.S. 471, 484, n.2 (1945) (internal quotation marks omitted). The writ appeared in English law several centuries ago, became "an integral part of our common-law heritage" by the time the Colonies achieved independence and received explicit recognition in the Constitution, which forbids suspension of "[t]he Privilege of the Writ of Habeas Corpus ... unless when in Cases of Rebellion or Invasion the public Safety may require it," Art. I, § 9, cl. 2.

As it has evolved over the past two centuries, the habeas statute clearly has expanded habeas corpus "beyond the limits that obtained during the 17th and 18th centuries." *Swain v. Pressley*, 430 U.S. 372, 380, n.13 (1977). But "[a]t its historical core, the writ of habeas corpus has served as a means of reviewing the legality of Executive detention, and it is in that context that its protections have been strongest." *INS v. St. Cyr*, 533 U.S. 289, 301 (2001); *see also Brown v. Allen*, 344 U.S. 443, 533 (1953) (Jackson, J., concurring in result) ("The historic purpose of the writ has been to relieve detention by executive authorities without judicial trial."). As Justice Jackson wrote in an opinion respecting the availability of habeas corpus to aliens held in U.S. custody:

> "Executive imprisonment has been considered oppressive and lawless since John, at Runnymede, pledged that no free man should be imprisoned, dispossessed, outlawed, or exiled save by the judgment of his peers or by the law of the land. The judges of England developed the writ of habeas corpus largely to preserve

these immunities from executive restraint." *Shaughnessy v. United States ex rel. Mezei*, 345 U.S. 206, 218-219 (1953) (dissenting opinion).

Consistent with the historic purpose of the writ, this Court has recognized the federal courts' power to review applications for habeas relief in a wide variety of cases involving executive detention, in wartime as well as in times of peace. The Court has, for example, entertained the habeas petitions of an American citizen who plotted an attack on military installations during the Civil War and of admitted enemy aliens convicted of war crimes during a declared war and held in the United States.

The question now before us is whether the habeas statute confers a right to judicial review of the legality of executive detention of aliens in a territory over which the United States exercises plenary and exclusive jurisdiction, but not "ultimate sovereignty."

III

Respondents' primary submission is that the answer to the jurisdictional question is controlled by our decision in *Eisentrager.* In that case, we held that a Federal District Court lacked authority to issue a writ of habeas corpus to 21 German citizens who had been captured by U.S. forces in China, tried and convicted of war crimes by an American military commission headquartered in Nanking, and incarcerated in the Landsberg Prison in occupied Germany. The Court of Appeals in *Eisentrager* had found jurisdiction, reasoning that "any person who is deprived of his liberty by officials of the United States, acting under purported authority of that Government, and who can show that his confinement is in violation of a prohibition of the Constitution, has a right to the writ." In reversing that determination, this Court summarized the six critical facts in the case:

> "We are here confronted with a decision whose basic premise is that these prisoners are entitled, as a constitutional right, to sue in some court of the United States for a writ of *habeas corpus.* To support that assumption we must hold that a prisoner of our military authorities is constitutionally entitled to the writ, even though he (a) is an enemy alien; (b) has never been or resided in the United States; (c) was captured outside of our territory and there held in military custody as a prisoner of war; (d) was tried and convicted by a Military Commission sitting outside the United States; (e) for offenses against laws of war committed outside the United States; (f) and is at all times imprisoned outside the United States." 339 U.S. at 777.

On this set of facts, the Court concluded, "no right to the writ of *habeas corpus* appears." *Id.* at 781.

Petitioners in these cases differ from the *Eisentrager* detainees in important respects: They are not nationals of countries at war with the United States, and they deny that they have engaged in or plotted acts of aggression against the United States; they have never been afforded access to any tribunal, much less charged with and convicted of wrongdoing; and for more than two years they have been imprisoned in territory over which the United States exercises exclusive jurisdiction and control.

Not only are petitioners differently situated from the *Eisentrager* detainees, but the Court in *Eisentrager* made quite clear that all six of the facts critical to its disposition were relevant only to the question of the prisoners' *constitutional* entitlement to habeas corpus. *Id.* at 777. The Court had far less to say on the question of the petitioners' *statutory* entitlement to habeas review. Its only statement on the subject was a passing reference to the absence of statutory authorization: "Nothing in the text of the Constitution extends such a right, nor does anything in our statutes." *Id.* at 768.

Reference to the historical context in which *Eisentrager* was decided explains why the opinion devoted so little attention to the question of statutory jurisdiction. In 1948, just two months after the *Eisentrager* petitioners filed their petition for habeas corpus in the U.S. District Court for the District of Columbia, this Court issued its decision in *Ahrens v. Clark*, 335 U.S. 188 (1948), a case concerning the application of the habeas statute to the petitions of 120 Germans who were then being detained at Ellis Island, New York, for deportation to Germany. The *Ahrens* detainees had also filed their petitions in the U.S. District Court for the District of Columbia, naming the Attorney General as the respondent. Reading the phrase "within their respective jurisdictions" as used in the habeas statute to require the petitioners' presence within the district court's territorial jurisdiction, the Court held that the District of Columbia court lacked jurisdiction to entertain the detainees' claims. *Id.* at 192. *Ahrens* expressly reserved the question "of what process, if any, a person confined in an area not subject to the jurisdiction of any district court may employ to assert federal rights." *Id.* at 192, n. 4. But as the dissent noted, if the presence of the petitioner in the territorial jurisdiction of a federal district court were truly a jurisdictional requirement, there could be only one response to that question. *Id.* at 209 (opinion of Rutledge, J.).

When the District Court for the District of Columbia reviewed the German prisoners' habeas application in *Eisentrager*, it thus dismissed their action on the authority of *Ahrens*. *See Eisentrager*, 339 U.S. at 767, 790. Although the Court of Appeals reversed the District Court, it implicitly conceded that the District Court lacked jurisdiction under the habeas statute as it had been interpreted in *Ahrens*. The Court of Appeals instead held that petitioners had a constitutional right to habeas corpus secured by the Suspension Clause reasoning that "if a person has a right to a writ of habeas corpus, he cannot be deprived of the privilege by an omission in a federal jurisdictional statute." In essence, the Court of Appeals concluded that the habeas statute, as construed in *Ahrens*, had created an unconstitutional gap that had to be filled by reference to "fundamentals." In its review of that decision, this Court, like the Court of Appeals, proceeded from the premise that "nothing in our statutes" conferred federal-court jurisdiction, and accordingly evaluated the Court of Appeals' resort to "fundamentals" on its own terms.

Because subsequent decisions of this Court have filled the statutory gap that had occasioned *Eisentrager's* resort to "fundamentals," persons detained outside the territorial jurisdiction of any federal district court no longer need rely on the Constitution as the source of their right to federal habeas review. In *Braden v. 30th Judicial Circuit Court of Ky.*, 410 U.S. 484, 495 (1973), this Court held, contrary to *Ahrens*, that the prisoner's presence within the territorial jurisdiction of the district court is not "an invariable prerequisite" to the exercise of district court jurisdiction under the federal habeas statute. Rather, because "the writ of habeas corpus does not act upon the prisoner who seeks relief, but upon the person who holds him in what is alleged to be unlawful custody," a district court acts "within [its] respective jurisdiction" within the meaning of § 2241 as long as "the custodian can be reached by service of process." 410 U.S. at 494-495. *Braden* reasoned that its departure from the rule of *Ahrens* was warranted in light of developments that "had a profound impact on the continuing vitality of that decision." 410 U.S. at 497. These developments included, notably, decisions of this Court in cases involving habeas petitioners "confined overseas (and thus outside the territory of any district court)," in which the Court "held, if only implicitly, that the petitioners' absence from the district does not present a jurisdictional obstacle to the consideration of the claim." *Braden* thus established that *Ahrens* can no longer be viewed as establishing "an inflexible jurisdictional rule," and is strictly relevant only to the question of the appropriate forum, not to whether the claim can be heard at all. 410 U.S. at 499-500.

Because *Braden* overruled the statutory predicate to *Eisentrager's* holding, *Eisentrager* plainly does not preclude the exercise of § 2241 jurisdiction over petitioners' claims.

IV

Putting *Eisentrager* and *Ahrens* to one side, respondents contend that we can discern a limit on § 2241 through application of the "longstanding principle of American law" that congressional legislation is presumed not to have extraterritorial application unless such intent is clearly manifested. *EEOC v. Arabian American Oil Co.*, 499 U.S. 244, 248 (1991). Whatever traction the presumption against extraterritoriality might have in other contexts, it certainly has no application to the operation of the habeas statute with respect to persons detained within "the territorial jurisdiction" of the United States. *Foley Bros. Inc. v. Filardo*, 336 U.S. 281, 285 (1949). By the express terms of its agreements with Cuba, the United States exercises "complete jurisdiction and control" over the Guantánamo Bay Naval Base, and may continue to exercise such control permanently if it so chooses. 1903 Lease Agreement, Art. III; 1934 Treaty, Art. III. Respondents themselves concede that the habeas statute would create federal-court jurisdiction over the claims of an American citizen held at the base. Considering that the statute draws no distinction between Americans and aliens held in federal custody, there is little reason to think that Congress intended the geographical coverage of the statute to vary depending on the detainee's citizenship. Aliens held at the base, no less than American citizens, are entitled to invoke the federal courts' authority under § 2241.

Application of the habeas statute to persons detained at the base is consistent with the historical reach of the writ of habeas corpus. At common law, courts exercised habeas jurisdiction over the claims of aliens detained within sovereign territory of the realm, as well as the claims of persons detained in the so-called "exempt jurisdictions," where ordinary writs did not run, and all other dominions under the sovereign's control. As Lord Mansfield wrote in 1759, even if a territory was "no part of the realm," there was "no doubt" as to the court's power to issue writs of habeas corpus if the territory was "under the subjection of the Crown." Later cases confirmed that the reach of the writ depended not on formal notions of territorial sovereignty, but rather on the practical question of "the exact extent and nature of the jurisdiction or dominion exercised in fact by the Crown."

In the end, the answer to the question presented is clear. Petitioners contend that they are being held in federal custody in violation of the laws of the United States. No party questions the District Court's jurisdiction over petitioners' custodians. Section 2241, by its terms, requires nothing more. We therefore hold that § 2241 confers on the District Court jurisdiction to hear petitioners' habeas corpus challenges to the legality of their detention at the Guantánamo Bay Naval Base.

V

[The Court then discusses the petitioners non-habeas claims and holds that there is no bar to them either.]

* * *

VI

Whether and what further proceedings may become necessary after respondents make their response to the merits of petitioners' claims are matters that we need not address now. What is presently at stake is only whether the federal courts have jurisdiction to determine the legality of the Executive's potentially indefinite detention of individuals who claim to be wholly innocent of wrongdoing. Answering that question in the affirmative, we reverse the judgment of the Court of Appeals and remand these cases for the District Court to consider in the first instance the merits of petitioners' claims.

It is so ordered.

Justice KENNEDY, concurring in the judgment.

The Court is correct, in my view, to conclude that federal courts have jurisdiction to consider challenges to the legality of the detention of foreign nationals held at the Guantánamo Bay Naval Base in Cuba. While I reach the same conclusion, my analysis follows a different course. Justice SCALIA exposes the weakness in the Court's conclusion that *Braden v. 30th Judicial Circuit Court of Ky.*, 410 U.S. 484 (1973), "overruled the statutory predicate to *Eisentrager's* holding." As he explains, the Court's approach is not a plausible reading of *Braden* or *Johnson v. Eisentrager*, 339 U.S. 763 (1950). In my view, the correct course is to follow the framework of *Eisentrager.*

Eisentrager considered the scope of the right to petition for a writ of habeas corpus against the backdrop of the constitutional command of the separation of powers. The issue before the Court was whether the Judiciary could exercise jurisdiction over the claims of German prisoners held in the Landsberg prison in Germany following the cessation of hostilities in Europe. The Court concluded the petition could not be entertained. The petition was not within the proper realm of the judicial power. It concerned matters within the exclusive province of the Executive, or the Executive and Congress, to determine.

The Court began by noting the "ascending scale of rights" that courts have recognized for individuals depending on their connection to the United States. *Id.* at 770. Citizenship provides a longstanding basis for jurisdiction, the Court noted, and among aliens physical presence within the United States also "gave the Judiciary power to act." *Id.* at 769, 771. This contrasted with the "essential pattern for seasonable Executive constraint of enemy aliens." *Id.* at 773. The place of the detention was also important to the jurisdictional question, the Court noted. Physical presence in the United States "implied protection," *id.* at 777-778, whereas in *Eisentrager* "th[e] prisoners at no relevant time were within any territory over which the United States is sovereign." *Id.* at 778. The Court next noted that the prisoners in *Eisentrager* "were actual enemies" of the United States, proven to be so at trial, and thus could not justify "a limited opening of our courts" to distinguish the "many [aliens] of friendly personal disposition to whom the status of enemy" was unproven. *Ibid.* Finally, the Court considered the extent to which jurisdiction would "hamper the war effort and bring aid and comfort to the enemy." *Id.* at 779. Because the prisoners in *Eisentrager* were proven enemy aliens found and detained outside the United States, and because the existence of jurisdiction would have had a clear harmful effect on the Nation's military affairs, the matter was appropriately left to the Executive Branch and there was no jurisdiction for the courts to hear the prisoner's claims.

The decision in *Eisentrager* indicates that there is a realm of political authority over military affairs where the judicial power may not enter. The existence of this realm acknowledges the power of the President as Commander in Chief, and the joint role of the President and the Congress, in the conduct of military affairs. A faithful application of *Eisentrager,* then, requires an initial inquiry into the general circumstances of the detention to determine whether the Court has the authority to entertain the petition and to grant relief after considering all of the facts presented. A necessary corollary of *Eisentrager* is that there are circumstances in which the courts maintain the power and the responsibility to protect persons from unlawful detention even where military affairs are implicated. *See also Ex parte Milligan*, 71 U.S. 2,4 Wall. 2, 18 L.Ed. 281 (1866).

The facts here are distinguishable from those in *Eisentrager* in two critical ways, leading to the conclusion that a federal court may entertain the petitions. First, Guantánamo Bay is in every practical respect a United States territory, and it is one far removed from any hostilities. The opinion of the Court well explains the history of its possession by the United States. In a formal sense, the United States leases the Bay; the 1903 lease agreement states that Cuba retains "ultimate sovereignty" over it. At the same time, this lease is no ordinary lease. Its term is indefinite and at the discretion of the United States. What matters is the unchallenged and indefinite control that the United States has long exercised over Guantánamo Bay. From a practical perspective, the indefinite lease of Guantánamo Bay has produced a place that belongs to the United States, extending the "implied protection" of the United States to it. *Eisentrager*, *supra*, at 777-778.

The second critical set of facts is that the detainees at Guantánamo Bay are being held indefinitely, and without benefit of any legal proceeding to determine their status. In *Eisentrager*, the prisoners were tried and convicted by a military commission of violating the laws of war and were sentenced to prison terms. Having already been subject to procedures establishing their status, they could not justify "a limited opening of our courts" to show that they were "of friendly personal disposition" and not enemy aliens. 339 U.S. at 778. Indefinite detention without trial or other proceeding presents altogether different considerations. It allows friends and foes alike to remain in detention. It suggests a weaker case of military necessity and much greater alignment with the traditional function of habeas corpus. Perhaps, where detainees are taken from a zone of hostilities, detention without proceedings or trial would be justified by military necessity for a matter of weeks; but as the period of detention stretches from months to years, the case for continued detention to meet military exigencies becomes weaker.

In light of the status of Guantánamo Bay and the indefinite pretrial detention of the detainees, I would hold that federal-court jurisdiction is permitted in these cases. This approach would avoid creating automatic statutory authority to adjudicate the claims of persons located outside the United States, and remains true to the reasoning of *Eisentrager*. For these reasons, I concur in the judgment of the Court.

[Dissenting opinion by Justice SCALIA, joined by the Chief Justice and Justice THOMAS, omitted.]

Notes

1. *Subsequent case history*

On April 20, 2004, while *Rasul* was pending before the Supreme Court, petitioners Shafiq Rasul and Asif Iqbal were released to the United Kingdom—their native country. Upon arrival in the UK they were freed. Brian Duignan, *Rasul v. Bush*, Encyclopædia Britannica Online, http://www.britannica.com/EBchecked/topic/1513557/Rasul-v-Bush. Of the two Australians who originally were joined as petitioners, Mamdouh Habib was returned to Australia in January of 2005 after the Government dropped all charges against him. He subsequently tried to bring charges against the Australian government for torture and mistreatment he claims he suffered while detained in both Pakistan and Guantánamo. *Habib Taken to Government Building in Pakistan*, The Sydney Morning Herald, April 16, 2007. David Hicks, the other Australian petitioner also was returned to Australia in April of 2007 but was incarcerated there until December of the same year when he was released from prison. Jane Holroyd, *David Hicks freed from jail*, The Sydney Morning Herald, Dec. 29, 2007.

2. *The suspension of the Great Writ*

As noted in the introduction, while appeals were pending from the decision of *Rasul* on remand, Congress passed the Detainee Treatment Act which stated "no court, justice, or judge shall have jurisdiction to hear or consider ... an application for a writ of habeas corpus filed by or on behalf of an alien detained by the Department of Defense at Guantánamo Bay, Cuba."

This provision was at issue in *Hamdan v. Rumsfeld*, 548 U.S. 557 (2006) and the Court ultimately held, after extensive statutory analysis, that the DTA's removal from federal courts of the power to hear Guantánamo detainees' habeas petitions did not apply retroactively or to pending cases, and thus it did not apply in *Hamdan*. In response, Congress passed the Military Commissions Act of 2006 which specified:

> No court, justice, or judge shall have jurisdiction to hear or consider an application for a writ of habeas corpus filed by or on behalf of an alien detained by the United States who has been determined ... to have been properly detained as an enemy combatant or is awaiting such determination.

28 U.S.C.A. § 2241(e) (Supp.2007). The MCA also specified that this should

> take effect on the date of the enactment of this Act, and shall apply to all cases, without exception, pending on or after the date of the enactment of this Act which relate to any aspect of the detention, transfer, treatment, trial, or conditions of detention of an alien detained by the United States since September 11, 2001.

120 Stat. 2636. It is these provisions of the MCA that became the subject of the Court's decision in *Boumediene* below.

3. *U.S. citizens as "enemy combatants"*

While both *Rasul* and *Hamdan* dealt with habeas petitions filed by non-citizens, there is another line of cases dealing with the rights of U.S. citizens detained as enemy combatants. While these cases came to the Court in the form of habeas petitions, the petition sometimes simply is a vehicle to challenge fundamental concerns such as due process or the lack of it. There never has been any question as to the rights of citizens to have access to federal courts through the writ of habeas corpus, and neither the DTA nor the MCA suspended habeas for U.S. citizens.

A. *Rumsfeld v. Padilla*, 542 U.S. 426 (2004)

Jose Padilla was the first United States citizen to be designated an enemy combatant. He was arrested in Chicago in May 2002, and taken to a Navy prison in Charleston, South Carolina. Eventually, he was taken out of military custody and sent to Miami, where he was arrested and convicted on charges that he conspired to kill Americans here and abroad. In January of 2008, he was sentenced to seventeen years and four months in prison by a federal district court judge.

His case reached the Supreme Court through a habeas petition. Ultimately the Court decided against him on procedural grounds, holding that Secretary of Defense Rumsfeld was not a proper party to be joined. The Court found that the commander of the military base, who was the one actually confining Padilla, was the proper party. The Court also held that the traditional rule is that the proper place for filing a petition for habeas is in the jurisdiction of confinement. Since Padilla's petition was made in the Southern District of New York, rather than his place of confinement, South Carolina, this too was incorrect. The Court therefore remanded with an order to dismiss.

Justice Stevens, however, representing a four member minority, wrote:

> The petition for a writ of habeas corpus filed in this case raises questions of profound importance to the Nation. The arguments set forth by the Court do not justify avoidance of our duty to answer those questions. It is quite wrong to char-

acterize the proceeding as a "simple challenge to physical custody," that should be resolved by slavish application of a "bright-line rule," designed to prevent "rampant forum shopping" by litigious prison inmates. As the Court's opinion itself demonstrates, that rule is riddled with exceptions fashioned to protect the high office of the Great Writ. This is an exceptional case that we clearly have jurisdiction to decide.

* * *

In the Court's view, respondent's detention falls within the category of "core challenges" because it is "not unique in any way that would provide an arguable basis for a departure from the immediate custodian rule." It is, however, disingenuous at best to classify respondent's petition with run-of-the-mill collateral attacks on federal criminal convictions. On the contrary, this case is singular not only because it calls into question decisions made by the Secretary himself, but also because those decisions have created a unique and unprecedented threat to the freedom of every American citizen.

* * *

Executive detention of subversive citizens, like detention of enemy soldiers to keep them off the battlefield, may sometimes be justified to prevent persons from launching or becoming missiles of destruction. It may not, however, be justified by the naked interest in using unlawful procedures to extract information. Incommunicado detention for months on end is such a procedure. Whether the information so procured is more or less reliable than that acquired by more extreme forms of torture is of no consequence. For if this Nation is to remain true to the ideals symbolized by its flag, it must not wield the tools of tyrants even to resist an assault by the forces of tyranny.

B. *Hamdi v. Rumsfeld*, 542 U.S. 507 (2004)[1]

Hamdi also reached the Court through a habeas action. In writing for the Court, Justice O'Connor made clear that the AUMF did in fact authorize the detention of U.S. citizens as "enemy combatants," but that absent the suspension of habeas corpus (which had not even occurred for non-citizens at that point), due process concerns demanded that such citizens still be given the opportunity to contest the factual bases for their detentions before neutral decision makers. The Court also held that notice of the factual basis for the charges against them was required, as was the individual's access to counsel. Justice O'Connor wrote:

> In sum, while the full protections that accompany challenges to detentions in other settings may prove unworkable and inappropriate in the enemy-combatant setting, the threats to military operations posed by a basic system of independent review are not so weighty as to trump a citizen's core rights to challenge meaningfully the Government's case and to be heard by an impartial adjudicator.

* * *

1. The correct spelling of the petitioner's name is Himdy. Improper transliteration from Arabic to English on the petitioner's passport led to the mistake which never was corrected. Joel Brinkley, *A Father Waits as the U.S. and the Saudis Discuss His Son's Release*, N.Y. Times, Oct. 10, 2004.

> Because we conclude that due process demands some system for a citizen-detainee to refute his classification, the proposed "some evidence" standard is inadequate. Any process in which the Executive's factual assertions go wholly unchallenged or are simply presumed correct without any opportunity for the alleged combatant to demonstrate otherwise falls constitutionally short. * * *
>
> * * *
>
> There remains the possibility that the standards we have articulated could be met by an appropriately authorized and properly constituted military tribunal. * * * In the absence of such process, however, a court that receives a petition for a writ of habeas corpus from an alleged enemy combatant must itself ensure that the minimum requirements of due process are achieved. * * *

Nine days after the Court's decision in *Hamdi*, combatant status review tribunals were established in an effort to afford detainees the constitutionally mandated minimum due process the Court held was required. However, the Court in *Boumediene*, 128 S.Ct. at 2260, presented below, expressed deep concern about the constitutional adequacy of the CSRTs.

C. *Munaf v. Geren*, 553 U.S. 674 (2008)

In *Munaf*, the Court held that United States courts have jurisdiction over habeas petitions filed on behalf of American citizens being held abroad in detainee camps. This decision was most applicable to those U.S. citizens confined in a detainee camp operated by the Multinational Force-Iraq (MNF-I). The MNF-I is an international coalition force that operates in Iraq under the unified command of U.S. military officers in accordance with United Nations Security Council Resolutions.

4. *Torture*

In April 2009, President Obama released to the public four top secret memoranda issued by the Bush Administration's Office of Legal Counsel between 2002 and 2005. These memoranda, commonly known as the "Torture Memos," detailed the techniques used for interrogation of detainees held at Guantánamo Bay and at other detention centers around the world. Among the methods approved for use against detainees were attention grasp, walling (in which the suspect could be pushed into a wall), facial holds, facial slaps, cramped confinement, wall standing, sleep deprivation, insects placed in a confinement box, and water-boarding.

President Obama has said that the CIA operatives who participated in these torture techniques will not be subjected to criminal prosecution. He reasoned that they should not be prosecuted for actions they took pursuant to the guidelines set by the Bush Administration. Do you agree with the President's decision? For discussion about the ethical issues raised by the torture memos, see Kathleen Clark, *Ethical Issues Raised by the OLC Torture Memorandum*, 1 J. NAT'L SEC. L. & POL. 455 (2005), and THE TORTURE MEMOS; RATIONALIZING THE UNTHINKABLE (David Cole ed., 2009).

5. *The consequences of Guantánamo habeas jurisprudence*

The Court in *Rasul* traced the history of the writ of habeas corpus and its availability to different types of petitioners (citizens and non-citizens) and the effect of the place of their incarceration (sovereign territory, non-sovereign territory still under the complete control of the detaining government, and foreign countries). If Guantánamo habeas jurisprudence has any lasting legacy, perhaps it is in the form of a more clarified set of situations in which is or is not available. Consider this and the contribution *Boumediene* might have, if any, to this further clarification.

Boumediene v. Bush

553 U.S. 723 (2008)

Justice KENNEDY delivered the opinion of the Court.

Petitioners are aliens designated as enemy combatants and detained at the United States Naval Station at Guantánamo Bay, Cuba. There are others detained there, also aliens, who are not parties to this suit.

Petitioners present a question not resolved by our earlier cases relating to the detention of aliens at Guantánamo: whether they have the constitutional privilege of habeas corpus, a privilege not to be withdrawn except in conformance with the Suspension Clause, Art. I, § 9, cl. 2. We hold these petitioners do have the habeas corpus privilege. Congress has enacted a statute, the Detainee Treatment Act of 2005 (DTA), that provides certain procedures for review of the detainees' status. We hold that those procedures are not an adequate and effective substitute for habeas corpus. Therefore § 7 of the Military Commissions Act of 2006(MCA), 28 U.S.C.A. § 2241(e), operates as an unconstitutional suspension of the writ. * * *

I

[The Court began with a recitation of the relevant Guantánamo habeas law, which is omitted.]

Petitioners' cases were consolidated on appeal, and the parties filed supplemental briefs in light of our decision in *Hamdan*. The Court of Appeals' ruling is the subject of our present review and today's decision.

The Court of Appeals concluded that MCA § 7 must be read to strip from it, and all federal courts, jurisdiction to consider petitioners' habeas corpus applications, that petitioners are not entitled to the privilege of the writ or the protections of the Suspension Clause, and, as a result, that it was unnecessary to consider whether Congress provided an adequate and effective substitute for habeas corpus in the DTA.

We granted certiorari.

II

As a threshold matter, we must decide whether MCA § 7 denies the federal courts jurisdiction to hear habeas corpus actions pending at the time of its enactment. We hold the statute does deny that jurisdiction, so that, if the statute is valid, petitioners' cases must be dismissed.

As amended by the terms of the MCA, 28 U.S.C.A. § 2241(e) now provides:

> "(1) No court, justice, or judge shall have jurisdiction to hear or consider an application for a writ of habeas corpus filed by or on behalf of an alien detained by the United States who has been determined by the United States to have been properly detained as an enemy combatant or is awaiting such determination.
>
> "(2) Except as provided in [§§ 1005(e)(2) and (e)(3) of the DTA] no court, justice, or judge shall have jurisdiction to hear or consider any other action against the United States or its agents relating to any aspect of the detention, transfer, treatment, trial, or conditions of confinement of an alien who is or was detained by the United States and has been determined by the United States to have been properly detained as an enemy combatant or is awaiting such determination."

Section 7(b) of the MCA provides the effective date for the amendment of § 2241(e). It states:

> "The amendment made by [MCA § 7(a)] shall take effect on the date of the enactment of this Act, and shall apply to all cases, without exception, pending on or after the date of the enactment of this Act which relate to any aspect of the detention, transfer, treatment, trial, or conditions of detention of an alien detained by the United States since September 11, 2001."

There is little doubt that the effective date provision applies to habeas corpus actions. Those actions, by definition, are cases "which relate to ... detention." Petitioners argue, nevertheless, that MCA § 7(b) is not a sufficiently clear statement of congressional intent to strip the federal courts of jurisdiction in pending cases. We disagree.

Their argument is as follows: Section 2241(e)(1) refers to "a writ of habeas corpus." The next paragraph, § 2241(e)(2), refers to "any other action ... relating to any aspect of the detention, transfer, treatment, trial, or conditions of confinement of an alien who ... [has] been properly detained as an enemy combatant or is awaiting such determination." There are two separate paragraphs, the argument continues, so there must be two distinct classes of cases. And the effective date of subsection MCA § 7(b), it is said, refers only to the second class of cases, for it largely repeats the language of § 2241(e)(2) by referring to "cases ... which relate to any aspect of the detention, transfer, treatment, trial, or conditions of detention of an alien detained by the United States."

Petitioners' textual argument would have more force were it not for the phrase "other action" in § 2241(e)(2). The phrase cannot be understood without referring back to the paragraph that precedes it, § 2241(e)(1), which explicitly mentions the term "writ of habeas corpus." The structure of the two paragraphs implies that habeas actions are a type of action "relating to any aspect of the detention, transfer, treatment, trial, or conditions of confinement of an alien who is or was detained ... as an enemy combatant." Pending habeas actions, then, are in the category of cases subject to the statute's jurisdictional bar.

We acknowledge, moreover, the litigation history that prompted Congress to enact the MCA. We cannot ignore that the MCA was a direct response to *Hamdan*'s holding that the DTA's jurisdiction-stripping provision had no application to pending cases. The Court of Appeals was correct to take note of the legislative history when construing the statute, and we agree with its conclusion that the MCA deprives the federal courts of jurisdiction to entertain the habeas corpus actions now before us.

III

In deciding the constitutional questions now presented we must determine whether petitioners are barred from seeking the writ or invoking the protections of the Suspension Clause either because of their status, *i.e.*, petitioners' designation by the Executive Branch as enemy combatants, or their physical location, *i.e.*, their presence at Guantánamo Bay. The Government contends that noncitizens designated as enemy combatants and detained in territory located outside our Nation's borders have no constitutional rights and no privilege of habeas corpus. Petitioners contend they do have cognizable constitutional rights and that Congress, in seeking to eliminate recourse to habeas corpus as a means to assert those rights, acted in violation of the Suspension Clause.

* * *

A

[*The Court began with an account of the history and origins of the write, which is omitted.*]

That the Framers considered the writ a vital instrument for the protection of individual liberty is evident from the care taken to specify the limited grounds for its suspension: "The Privilege of the Writ of Habeas Corpus shall not be suspended, unless when in Cases of Rebellion or Invasion the public Safety may require it." Art. I, § 9, cl. 2. * * *

* * *

B

The broad historical narrative of the writ and its function is central to our analysis, but we seek guidance as well from founding-era authorities addressing the specific question before us: whether foreign nationals, apprehended and detained in distant countries during a time of serious threats to our Nation's security, may assert the privilege of the writ and seek its protection.

To support their arguments, the parties in these cases have examined historical sources to construct a view of the common-law writ as it existed in 1789.... * * * In none of the cases cited do we find that a common-law court would or would not have granted, or refused to hear for lack of jurisdiction, a petition for a writ of habeas corpus brought by a prisoner deemed an enemy combatant, under a standard like the one the Department of Defense has used in these cases, and when held in a territory, like Guantánamo, over which the Government has total military and civil control.

We know that at common law a petitioner's status as an alien was not a categorical bar to habeas corpus relief. We know as well that common-law courts entertained habeas petitions brought by enemy aliens detained in England—"entertained" at least in the sense that the courts held hearings to determine the threshold question of entitlement to the writ.

We find the evidence as to the geographic scope of the writ at common law informative, but, again, not dispositive. Petitioners argue the site of their detention is analogous to two territories outside of England to which the writ did run: the so-called "exempt jurisdictions," like the Channel Islands; and (in former times) India. There are critical differences between these places and Guantánamo, however.

As the Court explained in *Rasul*, common-law courts granted habeas corpus relief to prisoners detained in the exempt jurisdictions. But these areas, while not in theory part of the realm of England, were nonetheless under the Crown's control. And there is some indication that these jurisdictions were considered sovereign territory. Because the United States does not maintain formal sovereignty over Guantánamo Bay, the naval station there and the exempt jurisdictions discussed in the English authorities are not similarly situated.

* * *

The Government argues, in turn, that Guantánamo is more closely analogous to Scotland and Hanover, territories that were not part of England but nonetheless controlled by the English monarch. [A]t the time of the founding, English courts lacked the "power" to issue the writ to Scotland and Hanover, territories ... referred to as "foreign." ... [T]he common-law courts' refusal to issue the writ to these places was motivated not by formal legal constructs but by what we would think of as prudential concerns. * * *

* * *

The prudential barriers that may have prevented the English courts from issuing the writ to Scotland and Hanover are not relevant here. We have no reason to believe an order from a federal court would be disobeyed at Guantánamo. No Cuban court has jurisdiction to hear these petitioners' claims, and no law other than the laws of the United States applies at the naval station. The modern-day relations between the United States and Guantánamo thus differ in important respects from the 18th-century relations between

England and the kingdoms of Scotland and Hanover. This is reason enough for us to discount the relevance of the Government's analogy.

* * *

IV

Drawing from its position that at common law the writ ran only to territories over which the Crown was sovereign, the Government says the Suspension Clause affords petitioners no rights because the United States does not claim sovereignty over the place of detention.

Guantánamo Bay is not formally part of the United States. And under the terms of the lease between the United States and Cuba, Cuba retains "ultimate sovereignty" over the territory while the United States exercises "complete jurisdiction and control." Under the terms of the 1934 Treaty, however, Cuba effectively has no rights as a sovereign until the parties agree to modification of the 1903 Lease Agreement or the United States abandons the base.

The United States contends, nevertheless, that Guantánamo is not within its sovereign control. This was the Government's position well before the events of September 11, 2001. And in other contexts the Court has held that questions of sovereignty are for the political branches to decide. Even if this were a treaty interpretation case that did not involve a political question, the President's construction of the lease agreement would be entitled to great respect.

We therefore do not question the Government's position that Cuba, not the United States, maintains sovereignty, in the legal and technical sense of the term, over Guantánamo Bay. But this does not end the analysis. Our cases do not hold it is improper for us to inquire into the objective degree of control the Nation asserts over foreign territory. As commentators have noted, " '[s]overeignty' is a term used in many senses and is much abused." When we have stated that sovereignty is a political question, we have referred not to sovereignty in the general, colloquial sense, meaning the exercise of dominion or power, but sovereignty in the narrow, legal sense of the term, meaning a claim of right. Indeed, it is not altogether uncommon for a territory to be under the *de jure* sovereignty of one nation, while under the plenary control, or practical sovereignty, of another. This condition can occur when the territory is seized during war, as Guantánamo was during the Spanish-American War. Accordingly, for purposes of our analysis, we accept the Government's position that Cuba, and not the United States, retains *de jure* sovereignty over Guantánamo Bay. [H]owever, we take notice of the obvious and uncontested fact that the United States, by virtue of its complete jurisdiction and control over the base, maintains *de facto* sovereignty over this territory.

Were we to hold that the present cases turn on the political question doctrine, we would be required first to accept the Government's premise that *de jure* sovereignty is the touchstone of habeas corpus jurisdiction. This premise, however, is unfounded. For the reasons indicated above, the history of common-law habeas corpus provides scant support for this proposition; and, for the reasons indicated below, that position would be inconsistent with our precedents and contrary to fundamental separation-of-powers principles.

A

The Court has discussed the issue of the Constitution's extraterritorial application on many occasions. These decisions undermine the Government's argument that, at least as applied to noncitizens, the Constitution necessarily stops where *de jure* sovereignty ends.

The Framers foresaw that the United States would expand and acquire new territories. Article IV, § 3, cl. 1, grants Congress the power to admit new States. Clause 2 of the same section grants Congress the "Power to dispose of and make all needful Rules and Regulations respecting the Territory or other Property belonging to the United States." Save for a few notable exceptions, throughout most of our history there was little need to explore the outer boundaries of the Constitution's geographic reach. When Congress exercised its power to create new territories, it guaranteed constitutional protections to the inhabitants by statute. In particular, there was no need to test the limits of the Suspension Clause because, as early as 1789, Congress extended the writ to the Territories.

Fundamental questions regarding the Constitution's geographic scope first arose at the dawn of the 20th century when the Nation acquired noncontiguous Territories: Puerto Rico, Guam, and the Philippines–ceded to the United States by Spain at the conclusion of the Spanish-American War—and Hawaii—annexed by the United States in 1898. At this point Congress chose to discontinue its previous practice of extending constitutional rights to the territories by statute.

In a series of opinions later known as the Insular Cases, the Court addressed whether the Constitution, by its own force, applies in any territory that is not a State. The Court held that the Constitution has independent force in these territories, a force not contingent upon acts of legislative grace. Yet it took note of the difficulties inherent in that position.

* * * The Court thus was reluctant to risk the uncertainty and instability that could result from a rule that displaced altogether the existing legal systems in these newly acquired Territories.

These considerations resulted in the doctrine of territorial incorporation, under which the Constitution applies in full in incorporated Territories surely destined for statehood but only in part in unincorporated Territories. As the Court later made clear, "the real issue in the *Insular Cases* was not whether the Constitution extended to the Philippines or Puerto Rico when we went there, but which of its provisions were applicable by way of limitation upon the exercise of executive and legislative power in dealing with new conditions and requirements." It may well be that over time the ties between the United States and any of its unincorporated Territories strengthen in ways that are of constitutional significance. But, as early as *Balzac* in 1922, the Court took for granted that even in unincorporated Territories the Government of the United States was bound to provide to noncitizen inhabitants "guaranties of certain fundamental personal rights declared in the Constitution." Yet noting the inherent practical difficulties of enforcing all constitutional provisions "always and everywhere," the Court devised in the Insular Cases a doctrine that allowed it to use its power sparingly and where it would be most needed. This century-old doctrine informs our analysis in the present matter.

Practical considerations likewise influenced the Court's analysis a half-century later in *Reid v. Covert*, 354 U.S. 1 (1957). The petitioners there, spouses of American servicemen, lived on American military bases in England and Japan. They were charged with crimes committed in those countries and tried before military courts. Because the petitioners were not themselves military personnel, they argued they were entitled to trial by jury.

* * *

That the petitioners in *Reid* were American citizens was a key factor in the case and was central to the plurality's conclusion that the Fifth and Sixth Amendments apply to American civilians tried outside the United States. But practical considerations, related not to the petitioners' citizenship but to the place of their confinement and trial, were relevant to each Member of the *Reid* majority. And to Justices Harlan and Frankfurter (whose votes were necessary to the Court's disposition) these considerations were the decisive factors in the case.

* * * The key disagreement between the plurality and the concurring Justices in *Reid* was over the continued precedential value of the Court's previous opinion in *In re Ross*, 140 U.S. 453 (1891), which the *Reid* Court understood as holding that under some circumstances Americans abroad have no right to indictment and trial by jury. * * *

* * * Justices Harlan and Frankfurter, while willing to hold that the American citizen petitioners in the cases before them were entitled to the protections of Fifth and Sixth Amendments, were unwilling to overturn *Ross*. Instead, the two concurring Justices distinguished *Ross* from the cases before them, not on the basis of the citizenship of the petitioners, but on practical considerations that made jury trial a more feasible option for them than it was for the petitioner in *Ross*. If citizenship had been the only relevant factor in the case, it would have been necessary for the Court to overturn *Ross*....

Practical considerations weighed heavily as well in *Johnson v. Eisentrager*, 339 U.S. 763 (1950), where the Court addressed whether habeas corpus jurisdiction extended to enemy aliens who had been convicted of violating the laws of war. The prisoners were detained at Landsberg Prison in Germany during the Allied Powers' postwar occupation. The Court stressed the difficulties of ordering the Government to produce the prisoners in a habeas corpus proceeding. It "would require allocation of shipping space, guarding personnel, billeting and rations" and would damage the prestige of military commanders at a sensitive time. In considering these factors the Court sought to balance the constraints of military occupation with constitutional necessities.

True, the Court in *Eisentrager* denied access to the writ, and it noted the prisoners "at no relevant time were within any territory over which the United States is sovereign, and [that] the scenes of their offense, their capture, their trial and their punishment were all beyond the territorial jurisdiction of any court of the United States." The Government seizes upon this language as proof positive that the *Eisentrager* Court adopted a formalistic, sovereignty-based test for determining the reach of the Suspension Clause. We reject this reading for three reasons.

First, we do not accept the idea that the above-quoted passage from *Eisentrager* is the only authoritative language in the opinion and that all the rest is dicta. * * *

Second, because the United States lacked both *de jure* sovereignty and plenary control over Landsberg Prison, it is far from clear that the *Eisentrager* Court used the term sovereignty only in the narrow technical sense and not to connote the degree of control the military asserted over the facility. The Justices who decided *Eisentrager* would have understood sovereignty as a multifaceted concept. * * * That the Court devoted a significant portion of Part II to a discussion of practical barriers to the running of the writ suggests that the Court was not concerned exclusively with the formal legal status of Landsberg Prison but also with the objective degree of control the United States asserted over it. Even if we assume the *Eisentrager* Court considered the United States' lack of formal legal sovereignty over Landsberg Prison as the decisive factor in that case, its holding is not inconsistent with a functional approach to questions of extraterritoriality. The formal legal status of a given territory affects, at least to some extent, the political branches' control over that territory. *De jure* sovereignty is a factor that bears upon which constitutional guarantees apply there.

Third, if the Government's reading of *Eisentrager* were correct, the opinion would have marked not only a change in, but a complete repudiation of, the Insular Cases' (and later *Reid*'s) functional approach to questions of extraterritoriality. We cannot accept the Government's view. Nothing in *Eisentrager* says that *de jure* sovereignty is or has ever been the only relevant consideration in determining the geographic reach of the Constitution or of habeas corpus. Were that the case, there would be considerable tension between *Eisentrager*, on the one hand, and the Insular Cases and *Reid*, on the other. Our cases need not be read to conflict in this manner. A constricted reading of *Eisentrager* overlooks what we see as a common thread uniting the Insular Cases, *Eisentrager*, and *Reid*: the idea that questions of extraterritoriality turn on objective factors and practical concerns, not formalism.

B

The Government's formal sovereignty-based test raises troubling separation-of-powers concerns as well. The political history of Guantánamo illustrates the deficiencies of this approach. The United States has maintained complete and uninterrupted control of the bay for over 100 years. At the close of the Spanish-American War, Spain ceded control over the entire island of Cuba to the United States and specifically "relinquishe[d] all claim [s] of sovereignty ... and title." From the date the treaty with Spain was signed until the Cuban Republic was established on May 20, 1902, the United States governed the territory "in trust" for the benefit of the Cuban people. And although it recognized, by entering into the 1903 Lease Agreement, that Cuba retained "ultimate sovereignty" over Guantánamo, the United States continued to maintain the same plenary control it had enjoyed since 1898. Yet the Government's view is that the Constitution had no effect there, at least as to noncitizens, because the United States disclaimed sovereignty in the formal sense of the term. The necessary implication of the argument is that by surrendering formal sovereignty over any unincorporated territory to a third party, while at the same time entering into a lease that grants total control over the territory back to the United States, it would be possible for the political branches to govern without legal constraint.

Our basic charter cannot be contracted away like this. The Constitution grants Congress and the President the power to acquire, dispose of, and govern territory, not the power to decide when and where its terms apply. Even when the United States acts outside its borders, its powers are not "absolute and unlimited" but are subject "to such restrictions as are expressed in the Constitution." Abstaining from questions involving formal sovereignty and territorial governance is one thing. To hold the political branches have the power to switch the Constitution on or off at will is quite another. The former position reflects this Court's recognition that certain matters requiring political judgments are best left to the political branches. The latter would permit a striking anomaly in our tripartite system of government, leading to a regime in which Congress and the President, not this Court, say "what the law is."

These concerns have particular bearing upon the Suspension Clause question in the cases now before us, for the writ of habeas corpus is itself an indispensable mechanism for monitoring the separation of powers. The test for determining the scope of this provision must not be subject to manipulation by those whose power it is designed to restrain.

C

As we recognized in *Rasul*, the outlines of a framework for determining the reach of the Suspension Clause are suggested by the factors the Court relied upon in *Eisentrager*. In addition to the practical concerns discussed above, the *Eisentrager* Court found relevant that each petitioner:

> "(a) is an enemy alien; (b) has never been or resided in the United States; (c) was captured outside of our territory and there held in military custody as a prisoner of war; (d) was tried and convicted by a Military Commission sitting outside the United States; (e) for offenses against laws of war committed outside the

United States; (f) and is at all times imprisoned outside the United States." 339 U.S., at 777.

Based on this language from *Eisentrager*, and the reasoning in our other extraterritoriality opinions, we conclude that at least three factors are relevant in determining the reach of the Suspension Clause: (1) the citizenship and status of the detainee and the adequacy of the process through which that status determination was made; (2) the nature of the sites where apprehension and then detention took place; and (3) the practical obstacles inherent in resolving the prisoner's entitlement to the writ.

Applying this framework, we note at the onset that the status of these detainees is a matter of dispute. The petitioners, like those in *Eisentrager*, are not American citizens. But the petitioners in *Eisentrager* did not contest, it seems, the Court's assertion that they were "enemy alien[s]." In the instant cases, by contrast, the detainees deny they are enemy combatants. They have been afforded some process in CSRT proceedings to determine their status; but, unlike in *Eisentrager*, there has been no trial by military commission for violations of the laws of war. The difference is not trivial. The records from the *Eisentrager* trials suggest that, well before the petitioners brought their case to this Court, there had been a rigorous adversarial process to test the legality of their detention. The *Eisentrager* petitioners were charged by a bill of particulars that made detailed factual allegations against them. To rebut the accusations, they were entitled to representation by counsel, allowed to introduce evidence on their own behalf, and permitted to cross-examine the prosecution's witnesses.

In comparison the procedural protections afforded to the detainees in the CSRT hearings are far more limited, and, we conclude, fall well short of the procedures and adversarial mechanisms that would eliminate the need for habeas corpus review. Although the detainee is assigned a "Personal Representative" to assist him during CSRT proceedings, the Secretary of the Navy's memorandum makes clear that person is not the detainee's lawyer or even his "advocate." The Government's evidence is accorded a presumption of validity. The detainee is allowed to present "reasonably available" evidence, but his ability to rebut the Government's evidence against him is limited by the circumstances of his confinement and his lack of counsel at this stage. And although the detainee can seek review of his status determination in the Court of Appeals, that review process cannot cure all defects in the earlier proceedings.

As to the second factor relevant to this analysis, the detainees here are similarly situated to the *Eisentrager* petitioners in that the sites of their apprehension and detention are technically outside the sovereign territory of the United States. * * *

As to the third factor, we recognize, as the Court did in *Eisentrager*, that there are costs to holding the Suspension Clause applicable in a case of military detention abroad. Habeas corpus proceedings may require expenditure of funds by the Government and may divert the attention of military personnel from other pressing tasks. While we are sensitive to these concerns, we do not find them dispositive. Compliance with any judicial process requires some incremental expenditure of resources. Yet civilian courts and the Armed Forces have functioned along side each other at various points in our history. The Government presents no credible arguments that the military mission at Guantánamo would be compromised if habeas corpus courts had jurisdiction to hear the detainees' claims. And in light of the plenary control the United States asserts over the base, none are apparent to us.

* * *

There is no indication, furthermore, that adjudicating a habeas corpus petition would cause friction with the host government. No Cuban court has jurisdiction over American military personnel at Guantánamo or the enemy combatants detained there. While obligated to abide by the terms of the lease, the United States is, for all practical purposes, answerable to no other sovereign for its acts on the base. Were that not the case, or if the detention facility were located in an active theater of war, arguments that issuing the writ would be "impracticable or anomalous" would have more weight. Under the facts presented here, however, there are few practical barriers to the running of the writ. To the extent barriers arise, habeas corpus procedures likely can be modified to address them.

It is true that before today the Court has never held that noncitizens detained by our Government in territory over which another country maintains *de jure* sovereignty have any rights under our Constitution. But the cases before us lack any precise historical parallel. They involve individuals detained by executive order for the duration of a conflict that, if measured from September 11, 2001, to the present, is already among the longest wars in American history. The detainees, moreover, are held in a territory that, while technically not part of the United States, is under the complete and total control of our Government. Under these circumstances the lack of a precedent on point is no barrier to our holding.

We hold that Art. I, § 9, cl. 2, of the Constitution has full effect at Guantánamo Bay. If the privilege of habeas corpus is to be denied to the detainees now before us, Congress must act in accordance with the requirements of the Suspension Clause. This Court may not impose a *de facto* suspension by abstaining from these controversies. The MCA does not purport to be a formal suspension of the writ; and the Government, in its submissions to us, has not argued that it is. Petitioners, therefore, are entitled to the privilege of habeas corpus to challenge the legality of their detention.

V

In light of this holding the question becomes whether the statute stripping jurisdiction to issue the writ avoids the Suspension Clause mandate because Congress has provided adequate substitute procedures for habeas corpus. The Government submits there has been compliance with the Suspension Clause because the DTA review process in the Court of Appeals provides an adequate substitute. Congress has granted that court jurisdiction to consider

> "(i) whether the status determination of the [CSRT] ... was consistent with the standards and procedures specified by the Secretary of Defense ... and (ii) to the extent the Constitution and laws of the United States are applicable, whether the use of such standards and procedures to make the determination is consistent with the Constitution and laws of the United States." § 1005(e)(2)(C).

The Court of Appeals, having decided that the writ does not run to the detainees in any event, found it unnecessary to consider whether an adequate substitute has been provided. * * *

* * *

Under the circumstances we believe the costs of further delay substantially outweigh any benefits of remanding to the Court of Appeals to consider the issue it did not address in these cases.

A

Our case law does not contain extensive discussion of standards defining suspension of the writ or of circumstances under which suspension has occurred. This simply confirms the care Congress has taken throughout our Nation's history to preserve the writ and its function. Indeed, most of the major legislative enactments pertaining to habeas corpus have acted not to contract the writ's protection but to expand it or to hasten resolution of prisoners' claims.

There are exceptions, of course. Title I of the Antiterrorism and Effective Death Penalty Act of 1996 (AEDPA), contains certain gatekeeping provisions that restrict a prisoner's ability to bring new and repetitive claims in "second or successive" habeas corpus actions. We upheld these provisions against a Suspension Clause challenge in *Felker v. Turpin*, 518 U.S. 651, 662-664 (1996). The provisions at issue in *Felker*, however, did not constitute a substantial departure from common-law habeas procedures. The provisions, for the most part, codified the longstanding abuse-of-the-writ doctrine. AEDPA applies, moreover, to federal, postconviction review after criminal proceedings in state court have taken place. As of this point, cases discussing the implementation of that statute give little helpful instruction (save perhaps by contrast) for the instant cases, where no trial has been held.

* * *

[H]ere we confront statutes, the DTA and the MCA, that were intended to circumscribe habeas review. Congress' purpose is evident ... from the unequivocal nature of MCA § 7's jurisdiction-stripping language.... When interpreting a statute, we examine related provisions in other parts of the U.S. Code. When Congress has intended to replace traditional habeas corpus with habeas-like substitutes, it has granted to the courts broad remedial powers to secure the historic office of the writ. In the § 2255 context, for example, Congress has granted to the reviewing court power to "determine the issues and make findings of fact and conclusions of law" with respect to whether "the judgment [of conviction] was rendered without jurisdiction, or ... the sentence imposed was not authorized by law or otherwise open to collateral attack." * * *

In contrast the DTA's jurisdictional grant is quite limited. The Court of Appeals has jurisdiction not to inquire into the legality of the detention generally but only to assess whether the CSRT complied with the "standards and procedures specified by the Secretary of Defense" and whether those standards and procedures are lawful. If Congress had envisioned DTA review as coextensive with traditional habeas corpus, it would not have drafted the statute in this manner. * * * [T]here has been no effort to preserve habeas corpus review as an avenue of last resort. No saving clause exists in either the MCA or the DTA. And MCA § 7 eliminates habeas review for these petitioners.

The differences between the DTA and the habeas statute that would govern in MCA § 7's absence, 28 U.S.C. § 2241, are likewise telling. In § 2241 Congress confirmed the authority of "any justice" or "circuit judge" to issue the writ. That statute accommodates the necessity for factfinding that will arise in some cases by allowing the appellate judge or Justice to transfer the case to a district court of competent jurisdiction, whose institutional capacity for factfinding is superior to his or her own. By granting the Court of Appeals "exclusive" jurisdiction over petitioners' cases, Congress has foreclosed that option. This choice indicates Congress intended the Court of Appeals to have a more limited role in enemy combatant status determinations than a district court has in habeas corpus proceedings. The DTA should be interpreted to accord some latitude to the Court of Appeals to fashion procedures necessary to make its review function a meaningful one, but, if congressional intent is to be respected, the procedures adopted cannot be as extensive or as protective of the rights of the detainees as they would be in a § 2241 proceeding. Otherwise there would have been no, or very little, purpose for enacting the DTA.

To the extent any doubt remains about Congress' intent, the legislative history confirms what the plain text strongly suggests: In passing the DTA Congress did not intend to create a process that differs from traditional habeas corpus process in name only. It intended to create a more limited procedure. It is against this background that we must interpret the DTA and assess its adequacy as a substitute for habeas corpus.

B

We do not endeavor to offer a comprehensive summary of the requisites for an adequate substitute for habeas corpus. We do consider it uncontroversial, however, that the privilege of habeas corpus entitles the prisoner to a meaningful opportunity to demonstrate that he is being held pursuant to "the erroneous application or interpretation" of relevant law. And the habeas court must have the power to order the conditional release of an individual unlawfully detained—though release need not be the exclusive remedy and is not the appropriate one in every case in which the writ is granted. These are the easily identified attributes of any constitutionally adequate habeas corpus proceeding. But, depending on the circumstances, more may be required.

Indeed, common-law habeas corpus was, above all, an adaptable remedy. Its precise application and scope changed depending upon the circumstances. * * *

* * *

The idea that the necessary scope of habeas review in part depends upon the rigor of any earlier proceedings accords with our test for procedural adequacy in the due process context. This principle has an established foundation in habeas corpus jurisprudence as well.... * * *

Accordingly, where relief is sought from a sentence that resulted from the judgment of a court of record ... considerable deference is owed to the court that ordered confinement. Likewise in those cases the prisoner should exhaust adequate alternative remedies before filing for the writ in federal court. Both aspects of federal habeas corpus review are justified because it can be assumed that, in the usual course, a court of record provides defendants with a fair, adversary proceeding. In cases involving state convictions this framework also respects federalism; and in federal cases it has added justification because the prisoner already has had a chance to seek review of his conviction in a federal forum through a direct appeal. The present cases fall outside these categories, however; for here the detention is by executive order.

Where a person is detained by executive order, rather than, say, after being tried and convicted in a court, the need for collateral review is most pressing. A criminal conviction in the usual course occurs after a judicial hearing before a tribunal disinterested in the outcome and committed to procedures designed to ensure its own independence. These dynamics are not inherent in executive detention orders or executive review procedures. In this context the need for habeas corpus is more urgent. The intended duration of the detention and the reasons for it bear upon the precise scope of the inquiry. Habeas corpus proceedings need not resemble a criminal trial, even when the detention is by executive order. But the writ must be effective. The habeas court must have sufficient authority to conduct a meaningful review of both the cause for detention and the Executive's power to detain.

To determine the necessary scope of habeas corpus review, therefore, we must assess the CSRT process, the mechanism through which petitioners' designation as enemy combatants became final. Whether one characterizes the CSRT process as direct review of the Executive's battlefield determination that the detainee is an enemy combatant—as the parties have and as we do—or as the first step in the collateral review of a battlefield determination makes no difference in a proper analysis of whether the procedures Congress put in place are an adequate substitute for habeas corpus. What matters is the sum total of procedural protections afforded to the detainee at all stages, direct and collateral.

Petitioners identify what they see as myriad deficiencies in the CSRTs. The most relevant for our purposes are the constraints upon the detainee's ability to rebut the factual basis for the Government's assertion that he is an enemy combatant. As already noted, at the CSRT stage the detainee has limited means to find or present evidence to challenge the Government's case against him. He does not have the assistance of counsel and may not be aware of the most critical allegations that the Government relied upon to order his detention. The detainee can confront witnesses that testify during the CSRT proceedings. But given that there are in effect no limits on the admission of hearsay evidence—the only requirement is that the tribunal deem the evidence "relevant and helpful,"—the detainee's opportunity to question witnesses is likely to be more theoretical than real.

* * *

Even if we were to assume that the CSRTs satisfy due process standards, it would not end our inquiry. Habeas corpus is a collateral process that exists, in Justice Holmes' words, to "cu[t] through all forms and g[o] to the very tissue of the structure. It comes in from the outside, not in subordination to the proceedings, and although every form may have been preserved opens the inquiry whether they have been more than an empty shell." Even when the procedures authorizing detention are structurally sound, the Suspension Clause remains applicable and the writ relevant. * * *

Although we make no judgment as to whether the CSRTs, as currently constituted, satisfy due process standards, we agree with petitioners that, even when all the parties involved in this process act with diligence and in good faith, there is considerable risk of error in the tribunal's findings of fact. This is a risk inherent in any process that is "closed and accusatorial." And given that the consequence of error may be detention of persons for the duration of hostilities that may last a generation or more, this is a risk too significant to ignore.

For the writ of habeas corpus, or its substitute, to function as an effective and proper remedy in this context, the court that conducts the habeas proceeding must have the means to correct errors that occurred during the CSRT proceedings. This includes some authority to assess the sufficiency of the Government's evidence against the detainee. It also must have the authority to admit and consider relevant exculpatory evidence that was not introduced during the earlier proceeding. Federal habeas petitioners long have had the means to supplement the record on review, even in the postconviction habeas setting. Here that opportunity is constitutionally required.

* * *

The extent of the showing required of the Government in these cases is a matter to be determined. We need not explore it further at this stage. We do hold that when the judicial power to issue habeas corpus properly is invoked the judicial officer must have adequate authority to make a determination in light of the relevant law and facts and to formulate and issue appropriate orders for relief, including, if necessary, an order directing the prisoner's release.

C

We now consider whether the DTA allows the Court of Appeals to conduct a proceeding meeting these standards. "[W]e are obligated to construe the statute to avoid [constitutional] problems" if it is " 'fairly possible' " to do so. There are limits to this principle, however. The canon of constitutional avoidance does not supplant traditional modes of statutory interpretation. We cannot ignore the text and purpose of a statute in order to save it.

The DTA does not explicitly empower the Court of Appeals to order the applicant in a DTA review proceeding released should the court find that the standards and procedures used at his CSRT hearing were insufficient to justify detention. This is troubling. Yet, for present purposes, we can assume congressional silence permits a constitutionally required remedy. In that case it would be possible to hold that a remedy of release is impliedly provided for. The DTA might be read, furthermore, to allow the petitioners to assert most, if not all, of the legal claims they seek to advance, including their most basic claim: that the President has no authority under the AUMF to detain them indefinitely. * * *

The absence of a release remedy and specific language allowing AUMF challenges are not the only constitutional infirmities from which the statute potentially suffers, however. The more difficult question is whether the DTA permits the Court of Appeals to make requisite findings of fact. The DTA enables petitioners to request "review" of their CSRT determination in the Court of Appeals; but the "Scope of Review" provision confines the Court of Appeals' role to reviewing whether the CSRT followed the "standards and procedures" issued by the Department of Defense and assessing whether those "standards and procedures" are lawful. Among these standards is "the requirement that the conclusion of the Tribunal be supported by a preponderance of the evidence ... allowing a rebuttable presumption in favor of the Government's evidence."

Assuming the DTA can be construed to allow the Court of Appeals to review or correct the CSRT's factual determinations, as opposed to merely certifying that the tribunal applied the correct standard of proof, we see no way to construe the statute to allow what is also constitutionally required in this context: an opportunity for the detainee to present relevant exculpatory evidence that was not made part of the record in the earlier proceedings.

* * *

Under the DTA the Court of Appeals has the power to review CSRT determinations by assessing the legality of standards and procedures. This implies the power to inquire into what happened at the CSRT hearing and, perhaps, to remedy certain deficiencies in that proceeding. But should the Court of Appeals determine that the CSRT followed appropriate and lawful standards and procedures, it will have reached the limits of its jurisdiction. There is no language in the DTA that can be construed to allow the Court of Appeals to admit and consider newly discovered evidence that could not have been made part of the CSRT record because it was unavailable to either the Government or the detainee when the CSRT made its findings. This evidence, however, may be critical to the detainee's argument that he is not an enemy combatant and there is no cause to detain him.

* * *

By foreclosing consideration of evidence not presented or reasonably available to the detainee at the CSRT proceedings, the DTA disadvantages the detainee by limiting the scope of collateral review to a record that may not be accurate or complete. In other contexts, *e.g.*, in post-trial habeas cases where the prisoner already has had a full and fair opportunity to develop the factual predicate of his claims, similar limitations on the scope of habeas review may be appropriate. In this context, however, where the underlying detention proceedings lack the necessary adversarial character, the detainee cannot be held responsible for all deficiencies in the record.

The Government does not make the alternative argument that the DTA allows for the introduction of previously unavailable exculpatory evidence on appeal. It does point out, however, that if a detainee obtains such evidence, he can request that the Deputy Secretary of Defense convene a new CSRT. Whatever the merits of this procedure, it is an insufficient replacement for the factual review these detainees are entitled to receive through habeas corpus. The Deputy Secretary's determination whether to initiate new proceedings is wholly a discretionary one. And we see no way to construe the DTA to allow a detainee to challenge the Deputy Secretary's decision not to open a new CSRT.... Congress directed the Secretary of Defense to devise procedures for considering new evidence, but the detainee has no mechanism for ensuring that those procedures are followed. * * *

We do not imply DTA review would be a constitutionally sufficient replacement for habeas corpus but for these limitations on the detainee's ability to present exculpatory evidence. For even if it were possible, as a textual matter, to read into the statute each of the necessary procedures we have identified, we could not overlook the cumulative effect of our doing so. To hold that the detainees at Guantánamo may, under the DTA, challenge the President's legal authority to detain them, contest the CSRT's findings of fact, supplement the record on review with exculpatory evidence, and request an order of release would come close to reinstating the § 2241 habeas corpus process Congress sought to deny them. The language of the statute, read in light of Congress' reasons for enacting it, cannot bear this interpretation. Petitioners have met their burden of establishing that the DTA review process is, on its face, an inadequate substitute for habeas corpus.

Although we do not hold that an adequate substitute must duplicate § 2241 in all respects, it suffices that the Government has not established that the detainees' access to the statutory review provisions at issue is an adequate substitute for the writ of habeas corpus. MCA § 7 thus effects an unconstitutional suspension of the writ. In view of our holding we need not discuss the reach of the writ with respect to claims of unlawful conditions of treatment or confinement.

VI

A

In light of our conclusion that there is no jurisdictional bar to the District Court's entertaining petitioners' claims the question remains whether there are prudential barriers to habeas corpus review under these circumstances.

The Government argues petitioners must seek review of their CSRT determinations in the Court of Appeals before they can proceed with their habeas corpus actions in the District Court. As noted earlier, in other contexts and for prudential reasons this Court has required exhaustion of alternative remedies before a prisoner can seek federal habeas relief. * * * [W]e have extended this rule to require defendants in courts-martial to exhaust their military appeals before proceeding with a federal habeas corpus action.

* * *

In cases involving foreign citizens detained abroad by the Executive, it likely would be both an impractical and unprecedented extension of judicial power to assume that habeas corpus would be available at the moment the prisoner is taken into custody. If and when habeas corpus jurisdiction applies, as it does in these cases, then proper deference can be accorded to reasonable procedures for screening and initial detention under lawful and proper conditions of confinement and treatment for a reasonable period of time. * * * Here, as is true with detainees apprehended abroad, a relevant consideration in determining the courts' role is whether there are suitable alternative processes in place to protect against the arbitrary exercise of governmental power.

The cases before us, however, do not involve detainees who have been held for a short period of time while awaiting their CSRT determinations. * * * In some of these cases six years have elapsed without the judicial oversight that habeas corpus or an adequate substitute demands. And there has been no showing that the Executive faces such onerous burdens that it cannot respond to habeas corpus actions. To require these detainees to complete DTA review before proceeding with their habeas corpus actions would be to require additional months, if not years, of delay. * * * While some delay in fashioning new procedures is unavoidable, the costs of delay can no longer be borne by those who are held in custody. The detainees in these cases are entitled to a prompt habeas corpus hearing.

Our decision today holds only that the petitioners before us are entitled to seek the writ; that the DTA review procedures are an inadequate substitute for habeas corpus; and that the petitioners in these cases need not exhaust the review procedures in the Court of Appeals before proceeding with their habeas actions in the District Court. The only law we identify as unconstitutional is MCA §7, 28 U.S.C.A. §2241(e). Accordingly, both the DTA and the CSRT process remain intact. Our holding with regard to exhaustion should not be read to imply that a habeas court should intervene the moment an enemy combatant steps foot in a territory where the writ runs. The Executive is entitled to a reasonable period of time to determine a detainee's status before a court entertains that detainee's habeas corpus petition. The CSRT process is the mechanism Congress and the President set up to deal with these issues. Except in cases of undue delay, federal courts should refrain from entertaining an enemy combatant's habeas corpus petition at least until after the Department, acting via the CSRT, has had a chance to review his status.

B.

* * *

The determination by the Court of Appeals that the Suspension Clause and its protections are inapplicable to petitioners was in error. The judgment of the Court of Appeals is reversed. The cases are remanded to the Court of Appeals with instructions that it remand the cases to the District Court for proceedings consistent with this opinion.

It is so ordered.

[Concurring opinion by Justice SOUTER, and dissenting opinions by Chief Justice ROBERTS and Justice SCALIA, are omitted.]

Notes

1. *Subsequent case history*

The six *Boumediene* plaintiffs were seized in Bosnia by American agents and taken to Guantánamo Bay in January 2002, after the U.S. embassy in Sarajevo asked the Bosnian government to arrest them on suspicion of involvement in a plot to bomb the U.S. embassy. This occurred after a three-month investigation during which the Bosnians found no evidence of such involvement, and after the Bosnian Supreme Court ordered the men released. Once at Guantánamo, the men were accused of being associated with al-Qaeda.

After the U.S. Supreme Court's holding in *Boumediene*, a district court judge ordered the release of five of the six plaintiffs in the case in November 2008. The judge declared that the government "failed to establish by a preponderance of the evidence the plan that is the exclusive basis for the government's claim that [plaintiffs] are enemy combatants."

2. *On remand*

Notice in *Boumediene* that the Court did not address whether the President has the authority to detain the petitioners. Rather, it left questions regarding the legality of the detention to be resolved by the district court.

3. Boumediene's *legacy*

Today, any person held at Guantánamo Bay, whether a U.S. citizen or not, has the right of habeas corpus to challenge the legality of his or her detention. On January 22, 2009 President Obama issued three executive orders that (1) required that the Guantánamo Bay detention facility be closed within one year; (2) formally banned torture; and, (3) established an inter-agency task force to lead a systematic review of detention policies and procedures and a review of all individual cases. The detention center did not close within the one year time frame, however. What would the closing of Guantánamo mean for a petitioner's standing to file for habeas relief? Would these judicial decisions no longer be important?

4. *Housing detainees outside Guantánamo*

Once President Obama issued an executive order on January 22, 2009, to close Guantánamo Bay, he faced the problem of where to send the almost 250 detainees being held there. Many of them have been cleared for release, but the U.S. has had difficulty in finding countries willing to accept them into their borders. The U.S. will not accept most of them into its borders either. Some detainees are unable to return to their countries of origin because they need asylum protection. *Guantanamo Bay history*, available at http://cbc.ca/world/story/2009/01/22/f-gitmo.html; *Guantanamo Bay Fact Sheet*, available at www.amnestyusa.org/america/FactSheet.pdf. How to resolve the cases of the remaining detainees who have not been cleared for release has proven to be both controversial and challenging. The Obama Administration has considered reinstituting trials by military tribunals for some of the detainees. Kim Chapman, *Obama to Resume Military Tribunals for Some Detainees* (Update3) Bloomberg, May 15, 2009, available at http://www .bloomberg.com/apps/news?pid=newsarchive&sid=aCF1J2FLXuyA. The administration is also proceeding with plans to prosecute some of the detainees in civilian courts in the United States. Benjamin Weiser, *Judge Bars Major Witness From Terrorism Trial*, New York Times, October 6, 2010, available at http://www.nytimes.com/2010/10/07nyregion/07/ ghailani.html. Opponents of civilian trials have argued that an entirely new legal system should be created in order to accomplish this. Richard Bernstein, *Balancing Civil Liberties and Warfare*, New York Times, October 20, 2010, available at http://www.nytimes.com/ 2010/10/21/us/2liht-letter.html?ref=ahmed_khalfan_ghailani. What solutions can you think of for this complex issue?

Reflections from a Guantanamo Detainee Lawyer

By Leonard Goodman

In mid-2007, I took on the representation of an Afghan man named Shawali Khan. Khan had been detained at "Gitmo" since February 2003, without any charges or legal representation. He was in his mid-40s, grew up on a fruit orchard outside of Kandahar, Afghanistan, and had no formal education.

In 2000, there had been a drought on the farm and Khan had moved with his father and brother to Kandahar City where they opened a shop selling petrol products. When

U.S. forces invaded Afghanistan in 2001, Khan continued to run his oil shop and even worked, for a short time, for the Karzai government as a driver.

In November, 2002, Khan was captured by some Afghan men who worked for a local warlord. Khan's captors told U.S. officials that Khan was a terrorist, plotting against U.S. interests in and around Kandahar. (It is almost certain that the U.S. paid a bounty to Khan's captors but this cannot be confirmed because, while the U.S. admits paying large cash bounties to warlords who turned in "al Qaeda and Taliban fighters," it has refused to release any of these files.)

Khan was sent to the U.S. air base at Bagram where he repeatedly told his interrogators that he and his family had an oil shop in Kandahar and were not enemies of the Americans. Although the interrogators wrote in their reports that Khan appeared honest, he was sent to Gitmo where he remains to this day.

The U.S. requires any lawyer or translator working with a Gitmo detainee to have a secret security clearance, which takes at least six months to obtain. I received mine in the summer of 2008 and was finally approved (by the Department of Defense) for a Gitmo visit in the fall. To get to Gitmo, you take a three-hour flight on a small commuter plane from Fort Lauderdale, Florida, to the Guantánamo Bay Naval Base on the south-eastern tip of Cuba. Lawyers and translators sleep in the "combined bachelor quarters." For each of my four visits to the base, I was accompanied by Tariq, my Pashto translator.

On the morning of a visit, lawyers and translators take a ferry across the bay to the prison side of the base. Detainees are transported from their cells to a special interview room where they must remain shackled to the floor. Lawyers cannot share classified information with their clients but can only show them approved materials. We may bring them food (usually meatless Egg McMuffins from the McDonalds on the base), but any food items must be fully consumed during the visit. Lawyers may not leave any items with their clients—no food, books, magazines, or even materials relating to their case. Any notes which a lawyer takes during the visit are confiscated, reviewed and later faxed back to the attorney with any items deemed sensitive redacted out.

Most of the evidence against Khan (and against all detainees) is classified. To view this evidence or just about any item associated with the case, counsel must go to the "Secure Facility" located near Alexandria, Virginia. In addition, nearly all pleadings in the case must be viewed, composed and filed from the Secure Facility.

By far, the most frustrating part about representing a Gitmo detainee is that there is so little lawyers can do for their clients. In June, 2008, right after Boumediene, I filed a habeas corpus petition in the D.C. District Court demanding an evidentiary hearing and Khan's release. During my first visit in the fall of 2008, I excitedly told Khan about this petition and about the great writ of habeas corpus. During my second visit, in January 2009, I again told Khan about the virtues of habeas corpus. I explained that his case was pending before a real federal judge and that he would have a real hearing where the government would have to produce real evidence to justify his continued detention (unlike the Mickey Mouse CSRT hearings Khan had already received at Gitmo). I further explained that Khan would have an opportunity to testify at his hearing via video conference.

Khan agreed to participate and requested that this hearing be held as soon as possible. I promised to push the judge for the earliest hearing date.

During my next visit in mid-2009, I had to explain to Khan that the court had granted the government's request for a stay of all habeas proceedings while it conducted a new search through archived intelligence files for additional evidence against Khan. Khan was angry and frustrated. The fact that I shared his frustration did not comfort him.

That fall, the court finally set Khan's case for a merits hearing. I wrote to Khan to tell him the good news. But then, in December, the government again successfully moved, over my strenuous objection, to stay the merits hearing. In January 2010, I visited Khan for the fourth time and delivered the bad news that his hearing had again been postponed. (Shortly after this visit, Khan fired me but then later agreed to let me represent him at his hearing.)

In February 2010, the court lifted the stay and reset the merits hearing, acknowledging perhaps that the government was merely stalling for time. On May 13, 2010, Khan's hearing commenced, closed to the press and the public.

The government produced no live witnesses at the merits hearing. Instead, it offered classified documents from U.S. intelligence officers reporting that certain unidentified Afghan informants had named Khan as an anti-U.S. insurgent. In response, the defense offered nine sworn declarations from Khan's family and neighbors, all of which refuted the charge that Khan was a terrorist. The defense also presented the live testimony of a professor and expert on Afghan terror groups and the published memoir of a U.S. journalist who lived in Kandahar during 2002, each of which supported the defense claim that the allegations against Khan were fabricated by bounty hunters.

The merits hearing began on a Thursday and was scheduled to conclude that Friday with Khan's testimony via video link. Unable to be in two places at one time, I enlisted a colleague, fellow Gitmo attorney Candace Gorman, to travel to the base and conduct the direct examination of Khan.

The U.S. considers any utterance of Mr. Khan a threat to national security and thus requires all transmissions to the courtroom go through a secure and encrypted video link. On the Friday of Khan's scheduled testimony, this encryption technology mysteriously malfunctioned. Fortunately, Ms. Gorman and Tariq agreed to spend the weekend at the base and, on the following Monday, Khan was able to take the oath and tell the court that he was a shopkeeper and not a terrorist or enemy of the United States.

Following closing arguments, the court took the case under advisement. On September 3, 2010, Judge John Bates of the D.C. District Court issued an order denying Khan's habeas petition. I have written Mr. Khan to inform him of the bad news and am presently working on his appeal.

Notes

1. *Effective assistance of counsel*

Given the difficulty of representing a detainee at Guantánamo—not being able to see your client easily, not being able to give your client materials that are relevant to his case, and not being able to take your notes with you when you leave—how do you think the constitutional standard of adequate representation is affected by the limiting circumstances of Guantánamo?

2. *The reach of habeas*

What do you think of the Bagram Airbase interrogators who stated that Khan "appeared honest?" What do you think of the propriety of imprisoning a man for the length of time that Khan has been imprisoned without a proper trial? Isn't this exactly the type of situation the writ of habeas corpus is meant to address?

Table of Cases

Index

– Q –

– R –